T0217126

Lecture Notes in Computer Science 503

Edited by G. Goos and J. Hartmanis

Advisory Board: W. Brauer D. Gries J. Stoer

Parallel Database Systems

PRISMA Workshop
Noordwijk, The Netherlands, September 24–26, 1990
Proceedings

Springer-Verlag
Berlin Heidelberg New York
London Paris Tokyo
Hong Kong Barcelona
Budapest

Pierre America (Ed.)

Parallel Database Systems

PRISMA Workshop
Noordwijk, The Netherlands, September 24-26, 1990
Proceedings

Springer-Verlag
Berlin Heidelberg New York
London Paris Tokyo
Hong Kong Barcelona
Budapest

Series Editors

Gerhard Goos
GMD Forschungsstelle
Universität Karlsruhe
Vincenz-Priessnitz-Straße 1
W-7500 Karlsruhe, FRG

Juris Hartmanis
Department of Computer Science
Cornell University
Upson Hall
Ithaca, NY 14853, USA

Volume Editor

Pierre America
Philips Research Laboratories
P.O. Box 80.000, 5600 JA Eindhoven, The Netherlands

CR Subject Classification (1991): H.2.4, C.1.2, D.1.3

ISBN 3-540-54132-2 Springer-Verlag Berlin Heidelberg New York
ISBN 0-387-54132-2 Springer-Verlag New York Berlin Heidelberg

This work is subject to copyright. All rights are reserved, whether the whole or part of
the material is concerned, specifically the rights of translation, reprinting, re-use of
illustrations, recitation, broadcasting, reproduction on microfilms or in other ways, and
storage in data banks. Duplication of this publication or parts thereof is only permitted
under the provisions of the German Copyright Law of September 9, 1965, in its current
version, and a copyright fee must always be paid. Violations fall under the prosecution
act of the German Copyright Law.

© Springer-Verlag Berlin Heidelberg 1991
Printed in Germany

Printing and binding: Druckhaus Beltz, Hemsbach/Bergstr.
2145/3140-543210 - Printed on acid-free paper

Preface

This volume constitutes the proceedings of the Workshop on Parallel Database Systems organized by the PRISMA (Parallel Inference and Storage Machine) Project, and held in Noordwijk on the Dutch North Sea coast, September 24–26, 1990. It contains contributions from invited speakers as well as from the organizing PRISMA Project. The invited speakers, all recognized experts in their fields, present their views on several subjects that are closely related to the title of the workshop. The PRISMA papers, taken together, give an in-depth overview of the PRISMA system. This system is based on a parallel machine, where the individual processors each have their own local memory and communicate with each other over a packet-switched network. On this machine a parallel object-oriented programming language, POOL-X, has been implemented, which provides dedicated support for database systems as well as general facilities for parallel programming. This POOL-X system then serves as a platform for a complete relational main-memory database management system, which uses the parallelism of the machine to speed up significantly the execution of database queries. The presentation of the PRISMA system, together with the invited papers, gives a broad overview of the state of the art in parallel database systems.

The workshop marked the end of the PRISMA Project, which started in October 1986. The project was a cooperation of Philips Research Laboratories, Eindhoven, the Netherlands, with the Centre for Mathematics and Computer Science (CWI) in Amsterdam and the Universities of Amsterdam, Twente, Leiden, and Utrecht. It was sponsored by the Dutch 'Stimuleringsprojectteam Informatica-onderzoek' (SPIN).

The contributions were selected by the programme committee, consisting of

> Pierre America (Philips Research Laboratories, chair)
> Peter Apers (University of Twente)
> Bob Hertzberger (University of Amsterdam)
> Martin Kersten (CWI, Amsterdam)

These proceedings were edited by Pierre America.

I would like to take this opportunity to thank the many persons who have contributed to PRISMA, both within the project and through interaction from related research. They are too numerous to mention in this preface, but many of them are authors of articles in these proceedings or are referenced therein. One person, however, deserves special mention here: Fred Robert, who diligently took care of logistic arrangements throughout PRISMA and this workshop.

February 1991

H. H. Eggenhuisen
PRISMA Project Leader

Contents

Invited Presentations

Languages for Parallel Programming

Henri E. Bal

Dept. of Mathematics and Computer Science
Vrije Universiteit
Amsterdam

ABSTRACT

Many different paradigms for parallel programming exist, nearly each of which is employed in dozens of languages. Several researchers have tried to compare these languages and paradigms by examining the expressivity and flexibility of their constructs. Few attempts have been made, however, at *practical* studies based on actual programming experience with multiple languages. Such a study is the topic of this paper.

We will look at five parallel languages, all based on different paradigms. The languages are: SR (based on message passing), Emerald (concurrent objects), Parlog (parallel Horn clause logic), Linda (Tuple Space), and Orca (logically shared data). We have implemented the same parallel programs in each language, using real parallel machines. The paper reports on our experiences in implementing three frequently occurring communication patterns: message passing through a mailbox, one-to-many communication, and access to replicated shared data.

1. INTRODUCTION

During the previous decade, a staggering number of languages for programming parallel and distributed systems has emerged.[5, 12] These languages are based on widely different programming paradigms, such as message passing, concurrent objects, logic, and functional programming. Both within each paradigm and between paradigms, heated discussions are held about which approach is best.[19, 29, 33]

The intent of this paper is to cast new light on these discussions, using a practical approach. We have implemented a number of parallel applications in each of several parallel languages. Based on this experience, we will draw some conclusions about the relative advantages and disadvantages of each language. So, unlike most of the discussions in the literature, this paper is based on actual programming experience in several parallel languages on real parallel systems.

The languages studied in this paper obviously do not cover the whole spectrum of design choices. Still, they represent a significant subset of what we feel are the most important paradigms for parallel programming. We discuss only a single language for each paradigm, although other languages may exist within each paradigm that are significantly different.

This research was supported in part by the Netherlands Organization for Scientific Research (N.W.O.).

Language	Paradigm	Origin
SR	Message passing	University of Arizona
Emerald	Concurrent object-based language	University of Washington
Parlog	Concurrent logic language	Imperial College
Linda	Tuple space	Yale University
Orca	Distributed shared memory	Vrije Universiteit

Table 1. Overview of the languages discussed in the paper.

The languages that have been selected for this study are: SR, Emerald, Parlog, Linda, and Orca (see Table 1). SR represents message passing languages. It provides a range of message sending and receiving constructs, rather than a single model. Emerald is an object-based language. Parlog is a concurrent logic language. Linda is a set of language primitives based on the Tuple Space model. Orca is representative of the Distributed Shared Memory model. The languages will be discussed in more detail in Section 2.

We focus on languages for parallel applications, where the aim is to achieve a speedup on a single application. These applications can be run on either *multiprocessors* with shared memory or *distributed* systems without shared memory. We have selected only languages that are suitable for both architectures. So, we do not discuss shared-variable or monitor-based languages, since their usage is restricted to shared-memory multiprocessors. Functional languages are not discussed either. Most functional languages are intended for different parallel architectures, (e.g., dataflow or graph reduction machines) and often try to hide parallelism from the programmer. This makes an objective comparison with the other languages hard. We also do not deal with distributed languages based on atomic transactions (e.g., Argus[31]), since these are primarily intended for fault-tolerant applications. The issue of fault-tolerant parallel programming is discussed in a separate paper.[9]

2. THE LANGUAGES

The languages studied in this paper have all been described in a recent survey paper,[12] so we will be brief here. We discuss only the main characteristics of each language. In addition, we give some background information about the implementation, usage, and availability of the languages.

Synchronizing Resources (SR)

SR[3, 4] is a language for writing distributed programs, developed by Greg Andrews, Ron Olsson, and their colleagues at the University of Arizona and the University of California at Davis. The language supports a wide variety of message passing constructs, including shared variables (for processes on the same node), asynchronous message passing, rendezvous, remote procedure call, and multicast.

The idea behind SR is that no single communication primitive will be ideally suited for all applications, hence the rich choice of primitives. On the other hand, one can argue that a language with so many features will also be complex and hard to learn. For this aspect of the language, we refer the reader to a separate paper.[6] For the present paper, we can safely assume that SR is one of the most expressive message passing languages around. Most other languages in this category (e.g., Ada®, Concurrent C, occam) provide a subset of SR's communication facilities.

SR has been used for a parallel Prolog-interpreter, a file system, and several other applications. The language has been implemented on a range of multiprocessors (Encore, Sequent Balance, Sequent Symmetry) and distributed systems (homogeneous networks of VAXes, Sun-3s, Sun-4s, and others). The compiler and run time system are available from the University of Arizona.

Emerald

Emerald[15,26] is an object-based language, originally designed at the University of Washington by Andrew Black, Norman Hutchinson, Eric Jul, and Henry Levy. Emerald is now being further developed at the University of Arizona, the University of Copenhagen, and elsewhere.

An object in Emerald encapsulates both static data and an active process. Objects communicate by invoking each other's operations. There can be multiple active invocations within one object, which synchronize through a *monitor*. The remote invocation mechanism is *location transparent*.

Central to Emerald's design is the concept of *object mobility*. An object may migrate from one processor to another, as initiated either by the programmer or the system. Emerald uses a novel parameter mode, *call-by-move*. This mode has similar semantics as call-by-reference, but additionally moves the object parameter to the node of the invoked object.

A prototype implementation of Emerald exists on networks of VAXes or Sun-3 workstations, connected by an Ethernet. This implementation has been used for a distributed mail system, a replicated name server, and some other applications. The Emerald system is not yet available to other users.

Although Emerald is probably the best known language based on concurrent objects, many other languages exist that are significantly different.[12] These languages may, for example, support different synchronization mechanisms and inheritance.

Parlog

We have chosen Parlog[21,22,23,25] as representative for the large class of concurrent logic languages. Parlog has been developed at Imperial College, London, by Keith Clark, Steve Gregory, and their colleagues.

The language is based on AND/OR parallelism and committed-choice nondeterminism. The user can specify the order (parallel or sequential) in which clauses are to be evaluated. For this purpose, sequential and parallel conjunction and disjunction operators can be used.

An interpreter for Parlog has been implemented on several shared-memory multiprocessors (Sequent Balance and Symmetry, Butterfly). A commercially available subset of Parlog, called Strand, has also been implemented on distributed systems (hypercubes, networks). Parlog has been used for discrete event simulation, natural-language parsing, the specification and verification of communication protocols, and several other applications. The Parlog system is available from Imperial College.

Linda

Linda is a set of language primitives developed by David Gelernter and colleagues at Yale University.[1, 18, 19] Linda is based on the Tuple Space model of communication. The Tuple Space is a global memory consisting of tuples (records) that are addressed associatively. Three atomic operations are defined on Tuple Space: **out** adds a tuple to TS; **rd** reads a tuple contained in TS; **in** reads a tuple and also deletes it from TS, in one atomic action.

The Tuple Space model can be embedded in an existing language (e.g., C, Modula-2, or Lisp), resulting in a parallel language. C/Linda is the senior member of this family.

Linda has been implemented on many parallel machines, both with and without shared memory, and has been used for numerous applications.[19] The system is distributed as a commercial product.

Orca

Orca is a language for implementing parallel applications on distributed systems. Orca was designed at the Vrije Universiteit in Amsterdam.[7, 10, 11, 13]

The programming model of Orca is based on logically shared data. The language hides the physical distribution of the memory and allows processes to share data even if they run on different nodes. In this way, Orca combines the advantages of distributed systems (good price/performance ratio and scalability) and shared-memory multiprocessors (ease of programming).

The entities shared among processes are data objects, which are variables of user-defined abstract data types. These data objects are replicated in the local memories, so each process can directly read its own copy, without doing any communication. The language run time system atomically updates all copies when an object is modified.

This model is similar to that of Distributed Shared Memory (DSM) systems.[30] In Orca, however, the unit of sharing is a logical (user-defined) object rather than a physical (system-defined) page, which has many advantages.[7]

Orca has been implemented on top of Amoeba[32] as well as on a collection of MC68020s connected through an Ethernet. The latter implementation uses the physical multicast capability of the Ethernet. The language has been used for several small to medium size parallel applications. The Orca implementation is being distributed as part of the Amoeba system.

Discussion

There are many ways to compare parallel languages. One way is a theoretical study of the expressiveness of their primitives. This works well for languages using the same paradigm (e.g., message passing), but is more problematic for comparison between different paradigms. Comparing, say, remote procedure calls and shared logical variables is not a trivial task.

Another approach is to take a small example problem, implement it in each language, and compare the resulting programs. All too often, the example problem turns out to be the dining philosophers problem, or one of its many variants. Language designers are well aware of this fact and always make sure that the dining philosophers problem can be solved in an elegant way. (The point also applies to the producer/consumer problem.)

The approach taken in this paper is to implement a set of small, yet realistic, problems in each language. The example problems we have studied are: matrix multiplication, the all-pairs shortest paths problem, branch-and-bound, game tree search, and successive overrelaxation. Space limitations do not permit us to discuss all these programs in detail here, let alone give their source code. Rather, we will look at certain aspects of each problem that are interesting from a parallel programming point of view. Frequently, a parallel problem calls for a certain type of *communication pattern* (or stereotype), and it is these patterns that we will discuss in the rest of this paper. For more details about the applications and the algorithms used for them, see reference 7.

To be more concrete, the communication patterns that we will look at are:

- Message passing through a mailbox.
- One-to-many communication.
- Access to shared data.

Each of these patterns occurs one or more times in our applications. For each pattern, we discuss how easy it is to express in the five languages. Based on this study, we will draw some conclusions about the advantages and disadvantages of the different approaches to parallel programming.

In each of the following three sections, we will discuss one communication pattern. For each pattern, we present several solutions. We start with what we think is the simplest solution, so the subsections are ordered by increasing complexity, rather than by a fixed language order. As we will see, different languages may sometimes take the same approach for dealing with a given communication pattern, although no two languages use the same approach for all three patterns (see Table 2 in Section 6).

3. MAILBOXES

The first communication pattern that we study is passing messages through a mailbox. A mailbox is a communication port with **send** (nonblocking) and **receive** operations that can be invoked by multiple processes.[12] Mailboxes can be contrasted with direct message passing, in which the sender always specifies the destination process (receiver) of the message. With mailboxes, any process that can access the mailbox can receive a message sent to it. So, each message sent to a mailbox is handled by one process, but it is not determined in advance which process will accept the message.

Mailboxes are useful, for example, in programs based on the replicated workers paradigm.[2, 20] In such programs, a process that has computed a new job (to be executed in parallel) can send it to a mailbox, where it will eventually be picked up by an idle worker process. Since it is not known in advance which worker will execute which jobs, a mailbox is much more useful than direct message passing. In our case, the branch-and-bound and game tree search programs both use this approach.

None of the languages we study have built-in mailboxes. Linda and Orca do not support message passing at all. Emerald provides only synchronous operation invocations on objects, so the receiver is fixed and the sender blocks during the invocation. SR provides asynchronous message passing, but the receiver of a message is fully determined when the message is sent. Parlog supports message passing through *streams*, which are built from shared logical variables. The receiving end of a stream can scan over the stream, but it cannot remove items from it.[19] Streams are useful if each receiver accepts all messages, but this is fundamentally different from mailboxes.

In the following subsections, we will discuss how the **send** and **receive** can be simulated in the different languages. We will look at three different methods, in order of increasing complexity:

- Distributed data structures (used in Linda)
- Shared objects (Orca and Emerald)
- Buffer processes (SR and Parlog).

Distributed Data Structures (Linda)

In Linda, the simulation is almost trivial. A mailbox is represented as a distributed data structure[20] in Tuple Space. The **send** and **receive** primitives are implemented as shown below:

```
send msg to MB ≡
     out("MB", msg)          # put a message in Tuple Space

receive msg from MB ≡
     in("MB", ? &msg)        # fetch a message from Tuple Space
```

Linda's **in** operation blocks until a matching tuple is found. Next, it assigns the formal parameters of the **in** (denoted by a "?") the corresponding values of the tuple. Finally, it deletes the tuple from Tuple Space. All of this is done atomically. In the code above, the message is stored in a local variable, whose address is passed as formal parameter to the **in**.

The above implementation of **send** and **receive** does not preserve the ordering of the messages. If the order is important, a sequence number could be added to each message. The sequence number of the next message to accept should be stored in an extra tuple, resulting in the following code:

```
send msg to MB ≡
     out("MB", msg, seqno);   # put message with sequence number in TS
     seqno = seqno + 1;       # increment sequence number for next message

receive msg from MB ≡
     in("seqno", ? &next);    # first obtain next sequence number
     out("seqno", next+1);    # put sequence-number tuple back in TS
     in("MB", ? &msg, next);  # now fetch message with right sequence number
```

In the first solution, the message tuples can be thought of as forming an unordered *bag*. In the second solution, they constitute an ordered *queue*.

Shared Objects (Orca and Emerald)

In both Emerald and Orca, similar (although more verbose solutions) are possible. In these languages, a mailbox can be implemented as a shared object containing a message queue or bag. In Orca, a generic message queue object can be specified as follows:

```
generic (type T)
object specification GenericMsgQueue;
     operation AddMsg(msg: T);   # Add a message to the tail of the queue
     operation GetMsg(): T;      # Fetch a message from the head of the queue.
end generic;
```

Here, *T* is a formal type parameter; an instantiation of this generic type should provide an actual type for *T*. The implementation of the generic type requires just one page of Orca code.[7]

Given this object type, the ordered **send** and **receive** can be implemented as follows:

send msg **to** MB ≡ MB$AddMsg(msg)

receive msg **from** MB ≡ msg := MB$GetMsg()

Here, *MB* is a shared object; its type is an instantiation of the *GenericMsgQueue* type.

In Emerald, a similar (polymorphic) object type can be defined and implemented. The Emerald version is more cumbersome, because the operations need to synchronize through monitors. In Orca, the run time system automatically synchronizes operations.

Buffer Processes (SR and Parlog)

SR and Parlog do not support shared objects. In these languages, an extra buffer process is needed for maintaining the messages. This intermediary process has to respond to requests to deposit and retrieve messages. This scheme can be implemented in SR and Parlog, but it has a significant programming overhead.

Our implementation of replicated workers in SR and Parlog[6, 8] uses a simpler but less efficient solution. The master generates only one job at a time and then waits until a worker asks for it. As a disadvantage, parallelism between the master and workers is almost eliminated. If multiple workers request a job, nearly all of them will be delayed until the master has computed enough jobs. For the applications we have studied, this is not a major problem, because job generation is computationally inexpensive. For other applications, buffering may be more critical.

Summary

In Linda, Orca, and Emerald, mailboxes can easily be simulated. Unarguably, the Linda version is shorter, due to the powerful associative addressing capability of the Tuple Space. On the other hand, the Orca/Emerald message queue object type need be implemented only once, and can be reused in other applications (especially since the type is generic/polymorphic).

Linda requires *three* operations on Tuple Space for retrieving a message from an ordered queue: two for bumping the index counter and one for fetching the message tuple. In Orca and Emerald, on the other hand, the message queue manipulations are naturally expressed with single operations. The communication overhead in Linda will therefore be higher, unless extensive optimizations are applied.

In SR and Parlog, the communication pattern is harder to express. A separate buffer process is needed for storing the messages. The extra programming overhead can be avoided by simplifying the solution, at the cost of less parallelism between the master and workers.

4. ONE-TO-MANY COMMUNICATION

The second communication pattern we study transmits data from one process to many others, *all* of which use these data. (In contrast, a message sent to a mailbox is used by only *one* process.) This pattern occurs in our All-pairs Shortest Paths (ASP) programs, which compute the lengths of the shortest paths between each pair of nodes in a given graph. The same communication pattern also occurs in Gaussian elimination programs.

Our ASP programs use a parallel version of Floyd's iterative algorithm.[24] Before each iteration, one row of the distances matrix is selected as *pivot* row. Next, all rows of the matrix are updated, using the pivot row. This general structure is illustrated by the code fragment of Figure 1. In ASP, the pivot row for iteration k is row k. The function *update* used in this figure computes the new value for a given row, using only the old value and the pivot row as input.

```
D: array[1 .. N] of array[1 .. N] of element;   # the distances matrix

for k := 1 to N do
        PivotRow := D[k];   # make copy of pivot row
        for i := 1 to N do   # update all rows
                D[i] := update(D[i], PivotRow);
```

Figure 1. Structure of the sequential (Floyd) ASP algorithm.

To parallelize this code, the updates of the rows (i.e., the inner loop) can be done concurrently. Note that the new value for row i only depends on the old value of row i and on the pivot row. So, the only data dependency is the pivot row.

Below, we will first look at our Parlog implementation of ASP, which uses fine-grained parallelism. The one-to-many communication is implicit in this program. Next, we will discuss more large-grained parallel implementations, using explicit multicast communication.

A Solution with Fine-grained Parallelism (Parlog)

In Parlog, the parallel version of Floyd's algorithm is very easy to express. Figure 2 shows part of the Parlog code for ASP. It is a straightforward translation of the code fragment above, using recursion instead of iteration.

```
mode asp(Size?, InitialDistances?, Iter?, ShortestPaths^).
asp(N, D, K, D) <- K > N: true.            % terminate after Nth iteration
asp(N, D, K, NewD) <- K =< N:
        get_elt(D, K, PivotRow) &                  % PivotRow := row K of matrix D
        update_matrix(D, K, PivotRow, D_next) &   % update all rows of D, yielding D_next
        K_next is K + 1 &                          % bump iteration counter
        asp(N, D_next, K_next, NewD).              % do next iteration

mode update_matrix(Matrix?, K?, PivotRow?, NewMatrix^).
update_matrix([], _, _, []).
update_matrix([R|Rs], K, PivotRow, [Q|Qs]) <-
        update_row(R, PivotRow, Q),      % update all rows of the matrix in parallel
        update_matrix(Rs, K, PivotRow, Qs).

mode update_row(Row?, PivotRow?, NewRow^).
        compute new value of the given row, using the old value and the pivot row
```

Figure 2. Part of the Parlog code for ASP. The "?" in mode declarations indicates that the parameter is input; the call blocks until the actual parameter is bound to a value. The "^" indicates an output parameter.

The first predicate (*asp*) implements the outer for-loop; the *update_matrix* predicate implements the inner loop. Concurrency is expressed through parallel conjunctions (the "," operator) in the latter predicate.

The Parlog program allocates *N* new AND-parallel processes during each iteration, and passes the pivot row as a parameter to each of them. This solution employs fine-grained parallelism. The shared-memory implementation of Parlog is tuned to this type of parallelism and achieves reasonable speedups. (For ASP, we have measured speedups of 5.3 on a 6-CPU Sequent Balance and 8.6 on a 12-CPU Sequent Symmetry.)

Large-grained Parallel Implementations of ASP

The other languages are less suitable for fine-grained parallelism. For these languages we use a fixed number of processes (one per processor), each containing a portion of the distances matrix. Each process executes the iterative algorithm shown in Figure 3.

```
for k := 1 to N do
    if k ∈ [lb .. ub] then       # do I have the pivot row?
        PivotRow := D[k];         # yes, copy it and multicast it
        multicast SendPivotRow(k, PivotRow) to all other processes
    else
        PivotRow := receive SendPivotRow(k) # no, fetch it from someone else
    for i := lb to ub do   # update all my rows
        D[i] := update(D[i], PivotRow);
```

Figure 3. Algorithm for the ASP process containing rows *lb* to *ub*.

At the beginning of each iteration, one process decides that it has the pivot row. This process sends its pivot row to all the other processes. Next, all processes update their portion of the matrix. The one-to-many communication style is more explicit in this code fragment, as shown by the usage of **multicast**. The communication pattern is illustrated further in Figure 4.

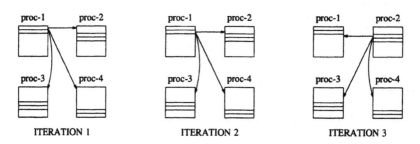

Figure 4. Communication pattern of the parallel ASP programs, using 4 processes, each containing 2 rows. During the first quarter of the computation (i.e., the first two iterations), all processes need pivot rows computed by the first process. During the second quarter, they need pivot rows from the second process, and so on.

One subtle point in the algorithm is that the ASP processes may be working on different iterations. In Figure 4, for example, Process 1 can start the second iteration before the others have finished the first.

In the following subsections we will discuss one-to-many communication in Orca, Linda, SR, and Emerald. The ASP programs in all these languages have the same structure—they all use the ASP processes defined in Figure 3—but they differ in their implementation of one-to-many communication. There are in fact two issues to be considered: how this pattern is *expressed* in the language and how it is *implemented* in the system. For efficiency, it is highly desirable that the implementation uses physical (hardware) multicast, if available. The solutions we will look at are:

- Shared data (Orca, Linda)
- Concurrent messages (SR)
- Point-to-point messages (Emerald)

One-to-many Communication with Shared Data (Linda and Orca)

Linda and Orca support the sharing of data among multiple processes. Data generated by one process can be read by multiple processes, so this is inherently one-to-many communication. In contrast, sending a message from one process to another is inherently one-to-one (or point-to-point) communication.

In Linda, the process containing the pivot row for iteration k simply puts it in Tuple Space, where it can be read by all other processes. So, the **multicast** and **receive** operations of Figure 3 are implemented as follows in Linda:

```
multicast SendPivotRow(k, row) ≡
    out("PivotRow", k, row)       # put row for iteration k in Tuple Space

row := receive SendPivotRow(k) ≡
    rd("PivotRow", k, ? &row)     # read pivot row
```

Note that the **rd** (read) operation contains an actual parameter for the iteration number (k) but a formal parameter for the row. The operation finds the tuple with the given iteration number and retrieves the row stored in that tuple. The tuple itself is unaffected.

The Orca solution is similar, except that the rows are put in an object shared among all processes. The specification of the object's type is shown below:

```
object specification RowCollection;
    operation AddRow(iter: integer; R: RowType);
        # Add the pivot row for the given iteration number
    operation AwaitRow(iter: integer): RowType;
        # Wait until the pivot row for the given iteration is available, then return it.
end;
```

The implementation of this object type is about half a page of Orca code.[7] With this object type, the **multicast** and **receive** operations are implemented as:

```
multicast SendPivotRow(k, row) ≡       PivotRows$AddRow(k, row);

row := receive SendPivotRow(k) ≡       row := PivotRows$AwaitRow(k);
```

Here, *PivotRows* is the shared data-object containing the pivot rows.

Expressing one-to-many communication in Linda and Orca is easy. A key question that remains, however, is what *really* happens in these systems. For efficiency, it makes considerable difference whether the pivot row is transferred through a real multicast protocol or not.

For Orca, there are two implementations to consider: one using true Ethernet multicast, the other using Amoeba RPC. If a new pivot row is generated, the first system will use a hardware multicast to send the *AddRow* operation to all processors. The second system will simulate multicast using multiple overlapping RPCs. The differences in performance between the two implementations are considerable.[7] The multicast system obtains a speedup of 9.2 on 10 processors. With exactly the same hardware, the RPC system only obtains a maximal speedup of 5.7. In the latter case, the communication overhead is linear to the number of processors, which prevents better speedups. With real multicast, the communication costs hardly depend on the number of receivers.[28]

For Linda, there are many different implementations to consider. The S/Net system replicates all tuples everywhere, using the S/Net broadcast capability.[17] The hypercube and Transputer implementations of Linda, on the other hand, hash each tuple onto one specific processor and do not replicate tuples.[14, 34] In this case, the communication overhead will be linear in the number of processors used. In theory, a broadcast to P processors can be done in $O(\log P)$ time on a hypercube and $O(sqrt(P))$ on a grid, so these two Linda implementations are far from optimal.

One-to-many Communication with Concurrent Messages (SR)

SR has a special language construct for sending a message concurrently to several processes. This **co** construct can be use to implement the **multicast** operation:

```
multicast SendPivotRow(k, row) ≡
    co (i := 1 to P)
            send receiver[i].PivotRow(k, row)
    oc
```

This approach to multicasting has three disadvantages:

1. The identities of all the receivers must be known in advance. In the example above, the identities are stored in an array.

2. If two SR processes multicast two messages, these messages need not arrive in the same order everywhere. In other words, multicast in SR is not *indivisible*.

3. The **co** statement currently is not implemented as a true (physical) multicast.

The first problem can be solved at some programming overhead, by supplying each ASP process the identities of its collaborators. Still, it shows a disadvantage of SR over Linda and Orca, which do not have this problem at all.

The second problem is subtler. Since the ASP processes may be working on different iterations, there may be multiple pending multicast messages. The receivers should accept these messages in the right order. Fortunately, SR supports *conditional* message acceptance, which allows the receivers to pick the right message. The **receive** primitive can be implemented as follows in SR:

```
row := receive SendPivotRow(k) ≡
    in PivotRow(iter, r) st iter = k ->
        row := r
    ni
```

The **in** statement accepts the pivot row only if the iteration number (passed as first argument) is right. In this way, the messages are accepted in the right order.

The SR multicast primitive is currently implemented with multiple point-to-point messages. The ASP program does not obtain a linear speedup. On a 6-CPU Sequent Symmetry, for example, we have measured a speedup of 4.1.

One-to-many Communication with Point-to-point Messages (Emerald)

Finally, we will consider the implementation of one-to-many communication in Emerald, which lacks a multicast facility. The process containing the pivot row therefore sends it using a sequence of point-to-point messages.

The only way in Emerald to transfer information between processes (active objects) is through operation invocations. The sender of the pivot row has to know the identities of all the other processes, as in SR. It invokes a *SendPivotRow* operation on each of them, one at a time, passing the pivot row as parameter. A subtle problem arises here, however, that does not occur in the other languages, as explained below.

Emerald provides a uniform parameter mechanism: all objects are passed by reference, no matter where the sender and receiver are located. This model is clean and useful for distributed applications where shared objects are moved around but not copied (e.g., a mailbox in an electronic mail system). For parallel applications such as ASP, however, the model is less appropriate. Each ASP process should be given a *copy* of the pivot row, not a remote reference to it, because that would be unacceptably inefficient. What is needed here is call-by-value semantics, which is not supported in Emerald.

Thus, the sender must copy the pivot row explicitly and pass this copy as call-by-move parameter to the *SendPivotRow* operation, causing it to be moved to the receiver's node. A distinct copy must be made for every receiver. So the **multicast** is implemented as follows in Emerald:

```
multicast SendPivotRow(k, row) ≡
     for all receivers r do
          r.SendPivotRow[k, move copy[PivotRow]]
```

Here, *copy* is a user-defined procedure that copies an array object.

Let us now see what happens at the receiving side. An operation invocation in Emerald is handled implicitly and creates a new thread within the receiving object. So, the *SendPivotRow* operation is serviced immediately, irrespective of whether the receiver has any use for the pivot row yet. It may have been waiting for this row to arrive, or it may still be working on an earlier iteration.

In any case, the pivot row is stored in a table, indexed by iteration number. In addition, an array of *condition variables* (also indexed by iteration number) is used to get the synchronization right. If an ASP process starts working on iteration k, it checks the first table to see if the pivot row for iteration k is available yet. If not, it blocks by doing a *wait* on the kth entry of the second table:

```
row := receive SendPivotRow(k) ≡
     if PivotRow(k) not yet available then
          wait PivotWait(k)      % wait on condition variable
     end if
     row <- PivotRows(k)         % assign PivotRows(k) to row
```

This entry will be *signaled* by the arrival of the pivot row. These tables and the operations on them are encapsulated in a monitor.

All in all, the Emerald implementation of ASP is far more complex than the other ones. In addition, the solution is far from efficient. Not only does it refrain from using physical multicast, but it also forces the sender to copy the pivot once for every receiver, which may become a sequential bottleneck.

Summary

We have looked at four different ways to implement the one-to-many communication style needed by programs such as ASP and Gaussian elimination. The Parlog solution is by far the simplest; it is hardly more complicated than the sequential algorithm. On the other hand, this solution employs rather fine-grained parallelism and will be inefficient on distributed hardware.

The three other solutions have a larger grain size. In Linda and Orca, one-to-many communication is expressed implicitly, by having one process generate data for multiple receivers. It depends on the implementation of the language whether real (hardware) multicast is used. In many cases, multicast will be simulated in software through multiple point-to-point messages, which is less efficient.

In both SR and Emerald, one-to-many communication is expressed through point-to-point messages. In SR, they are invoked concurrently, in Emerald sequentially. In neither case does the implementation use hardware multicast. In Emerald, there is an additional problem due to the lack of a call-by-value parameter mode.

5. ACCESS TO REPLICATED SHARED DATA

The third communication pattern we will study is that of distributed processes accessing shared data. Of course, in a distributed system there is no true shared memory, so for such architectures, the sharing is logical rather than physical.

The particular example we will look at is a shared variable that is read frequently and written infrequently. Such a variable can be implemented efficiently on a distributed system by replicating it in the local memories of the processors. Each processor can directly read the variable. Physical communication only occurs when the variable is written. Since we assume that the read/write ratio is very high, the communication overhead will be low.

This example occurs in parallel branch-and-bound algorithms, where the bound is a globally-shared variable. In the Traveling Salesman Problem (TSP), for example, the bound is the length of the shortest route for the salesman found so far. It is used for pruning partial solutions whose initial paths are already longer than the current best full route. This value is usually changed (improved) only a few times, but may be used millions of times by each processor. For TSP, we need the following two operations on a shared integer:

    update(value);   # store minimum of current and new value in the variable
    value := **read**();   # obtain current value of variable

The value of the global bound is monotonically decreasing, so the **update** operation should never increase the value. Also note that the operations must be *atomic*. The effect of simultaneous updates must be the same as that of consecutive updates (i.e., the result must be serializable).

Simple though it may seem, for many languages this communication pattern is hard to implement efficiently. Below, we will look at four different solutions of increasing complexity:

- Distributed shared memory (Orca)
- Simulating shared variables with tuples (Linda)
- Simulating shared variables with implicitly received messages (SR and Emerald)
- Simulating shared variables with explicitly received messages (Parlog)

Distributed Shared Memory Solution (Orca)

By far the simplest solution is obtained in Orca, which supports a Distributed Shared Memory model. The shared variable is put in a data object shared among all processes. The run time system automatically replicates the object in the local memories, so processes can directly read the value. Whenever the object is changed, all copies are updated immediately, by broadcasting the new value. Moreover, atomicity of the operations is already guaranteed by the language. The Orca code for updating and reading the shared object looks like this:

```
update(value) ≡      min$update(value);
value := read() ≡    value := min$read();
```

where *min* is the shared object containing the global bound. The implementation of this object is trivial.

This solution is both simple and efficient. The only overhead in reading the value is that of a local operation invocation. When the variable is changed, its new value is broadcast to all processors containing a copy.

The other languages do not support Distributed Shared Memory. SR only allows processes on the same machine to share variables. Parlog provides shared logical variables, but these can be assigned only once. Emerald provides a shared address space for all its objects, but it does not replicate mutable objects. Clearly, storing the variable in one object (and thus on one processor) would be highly inefficient. Finally, Linda comes closest to the DSM model, by providing a global Tuple Space with operations to add, read, and delete elements. Below, we will look at different ways of simulating shared variables in these other languages, starting with Linda.

Simulating Shared Variables with Tuples (Linda)

In theory, a shared variable can be simulated in Linda by storing it in Tuple Space. The atomic **update** operation can then be implemented as:

```
update(value) ≡
    in("minimum", ? &min);        # read and delete tuple
    if (value < min) min = value;  # is the new value really better ?
    out("minimum", min);           # put new minimum back in Tuple Space
```

The variable can be read by reading the tuple:

```
value := read() ≡    rd("minimum", ? &value);    # read current minimum,
                                                   # leaving the tuple unaffected
```

This simple solution makes heavy demands on the implementation of Tuple Space, however. Since the global bound is read millions of times, the overhead of reading it must be very low. This means that each processor should have a local copy of the tuple. Not all Tuple Space implementations have this property. The hypercube and Transputer implementations mentioned above, for example, store each tuple on only a single processor. An additional performance problem is the associative addressing of Tuple Space. Part of this overhead can be optimized away,[16] but it is not clear whether it can be eliminated entirely. So, whether or not the above solution is practical, depends on the implementation.

Simulating Shared Variables with Implicitly Received Messages (SR and Emerald)

In languages that do not support shared data at all, the shared variable will have to be simulated through message passing. Each processor can keep its own local copy, which is used for reading. Whenever the variable is written, all these copies have to be updated in a consistent way. One simple solution is to send updates through a central *BoundManager* process, which forwards them as *UpdateCopy* messages to all other processes.

A problem with this scheme is the asynchronous nature of updates. Assume that we have one computational process per processor (as in the replicated workers style). This process may receive *UpdateCopy* messages at any point of time. For languages providing *implicit* message receipt, this is no problem, since a new process will be created for handling the message. In SR, for example, the following operation can be used for handling *UpdateCopy* messages:

```
proc UpdateCopy(Value)      # update local copy of the bound
    P(mutex)                    # lock the copy, using a semaphore
    if value <= minimum ->      # ignore higher values
        minimum := value        # "minimum" is the local copy
    fi
    V(mutex)                    # unlock copy
end UpdateMinimum
```

Whenever this operation is invoked, a new process will be created to handle it. This process runs in parallel with the computational process. They can both access the local copy of the shared variable. To prevent race conditions, this variable is protected by a lock (mutex). The new process first locks the local copy of the variable, then updates it, and finally unlocks it.

In Emerald, a similar solution is possible, since operations in Emerald are also handled implicitly. The main difference with the SR solution is the usage of a monitor (rather than locks) for synchronizing access to the local copy of the shared variable.

Simulating Shared Variables with Explicitly Received Messages (Parlog)

In languages where messages can be accepted only explicitly (by an existing process) a different approach is required. One obvious solution is to use an extra local process for handling all incoming *UpdateCopy* messages. However, this solution is only applicable if the extra process and the computational process can share variables. So, some form of light-weight threads is needed. In languages lacking this support (and also lacking implicit message receipt), this approach clearly does not work.

A solution is to let the computational process itself periodically check for incoming messages. For example, in a TSP program using replicated workers style parallelism, a worker could check before starting a new job. If an *UpdateCopy* message comes in during execution of the job, it will not be noticed until the next job is started.

This solution is employed in our Parlog TSP program.[8] The global bound is represented as a stream of decreasing values. To update the bound, a new value is appended to the end of the stream. If a process needs to know the current best value, it scans the stream until the end. Since scanning the stream is expensive, it is done only occasionally (e.g., when starting a new job).

Unfortunately, delaying the updates of the local copy has a high penalty: the search overhead is increased considerably.[7] Because workers temporarily use inferior values for the global bound, they will do less pruning and search more paths than necessary. To compensate, the frequency of checking for updates can be increased, although this will incur a computational overhead.

Summary

Orca has the support for logically shared data as a design goal, so it is no surprise that communication through shared data is easy to express in this language.

For Linda, we represent the shared variable as a tuple in TS. Unlike regular shared variables, however, tuples are addressed associatively. It depends on the TS implementation strategy whether the same efficiency as for Orca is obtained. If, for example, a **rd** on TS involves communication, this approach is unlikely to be efficient.

In the other languages, shared variables can be simulated through message passing, by replicating them in the local memories. The ability to accept messages implicitly was shown to be useful here. In the absence of implicit message receipt, the computational process must occasionally check for update messages, with the risk of delaying updates. Note that Linda does not have this facility, so if the solution described earlier is inefficient, programmers will have to resort to periodic checks.

6. DISCUSSION

In the previous three sections we have looked at how the five languages deal with three example communication patterns. The results of this study are summarized in Table 2.

	Mailboxes	One-to-many communication	Replicated shared data
SR	Buffer process	Concurrent send	Messages with implicit receive
Emerald	Shared-object message queue	Point-to-point messages	Messages with implicit receive
Parlog	Buffer process	Solution with fine-grained parallelism	Messages with explicit receive
Linda	Distr. data structure message queue	Shared data	Shared tuple (or m.p. with explicit receive)
Orca	Shared-object message queue	Shared data	Distributed shared memory

Table 2. Summary of the solutions taken for all five languages to the three communication patterns.

Of course, there are far more patterns we could have looked at. A recent survey paper by Andrews mentions the following other paradigms for distributed process interactions: filters, heartbeat, probe/echo, and token-passing.[2] Even though our list of communication patterns necessarily is incomplete, we think we can draw some interesting conclusions about the languages we have studied. In this section, we will re-examine all five languages and discuss what we feel are their most profound strengths and weaknesses. In addition, we will address one other important issue: the ease of learning each language.

Synchronizing Resources (SR)

Given its ambitious goal of supporting many communication models, it is not surprising that SR is a fairly large language. Yet, we found it reasonably easy to learn. With regard to the sequential parts, the syntax, type system, and module constructs are different from most other languages. Nevertheless, these were fairly easy to learn, although the type system is far from perfect.[6]

SR tries to reduce the number of concepts for distributed and parallel programming by using an *orthogonal* design. There are two ways for sending messages (blocking and nonblocking) and two ways for accepting messages (explicit and implicit). These can be combined in all four ways, yielding four different communication mechanisms. We agree with the designers that this orthogonality principle simplifies SR's design. Unfortunately, there also are some less elegant design features. The concurrent-send (co) command, for example, is a rather ad-hoc extension of the basic model, with specialized syntax rules.

Since SR provides so many communication primitives, it is a flexible language. It is also more expressive than most other message passing languages. For example, SR allows messages to be accepted conditionally or in a certain order, both based on the message's parameters. For certain algorithms (e.g., disk scheduling) this is more expressive than, say, Ada's **accept** statement, which does not allow the guards to use the parameters of incoming messages.

It can be argued, however, that message passing is a low level of abstraction. Indeed, for several applications, other mechanisms are simpler to use than message passing. These higher-level mechanisms are frequently more expressive yet less flexible. In conclusion, SR is reasonably suited for virtually all applications. It is seldom spectacularly good or bad for any application.

Emerald

Emerald is an object-based language. It treats all entities as objects, but, unlike object-*oriented* languages, it does not support inheritance. Nonwithstanding its object-based nature, Emerald contains many constructs also found in procedural languages (e.g., nested scopes, functions, expressions, assignment and control statements). The type system is one of the more important contributions of the language. It is not easy to get used to, but it is flexible and features static type checking and polymorphism.

Support for parallel and distributed programming in Emerald is best understood using two levels of abstraction. At the highest level, we have concurrent objects that invoke each other's operations in a synchronous (blocking) way, certainly a nice and simple abstraction. To see what is really going on, we need to look at how invocations are implemented and synchronized. Here, we are at the level of *monitors*, which, although well understood, cannot be regarded as a high-level abstraction by today's standards. This clearly shows of in the implementation code: most of our Emerald programs are significantly longer than their counterparts in the other languages.

For parallel programming, Emerald is less flexible than SR. It provides only one form of interprocess communication: synchronous remote procedure calls that are accepted implicitly. The parameter mechanism is simple and consistent (call-by-reference is used throughout), but copying parameters is a nuisance. In principle, call-by-value parameters could have been allowed for passive objects (not containing a process). This extension would have made the parameter mechanism less uniform, however, and would have created a distinction between active and passive objects.

Emerald probably is more suitable for distributed applications (e.g., electronic mail, name servers) than for parallel applications. For such distributed applications, features like object migration and location independent invocations are more beneficial and the need for copying objects (e.g., electronic mailboxes) will be less.

Parlog

The time needed for learning Parlog depends entirely on ones background education in concurrent logic programming. The language itself is quite simple. In addition, there are certain programming idioms one should master, such as streams and objects built with shared logical variables.

The shared logical variable is at a higher level of abstraction than message passing. For some applications, it is spectacularly expressive. Our Parlog program for ASP, for example, is just as simple as the original *sequential* algorithm. The synchronization of the parallel tasks is done implicitly, using suspension on unbound logical variables. On the negative side, it is not clear whether the program will run efficiently on a realistic large-scale parallel system.

For other applications, shared logical variables are less suitable, but one can then fall back on message passing through streams, which is easy to implement in logic languages. The resulting programs frequently have a structure similar to those written in a message passing language.

Linda

Of all five languages discussed in this paper, Linda undoubtedly is the simplest one to learn. It adds only a few simple primitives to an existing base language. Despite this simplicity, Linda also is fairly flexible. Most communication patterns are easy to express in the language.

Most of the criticism in the literature on Linda is related to efficiency. The associative addressing and global visibility of the Tuple Space have led many people to believe that Linda cannot be implemented efficiently. However, its implementors have made considerable progress during the past few years in optimizing the performance on several machines. The **rd** operation, for example, hardly ever scans the entire Tuple Space, but typically uses hashing or something even more efficient. Just as with virtual memory, however, there will probably always remain cases where the high-level easy-to-program approach will not be optimal.

An important decision in Linda (and Orca) is to hide the physical distribution of data from the user. In contrast, Emerald gives the programmer control over the placement of data, by supporting user-initiated object migration. The Linda approach is simpler, but it makes heavier demands on the implementation. Again, the transparent approach will sometimes be less efficient, but it remains to be seen how big the differences in performance are for actual programs.

Orca

Orca is a new language rather than an extension to an existing sequential language. An important disadvantage of extending a base language is the difficulty of implementing pointers and global variables on systems lacking shared memory. These problems can more easily be avoided if the language is designed from scratch. Orca, for example, supports first-class *graph* variables rather than pointers. Unlike pointers, graphs can freely be moved or copied from one machine to another. Of course, this also implies that programmers have to learn a new language. The design of Orca has been kept as simple as possible, however, so this disadvantage should not be overestimated.

Orca is *not* an object-based language; it merely provides abstract data types. It supports both active processes and passive data-objects. Since objects in Orca are purely passive, they can be replicated, which is a very important goal in the implementation.

An important difference with Linda is the support for user-defined, high-level operations on shared data.[27] Linda only provides a fixed number of built-in operations on tuples, but Orca allows programmers to construct their own atomic operations, which can be of arbitrary complexity. Unlike Linda, Orca uses direct rather than associative addressing of shared data, and thus avoids any problems with associative addressing.

For some applications, Orca has important advantages over most other languages. Programs that need logically shared data are easy to implement in Orca and are very efficient. Orca also is one of the few languages that uses physical broadcasting in its implementation. As we have seen, for ASP this is of critical importance. On the other hand, there also are cases where the model is less efficient, for example when plain point-to-point message passing is required.

ACKNOWLEDGEMENTS

The author is grateful to the Department of Computer Science at the University of Arizona and the Department of Computing at Imperial College for receiving him as an academic visitor. Also, he would like to thank Nick Carriero, Greg Andrews, Dave Bakken, Gregg Townsend, Mike Coffin, Norman Hutchinson, Keith Clark, Jim Crammond, and Andrew Davison for the discussions on their languages. The work on Linda has been done in cooperation with Frans Kaashoek. Erik Baalbergen, Arnold Geels, Frans Kaashoek, and Andy Tanenbaum provided useful comments on the paper.

REFERENCES

1. Ahuja, S., Carriero, N., and Gelernter, D., "Linda and Friends," *IEEE Computer* 19(8), pp. 26-34 (Aug. 1986).

2. Andrews, G.R., "Paradigms for Process Interaction in Distributed Programs," TR 89-24, University of Arizona, Tucson, AZ (Oct. 1989).

3. Andrews, G.R. and Olsson, R.A., "The Evolution of the SR Programming Language," *Distributed Computing* 1, pp. 133-149 (July 1986).

4. Andrews, G.R., Olsson, R.A., Coffin, M., Elshoff, I., Nilsen, K., Purdin, T., and Townsend, G., "An Overview of the SR Language and Implementation," *ACM Trans. Program. Lang. Syst.* 10(1), pp. 51-86 (Jan. 1988).

5. Andrews, G.R. and Schneider, F.B., "Concepts and Notations for Concurrent Programming," *ACM Computing Surveys* 15(1), pp. 3-43 (March 1983).

6. Bal, H.E., "An Evaluation of the SR Language Design," IR-219, Vrije Universiteit, Amsterdam, The Netherlands (August 1990).

7. Bal, H.E., *Programming Distributed Systems,* Silicon Press, Summit, NJ (1990).

8. Bal, H.E., "Heuristic Search in PARLOG using Replicated Worker Style Parallelism," Research Report, Vrije Universiteit, Amsterdam, The Netherlands (May 1990).

9. Bal, H.E., "Fault-tolerant Parallel Programming in Argus," IR-214, Vrije Universiteit, Amsterdam, The Netherlands (May 1990).

10. Bal, H.E., Kaashoek, M.F., and Tanenbaum, A.S., "A Distributed Implementation of the Shared Data-object Model," *USENIX/SERC Workshop on Experiences with Building Distributed and Multiprocessor Systems*, Ft. Lauderdale, FL., pp. 1-19 (Oct. 1989).

11. Bal, H.E., Kaashoek, M.F., and Tanenbaum, A.S., "Experience with Distributed Programming in Orca," *Proc. IEEE CS 1990 Int. Conf. on Computer Languages*, New Orleans, LA, pp. 79-89 (March 1990).

12. Bal, H.E., Steiner, J.G., and Tanenbaum, A.S., "Programming Languages for Distributed Computing Systems," *ACM Computing Surveys* 21(3), pp. 261-322 (Sept. 1989).

13. Bal, H.E. and Tanenbaum, A.S., "Distributed Programming with Shared Data," *Proc. IEEE CS 1988 Int. Conf. on Computer Languages*, Miami, FL, pp. 82-91 (Oct. 1988).

14. Bjornson, R., Carriero, N., and Gelernter, D., "The Implementation and Performance of Hypercube Linda," Report RR-690, Yale University, New Haven, CT (March 1989).

15. Black, A., Hutchinson, N., Jul, E., Levy, H., and Carter, L., "Distribution and Abstract Types in Emerald," *IEEE Trans. Softw. Eng.* SE-13(1), pp. 65-76 (Jan. 1987).

16. Carriero, N., "The Implementation of Tuple Space Machines," Research Report 567 (Ph.D. dissertation), Yale University, New Haven, CT (Dec. 1987).

17. Carriero, N. and Gelernter, D., "The S/Net's Linda Kernel," *ACM Trans. Comp. Syst.* 4(2), pp. 110-129 (May 1986).

18. Carriero, N. and Gelernter, D., "How to Write Parallel Programs: A Guide to the Perplexed," *ACM Comp. Surveys* 21(3), pp. 323-357 (Sept. 1989).

19. Carriero, N. and Gelernter, D., "Linda in Context," *Commun. ACM* 32(4), pp. 444-458 (April 1989).

20. Carriero, N., Gelernter, D., and Leichter, J., "Distributed Data Structures in Linda," *Proc. 13th ACM Symp. Princ. Progr. Lang.*, St. Petersburg, FL, pp. 236-242 (Jan. 1986).

21. Clark, K.L., "PARLOG and Its Applications," *IEEE Trans. Softw. Eng.* **SE-14**(12), pp. 1792-1804 (Dec. 1988).

22. Clark, K.L. and Gregory, S., "PARLOG: Parallel Programming in Logic," *ACM Trans. Program. Lang. Syst.* **8**(1), pp. 1-49 (Jan. 1986).

23. Conlon, T., *Programming in PARLOG,* Addison-Wesley, Wokingham, England (1989).

24. Floyd, R.W., "Algorithm 97: Shortest Path," *Commun. ACM* **5**, p. 345 (1962).

25. Gregory, S., *Parallel Logic Programming in PARLOG,* Addison-Wesley, Wokingham, England (1987).

26. Jul, E., Levy, H., Hutchinson, N., and Black, A., "Fine-Grained Mobility in the Emerald System," *ACM Trans. Comp. Syst.* **6**(1), pp. 109-133 (Feb. 1988).

27. Kaashoek, M.F., Bal, H.E., and Tanenbaum, A.S., "Experience with the Distributed Data Structure Paradigm in Linda," *USENIX Workshop on Experiences with Building Distributed and Multiprocessor S ystems*, Ft. Lauderdale, FL., pp. 175-191 (Oct. 1989).

28. Kaashoek, M.F., Tanenbaum, A.S., Flynn Hummel, S., and Bal, H.E., "An Efficient Reliable Broadcast Protocol," *Operating Systems Review* **23**(4), pp. 5-20 (Oct. 1989).

29. Kahn, K. M. and Miller, M.S., "Technical Correspondence on "Linda in Context"," *Comm. ACM* **32**(10), pp. 1253-1255 (Oct. 1989).

30. Li, K. and Hudak, P., "Memory Coherence in Shared Virtual Memory Systems," *ACM Trans. Computer Systems* **7**(4), pp. 321-359 (Nov. 1989).

31. Liskov, B., "Distributed Programming in Argus," *Commun. ACM* **31**(3), pp. 300-312 (March 1988).

32. Mullender, S.J., Rossum, G. van, Tanenbaum, A.S., Renesse, R. van, and Staveren, H. van, "Amoeba: A Distributed Operating System for the 1990s," *IEEE Computer* **23**(5), pp. 44-53 (May 1990).

33. Shapiro, E., "Technical Correspondence on "Linda in Context"," *Comm. ACM* **32**(10), pp. 1244-1249 (Oct. 1989).

34. Zenith, S.E., "Linda Coordination Language; Subsystem Kernel Architecture (on Transputers)," RR-794, Yale University, New Haven, CT (May 1990).

RELATIONAL ALGEBRA OPERATIONS

Kjell Bratbergsengen
Department of Computer Science
The Norwegian Institute of Technology
University of Trondheim
NORWAY[1]

1.   INTRODUCTION

This work is done through a long period beginning in 1977. The new methods, based on hashing - for realizing relational algebra operations were presented in the Singapore [Brat84] in 1984. They were also briefly mentioned in a paper on network topologies presented in 1980 [Brat80]. The methods had by then been programmed into the TechRa database system, [Brat83], [Tech85]. The fundamental problem of all relational algebra operations, except selection - is to find matching records within one operand or two different operands. The relational algebra operations differ in the way resulting records are selected.

In this paper a compact and systematic method of realizing relational algebra operations is described. The methods have been realized and tested on two parallel computers, the CROSS8 and the HC16-186 . The CROSS8 project started in 1985 and the major tests were run during spring and summer 1987. The results were presented in [Brat87]. This paper also describes the CROSS8 hardware. CROSS8 consisted of 8 nodes each built around the Intel 186 processor. CROSS8 had a direct connection between all nodes. Building the HC16-186 started in 1987 and was finished a year later. This was a 16 node system and they were now interconnected through a hypercubic network. The relational algebra programs were ported to the HC16-186 and a new set of tests were taken. These results are presented in [Brat89], [Brat89b] and [BraGje89]. O ne motive for building another parallel machine was to see whether the methods scaled well for larger networks. Another motive was to test the hypercube network and it's capacity for relocating records.

A number of other algorithms has been implemented and tested on CROSS8 and HC16-186. Especially we would like to mention the parallel sorting programs developed by Jarle Greipsland and Bjørn A. Baugstø. Their work is described in a number of published papers, among others [BaGr89] and [BaGrKa90]

2.   DEFINITION OF A SET OF RELATIONAL ALGEBRA OPERATIONS

CROSS8, HC16-186 and HC-386 are relational algebra computers. Their instruction set is relational algebra operations. The array of node computers are controlled by a supervisory computer. The supervisor will get SQL statements from a host computer. The supervisor will do the parsing of the SQL - statements and translate SQL into a partially ordered sequence of relational algebra operations - the algebra tree. Later the algebra tree may be optimized, i.e. finding equivalent algebra trees which is faster to execute. The supervisor might also get algebra trees directly from the host computer.

We will not handle optimization in this paper, rather we will emphasize on the set of relational algebra operations and methods for their execution on a parallel database computer.

1 This work has been supported by The Royal Norwegian Council for Scientific and Industrial Research (NTNF), Intel Norway AS, Nordisk Elektronik AS and Eltron AS.

2. 1 The Basic Relational Algebra Operations

We have to define a useful set of relational algebra operations. First we describe a set of more or less standard operations, then we extend this set to more powerful routines.

Selection   R = A[P]. Select records satisfying a given predicate, P.

Projection   R = A {C}. Remove fields not named in C from result records. If C excludes key attributes then duplicate records must be searched for and removed from R.

Join   R = A ⊗ B. Equi join.

Union   R=A ∪ B. The two operands must at least have the key attributes in common.

Difference   R=A - B. The two operands are in principle of the same type. A more flexible interpretation of the operation is to demand that the B records contains at least a set of compatible key attributes. Only records from the A operand are transferred to R.

Intersection   R = A ∩ B. Only identical records are transferred to the result table. A more relaxed interpretation is to copy records from A to R and then delete records in R are not found in B.

Cross   R = A × B. Cross product. All combinations are of A and B records are added to R.

Division   R = A + B. This is a grouping operation. Records in A are grouped on certain attributes. Records in R contain grouping attributes and to become a result record all B records must be found in the group.

Aggregate   R = A(G,S). Aggregation is related to the division operation. Records with the same key values are forming a group. The key attributes are defined in G. What to do with the records within a group is defined in S.

Included   b = A ⊆ B This and the next operation are different. The result is a boolean value not a table. b is set to true if all records in A are found in B. The operation must also define a set of compatible attributes. The other attributes are not used in the operation.

Equal   b = A ≡ B . b is true if the two operands are identical, the same number of records and the same set of records are found in both operands.

The description and notation above is not complete. Instead of refining the above descriptions we would like to redefine and extend the functionality of the operations. One main cost factor in query execution is to move records from one table to another table. We would try to minimize the number of table moves and this can be done by combining operations. A selection can be applied at every point where data are flowing by. The same is true for projection, or more precisely projection without duplicate removal. To distinguish between true projection and stripping off attributes without duplicate removal we denote the latter **reduction**. It is important to apply reduction where possible to reduce the volume of data as early as possible. In our set of extended operations, selection and reduction is applied to all input tables and all output tables.

2. 2 A Set of Composite Relational Algebra Procedures.

A composite relational algebra procedure allows for selection and reduction on all input and output tables. A table is then described in this way: T:s:r. T is the table name, s is a selector or predicate on record attributes and constants and r is a list of attribute names or column names. Attribute names are separated by one or more spaces. If one wants to change the attribute name the new name follows a slash. Each algebra procedure is in itself now a rather powerful primitive. Using the familiar database in C.J. Date's book, [Date90] the SQL statement:

SELECT SNO FROM SP WHERE QTY > 300
UNION[1]
SELECT SNO FROM S WHERE CITY = "Trondheim" ;

can be translated into one composite algebra procedure call:

UNION (SP: QTY>300: SNO: *, S: CITY="Trondheim": SNO: *, R);

The star (*) denotes all attributes. Attributes named in the third :field are key attributes or the part of the record used when checking for duplicates.

When appropriate we also have to define key attributes, grouping attributes, comparing attributes, etc. in the different operations. We will now define a set of routines and explain the different parameters as they appear.

2. 3　　　　　　　　　　Composite Procedure Definitions

PROJECT (A:s:r, R::r);

It is not reasonable to allow selection on the output table because this selection is done on the input table. Reduction applies strangely enough. Duplicates are removed based on attributes of the reduced input table, R might be further reduced, but no possible new duplicates are removed this time.

SELECT (A:s:r, R);

No selection or reduction is applicable to the output operand. Renaming of attributes could be allowed, however.

Example:

SELECT (SP: SNO>123 AND QTY >= 400: *,

　　　　TSP: : SNO/SUPPLIERNO PNO/PARTNO QTY/QUANTITY);

There is no need to have a separate SELECT procedure as it is directly replaced by PROJECT.

JOIN (A:s:r:k, B:s:r:k, R:s:r) ;

Another attribute list is appended to the two input operands. The join keys of the two operands has to be named. Quite complex SQL statements can be executed by only one composite JOIN operation.

Example:

SELECT PNO, COLOR , QTY, INSTOCK
　　　FROM SP, P
　　　WHERE P.WEIGHT > 12.5 AND QTY > INSTOCK AND SP.PNO = P.PNO;

This composite algebra procedure will do the processing:

JOIN　　　(P: WEIGHT > 13.5: PNO COLOR WEIGHT INSTOCK: PNO,
　　　　　SP: : PNO QTY: PNO,
　　　　　T: QTY > INSTOCK: PNO COLOR QTY INSTOCK);

UNION (A:s:r:k, B:s:r:k, R:s:r);

k is a list of attribute names. The two lists A:k and B:k must define compatible attributes. Another problem here is whether we should assume A and B to be free from duplicates at the outset. The answer is simple however, after applying both a selector s, and a reducer r to the input tables it is not reasonable to assume them to be duplicate free. UNION is then programmed as a PROJECT but with the input file com-

---

[1] Remember that UNION automatically deletes duplicates in SQL. To keep duplicates use UNION ALL. This is different from SELECT as SELECT does not by default delete duplicates.

ing from two different tables. It is tempting to generalize UNION to an arbitrary number of input files, varying from 1 to n. This generalized UNION replaces PROJECT and SELECT.

DIFF (A:s:r:k, B:s:r:k, R:s:r);

Only records from A are moved to R. A:k and B:k are the attributes tested for equality. Therefore it is meaningless to have B:r <> B:k

INTERSECT (A:s:r:k, B:s:r:k, R:s:r);

We interpret this function to let only A records be included in R. Only records found in both tables are included. The set of attributes tested is A:k and B:k. As for DIFF it is also here meaningless to let B:k<> B:r.

CROSS (A:s:r, B:s:r, R:s:r);

The cross product will need a selector on all tables. A SQL statements which can be translated to a CROSS operation is:

        SELECT SNO, SNAME, PNO, S.CITY, P.CITY
            FROM P, S
                WHERE P.CITY < S.CITY;

This is translated into:

CROSS (S: : SNO SNAME CITY/SCITY, P: : PNO CITY/PCITY, T: PCITY < SCITY :);

DIVIDE (A:s:r:g:c, B:s:r:c, R:s:r) ;

Two new lists are introduced. g represents the grouping attributes and c the set of attributes which has to be found within each group. Division is used to find objects which are related to a group of other objects.

Example:

Find supplier number for suppliers who supply all parts.

        SELECT DISTINCT SNO FROM SP
            WHERE NOT EXISTS
                (SELECT * FROM P
                    WHERE NOT EXISTS
                        (SELECT * FROM SP
                            WHERE SP.PNO = P.PNO));

This expression is translated to:

DIVIDE (SP:: SNO PNO:SNO: PNO, P::PNO:PNO, T::) ;

Only grouping attributes are included in the result table.

AGGREGATE(A:s:r:g:f, R:s:r) ;

As above g defines a set of grouping attributes. f is new and f defines a set of aggregate operations. f consists of an operator and a list of attribute names. The selector in the result table is used to execute HAVING clauses in SQL. The SQL statement:

        SELECT DISTINCT PNO, COUNT (*), MAX(QTY), SUM(QTY)
            FROM SP
            WHERE SNO > S10
            GROUP BY PNO
            HAVING SUM(QTY) > 1000 ;

is translated to:

AGGREGATE (SP: SNO>S10: PNO QTY : PNO: COUNT() MAX(QTY) SUM(QTY)/SUMQ,

      T: SUMQ>1000 :);

b = INCLUDED (A:s:k, B:s:k) ;

No new table is produced, only a boolean value b. b is true if all records in A:s:k is found in B:s:k, otherwise b is set to false. A:k and B:k have to denote a compatible set of attributes.

b = EQUAL (A:s:k, B:s:k) ;

The two tables must be identical to get a true b. The same conditions as for INCLUDE applies.

2. 4   Some More Elaborate Examples

Having defined a set of composite relational algebra operations we will demonstrate its power on a more complex example. We are still using the Date database. We will state a problem in prose, then present an answer to it in SQL and at last a translation of the SQL statement into a series of composite relational algebra operations.

Problem 1:

Find supplier names for those who supplies yellow parts.

SQL:

SELECT SNAME

    FROM S, SP, P

        WHERE COLOR = "Yellow" AND P.PNO= SP.PNO AND SP.SNO = S.SNO ;

Composite algebra:

JOIN (P:COLOR="Yellow":PNO: PNO, SP::SNO PNO: PNO, TEMP::SNO) ;

JOIN (TEMP:::SNO, S::SNO SNAME: SNO, RESULT::SNAME);

Problem 2:

Find supplier names for those who do not supply part P2 or any part at all.

SQL:

SELECT SNAME FROM S

    WHERE NOT EXISTS

        (SELECT * FROM SP

            WHERE S.SNO=SP.SNO AND SP.PNO="P2") ;

Composite algebra:

PROJECT (SP:PNO="P2":SNO PNO, TEMP::SNO);

DIFF (S::SNO SNAME: SNO, TEMP:::SNO, RESULT::SNAME);

First we find all suppliers of P2. This list is stored in TEMP. Then we use this list for removing all records from the S table which is also found in TEMP. At this point we see the usage of the composite difference function where we can specify distinct lists for "projection" (reduction) and operand keys.

3. THE EXECUTION OF RELATIONAL ALGEBRA OPERATIONS, OVERALL STRATEGY

3.1 The Basic Problem

The fundamental problem for all the traditionally "heavy" algebra operations are to find matching records. This is true for projection (delete matching records), join (concatenate matching records), union and difference (delete matching records), intersection (keep matching records) and for division and aggregation (group matching records). Selection and insertion, update and deletion of *single* records are regarded as simple operations which are also easy to parallelize.

When choosing a general strategy we should also consider load distribution and load balancing in a parallel system. Simple operations like insertion and deletion of single records should both go fast and use few resources. Heavy operations should employ all nodes in a balanced manner. Our basic algorithms for doing relational algebra operations on a parallel computer system were developed during the years 1977 to 1980 in the ASTRA project [SmiBro83].

3.1.1 A Classical Split and Conquer Algorithm

To find matching keys we use a traditional split and conquer algorithm. Records of a table are spread out evenly on each node. When we want to test whether two records have equal values in some given fields we let them meet on the same node. Which node - is computed using a hash formula with the operation key as hash key. Using this technique we know for certain that if two records have the same operation key they will eventually end up at the same node. We might call this strategy a *rendez vous* method or a partitioning hash method, the former is preferred. With this strategy we have to reallocate all but 1/n of all records of the operands. n is the umber of nodes. After redistribution, the actual algebra operation can be completed locally within one node without further communication with neighboring nodes.

The original problem is converted to n smaller problems, each of size $\frac{V}{n}$ if V represents the size of the original problem. The extra cost of partitioning, mainly reallocating records - is of order $O\left(\frac{V}{n}\right)$. Cost reduction because of reduced problem size is depending on the cost of the basic method - the same method we are using in each node. The worst methods makes better use of partitioning, relatively speaking. However they have a worse starting point. For instance will $O(V)$-methods be best compared with $O(V^2)$-methods while $T_{nl} < T_{hj}$, i. e. $\frac{c \times V^2}{n^2} < \frac{c \times V}{n} \rightarrow V < n$ assuming the constant factor to be the same for both methods.

	1 processor	n node processors	improvement factor
Nested loop methods	$O(V^2)$	$O\left(\frac{V}{n}\right)^2$	n^2
Sort based methods	$O(V \times \log_2 V)$	$O\left(\frac{V}{n} \times \log_2 \frac{V}{n}\right)$	$\dfrac{n \times \log_2 V}{\log_2 V - \log_2 n}$
Hash based methods	$O(V)$	$O\left(\frac{V}{n}\right)$	n

Table 1   Time consumption for different groups of algebra methods. Their relative improvement used at a monoprocessor system to a multi processor system is shown. The improvement is due to partitioning the original problem.

3. 2 Data Distribution

Relations are distributed evenly to all nodes. A hash formula is currently used to determine the resident node, but other methods could as well be used. The hash function is applied to the primary key of the records. Storing records will engage only one node, the target node. Searching for records when the exact value of primary key is known is also engaging only the target node. This opens up for parallel insertion, update and deletion of single records with primary key given. HC16-186/386 performance of transaction type processing should then be greatly enhanced compared to traditional systems. This is now more or less a traditional way of distributing records. This method has been proven by many researchers, see for instance [Cope88].

3. 3 Indexes Are Mostly Used for Selection

The most time consuming algebra operations requires a complete scan of both (only one operand in the case of projection and aggregate) operands. This may be avoided if we have an index on at least one of the fields in the selection predicate. Index fields are not used for complex algebra operations. Indexes are only utilized for selection. Therefore, indexes does not play an important role except for selection. Then there is very little difference between worst case and best case for relational algebra operations. The methods described *are* actually worst case methods, but these methods are so fast that they could be used generally and still outperform leading systems like INGRES [Astr79] and IDM [Ubel85].

3. 4 The Algorithm Is Parallel and Automatically Load Balancing

The method just described has some very nice properties. It is parallel in two dimensions. All nodes are working simultaneously, this is one dimension. Each record goes thru 4 steps. It is read from disk, it is reallocated, it is subject to a local algebra operation and at last, result records are written to disk. All these 4 steps are executed in parallel on each node. This is the second dimension of parallelism.

The first step in load balancing is the record distribution. Records are evenly spread out on all nodes. But the selection of input operands might disturb the uniform distribution. The reallocation will again try to spread the records thereby balancing the load. The worst case will be if the operation keys are all the same or limited to a few values. Then all records end up at the same node and local algebra and writing result records has to be done from the same node. However, this situation is not likely to occur for large operands. One should notice that there is no work wasted on special load balancing computations, load balancing is intrinsic to the method.

4. A BRIEF DESCRIPTION OF THE HC16-x86 HARDWARE PLATFORMS

Each node is a conventional single board computer based on one of the standard Intel processors. HC16-186 is using the Intel 186 with 10 MHz clock. It has 1MB of dynamic RAM, a SCSI disk interface and dual port RAMs for communication between nodes and communication between each node and a host computer. Each dual port RAM module is 2KB. The only special feature of the HC16-186 is the communication system based on dual ported RAM. The connection topology for internode communication is a hypercube. The hypercube is a good compromise between cost (number of lines) and connectivity or capacity. The only drawback with dual port RAM is that the local system bus has to be used for transporting data. This takes away processing capacity. We have considered to put an extra communication processor on each node, but the idea has been abandoned. It is better and more in the spirit of parallel systems to increase the number of nodes in stead of increasing the power of each node. The flexibility and versatility of dual ported RAM far outweigh the drawbacks. The communication capacity is closely connected to prcessor speed and the communication capacity automatically upgrade with processor speed.

The dual port hypercube interconnection system is easyly scalable from 4 nodes to large systems with 1024 nodes. With todays processor chips we can build database computers with up to 20000 MIPS processing capacity.

4. 1   Disk Transfer and Disk Storage Capacity

It is our policy to use high end mass produced disks. Each disk might have lower specifications than the more advanced disks, but we will build the necessary capacity by employing more disks. Mass produced disks has the lowest price/performance ratio. Getting data off the disks can often become a bottleneck. It has been made disks with parallel track read/write capabilities, see [AMPE78]. However, they are more expensive, less reliable and less flexible in use than standard disks. During the last three years disk technology is almost revolutionized. Price/performance ratio has sunken dramatically, and it is now technically and economically feasible to use large number of small and medium sized disks to get a high transfer rate.

We are of course not limited to have one disk or one SCSI interface for each node. Disk arrays where a number of disks are operated as one gives higher bandwidth and more reliable storage [PaGiKa88]. Still however, each disk has a transfer rate from 0.7 to 2.5 MB/s depending on disk type. This must be compared with node bus capacity which also has improved dramatically over the last years. For HC16-186 it was 2.5 MB/s, on HC16-386 it has increased to 13.3 MB/s and on HCxx-486 it can be somewhere between 33 and 80 MB/s. Disks are getting relatively slower!

To days mass produced, high end disks stores up to 1 GB. In a given system one should taylor the disk capacity to the user needs. Relatively small disks might be employed to reach the required access and data transfer capacity in an on line transaction processing system.

4. 2   Record Reallocation and Interconnection Network Capacity

After the records are transferred to memory, they may still have to be transferred to another node. Therefore the node interconnection network has to be powerful enough not to make this the bottleneck. Both the CROSS8 and the HyperCube networks are strong on redistribution capacity. The accumulated relocation capacity of the CROSS8 network was 5.3 MB pr. second, on the HC16-186 it is 13.3 MB/s and on the HC16-386 it is increased to 42.7 MB/s.

Dual port RAM is memory shared by neighbors. The bus to this common memory is 16 bits wide. Having a 32 bit local bus we can write a formula for the theoretical absolute maximum relocation capacity.

The relocation capacity is: $R = \dfrac{2^{D+1}}{t \times (D+1)}$ D is the number of dimensions and t is the main memory access cycle time. Table 1 is showing the relocation capacity for different hypercubes and memory acces times.

Memory acces time in ns	D=number of hypercube dimensions								
	2	3	4	5	6	7	8	9	10
	4	8	16	32	64	128	256	512	1024
50	53	80	128	213	366	640	1138	2048	3724
100	27	40	64	107	183	320	569	1024	1862
150	18	27	43	71	122	213	379	1536	1241

Table 2   Relocation capacity (upper bound) in MB/s as a function of memory acces time and hypercube dimensions. The dual port RAM is 16 bits wide and the local system bus on each node is 32 bits wide. The memory access time is the same in both the main memory and the dual port memory

More data is normally transferred between disk and memory than between nodes. At least some part of the data are at the correct node from the beginning. Parts of records are projected out, and records are selected out after they are read from disk. With one disk on each node the accumulated disk transfer capacity is 24 MB/s on a 16 node system. This is relatively balanced for a HC16-386 system. Not all the CPU capacity should be used for reallocation alone.

In a database system for on line transaction processing (OLTP) the networks ability to conwey short and frequent messages might be of greater importance to performance than raw redistribution capacity. Several tests on the Hypercube interconnection system have been done and the interested reader is asked to see [AsTo90]. From their work we can see that the dual port RAM system compares very favourably with other hypercube systems, both on high bandwidth even for short messages and low latency.

5. THE SET OF BASIC OPERATIONS

5. 1 Finding Matching Records

The overall strategy is described in chapter 3. We are now left with the problem of performing relational algebra operations locally on each node.The basic methods are described in several papers, [BRAT84], [DeWi85] and [RiLuMi87]. The superiority of hashbased methods over sortbased methods is well accepted. Records from one operand are read into main memory or workspace. Then records are read one by one from the other operand and it is checked whether records stored in the workspace have the same key value or not. The search in the workspace can then be done in three principally different ways:

- 1. linear search
- 2. binary search if the work space is stored in a sorted order, or as a binary tree
- 3. hash lists, or hash tables.

The search times are of order $O(n)$, $O(\log_2 n)$ and $O(1)$ respectively. n is now the number of records in the work space, and n can be large because a large workspace gives good overall performance.

The different algebra operations are implemented using finite state machines. The description of each operation is also done this way. There is a set of elementary input or state transition conditions which must be described.

Input conditions to the finite state machine are:

normal	A record is available from the input file, and there is available space in work space area.
eof /eos	End of file on input file or input stream.
wsf	Work space is full.

The abnormal inputs, *eof/eos* and *wsf* trigger a state transition, the normal input condition does not. The actions taken during state transition vary from operation to operation. It is a rather well defined set of small operations, examples are: *switch to a new input file, initialize work space* or *write records in work space to result file*.

5. 2 Workspace

The workspace is a reservoir of records. Records in workspace are organized so it is easy and fast to find a record with a certain key or find records having keys within given limits. The data structure of the workspace may vary depending on the operation it is used for. If it is used for an equi join then some sort of hashed organization is preferred. Then we have to find records based on exact key values. If the operation is a more general join, some type of sorted order like binary trees would be better.

The organization of workspace might not be critical. More important is the size of the workspace. The workspace contains those records which are handled during one scan of some operand. If the workspace is small the same operand has to be scanned a number of times. Workspace for relational algebra operations is as important as sorting space is for sorting operations.

5. 2. 1   Operations on workspace

A number of operations can be defined on workspace. They can be grouped in two: operations at the record level and operations at the workspace level. Operations at the workspace level will involve all records in the workspace or the workspace organization itself.

Record level

At the record level, records are inserted and deleted. Records are found, their fields are combined with fields from other record and a resulting record is formed. Very often are different actions taken whether the new record already has a duplicate record in the workspace or not. Therefore we have defined at function

RelOp (MatchActions, NoMatchActions, Record)

which generalize most actions taken to workspace.These are:

Store	Record is stored in workspace.
Delete	If record is found in workspace it is deleted.
Make	Make a result record of the stored record and the new record. Write the composed record to the result file. Only at most one record is made, and which part of the two originals are found in descriptors.
MakeAll	The same as above, but all records matching the key of the input record are used as a source for composing new records. This operation is typically used in the join operation.
MakeDel	Make and delete. The matching record is used as a source, but then it is finito. It is deleted from workspace.
MakeGroup	Establish a new aggregate group in workspace. Used for aggregate operations
Aggregate	Do the aggregate operations on an identified aggregate group.
MakeTable	Establish a table of members from a stack of identifiers. Used in division.
Push	Push new member to the stack of identifiers. Used in division.
MarkGroup	The identified group has registered a new member. Used in division.
DelNCGroup	Delete non complete groups. Groups not having all their members registered are deleted. Used in division.
AddGroup	Add a new group. Used in division.

Workspace level

At the workspace level we have operations on the workspace as such or all records in the workspace. Defined operations are:

Iws	Initialize workspace.
Wws	Write workspace. All records of the workspace are written to the result file.
Sws	Sort workspace. All records of the workspace are sorted.

| Ppws | A special post processing stage. This routine is used for aggregate functions. When for example the aggregate function is to compute the average value of some field, the actions taken for each new record was to increase the number of records counted and add the field value to a sum. Before the work space records are written the average has to be computed and the record format justified. |

Input output operations

In the description of the actual algebra operations we generalize input and output. The first time a record is input to the algebra engine it is entered through the general input stream. The general input stream may consist of records from other nodes or from the disk on the local node. We handle this input stream as a file. The result records are also give to a generalized output stream. It is the stream handler which later determines whether this stream is to be sent to an other node or whether it is written to the local disk.

Records written to temporary files are handled by traditianal file functions.

Stream and file functions are:

OpenInput (T)	Open input stream for table records T
OpenOutput (T)	Open output stream, writing records to table T.
Input(t)	Read record from T
Output(t)	Write record to stream T
Open (F)	Open file F
Close (F)	Close file F
Erase (F)	Delete file F
Read (F,f)	Read record from F
Write (F,f)	Write f to file F
Mark (F)	Set a marker before current record on file F. Used by Pos(F)
Pos(F)	Position to last file mark set by Mark. Used for rereading a file
Reset(F)	Reset record pointer to first record. reread file from the beginning.

5. 2. 2 Use of Descriptors

In a real system record descriptors will be extensively used for describing which part of the record is the key, which parts are to be included in the resulting record, etc. Setting up descriptors is the responsibility of the supervisory program. A complete package of routines for moving and comparing records according to operation descriptors has to be available to the system implementor.

6. A DETAILED DESCRIPTION OF SOME SELECTED RELATIONAL ALGEBRA OPERATIONS

6. 1   Projection

Duplicate records are deleted. If two records have the same key one of these records is deleted. In phase 1 workspace is filled with records. During this process each new entry is checked for duplicates. If the new entry is a duplicate it is not stored. If the input table is empty before the workspace runs full, the workspace is written to the output table and the projection is complete. In this case the first duplicate record is the one stored. If the workspace becomes filled before all input records have been read, the projection proceeds differently. The remaining records of the input file are read and checked against the workspace. If a duplicate record is not found in workspace, the read record is written to a temporary file. When all records from the original input file is read, then the remaining records in the workspace is written to the result file.

We now have to remove duplicates from the temporary file. The temporary file is local and we should avoid rewriting of the temporary file if possible. We assume that the temporary file is so large that it may be read in several rounds. Again we start with filling workspace and at the same time throwing away duplicate records. The phase two is slightly different compared to the first scan of the file. We do not write input records to a new temporary file.

Instead we reread the temporary file from the first record which did not find space in the workspace in the preceding scan. As we are not able to exclude duplicates from the temporary file we are deleting duplicates from the workspace in stead. This strategy is profitable if the number of duplicates are small. If most records are duplicates it would have been better to write a new temporary file.

The transported volume in this operation is V. Let A be the volume of table A, R the volume of table R and M the size of workspace.

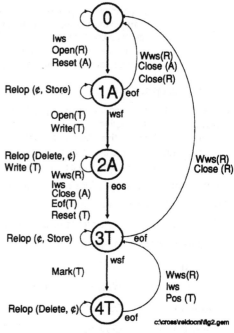

Fig. 1   State machine for multicomputer projection

A is read one time.

If A is larger than M then the temporary file T is written. T = A-M. Then T is repeatedly read, the first time all records in T, the second time T-M records are read, the third time T-2M and so on until all parts of T has been stored in workspace. The upper limit of repeatedly reading T is $V = \frac{A}{2}(\frac{A}{M} - 1)$.

The total disk transportation volume for doing projection is:

If A <= M: $V_{pro} = A + R$

MULTICOMPUTER PROJECTION						
STATE	INPUT STATE	NEW STATE	INPUT FILE	MATCH ACTION	MOMATCH ACTION	STATE CHANGE ACTIONS
0	normal	1	A	Ø	Store	Iws, Open (R), ReSet (A)
1	normal	1	A	Ø	Store	
1	eos	0	A			Wws(R), Close (A), Close (R)
1	wsf	2	A			Open (T), Write(T)
2	normal	2	A	Delete	ø	Write(T)
2	eos	3	A			Wws(R), Iws, Close (A), Eof(T), Reset (T)
3	normal	3	T	Ø	Store	
3	eof	0	T			Erase (T), Wws(R), Close (R)
3	wsf	4	T	Delete	Ø	Mark(T)
4	normal	4	T	Delete	Ø	
4	eof	3	T	-	-	Wws(R), Iws, Pos(T)

Table 3   State machine for the multicomputer projection. The column for nomatch and match contains actions which are depending on whether matching records are found or not in the workspace.

When A > M: $\quad V_{pro} = \dfrac{A}{2}(\dfrac{A}{M}+3) - M + R$

So far, we have described a basic nested loop algorithm. When A > 3M we should use local partitioning, see chapter 8. If local partitioning is employed and we use only one partitioning level, then

$V_{pro} = 3A - 2M + R \approx 3A + R$

All formulas for V represent upper limits since reduction in volume due to duplicates are not counted for.

Doing relational algebra, time is spent on three main tasks: disk I/O, relocation and computations. On our two first prototypes all of these operations tied up the local system bus. Hence there was no true overlapping of operations. This picture is somewhat changed on our last prototype the HC16-386. This computer has an improved disk interface and very high bus capacity so disk I/O transfer is almost negligible as far as bus capacity is concerned. However we have not yet done any performance measurements on HC16-386.

6.2 Join

A is supposed to be the smallest operand. The operation starts with A records streaming to their target node. There they are filled into the workspace and no records are deleted. If the workspace is full before all A records are received, streaming continues until all A records are at their target node. Those records which do not find room in workspace are stored on temporary file TA.

At this point we can start streaming B records. If a temporary file was created (TA) then we also create a temporary file TB containing all B records. Received B records are always checked against workspace and result records are made for all matching records. These records are given to the output stream.

When end of stream for B operands is reached the operation is finished if no temporary files exist. However, if they exist the join is now completed locally. The TA file is loaded into workspace part by part and every time checked against B records. This is repeated TA/M times.

Then phase two starts reading B records. If the work space is full, also B must be stored at the target nodes because they will be read many times while the remaining A records are read. Sending records between nodes is expensive and only those parts of the records which is either part of result or part of the operation is sent.

When the join attribute is a key of either A or B then relocation of this table is unnecessary. Only the table where the join attribute is a non key should be relocated.

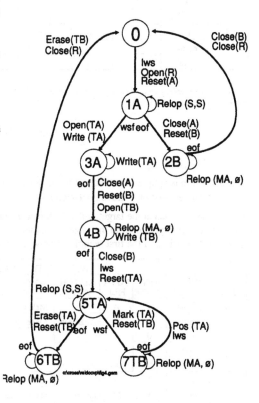

Figure 2   State diagram for multiprocessor join.
Relop(MA,ø) will search workspace for all matching records and write a result record to the R output buffer.

						MULTICOMPUTER JOIN
STATE	INPUT STATE	NEW STATE	INPUT FILE	MATCH ACTION	NOMATCH ACTION	STATE CHANGE ACTIONS
0	normal	1	A	Store	Store	Iws, Open (R), Reset (A)
1	normal	1	A	Store	Store	
1	eof	2	A			Reset (B), Close (A)
1	wsf	3	A			Open (TA), Write(TA)
2	normal	2	B	MakeAll		
2	eof	0	B			Close (B), Close(R)
3	normal	3	A			Write (TA)
3	eof	4	A			Reset(B), Close (A), Open (TB)
4	normal	4	B	MakeAll		Write(TB)
4	eof	5	B			Reset(TA), Iws, Close(B)
5	normal	5	TA	Store	Store	
5	eof	6	TA			Reset (TB), Erase (TA)
5	wsf	7	TA			Reset(TB), Mark (TA)
6	normal	6	TB	MakeAll		
6	eof	5	TA			Pos (TA), Iws
7	normal	7	TB	MakeAll		
7	eof	0	TB			Erase (TB), Close(R)

Table 5   State table, join on a multiprocessor system. The difference from a mono system is that overflow A records are stored locally on target node. So are also the B records if there are local overflow records from A in store.

6.3   Aggregate Functions

The naive algorithm

This algorithm is simple to realize and works well for even larger operands. It's weak point is that more records than necessary are moved between nodes.

Records are grouped at the target node. Each record is individually hashed on the grouping attributes and relocated to the target node. In the target node there is established one record in workspace for each group. At the arrival of the first record in a new group the new group record is established. When more

						AGGREGATION, BASIC ALGORITHM
STATE	INPUT STATE	NEW STATE	INPUT FILE	MATCH ACTION	NOMATCH ACTION	STATE CHANGE ACTIONS
0	normal	1	A		MakeGroup	Iws, Reset (A)
1	normal	1	A	Aggregate	MakeGroup	
1	eof	0	A	-	-	Close(A), Ppws, Open (R), Wws, Close(R)
1	wsf	2	A			Open (TA), Write (TA)
2	normal	2	A	Aggregate		Write (TA)
2	eof	3	A			Close(A), Reset(TA), Ppws, Open(R),Wws, Iws
3	normal	3	TA	Aggregate	MakeGroup	
3	eof	0	TA			Ppws, Wws, Erase (TA), Close(R)
3	wsf	4	TA			Open (TB), Write(TB)
4	normal	4	TA	Aggregate		Write(TB)
4	eof	3	TA			Ppws, Wws, Iws, Erase (TA), Swap(TA,TB), Reset (TA)

Table 4   State transition table for aggregation, the naiv algorithm.

records of the group arrives the group record is updated according to the set of aggregate functions which applies.

If the number of groups (aggregate records in workspace) is so large that there is not room in workspace, some records are scanned two or more times. Records that do not find their matching record in the work-space are written to a local temporary file, see state 2. The temporary file is used as input file in the next pass, see state 3 and if necessary a new temporary file is written see state 4.

The naive algorithm is the only one realized in CROSS8/HC16 so far. HC16-186 aggregates about 4 MB/s.

Distributed aggregation

The preceding algorithm does not take advantage of the possibilities for local aggregation. Especially if there are large groups (many records in each group) the data volume transferred between nodes can be considerably reduced. The simplest version of this algorithm will make a complete local aggregation in step one. This is very efficient if all groups are stored in workspace. If the local aggregation needs more space, intermediate files are established. States 1, 2, 3 and 4 pertains to local aggregation. If all groups have room in workspace only state 1 is activated. States 5, 6, 7 and 8 are for global aggregation.

After all local aggregations are finished we do a global aggregation following the same pattern as in the naive algorithm. We have now reduced the number of records to at least one per group from each node. The post processing step should be skipped for local aggregates it is sufficient to to a common post pro-cessing in the global aggregation.

Local aggregation does not contribute to load distribution if the nodes are unevenly loaded at the outset.

						AGGREGATION, DISTRIBUTED PRE GLOBAL AGGREGATION
STATE	INPUT STATE	NEW STATE	INPUT FILE	MATCH ACTION	NOMATCH ACTION	STATE CHANGE ACTIONS
0	normal	1	A		MakeGroup	Iws, Reset (A)
1	normal	1	A	Aggregate	MakeGroup	
1	eof	5	A			Close(A), Open (RT), Wws(RT), Iws, Reset(RT)
1	wsf	2	A			Open (TA), Write (TA)
2	normal	2	A	Aggregate		Write (TA)
2	eof	3	A			Close(A), Reset(TA), Open(RT),Wws(RT), Iws
3	normal	3	TA	Aggregate	MakeGroup	
3	eof	5	TA			Wws(RT), Erase (TA), Iws, Reset(RT)
3	wsf	4	TA			Open (TB), Write(TB)
4	normal	4	TA	Aggregate		Write(TB)
4	eof	3	TA			Wws(RT), Iws, Erase (TA), Swap(TA,TB), Reset (TA)
5	normal	5	RT	Aggregate	Makegroup	
5	eof	6	RT			Erase(RT), Ppws, Open(R), Wws(R), Close(R)
5	wsf	7	RT			Open (TA), Write(TA)
6	normal	6	RT	Aggregate	Write(T)	
6	eof	7	RT			Open (R), Wws (R), Erase(RT), Reset(T), Iws
7	normal	7	T	Aggregate	MakeGroup	
7	eof	0	T			Erase(T), Ppws, Wws(R), Close(R)
7	wsf	8	T			Open (TT), Write(TT)
8	normal	8	T	Aggregate	Write(TT)	
8	eof	7	T			Erase(T), Ppws, Wws(R), T=TT, Iws

Table 6   Distributed aggregation. Groups are aggregated locally before they are redistributed in a global aggregation.

6. 4   Division

To illustrate a complex function we will describe division. The function was defined as:

DIVIDE (A:s:r:g:c, B:s:r:c, R:s:r) ;

All A records are grouped on g. If all values B:c are found in group A:g then A:g is moved to R. A distributed algorithm for computing R is as follows. The numbers indicate state values for which the operations described are done:

1. Relocate B records based on B:c as operation key. Node k contains B_k records. The set of B records in each node is now ready to be tested by all A records. If B contains more records than can be stored in workspace then the operation is aborted. This should be very unlikely.

				DISTRIBUTED DIVISION		
STATE	INPUT STATE	NEW STATE	INPUT FILE	MATCH ACTION	NOMATCH ACTION	STATE CHANGE ACTIONS
0	normal	1	B			Iws(B), Push(B)
1	normal	1	B		Push(B)	
1	eof	2	B			Close(B), MakeTable(B), Iws(A)
1	wsf	0	B			Error, not defined
2	normal	2	A	if A:c in B: MarkGroup	if A:c in B: AddGroup	
2	eof	6	A			Close(A), DelNCGroup, Open(RT), Wws(RT), Eof(RT), Reset(RT), Iws
2	wsf	3	A			Open(T), Write(T)
3	normal	3	A	if A:c in B: MarkGroup	if A:c in B Write(T)	
3	eof	4	A			DelNCGroup, Open (RT), Wws (RT), Iws(A), Eof(T), Reset (T)
4	normal	4	T	MarkGroup	AddGroup	
4	eof	6	T			Delete (T), DelNCGroup, Wws(RT), Eof(RT), Reset(RT), Iws
4	wsf	5	T			Open(TT), Write(TT)
5	normal	5	T	MarkGroup	Write(TT)	
5	eof	4	T			Delete(T), DelNCGroup, Wws(RT), Eof (TT), Reset (TT), T = TT, Iws
6	normal	6	RT	CountGroup	AddGroup	
6	eof	0	RT			Delete (RT), Open (R), DelNCgroup, Wws (R), Close (R)
6	wsf	7	RT			Open (T), Write(T)
7	normal	7	RT	CountGroup	Write(T)	
7	eof	8	RT			Delete(RT), Open(R), DelNCGroup, Wws(R), Eof(T), Reset(T), Iws
8	normal	8	T	CountGroup	AddGroup	
8	eof	0	T			Delete(T), DelNCGroup, Wws(R), Close(R)
8	wsf	9	T			Open(TT), Write(TT)
9	normal	9	T	CountGroup	Write(TT)	
9	eof	8	T			Delete(T), DelNCGroup, Wws(R), Eof(TT), Reset(TT), T=TT, Iws

Table 7   State diagram for distributed division. States 1 to 5 are for testing against membership in subgroups. States 6 to 9 checks for membership in all groups. Only A records with B members are stored temporarily. All other A records are discarded from further processing.

2. Relocate A records based on A:c as operation key. If A:c is found among the B records on the target node this record takes part in an "aggregation", otherwise it is discarded. The aggregation is special - tick off position A:c and A:g in a two dimensional matrix, where A:c determines B record position and A:g the group identifier. When all A records are processed we are checking all groups in workspace. Only groups with all B records are complete, and only group identifiers for complete groups are saved to a temporary file RT.

3,4, and 5. If A contains more groups than can be stored in workspace, then records belonging to the extra groups, must be temporarily stored on a local file T. Only records having a matching field in B are stored. When all input records are processed we apply the same post processing as for state 2.

6. The RT file in every node now contain identifiers of complete subgroups. To be a result record the same group identifier must exist on every node. We relocate group identifiers with the group identifier as the relocation key. At the target node, the number of group identifier records are counted within each group. Only identifiers of complete groups are written to the result file.

7, 8 and 9. If there are more group identifiers than can be stored in workspace they are written to a temporary file.

The total work for this operation is one relocation of B, one relocation of A and a second relocation of some part of A. The first reduction step is that only A records with c values found in B are relocated the second time. The second reduction factor is that subgroups should be complete if A is be reallocated. This is very data dependent and it is also inversely proportional with the number of nodes. Let A and B denote the volume of the corresponding operands. For operand volumes A<M relocation work is probably closer to B+A than B+2A. For volumes larger than M, parts of A has to be scanned several times. We are not considering operands where B>M. This situation would be very unlikely.

To check against B we organize all B records in a combined stack and hash list. Which B records which have been found for a certain group is marked in a bit vector. There is one bit vector for each group. Access to the group identifiers is also done through a hash list.

7.   USAGE OF FILTERS

Filters are implemented as bit vectors and the effect of filters is described among other places in [Brat84]. The best effect of filters is when operands can be eliminated at an early stage in the process. Then we can save both transportation time, CPU time, disk IO time and space. The cost of using filters are coupled to filter creation, filter distribution and filter discrimination. In some cases data has to be scanned twice, one for creating the filter and the second time for exploiting it.

The usage of filters is very much depending on the actual operation. The effect of filters are also depending on hardware characteristics. If record relocation is very costly filters could be used to reduce the volume.

Filters in projection

We will try to reduce to a minimum the number of records relocated. This algorithm will work:

1. Start with a blank filter

2. Read all A records and mark the computed bit position.

3. Send all filters to one node and construct a global mask with ones only in positions where two or more filters have corresponding ones. This global mask is then broadcast to all nodes.

4. Scan all A records once more. Records with zero in the global mask does not have a duplicate and are written directly to the output file. If a bit is set, this record might have a duplicate. Therefore, this record is relocated to a target node. There it will "meet" possible duplicates.

To be effective, this algorithm requires a filter in each node which contains at least twice as many bits as there are records in A (in total). An increasing number of nodes requires relatively more space for filters.

Filters in join

Filters in join can be very beneficial. Filters are created when the A operand is relocated at the target node. A B record is only interesting if it finds a matching bit in the filter. The simplest way of applying the filter is to use it at the node of record entry. Then we avoid any duplication of filters. With this strategy we do not avoid relocation of "blind" records, we are saving only the final processing - and for large operands; temporary storage of non-interesting records. To avoid relocation of non-interesting records we should move the filter to the sending nodes. This means that all filters are broadcast and stored in every node.

Filters in aggregation

It is not obvious how filters can be useful in aggregation

Filters in division

A filter of the B operand should be ready at the end of the first relocation. This will give one filter for each subgroup. These filters are broadcast to all nodes and used during the relocation of A records. Only records with a corresponding bit set in the filter should be relocated. This could possibly save a lot of relocation work since A normally is much larger than B and many records in A do not find a matching value in B.

8. PARTITIONING AT THE LOCAL LEVEL

Partitioning has been used all through this paper. We have had one partition for each node. For very large operands this might not be enough. The effect of local partitioning is also described in [Brat84]. How large is large? Nested loop join which we have used locally are better than partitioned hash join as long as the smallest operand A is less than 3M to 5M depending on the relative size of A and B. On a HC16-386 the total memory is 32MB and up - workspace might be several tens of megabytes. Nested loop joins should be fairly efficient for total operands less than one GB. However there is no need to fear even much larger operands. We use join as an example.

When workspace is full in state 3, see table 3 - we are writing the A records to a temporary and local file TA. At this point we can partition A into as many groups as we can afford extra outbuffers. We do not know the exact size of A, only an upper limit - if A is a stored table in the database. Each partition need not be much smaller than M, and limiting the number of partitions is beneficial because the extra out-buffers are taken from the same memory as M - the workspace. Partitioning in one level should suffice. 10 extra outbuffers each 8KB is only taking 80 KB from workspace likely to be larger than 1 MB. In this way operations on 100 GB on a 16 node systems will be quite efficient.

ACKNOWLEDGMENTS

This work is heavily dependent on work of others. First of all I would thank Torgrim Gjelsvik who built or finished all our parallel computers. He also programmed them and ran the benchmark tests. Øystein Torbjørnsen has been of great help on all difficult programming problems and he also set up a basic library of communication and support routines. Svein-Arne Solbakk and Tor Eivind Johansen were the first to work on the project and they started to build both the hardware and the software for CROSS8. We would also like to mention Intel Norway AS, Nordisk Elektronikk AS and Eltron AS. They have been of great help and we have gotten their products to very favourable prices. Last, but not least there would have been no project without the support from NTNF.

REFERENCES

[AMPE78] AMPEX Corp. "PTD-930x Parallel Transfer Drive, Product Description 3308829-01, October 1978.

[AsTo90] Ole John Aske and Øystein Torbjømsen: "Communication on HC16-186 - A Study of Methods and Performance in a Hypercubic Network Based on Dual Port RAM.", The Fifth Distributed Memory Computing Conference, Charleston, South Carolina April 1990.

[Astr79] Astrahan M.M, et al. "System R A Relational Database Management System", IEEE Computer Vol. 12, No 5, May 1979.

[BauGre89] Bjørn Arild W. Baugstø and Jarle Greipsland: "Parallel Sorting Methods for Large Data Volumes on a Hypercube Database Computer", The Sixth International Workshop on Database Computers, France, June 1989

[BaGrKa90] B.A.W. Baugstø, J.F. Greipsland and J. Kamerbeek: "Sorting Large Data Files on POOMA", Conpar, Sept. 1990.

[BiDeTu83] D.Bitton, D. DeWitt and C. Turbyfill "Benchmarking Database Systems. A Systematic Approach", The 9th International Conference on Very Large Data Bases, Florence Oct. 1983.

[BorDew81] Haran Boral and David DeWitt "Processor Allocation Strategies for Multiprocessor Database Machines", ACM TODS Vol. 6, No. 2, 1981.

[Bra80] Kjell Bratbergsengen, Rune Larsen, Oddvar Risnes and Terje Aandalen "Neighbor Connected Processor Network for Performing Relational Algbra Operations" The 5th Workshop on Computer Architecture for Non-Numeric Processing, March 11-14, 1980 Pacific Grove, Ca.

[Bra83] Kjell Bratbergsengen "Data Base Management Systems for Engineering Applications. Requirements Specification", Kongsberg Vaapenfabrikk, avd. Trondheim, July 1983.

[Bra84] Kjell Bratbergsengen "Hashing Methods and Relational Algbra Operations", The 10th Conference on Very Large Data Bases, Singapore Aug. 1984.

[Bra87] Kjell Bratbergsengen "Algebra Operations on a Parallel Computer - Performance Evaluation" Dept. of Computer Science Report No. 14, May 1987. The 5th International Workshop on Database Machines, Oct 5-8 1987 Karuizawa Japan.

[Bra89] Kjell Bratbergsengen: "The Development of Database Computers", SIBUG, Bergen 7-8 feb. 1989.

[Bra89b] Kjell Bratbergsengen: "The Development of the Parallel Database Computer HC16-186", Fourth Conference on Hypercubes, Concurrent Computers and Applications, Monterey, Ca, March 6-8, 1989.

[BraGje89] Kjell Bratbergsengen and Torgrim Gjelsvik "The Development of the CROSS8 and HC16-186 Parallel (Database) Computers", Division of Computing Systems and Telematics, The Norwegian Institute of Technology, The Sixth International Workshop on Database Machines, France June 19-23, 1989.

[Cope88] G. Copeland, W. Alexander, E. Boughter and T. Keller "Data Placement in Bubba", ACM Sigmod Vol. 17, Number 3, September 1988.

[Date90] C.J. Date "An Introduction to Database Systems" Volume I, Fifth Edition, Addison-Wesley 1990.

[DeWi85] D.J. DeWitt and R. Gerber "Multiprocessor Hash-Based Join Algorithms", Proceedings of the 1985 VLDB Conference, Stockholm August 1985.

[DeWi87] D.J. DeWitt, S. Ghandeharizadeh, D. Schneider, R. Jauhari, M. Muralikrishna and A. Sharma "A Single User Evaluation of The Gamma Database Machine", Proceedings of the 5th Inernational Workshop on Database Machines, Japan, October 1987.

[DeWi88] D.J. DeWitt, S. Ghandeharizadeh, D. Schneider "A Performance Analysis of the Gamma Database Machine", ACM Sigmod Vol. 17, Number 3, September 1988.

[Gra90] Goetz Graefe "Encapsulation of Parallelism in the Volcano Query Processing System", ACM Sigmod, Vol. 19, Issue 2 June 1990.

[Nech84] Philip M. Neches "Hardware Support for Advanced Data Management Systems", IEEE Computer, Vol 17, No 11, Nov. 1984.

[PaGiKa88] D.A. Patterson, G. Gibson and R.H. Katz "A Case for Redundant Arrays of Inexpensive Disks (RAID)", ACM Sigmod, Vol. 17, Number 3, September 1988.

[RiLuMi87] J.R. Richardson, H. Lu and K. Mikkilineni "Design and Evaluation of Parallel Join Algorithms", ACM Sigmod Conference Proceedings, Vol. 16. No. 3, December 1987.

[SheNe84] "The Genesis of a Database Computer: A Conversation with Jack Shemer and Phil Netches of Terabyte Corporation", IEEE Computer, Vol 17, No 11, Nov. 1984.

[SoJo85] Svein-Arne Solbakk og Tor Eivind Johansen "DELTA databasemaskin for relasjonsdatabaser", Prosjektarbeider i databehandling ved IDB NTH, mai 1985 (In Norwegian).

[SmiBro83] J. Smith and M. Brodie (eds) "Relataional Database Systems. Analysis and Comparison" Springer Verlag 1983

[Ston76] Stonebraker M. et al. "The Design and Implementation of INGRES", TODS 2, sept. 1976.

[TECH84] TECHRA User Manual. Kongsberg Vaapenfabrikk avd. Trondheim, 1984.

[Ubel85] Michael Ubell "The Intelligent Database Machine (IDM)", Query Processing in Database Systems, Kim, Reiner & Batory; Eds., Springer Verlag 1985. may

An Overview of Parallel Strategies for Transitive Closure on Algebraic Machines *

Filippo Cacace
Dipartimento di Elettronica, Politecnico di Milano

Stefano Ceri
Dipartimento di Matematica, Universita' di Modena

Maurice A.W. Houtsma
Department of Applied Mathematics, University of Twente

Abstract

An important feature of database technology of the nineties is the use of distributed computation for speeding up the execution of complex queries. Today, the use of parallelism is tested in several experimental database architectures and a few commercial systems for conventional select-project-join queries. In particular, hash-based fragmentation is used to distribute data to disks under the control of different processors, in multi-processor architectures without shared memory, in order to perform selections and joins in parallel.

With the development of new (logic) query languages and deductive databases, the new dimension of recursion has been added to query processing. Transitive closure queries, such as bill-of-material, allow important database problems to be solved by the database system itself; and more general logic programming queries allow us to study queries not considered before. Although recursive queries are very complex, their regular structure makes them particularly suited for parallel execution. Well-considered use of parallelism can give a high efficiency gain when processing recursive queries.

In this paper, we give an overview of approaches to parallel execution of recursive queries as they have been presented in recent literature. After showing that the most typical Datalog queries have exactly the same expressive power as the transitive closure of simple algebraic expressions, we focus on describing algebraic approaches to recursion.

To give a good overview of the problems that are inherent to parallel computation, we introduce a graphical formalism to describe parallel execution. This formalism enables us to clearly show the behaviour of parallel execution strategies. We first review algorithms developed in the framework of algebraic transitive closures that operate on entire relations; then we introduce fragmentation, distinguishing between hash-based and semantic fragmentation.

1 Introduction

Over the past few years, recursive queries have emerged as an important new class of complex queries. These queries enable solving classical database problems, such as the *bill-of-material* (finding all transitive components of a given part). This type of problems is classically managed in commercial applications by embedding queries within programming language interfaces, and then dealing with recursion by using the programming language constructs. However, these applications are both

---

*This research is partially supported by the LOGIDATA+ Project of the National Research Council of Italy

unefficient and hard to program. Database languages of the future will be able to express simple types of recursion, such as transitive closure, within their query languages; and logic programming interfaces to databases will be able to express general recursion. These queries are intrinsically much more complex than conventional queries, because they require iterating the application of operations until termination (fixpoint) conditions are met. Though in general the finiteness of the computation is certain, the number of iterations is not known a-priori. Thus, there is a definite need for the development of new optimization strategies and techniques to deal efficiently with recursive queries.

During the past decade, much effort has been put into the development of new techniques for more efficient processing of conventional relational queries. These techniques range from the use of efficient physical data structures, to a clear separation between *clients* and *servers*, and to the use of multi-tasking and multi-threading within advanced architectures for database servers. Although these techniques can be supported in a conventional single-processor environment, they are particularly suited for multi-processor architectures. These architectures are becoming more and more widespread, be it in the context of distributed systems or in the context of advanced multi-processor machines. Indeed, database access is particularly suited for distributed (parallel) execution, because it adds the dimension of *data distribution* to processing distribution, thus allowing a combination of these two dimensions to generate very efficient execution strategies.

We may distinguish two types of parallelism in databases. *Inter-query parallelism* enables multiple small queries to be executed in parallel; this notion of parallelism is used for building systems capable of running hundreds or even thousands of small transactions per second against a large, shared database. In this case, efficiency is mainly achieved by building servers that are very fast in processing each request; parallelism is the consequence of the concurrent presentation of requests from multiple sources, which are served concurrently by a complex process architecture; the database itself may or may not be distributed. In the rest of the paper, we will not consider this type of parallelism.

In this paper we concentrate on the second type of parallelism, called *intra-query parallelism*, which enables the distribution of complex queries to multiple processors. Intra-query parallelism aims at minimizing the response time of a query by sharing the heavy processing load on multiple processors, in this case each processor is typically dedicated to the query.

Intra-query parallelism has been considered as an important feature in query optimization since many years. Relational query optimizers try to exploit parallelism by detecting the parts of a query plan that can be executed in parallel; asynchronous models of execution are typically used even within a centralized database architecture in order to enable the concurrent execution of parts of an access plan. In distributed databases, intra-query parallelism has been considered as an underlying, implicit assumption of many theoretical approaches to query optimization developed in the late seventies and early eighties, which were building fast execution plans by postulating that each part of the plan could be executed in parallel [2, 16].

Intra-query parallelism has become feasible only very recently. And although many systems support parallelism in query execution, they do not yet support fragmentation; only few commercial systems support fragmentation, including Teradata and Tandem [29]. Advanced techniques based on data fragmentation and performance measurements for comparing them have been developed in a few research environments; among them, the *Prisma* machine, developed at Philips and several Dutch universities [4, 24], the *Delta* machine, developed at Wisconsin University [14, 28], and the *Bubba* machine, developed at MCC [13].

Especially data fragmentation is an essential ingredient for parallelism, as it enables a natural partitioning of query processing. Each processor controls a disk which stores fragments of relations. With this architecture, it is possible to execute selections, projections, and some joins in a distributed way on each processor, and collect from each processor the result of these operations [10]. Due to the importance of fragmentation for intra-query parallelism, we will in our overview of parallel strategies separate methods operating on fragments from those operating on complete relations.

In this paper, we survey parallel techniques for executing recursive queries on algebraic machines. Section 2 presents some preliminary foundations, and in particular builds the bridge between research on transitive closure for algebraic expressions and research on Datalog and logic programming. We show that these two research fields, though apparently different, are indeed two sides of the same coin. After having shown this, we may freely mix logic and algebraic formalisms for expressing recursive queries and evaluation strategies. We also introduce a graphical representation of algorithms, highlighting regularities in the computation and clearly showing the parallel behaviour of the evaluation strategies to be discussed.

In Section 3, we describe research focused on parallel execution of transitive closure. First, we discuss methods which do not use fragmentation, then we discuss hash-based fragmentation, and finally we discuss fragmentation that is based on the semantic content of data.

2 Preliminary foundations

When we consider research for the optimization of recursive queries, we note that the problem is approached from two different perspectives: algebraic optimization and logic optimization. Examples of research on algebraic optimization may be found in [3, 9, 12, 18, 31], examples of logic optimization may be found in [15, 22, 26, 32, 33]. These two approaches are actually equivalent; this is illustrated in [7, 8], where it is described how to transform Datalog programs into equations of positive Relational Algebra (RA+), and *vice versa*.

Let us show this equivalence in detail. The transitive closure of a binary relation R is expressed by the following formula, for some finite number n:

$$R^* = R \cup R^2 \cup R^3 \cup \ldots \cup R^n$$

Note that in this formula $R^2 = \pi_{1,4}(R \underset{2=1}{\bowtie} R)$, $R^3 = \pi_{1,4}(R^2 \underset{2=1}{\bowtie} R)$, etc. The solution of this expression is equivalent to the minimal model of the following Datalog program (where lower case letters denote Datalog predicates, relations corresponding to these predicates are denoted by upper case letters):

$$p(X,Y) :- r(X,Y).$$
$$p(X,Y) :- r(X,Z), p(Z,Y).$$

Of course, this also holds in the other direction. Consider the following Datalog program:

$$p(X,Y) :- r(X,Y).$$
$$p(X,Y) :- s(X,S), t(S,T), p(T,Y).$$

This program consists of one linear stable recursive rule and one non-recursive rule; it is called a *linear sirup* in logic programming terminology. The minimal model of this program can be computed by unfolding the recursive rule until no more new tuples are derived. Hence, in the first step we get:

$$p(X,Y) :- s(X,S), t(S,T), r(T,Y)$$

which is equivalent to:

$$\pi_{1,4}(\pi_{1,4}(S \underset{2=1}{\bowtie} T) \underset{2=1}{\bowtie} R)$$

In the second step we get:

$$p(X,Y) :- s(X,S), t(S,T), s(T,U), t(U,V), r(V,Y)$$

which is equivalent to

$$\pi_{1,4}(\pi_{1,4}(\pi_{1,4}(S \underset{2=1}{\bowtie} T) \underset{2=1}{\bowtie} \pi_{1,4}(S \underset{2=1}{\bowtie} T)) \underset{2=1}{\bowtie} R) = \pi_{1,4}((\pi_{1,4}(S \underset{2=1}{\bowtie} T))^2 \underset{2=1}{\bowtie} R)$$

and so on. By unfolding the definition in this way and translating it to Relational Algebra, we compute $(\pi_{1,4}(\pi_{1,4}(S \underset{2=1}{\bowtie} T))^* \underset{2=1}{\bowtie} R)$; this is an ordinary transitive closure.

Summarizing, the following proposition holds:

```
power := R;
union := R;
repeat
        old_union := union;
        power := π (power ⋈ R);
        union := union ∪ power
until union = old_union

delta := R;
union := R;
repeat
        power := π (delta ⋈ R);
        delta := power - union;
        union := union ∪ delta
until delta = ∅
```

Figure 1: Naive and semi-naive algorithm

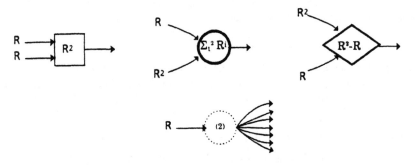

Figure 2: Building blocks of the graphical model

- Each linear sirup in Datalog is equivalent to a transitive closure operation.

Since transitive closure and linear sirups in Datalog are equivalent, we may use the same procedure for computing them. The two most well-know methods are called *naive* and *semi-naive*; they are shown in Fig. 1. Their relative merit is discussed, for instance, in [8]. Briefly, semi-naive evaluation is more efficient than naive evaluation, because at each iteration only the difference term *delta* is joined, instead of the entire term *power*. Semi-naive evaluation can be applied to linear Datalog programs (and therefore to sirups) but it cannot be applied to general Datalog programs.

Knowing that Datalog and positive Relational Algebra may be easily translated into each other, in the rest of this paper we freely mix the two formalisms; in general, we use Datalog to express queries and Relational Algebra for describing evaluations. To improve and clarify the description of algorithms, we introduce a graphical model to represent algebraic expressions; the graphic representation highlights the structure of parallel computation.

The building blocks of the graphical model are graphic symbols, each corresponding to either an algebraic operation or to a hashing operation. Input operands for the operations are represented by input edges, while the result produced by the operation is represented by an output edge. The label inside the building block indicates the operation performed. The following graphic symbols, as shown in Fig. 2, are used:

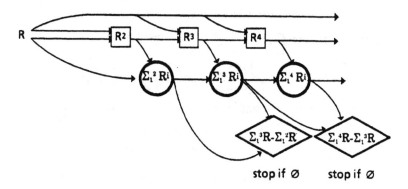

Figure 3: Graphic representation of naive evaluation

Squares are used to denote *joins*. Each join has two operands and produces one result. In Fig. 2 we see a join having a relation R as both inputs and producing R^2 as result. If R represents connections (of length 1), then R^2 represents paths of length 2.

Circles are used to denote *unions*. Each union has several operands and produces one result. In Fig. 2 we see the union $R \cup R^2$, giving all all paths of either length 1 or length 2.

Diamonds are used to denote *set differences*. Each difference has two operands and produces one result. In Fig. 2 we see the set difference $R^2 - R$, giving all paths of length 2 that do not already appear as direct connections.

Dashed circles are used to denote data redistribution by *hashing*. Each hashing operation has one input operand and produces an output operand. The label inside the block indicates the hashing criterion; in Fig. 2 we see that the relation R is hashed on its second attribute.

Fig. 3 presents the naive evaluation of transitive closure queries which was described in an algorithmic way in Fig. 1. The figure clearly shows that three types of operations are involved: joins to compute subsequent powers of R, unions to gather the results, and set differences to test for termination of the computation.

3 Parallel algorithms for transitive closure

In this section we first discuss several variations to naive evaluation that were not designed for parallel evaluation, but are nevertheless instructive to analyse. We then discuss parallel naive evaluation, hash-based fragmentation, and finally fragmentation based on semantic content of data.

3.1 Variations to naive evaluation

Throughout this subsection, we consider variations to the naive evaluation which try to improve its performance by either reducing the number of tuples considered at each iteration (through the semi-naive approach) or by generating several powers of R at each iteration, thus reducing the total number of required iterations (through the square, smart, and "minimal" approach). These algorithms were not designed for parallel evaluation, but their analysis is instructive because it indicates intrinsic limits to parallelism, thus enabling us to identify the features that lead to an inherently sequential behaviour and preventing parallel evaluation.

Algorithms evaluate the extension of the predicate p defined as follows:

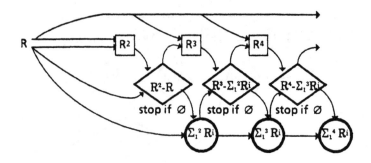

Figure 4: Semi-naive evaluation

$$p(X,Y) \; : - \; r(X,Y).$$
$$p(X,Y) \; : - \; r(X,Z), \; p(Z,Y).$$

Such an extension is given by all the tuples belonging to the subsequent powers R^n of the relation R, as discussed in Section 2.

One way of introducing parallelism in the evaluation consists in assigning a specialized processor to each *type of operation*. For instance, one processor performs joins, a second one performs unions, a third one performs differences. In this case, there is a strict sequentialization between operations of the same kind, but operations of different kinds can sometimes occur in parallel. Typically, they are done in parallel if they use the same input relations.

The second approach to parallelism (a brute-force one) consists in assigning a new processor to the evaluation of *each iteration*, until processors are exhausted; in this case, it is essential to use pipelining, so that each processor starts as soon as possible, namely, when its first input tuples are produced by the predecessor processors. Note that set difference is peculiar, because it cannot produce output tuples until its second operand is complete, thus breaking the flow of pipelining. When set differences are only used for the termination test, it may be convenient to perform them asynchronously, so that processes are not slowed down. However, this approach incurs the risk of replicated or superfluous computation, because iterations may be activated also subsequent to a successful termination test: the test becomes known after processing has already occurred. This may cause a dramatic increase of the global amount of work performed, while the reduction of delay might be minimal.

3.1.1 Naive evaluation

Let us reconsider Fig. 3. Unions, joins, and differences may be assigned to a different processor or to a different class of processors. In the naive approach, many duplicate tuples may be generated; this may lead to a high overload of tuples sent across the network. Since set difference determines the termination of the computation, it acts as a synchronization point. Join processors may be slowed until difference is terminated, or instead they can proceed at the risk of performing unnecessary computation. In conclusion, naive evaluation is not very well suited for parallel computation.

3.1.2 Semi-naive evaluation

Fig. 4 shows the semi-naive evaluation of transitive closure queries, which was described before in an algorithmic way in Fig. 1. The graphical presentation clearly shows that also semi-naive algorithm is hardly suited for parallel computation. At each step, a set difference operation is required before the join operation; this operation eliminates duplicates from the computation. Therefore, join and set difference operations are strongly synchronized. The union that builds the final results may

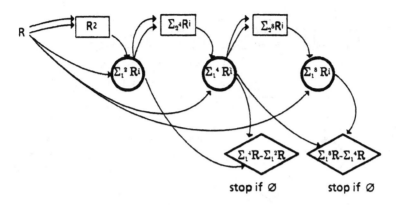

Figure 5: Squaring evaluation

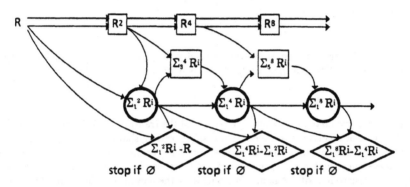

Figure 6: "Smart" evaluation

be done asynchronously on a separate processor, but this does not lead to major improvements in performance. In summary, due to the synchronization imposed by the set difference, the resulting semi-naive evaluation is essentially a sequential process.

3.1.3 Squaring evaluation

Squaring evaluation, introduced by Apers et al. [3] (and others), is shown in Fig. 5. This method reduces the number of iterations required to compute the transitive closure by subsequently squaring the result from the previous iteration. Hence, first paths of length up to 2 are computed, then paths of length up to 4, then paths of length up to 8, and so on. The graphical representation clearly shows that joins and unions are interleaved, while set differences are only performed for testing termination, and can be done asynchronously.

3.1.4 Smart evaluation

"Smart" evaluation, introduced by Ioannidis [23], uses an improved variation of the squaring approach, by considering at each iteration the paths of length 2, 4, 8, etc. to create new tuples. The computation of the subsequent powers of R (R^2, R^4, R^8, etc.) may be done on a separate processor or processor class without synchronizing with the rest of the computation, but unions and other joins

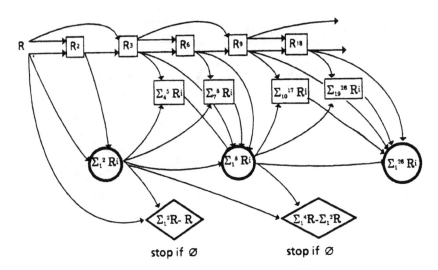

Figure 7: "Minimal" evaluation

required for producing the result must be synchronized with the power joins. Set differences are only used for testing termination and they can be done asynchronously.

3.1.5 Minimal evaluation

Besides the "smart" evaluation, some other rewritings of the transitive closure are also introduced by Ioannidis [23]. One of them is the so-called "minimal" algorithm, shown in Fig. 7. It is called minimal because it requires the minimal number of operations for computation of the transitive closure. Obviously, these operations are in general very complex, so the gain in number of operations is outbalanced by their complexity. Again, joins computing the powers of R do not need to synchronize with other operations, while the other join and union need to. The set difference operation is used only for testing termination.

3.1.6 Concluding remarks

In this section we have shown that standard algorithms for computation of the transitive closure operation are very hard to parallelize. These algorithms were defined in order to compute the entire transitive closure; they can also be used for queries having the first argument of the predicate p bound to a constant, e.g., $? - p(a, X)$. or $? - p(X, a)$; let R_{bf} and R_{fb} denote the results of these queries.

The straightforward approach for solving these queries is to apply a final selection on R^*; however, the most efficient method consists in anticipating the selection. The method of *variable reduction* [8] allows to simplify the query $? - p(X, a)$ on the program:

$$p(X, Y) :- r_1(X, Y).$$
$$p(X, Y) :- r_2(X, Z), \ p(Z, Y).$$

As it follows:

$$R_{fb} = \sigma_{2=a} R^k = \pi_{14}(R^{k-1} \underset{2=1}{\bowtie} \sigma_{2=a} R)$$

Where k is the iteration number at which the fixpoint is reached, i.e. $R^* = R^k$. This formula, evaluated from right to left, allows computing the first join by using $\sigma_{2=a} R$ as an operand, instead of R. This corresponds to the conventional anticipation of selections wrt. joins in query processing practice.

The query $?- p(a, X)$. cannot be simplified in the same way; however, if we consider the equivalent program:

$$p(X, Y) :- r_1(X, Y).$$
$$p(X, Y) :- p(X, Z), \ r_2(Z, Y).$$

Then we have:

$$R_{bf} = \sigma_{1=a} R^k = \pi_{14}(\sigma_{1=a} R \underset{2=1}{\bowtie} R^{k-1})$$

This formula, evaluated from left to right, allows computing the first join by using $\sigma_{1=a} R$ as an operand, instead of R.

Performance comparisons between the algorithms discussed in this subsection and the semi-naive method, presented in [23], show in general better performances; however, they use only relations corresponding to trees and list, whereas graphs would be subject to the severe problem of dealing with duplicate tuples in the computation. Thus, real gains of algorithms square, smart, and minimal with cyclic databases are questionable.

3.2 Parallel naive evaluation

In this section we discuss a parallel version of naive evaluation as described by Raschid and Su [27]. They consider again the recursive program:

$$p(X, Y) :- r(X, Y).$$
$$p(X, Y) :- r(X, Z), \ p(Z, Y).$$

They concentrate on the query $? - r(a, b)$., characterized by having both arguments bound to a constant; let R_{bb} denote the relation produced as result. Note that, for a particular choice a and b of bindings, R_{bb} returns the tuple (a, b) if $r(a, b)$ can be proved, the empty relation otherwise. We further denote as R_{bb}^i the tuples produced at the $i - th$ iteration for solving the R_{bb} query, and similarly for R_{bf}^i and R_{fb}^i; finally, the summation: $\Sigma_1^k R_{bb}^i$ gives all the result tuples for the query R_{bb} after k iterations.

Fig. 8 shows the algorithm of Raschid and Su [27]. Though in principle this architecture is capable of solving the R_{bf} and R_{fb} queries, in practice the architecture degenerates to the naive evaluation in those cases (assume the R_{bf} query and the first line of joins, unions, and differences for R_{bf} terms with the naive evaluation shown in Fig. 3; the other blocks of this architecture do not produce useful tuples). Thus, this architecture applies successfully only to the R_{bb} query.

Based on the bindings in the query, they start by evaluating R_{bf}, R_{fb} and R_{bb}: we have $R_{bf} = \sigma_{1=a} R$, $R_{fb} = \sigma_{2=b} R$, $R_{bb} = \sigma_{1=a,2=b} R$. Then, at each iteration four terms are computed through join operations: R_{bf}^i, R_{fb}^i, R_{bb}^{2i-1}, and R_{bb}^{2i} (the last term is omitted at the first iteration). In the figure, the four terms are shown for the first three iterations (note a 3×4 matrix of joins); the reader can thus perceive the regularity of the computation.

At each iteration, three union operations are also required: $\bigcup_i R_{bf}^i$, $\bigcup_i R_{fb}^i$, and $\bigcup_i R_{bb}^i$. Additionally, two differences compute the increment of tuples solving the queries R_{bf} and R_{fb}. The query R_{bb} is solved when $\bigcup_i R_{bb}^i$ produces one tuple. It is also solved negatively, in the sense that the answer is the empty relation, when either of the differences is empty; that means that no additional tuples are or will be produced that were not considered at the previous iteration.

When we consider the number of processors to be used in this evaluation mechanism, we may note the following. The four join operations should be done in parallel, and similarly the three unions. The set difference operations are best implemented on the same processors as the corresponding unions. Therefore, the suggested optimal number of processor is seven.

Although parallelism is clearly achieved by this method, some critical remarks should be made. First, the considered query is rather peculiar (R_{bb}); since the computation may be halted after the

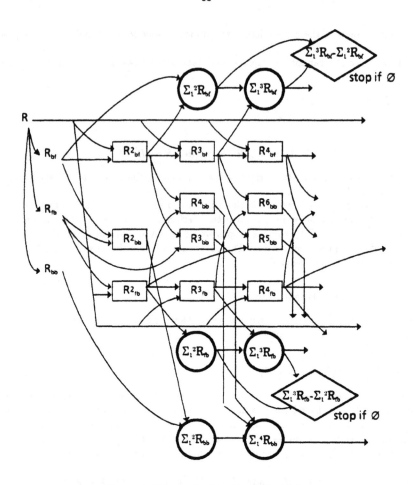

Figure 8: The method by Raschid and Su

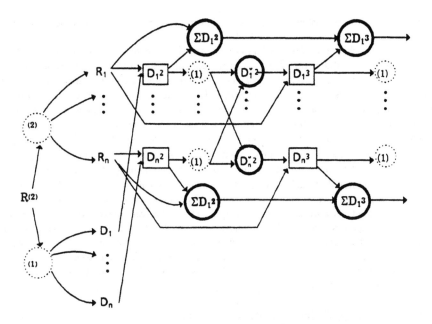

Figure 9: The method by Valduriez and Khosafian

first tuple that answers the query is produced, this approach is rather like cracking a nut with a sledgehammer. Second, parallelism comes together with massive interprocessor communication, and this is rather costly. In [17, 18, 25] it was reported that simulations of this method on a model of the *Prisma* database machine actually showed a negative speed-up, due to synchronization and communication costs. This parallel strategy turned out to be slower than smart single-processor strategies.

3.3 Hash-based fragmentation

In this section we study methods for parallel execution of recursive queries which use hash-based fragmentation. The basic idea behind these strategies is to use fragmentation of relations R and S in order to compute $R \bowtie S$ as $R_1 \bowtie S_1 \cup \ldots \cup R_n \bowtie S_n$. This approach is called *simple distributed join* in [10], where applicability and correctness conditions are discussed.

We consider a fragmentation of R into $R_1, \ldots R_n$ and the iterative join of R with itself in order to solve the usual recursive problem:

$$p(X, Y) \ :- r(X, Y).$$
$$p(X, Y) \ :- r(X, Z), \ p(Z, Y).$$

We start by discussing the approach of Valduriez and Khosafian [31], then we discuss a straightforward extension of this approach described by Cheiney and de Maindreville [12].

3.3.1 The method by Valduriez and Khosafian

The method by Valduriez and Khoskafian [31] is shown in Fig. 9. The strategy starts by hashing the relation R on its *second* attribute and distributing it to n processors. A second copy of R, called

D, is then hashed on its *first* attribute and distributed to processors; this copy represents the *delta* relation.

This fragmentation has to be fully understood: in practice, the domain *dom* of the join columns of R is partitioned into subdomains dom_i, and each domain is assigned to a processor; then, that processor receives the fragments R_i of R and D_i of D corresponding to that subdomain dom_i. In this way, the join between the second and first column of R can take place in parallel on each processor. However, fragments might be unbalanced; there is no guarantee that, by partitioning the domain and then by building the fragmentation, fragments will be of the same size.

On each processor i, the fragments of R_i and D_i are joined, generating the results: $D_i^2 := R \underset{2=1}{\bowtie} D_i$. This result has to be re-hashed on the first column. Re-hashing is done locally on each processor, and the results are sent to the appropriate processor for the next join ($D_i^3 := R_i \underset{2=1}{\bowtie} D_i^2$). At each step, deltas are accumulated at each processor by means of a union. Note that in this strategy the same tuple may appear in several deltas, thus leading to unnecessary, redundant computations.

When R corresponds to a directed acyclic graph (DAG), the computation ends when all deltas are empty. When instead R corresponds to a relation with cycles, then the union of deltas produced after each iteration at all processors and a set difference with the union produced at the previous iteration are required for detecting termination. In Fig. 9 we only show the accumulation of deltas at each processor; a last step (not shown in Fig. 9) is to gather all accumulated deltas on a single processor by a final union operation.

3.3.2 The method by Cheiney and de Maindreville

In [12], Cheiney and de Maindreville show a simple extension of this evaluation strategy that avoids rehashing deltas at each iteration step. This strategy is shown in Fig. 10; it differs from the approach described in [31] only for one feature: after the hashing of R_i on the second attribute, the resulting n fragments are further hashed on their first attribute. Each of the n fragments R_i is thus conceptually divided into n sub-fragments R_{ij}. After joining with the delta fragments at each iteration k, the second hashing is used to pre-determine where tuples of delta relations D_i^k need to be sent, without need for their rehashing. Figure 10 shows this algorithm.

Note that this approach can be even further extended by assigning a processor to each sub-fragment R_{ij} instead of assigning a processor to each fragment $R_i = \bigcup_j R_{ij}$. In this way, n^2 processors are used instead of n, each performing a smaller fraction of work.

3.3.3 Concluding remarks

Approaches presented in this section extend to recursive query processing the work currently being done for applying *intra-query parallelism* to joins [14, 13, 29]. As we noted in the introduction, recursive queries present a repeating pattern of join operations, hence parallelism has great potential.

The effectiveness of the evaluation strategies presented in this section depends crucially on an even distribution of the workload. This requires an even distribution of tuples to fragments and an even redistribution of resulting tuples into fragments at each iteration. Such situation can be produced only with a uniform distribution of values within join columns, while skewed distributions are likely to produce unbalanced fragments. A problem which is common to both approaches is that of duplicate elimination. The evaluation method described in [31] lacks a global union of deltas D_i, this means that duplicate tuples are not detected. In [12], a local union is performed with all incoming tuples of D_i, thus detecting duplicates produced at the same iteration, but no global union is done. The presence of duplicates creates unnecessary redundant computation.

Both [31] and [12] present an analysis of performance, based on a cost model described in [31]. This model assumes an architecture without shared memory (also called message-passing architecture). The time to produce new tuples is considered to be constant, and details about join and union algorithms are therefore not given. Relations are assumed to be acyclic. Analytic performance analysis, both in [31] and [12], demonstrate a strong advantage of the proposed methods in terms

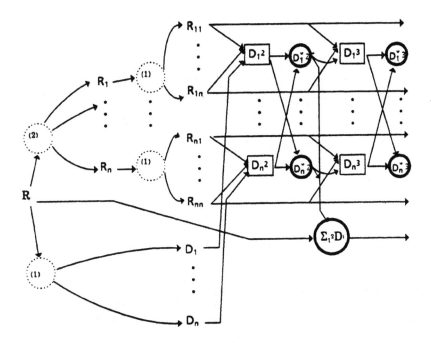

Figure 10: The method by de Maindreville and Cheiney

of computation speedup, thus confirming the intuition that hash-based fragmentation may be very efficient. However, these results rely heavily on the assumptions of uniform distribution and absence of duplicates within produced fragments; these assumptions do not hold in many applications. In the next section, we discuss an approach that uses a fragmentation derived from the semantics of the application domain.

3.4 Semantic fragmentation

The approach of Houtsma, Apers and Ceri, discussed in [17, 18, 20], builds a fragmentation specifically tailored to parallel execution of recursive queries. Such fragmentation, however, is also used in practice: the approach was suggested by real-world observations. Also in this case, the approach was developed in two stages; we describe the *disconnection set approach*, and then its generalization to *hierarchical fragmentation*.

3.4.1 Disconnection set approach

The basic idea that underlies the disconnection set approach can best be illustrated by an example. Consider a railway network connecting cities in Europe, and a question about the shortest connection between Amsterdam and Milan [1]

This question can be split into several parts: find a path from Amsterdam to the eastern Dutch border, find a path from the Dutch border to the southern German border, find a path from the German border to the Italian border, and find a path from the Italian border to Milan. We assume that data are naturally fragmented by state (e.g., there is a Dutch, a German, and an Italian database

---

[1] In pure Datalog this request cannot be expressed; however, several extensions of Datalog exist which provide the required features for this recursive query, among them the language Logres [5].

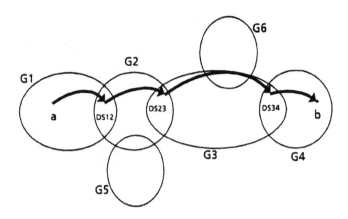

Figure 11: The disconnection set approach

which can be accessed through a common distributed database system). Moreover, we also assume that the points where one can cross a border are relatively few.

This fragmentation leads to a highly selective search process, consisting in determining the properties of connections from the origin to the first border, then between borders of two subsequent intermediate fragments, and finally from the last border to the destination city. These queries have the same structure; they apply only to a fragment of the database, and can be executed in parallel. The approach is sketched in Fig. 11.

The connection information is stored into a relation R; each tuple corresponds to an arc of the graph G, which can have cycles. By effect of the fragmentation, R is partitioned into n fragments $R_i, 1 \leq i \leq n$, each stored at a different computer or processor. This fragmentation induces a partitioning of G into n subgraphs $G_i, 1 \leq i \leq n$. Disconnection sets DS_{ij} are given by $G_i \cap G_j$. We assume that the number of nodes belonging to disconnection sets is much less than the total number of nodes in G.

In order to make the above approach feasible, it is required to store in addition some *complementary information* about the identity of border cities (i.e. the nodes in the disconnection set) and the properties of their connections; these properties depend on the particular recursive problem considered. For instance, for the shortest path problem it is required to precompute the shortest path among any two cities on the border between two fragments. This complementary information about the disconnection set DS_{ij} is stored at both sites storing the fragments i and j.

An important property of fragmentation is to be *loosely connected*: this corresponds to having an acyclic graph G' of components G_i. Formally, $G' = < N, E >$ has a node N_i for each fragment G_i and an edge $E_{ij} = (N_i, N_j)$ for each nonempty disconnection set DS_{ij}. Intuitively, if the fragmentation graph is loosely connected, then it is easier to select fragments involved in the computation of the shortest path between two nodes; in particular, for any two nodes, there is only one chain of fragments such that the first one includes the first node, the last one includes the last node, and remaining fragments in the chain connect the first fragment to the last fragment. However, for many practical problems (such as the European railway network) such a property does not hold.

In [18] it is shown that, if the fragmentation is loosely connected, then the shortest path connecting any two cities is found by involving in the computation only the computers along the chain of fragments connecting them [2]. Obviously, if the source and destination are within the same fragment, then the query can be solved by involving only the computer storing data about that fragment, in-

---

[2]Note that the shortest path might include nodes *outside* the chain, however their contribution is precomputed in the complementary information.

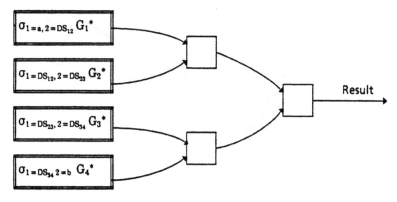

Figure 12: Example of query with the disconnection set approach

cluding all complementary information about disconnection sets stored at that fragment. In practice, this has the nice implication that queries about the shortest path of two cities in Holland can be answered by the Dutch railway computer system alone, even if the path goes outside the Dutch border. If instead the fragmentation is not loosely connected, then it is required to consider all possible chains of fragments independently for solving the query.

Along one chain of length n, query processing is performed in parallel at each computer; each subquery determines independently a shortest path (at the first fragment, between the start city and the first disconnection set; at the last fragment, between the last disconnection set and the destination city; at an intermediate fragment, between the input and output disconnection sets). Note that disconnection sets introduce additional selections in the processing of the recursive query, as they act as intermediate nodes that must be mandatorily traversed. These shortest paths are computed by considering also the complementary information. The final processing requires to combine all shortest paths obtained from the various processors with the complementary information, thus computing various "candidate" short paths, and selecting the shortest one among them. This process is shown in Fig. 12.

3.4.2 Parallel hierarchical evaluation

Houtsma, Cacace, and Ceri present in [21] a generalization of the disconnection set approach, called *parallel hierarchical evaluation*. This approach is inspired by real-life observations concerning transport problems. If we consider, for instance, the railroad network in Italy, we note that it is subdivided into geographical regions. Slow trains running inside regions stop at every station; inter-city trains connecting remote regions stop only at few stations, typically at the major cities of each region. Therefore, for long-distance travels, it makes sense to use the regional network around the departing city for connecting to the high-speed network of inter-city trains, then use inter-city trains, and finally use the regional network around the destination city in order to reach destination. This general rule may have an exception when start and destination cities are in adjacent fragments; in that case, the use of slow trains connecting the two regional networks may give the best solution.

The parallel hierarchical evaluation works exactly in this way. A subset of the connections are declared to be at high-speed, and form a fragment *HS*. All other connections are partitioned into n fragments $G_i, 1 \leq i \leq n$. The tuples of *HS* are stored on a separate computer together with complementary information about disconnection sets DS_i between *HS* and the various fragments G_i. Each fragment G_i is stored at a different computer together with complementary information of their disconnection sets. Any two fragments G_i and G_j are declared as either adjacent or nonadjacent. If two fragments G_i and G_j are *adjacent*, they are stored together with the complementary information

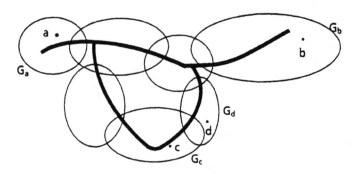

Figure 13: Parallel hierarchical evaluation

regarding their disconnection set DS_{ij}. Further, it is required that the shortest path between any two cities in G_i and G_j does not use connections of a different fragment, while it may use connections in HS. If two fragments G_i and G_j are *nonadjacent*, then the shortest path connecting any two cities of G_i and G_j should use the connections in G_i, G_j, and HS, but no other connection.

When these conditions hold, the computation of shortest paths connecting any two cities can be performed in parallel using three processors. If fragments are nonadjacent, the solution is found by composing shortest paths between the start city and DS_i in the processor storing G_i, between DS_i and DS_j in HS, and between DS_j and the destination city in G_j. If fragments are adjacent, then also the alternative of connecting the start city to DS_{ij} in G_i and DS_{ji} to the destination city in G_j must be evaluated and compared with the best solution which uses HS. Final post-processing for computing the total distance of the shortest path is performed exactly in the same way as in the disconnection set approach. An example of fragmentation with HS network is given in Fig. 13.

In [21], a procedure is defined for building a fragmentation that satisfies the applicability conditions of the method, starting from given centers of regions. Starting from these centers, an initial HS fragment is computed that includes the edges of the shortest paths between the centers. Then the fragments are gradually built by including edges with minimal distance from the centers into the appropriate fragments. Finally, the HS is suitably modified so that each pair of fragments is either adjacent or non-adjacent.

3.4.3 Concluding remarks

The disconnection set and the hierarchical approach are successful in partitioning the computation of one recursive query over a large relation R into several recursive queries over small relations R_i. One important speed-up factor is due to the reduced number of iterations required to compute each recursive query independently. Recall that the number of iterations required before reaching a fixpoint is given by the maximum diameter of the graph; if the graph is fragmented in n fragments G_i of equal size, then the diameter of each subgraph is highly reduced, hence giving efficient fixpoint evaluation.

Note that neither communication nor synchronization is required during the first phase of the computation; for evaluating the recursive subquery on a fragment any suitable single-processor algorithm may be chosen [1]; it is also possible to use some other parallel method. Only at the end of the computation, some communication is required for computing the final joins. These joins will have relatively small operands (since the disconnection sets are small) and pipelining may be used for their computation.

The disadvantage of the disconnection set approach is mainly due to the pre-processing required for building the complementary information and to the careful treatment of updates. Complementary information is different for each type of transitive closure query: in [19] the considered queries are connectivity, shortest path, and bill of material. However, as long as updates are not too complex and not too frequent, this cost may be amortized over many queries.

4 Conclusions

This paper has presented an overview of techniques for parallel evaluation of recursive queries. First we have shown the equivalence between transitive closure of relational expressions and a subclass of logic queries; this equivalence allows developing a general reference framework, where logic programming is used uniformly to express recursive programs and queries, and both *algebraic* and *logic* solution methods may be used to evaluate them. Furthermore, we have developed a graphical representation of algorithms, to show their characteristics when executed in parallel.

We have concentrated on giving an overview of algebraic methods for parallel execution of recursive queries (an overview of logic methods is included in [6]). Algebraic methods are essentially *evaluation* methods; they include the standard naive and semi-naive methods, but also several other methods. Some of them alter the basic structure of naive and semi-naive evaluation to build larger intermediate relations with fewer iterations; other methods use hash-based fragmentation to achieve parallelism; finally, other algebraic methods use semantic fragmentation to achieve efficient computation of special queries.

Processing of recursive queries is very hard; as such, recursive queries are particularly suited to parallel execution. The regular structure of recursion and the possibilities offered by hash-based or semantic fragmentation make parallel execution of recursive queries potentially very efficient.

References

[1] AGRAWAL R. AND JAGADISH H.V. "Direct algorithms for computing the transitive closure of database relations", in *Proc. 13th Int. Conference on Very Large Data Bases*, Brighton, 1987, pp. 255–266.

[2] APERS P.M.G., HEVNER A., AND YAO B., "Optimization algorithms for distributed queries", *IEEE-Transactions on Software Engineering*, SE9:1, 1983.

[3] APERS P.M.G., HOUTSMA M.A.W., AND BRANDSE F. "Processing recursive queries in relational algebra," in *Data and Knowledge (DS-2), Proc. of the 2nd IFIP 2.6 Working Conference on Database Semantics, Albufeira, Portugal, Nov. 3–7, 1986*, R.A. Meersman and A.C. Sernadas (eds.), North Holland, 1988, pp. 17–39.

[4] APERS P.M.G., KERSTEN M. L., AND H. OERLEMANS, "PRISMA database machine: a distributed main-memory approach," in *Advances in Database Technology*, Proc. Int. Conference Extending Database Technology (EDBT), 1988, pp. 590–593.

[5] CACACE F., CERI S., CRESPI-REGHIZZI C., TANCA L., AND ZICARI R. "Integrating object oriented data modeling with a rule-based programming language", in *Proc. ACM-Sigmod Conference*, Atlantic City, May 1990, pp. 225–236.

[6] CACACE, F., CERI, S., AND HOUTSMA, M.A.W. "A survey of parallel execution strategies for transitive closure and logic programs," Technical Report university of Twente–Politecnico Milano, Nov. 1990. Submitted for publication.

[7] CERI S., GOTTLOB G., AND LAVAZZA L. "Translation and optimization of logic queries: the algebraic approach", in *Proc. of the 12th Int. Conf. on Very Large Data Bases*, Kyoto, pp. 395-403, August 1986.

[8] CERI S., GOTTLOB G., AND TANCA L. *Logic Programming and Databases*, Springer-Verlag, 1990.

[9] CERI S., GOTTLOB G., TANCA L., AND WIEDERHOLD G., "Magic Semi-joins", *Information Processing Letters*, 33:2, 1989.

[10] CERI S. AND PELAGATTI G. *Distributed Databases: Principles and Systems*, Computer Science Series, McGraw-Hill, 1984.

[11] CERI S. AND TANCA L. "Optimization of systems of algebraic equations for evaluating Datalog queries," in *Proc. 13th Int. Conf. on Very Large Data Bases*, Brighton, Sept. 1987, pp. 31–42.

[12] CHEINEY J.P. AND DE MAINDREVILLE C. "A parallel strategy for transitive closure using double hash-based clustering," *Proc. 16th Int. Conf. on Very Large Data Bases*, Brisbane, Aug. 1990, pp. 347–358.

[13] COPELAND G., ALEXANDER W., BOUGHTER E., AND KELLER T. "Data placement in Bubba," *Proc ACM-Sigmod Conference*, 1988, pp. 99-108.

[14] DE WITT D. J., GHANDEHARIZADEH S., AND SCHNEIDER D. "A performance analysis of the Gamma database machine," *Proc. ACM-Sigmod Conference*, 1988, pp. 350–360.

[15] GANGULY S., SILBERSCHATZ A., AND TSUR S. "A framework for the parallel processing of Datalog queries," *Proc. ACM-Sigmod Conference*, Atlantic City, May 1990, pp. 143–152.

[16] GOODMAN N., BERNSTEIN P.A., WONG E., REEVE C.L., ROTHNIE J.B. "Query processing in SDD-1 - A system for Distributed Databases", *ACM-Transactions on Database Systems*, 6:4, 1981.

[17] HOUTSMA M.A.W. *Data and Knowledge Base Management Systems: Data Model and Query Processing*, Ph.D. Thesis, University of Twente, Enschede, the Netherlands, Nov. 1989.

[18] HOUTSMA M.A.W., APERS P.M.G., AND CERI S. "Distributed transitive closure computation: the disconnection set approach," *Proc. 16th Int. Conf. on Very Large Data Bases*, Brisbane, Aug. 1990, pp. 335–346.

[19] HOUTSMA M.A.W., APERS, P.M.G., AND CERI S. "Parallel computation of transitive closure queries on fragmented databases," Technical report INF88-56, University of Twente, the Netherlands, Dec. 1988.

[20] HOUTSMA, M.A.W., APERS, P.M.G., AND CERI, S. "Complex transitive closure queries on a fragmented graph," *Proc. 3rd Int. Conf. on Database Theory*, Lecture Notes in Computer Science, Springer-Verlag, Dec. 1990.

[21] HOUTSMA M.A.W., CACACE F., AND CERI S. "Parallel hierarchical evaluation of transitive closure queries," in preparation.

[22] HULIN G., "Parallel processing of recursive queries in distributed architectures," *Proc. 15th Int. Conf. Very Large Data Bases*, Amsterdam 1989, pp. 87–96.

[23] IOANIDIS Y. "On the computation of the transitive closure of relational operators," *Proc. 12th Int. Conf. on Very Large Data Bases*, Kyoto 1986, pp. 403–411.

[24] KERSTEN, M.L., APERS, P.M.G., HOUTSMA, M.A.W., VAN KUIJK, H.J.A., AND VAN DE WEG, R.L.W. "A distributed, main-memory database machine," in *Proc. of the 5th Int. Workshop on Database Machines*, Karuizawa, Japan, Oct. 5–8, 1987; and in *Database Machines and Knowledge Base Machines*, M. Kitsuregawa and H. Tanaka (eds.), Kluwer Academic Publishers, 1988, pp. 353–369.

[25] KLEINHUIS G. AND OSKAM K.R. "Evaluation and simulation of parallel algorithms for the transitive closure operation," M.Sc. Thesis, University of Twente, the Netherlands, May 1989.

[26] NEJDL W., CERI S., AND WIEDERHOLD G. "Evaluating recursive queries in distributed databases," Tech. Rep. 90-015, Politecnico di Milano, submitted for publication.

[27] RASCHID L. AND SU S.Y.W. "A parallel strategy for evaluating recursive queries," *Proc. 12th Int. Conf. on Very Large Data Bases*, Kyoto 1986, pp. 412–419.

[28] SCHNEIDER D. A. AND DE WITT D. J. "A performance analysis of four parallel join algorithms in a shared-nothing multiprocessor environment," in *Proc. ACM-Sigmod Conference*, 1989, pp. 110–121.

[29] TANDEM DATABASE GROUP, "NonStop SQL: a distributed, high-performance, highly-availability implementation of SQL", in *High Performance Transaction Systems*, Lecture Notes in Computer Science, Springer-Verlag, 1987.

[30] ULLMAN J.D. *Principles of Data and Knowledge-Based Systems"*, Computer Science Press, 1989.

[31] VALDURIEZ P. AND KHOSKAFIAN S. "Parallel Evaluation of the Transitive Closure of a Database Relation," Int. Journal of Parallel Programming, 17:1, Feb. 1988.

[32] VAN GELDER A., "A message passing framework for logical query evaluation," in *Proc. ACM-Sigmod Conference*, 1986, pp. 155–165.

[33] WOLFSON O. "Sharing the load of logic program evaluation," *Int. Symp. on Database in Parallel and Distributed Systems*, Dec. 1988, pp. 46–55.

Data Management with Massive Memory: A Summary [†]

Hector Garcia-Molina, Robert Abbott,
Christopher Clifton, Carl Staelin, Kenneth Salem [††]

Department of Computer Science
Princeton University
Princeton, N.J. 08544   U.S.A.

1. Introduction

The Massive Memory Machine Project (MMM) was started at Princeton around 1983. Year by year, semiconductor memory was becoming cheaper (and still is) and memory chip densities were increasing dramatically. We were interested in studying how availability of very large amounts of memory would change the way data intensive problems could be solved. We believed that just like parallel computer architectures could speed up scientific computations, computer architectures and software that exploited massive main memories could yield oder-of-magnitude performance improvements on many important computations.

By the end of 1985 we had received joint funding from the U.S. National Science Foundation and the Defense Advanced Research Projects Agency. This formal project has two main goals. One was to study key data intensive applications and to develop strategies for effectively utilizing large memories. The second was to design, implement, and test computer architectures that could support fast access to very large memories.

In this paper we will briefly summarize four of the MMM sub-projects having to do with data processing applications. For one sub-project, we implemented a memory resident transaction processing system (System M), of the type that might be used in an airline reservation or banking application. The second sub-project is an advanced file management system (iPcress). A third sub-project (HyperFile) involves a document management system that can be used to support hypertext style applications. Since memory resident data can be accessed very fast, a fourth sub-project studied real-time database management techniques.

[†] This research was supported by the Defense Advanced Research Projects Agency of the Department of Defense and by the Office of Naval Research under Contracts Nos. N00014-85-C-0456 and N00014-85-K-0465, and by the National Science Foundation under Cooperative Agreement No. DCR-8420948. The views and conclusions contained in this document are those of the authors and should not be interpreted as necessarily representing the official policies, either expressed or implied, of the Defense Advanced Research Projects Agency or the U.S. Government.

[††] Robert Abbott is now with Digital Equipment Corporation, Littleton, MA.; Kenneth Salem is with the University of Maryland, College Park, MD.

This is not a complete summary of the MMM activities, as there were other projects in the architecture and performance evaluation areas. In addition to the authors of this paper, there were other individuals who contributed to the project in general and to the data management sub-projects. These include Rafael Alonso, Daniel Barbara, Richard Lipton, Arvin Park, Jonathan Sandberg, and Jacobo Valdes.

As part of our summary we will reference various papers we have written that give more details and results. These papers discuss in detail the relationship to other work in these areas, so to avoid repetition, we will not include here references to this other related work. We also note that even though NSF and DARPA funding for MMM ends in 1990, some of our sub-projects are continuing with other funding. In particular, we are currently actively working on the iPcress and HyperFile systems. We also have a strong interest in continuing to study real time and transaction processing issues related to massive memory.

2. System M

System M is an experimental transaction processing system with a memory resident database. System M was built with three goals in mind:

(1) *To evaluate the potential gains of memory resident databases.* Given the current costs of memory, it is now feasible to store in main memory realistically large databases. The improvements in performance can be great: I/O is substantially reduced, transaction context switches (and associated CPU cache flushes) are cut, lock contention is decreased, more efficient memory search structures and query processing can be used, and so on.

(2) *To explore the architecture and algorithms best suited for memory resident databases.* A memory-resident transaction processing system (MTPS) could be implemented simply as a disk-based system (DTPS) with a buffer that happens to be large enough to hold the entire database. This approach fails to capitalize on many of the potential advantages that memory residence offers. System M, on the other hand, has been implemented from scratch with memory residence in mind, leading to a novel internal process architecture and recovery strategies.

(3) *To provide and experimental testbed for comparing algorithms.* In particular, System M implements several checkpointing and logging strategies. (The checkpointer is the component that periodically sweeps memory, propagating changes to the backup database on disk.)

We focused on checkpointing and logging because we believe they are the major performance issues in a MTPS. In other words, *conceptually*, the data management algorithms for a MTPS and a DTPS are similar. Both types of systems have data in memory and on disk, and must propagate the updated data to disk. Both mechanisms must have concurrency control mechanisms. However, a MTPS will do many fewer I/O operations: the only I/O is to maintain transaction durability. This implies that recovery I/O (for durability) is relatively much *more* important than in a DTPS. Recovery I/O requirements should be satisfied without sacrificing the advantages that memory resident data can bring.

To achieve this, it is essential to decouple the checkpointing and logging components as much as possible from the rest of the system, so that transaction processing rarely has to wait for them. It is also important that the checkpointer's updates to the backup database follow a sweep pattern, avoiding random I/O and larger seek times. Some high performance commercial systems batch together disk writes to achieve a good access pattern. So the idea of using a sweep checkpointer is not new. What is new is the desire to evaluate the performance of such checkpointers carefully, in light of the criticality of I/O costs in a MTPS.

System M is implemented in C on a VAX 11/785 with a 128 megabytes main memory[†] and running the Mach operating system. The main process types in System M are (1) a message server that generates new transactions; (2) a transaction server that runs the transactions; (3) a log server that manages the log; (4) and a checkpointer. There is only one log and one checkpointer process. In most cases, a transaction server can run a complete transaction with no interruptions (all of its data is in memory). Thus, it is usually advantageous to have a single transaction server, so that transaction are run serially. The checkpointer can run three types of algorithms: a fuzzy checkpoint one, a copy-on-update one, and a black-and-white one. The log manager can use value, action or transaction logging. To evaluate System M, a realistic credit card application was implemented. Typical transactions check the validity of a credit card, record a purchase, report a stolen card, and so on.

A detailed description of System M and its performance is given in [Sale90]. Some additional analytical results are presented in [Sale89]. One illustrative result is the following one. A disk based system typically requires about 100,000 instructions to process a transaction such as the ones in our credit card application. Currently, System M requires roughly 12,000 instructions. Thus, not only is the I/O load reduced due to memory residence, but the CPU requirements can be cut by an order of magnitude. This is due mainly to the simplified nature of a MTPS. Of course, this rough comparison must be treated with caution since commercial system provide more functionality than System M. But on the other hand, System M's performance is the result of only two man-years of implementation work.

3. The iPcress File System

In 1987 we initiated a joint study with Dieter Gawlick and Richard Wilmont of Amdahl Corporation to understand data access patterns of real applications. We looked at I/O operations on very large file systems (on the order of one terra byte) at several Amdahl customer locations. (Our results are presented in detail in [Stae88].) We observed that even for such huge file systems, there was relatively good locality of reference. If the file system could have on the order of a gigabyte of main memory buffers, then a large majority of all file accesses could be satisfied without going to disk. Furthermore, we discovered that certain file statistics could help in predicting future file usage. If these statistics were kept by the file system and used in caching decisions, the hit ratio could be improved further.

This suggested to us a novel type of file system, where frequently accessed files would reside permanently in memory. Decoupled from normal file activity, the system would analyze its file statistics and decide what files could migrate to disk. When a disk file were referenced, the system could decide to stage in the entire file and make it memory resident.

---

†   When we bought our VAX in 1985, 128 megabytes was considered a substantial main memory.

Based on these ideas, we designed the iPcress File System. We desired a general purpose file system that could replace the UNIX file system, perform much better and also address some of UNIX's other shortcomings. In particular, we wanted to utilize existing hardware and I/O bandwidth more effectively. We also wanted to provide better reliability and recovery than that afforded by UNIX. Additionally, we wanted it to be able to integrate all secondary storage devices for a host, such as disks, electronic disks and video jukeboxes, into a single file system. However, the basic UNIX file system interface, with its view of files as a stream of bytes, is a very fundamental and useful abstraction. Consequently, the iPcress file system keeps the simple UNIX interface, but it completely discards the UNIX implementation of the file system.

The iPcress file system is also being implemented on our VAX 11/785 running MACH. It uses MACH threads, ports, and shared memory facilities. The file system is run as a user process and it communicates with its clients using ports. This means that iPcress will be very portable. File data is transferred between client and server via shared memory. The system was written in GNU C++, and uses the GNU C++ library and generic facilities.

As part of the design, we decided that each host should have a single file system that includes all secondary storage for the machine. This is a very fundamental change from the UNIX file system, which places a separate file system on each device. It also allows us to add several important features, such as mirrored files, in a natural way. In addition, it implies that the system should be insensitive to the loss of any given device. Finally, it allows the system to monitor and control all file operations and secondary storage for the whole system.

We also decided to use a file cache, rather than a block cache. A file cache will stage and flush complete files, unless the file is very large. If files are usually contained in a single extent, then the available bandwidth to disk is utilized as effectively as possible. In addition, if the file system were to keep statistics for each file regarding past file access patterns, then the file cache (and the secondary storage manager) could attempt to optimize its behavior. Most heavily accessed files should live within the cache, and most read requests should be fulfilled from the cache rather than disk.

In order to optimize performance, we use a variable size blocking scheme, so that most files could be contained within a single contiguous block of storage (extent). We use the buddy system for both memory and disk management because of its simplicity and performance. The buddy system allocates blocks in sizes which are a power of two, which can result in large internal fragmentation costs. Therefore we decided to use a variant on the buddy system similar to that used in the DTS file system at Dartmouth, which reduces internal fragmentation by splitting some files into several extents.

One technique unique to iPcress is the online internal collection of file access statistics by the file system. The file system keeps a set of statistics for each file regarding that file's access patterns. This is useful for a variety of optimization techniques. First of all, it may be used to balance disk loads, or to influence the layout of files within a disk. It may also be used to detect which files may be split into several extents without greatly impacting system performance.

The prototype of iPcress is currently working as a single threaded user-level NFS server. This working prototype does not yet include optimizations such as dynamic file placement and layout. The code itself has not yet been tuned to improve performance. The key features of iPcress which have been implemented are:

- Large file cache
- Variety of storage techniques and caching algorithms
- Variable size blocks in both memory and secondary storage
- Multiple devices within a single file system
- Runs under MACH

Currently iPcress supports three basic types of file layout: data is contained within the inode, data is contained within a single disk block, and data is contained in several disk blocks. iPcress also supports three distinct caching algorithms: predictive caching of a whole file, caching whole (variable sized) disk blocks on demand, and caching sectors (typically much smaller than an iPcress disk block) on demand.

The initial iPcress prototype has been evaluated and compared to a commercial NFS server, using the Andrew Benchmark, designed by M. Satyanarayanan at Carnegie Mellon University. The experiments were done using a VAX 11/785 as the NFS file server and an IBM RT as the NFS client. The results indicate that this first iPcress prototype performs as well as the NFS server [Stae90]. This indicates that at least the redesign of the file system did not introduce any critical inefficiencies. It also leads us to believe that when the optimizations are added to iPcress, and that when tests are run on large files, iPcress will perform substantially better that current file systems.

4. HyperFile, A Document Database

Traditional database management systems are designed for information which consists of large numbers of identically structured *records*. Much of the data which can be stored and accessed using a computer does not fit cleanly into such a structure. In particular many documents, involving text as well as pictures, graphs, and other media, are now created and stored on computers. Currently such information is stored in file systems and does not benefit from the access and reliability technology which has been developed in the Database Management field.

One model for electronic documents which is growing in popularity is *hypertext*. In this model, nodes containing information are connected by links, and the user "reads" a document by following these links. This model has a problem scaling to large collections of documents. Although it is nice to use if one knows how to get to a document, it can be difficult to find information if one does not know which links to follow. We have developed a query language which supports the hypertext-style browsing interface, and integrates this with non-navigational queries. We view this query language as an interface between an application which presents the document, and a "document server" which provides storage, reliability, sharing, and other facilities offered by traditional databases. An overview of this approach is given in [Clif88].

We are looking at a number of issues that arise in such a system. One example is *indexing*. In our system queries may only operate on a portion of the database determined by the links between documents. Indexes must take into account these links when defining the *scope* of the index. This is in contrast to a relational system where the scope of an index is a relation or view, which is defined independent of the database content. A number of approaches for indexing in this environment are described and analyzed in [Clif90]. These involve "hierarchies" of indexes associated with different locations in the database. Each index is responsible for documents in a subset of the database, and queries which access areas of the database containing many indexes make use of all of them in a coherent manner. This work may have applications in other hypertext systems as well as in object-oriented databases.

Another issue is distributed HyperFile. In many cases a single document server may not be appropriate, for example an archival server may not want to contain works in progress, and users may want documents which they "own" to be stored locally. We support distributed queries in a simple and efficient manner, which scales well to large and geographically distributed systems.

We have built a prototype database manager based on these ideas. Current work with this prototype involves experiments with distributed queries, and the development of a user interface which provide a hypertext-style browsing "look and feel" for composing non-navigational queries.

The prototype is implemented as part of the MMM Project, efficiently utilizing the available large memory. Our initial strategy is to cache in memory only the structured portion of documents, leaving text data on secondary storage. With a simple and regular document model we expect to be able to store the in memory portion of the documents very compactly. This in turn means that for many queries all of the search data (e.g., keywords, pointers) will be memory resident, making it possible to examine vast numbers of documents. Only when the desired documents are identified, would access to secondary storage be needed to retrieve the bulky parts such as contents of a paper, pictures, etc.

5. Real Time Database Processing

Many applications have at the same time real-time constraints and large data needs (e.g., aircraft tracking, hospital monitoring, reservations systems). A memory-resident database system could provide the required response time. However, existing database management systems do not provide real-time services. They process transactions as quickly as they can, but they do not guarantee that a transaction will meet its deadline. Furthermore, most users cannot even tell the system what priority their request has. Hence, all transactions are treated as equal.

We have started to investigate real-time database systems, as an application for a massive memory machine. Such systems would provide facilities for processing database requests within given deadlines. The first problem we have addressed in this area is that of transaction scheduling. In the future we plan to study additional issues like the general architecture, how to trigger events efficiently, and the appropriate user interface.

Real time transaction scheduling differs from conventional scheduling in that the transactions (or tasks) make *unpredictable* resource requests, mainly requests to read or write the database. In our case, the scheduling algorithm must be combined with the concurrency control algorithm (which guarantees that executions are serializable). To illustrate the interaction, consider a transaction T_1 that is being executed because its deadline is the nearest. Now assume that T_1 requests a lock that is held by transaction T_2. What should the system do? Abort T_2 so that the lock is released and T_1 can proceed? Or maybe suspend T_1 so that T_2 can complete and release its lock? Or maybe it is best to let T_1 proceed without aborting T_2, hoping that the schedule will still be serializable (optimistic control)?

In a first study we developed a family of locking-based scheduling algorithms for memory resident real-time database systems [Abbo88a]. Each algorithm has three components: a policy to determine which tasks are eligible for service, a policy for assigning priorities to tasks, and a concurrency control mechanism. The eligibility policy determines whether a transaction that has already missed its deadline (or is about to) can be aborted and not performed at all. The priority policy orders the ready transactions according to their deadline, the slack time, or the arrival time. The concurrency control policy specifies the action to take when lock conflicts occur.

We studied the performance of the scheduling algorithms via a detailed event-driven simulation [Abbo88b]. The parameters in the model include the arrival rate of transactions, the average number of objects updated, the available slack for meeting the transaction's deadline, and the possible error in the transaction's running time estimate. The performance metrics we studied were the number of missed deadlines, the transaction throughput, and the number of aborted (and restarted) transactions.

In a second study we expanded our model to include disk resident database systems and both shared and exclusive locks [Abbo89]. Of course, in a large memory environment, disk resident databases are less of interest, but we felt that studying this case would shed light into the memory-disk tradeoffs. We developed two different ways in which to schedule IO requests at the disk. We also examined two additional concurrency control algorithms including one which promotes the priority of a transaction which is blocking a higher priority transaction from executing.

The algorithms were evaluated via a detailed event-driven simulation. Some of the new parameters in the model were size of the database, average number of objects locked exclusively and the speed of the disk server. The performance metrics used to rate the different algorithms were number of missed deadlines, average tardy time of transactions, and number of aborted (and restarted) transactions. We also studied the algorithms under a simulated load spike, or the introduction of a flurry of jobs in an otherwise lightly loaded system.

6. References

[Abbo88a] R. Abbott and H. Garcia-Molina, "Scheduling Real-Time Transactions," *ACM SIGMOD Record*, Vol. 17, No. 1, March 1988, pp. 71-81.

[Abbo88b] R. Abbott and H. Garcia-Molina, "Scheduling Real Time Transactions: A Performance Evaluation," *Proc. 14th VLDB Conference*, Long Beach, California, August 1988.

[Abbo89] R. Abbott and H. Garcia-Molina, "Scheduling Real-Time Transactions with Disk Resident Data," *Proc. 15th VLDB Conference*, Amsterdam, August 1989, 385-396.

[Clif88] Chris Clifton, Hector Garcia-Molina, and Robert Hagmann, "The Design of a Document Database," *Proceedings of the Conference on Document Processing Systems,* pp. 125-134, ACM, Santa Fe, New Mexico, December 5-9, 1988.

[Clif90]   Chris Clifton and Hector Garcia-Molina, "Indexing in a Hypertext Database," *Proceedings of the 1990 International Conference on Very Large Databases,* Brisbane, Australia, August 13-16, 1990, pp. 36-49.

[Sale89]   K. Salem, H. Garcia-Molina, "Checkpointing Memory-Resident Databases," *Proc. IEEE Database Engineering Conference*, February 1989.

[Sale90]   K. Salem, H. Garcia-Molina, "System M: A Transaction Processing Testbed for Memory Resident Data," *IEEE Transactions on Knowledge and Data Engineering*, Vol. 2, No. 1, March 1990, pp. 161-172.

[Stae88]   Carl Staelin, File Access Patterns, Technical Report CS-TR-179-88, Department of Computer Science, Princeton University, September 1988.

[Stae90]   C. Staelin, H. Garcia-Molina, "File System Design Using Large Memories," *Proc. 5th Jerusalem Conference on Information Technology*, Jerusalem October 1990. (Also Technical Report CS-TR-246-90, CS Dept., Princeton University.)

An Approach to Implement Dynamically Defined Complex Objects

T. Härder

University of Kaiserslautern, Dept. of Computer Sciences, D-6750 Kaiserslautern, West Germany

Abstract

Conventional data models embodied by current database management systems (DBMS) do not provide satisfactory support for emerging applications. A major reason for this deficiency is the absense of concepts for complex object processing. In this paper, we explain the motivation and key properties of a new data model explicitly designed for the management of complex objects. Furthermore, the most important design decisions and implementation concepts for complex objects are discussed, as far as they were realized in the PRIMA project. Finally, we describe a nested transaction concept enabling intra-transaction parallelism when complex objects have to be retrieved or manipulated.

1. Introduction

Today's DBMS are unable to meet the increasing requirements of emerging applications that would like to use a DBMS. Such applications including CAD, VLSI design, geographic information management, etc. are often called non-standard applications. To improve this situation, a new generation of DBMS architectures adjusted to the demands of the applications has to be developed.

For this purpose, many researchers have analysed the data management needs of a spectrum consisting mainly of engineering applications and have encountered both a modeling and a processing problem in today's DBMS [Da86, DD86, DE84, LK84, SR86, WSSH88]. An important reason for both problems is the lack of adequate support for complex objects [". . . support for molecular objects should be an integrate part of future DBMSs . . ." [BB84]). For our discussion, the notion of complex objects (molecules) is used to indicate that such objects have an internal structure maintained by the DBMS and that access to the object is provided as a whole as well as to its components.

[BB84] has classified the 'molecular' objects according to their structure, leading to disjoint/non-disjoint and recursive/non-recursive complex objects. We have argued elsewhere [HMMS87, Hä89, Mi89] that the least restrictive or most general classification properties **non-disjoint/recursive** are indispensable for a data model sufficiently useful for the broad class of non-standard applications. In order to achieve refined and accurate modeling as well as efficient processing for complex objects, the data model and its implementation should offer [HMS90]

- genuine and symmetric support for **network structures** (sharing of sub-objects in contrast to hierarchical structures, which are just special cases thereof), or even recursive structures,

- support for **dynamic** object definition in combination with

- **powerful**, yet **efficient manipulation** facilities.

Before we outline the molecule-atom data model (MAD model) as our solution to the handling of complex objects in sect. 3, we explain why the relational model fails to provide the above mentioned capabilities. Sect. 4 discusses the major implementation problems related to complex objects within the architectural framework of the PRIMA project [Hä88]. The main properties of a nested transaction concept are sketched in sect. 5, which supports parallelism in operations on complex objects motivated in sect. 6. Finally, we present some conclusions and give an outlook as to our current application areas.

2. Why not the relational model ?

In order to investigate the weaknesses of the relational model for engineering applications, we start with a simplified example from solid modeling. Fig. 1 illustrates the Entity/Relationship diagram [Ch76] and a mapping example for the representation of 3D-objects. Note, we have skipped a number of additional entity types such as track and relationship types (between Point and Face or Point and Volume) to keep the example tractable. The recursive relationship on Volume is only used to demonstrate the mapping of recursive structures to the data model. In the following, we mainly focus on the non-recursive part (from Volume to Point).

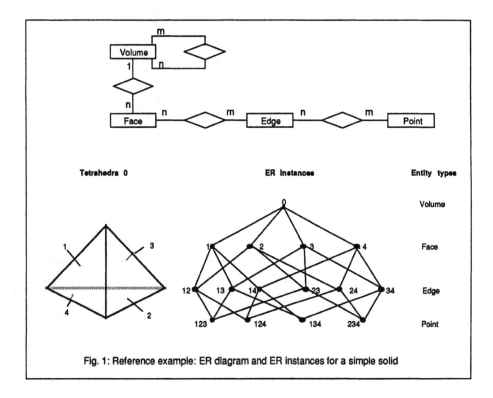

Fig. 1: Reference example: ER diagram and ER instances for a simple solid

The relational model offers the concept of normalized relations, primary key, and foreign key to map entity and relationship types. Primary/foreign key pairs are used to represent the relationships in the model. Since only functional relationships may be covered by primary/foreign key pairs, every (n:m)-relationships has to be replaced by two (artificial) (1:n)-relationships. Such keys are always symbolic values (user-defined) which may have some critical impact on join, integrity checking, or search operations. As far as model-inherent integrity preservation is concerned, the so-called relational invariants should be guaranteed by the system.

Our reference example of Fig. 1 may be syntactically translated into a relation DB schema by assigning each entity type and each (n:m)-relationship type to a separate relation and by representing each (1:n)-relationship type by a pair of primary/foreign keys. The result is shown in Fig. 2 together with a sample database for the representation of the simple solid Tetrahedra 0. To indicate the functional relationships established by primary/foreign keys, we have used dotted lines at the instance and at the type level.

Schema definition statements

```
CREATE TABLE Volume
    (vid          :  INTEGER,
    descriptor    :  CHAR(20),
    numfaces      :  INTEGER,
    usage         :  CHAR(25),
    PRIMARY KEY (vid));


CREATE TABLE Face
    (fid          :  INTEGER,
    forientation  :  INTEGER,
    numedges      :  INTEGER,
    vref          :  INTEGER,
    PRIMARY KEY (fid),
    FOREIGN KEY (vref) REFERENCES Volume);


CREATE TABLE Edge
    (eid          :  INTEGER,
    etype         :  CHAR(5),
    PRIMARY KEY (eid));


CREATE TABLE Point
    (pid          :  INTEGER,
    x, y, z       :  INTEGER,
    PRIMARY KEY (pid));
```

```
CREATE TABLE VolStructure
    (u_vid        :  INTEGER,
    l_vid         :  INTEGER,
    PRIMARY KEY (u_vid, l_vid),
    FOREIGN KEY (u_vid) REFERENCES Volume,
    FOREIGN KEY (l_vid) REFERENCES Volume);


CREATE TABLE FE_Rel
    (fid          :  INTEGER,
    eid           :  INTEGER,
    PRIMARY KEY (fid, eid),
    FOREIGN KEY (fid) REFERENCES Face,
    FOREIGN KEY (eid) REFERENCES Edge);


CREATE TABLE EP_Rel
    (eid          :  INTEGER,
    pid           :  INTEGER,
    PRIMARY KEY (eid, pid),
    FOREIGN KEY (eid) REFERENCES Edge,
    FOREIGN KEY (pid) REFERENCES Point);
```

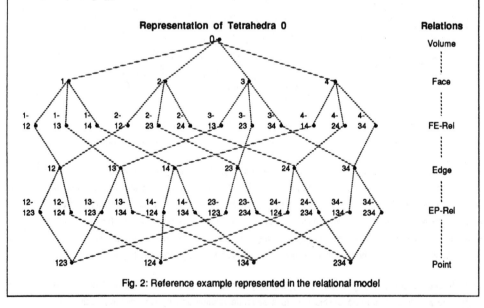

Fig. 2: Reference example represented in the relational model

As one can see even in this simplified example, the tuples representing Tetrahedra 0 are spread across many (six) relations. More complex CAD objects would require the use of about 20 or more relations [Hä89]. Since the data model knows only relations as objects, more complex structures cannot be dealt with. It can only pro-vide an 'atomized' view of the application entities, that is, all model-inherent operations deal with tuples and relations (closure property), but cannot derive structured objects. For example, the view of the solid as an integral object including its representation, manipulation, and integrity preservation has been lost. When complex objects have to be handled, a component above the data model interface (e.g. application) has to perform this task using relational operations.

For this reason, access to complex objects has to be simulated by means of SQL operations applied to sets of independent relations. Let us assume that the Face object with fid = 2 together with the related Edges and Points has to be fetched. Since the result of an SQL operation is a (homogeneous) relation, such a request is not feasible (without loosing the object structure). But we may, for example, obtain all Points belonging to Face objects (with F.fid < 3), thereby explicitly reconstructing the complex Face object by means of user-specified joins:

```
SELECT    F.fid, F.forientation, F.numedges P.x, P.y, P.z
FROM      Point P, EP-Rel S, Edge E, FE_Rel T, Face F
WHERE     F.fid < 3
   AND    P.pid = S.pid          /*  reconstruction of  */
   AND    S.eid = E.eid          /*  complex objects    */
   AND    E.eid = T.eid          /*  at                 */
   AND    T.fid = F.fid;         /*  run time           */
```

The relational model permits the use of relationships in both directions. If we want to access all Faces associated with Point (50,44,75), we cannot refer to the corresponding Point object with all related Edges and Faces (a complex object with inverse nesting as compared to the previous case), but we may again derive the object structure explicitly:

```
SELECT    F.fid, F.forientation, F.numedges
FROM      Point P, EP-Rel S, Edge E, FE_Rel T, Face F
WHERE     P.x = 50 AND P.y = 44 AND P.z = 75
   AND    P.pid = S.pid          /*  reconstruction of  */
   AND    S.eid = E.eid          /*  complex objects    */
   AND    E.eid = T.eid          /*  at                 */
   AND    T.fid = F.fid;         /*  run time           */
```

It is interesting to note that the same sequence of join operations has to be used in both cases, although both object structures (Face-Edge-Point and Point-Edge-Face nesting) are quite different.

More arguments and observations may be found for modeling and processing weaknesses of the relational model. To shorten the discussion, let us summarize our criticism:

- The structure of complex objects is not preserved when mapped to relations; hence, it cannot be used for retrieval, update, or integrity checking.
- (n:m)-relationships cannot be directly represented; their replacement by two (1:n)-relationships leads to ponderous modeling and increase of type-crossing operations.
- Referential integrity checking may be expensive due to missing operational support.

- Explicit reconstruction of complex objects at run-time causes significant overhead due to the number and type of join-operations (based on symbolic values).

- Neither recursive object structures nor recursive search operations (e.g. transitive closure) are supported.

As a consequence, the application has to do almost everything in a very expensive way as far as complex object handling is concerned.

3. A Data Model for Complex Objects

So far we have explained why complex object management is not possible in the relational model because of inadequate operations and missing structures to support object orientation. Simulation of an equivalent behavior, however, is incomplete (lack of structure) and neither effective nor efficient as shown in [Hä89]. For this reason, we advocate a powerful data model supporting complex objects; its key properties were encountered by several prototype studies which were directed towards database requirements for engineering applications.

3.1 Desired Data Model Properties

Our data model should exhibit structural object orientation allowing the system to utilize the structure information to derive or manipulate the complex object as a unit and to maintain the referential integrity of the structure. The integration of application-oriented (behavioral) semantics and integrity into the model was not considered in order to avoid overloading the model with application-specific aspects; it could be added by a so-called application layer operating on top of the data model interface [HM90]. The result of our prototype studies revealed important access and processing characteristics of engineering applications [Hä89] which influenced the design objectives of our data model:

- **Non-disjoint object representation:** Complex objects may share common subobjects. Whenever a relationship is of type (n:m), such component sharing occurs. This type of relationship is frequent in engineering applications and, therefore, critical for modeling tasks. If relationship representation is restricted to functional ones (1:1, n:1), object representation is disjoint; however, modeling accuracy and completeness are by no means satisfying the requirements of advanced applications. Hence, non-disjoint object representation is essential.

- **Recursive objects:** Complex objects are called recursive if they are composed of objects of the same type, e.g. solids are built using previously constructed solids. Besides (n:m)-relationships recursiveness seems to be a distinct characteristic of engineering applications. Hence, recursive object definition as well as object manipulation by the system avoids tedious and ineffective object manipulation by the application.

- **Dynamic definition of complex objects:** Static definition of complex objects means that they are defined in the DB schema (frozen at schema definition time). Such static objects are considered to occur rather infrequently. Typically, each algorithm has tailored views of the complex object it is processing. Some solid-construction algorithm may require a particular face object along with the corresponding edges and points (Face-Edge-Point), whereas another task may refer to just the inverse object nesting, i.e. a point object with its adjacent faces and edges (Point-Edge-Face). Hence, design flexibility is greatly enhanced by means of dynamic object definition, e.g. in the user query.

- **Symmetry of relationship representation:** Dynamic object definition implies dynamic object derivation. Since all relationships specified in the DB schema may be used in either direction for object definition, all of them should be represented in such a way that they can be efficiently traversed in both directions (symmetrical representation). For performance reasons, (n:m)-relationships should be mapped directly (without special connection record) to minimize type-crossing operations (e.g. joins).

It was our main goal to incorporate all these properties in our data model.

3.2 The Molecule-Atom Data Model

In the following, we introduce the essential characteristics of the molecule-atom data model (MAD model [Hä88]) and show how the design objectives were obtained. The concepts of the relational model help us to explain similarities and differences, when mapping entity and relationship types of the real world using the concepts of the data model:

- Relations are named **atom types** and tuples are now called **atoms**, which represent entities of the real world.

- All relevant relationships between entity types are explicitly specified in the DB schema and represented in the DB. As opposed to this, the relational model relies on the foreign key/primary key concept.

- Relationship types, simply called **link types**, are represented in an explicit and symmetrical way. As a result, the DB schema consists of undirected networks of atom types.

- Atoms are connected to one another by **links** according to the link types specified in the DB schema. As an important consequence, the DB can be viewed as an undirected network of atoms.

- Atoms consist of **attributes** of various data types, are uniquely identifiable, and belong to their corresponding atom types. The data types of the attributes, however, can be chosen from a richer selection than those in the relational model. The types **RECORD, ARRAY,** and the repeating-group types **SET** and **LIST** yield a powerful structuring facility at the attribute level.

- Two special types serve for the realization of links between atoms. Atom identification is achieved by the **IDENTIFIER** type which is implemented by a system-supplied surrogate concept. Based on this type the **REFERENCE** type was defined and provides a list of identifier values belonging to atoms of exactly one atom type.

Fig. 3 illustrates as an example, the schema definition for solids and an atom network representing the simple solid Tetrahedra 0 (the recursive relationships on Volume atoms are not shown). By comparing it with Fig. 1, it becomes obvious that the MAD model can be perceived as a direct mapping (implementation) of the ER model. As illustrated by the schema definition, each link type (e.g. between atom types Volume and Face) is specified by a pair of REFERENCE_TO attributes, one in each atom type involved (e.g. attribute fref of Volume and attribute vref of Face). A link between two atoms (e.g. between 0 and 3) is represented by the corresponding values of the REFERENCE_TO attributes forming the link type; they contain the IDENTIFIER values of the atoms they are referencing (e.g. vref of atom 3 stores the vid value of atom 0 and, in turn, fref of atom 0 the fid value of atom 3 and, of course, 1,2,4). As indicated by the example, our data model supports the concept of cardinality restrictions for link types. An AT_LEAST and an AT_MOST value specify the minimum and maximum number of references which each atom may contain for the corresponding link type.

Obviously, all kinds of relationships (1:1, 1:n, n:m) as well as recursive relationships on the same entity type (e.g. on Volume) can be directly mapped by this concept. Hence, (n:m)-relationships no longer require a decomposition and two (1:n)-mappings, as is necessary in the relational model. Furthermore, convenient information such as numfaces and numedges in the relational DB schema (see Fig. 2) is redundant in the sense that the number of faces and edges can be extracted by searching the Face and FE-Rel relations respectively. As a consequence of our link representation, we do not need to represent this information by attributes; the operation COUNT applied to V.fref and F.eref quickly delivers the current values thereby avoiding the introduction of hidden redundancy. As far as referential integrity is concerned, the system controls all defined link types (pairs of REFERENCE_TO attributes) together with the associated cardinality restrictions. If a link is inserted, modified or deleted by updating the corresponding REFERENCE_TO attribute value, the appropriate back references are automatically adjusted. The specification of the counterpart attribute in the REFERENCE_TO clause is not necessary if only a single link is involved in an atom type. If multiple links are present, this specification is needed to avoid ambiguities. It permits the fast location of the corresponding counter references necessary for checking the cardinality restrictions and for link modification operations.

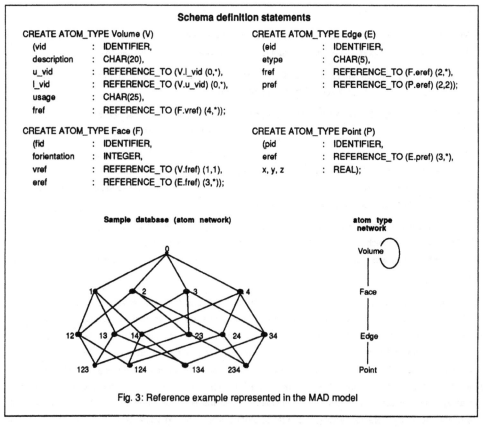

Schema definition statements

CREATE ATOM_TYPE Volume (V)
(vid	:	IDENTIFIER,
description	:	CHAR(20),
u_vid	:	REFERENCE_TO (V.l_vid (0,*),
l_vid	:	REFERENCE_TO (V.u_vid) (0,*),
usage	:	CHAR(25),
fref	:	REFERENCE_TO (F.vref) (4,*));

CREATE ATOM_TYPE Edge (E)
(eid	:	IDENTIFIER,
etype	:	CHAR(5),
fref	:	REFERENCE_TO (F.eref) (2,*),
pref	:	REFERENCE_TO (P.eref) (2,2));

CREATE ATOM_TYPE Face (F)
(fid	:	IDENTIFIER,
forientation	:	INTEGER,
vref	:	REFERENCE_TO (V.fref) (1,1),
eref	:	REFERENCE_TO (E.fref) (3,*));

CREATE ATOM_TYPE Point (P)
(pid	:	IDENTIFIER,
eref	:	REFERENCE_TO (E.pref) (3,*),
x, y, z	:	REAL);

Sample database (atom network)

atom type network

Volume
Face
Edge
Point

Fig. 3: Reference example represented in the MAD model

The direct and symmetric representation of relationships by bidirectional links establishes the basis for the model's flexibility. Based on the atom networks, complex objects (molecules) are dynamically definable as higher level objects which are viewed as structured sets of interconnected and possibly heterogeneous atoms. Their structure is described by a directed connected subgraph of the DB schema whose nodes are the atom types involved and whose edges are the link types to be used. For example, Face-Edge-Point specifies the structure of molecules where the relationships Face-Edge and Edge-Point are exploited to derive the molecule set. The structure graph must have one designated node (the **root**) from which all other nodes can be reached. Only in the case of recursive molecules is this structure graph allowed to be cyclic (e.g. Bill-of-Materials problem).

At least at the conceptual level, the dynamic derivation of the molecules proceeds in a straightforward way using the molecule structure as a kind of template, which is laid over the atom networks: for each atom of the root atom type, a molecule is derived following all links determined by the link types of the molecule structure until the leaves are reached. Hence, for each root atom a single molecule is derived (see Fig. 4). Both the molecule structure together with the corresponding set of molecules are denoted **molecule type**.

3.3 Query Facilities in MQL

The operational power of the MAD model is gained by the molecule query language (MQL) and its facilities for molecule processing. A detailed description of it may be found in [Mi88]. Here, we have to restrict ourselves to a short summary. Similar to SQL, MQL is subdivided into three parts dedicated to data definition (DDL), load definition (LDL), and data manipulation (DML). To indicate the power of the language, we illustrate some query facilities.

Analogous to SQL, there are three basic language constructs:

* The *FROM* clause specifies the molecule type to be worked with.

* The *WHERE* clause allows for the restriction of the corresponding molecule set.

* The projection clause (i.e. the *SELECT* clause in the case of retrieval statements) defines the set of the molecule's atoms to be retrieved and is responsible for proper molecule projection.

Compared to SQL, these constructs exhibit extended semantics and syntax in accordance to the more complex objects which have to be dealt with. They form the basis of all DML-statements offered. The result of each query is also a molecule type. Thus, it can be shown [Mi89] that the closure of the MAD model under its molecule operations is guaranteed. This is a very important fact, which allows the nesting of molecule queries; each molecule-type specification can be replaced by a molecule query.

In the following, we wish to demonstrate how the key properties of the MAD model are available through MQL statements. Dynamic object definition is achieved by means of the FROM clause which determines the molecule structure to be operated upon. Fig. 4a shows the result of an MQL query which was derived from the atom network of Fig. 3. In addition, Fig. 4b illustrates the aspect of symmetric relationship representation, where Point-Edge-Face was used instead of Face-Edge-Point in the previous example.

The molecule structures in Fig. 4 form (simple) hierarchies; in the same way, network structures may be specified, e.g. the molecule type A-(B,C)-D corresponds to a diamond structure at the type level. Even recursion along a link type can be easily specified by an MQL query. One of the directed links selected for the molecule type definition is used to form a cycle in the molecule structure. Hence, the definition of a recursive molecule type consists of a subgraph called **component molecule type** and the recursion defining relationship (indicated by the keyword RECURSIVE). Molecules of a recursive type are denoted **recursive molecules** [Sch89].

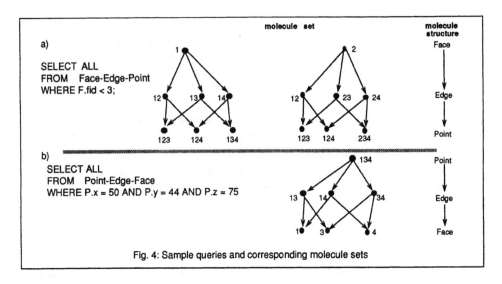

Fig. 4: Sample queries and corresponding molecule sets

Recursive molecules on atom type Volume may be defined via REFERENCE_TO attributes u_vid or l_vid by using the RECURSIVE clause, e.g.

- Volume RECURSIVE Volume.u_vid-Volume   (is-used-in relationships)
- Volume RECURSIVE Volume.l_vid-Volume   (is-composed-of relationships).

These molecule type definitions specify molecules which are tailored to solve problems of the Bill-of-Material type. They are derived from the atom network (of Volume atoms) in analogy to non-recursive molecules: Starting from the root atom a component molecule is built up (recursion level 0). For each leaf atom involved in the recursion defining relationship, new root atoms may be found. They trigger the derivation of the related component molecules (recursion level 1) which are appended to the resulting molecule. Depending on the network structure, this process allows for an unlimited depth of recursion. In order to guarantee termination, a component molecule belongs to a recursive molecule exactly once; if a component molecule is already in the resulting molecule, it is not included again. Furthermore, recursion depth can be controlled by special keywords referring to the recursion level or stop predicates [Sch89]. This recursive process leads to the realization of a transitive closure computation with a single starting point: A maximal directed acyclic subgraph of the atom network is formed.

Molecules representing transitive closures contain only minimal paths, which are not sufficient for the computation of some path problems (e.g. shortest paths, critical paths, etc.). For this reason, the expressiveness of MQL was extended by the REC_PATH clause and by special operators for aggregation and concatenation to specify and evaluate recursion paths. Path problems are computed by generating all maximal cycle-free paths according to the directed relationship specified in the REC_PATH clause (in place of the RECURSIVE clause). Instead of tracing all values of a REFERENCE_TO attribute at a time to derive the transitive closure, only one REFERENCE_TO value is followed for the path computation. As a result, each of the generated paths forms a molecule of its own. For details see [Sch89].

An example for recursive molecules is outlined in Fig. 5. The definition of the recursive molecule type consists of the component molecule type (A-B-C) and the recursion defining relationship (C-A). Molecule derivation is

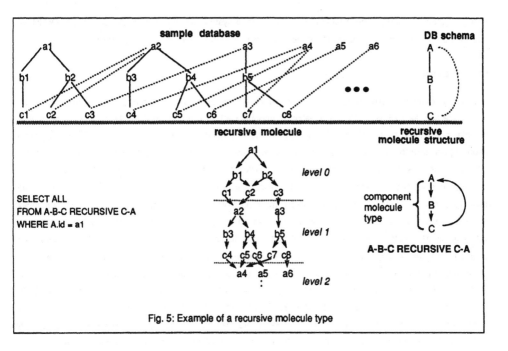

Fig. 5: Example of a recursive molecule type

sketched for a sample DB. In this example, recursion would proceed as long as new root atoms (of type A) are found during molecule materialization.

All examples so far reflect the property of non-disjoint representation of the atom networks and the derived molecules. A molecule set is dynamically obtained as the result of an MQL query: the corresponding sets of interrelated heterogeneous record structures are then passed on to the caller of the query.

Obviously, dynamic object derivation is a performance-critical issue. It should be noted, however, that atom-type crossing operations (hierarchical joins) are less frequent and more efficient than joins in the relational model due to direct (n:m)-relationship representation and system-controlled surrogates. Furthermore, cluster mechanisms at the physical level may speed-up such operations.

4. Implementation of complex objects

So far, we have outlined our view of dynamically derived structured objects. Furthermore, we have sketched some functions of the DML to define and manipulate such objects. With these concepts in mind we can begin discussing the major issues of a DBMS which implements such a powerful data model.

Every DBMS embodies a layered architecture which is in charge of dynamically mapping the physical objects on external storage devices to the objects (molecules) visible at the data model interface. At the bottom, the database is a very long bit string stored on disk which needs to be interpreted by the DBMS code. Proceeding from the bottom up, each layer derives objects containing more structures and allowing more powerful operations. Finally, the uppermost interface supports the objects, operations, and integrity constraints of the data model. Here we refer to a hierarchical architecture with three layers, which is common in many approaches (e.g. System R [As76]). These layers are called storage system, access system and data system which we describe from the bottom up along with their mechanisms related to complex objects implementation.

4.1 Storage system

The storage system is responsible for the management of the DB files on external storage and the DB buffer in main memory as well as for the propagation of updates back to external storage. The objects, or alternatively containers, offered by the storage system are segments divided into pages of equal size. Appropriate adaptation of page size to suit the objects to be stored will reduce I/O overhead, since pages are the unit of physical data transfer. A separate page size per object, however, is unmanageable and would cause a lot of fragmentation in the DB buffer and on disk. A different page size per segment (e.g. 2^n Kbyte, $1 \leq n \leq 5$), on the other hand, may be feasible and may relieve the mapping problem for larger objects. Accordingly, the mapping between pages and disk blocks as well as buffer replacement become more complicated. Buffer management with multiple page sizes [Si88] adds a lot of complexity to replacement decisions, even for restricted page lengths (2^n Kbyte). A single buffer may achieve better memory utilization as compared to schemes with multiple buffers of the same overall size where each buffer is used for a fixed page size. However, buffer fragmentation as well as stronger sensitivity of replacement decisions to reference patterns and page sizes, make the use of such schemes at least debatable. More robust and simple buffer management is therefore gained by a static buffer partitioning, where each of the multiple buffers may be managed by a page replacement algorithm tailored to the expected reference patterns. Lower memory utilization as an argument will become less valid with the growth of memory sizes and a decrease in memory costs.

Typically, the storage system interface offers a single page upon request of the access system. When accessing larger objects or object clusters, it may be advantageous to support the concept of page sequence (or virtual page) consisting of a header page and an arbitrary number of component pages. Reference to such a compound page enables the storage system to accomplish optimization measures when it has to be read or written (e.g. parallel disk access, chained I/O).

4.2 Access system

The access system stores and maintains records (atoms with set-valued variable-length attribute values) and a variety of access path structures to speed-up different types of access. For this purpose, it uses the services of the storage system (e.g. fix and unfix page or page sequence, etc.).

Storage of records

Atoms to be stored need a flexible storage structure supporting variable length, dynamic growth or shrinking, as well as stability of reference. In our context, the following properties for storage schemes are important [SS90]:

- Modification or direct access of atoms is always performed via surrogates. Hence, the corresponding values should make fast access possible.

- Physical movements of an atom should not invalidate its external address used for reference purposes.

- Computation of the position of an attribute value within a record is performance-critical, e.g. to enable efficient sorting.

- Fast access to a single attribute value should be supported independent of whether it has a defined value or not.

- Storage size of records should be kept as small as possible to reduce storage costs as well as I/O overhead.

- Dynamic extensions of existing atom types (e.g. addition of a new attribute) should be possible without immediate modifications in the records affected.

A flexible storage scheme satisfying these requirements was proposed in [SS90]; here, we only sketch the main ideas. The description of an atom type is kept in the meta-data managed by a dedicated component. Hence, attribute description such as name, type, fixed or variable length, single- or set-valued, etc. is available for all attributes, as well as information concerning their sequence, in the atom. In this way, all values belonging to an atom can be stored in form of byte strings (value), as illustrated in Fig. 6.

The first entry of each record contains the surrogate of the associated atom (access to the record via the surrogate value has to be organized efficiently, e.g. by a surrogate translation table). The defined values information implemented by a bitmap permits the skipping of undefined attributes values. Thus, only existing attribute values are stored in the sequence specified in the meta-data. To support position computation within a record, fixed-length attributes are directly stored, whereas variable-length attributes are represented by a management entry (of fixed length) which points to the corresponding value at the 'variable' part of the record. It should be noted that this scheme tries to minimize modification as well as expansion overhead, by using a starting offset (which changes when a new value its attached) and additional relative offsets (which may be influenced when variable-length values are updated). Furthermore, attribute expansions at the atom-type level do not have an impact on the record structure, the corresponding attribute value is considered undefined as long as the record has not received it (the length of the bitmap allows such a decision).

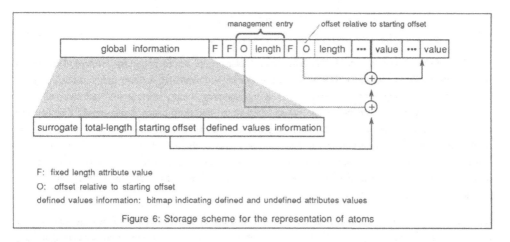

Figure 6: Storage scheme for the representation of atoms

Mapping a record to a page sequence

If the record length is smaller than the page size of the corresponding segment, it is stored within a single page and may share the page with other records. On the other hand, a record may exceed the page size which requires a page sequence to be used as a 'container' for such a record. A straightforward approach is to consider the page sequence as a single linear address space, i.e., a record is mapped onto the page sequence as if there were no page boundaries (except the intersperse of page headers). In this case, however,

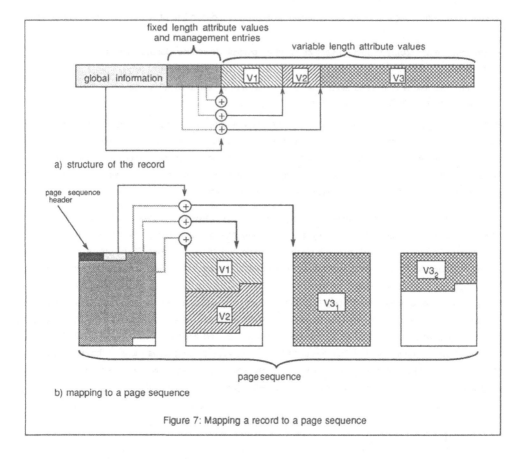

fixed length attribute values
and management entries

variable length attribute values

global information

a) structure of the record

page sequence header

page sequence

b) mapping to a page sequence

Figure 7: Mapping a record to a page sequence

record update may become very cumbersome when displacements across pages are involved. Therefore, a mixed strategy may be beneficial, to avoid excessive modification overhead. A 'fixed' part contains the global information, all fixed-length attribute values, and all management entries, whereas the 'variable' part at the end consists of all variable-length attribute values which would frequently cause displacements if represented as a contiguous byte sequence. As indiciated in Fig. 7, the fixed part is consecutively mapped to the page sequence disregarding the page boundaries. The attribute values of the variable part are then attached at the end of the fixed part. Each attribute value, however, is checked as to whether or not it fits entirely into a page. If not, one or sometimes even more new pages are allocated to accommodate the values. The details of this mapping may be found in [SS90].

Note that only one record is stored in a page sequence which strongly simplifies the management of 'long' records, especially their modifications. This storage scheme could also be extended to accommodate 'long fields' [CD86, LL89] which, however, does not directly address the issues of complex objects.

So far, we have outlined the storage structure when a single atom type is allocated to a segment. With appropriate access paths such as B*-trees, fast direct access to single atoms as well as efficient navigation through atom sets according to value-based sort orders may be accomplished. Fast access to a complex object as a whole, however, is not supported. Complex objects with a static structure (restricted to hierarchical relationships) can be easily allocated to enhance efficient access by clustering the object's components along its (unique) structure (e.g. NF^2 tuples [SPSW90]). Dynamic definition of complex objects, in contrast, leaves the selection of a particular object structure open until run-time; hence, the best we can expect is a more or less precise prediction of access characteristics to the database to define and establish appropriate storage structures (at schema definition time).

One concept to speed-up dynamic object derivation is the symmetrical relationship representation by surrogate-based links which allows for direct accessing of the counterparts in join operations; thus, it guarantees effective and relatively efficient hierarchical joins. If the atoms to be joined, however, are spread over multiple segments, quite a substantial I/O overhead has to be taken into account which makes object derivation (a multi-join process) time-comsuming. For this reason, a special storage structure useful for at least frequently requested complex objects should help to improve dynamic object derivation. In [SS89], a cluster mechanism is proposed that is expected to support the required flexibility and dynamism for complex object construction (as needed by the MAD model) with nearly the efficiency of static structure clustering.

A Storage structure for atom clusters

In order to achieve physical clustering for a set of atoms, we have to allocate them in an appropriate physical container, i.e. in a page sequence. If we cluster all atoms belonging to a specific molecule in such a physical container, molecule materialization is a perfectly local operation, that is, the page references for the required hierarchical joins are confined by the page sequence. Such a structure is called atom-cluster type; it obviously minimizes disk access time for the corresponding atom set. Hence, the key idea is to predefine atom-cluster types (by LDL statements) and to allocate the associated (heterogeneous) atom sets to page sequences such that frequently requested molecules are logically contained in these atom clusters. Here, we cannot discuss the question as to which atom-cluster types should be chosen to speed-up molecule materialization; such a decision needs a lot of application knowledge and must be addressed by the DB administrator.

Before we illustrate a storage structure for atom clusters, we wish to point out some consequences of the underlying concept. Fig. 8 and 9 show some examples of molecules which may be derived from our sample database in Fig. 3. For example, we may define an atom-cluster type Volume to Face, which clusters the atom set of Fig. 8. (An atom-cluster type is directed in the sense that the root atoms determine the atom set to be clustered.) Then, the molecule with the structure Volume-Face as well as those of Face-Volume can be derived using the atom cluster. In this case, the functional relationship between Volume and Face allows disjoint representation of atom clusters.

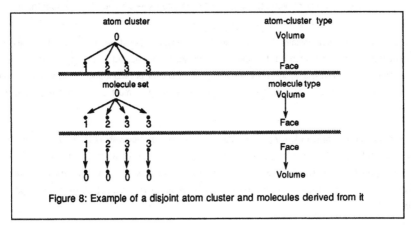

Figure 8: Example of a disjoint atom cluster and molecules derived from it

In Fig. 9, the atom-cluster type is again hierarchically structured, however, the relationships between Face and Edge as well as Edge and Point are (n:m). Such relationships to non-disjoint components cause redundant atom representation in the clustered atom sets. As illustrated in our example, molecule sets for molecule types Face-Edge-Point, Edge-Point and others can be materialized from the given atom-cluster type. Apparently, the molecule types Point-Edge or Point-Edge-Face cannot be completely derived by using a single atom cluster per molecule.

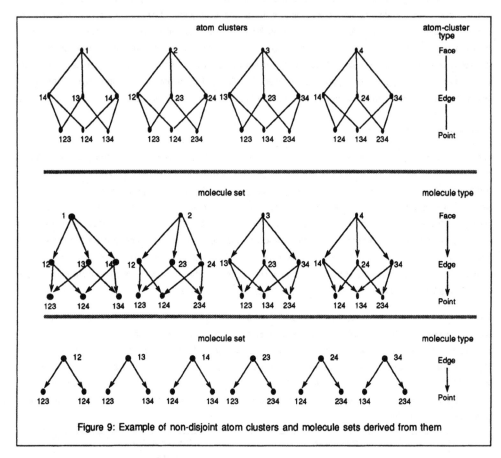

Figure 9: Example of non-disjoint atom clusters and molecule sets derived from them

[SS89] argues that only hierarchically structured atom-cluster types should be allowed; network-like or recursive type structures should be ruled out for operational reasons, complicated maintenance, and semantical interpretation problems. Nevertheless, the price for the cluster concept is redundancy maintenance if (n:m)-relationships are involved. Hence, the benefits of materialization support must outweigh the increased update costs.

Physical contiguity of all atoms belonging to an atom cluster can be effectively obtained by the following mapping (Fig. 10): Each atom cluster is described by a so-called characteristic atom which contains references to all atoms, grouped by atom types, belonging to the resp. atom cluster. Moreover, the characteristic atom keeps information for each reference to the contained atoms which is evaluated to determine update dependencies in the cluster.

Each atom cluster is mapped onto a so-called cluster record, i.e. a byte string of variable length containing the characteristic atom together with all atoms of the cluster. Although they may be referenced several times, all atoms are included only once.

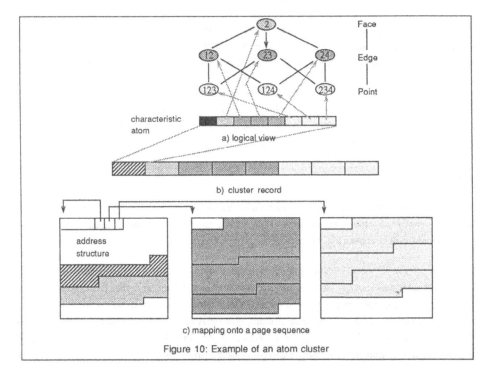

Figure 10: Example of an atom cluster

The cluster record, in turn, is mapped onto a page or a page sequence of the segment to which the atom-cluster type is assigned. If the entire cluster fits into a page, the cluster record can be stored as a byte string containing subrecords for each atom (according to the storage scheme in Fig. 6). Even multiple (small) atom clusters may be stored subsequently in a page, whereas a page sequence always contains only one atom cluster, that is, stores only a single cluster record. Such a mapping is more complicated: All atoms of a single atom type are placed into a subrecord; all subrecords are subsequently mapped onto pages thereby adjusting them to page boundaries, if necessary (see Fig. 10). Since atom clusters (or page sequences) may become large, additional address structures can help to quickly locate an atom. Single-page atom clusters are searched sequentially, whereas direct access to atoms is provided for larger clusters by keeping an address table for the subrecords in the header page of the page sequence. Subrecords which span multiple pages, in turn, have an address table for the atoms to avoid a sequential scan over these pages.

Replicated storage structures

To improve retrieval of dynamically defined sets of atoms, various forms of storage redundancy may be introduced. As explained above, atom-cluster types will cause atom representations to be replicated by a varying degree depending on the relationship structure. Furthermore, access paths such as B*-trees or grid files embody some kind of storage redundancy (at least at the level of attributes and identifiers). However, explicit replication of selected atom types may sometimes be useful to enhance retrieval performance. For example, the specification of a **sort order** provides a special storage structure keeping all atoms of an atom-type sorted according to some of its attributes; such sort orders are fully redundant because the basic storage structure (in system-defined order) always exists for an atom type.

As far as modification operations are concerned, storage redundancy has to be concealed by the access system. Hence, the update of an atom in one particular representation has to be automatically propagated to all its representations in a way that is transparent to all system components outside the access system.

Although the complexities involved in the maintenance of replicated storage structures have to be confined to the access system, the existence of such structures together with appropriate access primitives has to be made known to the data system. Otherwise the optimizer cannot select from the existing choices of access paths which would make storage redundancy useless.

The access system interface

The access system offers an atom-oriented interface which allows for navigational retrieval and modification of atoms. To satisfy the retrieval requirements of the data system, it supports **direct access** to single atoms as well as **atom-by-atom access** to either homogeneous or heterogeneous atom sets.

Scans are a concept to control a dynamically defined set of atoms, to hold a current position in such a set, and to successively deliver single atoms or only selected attributes thereof for further processing. A scan operation is linked to a certain storage structure or access path which determine sequence and result set of atoms to be retrieved. To increase the flexibility of scans, their result set can be restricted by a simple search argument solvable on each atom and/or start/stop conditions in the case of value-based ordering of atoms. The PRIMA access system supports the following scan operations at its interface:

- the atom-type scan based on a general basic storage structure
- different access path based scans (e.g. a scan based on B*-trees)
- scans guaranteeing a certain sort order, which may either be materialized or dynamically derived
- the atom-cluster scan which operates on clusters of heterogeneous atoms.

Whereas the first three scan types support 'horizontal' access to a homogeneous atom set belonging to one atom type, the last one allows for the 'vertical' access to a heterogeneous atom set across several atom types.

4.3 The data system

The data system has to fill in the gap between the atom-oriented interface of the access system and the data model interface, which deals with complex objects. Its main task is to map the objects and operations of the MAQ model to the primitives available at the access system interface. Hence, it is responsible for the dynamic construction of molecules and for the set-oriented delivery of result sets to the requesting component.

For this purpose, the data system implements all mechanisms of complex object processing which arise from the need to handle molecules dynamically defined at query time. It translates MQL queries into an internal representation called **query evaluation plan** (QEP), optimizes the QEP, and executes it by means of access system calls in order to compute the requested result. MQL statements are normally embedded in application programs which may be executed quite frequently. An interpreter approach would, therefore, repeatedly cause the full overhead of all query processing phases. To obtain the benefits of a 'compiled' approach [LW79], we separated compilation and optimization from execution leading to three distinct phases of complex object processing:

- Compilation of the MQL statement generates a valid, but not necessarily optimal query evaluation plan and stores it within an access module.

- Optimization transforms the QEP according to given heuristics and rules, in order to find the equivalent QEP which executes the query with minimal response time. This optimization phase includes the determination of evaluation strategies and the selection of access paths.

- Execution of the access module either retrieves or modifies atoms by means of access system calls according to the optimized QEP. Instead of generating code for the QEP, we designed an interpreter for QEPs, which contain the execution sequence in the form of access system calls. To handle retrieval requests, the data system maintains a main storage data structure where it inserts and combines the requested atoms in order to build up the query result. Upon completion, the derived molecule set is passed on to the caller in a set-oriented manner. Such an execution can be repeated independently of the first two phases.

In this paper, we cannot describe all the complexities of complex object processing [HMS90]. We would rather sketch some important issues by means of examples.

Compilation of a retrieval statement

The MQL compiler checks the user query for syntactic and semantic correctness, performs the so-called query standardization, and creates the initial QEP in an access module. Standardization includes

- the replacement of ALL in SELECT clauses by the corresponding set of attribute names.
- the resolution of molecule types predefined in the DB schema (FROM clauses)
- the representation of boolean expressions in conjunctive normal form as well as the expression completion of incompletely quantified expressions in the WHERE clauses.

Let us assume a rather simple query with qualified projection in the SELECT clause referring to the database in Fig. 3:

```
SELECT   Face, Edge, (SELECT Point
                      FROM RESULT
                      WHERE Point.x > 10)
FROM     Face-Edge-Point
WHERE    Face.fid < 3
```

The resulting QEP in Fig. 11 consists of an operator graph describing the execution plan. It serves as an easy--to-understand example which illustrates the principal ideas. Of course, such QEPs may be much more complex.

It is generally possible to divide all nodes of an operator graph into two classes: the **leaf nodes** are employed to construct the (simple) molecules, whereas the **inner nodes** subsequently operate on these molecules to derive more complex structures or properties, e.g. recursive molecules, qualified projection, aggregation etc.

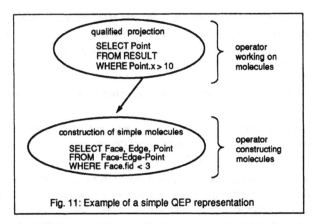

Fig. 11: Example of a simple QEP representation

All operators related to leaf nodes are of type CSM ('construction of simple molecules'); they can be used to derive molecules of the following form:

SELECT <unqualified projections>
FROM <one non-recursive, hierarchical molecule type>
WHERE <molecule qualification Q>

Hence, the CSM type is in charge of selecting the qualified atoms via access system operators and of building up the (initial) molecule set by using a main memory data structure. Since leaf-to-root evaluation is always applied to the operator graphs, the operators represented by the inner nodes work on this data structure thereby accomplishing the requested result set step by step.

Optimization considerations

The optimization phase includes simplification, amelioration and finally refinement of a query [JK84]. Query refinement which is most important to our discussion considers alternative strategies for the execution of the operators in the QEP in order to find the cheapest execution plan. It should be clear so far that CSM is a performance-critical operator (besides the operator for the construction of recursive molecule) because it reads atoms from the database (as the only operator). Hence, the problem of access path selection and the algorithms for processing joins have to be considered.

We have pointed out for the relational model that reconstruction of complex objects has to be performed by general joins using primary/foreign key pairs. In our case, CSM executes specialized joins called hierarchical joins and evaluates conditions on the result. The molecule structure as specified in the FROM clause can be seen as a kind of join plan where atom types connected by a link type may be combined via the specified directed link. As opposed to the relational join, our hierarchical join is an (n:m)-join, that is, for example, each atom f of Face within a molecule Face-Edge may have several descendants e_i of type Edge which may be shared with other Face atoms. In this case, the join condition is "E.eid is contained in F.ref", where the REFERENCE_TO attribute F.ref points to atoms of type Edge. Hence, a nested loop algorithm may be efficiently applied:

```
Foreach atom f of type Face
  Foreach entry d in F.ref
    If atom e of type Edge with e.eid = d is not contained in the result's atom set
    call e from the access system via condition e.eid = d
```

Note that an atom may be shared among several molecules of a result set or may be a descendent of more than one atom within a molecule. Such cases give rise of the optimization in the inner loop.

It is clear that all atoms participating in a hierarchical join have to be fetched via access system calls. To minimize the number of these calls, the evaluation of the WHERE-clause conditions should be performed as early as possible to restrict the atom set to be investigated. Since restrictions may apply to every atom type appearing in the molecule structure, restriction evaluation is not straightforward. For a refined discussion, we refer to [HMS90]. Furthermore, the speed of a hierarchical join depends on the access paths and clusters to be used in locating the atoms in the database. Hence, CSM optimization has to perform the selection of the best available scans on existing storage structures for each of the hierarchical joins. Obviously, the use of atom-cluster scans which are tailored to the execution of hierarchical joins will greatly accelerate CSM operation.

Execution of an access module

Query optimization yields the 'best' QEP in form of an operator graph which specifies the execution plan of the query still at quite an abstract level. Query execution is then performed by interpreting the operator graph node by node under control of the data system. Again, various strategies concerning sequential, pipelined, or even concurrent executing of nodes are applicable (see [HSS88]).

As mentioned earlier, the result set of a query is built up in a main memory data structure. Since distinct molecules are derived, one may get a substantial degree of storage redundancy for the representation of atoms due to the (n:m)-relationship involved. To avoid multiple copies of the same data in the resulting molecule set, we separated the representation of the molecule structure from the representation of its data (see Fig. 12). Hence, only REFERENCE_TO values of atoms are included several times to establish the structural view. To guarantee fast access to all elements, structure and atom data are organized in two tables based on extendible hashing.

Let us finish the discussion of the data system with some remarks on the materialization of recursive molecules. Each component molecule is derived just like a regular molecule using hierarchical joins, etc. These component molecules are then combined according to the recursion defining links. The hash-based data structures (Fig. 12) greatly facilitate the detection of loops in the recursion, since component molecules may be identified

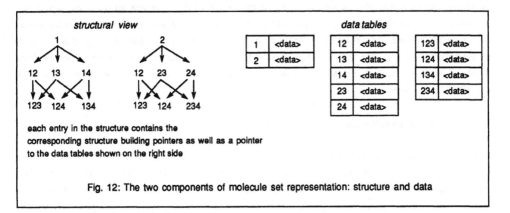

Fig. 12: The two components of molecule set representation: structure and data

by their root atoms. Hence, it is sufficient to check for the non-existence of the root atom in the resulting molecule, before the corresponding molecule component is materialized.

All further transformations and manipulations on recursive molecules are performed by operators corresponding to inner nodes of a QEP (see Fig. 11). Obviously, the availability of sufficient storage space in main memory determines the performance of these QEP operations.

5. Transaction Concept for Processing Complex Objects

In the previous section, we have described which implementation concepts support the requirements of complex object management and how they fit in a layered DBMS architecture. Now, we will discuss the principles of the dynamics of query processing for complex objects, that is, the transaction concept [BKK85, Gr81, KLMP84] to be employed, and some hints related to its implementation. A major objective of the transaction concept design was the desire to exploit the inherent parallelism when processing MQL operations (see sect. 6). Thus, the transaction concept should enable concurrent operations in the various DBMS layers thereby reducing the response time for a given MQL request [WS84].

Flat transactions do not provide any intra-transaction control structure to enable cooperation and isolation on shared resources and to conceal the impact of failing activities. For this reason, nested transactions [Mo81] were proposed as a control structure to achieve a safe and robust run-time environment for parallel and/or distributed processing within a transaction. A transaction is recursively decomposed into subtransactions resulting in a transaction tree with the so-called TL-transaction (top level) as the root. These subtransactions control all activities in the system. Accordingly, they can be used as the units of concurrency control as well as recovery. A suitable transaction nesting may obtain sufficiently small granules of concurrency control (e.g. locking) to enable significant intra-transaction concurrency in a safe way. On the other hand, such a transaction nesting enables intra-transaction recovery where a subtransaction (and its subordinates) can be aborted and rolled back without any side-effects to others.

Flat transactions observe the ACID principle [HR83]. As the unit of Atomicity, Consistency, Isolation and Durability, a transaction guarantees concurrency transparency among transactions as well as failure transparency. These properties must also be realized by the TL-transaction as the outermost sphere of transaction control, whereas weaker properties may be provided by subtransactions. Atomicity and isolated execution remain key properties of each subtransaction; consistency control and the responsibility for the persistence of its modified data (durability), however, may be delegated by a subtransaction to its parent transaction (and ultimately to the TL-transaction). For further discussion of nested transaction properties, we refer to the literature [HR87,Mo81,We86].

A model for nested transactions

How can we apply the transaction nesting to the complex object processing? The dynamical flow of control during the execution of a DBMS request may be characterized as a tree of procedure activations; for example, each operator within a layer or at its interface embodies such a procedure. A closer look at the typical workloads of engineering applications [Hä89] reveals that the operator trees spanned by typical requests may obtain a very large fan-out at each of our system layers. For example, consider even the simple query of Fig.

11 and assume that the CSM operator performs some atom-type scans. Obviously, subgraphs of our operator graph have to be guarded by subtransactions. The critical question is what are the appropriate granules (subgraph sizes) to balance the overhead of transaction management with the benefits of fine-grained control structures (concurrency, failure isolation). The model of nested transactions itself does not restrict the use of subtransactions to a minimum granule. Hence, we may allocate multiple transaction levels within a single system layer or we may even bracket execution paths across layer boundaries. It is, however, a good design principle to observe layer boundaries within the transaction hierarchy. Therefore, we do not permit transactions to span multiple system layers. Hence, transaction properties (atomicity, isolation) may be used to control clean and safe cooperation across layer boundaries.

Our nested transaction model is illustrated in Fig. 13. The TL-transaction consists of a sequence of MQL queries where each of them is guarded by an MQL transaction. This, in turn, can be decomposed into multiple data system transactions (depending on optimizer decisions and the inherent potential of intra-operation concurrency). Each data system transaction may invoke many access system transactions each fetching or modifying a single atom (if maximum parallelism should be achieved). On the other hand, an entire scan operation may be enclosed by a single access transaction (with a conversational interface to the parent transaction).

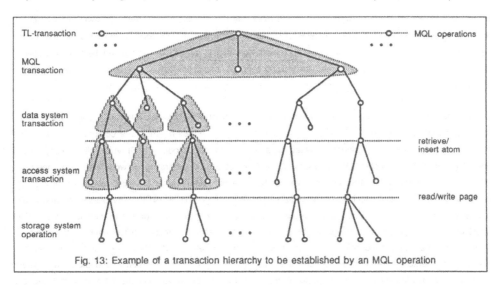

Fig. 13: Example of a transaction hierarchy to be established by an MQL operation

As indicated in Fig. 13, storage system operations are not organized as separate subtransactions, that is, I/O operations within an access system transaction are not performed in parallel. Hence, as far as concurrency and recovery issues of them are concerned, access system transactions will provide the necessary functions [HPS90].

In our PRIMA implementation, we decided to group all transaction-related services in a so-called transaction management subsystem (see Fig. 14). It consists of four major components which are jointly responsible for preserving the ACID properties during transaction execution. The transaction manager is responsible for the management of the transaction hierarchies and for accomplishing the atomicity property. Furthermore, it is acting as a coordinator to distribute information or to obtain general agreement, e.g. during commit or abort. Consistency is controlled by the consistency manager whereas concurrency control performed by the lock manager takes care of isolated execution. Finally, durability of database updates is guaranteed by the recovery manager which collects log information to cope with various failure types. For performance reasons, the services of these managers are directly invoked by a transaction as long as it proceeds normally. In the case of special events, however, all managers have to be synchronized by the transaction manager to do their job.

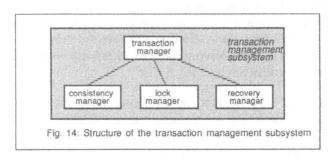

Fig. 14: Structure of the transaction management subsystem

Implementation issues of nested transaction management

In our context, we will limit our discussion to the most relevant aspects which affect complex object processing. The transaction manager offers general functions to create, commit, or abort a transaction in the framework of nested transactions. Hence, their implementation has to reflect the anticipated type of processing, that is, highly dynamic transaction trees embodying a lot of concurrent activities have to be efficiently maintained by m-ary trees (e.g. mapped to binary trees adjusted to specific traversal requirements).

Concurrency control is more strongly influenced by the properties of complex objects. If only static objects (defined in the DB schema) are involved, the checking of synchronization conflicts is comparably simple. For example, [He89] proposes an algorithm based on a hierarchical data model [SS86] which allows easy detection of common subhierarchies. With dynamically defined objects incorporating network structures, however, there is hardly a chance to find an effective conflict detection algorithm at the type level. Synchronization which is based on conflict checking of molecule structures (type graphs) would be very pessimistic and would mostly detect phantom conflicts. Similar arguments apply if the predicates (together with the type definitions) of the MQL queries are utilized. (Note, molecules are 'elusive' as far as conflict checking is concerned. They have to be materialized before component overlap can be determined.) Therefore, the only realisitic approach with tolerable performance characteristics seems to employ synchronization at the atom level. Thus, we have implemented an R-X locking protocol (with lock inheritance) which requires an explicit lock request for each atom involved in a complex object operation. When a page is accessed to fetch or modify an atom, an appropriate short-term lock (fix-phase) is acquired for the entire page or page sequence in order to prevent side-effects due to page modifications. Thus, concurrent operations of multiple subtransactions (or independent transactions) in a page are supported by our locking protocol (excluding only fix-phases).

Consistency control [Es76] becomes more and more important even in conventional DBMS, e.g. the preservation of referential integrity. This is particularly true for complex object processing where the system must guarantee consistency in situations with much more elaborate objects and operations. As indicated in sect. 4, our system provides increasing levels of abstraction where the objects, operations and integrity constraints grow more complex with each layer. Hence, our framework of nested transactions seems to fit nicely the requirements of this level-to-level control of integrity. We mentioned earlier that a subtransaction may delegate its responsibility for integrity preservation to its parents. This fact allows more complex integrity conditions to be controlled and optimized. Consider the deletion of a molecule where multiple atoms with their references and counter-references have to be deleted. Since referential integrity cannot be guaranteed for each single delete of an atom, the corresponding check operation must be deferred.

Another example is the control of the cardinality restrictions for links which sometimes require several modification operations before they satisfy their specification. In such situations, a consistency control component [Sch90] can be used to collect the resp. information relevant for integrity control and to optimize the checking and modification overhead, e.g. an atom to be addressed by multiple references has to be located only once. The transaction hierarchy then allows flexible control for such deferred checks.

Finally, let us highlight our design decisions in the case of the recovery component. Buffer management applies a NOSTEAL policy [HR83]; thus, the abort operation of a subtransaction is a in-memory rollback by using a log of inverse operations at the atom level. To speed-up commit processing, we employ a NOFORCE scheme, which requires partial REDO of committed transactions when a system crash occurs. For this purpose, we keep a REDO log on disk; since we use atom locking (and the log granularity cannot be larger than the lock granularity), physical entry logging based on atoms was chosen. Hence, our NOSTEAL/NOFORCE scheme optimizes the normal case (and not the crash recovery) by avoiding synchronous I/O as far as possible.

6. Using Parallelism In Complex Object Management

Our design decision for the nested transaction concept was explicitly motivated by the desire to achieve intra-transaction parallelism in various tasks of complex object management. As illustrated by Fig. 13, the transaction framework allows the exploitation of inherent parallelism and the control of medium or even fine grained parallel activities in several system layers.

As discussed elsewhere [Du87, HSS89], suitable hardware configuration and run-time environments are a prerequisite for implementing these concepts. In our case, we assume a tightly or closely coupled multiprocessor architecture where database buffer, lock and log information, as well as other common data may be efficiently shared among the various processes distributed across the processors. In order to simulate such an environment in a network of SUN workstations, we have implemented the RC-System (remote cooperation) which allows efficient location-transparent communication among processes configurated as a system [HKS90].

Intra-operation parallelism

In this section, we will briefly identify the DBMS functions where it pays to generate parallel activities. Obviously, retrieval of atoms and the subsequent molecule materialization is a promising area. Since an MQL query specifies a set of molecules, one strategy is to derive all molecules in parallel (inter-molecule parallelism), that is, each molecule is handled by an own process or task. Another strategy could derive the molecule's components concurrently (intra-molecule parallelism). This strategy is enabled by our link concept where the REFERENCE_TO attribute of an atom contains the set of identifiers of atoms it is linked to. Hence, the traversal of subgraphs in the atom network may be performed in parallel. Depending on the specific molecule qualification (WHERE clause), various optimizations of search strategy are conceivable [HSS88].

Similar efforts can be employed to manipulation operations and consistency management. Again, the link concept supports concurrent activities in an obvious way. For example, the deletion of a molecule or checking of referential integrity could proceed in parallel.

Finally, the maintenance of redundancy is an area we have designed parallel algorithms for. In sect. 4, we have advocated the use of replicated atom representations (e.g. sort orders) or atom-clusters provoking redundant storage structures in order to speed-up retrieval operations and, of course, dynamic materialization of molecules.

Deferred update of replicated storage structures

The maintenance of replicated storage structures could easily cause a performance bottleneck if update operations occur too frequently. Therefore, the concept of deferred update was proposed in the literature [DLPS85] to avoid response time penalties. However, this concept requires replicated copies to be invalidated as long as they do not represent the latest value; depending on the number and type of replication, the implementation of a practical invalidation scheme may turn out to be cumbersome.

Concurrent update [HSS88] avoids the problem of maintaining invalid storage structures. Parallelism in the access system is used to keep all replicas of a modified atom up-to-date. For this purpose, an evaluation component identifies update calls to the access system and invokes concurrent operations on the various redundant structures. Hence, response time of such a call should not be strongly increased as compared to the non-redundant case.

7. Conclusions and Outlook

The data model plays a key role in any DBMS application. This fact is particularly true, if complex objects, e.g. in engineering applications, have to be processed. Although once faithful believers in the relational model, we now feel that this simple model is too simple, at least as far as advanced applications are concerned. For this reason, we were converted more and more to another 'kind of religion' and advocate the MAD model. This data model allows for dynamically defined and recursive complex objects with non-disjoint components which are derived from atom networks incorporating symmetrical relationship representation. Recursion definition enables the solution of transitive closure as well as path problems which may be directly specified by means of MQL queries.

For the implementation, we have outlined a number of important concepts. We aimed to increase the freedom in defining segments with page sizes tailored to the atom type to be stored as well as in page sequences in order to reduce the I/O problem. The mapping of atoms to records was achieved by a flexible storage scheme which guarantees fast access to any field position and limits the overhead/displacement of updates directed to variable length fields. Atom clusters were introduced to speed-up materialization of molecules which are frequently referenced. Since atoms are clustered in physical contiguity according to the molecules to be derived, 'non-disjoint atoms' have to be stored redundantly. Generally, replication was proposed as a concept to accelerate dynamical object derivation.

The materialization of complex objects is achieved by compiling MQL queries into operator graphs which are optimized according to the available access paths and storage structures. Execution of such operator graphs is then performed by an interpreter which uses a hash-based main memory data structure to represent the result molecule set.

A nested transaction concept was designed to employ parallel algorithms when processing MQL queries. By the decomposition of the dynamical execution trees of such queries into hierarchically nested subtransactions, medium or even fine grained parallelism may be achieved. This parallelism within complex object processing can be applied to retrieval as well as update operations of molecules in order to speed-up molecule materialization or the maintenance of replicated storage structures.

The stepwise abstraction process realized by the various layers of our system leads to structure-oriented complex objects; that is, the result of an MQL query is a set of molecules which, in turn, consist of a set of interconnected heterogeneous atoms without any specific application semantics. We expect that advanced DBMS applications will primarily take place in workstation/server environments where the application-oriented processing is carried out in the workstations. For this reason, our molecules are transferred across a set-oriented interface to a so-called application layer located at the workstation where they are stored in an object buffer to obtain 'nearby the application' locality. The application, e.g. a solid modeler, can then manipulate these data structures via a predefined interface which offers operations tailored to the resp. application (e.g. in the form of ADTs). Hence, the application layer may be equipped with concepts and mechanisms to overlay application-oriented semantics [BM86] to the more structure-oriented molecules of the MAD model. This approach avoids the overloading of the complex object data model by application specific aspects.

Based on this architectural framework, we have implemented a technical modeler (TechMo), a VLSI design application, and a knowledge base management system KRISYS [DHMM89, Ma89]. The former two application refer to tailored ADT interfaces which are realized by specific application layers. KRISYS, in turn, can be perceived as a (generic) modeling system which allows the specification of rich facilities and abstraction concepts for application support [Ma88]. Quite a number of applications in the areas of expert systems and intelligent CAD are currently being investigated.

Acknowledgements

We would like to thank H. Schöning for his careful reading and useful hints concerning the paper.

8. References

As76   Astrahan, M.M., et al.: SYSTEM R: A Relational Approach to Database Management, in: ACM TODS, Vol. 1, No. 2, 1976, pp. 97-137.

BB84   Batory, D.S., Buchmann, A.P.: Molecular Objects, Abstract Data Types and Data Models; A Framework, in: Proc. 10th VLDB Conf., Singapore, 1984, pp. 172-184.

BKK85   Bancilhon, F., Kim, W., Korth, H.F.: A Model of CAD Transactions, in: Proc. 11th Int. Conf. on VLDB, Stockholm, Aug. 1985, pp. 25-33.

BM86   Brodie, M.L., Mylopoulos, J. (eds.): On Knowledge Base Management Systems (Integrating Artificial Intelligence and Database Technologies), Topics in Information Systems, Springer-Verlag, New York, 1986.

CD86   Carey, M.J., DeWitt, D.J., et al.: The Architecture of the EXODUS Extensible DBMS, in: Proc. int. Workshop on Object-Oriented Database Systems, Pacific Grove, 1986, pp. 52-65.

Ch76   Chen, P.P.: The Entity-Relationship-Model - Toward a Unified View of Data, in: Proc. ACM TODS, Vol. 1, No. 1, 1976, pp. 9-36.

Da86   Dadam, P., et al.: A DBMS Prototype to Support Extended NF^2-Relations: An Integrated View on Flat Tables and Hierarchies, in: Proc. ACM SIGMOD Conf., Washington, D.C., 1986, pp. 356-367.

DD86   Dittrich, K.R., Dayal, U. (eds.): Proc. Int. Workshop on Object-Oriented Database Systems, Pacific Grove, 1986.

DE84   Special Issue on Engineering Design Databases, IEEE Database Engineering, Vol. 7, No. 2, June 1984.

DHMM89   Deßloch, S., Härder, T., Mattos, N., Mitschang, B.: KRISYS: KBMS Support for Better CAD Systems, in: Proc. 2nd International Conference on Data and Knowledge Systems for Manufacturing and Engineering, Gaithersburg - Maryland, Oct. 1989, pp.172-182.

DLPS85   Dadam, P., Lum, V.Y., Prädel, U.: Schlageter, G.: Selective Deferred Index Maintenance and Concurrency Control in Integrated Information Systems, in: Proc. 11th VLDB Conf., Stockholm, 1985, pp. 142-150.

Du87   Duppel, N., Peinl, P., Reuter, A., Schiele, G., Zeller, H.: Progress Report #2 of PROSPECT, Research Report, University of Stuttgart, 1987

Es76   Eswaran, K.P.: Aspects of a Trigger Subsystem in an Integrated Database System, in: 2nd Int. Conf. on Software Engineering, 1976, pp. 243-250.

Gr81   Gray, J.N.: The Transaction Concept: Virtues and Limitations, Proc. 7th Int. Conf. on VLDB, Cannes, Nov. 1981, pp. 144-154.

Hä88   Härder, T. (ed.): The PRIMA Project Design and Implementation of a Non-Standard Database System, SFB 124 Research Report No. 26/88, University of Kaiserslautern, 1988.

Hä89   Härder, T.: Engineering Applications - a Challenge for the Next Generation of DBMS, Internal Report ZRI 3/89, University of Kaiserslautern, 1989.

He89   Herrmann, U., et al.: A Lock Technique for Disjoint and Non-Disjoint Complex Objects, Fern-Universität Hagen, Informatik Berichte, Nr. 85, 03.1989, 15 p.

HKS90   Hübel, Ch., Käfer, W., Sutter, B.: A Client/Server System as a Base Component for a Cooperating DBMS (in German), SFB 124, Research Report 26/90, University of Kaiserslautern, May 1990.

HM90   Härder, T., Mattos, N.M.: An Enhanced DBMS Architecture Supporting Intelligent CAD, in: Proc. Int. Conf. TECHNO-DATA'90, Berlin, Dec. 1990 (invited lecture).

HMMS87   Härder, T., Meyer-Wegener, K., Mitschang, B., Sikeler, A.: PRIMA - A DBMS Prototype Supporting Engineering Applications, SFB 124 Research Report No. 22/87, University of Kaiserslautern, 1987; in: Proc. 13th VLDB Conf., Brighton, UK, 1987, pp. 433-442.

HMS90   Härder, T., Mitschang, B., Schöning, H.: Query Processing for Complex Objects, submitted for publication, 1990.

HPS90   Härder, T., Profit, M., Schöning, H.: Supporting Parallelism in Engineering Databases by Nested Transactions, submitted for publication, 1990.

HR83   Härder, T., Reuter, A.: Principles of Transaction-Oriented Database Recovery, in: ACM Computing Surveys, Vol. 15, No. 4, 1983, pp. 287-317.

HR87   Härder, T., Rothermel, K.: Concepts for Transaction Recovery in Nested Transactions, in: Proc. ACM SIGMOD'87 Conf., San Francisco, May 1987, S. 239-248.

HSS88   Härder, T., Schöning, H., Sikeler, A.: Parallelism in Processing Queries on Complex Objects, in: Jajodia, S., Kim, W., Silberschatz, A. (eds.), Proc. Int. Symp. on Databases in Parallel and Distributed Computing, Austin, Texas (1988) 131-143.

HSS89   Härder, T., Schöning, H., Sikeler, A.: Parallel Query Evaluation: A New Approach to Complex Object Processing, in: IEEE Data Engineering, Vol. 12, No. 1, March 1989, pp. 23-29.

JK84   Jarke, M., Koch J.: Query Optimization in Database Systems, in: Computing Surveys 16 (1984) 111-152.

KLMP84   Kim, W., Lorie, R., McNabb, D., Plouffe, W.: Nested Transactions for Engineering Design Databases, in: Proc. 10th VLDB Conf., Singapore, 1984, pp. 355-362.

LK84   Lorie, R., Kim, W., et al.: Supporting Complex Objects in a Relational System for Engineering Databases, IBM Research Laboratory, San Jose, CA, 1984.

LL89   Lehman, T.J., Lindsay, B.G.: The Starburst Long Field Manager, in: Proc. 15th VLDB Conf., Amsterdam, Aug. 1989, pp. 375-384.

LW79   Lorie, R.A., Wade, B.W.: The compilation of a high level data language, IBM Research Report RJ 2589, San Jose, Calif. 1979.

Ma88   Mattos, N.M.: Abstraction Concepts: the Basis for Data and Knowledge Modeling, in: 7th Int. Conf. on Entity-Relationship Approach, Rom, Italy, Nov. 1988, pp. 331-350.

Ma89   Mattos, N.M.: An Approach to Knowledge Base Management - requirements, knowledge representation and design issues, Doctoral Thesis, University of Kaiserslautern, Computer Science Department, Kaiserslautern, 1989.

Mi88   Mitschang, B.: A Molecule-Atom Data Model for Non-Standard Applications - Requirements, Data model Design, and Implemlentation Concepts (in German), Doctoral Thesis, University of Kaiserslautern, Computer Science Department, Kaiserslautern, 1988.

Mi89   Mitschang, B.: Extending the Relational Algebra to Capture Complex Objects, in: Proc. of the 15th VLDB Conf., Amsterdam, 1989, pp. 297-306.

Mo81   Moss, J.E.B.: Nested Transactions: An Approach to Reliable Computing, M.I.T. Report MIT-LCS-TR-260, M.I.T., Laboratory of Computer Science, 1981.

Sch89   Schöning, H.: Integrating Complex Objects and Recursion, in: Proc. 1st Int. Conf. on Deductive and Object-Oriented Databases, Kyoto, Japan, Dec. 1989.

Sch90   Schöning, H.: Preserving Consistency in Nested Transactions, in: Proc. HICSS-23, Volume II, Hawaii, Jan. 1990, pp. 472-480.

Si88   Sikeler, A.: VAR-PAGE-LRU: A Buffer Replacement Algorithm Supporting Different Page Sizes, in: Proc. Int. Conf on Extending Database Technology (EDBT), Venice, Italy, 1988, Lecture Notes on Computer Science 303, pp. 336-351.

SPSW90 Schek, H.-J., Paul, H.-B., Scholl, M.H., Weikum,, G.: The DASDBS Project: Objectives, Experiences, and Future Prospects, in: IEEE Transactions on Knowledge and Data Engineering, Vol. 2, No. 1, March 1990, pp. 25-43.

SR86   Stonebraker, M., Rowe, L.A.: The Design of POSTGRES, in: Proc. ACM SIGMOD Conf., Washington, D.C., 1986, pp. 340-355.

SS86   Schek, H.-J., Scholl, M.H.: The Relational Model with Relation-Valued Attributes, in: Information Systems, Vol. 11, No. 2, 1986, pp.137-147.

SS89   Schöning, H., Sikeler, A.: Cluster Mechanisms Supporting the Dynamic Construction of Complex Objects, in: Proc. 3rd Int. Conf. on Foundations of Data Organization and Algorithms FODO'89, LNCS 367, Paris, France (1989) 31-46.

SS90   Schöning, H., Sikeler, A.: Design of Storage Schemes for Enhanced Database Management Systems, SFB 124 Research Report No 25/90, University of Kaiserslautern, 1990.

We86   Weikum, G.: A Theoretical Foundation of Multi-Level Concurrency Control, in: Proc. ACM SIGACT-SIGMOD: Symposium on Principles of Database Systems, Cambridge, March 1986, pp. 31-42.

WS84   Weikum, G., Schek, H.J.: Architectural Issues of Transaction Management in Multi-Layered Systems, in: Proc. 10th VLDB Conf., Singapore, 1984, pp. 454-465.

WSSH88 Wilms, P.F., Schwarz, P.M., Schek, H.-J., Haas, L.M.: Incorporating Data Types in an Extensible Database Architecture, in: Proc. 3rd Int. Conf on Data and Knowledge Bases, Jerusalem, 1988.

Experience with MIMD Message-Passing Systems: Towards General Purpose Parallel Computing

A. J. G. Hey

University of Southampton

Highfield, Southampton SO3 9AN

United Kingdom

Abstract

The paper discusses the parallel programming lessons learnt from the ESPRIT SuperNode project that developed the T800 Transputer. After a brief review of some purportedly portable parallel programming environments, the Genesis parallel benchmarking project is described. The next generation of Transputer components are being developed in the ESPRIT-2 PUMA project and the goals of this project are briefly outlined. The paper closes with some speculations on the possibility of truly general-purpose parallel computing and reviews the work of Valiant.

1 Introduction

Multiprocessor machines have now been convincingly shown to yield cost-effective solutions to a wide variety of problems [1,2]. Nevertheless, the fact that such machines cannot, in general, run standard sequential programs without significant modifications is preventing the widespread take-up of parallel hardware by industry. In this context, it should be remembered that it was not until efficient vectorising compilers appeared that manufacturers of pipelined vector machines were able to expand their marketing horizons significantly.

The problem of "parallelising" dusty deck sequential programs, usually written in Fortran or C, is generally not very popular with computer scientists, at least within Europe. By contrast, there are many computer scientists excited at the prospect of designing new languages for parallel machines. For example, Backus, who gave the world Fortran, now proposes the functional language FP as a possible answer to the problems of parallel programming [3]. Now it is undoubtedly true that new languages can and will make the effective exploitation of parallelism much easier and more controllable. However, there is an economic fact of life that cannot be ignored, namely, that large companies with many hundreds of man-years invested in sequential software will not invest substantially in parallel hardware until there is a convincing "migration route" to such machines.

A related problem concerns the plethora of parallel architectures at present on the market: even so-called experts are hard put to predict which ones will survive. The failures of the FPS T-Series, the Denelcor HEP and now, more recently, of the ETA-10 come immediately to mind. No major software company will invest large numbers of man-years in converting or producing code for one specific parallel machine unless there is some guarantee of *portability* —that their parallelised code will be readily portable to other parallel architectures— or of *generality* —that the particular parallel architecture will continue to be relevant for many years to come.

For the purposes of this paper it will be helpful to make some 'local' definitions of the terms that will be used to describe parallel systems. First, of course, we must define what we mean by a 'supercomputer'. In this paper, supercomputer is taken to mean any computer system capable of delivering Cray-1 performance on any given problem. For example, on vectorisable code this may mean 100 MFlops or so: on non-vectorisable problems much smaller performance figures are common.

Since there will soon be workstations providing this sort of performance, it is probably necessary to give some justification for basing our definition on the performance of a 15-year old machine. Firstly, the Cray-1 was the first commercially successful supercomputer: subsequent clock cycle reductions and design modifications have only achieved around a factor 10 speedup of a single vector pipe [4]. Secondly, the current generation of multi-processor vector supercomputers, although having an impressive total MFlop rating, are rarely used on a single application: the European Centre for Medium-Range Weather-Forecasting (ECMWF) in Reading is a notable exception. Lastly, the US Department of Commerce is now considering [5] a new definition of 'supercomputer' for supercomputer export licences to various friendly or not so friendly countries that makes use of multiples of 100 MFlop Cray-1 like units! The second term we shall need to define is 'special-purpose'. This is taken to mean a computer that is specifically designed to perform well on a 'single' problem: its architecture may well not be appropriate for other computer-intensive problems because of differing computer-communication ratios and so on.

Many parallel systems today are often described as being both 'high-performance' and 'general purpose'. We would like to be more specific in our use of the term 'general-purpose'. What vendors and enthusiasts of today's parallel machines mean by their use of the phrase 'general-purpose' is that the system may be used to deliver high-performance on many different types of problems. This is not, however, the same as what a user of a uni-processor machine would understand by the term 'general-purpose'. In this latter context, 'general-purpose' implies that the user has a very wide range of standard languages, libraries, applications packages, operating systems and tools at his or her disposal. Such truly portable software does not yet exist for parallel machines and we shall reserve the term 'general-purpose' to describe this nirvana-like state of affairs.

The paper is organised as follows. Section 2 summarises the results obtained in the ESPRIT SuperNode project and details the new aspects of parallel programming provided by Transputer systems. The next section makes some brief remarks about present day programming environments for multi-Transputer systems that make some claim towards portability. Section 4 describes the ESPRIT Genesis project parallel benchmark activity and Section 5 reviews the ESPRIT PUMA which should deliver the next generation of Transputer components from Inmos. The last section discusses the possibility of general purpose parallel computing and reviews some recent proposals of Valiant.

2 The ESPRIT SuperNode Project

In 1985 the ESPRIT-1 programme funded a three year-project led by RSRE (the Royal Signals and Radar Research Establishment at Malvern) to develop a low-cost, high-performance architecture capable of exploiting a new floating-point Transputer, to be developed by Inmos within the project. Southampton University provided the basic reconfigurable 'SuperNode' cluster architecture [6], with input from RSRE and other members of the collaboration. The other industrial partners were Thorn-EMI in the UK, and Apsis-Aptor and Telmat in France. IMAG at the University of Grenoble was one of the original partners and the University of Liverpool joined during the project to study the question of parallel numerical libraries. As is now well-known, Inmos were very successful in producing a competitive state-of-the-art microprocessor which was innovative in several respects, notably in incorporating the floating point co-processor on the same chip as the CPU, SRAM and communication hardware that comprised the T414 Transputer. The SuperNode architecture was also very powerful and flexible. It provided complete reconfigurability for any valid Transputer graph topology up to at least 1000 nodes. In addition to providing low-level software—such as the basic debugger which is now part of the standard Inmos software—a key belief of the project was that the architecture should be driven by real applications. Thus a wide spectrum of applications were implemented on the SuperNode [2] and its cost-effectiveness and competitive performance evaluated and established in several different fields. The SuperNode architecture is now marketed commercially by both Parsys, a spin-off company from Thorn-EMI, and by Telmat.

At this point we should give some details of the floating-point performance of the T800. The hardware incorporates a floating-point unit (FPU) together with a 10 (RISC) Mip CPU, 4 fast serial communication links and 4 kbytes of fast SRAM, all on a single chip. The links can support 2 Mbytes/sec bidirectional communication on each of the four links, concurrently with operation of the CPU and FPU. The concurrent operation of the FPU and CPU allows the 20 MHz version of the T800 to sustain 1.5 MFlops on Livermore Loop 7 [7] and the 30 MHz part, 2.25 MFlops. The performance of the T800 on Whetstone and Dhrystone benchmarks is discussed in the Inmos Technical note, entitled 'Lies, Damn Lies and Benchmarks' [8]. Recently, Roweth and Clarke have shown that the T800-20 achieves between 0.5 and 1.5 MFlops on the level 1 BLAS routines coded in assembler [9]. More typically, well-optimised Occam code can deliver around 1 MFlops performance on suitable applications. However, with the presently-available compilers, Fortran and C versions of the same applications are lucky if they can sustain more than 0.5 MFlops. For the T800-30, these numbers should all be scaled up appropriately.

The applications developed by the different partners within the project for evaluation purposes included both high-level and low-level signal and image processing, image synthesis by ray tracing, logic simulation and scientific and engineering applications. The applications and evaluation work was led by the University of Southampton and we found it useful to classify the application implementations into three broad computational paradigms: Geometric Parallelism, Algorithmic Parallelism and Processor Farms [10].

Geometric parallelism is also known as data parallelism or domain decomposition: it corresponds to distributing a large data structure amongst the processors. For scientific and engineering problems, this large array often corresponds to a physical grid of points and optimal distribution then involves a partitioning of the physical geometry of the problem. Such techniques have been well-studied on hypercubes and on SIMD machines such as the AMT DAP or TM's Connection Machine (CM). The novel feature of the reconfigurable Transputer MIMD architecture is the capability to tailor the topology to suit the problem —there are many ways to map 3 or 4 dimensional grids onto a 2 dimensional array of Transputers for example. The other new features, compared to the first generation hypercube machines, were the ability to overlap communications with calculation and use multi-tasking on a single node to hide communication latencies. The very low context switch time of the T800, and its small message startup time, both of the order of 1 or 2 microseconds, enabled applications programmers to make use of different programming styles since they were no longer obliged to code so that communications involved only long messages and occurred only infrequently. With large enough problems, very high efficiencies (well over 90%) may easily be obtained with this technique.

Algorithmic parallelism was a new degree of freedom available to reconfigurable Transputer systems and corresponds to the ability to design the topology of the network to match the particular algorithm. Instead of distributing the data, the algorithm is broken up in suitable size pieces and the data 'flows' through the network in a coarse-grain dataflow manner. A typical algorithmic network might incorporate a number of 'pipes' which branch and merge together with a small 'farm' structure such as a tree or a chain. For a very large problem, this whole structure could then be geometrically replicated as often as required —corresponding to a 'hybrid' use of our three paradigms. Allwright has successfully programmed a 1260 Transputer system at Southampton in this manner in his investigation of graph theory [11]. Needless to say, load-balancing issues and communication bottlenecks must be studied with care for these algorithmic implementations but reasonable efficiencies in excess of 60% or so can quite easily be obtained [10].

Processor Farm parallelism, also known as 'event' or 'task' parallelism is suitable for situations in which a problem may be broken up into many independent tasks. These may be allocated to processors by a 'farmer' controller and the results collected. Many image processing problems have this structure and a simple implementation of ray tracing, in which the database is replicated on each processor and independent rays distributed, can show spectacular speedups [12]. Such 'farms' are also suitable for increasing throughput: in this situation the farmer distributes independent runs of the same program with different data or, in the case of Monte Carlo simulations, different random numbers. With assistance from Meiko, Glendinning ran the first non trivial Fortran code on a Transputer and demonstrated the utility of such Fortran farms for High Energy Physics even for T414 arrays [13]. More recently, such farms have been demonstrated to be effective in Gamma Ray Astronomy applications [14] and CERN and other groups are looking at real codes and realistic configurations that can provide sufficient I/O bandwidth for their needs [15,16].

It should, of course, be said that there are many other attempts to classify the type of parallelism for implementation on distributed memory systems. The CalTech group, led by Fox —now at Syracuse— uses a classification based on the 'granularity' 'connectivity' and 'synchrony' of the application [1], and the CMU group led by H.T. Kung identifies nine useful computational models [17]. These classifications are not identical to ours but in many cases a correspondence in terminology can be found. Similarly, the Linda group at Yale under Gelernter use a classification based on what they call the 'result', 'activity' and 'structure' paradigms [18], which roughly correspond to our geometric, farm and algorithmic classification. The really new features of the SuperNode application and evaluation work were due both to the flexibility provided by the underlying Transputer hardware and to the Eulerian switch architecture [6] of the SuperNode. The architecture also allows dynamic reconfiguration as a program is running. Baker at RSRE has performed some very interesting experiments making use of this facility [19].

The SuperNode is scalable to the computational demands and financial requirements of the would-be purchaser. RSRE have a 256 T800 SuperNode system with a peak performance of over 350 MFlops. Southampton has a 128 T800 system which we have benchmarked at just over 1 MFlops per Transputer for a heat-bath QCD code written in Occam: the same application code using the 3L Fortran compiler achieves only about 40 MFlops [20]. However, although such systems could deliver 'supercomputer' performance the software was certainly not in a form likely to prove attractive to applications programmers brought up on a diet of Fortran or C, and UNIX or VMS, on machines like SUNs and VAXes. Initially, the only programming language available for the Transputer was Occam and TDS, the Transputer Development System, the only programming environment. It certainly required some dedication and belief that the Transputer route to parallel processing had the basics correct for an unsophisticated user to dive into a 'fold' of TDS and throw away his or her Fortran program. However, Transputer systems have the great merit of being very simple at the hardware level. Consequently, such systems were able to provide a low-cost entry to supercomputing for those who would otherwise not be able to afford the entry price. We briefly discuss the present state of Transputer environments in the following section.

3 Portable Programming Environments for Transputer Systems

One of the key requirements of users of the distributed memory MIMD systems, be they hypercubes, meshes or rings, with or without Transputers, is some guarantee of portability for their painfully parallelised code. This was realised early on by the CalTech Concurrent Computation Group led by Fox. As a result, the description of their work in the two volume book [1] has a surprising amount of generality and is largely independent of the specific hardware topology. There were two key aspects to their work. Firstly, the CrOS 'operating system' collected together interprocessor communication routines which provided basic read, write, shift, broadcast and combining functions between the nodes themselves and between nodes and the control process. In addition, routines were supplied to map the concurrent processor into the require decomposition topology. Secondly, their 'CUBIX' library attempted to provide the applications user with useful and standard concurrent I/O facilities. The CrOS communication routines were best suited to what Fox and his co-authors characterise as 'loosely synchronous' applications in which the pattern of the communication is known prior to run-time. The CrOS communication routines are also 'blocking', 'CSP-like' routines. The so-called Crystal Router algorithm was developed for irregular problems in which the message traffic changes dynamically and/or involves message passing between non-nearest neighbours. This algorithm can also be used to implement a non-blocking form of communication between arbitrary processors.

Parasoft's Express parallel programming environment represents a commercialisation of these ideas. The scope has been extended to include debugging and performance evaluation packages, and Parasoft have just announced 'ASPAR' —an automatic paralleliser that translates suitable existing sequential programs into parallel versions. How generally successful and useful such a compiler will be remains to be seen. One feature of Express that is readily demonstrable, however, is the portability of Express parallel programs from Intel iPSCs, to Ncubes, to Transputer systems. This sort of guarantee will undoubtedly be welcomed by users wishing to protect their investment of time and effort in producing parallelised code.

At least two other parallel programming environments available for Transputer systems deserve a mention, namely, Linda and Strand. Linda frees the user from hardware issues by introducing the notion of a 'tuple space' into which data items can be put and retrieved by any processor [18]. Carriero and Gelernter regard Linda as a 'coordination' language for gluing together active pieces of code written in some 'computational' language such as Fortran or C. They argue that Linda represents an elegant abstraction of parallel programming that offers portability to the user across shared and distributed memory multi-processor machines. What performance penalty is paid for this portability is not yet clear —in this respect both Express and Linda need a detailed evaluation. The last mention goes to Strand. This is a very different concurrent programming environment and the STRAND88 language is advertised as being "a modular language based on a simple computational model that includes data flow, synchronisation and dynamic process creation". User data types and code written in C or Fortran can be incorporated into the final Strand program. At first sight, the environment looks very unfamiliar to an imperative language programmer. However, it should be noted that the author has no first-hand experience with this type of environment nor with the Linda environment.

4 The Genesis Parallel Benchmarks

As a follow-on to the SuperNode project, Inmos were involved with Bull, Chorus, Siemens and Suprenum, as well as some other companies, research laboratories and universities, in an ESPRIT-2 project called Genesis. The first year of the project, 1988-9, comprised a pre-study phase in which the feasibility of building and marketing a competitive multi-processor machine for the 1990s was examined in detail. An important part of this pre-study work was an evaluation workpackage, led by Southampton University, tasked with assessing the present state-of-the-art in parallel systems and extrapolating into the future. As is well-known, benchmarking parallel machines is an almost impossible task at the best of times, even with unlimited time and resources: the Genesis pre-study had 6 months and very limited resources.

The evaluation group comprised Southampton and Liverpool universities, Bull, Siemens and Suprenum and the GMD in Bonn. In order to obtain some consistent and reproducible performance data over a range of different parallel machines, it was decided to develop a parallel benchmark suite within the project since no satisfactory suite of parallel benchmarks then existed. In fact, the CalTech Performance Evaluation Project was taking place at about the same time as this study, and their approach turned out to be similar in spirit (but different in detail) to ours. The CalTech group reported their results [21] at about the same time as the Genesis report [20]. Both these benchmark suites are directed more at highly parallel distributed memory MIMD systems than at vector supercomputers: in this sense they may be regarded as complementary to the PERFECT benchmark suite instigated by David Kuck and collaborators [22].

The Genesis benchmarks were required to be written in standard Fortran 77 and both sequential and distributed versions supplied, together with full documentation and a computation/communication analysis. In the distributed versions, a natural communications topology for the each application was described and the location of 'SEND/RECEIVE' communications indicated. The specific calls and implementations will, of course, differ from machine to machine.

It was decided to adopt a multi-level approach to parallel benchmarks with codes covering a range of complexity. Three levels of complexity/realism were identified:

1. Synthetic Code Fragments.

   These are short code segments that are believed to reflect programming constructs or work loads typical of some application area. These are recognised to be somewhat artificial but at the same time are relatively easy to understand and adapt for different systems.

2. Application Kernels.

   These codes are typically longer than the above and are the computationally-intensive kernels of a variety of different applications. These benchmarks are more complex to analyze but are likely to come closer to modelling the behaviour of full application programs.

3. Full Application Codes.

   It is essential to verify whether the supposed 'application kernel' is at all an accurate guide to the performance of full applications programs running on parallel machines. Often, for example, there are non-parallelisable data distribution and collection phases in the full codes, or perhaps the sheer size of real applications may result in memory and/or I/O bottlenecks. Thus implementation of full applications programs is a necessary step in a complete evaluation of a parallel system.

The time and manpower limitations of the pre-study restricted the focus to the first two levels of benchmarks: the third 'full application' level had to be deferred to the next phase. Some standard single node benchmarks —Livermore loops, Whetstone and NASA kernels (the latter a reduced form suitable for the node memory limitations of current machines)— were also implemented. There are currently 7 benchmark codes derived from a range of application areas:

- FFT: a non-vectorisable version of a 1-dimensional fast Fourier transform algorithm. A vectorisable algorithm is being included in the next phase.

- PDE1: a 3-dimensional Poisson solver using parallel red-black relaxation.

- PDE2: a 2-dimensional multigrid Poisson solver using a range of fine and coarse grids.

- QCD1: a 'pure gluon' SU(3) heat-bath lattice gauge theory simulation.

- QCD2: the kernels of SU(2) or SU(3) lattice gauge theory simulations with dynamical quarks involving the solution of a large sparse system of linear equations by conjugate gradient iteration.

- MD: a 3-sphere triangulation program that attempts to simulate the essential ingredients of a long-range molecular dynamics problem.

- GAUSS: a matrix equation solver for $Ax = b$ with multiple right hand sides. Note that the well-known LINPACK benchmark corresponds to a special case of this problem but the results are not directly comparable since different methods of solution are used.

A CFD benchmark for computational fluid dynamics and a 2-dimensional FFT benchmark were also planned but had to be omitted through lack of time: their omission will be rectified in the next phase.

The evaluation group had access to a wide range of machines with both Shared Memory (SM) and Distributed Memory (DM) architectures:

- SM Vector Supercomputers: Isis, Cray-XMP, ETA-10

- SM Multiprocessor: Alliant

- DM MIMD with scalar nodes: NCube, SuperNode/Meiko iPSC-2

- DM MIMD with vector nodes: iPSC-2, Ametek/Symult

It is important to emphasise some of the many limitations of this study:

- The benchmark codes were ported to the various machines by experienced parallel programmers. However, the programmers were not necessarily experts on the particular application nor on the hardware and detailed system features of the particular machine.

- The benchmarks evaluate some overall performance of 'architecture + operating system + compiler'. There was not time for an investigation of the effects of different details of memory organisation and so on.

- The benchmarks were ported in a few days to a week per machine and some effort made to optimise the performance, short of 'significant' re-writing of code. Given the inevitably large uncertainties involved, no attempt was made to quantify the amount of effort expended on optimisation: this is in contrast to the CalTech and PERFECT procedures. (One exception occurred for QCD2 code on the Alliant. The concurrent performance was severely crippled by the very short vectors produced by one particular subroutine: a modified version of this routine alleviated this particular problem).

It must also be remembered that parallel processor performance is characterised by more than a single parameter. This makes the results difficult to present and often makes it difficult for a would-be user to gain a fair impression of the performance of some particular parallel machine. Full details of the results of the Genesis Benchmark Study, together with discussion of the individual benchmarks are contained in the final report of the working group [20].

Before we attempt to draw some conclusions from this study, we should emphasise that we are trying to benchmark a moving target. During the course of the benchmarking exercise, two systems —the ETA-10 and the Ametek/Symult machine— were withdrawn from the market. Since the completion of the first phase of this study, some new, much more powerful 'second-generation' DM MIMD systems have appeared —iPSC/860, NCube-2 and Suprenum. Thus these conclusions only reflect the state-of-the-art a year ago —and a year is a long time in this business. With this caveat, plus the further caveat that the following opinions are not necessarily shared by all members of the Genesis evaluation group, we conclude:

1. At present, a single vector supercomputer 'node' can outperform DM MIMD systems on large vectorisable problems. This conclusion may need revision in the light of the new systems mentioned above.

2. Presently available DM MIMD systems with vector nodes are unimpressive. Only the Intel iPSC2 had a vectorising compiler available and it proved difficult to exceed more than 1 MFlop per vector node. Again, the new Suprenum system, the Intel iPSC/860 system and DARPA's Touchstone project [23] may change this situation.

3. For systems with high-performance vector nodes, the communication startup overhead translates to many floating-point operations. This mandates large granularities and relatively few, long messages. This implies that large problems are required to obtain high efficiencies.

4. Scalar node DM MIMD systems show less rapid fall-off in performance as the problem size is decreased than do vector nodes.

We are therefore led to speculate that machines with scalar nodes supporting fast context switching and with low communication startup overheads may be a more cost-effective route to better overall efficiencies on a wider range of problems and problem sizes than vector node machines.

5   The ESPRIT-2 PUMA Project

The major goal of this project is to develop the next generation of Transputer components capable of providing low-latency global communications. The industrial partners with Inmos are Siemens from Germany and Bull, Chorus and Syseca from France. RSRE are project managers and the GMD in Bonn and Southampton and Liverpool Universities are the academic partners. PUMA is an acronym derived from the full title of the project, Parallel Universal Message-passing Architectures. The project has two principal research themes:

1. the investigation of software techniques and applications based on the universal message-passing paradigm,

2. an exploration of the implementation of the shared memory P-RAM model of concurrent computation on such a distributed memory system and an evaluation of the performance of such models.

The rationale for the project is as follows. The first generation Transputer systems enabled users to exploit 'locality' —of processing, of memory and of communications. However, this physical locality constraint restricts the types of algorithms and system software that may be developed for such systems. Inmos intend that their next generation Transputer components will relax the constraint of local communications by:

1. allowing Transputer links to support many virtual channels,

2. embedding low-latency message switching into a new dynamic switch chip.

In as much detail as Inmos are prepared to release at present, the next Transputer —codenamed 'H1'— will have the following characteristics:

Processing Capabilities:

- a pipelined superscalar architecture capable of sustaining over 20 MFlops floating-point performance

- an on-chip FPU and CPU like the T800

- an on-chip instruction, data and workspace cache of 16 kbytes, switchable to ordinary memory

- some form of memory protection

Communication Capabilities:

- new high bandwidth links supporting a total of 80 Mbytes/sec bidirectionally

- an on-chip Virtual Channel Processor multiplexing logical links onto physical links

- off-chip message-routing supported by a low-latency, high bandwidth, dynamic routing switch

Inmos also promise support for mixed Tx/Hx systems with a link protocol conversion chip and binary code compatibility between the two types of Transputers. More details of the routing strategy Inmos are adopting may be found in the recent paper by May and Thompson [24].

It is clear that the arrival of such new components for building distributed memory message passing systems will have a major impact. Currently, the new generation of RISC chips —like the i860 or the IBM RS/6000— make the T800 look underpowered, but it is not yet clear how well these chips, with their inevitably high context switch costs and the real costs of constructing special-purpose routing systems, will perform in multi-processor systems. The new dynamic routing chip from Inmos will be a mass-produced, off-the-shelf component and, as for the first generation systems, it should be a straightforward engineering task to construct powerful multi-H1 systems. In the long run, however, it may not be these types of systems which are the major competitor to the H1. The first Intel iWARP system is promised for mid-1990 and iWARP chips —which like Inmos Transputers, integrate communication hardware, memory and processors— have now been successfully fabricated [25].

6 General-Purpose Parallel Computing

In the introduction to this paper we defined what we meant by the term 'general-purpose'. For the parallel computer industry to grow into a significant sector of the whole computing market, it is essential that parallel computing loses its special-purpose tag and looks at more than just the very high-performance end of the market. In principle, parallel computers offer the promise of scalable, general-purpose computing performance. However, in order for users to protect their parallel software investment and to make possible the growth of a significant 'third party' parallel software industry, it is essential to be able to guarantee portability and standard languages across a range of parallel hardware. A celebrated paper by Karp and Babb [26] is entitled 'A Comparison of 12 Parallel Fortran Dialects'! This is absolutely what the user or commercial software developer does not wish to see. Similarly, the sad list of failures of parallel processor startup companies lengthens year by year. What can be done?

It is clearly vital to be able to separate the parallel hardware concerns from the parallel software concerns. In the uni-processor case, the von Neumann model allows us to do just this. Can there ever be a similar parallel abstraction? Dally at MIT has proposed a primitive set of mechanisms that attempts to separate issues of programming models from issues of machine organisation. The Parallel Machine Interface (PMI) that Dally and Wills propose [27] is a compromise between what can easily be implemented in hardware and what is required to support different models of parallel computation —actors, dataflow and shared memory. Dally and his group are collaborating with Intel to build the J-machine, an experimental fine-grain concurrent computer consisting of 64K nodes configured as a 3-dimensional mesh. Intel are producing the node chip for the machine which is a message driven processor (MDP) comprising a specialised processor, four thousand 36 bit words of memory and a portion of the 3 dimensional mesh network. Again, like the iWARP, this chip has all the ingredients to be called a generic Transputer. Unlike the iWARP, however, the MDP chip will have a very fast context switch in order to implement the necessary PMI mechanisms efficiently. The J-machine will be a very interesting research machine.

Valiant is another who believes that such a separation of parallel hardware and software issues is possible [28]. Since Valiant's ideas are challenging and potentially of great importance to the future of parallel computing it is worthwhile to review his arguments in some detail. Valiant argues that the success of the Von Neumann model of computation is due, in part, to the concept of a universal sequential computer:

1. Turing demonstrated the universality of a sequential Turing machine in his classic 1936 paper [29].

2. It can be shown that there is a single general-purpose Turing machine which can simulate in time $0(T \log(T))$ every special-purpose time T Turing machine [3].

3. When the tape of the Turing machine is generalised to a Random Access Machine (RAM), the $\log(T)$ overhead can be reduced to a constant [31].

It is therefore interesting to ask the question of whether or not there is a similar 'universality' result for parallel computers. Valiant has answered this question in the affirmative and proved that an efficient general-purpose architecture for parallel computers is possible.

In order to discuss what Valiant has actually proved it is necessary to introduce some definitions [31]:

1. Realistic p-processor parallel computer:

This is assumed to be a set of p sequential processors and memories connected by a sparse communication network.

2. Idealised p-processor parallel computer:

This is a set of p processors and memories and no restrictions on communication between any of the processors.

The idealised p-processor machine leads to another idealisation —the PRAM or Parallel Random Access Machine. This is a model that is able to reflect the inherent logical parallelism in problems but ignores all communication overheads. It consists of a set of p synchronised processors, each with its own local memory. The processors are conventional sequential machines with their instruction set extended to include operations allowing interprocessor communication —reads and writes into other processor memories.

Valiant's principle result is as follows. If an algorithm takes time T on an idealised p-processor machine the operation count is said to be the product pT. Valiant shows that the ideally optimal pT product can be obtained to within a constant factor by a p-processor realistic parallel machine for all algorithms with sufficient "parallel slackness". This means the algorithms must be implementable on an idealised $p \log p$-processor machine in time $0(T/\log p)$. This excess concurrency —$\log p$ processes on each processor of the p-processor realistic machine— is the price that has to be paid for using implementable communication networks. An important ingredient in Valiant's proof is that the interconnection network must support communication with bounded delays so that message delivery is assured in $0(\log p)$ time even for heavily loaded networks. Valiant shows that networks and routing algorithms do exist which meet this requirement. It is in this technical sense, therefore, that Valiant has proved a parallel universality result.

It is perhaps worth saying a little more about the PRAM model. This was defined as a synchronous parallel machine in which each processor can access a common memory at each step of the computation. However, it is known that many results obtained for PRAMs can be applied to non-synchronous machines and to machines based on message-passing (MP-RAMs) rather than common memory access. Valiant also distinguishes 3 types of PRAM models [32]:

1. Seclusive PRAMs or SPRAMs:

Every processor accesses only one memory module at each step. In this case, Valiant's universality result applies directly.

2. Exclusive PRAMs or EPRAMs:

More than one processor can access the same memory module at once. In this case Valiant shows that universality still holds but that the data must be distributed sufficiently randomly throughout the modules. Hashing functions which achieve this are known to exist [32]. (Note that both the SPRAM and the EPRAM are special cases of an EREW PRAM).

3. Concurrent PRAMs or CPRAMs:

More than one processor is allowed to access the same store location at once. (This is also known as a CRCW PRAM). Universality can now be shown to hold if the communication network is enhanced with a combining capability. As an alternative to adding such a hardware option, Valiant has introduced the notion of a Bulk-Synchronous Parallel (BSP) computer [28]. In this model, the processors are synchronised after a "superstep" consisting of a number of instructions or sends and receives. It is possible to prove that such a bulk-synchronised seclusive PRAM (Valiant's XPRAM) can efficiently simulate a CPRAM.

These theoretical results are exciting and encouraging. However, to what extent such universality results may be achieved with real message-passing hardware rather than these idealised systems remains an open question. Moreover, the question of what are the "best" processor, memory and network components for building such truly general purpose parallel machines is also unanswered. The ESPRIT-2 GP-MIMD project is attempting to find answers to these questions. If successful, parallel computing may lose its special purpose tag and standard parallel languages and environments and third-party parallel software become a reality.

References

[1] G.C. Fox et al, "Solving Problems on Concurrent Processors", Prentice Hall 1988.

[2] A.J.G. Hey and D.J. Pritchard, "Parallel Applications on the RTP Supernode machine", invited paper in proceedings of "3rd International Conference on Supercomputing". L.P. Kartashev and S.I. Kartashev, Vol. II, 264, 1988.

[3] J. Backus, "Can Programming be Liberated from the Von Neumann Style? A Functional Style and its Algebra of Programs", Comm. of the ACM 21, 1978.

[4] R.W. Hockney and C.R. Jesshope, Parallel Computers 2, Adam Hilger 1988.

[5] Supercomputing Review, "For the Record", p.19, April 1990.

[6] D.A. Nicole, E.K. Lloyd and J.S. Ward, "Switching Networks for Transputer Links", Proceedings of 8th Occam User Group, Sheffield 1988.

[7] Transputer Applications Notebook—Architecture and Software, "IMS T800 Architecture", p.78, Inmos Databook Series 1989.

[8] Transputer Applications Notebook—Systems and Performance, "Lies, Damned Lies and Benchmarks", p.258 Inmos Databook Series 1989.

[9] D. Roweth and L.J. Clarke, unpublished.

[10] A.J.G. Hey, "Reconfigurable Transputer networks: practical concurrent computation", article in Scientific Applications of Multiprocessors, edited by R.J. Elliott and C.A.R. Hoare, Prentice Hall 1989.

[11] J. Allwright, Southampton CCG research report 1989, to be published.

[12] Transputer Applications Notebook—Architecture and Software, "Exploiting concurrency: a raytracing example", p.144, Inmos Databook Series 1989.

[13] I. Glendinning and A.J.G. Hey, Comp. Phys. Comm. 45 p.367, 1987.

[14] M.J. Gorrod, M.J. Coe and M. Yearworth, "Parallel processing of Monte Carlo simulations using a Transputer array", Southampton Astronomy Group research report 1989, to be published.

[15] J.M. Carter, M.G. Green and T. Medcalf, "Transparent use of Transputers for off-line computation", Royal Holloway and Bedford New College research report 1989.

[16] S. Booth et al., "Harnesses for running HEP Fortran programs on the Meiko Computing Surface", CERN research report 1989.

[17] H.T. Kung, "Computational models for parallel computers", article in Scientific Applications of Multiprocessors edited by R.J. Elliott and C.A.R. Hoare, Prentice Hall 1989.

[18] N. Carriero and D. Gelernter, "Linda in Context", Yale research report 1988.

[19] S. Baker, seminar in Southampton, 1989.

[20] A.J.G. Hey and C.J. Scott, "Report of the state of the art and evaluation workpackage", ESPRIT-2 project P2447 (Genesis pre-study), June 1989.

[21] P. Messina et al., "Benchmarking Advanced Architecture Computers", CalTech Report C3P 712, June 1989.

[22] M. Berry et al., "The PERFECT Club Benchmarks: Effective Performance Evaluation of Supercomputers", CSRD Report No. 827, November 1988.

[23] S. Lillevik, "Touchstone project Overview", to be published in the Proceedings of DMCC5, Charleston 1990.

[24] D. May and P. Thompson, "Transputers and Routers: Components for Concurrent Machines", to be published in the proceedings of the 3rd Transputer/Occam International Conference, Tokyo, May 1990.

[25] T. Gross, seminar at IBM Research 1990.

[26] A.H. Karp and R.G. Babb II, IEEE Software, September 1988.

[27] W.J. Dally and D.S. Wills, "Universal Mechanisms for Concurrency", MIT research report 1989.

[28] L.G. Valiant, "A Bridging Model for Parallel Computation", Communications of the ACM 33 (1990), 103.

[29] A.M. Turing, "On Computable Numbers with an Application to the Entscheidungs Problem", Proc. London Math. Soc. Ser. 2-42 (1936), 230.

[30] F.C. Hennie and R.E. Steans, "Two Tape Simulation of Multitape Machines", JACM 13:4 (1966), 533.

[31] S.A. Cook and R.A. Reckhow, "Time Bounded Random Access Machine", JCSS 7 (1973), 354.

[32] L.G. Valiant "General Purpose Parallel Architectures" in the Handbook of Theoretical Computer Science, J. van Leeuwen, ed. North Holland 1990.

PARALLEL ASSOCIATIVE PROCESSING FOR

KNOWLEDGE BASES

Simon Lavington
Dept. of Computer Science, University of Essex, UK.

Abstract.

Data structures such as sets, relations and graphs occur frequently in Artificial Intelligence applications. When these structures are large, as in deductive databases and knowledge bases, the performance of conventional computers is poor. The generic operations on these structures, such as pattern-directed search, set intersection and transitive closure, all involve associative matching of variable-length lexical strings. In this paper, which is an updated version of a recent UNICOM presentation, we describe novel add-on hardware which employs SIMD parallel techniques to achieve the required associative processing. The hardware is embedded in an architecture which allows knowledge bases to be stored and processed in situ. Performance figures are given.

1   Introduction

The generic operations of AI programs, such as pattern-directed searching, variable binding, set intersection and transitive closure, all take place on symbolic data. These operations depend upon the comparison of one data value with many other data values. More particularly, they involve the associative matching of variable-length lexical strings. Since the matching, or comparison, of symbolic data is so fundamental to information systems in general, it is natural to consider ways in which this activity could be speeded up by some form of associative hardware. The variable length of symbolic objects, and the potential overlap between the internal representation of strings, numerals, pointers, etc makes the design of general-purpose hardware support somewhat difficult.

Another difficulty lies in the management of associatively-accessed (ie content-addressable) memory. The data values referred to above are all part of user-defined structures such as sets, graphs, networks, tables and relations. Since graphs can be represented as relations, the super-type **relation** is a useful unifying conceptual framework. The super-type relation is a logical, rather than physical, object and so the memory-management strategy (ie 'paging and protection') used for knowledge bases should reflect this logical structure. Although memory management is not a main theme of this paper, we make reference to memory management requirements when presenting our analysis of the problems encountered in exploiting parallelism in knowledge bases.

Although there is much natural parallelism in database and knowledge base applications, the cost-effective exploitation of this parallelism is not easy. This is because conventional (von Neumann) computers, and their software, operate at a level of data granularity far finer than that implied by the above set and graph manipulations. Put another way, the primitive types found in most programming languages are not rich enough to support adequately the abstract data types desired by applications programmers. An exception is SETL (Ref. 1). This has the desired relational primitives, analagous to the matrix primitives in APL, but is very inefficient because of the mismatch between SETL primitives and the computational facilities offered by conventional hardware.

A new architectural approach is required. We address the central issue of data granularity. Related practical problems, familiar to all database practitioners, are how to localise searching and how to avoid the unnecessary movement of data. We tackle these problems with particular reference to Artificial Intelligence because the structural complexity of many AI applications is not readily tamed by conventional software strategies. When the volume of stored knowledge becomes significant, as in large knowledge-bases or persistent object systems, the performance of conventional computers leaves much to be desired. A call for two orders of magnitude improvement in performance in run times for AI applications is not uncommon (Ref. 2).

In Section 2 we introduce the architectural concept of **active memory**, as a means of improving the performance of conventional computing systems. Now that the object-oriented paradigm is being applied to databases, the requirements of persistent object management are included in an analysis of the active memory's advantages. More details are given in ref. 3. In Section 3 we state the desired functionality of an active memory from the users' viewpoint. This leads on to a discussion in Section 4 of low- level procedural interfaces and information representation. For these topics, we draw on our operational experience of an existing knowledge- base server. In Section 5 we outline the hardware implementation of an active memory from off-the-shelf components such as transputers, showing how SIMD-parallel techniques are used to provide both associative (ie content-addressable) memory and the desired structure manipulations - all in the one unit. The performance of this unit is described in Section 6, firstly in terms of the raw speed of generic operations such as search, insert and transitive closure. Finally, a case study is given which indicates a speed-up of up to three orders of magnitude when the SIMD parallel techniques are applied to a practical management information system.

2 The Concept of Active Memory

The programming community readily accepts the idea of add-on hardware support for certain well-defined tasks such as graphics and floating-point calculations. Such special-purpose hardware is acceptable because the cost-effectiveness is clear and because the functional interface is easy to use. We now introduce a new add-on device which we call an active memory unit. We justify this novel concept via an analysis of the shortcomings of conventional memory systems.

Figure 1(a) shows a conventional hierarchy of memory devices, M1 (faster, volatile) and M2 (slower, non volatile). For present purposes it is not necessary to know whether this hierarchy is connected to one or several processors. Although we ought strictly to refer to the locus of computational control, for simplicity we show the memory hierarchy controlled by a single box labelled CPU. In Figure 1(a) data processing can only proceed if the data to be processed is within the CPU's addressing range (here M1). Thus, persistent data structures are in general moved from M2 to M1, whereupon the CPU takes (reads) fine-grain elements of the data structure in order to operate upon them. There are three points to note about the conventional computing environment represented by Figure 1(a):

i)   A physical address-mapping is necessary between M_1 and M_2; this physical mapping does not normally reflect the logical structure of the data. Hence memory management ('paging and protection') is carried out with reference to coarse physical address boundaries.

ii)   The bandwidths of both interconnecting highways has to be high, if high overall performance is to be maintained.

iii)   All responsibility for the exploitation of parallelism resides within the CPU. Assuming CPU to be based on a general-purpose von Neumann computational model, responsibility for exploiting parallelism is actually moved into software (at the compiler and/or source program level) for most programming languages.

In Figure 1(b) the system has been augmented by the addition of an autonomous unit labelled Active Memory. This may also contain a hierarchy of devices, S1 (fastest, volatile) and S2 (slowest, non-volatile), but this internal arrangement is invisible to CPU. Both S1 and S2 have limited (i.e. special-purpose) computational ability in addition to their ability to store information. Apart from explicit insert and delete commands, data is persistent within the Active Memory. This property of persistence is extended to any new data structures created as a result of operations involving existing data structures. Such action has implications for data consistency, naming conventions and version control. These are issues which are the subject of current research.

The Active Memory has a number of other unusual properties, as follows. The Active Memory is associative, i.e. content-addressable. That is to say, CPU can only refer to a data object held within the Active Memory by a unique name. The term 'name' is taken to include 'descriptor', 'interrogand', or 'pattern', so that variables and wild cards are accommodated. A consequence of this is that named objects can have varying granularity. The hidden memory management within the Active Memory is also of variable granularity, being based on logical descriptors rather than on physical addresses. The data-manipulation commands built into the Active Memory reflect the common operations on frequently-used data structures such as relations, sets and graphs. Such operations exhibit much scope for parallelism. The repertoire of commands is discussed in Section 3; their hardware implementation is discussed in Section 5. Note that the Active Memory is primarily intended for structured data arising from a finite, but useful, sub-set of users' abstract data type declarations. Other (possibly un-structured) data may be held as usual in M1 and M2 in Figure 1(b). Since the Active Memory's commands are memory-mapped, it is open to the CPU's system software to integrate (M1 + M2) and (S1 + S2) into a one-level virtual store. It is, of course, not so easy to offer persistence within the (M1 + M2) section of this integrated virtual memory - though computers such as the MONADS do this via extremely large address spaces (Ref 4).

3   Functional Requirements

As was mentioned earlier, the structures which the active memory has to manipulate mainly consist of sets, relations and graphs. Generically, the super-type **relation** appears capable of describing all such structures. A list of suitable operations on these structures includes the following:

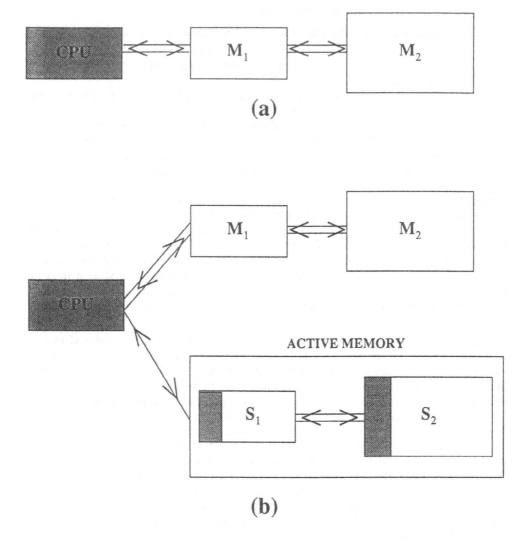

Figure 1: adding active memory to a conventional computer

(i) **relational and set primitives:** insert, delete, member, select, project, intersect, difference, union, join, duplicate removal.

(ii) **set aggregate primitives:** cardinality, maximum, minimum, average.

(iii) **recursive query primitives:** transitive closure of a relation, reachable node set, n^{th} wave of tuples, 'is there a path between two specified nodes?', return the path between two specified nodes, composition of relations.

(iv) **graph aggregate primitives:** shortest path, longest path, arc average, node average.

(v) **special primitives:** (yet to be decided, but possibly including: sort, modify, range search, fuzzy search, Euclidean distance, Hamming distance).

The third group needs more explanation. The intention is to support the evaluation of linearrecursive rules. Two types of linear recursive rule are considered: single-sided (single-chain) and double-sided (n-chain). The first type are transitive closure rules. Although the second type can be evaluated by one transitive closure query plus one or more non-recursive queries, this is generally not an efficient strategy. The provision of an 'nth wave' primitive allows much better performance. This returns the nth wave of nodes starting from a specified (variable binding) node set. Successor nodes are automatically re-cycled (n-1) times to discover the end of all n-step paths from the source nodes. Another of the above primitives that needs further explanation is 'reachable node set'. This returns the set of nodes to which paths exist from a specified initial binding set. This operation applies to a base relation. The corresponding set in a virtual relation p, defined by a chaining rule such as:

$$p(x,y) \;:\text{-}\; a(x,v),b(v,w),c(w,y).$$

can be produced without having to materialise the whole virtual relation. The active memory implements this by chaining responder sets through the base relations a, b, c, repeatedly. Further information is contained in ref. 5. Some specimen timings are given in Section 5.

Lest all this appear too biassed towards the deductive database paradigm, it should be noted that relational operations also seem to be at the heart of other popular AI paradigms. For example in production systems, a set of rules is applied to a set of facts by attempting to match the condition-part of a rule with fact patterns. Each of the conditions of a rule is a tuple whose terms may be values (ground term) or variables. A condition may be regarded as defining a relation, which is instantiated by a subset of zero or more facts in the factbase, a fact being a tuple of ground terms. Pattern matching can thus be defined as finding the join of the relations associated with all of the conditions of each rule. A rule is satisfied if its join is non-null.

As far as overall system requirements are concerned, we summarise here the desirable properties of the active memory which were hinted at in Section 2.

(a) **Memory management.** An active memory should provide hardware-assisted support for the 'paging' and protection of information within a hierarchy of volatile and non-volatile storage devices. These devices should be associative, ie content-addressable.

(b) **Persistence.** Through (a), the active memory should provide support for persistent objects so that any <type> system enforced by a programming language on short-term data in the active memory is also enforced on long-term data. Persistent stores require a large, uniform naming system which allows direct access to objects of various sizes, without requiring knowledge of their physical location. Any structural relationships ('cross-references') between persistent objects should be maintained.

(c) **Ease of integration and extension.** The procedural interface for the primitive operations given previously should be easy to integrate within the low-level software and hardware of a conventional computing system. The active memory should be modularly extendible.

(d) **Speed and size.** The speed of the active memory's primitive operations should at least be faster than could be achieved by hand-coded software running on a uniprocessor of compatible technology. This implies the use of parallel techniques. As far as capacity is concerned, the active memory should have a fast (semiconductor) section which is comparable in size with a normal RAM primary memory.

When sets and graphs arise indirectly, eg for control purposes, the quantification of size and speed is not so obvious. Examples are: lemma stores, fact dependency networks, constraint satisfaction, and truth maintenance systems. We take the latter two cases for illustration. Both constraint satisfaction (eg ref. 6) and truth maintenance (eg ref. 7) have been used in AI applications areas such as planning and scheduling, fault diagnosis, natural language processing, scene labelling in vision, etc. Both techniques attempt to control the problem-space by using derived information. In constraint satisfaction systems, it is convenient to represent domains of values as sets; similarly, the derived values of compositions of problem-variables can be represented as sets. Algorithms then make use of operations such as intersection to work towards the final problem solution. The amount of working space required by these algorithms can be considerable. One C S system, when solving the 10-Queens problem, starts with 10 sets of ten members each and then generates fewer but larger sets until the final solution set (of 700 elements) is reached. At one intermediate stage, 5 sets each of cardinality about 7500 are generated. In Truth Maintenance systems, networks (ie graphs) represented as tuples are searched for matches. Such networks can become quite large: a million-node network is regarded as a minimum realistic Truth Maintenance System.

The architectural requirements (a) and (b) above depend critically on the conventions adopted for the low-level representation of information. In the next Section we describe the conventions which have been developed for a knowledge-base server known as the Intelligent File Store (IFS) (Ref 2). An IFS/1 has been in use at a customer's site since December 1987. The IFS/1's storage conventions are being incorporated into a prototype active memory unit now under construction at the University of Essex.

4   Information Representation and Low-Level Interface

The active memory of Figure 1(b) must be semantics-free, in the sense of being able to support a variety of applications, programming languages and information models. As mentioned above, the active memory is associative. Except in the trivial case where all lines contain uniform objects, eg virtual addresses in a translation look-aside buffer, each entry in any associative memory must have a certain field that is invariant for that class of object. Furthermore, the accessing mechanism must take account of the fact that, in a general-purpose associative memory, different classes of stored object may have differing field formats. If a particular field-position for a given object can contain alternatives, as for example with union types, then some mechanism is also required which distinguishes primitive types during the associative match process. The underlying principle is that the comparison hardware must be certain that it is comparing like with like, when attempting to match an interrogand with a stored entry. Of course, there are occasions when a match is forced, for example when the stored entry contains a named variable or when the interrogand contains a wild card.

Within the foregoing framework, there are several possible conventions for low-level information representation in an associative memory. We describe the scheme we have used for the last few years for a knowledge-base server called the Intelligent File Store, IFS/1 (Lavington 1988);this scheme is also being used for our active memory. It should be mentioned that we are working on a revision that will permit a richer interpretation of the concept of type. In the existing IFS/ 1, it is convenient to describe each stored line as a tuple according to the following format:

<L><TF><T1><T2> ... <Tm><M1><M2> ... <Mn>

where:

<L> is an optional label (eg gödelisation)
<TF> is an invariant term for a particular tuple format
<T1><T2> ... are terms in a wff
<M1><M2> ... are optional modifiers for the <L> and <T> fields

The <terms> may be lexemes (eg character strings), integers, labels (eg gödel numbers), abstract nodes, named variables, etc. The <terms> are all mapped into fixed-length internal indentifiers (IDs). Thus, IDs are used to represent all primitive objects. To distinguish primitive types, each ID has the format:

<tag><unique sub_code>

<tag> is usually four bits. The total length of an ID is a system-configuration constant, set by software in the range two to eight bytes. For the rest of this paper we shall assume a typical ID length of four bytes.

For many user-defined primitive objects, the creation of the <unique sub-code> bits of an ID is simply achieved by maintaining a counter, updated each time a new ID of that <type> is allocated. For a <type> requiring much dynamic allocation and deallocation, a free list could also be maintained if the available space (max. 2^{60}) is not felt to be large enough. The IFS gives hardware support for three system-defined ID <types>, namely: numeric, label, and lexical. For <type> numeric, the <unique sub-code> is simply a two's complement integer. For <types> label and lexical, the <unique sub-code> is allocated in a manner which speeds up subsequent dereferencing.

From a system viewpoint, the existence of a typed ID space raises two implementation issues: how to map rapidly into and out of the ID space; how to manage the ID space so as to ensure uniqueness of encryption within any one <type> of object, in a multi-user environment. These issues are most acute in the case of lexical tokens, and justify the provision of hardware assistance. The task of a unit called a Lexical Token Converter (LTC) is therefore twofold: firstly, to translate from the lexemes (e.g. character strings) used in an AI program into and out of the ID space; secondly, to allocate and deallocate lexical IDs in a consistent manner, keeping a dictionary of all lexemes known to the system so far. The LTC is thus two-way associative memory with additional ID allocation/deallocation features. There are other desirable properties of the LTC such as the ability to perform fuzzy searches. A full discussion is given in Ref 8. In particular, it is shown that an LTC of between one and ten Mbytes total capacity should suffice for practical knowledge bases.

The above tuple format and ID conventions are assumed for all the hardware primitive operations described in Section 3. The active memory hardware primitives are presented to users via various levels of software, at the lowest level of which is an applications-independent and model-independent C procedural interface. There are procedures at this lowest level for all of the hardware actions listed in Section 3. For example, there are two main versions of the search (or select) command, the general forms of which are as follows:

> p-search(patt, A)
> r-search(patt, resp)

Both commands assume that the required C declarations have been made, and that 'patt' has been initialised to a desired interrogand pattern, including wild cards where desired. 'A' is the name by which the responder set will be known. 'resp' is an area in the user's memory to which responders may be returned. The first command, p-search, automatically inserts any responders back into the active memory, creating a persistent structure   named A.   There are, of course, some consequential issues concerning version-number to be resolved in practical database systems. Hardware support within the active memory for automatic versioning of structures is under consideration at the time of writing. The second command, r-search, is a variation which returns responders to the host processor into a buffer pointed to by resp. Above this lowest level, various software strategies are possible. We may, for example, wish to enrich the primitive types of the applications programming language by adding types which reflect the structure of the tuples we wish to store in the active memory.

5   Hardware Realisation

The underlying structure of the active memory follows that of the IFS/1 (Ref. 2) and the IFS/1's relational algebraic processor (Ref. 9). Both these units employ SIMD-parallel search engines and hardware-hashed RAM to give very rapid search rates. This permits associative matching tasks to be carried out over large volumes of information in a more cost-effective manner than would be possible with CAM chips. In the active memory the storage functionality and the relational processing activity are combined within the same hardware unit. The main difference between the former IFS/1 implementation and our active memory now under construction is that the latter uses transputers in place of PAL-based finite state machines for control purposes. Using several transputers for distributed control gives greater functional flexibility, better modular extensibility, and very much shorter development times. Since the data-intensive work is still carried out by special SIMD search engines, there is little degradation of overall performance compared with the IFS/1's MSI control hardware.

Figure 2 shows a section of the active memory now being built at Essex. The boxes T_{bf}, T_n and T_r are TRAMS - (transputer-plus-RAM modules). The subscripts bf,n and r respectively stand for: branch fan- out, node and root. The box labelled H alongside each node transputer is a memory-mapped hardware hasher. The search modules SM each consist of 1Mbyte of 80nsec. DRAM, a 32-bit wide search engine, and a small amount of organisational logic for masking, etc. The search modules are mapped into T_n's address space for control purposes. In the prototype there are four search modules per node, giving 12Mbytes of associative (ie content-addressable) memory in   Figure 2. This CAM is used both for structure storage and during the execution of the relational operations described in Sections 3. Each SM pcb contains about twice the number of

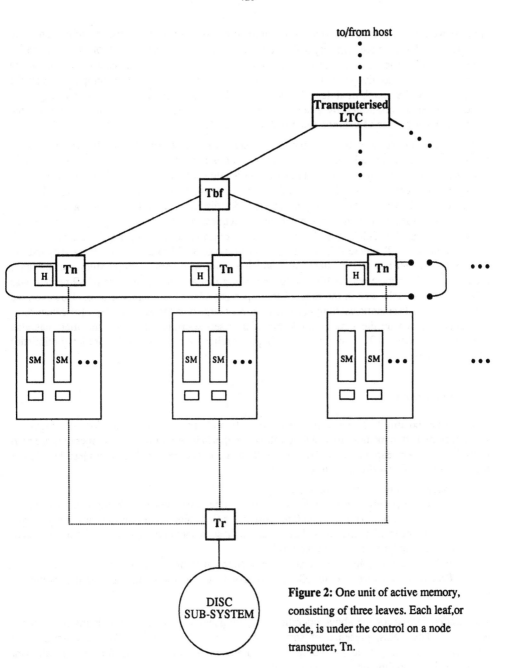

Figure 2: One unit of active memory, consisting of three leaves. Each leaf, or node, is under the control on a node transputer, Tn.

chips as would be the case if it was a conventional RAM board of the same capacity. Thus the cost per bit of the active memory's CAM is about twice the cost per bit of conventionally-accessed RAM. The memory per module, and the nodes in the tree, can easily be extended in future. Overflow is to disc(s), which are organised into logical hashing bins compatible with the organisation of the search modules. The box labelled trasputerised LTC is a similar arrangement of search modules controlled by a node transputer, as described in Ref 8. This implements the lexical token conversion functions described in Section 4.

The associatively-accessed disc in Figure 2 is naturally the non-volatile part of the active memory, for which the search modules appear as a cache. Data is moved between the disc(s) and cache in logical sets, according to a scheme known as semantic caching (Ref. 10). Cached sets, for example 'all people living in Ipswich', also have their set-descriptor (corresponding to <?><lives.in><Ipswich>) placed in the cache. As discussed in ref. 10, testing cached set-descriptors is sufficient to determine whether a requested set is totally, partly, or not at all contained within the cache. It is shown that the overheads of carrying out these tests is small provided that $R \gg 2^t$, where R is the performance ratio of RAM to disc (typically $> 10^4$) and t is the number of <terms> in the interrogand which are not wild cards. Initial studies of a binary relational database gave reasonable results, indicating that an average hit-rate of 89 percent was achieved with a cache size in the range 5 to 10 percent of the total database size. However, we have not yet used semantic caching in earnest on very large databases. A strategy for concurrent-user control based on the same variable-granularity set-descriptors for lock specifiers has also been proposed (Ref. 10). A combination of pre-conflict locking and post-conflict (optimistic) locking is envisaged.

6   Performance

Based on the existing IFS/1 performance (Refs. 2, 9) and upon Occam simulations of Figure 2, we expect the active memory to yield the following approximate timings when operands are held in the RAM-based search modules. (Note that these are times measured at the nodes; they do not include any transfers to/from the host).

> **Insert a tuple:** 60 microseconds.
> **Member operation:** 40 microseconds (fixed time, independent of relation cardinality).
> **Search with one wild card:** 400 microseconds (independent of relation cardinality; varies with number of responders, but assumes these responders are kept within the active memory and not returned to the host).
> **Join operation:** join of two 1000-tuple relations in about 5 milliseconds.
> **Transitive closure:** up to 600 microseconds for a 1000-node graph, depending on bushyness.

The relation format for the above operations is very general, no assumptions being made about position of key fields, presence of sorted values, etc. Hand-coded software, running on a uniprocessor of compatible technology, only offers competitive speeds for very small data structures of cardinality typically less than 20.

As a practical example of the potential use of the active memory in support of management information systems, we quote the results of an evaluation carried out by the Union Bank of

Switzerland (Ref 11). UBS used an IFS/1 to hold a relational database containing historical share-transaction information. In the first test, 100,000 5-field tuples were used to represent the following data for 87 stock titles:

trading day, year, stock title, average price on this trading day, volume traded on this day.

In a second test, two more fields were added to each tuple to give information on the highest price and lowest price for the trading day in question.

Specimen queries such as: 'return all entries for a given title over a given year', were carried out on the two sets of 100,000 tuples. When compared with two well-known relational database products running on an Apollo Workstation, the IFS/1 was observed to speed up queries by between 10 - 1000 times. The actual speed-up factor depended upon number of wild cards in the query, but was nearly independent of the position of the wild card in the interrogand. In Ref 11 the following additional comments are made by UBS about the IFS/1:

a) access is truly relational - the order of tuples does not matter;
b) no indices are necessary, hence inserts and updates are fast;
c) database tuning and query optimisation are unnecessary;
d) the IFS low-level procedural interface is easy to use.

Another comment of the potential for active memory comes from our collaboration with Hewlett Packard's Bristol Laboratories. Experiments are in progress to support Hewlett Packard's KBMS1 knowledge-base management system with an IFS/1 knowledge-base server. KBMS1 uses a Prolog computational model. For certain clause bases, the number of unifications required to answer a particular query can be reduced by over two orders of magnitude by letting the IFS/1 perform pre-unification filtering.

7   Conclusions

The processing of AI structures is a task ill-served by conventional architectures. An add-on unit called the **active memory** has been described which uses SIMD parallelism to speed up performance in a modularly-extensible, cost-effective, manner. The active memory offers a reasonably high level of functionality, well-suited to smart database and knowledge-base applications. This helps to remove some of the complexity from run-time software, by migrating tedious structure-manipulation tasks away from the CPU and into the special add-on unit. In other words, the natural data parallelism inherent in many AI structures is exploited automatically.

8   Acknowledgements

It is a pleasure to acknowledge the contribution of other members of the IFS team at Essex. The work described in this paper has been supported by SERC grants GR/E/05018 and GR/E/06319.

References

1   R B K Dewar ,E Schonberg and J T Schwartz 'High-Level Programming - An Introduction to the Programming Language SETL' *Courant Institue of Math Sciences,* New York 1983.

2   S H Lavington, 'Technical Overview of the Intelligent File Store'. *Knowledge-Based Systems,* Vol.1,No.3, June 1988, pages 166 - 172.

3   S H Lavington and R A J Davies 'Active Memory for Managing Persistent Objects'. Presented at the International Workshop on Computer Architectures to Support Security and Persistence, *Bremen, FRG,* May 1990. Proceedings to be published by Springer-Verlag.

4   J Rosenberg and J L Keedy 'Software Management of a Large Virtual Memory'. *Proceedings of the 4th. Australian Computer Science Conference,* Brisbane, February 1981, pages 171 - 183.

5   J Robinson and S H Lavington 'A Transitive Closure and Magic Functions Machine' *To be presented at the Second International Symposium on Databases in Parallel and Distributed Systems,* July 1990, Dublin.

6   C Freuder 'Synthesizing Constraint Expressions' *CACM* November 1978, Vol 21, No 11, 958-966.

7   J De Kleer 'An Assumption-Based TMS' *AI 28* (1986) 127-162.

8   C J Wang and S H Lavington 'SIMD Parallelism for Symbol Mapping'. To be presented at the *International Workshop on VLSI for AI and Neural Networks,* Oxford, September 1990.

9   S H Lavington, J Robinson and K Y Mok, 'A High Performance Relational Algebraic Processor for Large Knowledge Bases'. *Presented at the International Workshop on VLSI for Artificial Intelligence, Oxford,* July 1988. Published in: VLSI for Artificial Intelligence, eds. Delgado-Frias and Moore, Kluwer Academic Press, 1989, pages 133 - 143.

10   S H Lavington, M Standring, Y J Jiang, C J Wang and M E Waite, 'Hardware Memory Management for Large Knowledge Bases'. *Proceedings of PARLE, the conference on Parallel Architectures and Languages Europe,* Eindhoven, June 1987, pages 226 - 241. (Published by Springer-Verlag as Lecture Notes in Computer Science, Nos. 258 & 259).

11   H Walther 'Performance Measurement of the Associative Memory IFS at the Artificial Intelligence Applications Institute at Edinburgh, 13 November 1989 - 24 November 1989'. *UBILAB Report* February 1989, Union Bank of Switzerland, Zurich.

PERFORMANCE ESTIMATES OF A JOIN

Suresh Patel

ICL,
Wenlock Way, West Gorton,
MANCHESTER, M12 5DR.

Abstract.

The European Declarative System (EDS) project (ESPRIT II EP2025), supported by the Commission of the Europen Communities (CEC DG XIII/A/4) is developing a system supporting a parallel relational database, along with parallel LISP and PROLOG languages implementations. This paper describes a performance model for a JOIN under the relational database on the multi-processor distributed store EDS prototype machine. For the performance model we are interested in the data rates across the processing elements, as the data rates will form part of the requirement for the design of the EDS prototype machine architecture. We describe a number of algorithms and how they are executed. We are particularly interested in the algorithms that give the fastest JOIN timings.

1   INTRODUCTION

The architecture of the EDS prototype system is based on two main conclusions derived from a study of the trends in current hardware technologies. Firstly the bandwidth requirements of micro-processors will outstrip that of store. Secondly the cost/performance of semi-conductor store is declining faster than that of discs and will cross over in the late 1990s. In fact it can be argued that it has already occurred for very large systems. The design of the EDS prototype system architecture intercepts these trends in the following ways.

1. The EDS prototype machine will consist of processor-store units (called processing elements or PEs) where the processor is closely coupled to the local store, and the PEs are loosely connected by a network.

2. The design of the Database Server will support a two level stable store where the top level is RAM with battery back-up and the second level is disc storage. The design will be optimized for the situation where the database is held entirely in the RAM store.

The principle application of the system being developed in the ESPRIT II EDS Project will be the Database Server. This will provide an advanced relational database system providing high performance and functionality. The document [Watson 90] describes the EDS Parallel Relational Database System.

For our purpose we assume a distributed database where the database is a collection of data which belongs logically to the same system but is stored across a number of processing elements. Access to data from non local processing elements would involve message passing. We also assume the relational model of database where the database is stored in the form of relations. A relation may be thought of as a table with a fixed number of columns (attributes) and a variable number of rows (tuples). We describe the performance model for a join under this system (for a number of algorithms) and also briefly describe the join. The algorithms may vary in three ways

- The amount of the EDS relational database implementation included.

- The way in which the relational database is held in our system.

- The complexity of the JOIN we are performing.

1.1 Relations

A *relation* on domains D_1, D_2, ..., D_n (not necessarily all distinct) consists of a *heading* and a *body*.

- Heading. The *heading* consists of a fixed set of *attributes* A_1, A_2, ..., A_n, such that each attribute A_i corresponds to exactly one of the underlying domains D_i (i = 1, 2, ..., n).

- Body. The *body* consists of a set of *tuples*, where each tuple in turn consists of a set of attribute-value pairs $(A_i:v_i)$ (i = 1, 2, ..., n), one such pair for each attribute A_i in the heading. For any given attribute-value pair $(A_i:v_i)$, v_i is a value from the unique domain D_i that is associated with the attribute A_i.

The number of tuples in the relation is called the *cardinality* of the relation.

1.2 Joins

One of the most important operations of the relational systems and probably the most important limiting factor on their performance is the $\Theta - join$ operation. The $\Theta - join$ of a source relation S and a target relation T on attributes A from S, and B from T, is the relation R, obtained by concatenating each tuple $s \in S$ and each tuple $t \in T$ whenever $(s[A] \Theta t[B])$ is true. Θ is one of the operators $=, \neq, <, \leq, \geq, or >$. The $\Theta - join$ operation is generally needed for formulating queries which reference more than one relation. The most frequently used type of $\Theta - join$ operation is the equijoin, or simply join, where "Θ" is the operator "=".

Figure 1a shows the most common join, the natural join in diagramatic form. The relations are shown as tables. Figure 1b shows an equijoin in diagramatic form. Note the replication of the *B* attribute in the resulting relation *R*. The difference between the natural join and the equijoin is that in the natural join the *B* attribute is not replicated. So in the case of the equijoin, the tuple from relation *S* and the tuple from relation *T* are concatenated, where as for the natural join the tuples are concatenated but the attribute on which the relations are joined is only included once. Figure 1c shows an equijoin but in this case we have restricted the resultant relation so that it does not contain any tuples where the *X* attribute is either *X4* or *X7*. This case is slightly more complex than the equijoin described earlier and has been included here to illustrate complex joins.

Above we described a slightly more complex join than the equijoin, the definition of a complex join is contentious. We could define it to be a join where a number of selection criteria are applied or we could define it to be a join between many relations on a number of attributes or even define it to be set of join trees (i.e. a join result further joined to another relation, the result of which is again joined to some other relation etc). For our algorithms we will use equijoin as the normal case, so from now on where ever we mention either join or equijoin we mean the basic equijoin as illustrated in Figure 1b.

Fig a : Join (S[B] = T[B])

Relation S

A6	B8
A4	B4
A3	B3
A2	B2
A5	B5
A1	B1

Relation T

B1	X1
B5	X7
B3	X3
B4	X4
B6	X6
B2	X2

Relation R

A1	B1	X1
A5	B5	X7
A2	B2	X2
A4	B4	X4
A3	B3	X3

Fig a : Join (S[B] = T[B])

Relation S

A6	B8
A4	B4
A3	B3
A2	B2
A5	B5
A1	B1

Relation T

B1	X1
B5	X7
B3	X3
B4	X4
B6	X6
B2	X2

Relation R

A1	B1	B1	X1
A5	B5	B5	X7
A2	B2	B2	X2
A4	B4	B4	X4
A3	B3	B3	X3

Fig b : Equijoin (S[B] = T[B])

Relation S

A6	B8
A4	B4
A3	B3
A2	B2
A5	B5
A1	B1

Relation T

B1	X1
B5	X7
B3	X3
B4	X4
B6	X6
B2	X2

Relation R

A1	B1	B1	X1
A3	B3	B3	X3
A2	B2	B2	X2

Fig c : Equijoin above with SELECTION (R[X] <> {X4, X7})

Figure 1: The EQUIJOIN

2   MAIN FUNCTION

From the performance model we will extract the data rates between the processing elements, these will form part of the requirement for the design of the EDS prototype machine architecture.

The method we propose is :

- Identify the number of messages and their sizes to completion of the equijoin.

- Estimate the processing time taken at each stage. Hence the time between receiving the equijoin request and completion of the equijoin.

- We can then work out the amount of data that needs to be transmitted across the processors in the time taken between receiving the equijoin request and completion of the equijoin. Hence we can work out the average data rates required from the machine for the equijoins.

- We also work out the peak data rates and the intervals for which they need to be sustained.

- The average and peak data rates from above form part of the requirements for the EDS prototype machine network design.

3   OPTIONS CONSIDERED

In general, the execution of a JOIN algorithm by a multiprocessor machine can be decomposed into a number of phases. A typical phase is carried out by one processor and involves the joining (concatenating) of some source and target tuples. We describe in this document, algorithms for the EDS prototype machine, but at the same time avoid making our performance model complex by avoiding some of the optimisations that can be employed in implementing joins (e.g. Join Indices).

First we describe the way in which the data is organised.

We have based this model on the relation structure shown in Figure 2. The Data Manager has a pointer to the relation object. This object points to the top-level of the multi-way tree structure which holds the relation. The top-level consists of pointers to sub-trees, each pointing to a sub-tree in any particular processing element. The top-level of the local processing element consists of pointers to sub-trees, each pointing to a tuple, belonging to this relation. The tuple object also consists of pointers, each pointing to a structure containing an attribute from the tuple.

When a query needs an assurance that some object that it is interested in, typically a database record, will not change in some unpredictable manner while the query is doing some related computation, it acquires a lock on that object. The effect of the lock is to "lock other queries out of" the object, and thus in particular to prevent them from changing it. The first query is thus able to carry out its processing in the certain knowledge that the object in question will remain in a stable state for as long as that query wishes it to.

If a second query wishes to access an object which is locked by the first query and is still in a locked state, the second query will typically have to wait until the lock is released before commencing processing of that object. This is not always the case as objects may be "share locked" in certain cases. We note from the structure of our relation that we could lock the whole relation at the "relation object" level or even lock at the "local object" or "tuple object" level. There will be different locking levels, all depending on a number of factors eg. reading, writing, efficiency etc. We are not interested in the level at which our relation is locked but assume that whenever an object is accessed there is some amount of processing involved in checking and setting status values (i.e. shared lock). For our algorithms we will assume that none of the queries will have to wait until an object is released.

For our algorithms we make some assumptions about the way in which our source and target relations are distributed across the machine. Source relation S has an attribute A, target relation T has an attribute B. During creation/storage of the relations S and T, the Data Manager would run some function F_S, using attribute A for relation S and some function F_T, using attribute B for relation T as parameters, to determine which processing elements to store the particular tuples. The results of running these hash functions are stored in some form on all processors in the machine. We shall call this data Meta-data. The important point here is that each processor has access to the Meta-data for the relations in the machine.

We consider four different algorithms, for each we will keep the structure and size of the relation the same. The main characteristics of each algorithm are itemised below with detailed description in section 4.

- Algorithm A - We assume that we know which attributes the equijoin is to be performed on prior to generating the relations, hence we distribute the relations appropriately, by using the function F_S to distribute both S and T. The equijoin is then formed by collecting the results of all the local equijoins since $F_T = F_S$.

- Algorithm B - We assume that S is distributed using function F_S and T is distributed using function F_T. The equijoin is then formed by first getting all processing elements holding S to send the all the tuples of S, one tuple at a time, to all processing elements holding T. Each processing element holding T will form a local equijoin for each tuple received and sends the result to the parent processing element.

- Algorithm C - We assume that S is distributed using function F_S and T is distributed using function F_T. The equijoin is then formed by first getting all processing elements holding S to send the all the tuples of S to all processing elements holding T. Each processing element holding T will form a local equijoin for each set of tuples received and sends the result to the parent processing element. This option is the same as Algorithm B, but we have increased the granularity of the work done by each processing element by gathering all local tuples before sending out the message.

- Algorithm D - We assume that each processing element can derive the distribution information of our target relation by applying some function on the attribute to be used in the equijoin. We have also assumed that the processing element that initiates the equijoin knows the domain of the source relation. In this case we are using function F_T to redistribute S at run time.

4   ALGORITHMS

We describe the algorithms and the number of messages for each algorithm in this section, the processing times are described in section 5.

The following parameters of the relations are used for the performance estimates:

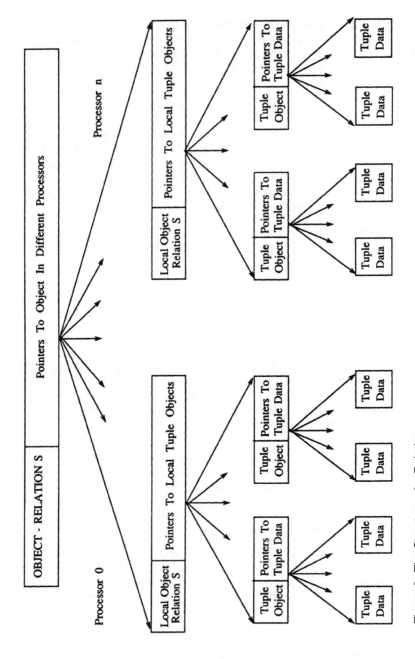

Figure 2: The Structure of a Relation

- Relation *T* is *CardT* records distributed across *ProcsT* processing elements.

- Relation *S* is *CardS* records distributed across *ProcsS* processing elements.

- Attribute *A* of relation *S* and attribute *B* of relation *T* are strings of fixed length 28 characters.

- The result of the join *R* contains *CardR* records.

- We assume that relation *S* and relation *T* are evenly distributed, hence each processing element holding relation *S* will hold *SonProc* records of relation *S* and each processing element holding relation *T* will hold *TonProc* records of relation *T*. ie. $CardT = TonProc \times ProcsT$ and $CardS = SonProc \times ProcsS$ etc.

For our estimate we use the following values :

- *CardS* is 1000.

- *CardT* is 12500.

- *CardR* is 250.

- *ProcsS* is 10.

- *ProcsT* is 50.

- *SonProc* is 100.

- *TonProc* is 250.

We only utilise 50 processing elements of the EDS prototype machine.

4.1 Join algorithm A

For this algorithm we have $F_S = F_T$. Since the same function is run on attribute *A* and attribute *B*, and we are interested in the equijoin ($S[A] = T[B]$) tuples of *S* and *T*, where $A = B$, get allocated the same processing element for storage. The join in this case means, broadcast to all processing elements containing *S* and *T*, to do local equijoins. The equijoin is then formed from the collection of all the local equijoins by the parent processor. We are distributing *T* using function F_S. This means that local equijoins will be formed on *ProcsS* processing elements.

Figure 3 shows the join in diagramatic form. The description of that join follows here.

- A message arrives from the Data Manager asking some query to be performed, which involves an equijoin between relation *S* and *T*. *(1 message)*.

- Processor P_X sends a message to processor P_S, asking it to distribute the equijoin-function to all the processors that hold the relation *S*. *(1 message)*.

- Processor P_S sends a message to each processor, which holds the relation *S*, asking local equijoins to be performed. Processor P_S also sends a *start* message, for each message to processors holding relation *S*, to processor P_X. *(2 times ProcsS messages)*.

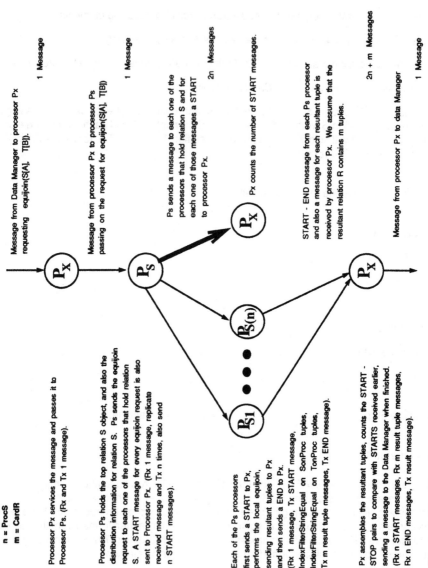

n = ProcS
m = CardR

Message from Data Manager to processor Px requesting equijoin(S[A], T[B]).

1 Message

Processor Px services the message and passes it to Processor Ps. (Rx and Tx 1 message).

Message from processor Px to processor Ps passing on the request for equijoin(S[A], T[B])

1 Message

Processor Ps holds the top relation S object, and also the distribution information for relation S. Ps sends the equijoin request to each one of the processors that hold relation S. A START message for every equijoin request is also sent to Processor Px. (Rx 1 message, replicate received message and Tx n times, also send n START messages).

Ps sends a message to each one of the processors that hold relation S and for each one of those messages a START to processor Px.

2n Messages

Px counts the number of START messages.

Each of the Ps processors first sends a START to Px, performs the local equijoin, sending resultant tuples to Px and then sends a END to Px. (Rx 1 message, Tx START message, IndexFilterStringEqual on SonProc tuples, IndexFilterStringEqual on TonProc tuples, Tx m result tuple messages, Tx END message).

START - END message from each Ps processor and also a message for each resultant tuple is received by processor Px. We assume that the resultant relation R contains m tuples.

Px assembles the resultant tuples, counts the START - STOP pairs to compare with STARTS received earlier, sending a message to the Data Manager when finished. (Rx n START messages, Rx m result tuple messages, Rx n END messages, Tx result message).

2n + m Messages

Message from processor Px to data Manager

1 Message

Figure 3: Algorithm A

- Each of the processors holding relation S sends a *start* message to P_X. *(ProcsS messages)*.

- Each of the processors holding relation S, performs local equijoins sending the resulting tuples to P_X. When there are no more resulting tuples remaining an *end* message is sent to P_X. *(ProcsS messages)*.

- Processor P_X, on receiving tuple data messages, collects and forms a new resultant relation R. *(CardR messages)*.

- Processor P_X, on receiving a *start - end*, messages from processors containing relation S, decrements the count (the summation of earlier *starts*). When the count is zero, the join is completed and the result is another relation R, a pointer to R is passed to the Data Manager. *(1 message)*.

4.2   Join algorithm B

For this algorithm we have S distributed using function F_S and T is distributed using function F_T. The equijoin is then formed by first getting all processing elements holding S to send the all the tuples of S, one tuple at a time, to all processing elements holding T. Each processing element holding T will form a local equijoin for each tuple received and sends the result to the parent processing element.

Figure 4 shows the join in diagramatic form . The description of that join follows here.

- A message arrives from the Data Manager onto processor P_X. *(1 message)*.

- Processor P_X sends a message to each processor, which holds the relation S, asking it to send all local tuples from relation S to each of the processors that holds tuples of relation T. *(ProcsS messages)*.

- Each one of the processors that hold relation S sends a *start* message to each of the processors that hold the relation T. *ProcsS* messages to each of *ProcsT* processors. *(ProcsS times ProcsT messages)*.

- Each one of the processors that hold relation S sends a message for each tuple with attribute A to each of the processors that hold the relation T. Let us assume that relation S has *MatchS* tuples that have attribute A, in most cases this will be all the tuples in relation S so *MatchS* will be equal to *CardS*, then *MatchS* times *ProcsT* messages are sent.   *(MatchS times ProcsT messages)*.

- Each one of the processors that hold relation S sends a *end* message to each of the processors that hold the relation T. *(ProcsS times ProcsT messages)*.

- Each one of the processors that hold relation S also sends a *start* to processor P_X for each of the *ProcsT* messages. *(ProcsS times ProcsT messages)*.

- Each one of the *ProcsT* processors receives *ProcsS start* messages, *ProcsS end* messages and *MatchS* tuple messages.

- Each one of the *ProcsT* processors sends a *start* message to processor P_X, then a message for each tuple which forms the result of the equijoin followed by a *end* message. *(2 times ProcsT + CardR messages)*.

n = ProcS

Message form Data Manager to processor Px requesting equijoin(S[A], T[B]). 1 Message.

Processor Px services the message and passes it to each Processor which holds relation S. (Rx 1 message, Tx n messages).

Px sends a message to each one of the processors that hold relation S, requesting the equijoin. n Messages.

Each of the processor which hold relation S, receives the request, sends a START, all local tuples of S and then a END to each one of the processors which holds relation T. (Rx 1 message, Tx ProcsT STARTs, IndexFilterStringEqual on local S, Tx SonProcs times ProcsT tuple messages, Tx ProcsT ENDs, Tx ProcsT STARTs).

Each of the Ps processors sends a START message, a message for each local tuple of relation S and a STOP message to each of the processors that hold relation T.

Each of the Ps processors also sends a START message for each START above to Px. 3n times ProcsT + CardS times ProcsT Messages.

Each of the Pt processors (Rx START, Tx START to Px, Rx CardS tuple messges, IndexFilterStringEqual on TonProc, Tx result tuple messages. Tx END to Px).

Each of the Pt processors sends a START message for each START it received to Px, followed by a message for each result tuple and then a END. 2n times ProcsT + CardR Messages.

Px (Rx n times ProcsT STARTs, Rx CardR tuple messages, Rx n times ProcsT ENDs, Tx result message to Data Manager).

Message from processor Px to the Data Manager. 1 Message

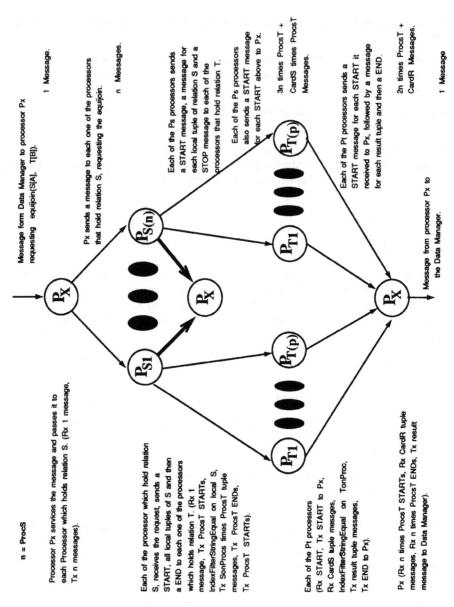

Figure 4: Algorithm B

- Processor P_X, on receiving a *end* decrements the count (the summation of *starts*), on receiving a *Resultant tuples*, adds the tuples received in the message to a new relation *R*. When the join is completed a pointer to *R* is passed to the Data Manager. *(1 message)*.

4.3   Join algorithm C

For this algorithm we have *S* distributed using function F_S and *T* is distributed using function F_T. The equijoin is then formed by first getting all processing elements holding *S* to send the all the tuples of *S* to all processing elements holding *T*. Each processing element holding *T* will form a local equijoin for each set of tuples received and sends the result to the parent processing element.

Figure 5 shows the join in diagramatic form . The description of that join follows here.

- A message arrives from the Data Manager onto processor P_X. *(1 message)*.

- Processor P_X sends a message to each processor, which holds the relation *S*, asking it to send all local tuples from relation *S* to each of the processor that holds tuples of relation *T*. *(ProcsS messages)*.

- Each one of the processors that hold relation *S*, gathers all the tuples of relation *S* and assembles a message.

- Each one of the processors that hold relation *S* sends a message to each of the processors that hold relation *T*. *(ProcsS times ProcsT messages)*.

- Each one of the processors that hold relation *S* also sends a *start* to processor P_X for each of the *ProcsT* messages. *(ProcsS times ProcsT messages)*.

- Each one of the *ProcsT* processors sends a *start* message to processor P_X, then a message for each tuple which forms the result of the equijoin followed by a *end* message. *(2 times ProcsT + CardR messages)*.

- Processor P_X, on receiving a *end* decrements the count (the summation of *starts*), on receiving a *Resultant tuples*, adds the tuples received in the message to a new relation *R*. When the join is completed a pointer to *R* is passed to the Data Manager. *(1 message)*.

4.4   Join algorithm D

For this algorithm we assume that each processor has access to the Meta-data as well as the functions F_S and F_T for the relations in the machine. The target relation is distributed by applying F_T on attribute *B*.

In this case since we are interested in an equijoin on attribute *A* of relation *S* and attribute *B* of relation *T* and all processors have access to the functions that are run to distribute the relations, all we need to do for any given *A* is to run function F_T on *A* to give us the processor on which there may be an attribute *B* of relation *T*, that will match *A*. We have said that there may be an attribute *B* of relation *T*, since we are not sure if that attribute and tuple exists, but if it did then we have determined which processor it will be on.

We have redistributed relation *S* using function F_T. This is similar to Algorithm A but this time the equijoins will be formed on *ProcsT* processing elements.

135

n = ProcS

Message form Data Manager to processor Px
requesting equijoin(S[A], T[B]).   1 Message.

Processor Px services the message and passes it to
each Processor which holds relation S. (Rx 1 message,
Tx n messages).

Px sends a message to each one of the processors
that hold relation S, requesting the equijoin.
                                              n Messages.

Each of the Ps processors sends
a message containing the request
for the equijoin and all local tuples
of relation S to each of the
processors that hold relation T.

Each of the Ps processors
also sends a START message
for each message above to Px.
                              2n times ProcsT
                              Messages.

Each of the processor which hold relation
S, receives the request, gathers all local
tuples and sends them as a message
to each one of the processors
which holds relation T.   Also sends
a START for each message to Px.
(Rx 1 message,
BagToSortedList on SonProc
tuples, Tx large message all
processors holding T,
Tx START for each large
message to Px).

Each of the Pt processors sends a
either a result relation message or an
END message for each tuple message
it received.

Each of the Pt processors
(Rx large message,
BagToSortedList on SonProc tuples,
IndexFilterStringEqual on TonProc,
BagToSortedList on result tuples,
Tx result tuple large message).
                                        n times ProcsT
                                        Messages.

Processor Px (Rx n times ProcsT STARTs messages,
Rx n times ProcsT tuple messages, Tx
message to Data Manager).

Message from processor Px to
the Data Manager.   1 Message

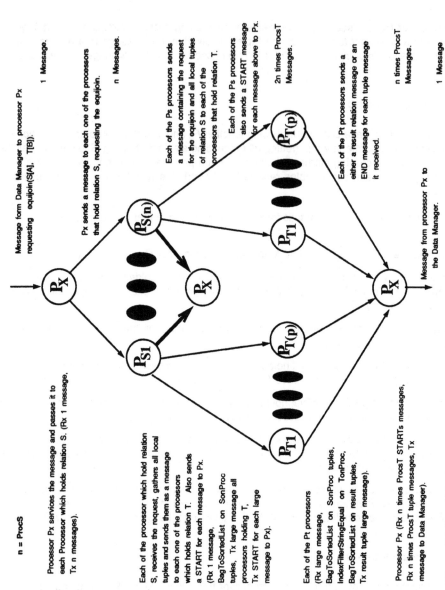

Figure 5: Algorithm C

Figure 6 shows the join in diagramatic form . The description of that join follows here.

- A message arrives from the Data Manager onto processor P_X, asking some query to be performed, which involves a join between relation S and T. *(1 message)*.

- Processor P_X sends a message to each processor, which holds the relation S, asking it to send all local tuples from relation S to the processor that holds the coresponding tuples of relation T. *(ProcsS messages)*.

- Each one of the processors that hold relation S, runs function F_T on attribute A for each tuple, sending that tuple to the processor yielded by the result of the function application. *(CardS messages)*.

- Each one of the processors that hold relation S also sends a *start* to processor P_X for each of the tuple messages. *(CardS messages)*.

- Each one of the *ProcsT* processors which receives tuple messages, will for each message it receives either send *Resultant tuples* or *end* message to processor P_X. The *Resultant tuple* is made up of the concatenation of the tuple received in the incoming message and the local relation T tuple, providing $t[A]$ exists. *(CardS messages)*.

- Processor P_X, on receiving a *end* decrements the count (the summation of *starts*), on receiving a *Resultant tuple*, adds the tuple received in the message to a new relation R and then decrements the count. When completed a pointer to R is passed to the Data Manager. *(1 message)*.

5   PERFORMANCE

5.1   Algorithm A performance

Number of messages for Algorithm A

We can now determine the number of messages for our join under our system. From above we have $1 + 1 + 2$ times $ProcsS + ProcsS + ProcsS + CardR + 1$ messages. *293 messages* for our join.

Processor Time for Algorithm A

The estimation of each bit of work is itemised below.

- Processor P_X.
  - Receive a message of size 128 bytes from the Data Manager. This message contains the packet/cell which is a function call to equijoin with pointers to the two relations and the attribute names with some pre and post amble.
  - Transmits a message of size 128 bytes to processor P_S.

- Processor P_S.
  - Receives a 128 byte message from processor P_X.

137

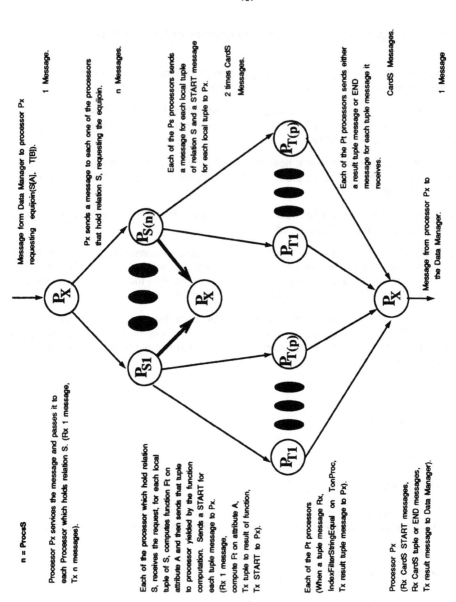

n = ProcsS

Processor Px services the message and passes it to each Processor which holds relation S. (Rx 1 message, Tx n messages).

Each of the processor which hold relation S, receives the request, for each local tuple of S, computes function Ft on attribute A and then sends that tuple to processor yielded by the function computation. Sends a START for each tuple message to Px.
(Rx 1 message,
compute Ft on attribute A,
Tx tuple to result of function,
Tx START to Px).

Each of the Pt processors
(When a tuple message Rx,
IndexFilterStringEqual on TonProc,
Tx result tuple message to Px).

Processor Px
(Rx CardS START messages,
Rx CardS tuple or END messages,
Tx result message to Data Manager).

Figure 6: Algorithm D

Message form Data Manager to processor Px requesting equijoin(S[A], T[B]).
1 Message.

Px sends a message to each one of the processors that hold relation S, requesting the equijoin.
n Messages.

Each of the Ps processors sends a message for each local tuple of relation S and a START message for each local tuple to Px.
2 times CardS Messages.

Each of the Pt processors sends either a result tuple message or END message for each tuple message it receives.
CardS Messages.

Message from processor Px to the Data Manager.
1 Message

- Transmits the received message to all 10 processors containing relation S.
- Transmits 10 *start* messages of size 64 bytes to processor P_X.

- Processor $P_S(n)$.

    - Receives a 128 byte message from processor P_S.
    - Transmits *start* message of size 64 bytes to processor P_X.
    - Performs a local equijoin, which we approximate to the function call *IndexFilterStringEqual* over an average of 100 tuples per processor plus the 100 function calls to *IndexFilterStringEqual* over an average of 250 tuples.
    - We assume that each processor which holds S will on average formulate *CardR divided by ProcsS* resultant tuples, and hence send *CardR divided by ProcsS* tuple messages. The size of the tuple message is important, we take a "intelligent" guess at the size, 8 attributes at 30 bytes each giving 240 bytes per tuple plus some pre and post amble giving us < 300 bytes but > 256 bytes. Thus sending 250 divided by 10 messages, each approximately 300 bytes to processor P_X.
    - Transmits *end* message of size 64 bytes to processor P_X.

- Processor P_X.

    - Receives 10 *start* messages.
    - Receives 250 tuple messages each of size 300 bytes.
    - Receives 10 *end* messages.
    - Transmits message of size 64 bytes as result of equijoin to Data Manager. We are only sending the pointer to the result object to the Data Manager. We ignore the cost of assembling the resultant relation.

Data rates for Algorithm A

MESSAGES	DM to P_X	P_X to P_S	P_S to P_X	P_S to $P_S()$	$P_S()$ to P_X	P_X to DM
No. Messages @ Size in Bytes	1 @ 128	1 @ 128	10 @ 64	10 @ 128	20 @ 64 250 @ 300	1 @ 64
Total Bytes	128	128	640	1280	76280	64

Total number of bytes transmitted is 78 kbytes.

Processor	Function Executed	Time
P_X	R_X 1 message (128 bytes)	1.5 μs
P_X	T_X 1 message (128 bytes)	3.6 μs
P_S	R_X 1 message (128 bytes)	1.5 μs
P_S	T_X 10 messages (128 bytes)	36.0 μs
P_S	T_X 10 messages (64 bytes)	36.0 μs
$P_S(n)$	R_X 1 message (128 bytes)	1.5 μs
$P_S(n)$	T_X 1 message (64 bytes)	3.6 μs
$P_S(n)$	IndexFilterStringEqual 100 Tuples	72.0 μs
$P_S(n)$	100 * IndexFilterStringEqual 250 Tuples	17900.0 μs
$P_S(n)$	T_X 25 messages (300 bytes)	90.0 μs
$P_S(n)$	T_X 1 message (64 bytes)	3.6 μs
P_X	R_X 10 messages (64 bytes)	15.0 μs
P_X	R_X 250 messages (300 bytes)	375.0 μs
P_X	R_X 10 messages (64 bytes)	15.0 μs
P_X	T_X 1 message (64 bytes)	3.6 μs
	TOTAL TIME FOR EQUIJOIN	18571.4 μs

During *18500 μs* we send *78 kbytes* of data, so this gives us a data rate of *4 Mbytes/sec.*

5.2   Algorithm B performance

Number of messages for Algorithm B

We can now determine the number of messages for our join under our system. From above we have *1 + ProcsS + (ProcsS times ProcsT) + (CardS times ProcsT) + (ProcsS times ProcsT) + (ProcsS times ProcsT) + (2 times ProcsT) + CardR + 1* messages.   *51862 messages* for our join.

Processor Time for Algorithm B

The estimation of each bit of work is itemised below.

- Processor P_X.

    - Receives a message of size 128 bytes from the Data Manager. This message contains the packet/cell which is a function call to equijoin with pointers to the two relations and the attribute names with some pre and post amble.

    - Transmits the received message to all 10 processors containing relation *S*.

- Processor $P_S(n)$.

    - Receives a 128 byte message from processor P_X.

    - Transmits 50 *start* message of size 64 bytes, one to each of the processors containing relation *T*.

    - Selects each tuple of relation *S* with attribute *A*, which we approximate to the function call *IndexFilterStringEqual* over an average of 100 tuples.

    - Transmits each one of those 100 tuples as a separate message to each one of the 50 processors that holds relation *T*, each message is 180 bytes.

- Transmits 50 *end* message of size 64 bytes, one to each of the processors containing relation *T*.
- Transmits 50 *start* messages of size 64 bytes to processor P_X.

- Processor $P_T(n)$.

  - Receives a *start* from each one of the 10 processors holding relation *S*.
  - Transmits 10 *start* messages of size 64 bytes to processor P_X, one for each *start* it received.
  - Receives 1000 tuples messages, 100 from each one of the 10 processors holding relation *S*.
  - Performs a equijoin for each tuple received, which we approximate to 1000 function calls to *IndexFilterStringEqual* over an average of 250 tuples.
  - Each processor holding relation *T* generates 5 resultant tuples, hence 5 result tuple messages of 300 bytes each are sent to P_X.
  - Transmits 10 *end* messages of size 64 bytes to processor P_X.

- Processor P_X.

  - Receives 500 *start* messages.
  - Receives 250 tuple messages each of size 300 bytes.
  - Receives 500 *end* messages.
  - Transmits message of size 64 bytes as result of equijoin to Data Manager. We are only sending the pointer to the result object to the Data Manager. We ignore the cost of assembling the resultant relation.

Data Rates for Algorithm B

MESSAGES	D M to P_X	P_X to $P_S()$	$P_S()$ to P_X	$P_S()$ to $P_T()$	$P_T()$ to P_X	P_X to D M
No. Messages @ Size in Bytes	1 @ 128	10 @ 128	500 @ 64	500 @ 64 50000 @ 180 500 @ 64	500 @ 64 250 @ 300 500 @ 64	1 @ 64
Total Bytes	128	1280	32000	9064000	139000	64

Total number of bytes transmitted is 9236 kbytes.

Processor	Function Executed	Time
P_X	R_X 1 message (128 bytes)	1.5 μs
P_X	T_X 10 messages (128 bytes)	36.0 μs
$P_S(n)$	R_X 1 message (128 bytes)	1.5 μs
$P_S(n)$	T_X 50 messages (64 bytes)	180.0 μs
$P_S(n)$	100 * IndexFilterStringEqual 100 Tuples	7200.0 μs
$P_S(n)$	T_X 5000 messages (180 bytes)	18000.0 μs
$P_S(n)$	T_X 50 messages (64 bytes)	180.0 μs
$P_S(n)$	T_X 50 messages (64 bytes)	180.0 μs
$P_T(n)$	R_X 10 messages (64 bytes)	15.0 μs
$P_T(n)$	T_X 10 messages (64 bytes)	36.0 μs
$P_T(n)$	R_X 1000 messages (180 bytes)	1500.0 μs
$P_T(n)$	1000 * IndexFilterStringEqual 250 Tuples	179000.0 μs
$P_T(n)$	T_X 5 messages (300 bytes)	18.0 μs
$P_T(n)$	T_X 10 messages (64 bytes)	36.0 μs
P_X	R_X 500 messages (64 bytes)	750.0 μs
P_X	R_X 250 messages (300 bytes)	375.0 μs
P_X	R_X 500 messages (64 bytes)	750.0 μs
P_X	T_X 1 message (64 bytes)	3.6 μs
	TOTAL TIME FOR EQUIJOIN	208262.6 μs

During *208000 μs* we send *9236 kbytes* of data, so this gives us a data rate of *44 Mbytes/sec*.

5.3   Algorithm C performance

Number of messages for Algorithm C

We can now determine the number of messages for our join under our system. From above we have *1 + ProcsS + (ProcsS times ProcsT) + (ProcsS times ProcsT) + (2 times ProcsT) + CardR + 1* messages. *1362 messages* for our join.

Processor Time for Algorithm C

The estimation of each bit of work is itemised below.

- Processor P_X.

  - Receives a message of size 128 bytes from the Data Manager. This message contains the packet/cell which is a function call to equijoin with pointers to the two relations and the attribute names with some pre and post amble.
  - Transmits the received message to all 10 processors containing relation S.

- Processor $P_S(n)$.

  - Receives a 128 byte message from processor P_X.
  - Gathers each tuple of relation S with attribute A, which we approximate to the function call BagToSortedList over an average of 100 tuples.
  - Transmits those 100 tuples as a message to each one of the 50 processors that holds relation T, each message is 18000 bytes.

- Transmits 50 *start* messages of size 64 bytes to processor P_X.

- Processor $P_T(n)$.

  - Receives 10 messages containing 100 tuples each from each one of the 10 processors holding relation S.
  - Picks each tuple at a time and performs a equijoin , which we approximate to 10 function calls to *BagToSortedList* for separating each tuple and a 1000 function calls to *IndexFilterStringEqual* over an average of 250 tuples for the equijoin.
  - Each processor holding relation T generates 5 resultant tuples, those 5 results are sent as one message hence a messages of 1500 bytes is sent to P_X.
  - Transmits 10-1 *end* messages of size 64 bytes to processor P_X.

- Processor P_X.

  - Receives 450 *end* messages.
  - Receives 50 tuple messages each of size 1500 bytes.
  - Transmits message of size 64 bytes as result of equijoin to Data Manager. We are only sending the pointer to the result object to the Data Manager. We ignore the cost of assembling the resultant relation.

Data Rates for Algorithm C

MESSAGES	D M to P_X	P_X to $P_S()$	$P_S()$ to P_X	$P_S()$ to $P_T()$	$P_T()$ to P_X	P_X to D M
No. Messages @ Size in Bytes	1 @ 128	10 @ 128	500 @ 64	500 @ 18000	450 @ 64 50 @ 1500	1 @ 64
Total Bytes	128	1280	32000	9000000	103800	64

Total number of bytes transmitted is 9137 kbytes.

Processor	Function Executed	Time
P_X	R_X 1 message (128 bytes)	1.5 µs
P_X	T_X 10 messages (128 bytes)	3.6 µs
$P_S(n)$	R_X 1 message (128 bytes)	1.5 µs
$P_S(n)$	BagToSortedList 100 Tuples	20440.0 µs
$P_S(n)$	T_X 50 messages (64 bytes)	180.0 µs
$P_S(n)$	T_X 50 messages (18000 bytes)	180.0 µs
$P_T(n)$	R_X 10 messages (18000 bytes)	15.0 µs
$P_T(n)$	10 * BagToSortedList 100 Tuples	204400.0 µs
$P_T(n)$	1000 * IndexFilterStringEqual 250 Tuples	179000.0 µs
$P_T(n)$	T_X 9 message (64 bytes)	32.4 µs
$P_T(n)$	T_X 1 message (1500 bytes)	3.6 µs
P_X	R_X 450 messages (64 bytes)	675.0 µs
P_X	R_X 50 messages (1500 bytes)	75.0 µs
P_X	T_X 1 message (64 bytes)	3.6 µs
	TOTAL TIME FOR EQUIJOIN	405011.3 µs

During *405000 µs* we send *9137 kbytes* of data, so this gives us a data rate of *23 Mbytes/sec.*

5.4 Algorithm D performance

Number of messages for Algorithm D

We can now determine the number of messages for our join under our system. From above we have *1 + ProcsS + CardR + CardR + CardR + 1* messages. *762 messages* for our join.

Processor Time for Algorithm D

The estimation of each bit of work is itemised below.

- Processor P_X.

  - Receives a message of size 128 bytes from the Data Manager. This message contains the packet/cell which is a function call to equijoin with pointers to the two relations and the attribute names with some pre and post amble.
  - Transmits the received message to all 10 processors containing relation *S*.

- Processor $P_S(n)$.

  - Receives a 128 byte message from processor P_X.
  - Selects each tuple of relation *S* with attribute *A* and computes a function F_T, which we approximate to 100 function calls to *BagToSortedList* over an average of 100 tuples.
  - Transmits those 100 tuples as a seperate messages, each one to a particular processor that holds relation *T*, each message is 180 bytes.
  - Transmits 100 *start* messages of size 64 bytes to processor P_X.

- Processor $P_T(n)$.

  - On average receives 20 messages containing 1 tuple.
  - Performs a equijoin , which we approximate 20 function calls to *IndexFilterStringEqual* over an average of 250 tuples.
  - Each processor holding relation *T* generates 5 resultant tuples, those 5 results are sent as messages hence 5 messages of 300 bytes are sent to P_X.
  - Transmits 20-5 *end* messages of size 64 bytes to processor P_X.

- Processor P_X.

  - Receives 750 *end* messages.
  - Receives 250 tuple messages each of size 300 bytes.
  - Transmits message of size 64 bytes as result of equijoin to Data Manager. We are only sending the pointer to the result object to the Data Manager. We ignore the cost of assembling the resultant relation.

Data Rates for Algorithm D

MESSAGES	D M to P_X	P_X to $P_S()$	$P_S()$ to P_X	$P_S()$ to $P_T()$	$P_T()$ to P_X	P_X to D M
No. Messages @ Size in Bytes	1 @ 128	10 @ 128	1000 @ 64	1000 @ 180	750 @ 64 250 @ 300	1 @ 64
Total Bytes	128	1280	64000	180000	123000	64

Total number of bytes transmitted is 368 kbytes

Processor	Function Executed	Time
P_X	R_X 1 message (128 bytes)	1.5 μs
P_X	T_X 10 messages (128 bytes)	3.6 μs
$P_S(n)$	R_X 1 message (128 bytes)	1.5 μs
$P_S(n)$	100 * IndexFilterStringEqual 100 Tuples	7200.0 μs
$P_S(n)$	T_X 100 messages (180 bytes)	360.0 μs
$P_S(n)$	T_X 100 messages (64 bytes)	360.0 μs
$P_T(n)$	R_X 20 messages (180 bytes)	30.0 μs
$P_T(n)$	20 * IndexFilterStringEqual 250 Tuples	3580.0 μs
$P_T(n)$	T_X 5 messages (300 bytes)	18.0 μs
$P_T(n)$	T_X 15 messages (64 bytes)	54.0 μs
P_X	R_X 250 messages (300 bytes)	375.0 μs
P_X	R_X 750 messages (64 bytes)	1125.0 μs
P_X	T_X 1 message (64 bytes)	3.6 μs
	TIME FOR EQUIJOIN	13112.2 μs

During *13000 μs* we send *368 kbytes* of data, so this gives us a data rate of *28 Mbytes/sec*

6   CONCLUSIONS

We have taken four different algorithms for analysis for the equijoin. Algorithm B and Algorithm C, which we would term worst cases and Algorithm A and Algorithm D which are the typical cases expected on our EDS prototype machine. The average and peak data rates across processing elements are tabulated below.

Algorithm	Total Data Transferred kbytes	Total Time for Equijoin secs	Total Data Rate Mbytes/sec
Algorithm A	78	0.019	4.2
Algorithm B	9236	0.210	44
Algorithm C	9137	0.400	23
Algorithm D	368	0.013	28

Peak Data Rate in Mbytes/s	Out of P_x	%	Out of $P_s()$	%	Out of $P_t()$	%
AlgorithmA	25 for 5μs	0.03	2.6 for 70 μs	0.4	0.5 for 18ms	97.3
AlgorithmB	34 for 38 μs	0.02	35 for 26 ms	12.5	0.015 for 0.2s	96.2
AlgorithmC	34 for 38 μs	0.01	44 for 20 ms	4.9	0.005 for 0.4s	98.8
AlgorithmD	34 for 38 μs	0.30	3 for 8 ms	61.5	0.7 for 3.7ms	28.5

The % figures give the % of the time for which this peak data rate needs to be sustained

Algorithm B and Algorithm C are very similar, but the data rates are different with Algorithm C showing a smaller data rate. The messages generated for Algorithm C range from 64 bytes to 18000 bytes. Our analysis uses the estimates for message passing of messages in the range 1 to 1K bytes. Since the long 18000 bytes messages make up approximately 30% of the messages, if the overheads for transmitting and receiving these messages is vastly different from the figures in Appendix A1, then our data rate would be wrong.

We also expect the performance to vary with the complexity of the equijoins.

We have estimated a number of data rates, from 4 Mbytes to 44 Mbytes which will be required to be supported by an EDS prototype network which connects 50 processing elements.

We have shown that

- Algorithm D is the fastest equijoin timing.

- Algorithm A is just slightly slower than Algorithm D but the data rates that need to be supported is substantially lower than Algorithm D's. We must remember that only 10 processing elements are involved for Algorithm A.

- The performance varies vastly depending on the characteristics of the data participating in the join operation.

7   ACKNOWLEDGEMENTS

The work presented in this paper has been carried out by a team based at ICL in Manchester.

8   REFERENCES

[Watson 90]   Paul Watson and Paul Townsend
                     The EDS Parallel Relational Database System
                     In this Volume (1990).

[Townsend 87]   Paul Townsend
                     Flagship Hardware and Implementation
                     ICL Technical Journal (May 1987).

[Ward 89]   Mike Ward
                     Processing Element Functional Specification
                     EDS project Internal Paper (1989)

A1   MESSAGE PASSING TIMINGS

The Processing Element Functional Specification *[Ward 89]* gives an estimate of the main processor's firmware overheads for transmitting and receiving messages. The Message Passing overheads are the same for both short 128-byte messages and long 1 kbyte messages.

The time given for transmitting a message is 3.6 μs and for receiving a message 1.5 μs.

A2   FLAGSHIP TIMINGS

The Flagship parallel processing machine has been built by ICL in conjunction with UK universities under an ALVEY contract and has been used extensively to obtain performance information. The Flagship machine is a 15 processing element machine similar in design to the EDS prototype machine. The Flagship machine uses 68020 processors while it is proposed to use SPARC processors for the EDS prototype machine. The paper [Townsend 87] describes the Flagship Hardware and Implementation.

The requirement here is that we need to time some experiments on the FLAGSHIP machine and use those results to project/extrapolate to the amount of processing time on the EDS prototype machine for the join algorithms.

We estimate the performance for each bit of work in units of average *SPARC* instructions, from which we can approximate to time as indicated below. The estimates are all based on the Flagship machine performance executing similar functions.

On average two *SPARC* instructions are equivalent to one Flagship machine instruction. The EDS prototype *SPARC* processor executes instructions at 20 times the rate of the FLAGSHIP machine, so if a particular function takes $t\ \mu\ seconds$ on the Flagship machine it will take $\frac{t}{10}\ \mu$ *seconds* on the *SPARC* processor.

Figure 7 shows the Structure of a Relation on Flagship that we have used to in our experiments. The functions we run on the Flagship machine are:

- BagToSortedList - This operator takes an existing relation and converts it to a list. The list will be formed from a left-to-right traversal of the relation tree, thus the list will be sorted in ascending order on the key used for ordering the bag. This is required for transmitting a local relation to another processor.

- IndexFilterStringEquals - This operator is used where we wish to return elements of an input relation which satisfy some test on an attribute of the input relation. In this case the text is the string equality of the given index and the attributes.

A2.1   Bag_To_Sorted_List

Our requirement is to estimate *BagToSortedList* for 100 tuples. For *BagToSortedList* on 100 tuples, timed on the Flagship machine, it takes 230K μs with 512 rewrites. Each rewrite has an overhead of 50 μs. This gives us 204.4K μs on the Flagship machine. This is converted to 20440 μs for *BagToSortedList* on 100 tuples for the EDS prototype machine, using the method described above.

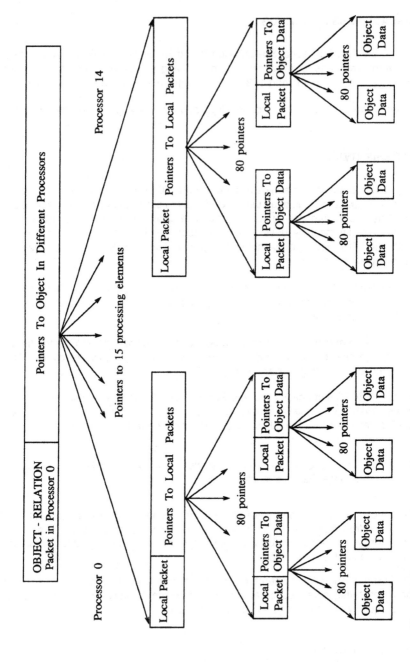

Figure 7: Structure of Relation on FLAGSHIP

A2.2   Index_Filter_String_Equals

Our requirement is to estimate *IndexFilterStringEquals* for 100 tuples and also for 250 tuples. We have assumed that each tuple has 4 attributes, this gives us for 100 tuples and 250 tuples, 400 and 1000 attributes respectively. We ran *IndexFilterStringEquals* to index 6000 elements on the Flagship machine. The execution time was 11.7K μs which included 4 rewrite overheads at 50 μs each, 2 copy request overhead at 250 μs each and 1 export request overhead at 250 μs.

This gives us 10.75K μs for 6000 elements, 1.79 μs for each element and hence 716 μs for 100 tuples, 1790 μs for 250 tuples for the Flagship machine. Converting for the EDS prototype machine gives us *IndexFilterStringEquals* on 100 tuples takes 72 μs and *IndexFilterStringEquals* on 250 tuples takes 179 μs.

The EDS Parallel Relational Database System

Paul Watson and Paul Townsend

ICL,
Wenlock Way, West Gorton,
MANCHESTER, M12 5DR.

Abstract.

This paper describes the parallel Relational Database Management System (RDBMS) currently being designed and built by the ESPRIT II EDS project. The system components include a high performance distributed store parallel machine consisting of up to 256 processing elements connected by a delta network, an operating system designed for the parallel system, and a RDBMS which exploits both inter and intra query parallelism. The paper examines a vertical slice through the system, showing how the RDBMS, operating system and hardware contribute to the efficient parallel execution of database queries.

1 INTRODUCTION

The European Declarative System (EDS) project (ESPRIT II EP2025), supported by the Commission of the European Communities (CEC DG XIII/A/4) is developing a system supporting a parallel relational database, along with parallel LISP and PROLOG languages implementations.

The project participants are Bull, ICL, Siemens, ECRC and their associates. They aim to apply the past research and industrial experience of the partners to meet their commercial objectives, emphasising efficiency and cost/performance. Some of the past work of the partners which has made a major contribution to the EDS system design includes the Bull Delta Driven Computer [1], ECRC PROLOG research [2], Siemens Lisp and machine design expertise, and two parallel distributed store machine projects in which ICL has been a partner: ALICE [3] and FLAGSHIP [4] [5].

The EDS project is concerned with developing parallel technology which can provide an evolutionary upgrade to users' IT systems and the application to Relational Database Management Systems (RDBMS) has been chosen by the partners as the prime focus of the project because it is a key component of their business.

Therefore, the main aim of EDS is to develop a prototype parallel RDBMS which can then be quickly further developed by the partners, separately or together. The project will produce a subset of a full parallel RDBMS back-end that will support a number of benchmarks, commercial applications and exemplars which will demonstrate its functionality and performance. Exploitation development activities, carried out by the individual partners to integrate EDS into their product lines, will be overlapped with the project.

A prime objective of the project is the use of parallelism to obtain performance scalable over a range from a few times to a few hundred times the performance of a single state-of-the-art microprocessor system with comparable cost performance ratio.

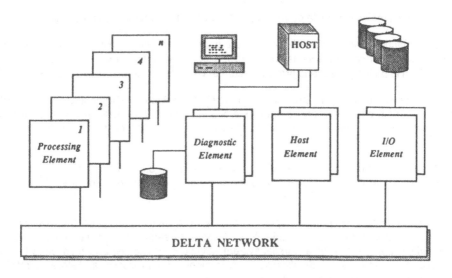

Figure 1: The EDS Machine Architecture

The corner-stone of the exploitation strategy is the conformance to the appropriate database language standards; the system must appear to users as an evolutionary step, and so support existing end-user and application interfaces.

Figure 1 is a diagram of the machine architecture. The system can have up to 256 Processing Elements (PEs) which consist of a large semiconductor store, a high performance processor, and a support unit for network communication. A Distributed Store design was chosen for its extensibility: by adding PEs both the processor power and store bandwidth of the system can be increased. In contrast, the performance of shared store systems is limited by their fixed store bandwidth.

The Distributed Store architecture has also fewer centralized resources than a Shared Store architecture and, as will be described later, this can be used to advantage in building a reliable RDBMS system. By configuring processing elements in and out under software control, the system's storage (both main store and disk), processing and external communications capability can be tested or upgraded while the machine is still running.

The system will provide high performance by efficiently utilizing the power of the parallel machine to exploit both inter and intra query parallelism. Relations will be distributed in an intelligent manner over the main RAM stores of several processing elements so that the relational operations can access and process different relations, and different parts of the same relation, in parallel. The system aims to efficiently support a mix of both data intensive, and concurrency intensive query profiles. The active part of the database will be held in stable semi-conductor storage, providing fast data accessing. Their is capability in the design to support a total database larger than the available stable semi-conductor store, through the use of magnetic discs and other backing storage media.

The network is designed to provide highly efficient message passing between processing elements to support communication between the parallel parts of the computation. For high performance, the system will compile queries into object code for direct execution by the processors.

The EDS machine can be hosted either by the partner's proprietary computer systems or Unix systems. Multiple host connections are supported, so allowing the communications bandwidth to the machine to be increased, and providing alternative paths to the machine to improve resilence.

The Diagnostic Element (DE) provides the hardware interface for diagnostics to the machine. As well as being connected to the network along with the PEs, the DE also has another, low bandwidth, direct connection to every PE. This is used for debugging and initialization of the system.

I/O elements can be added to the system to provide mass storage on disks and tapes. The architecture will also support local I-O connections on the PEs, so giving the PEs local disk storage.

The system has its own operating system, called *EMEX*, which is designed specifically to meet the requirements of the parallel architecture. In order to satisfy the special demands incurred when writing applications for a parallel system advanced debugging and monitoring tools are provided. Their facilities include allowing users to monitor the processor and store utilizations in the machine and to trace the execution of a program.

The aim of this paper is to examine a vertical slice through the EDS parallel system to show how it operates efficiently as a parallel RDBMS. The system's role of efficiently supporting PROLOG and LISP is not covered here. Section 2 presents an overview of the EDS RDBMS, describing its components and their functionality. Section 3 then introduces the computational model used to execute database queries in parallel. Section 4 describes the support provided by the *EMEX* operating system for the RDBMS. Section 5, does the same but for the hardware. In Section 6 we conclude by giving performance targets for the project, and discuss benchmarking and applications.

2   THE EDS RDBMS

A large parallel computer, such as the EDS machine, is not cost effective unless the computation to be performed can be efficiently mapped across its parallel resources. In the EDS RDBMS, the Relations are horizontally fragmented (i.e. by row) over a set of processing elements. This allows different queries, or different parts of the same query to process different fragments of a relation in parallel. The computational model will be described in detail in the next section, but this section will introduce the RDBMS components.

The EDS project is constructing the back-end of a relational database system, taking as input ESQL produced by the partner's strategic front-end tools and application interfaces. The RDBMS is divided into two major components: the Request Manager which compiles the database commands into native machine code, and the Data Manager which provides the run time library for the execution of those commands. These are supported by: the Object Manager which is an EDS system facility providing stable data storage and concurrency control; and a Session Manager which processes requests from application programs for connection to a database session, establishes the initial resources required by the session and reclaims them when the session ends. We now consider the database system components in more detail.

2.1   The Request Manager

The input to the Request Manager (RM) are commands in the database language *ESQL* [6]. This is a superset of SQL, designed to give more expressive power in areas which include: User Defined Abstract Data Types, Objects, Rules, Multi-Statement Queries, Integrity Constraints, Triggers, user Defined Aggregate Functions and the Expression of Parallelism. The RM first checks the syntax and semantics of a query, converting it into an internal language *LERA*, which is then optimized. There are 3 stages of optimization:

1. **Logical Optimization** This stage simplifies the input LERA program to produce a sequence of fewer operations. Syntactic optimization will reduce the input query to canonical form prior to subsequent optimizations. Algebraic transformations are used to optimize the effect of restrictions on the volume of recursion, following which common subexpressions are isolated and, where appropriate, eliminated (the optimizer will use heuristics to make the trade-off between repeated evaluation and increased communication). Integrity constraints are used to identify and eliminate subexpressions which are constrained to produce empty relations or their relative complements (except where this has arisen from the use of query modification in the analyzer to check constraints) and to augment the predicates of search expressions. Search predicates are further augmented by propagating constraints on attributes as far as possible, and simplified by using properties of the comparators involved (eg substitutivity of equality, transitivity of order, inheritance between classes), and a similar process applied to chains of user defined method applications when the properties concerned are known. Loops are replaced by LERA fixed-point operators for subsequent processing by the parallelizer optimization stage.

2. **Physical Optimization** Information concerning the physical schemata and the size and distribution of physical relations is used to decompose the query into operations on physical relations and select an optimal ordering for them. The optimizer will maintain estimates of the size and distribution of intermediate results, while the catalogue (described later) holds statistical information on base relations. Access methods, parallel algorithms for operations, and local algorithms for the local components of operations are selected, and the placement of operations in relation to the location of data is determined (so that the communication overhead of the query is established). Selection of storage methods for intermediate structures is made based on the cost of creation for a particular format. For accesses through indexes, selectivity estimates are made and used in conjunction with clash and deadlock statistics to determine whether a locking grain other than the default is appropriate. The choice between execution strategies and algorithms is based on a cost model which reflects the characteristics of the EDS Data Manager environment. The optimizer will determine cases where optimization choices should be left until run time (eg when there is good probability that some intermediate relation will exist in one processing element only, but this is not completely certain) and generate alternate subprograms together with the run-time tests needed to choose between them.

3. **Parallelization** The parallelizer converts the optimized query into a set of localized (to a PE) operations in which all inter-PE communication is explicit. It chooses the optimal algorithms for controlling the sequencing of operations, in particular for the detection of termination, and selects the mechanisms to be used for parameter passing between components of the query. It splits the (conceptually centralized) operations constructed by the previous optimization stages into localized operations within a control framework, respecting the choice of algorithms made by the physical optimization process. Local communication is recognised and represented as local pipes which may be implemented as procedure or co-routine

calls, and operations which share data are grouped to enable the code generator to identify store sharing requirements.

For precompiled queries, a bound on optimization time may be set (based on session parameters); otherwise an exhaustive search for the least cost form of the query is used. For ad-hoc queries, a more efficient search strategy is required (such as Monte-Carlo methods, simulated annealing, etc) and the optimization process must stop when the gains at execution time are likely to be outweighed by the losses at optimization time.

The output of the last stage of optimization (parallelization) is called LERA-par and is used as the input to the code generator, which in turn outputs executable code in the form of C++.

The *Catalogue* holds data describing the database. It is accessed via the Catalogue Manager which provides a simple procedural interface for use by the various components of the Request Manager. It records the dependencies of compiled code (queries and methods) on other catalogue data, so that modules can be invalidated when the need arises through changes to schemata, types, etc. Modules which are recompiled on next execution are distinguished from those which are to be recompiled as a background activity immediately upon being invalidated.

Data held in the catalogue includes:

- relational schemata.
- type definitions.
- view definitions.
- clustering information (distribution type and constraints, not physical mappings).
- source and object modules.
- dependency information.
- trigger definitions.
- constraint definitions.
- security data (principals[users] and their access capabilities, classification bounds, and trusts; access permissions and classifications for each attribute, view definition, query, type, and method).
- information (approximate) about
    - the size of each relation.
    - frequency distribution of attribute values.
    - clash and back-out rates for each access method.
    - access frequency for each access method.
- cost information for each access method.
- semantic identities for relations and functions on abstract domains.
- user identifier (name) to data manager identifier map for (physical) relations, types, methods, and queries.

- data manager identifiers for the built-in set of queries provided in the data manager.

For the size and frequency information, the catalogue manager will collect updates periodically from the data manager; the system administrator will have facilities to control the frequency.

A change to some catalogue data will trigger data manager functions (or require synchronization with other data manager activity); the catalogue manager will advise the data manager of all such changes at some point during the transaction in which the changes are made. An example of this is that if the method of fragmentation of a relation changes, then all subsequent accesses to that relation will need to use a different function for determining the location of tuples.

2.2   The Data Manager

The Data Manager executes the object programs produced by the Request Manager, and supports the data distribution, access methods and indexing techniques required by the optimizer. An instance of the Data Manager runs on each PE taking part in the execution of a query. The Data Manager has four main sub-components: the Relational Execution Model (REM), the Relation Access Manager (RAM), the Access Methods and the Basic Relational Execution Model (BREM).

The Relational Execution Model (REM)

The REM consists of the LERA-par operators. These are designed for a distributed mainstore database and fall into the following categories:

1. Control operations: to impose the correct ordering on relational operations, and detect termination.

2. Data Definition operations

3. Relational operations

4. The fixed point operator

5. Support for cursors

6. Support for triggers

These operators will be provided as a library of procedures which can be called by the object code.

The Relational Access Manager (RAM)

The REM operations access the tuples of a relation by calling the interface procedures of the Access Methods instances associated with the relation. The functions of the RAM are as follows.

- To provide the interface to the distribution information for the relation

- To provide a uniform interface to the underlying Access Method instances

- To provide an efficient mechanism for obtaining the local (to a PE) instance from the global identifier for an Access Method instance

- To maintain the consistency of the multiple instances of Access Methods for a relation in the presence of updates to the relation

The Access Methods

The Access Methods provide both the mechanisms for storing the tuples of a relation (the storage method) and the mechanisms for fast access to the tuples via a key (i.e. indexes). These mechanisms are Abstract Data Types consisting of the data structures and the interfaces for providing access to the relations. The Access Methods are optimized for working only on relations held in stable semi-conductor storage.

The RAM provides a mechanism whereby new types of access method can be incorporated into the system. This will allow the easy extension of the Database Server to provide access methods tailored to the users applications.

The Basic Relational Execution Model (BREM)

BREM provides an environment for the execution of parallel programs. This environment has been optimized for the execution of LERA-par programs, and the associated REM functions and access method functions. The LERA-par computational model is described in detail in the next chapter.

The Data Manager also provides the following miscellaneous functions: provision of an interface to Request Manager, loading of the code for LERA- par programs, garbage collection of query resources and support for session management.

2.3   The Object Manager

This is a general EDS system resource providing stable data storage and concurrency control. Consequently it removes some of the complexity from the Data Manager which is able to access data objects (which may be structured) through a high level interface.

Stable Object Storage

This component provides the abstraction of an object as a uniquely identifiable entity with an association to persistent data and a protocol for accessing and changing the data. Here persistent is used in the sense of persisting across system breaks. To achieve this persistence of data it must be held in some type of stable store. The Object Manager will support two types of stable store: semi-conductor based (for example RAM with a battery back-up) and discs. All database computations are designed to operate on data held in fast semiconductor storage. The Object Manager therefore not only manages the two forms of stable store, but also the migration of data between them so that the currently "active" part of the database is in semiconductor storage.

The object storage component also supports duplexing of data. There can be three different types of data duplexing in the EDS Database Server: duplexing in a different processing element on the same machine, duplexing in a stand-by machine, and duplexing on discs.

Concurrency Control and Resilience

This component covers concurrency control (including deadlock detection), logging, archiving, recovery and support for inter working. The concurrency control mechanisms supported are two-phase locking and more advanced mechanisms which allow the access methods to provide higher concurrency.

The resilience facilities of the Object Manager are required to be able to recover the database system from the following types of failure.

- Transient system breaks - no stable store data can be lost

- Hard system faults where a processing element is lost but the stable semi-conductor store is still accessible

- Semi-conductor stable store failure

- Disc media failure

The recovery mechanisms will be designed to exploit the semi-conductor stable store to minimize recovery time after a system break.

3   THE COMPUTATIONAL MODEL

In this section we describe how the Relational Execution Model performs the parallel evaluation of database queries. One of the main influences on its design was the Bubba project [7]. As was stated in the last section, the relations are horizontally fragmented over a set of processing elements. This set is called the *Home* of the relation. The size of the Home, and the algorithm by which the relation is fragmented can be defined by the user when the relation is created, otherwise they will be chosen by the Request Manager using statistical information from the catalogue: for example the range of attribute values and the relation size. Once the computational model has been described it will become clear why the choice of Home size and fragmentation algorithm are important for the efficient exploitation of parallelism.

Consider the SQL schema for a relation *scost*:

```
CREATE TABLE scost (
  share_id c4,
  cost integer2,
  currency c2);
```

(the ESQL CREATE TABLE command is extended to give the user the option of specifying a Home Size and fragmentation algorithm). The mapping of the Home of a relation onto a set of PEs is decided at execution time by the Data Manager utilizing information provided by the *EMEX* operating system on the loading (both store and processor) of all the PEs in the machine. As will be seen, the relational operations are performed on the fragmented tables in situ, and so the process of selecting the Home of a relation is an important part of the task of spreading processing evenly over the whole machine. As an example, the Request Manager, or user, may specify that *scost* is fragmented over 4 PEs by hashing on the *share_id* attribute. The Data Manager may then decide to map the Home of *scost* onto PEs 1,3,8 and 9.

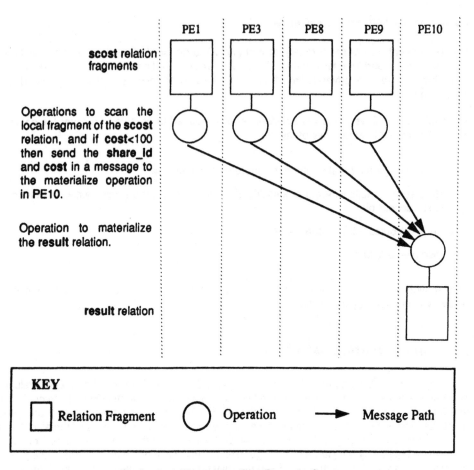

PE1   PE3   PE8   PE9   PE10

scost relation
fragments

Operations to scan the
local fragment of the **scost**
relation, and if **cost**<100
then send the **share_id**
and **cost** in a message to
the materialize operation
in PE10.

Operation to materialize
the **result** relation.

result relation

KEY

☐ Relation Fragment   ◯ Operation   ➤ Message Path

Figure 2: A Plan of the First Example Query

For queries which perform simple operations on relations (ex. Debit-Credit [12]) inter-query parallelism is exploited because different queries operating on fragments of a relation can be executed
on different PEs in parallel. For more complex queries, intra-query parallelism can be achieved
by decomposing the query into separate operations which are executed on different PEs. For
example, if the user submits the query:

```
SELECT share_id, cost
FROM scost
WHERE cost < 100
```

the Request Manager will use information in the catalogue on the fragmentation of *scost* to decide
how to compute the result. An operation will be created on each PE in the Home of *scost* to
perform the selection and projection on the fragment of *scost* stored in that PE.

Each operation can operate on the local fragment of *scost* at the same time. If *scost* is fragmented
evenly over the 4 PEs of its Home we would hope to achieve a speed-up close to 4 over a

single processor implementation of the selection and projection, assuming that each operation has roughly the same amount of processing to do.

Figure 2 shows a plan of this query execution. When each operation has completed, the result will itself be fragmented across the Home of *scost*. If may be desirable to collect the result in a single PE, perhaps so that it can be printed on the user's terminal. To achieve this, each local select operation sends the result of the selection and projection operations in messages to a *materialize* operation which simply stores them. If these result tuples are sent as soon as they are produced, rather than when the selection and projection operation has completed its work on the whole local fragment of *scost*, then the materialize operation can work in parallel with the local selection and projection operations.

This simple example illustrates the main principles of the computational model: operations execute at the Home of the data on which they operate; their inputs and outputs are either a stream of messages or a (fragment of a) stored relation. Two forms of intra-query parallelism are exploited:

- **Data Parallelism** Where an operation is performed on a relation, the relation is fragmented over a set of PEs and the operation is performed in parallel on each fragment.

- **Pipeline Parallelism** Where an operation produces a (fragment of a relation) which is consumed by another operation, if possible each tuple is forwarded as it is produced so that the consumer can compute in parallel with the producer.

In order to determine when the execution of a query has ended, control signals are added to the computation. Each operation produces a control output when it has completed its task. For an operation whose output is a stored relation, a special *END* signal is sent to any operation waiting for it to complete. In the above example, the operation which stores the result relation would send an *END* message (in this case to a special operation which notifies the Session Manager that the current query execution is completed). When an operation which produces a stream of messages has completed its task it sends an End Of Stream (*EOS*) message to any operation(s) consuming its output. The EOS sending mechanism ensures that all messages sent to the consumer have arrived and are queued before the EOS is received by it. The consumer will process all queued incoming messages before acting on the EOS, by itself sending an *END* or *EOS* to any waiting operations.

Some operations consume streams of messages from several producers. They therefore wait until an EOS has arrived from each stream, rather than act on just the first. The operation which stores the *result* relation falls into this category; it waits for 4 EOS's.

A more complex query is:

```
CREATE TABLE scost (
   share_id c4,
   cost integer2,
   currency c2);

CREATE TABLE exchange (
   currency c2,
   rate integer2);

SELECT share_id, cost, rate
FROM scost, exchange
```

```
WHERE cost < 100 AND scost.currency=exchange.currency
```

If the *exchange* relation is hashed on its currency attribute over PEs 4 and 5 then a plan of the computation is given in Figure 3.

The first layer of operations (labelled SEL) in the computational plan scan the local fragments of the *scost* relation and select any entries meeting the criteria *cost < 100*. These are sent, as they are discovered, in a message to the next layer of operations (labelled JOIN) which join them with the exchange relation on the currency attributes. Rather than send each entry to all PEs in the Home of *exchange*, if the hash function used to fragment the exchange relation is applied to the currency attribute of those entries, they can be sent just to the local operation which will be able to perform a successful join. This reduces processing and message passing. The successful tuples from the join operations are then sent to the *Materialize* operation which stores them in the *result* relation. As in the previous example, control operations are added to the computational plan to provide a termination indication.

The above examples illustrate the importance of selecting a sensible home size and fragmentation algorithm for a relation. Because computation is performed on relations in situ, these two parameters determine the parallelism achieved by operations performed on a relation. The home sizes in the examples have been kept artificially small and it may seem advantageous to always spread relations across all the processors in the machine, so allowing the maximum parallelism for operations on that relation. However, if a relation does not have many entries, or the operations on it are not very compute intensive, then the extra communication and control costs incurred by a large home size could reduce the performance over that which could be achieved by the selection of a smaller home.

It is inevitable that sometimes a relation will be badly distributed for the queries which access it. When this occurs, the system or user may choose to redistribute it. The choice of a new fragmentation algorithm may be influenced by statistical information gathered in the catalogue on patterns of access to the relation.

4   OPERATING SYSTEM SUPPORT FOR PARALLEL COMPUTATION

The parallel database computational model requires operating system support if it is to be efficiently implemented. Because no available operating system addressed all issues which are important for the performance of that model, one ('*EMEX*') was designed for the EDS machine. The Chorus Operating System [8] was used as a basis for the *EMEX* implementation. While many modules were replaced or modified, the project can still benefit from many Chorus Systemes developments, including their Unix subsystem.

In this section we examine those features of *EMEX* which are important to the performance of the computational model described in the last section.

4.1   Light Weight Threads

There are two sources of processable work during the execution of a query: that generated by the arrival of a message at an operation which consumes a stream of messages, and the execution of those operations which do not consume a stream of messages (for example those which operate on stored relations). The execution of an operation on a relation or message may have to wait for a lock to be released, or for data to be fetched from disk; to prevent this from introducing

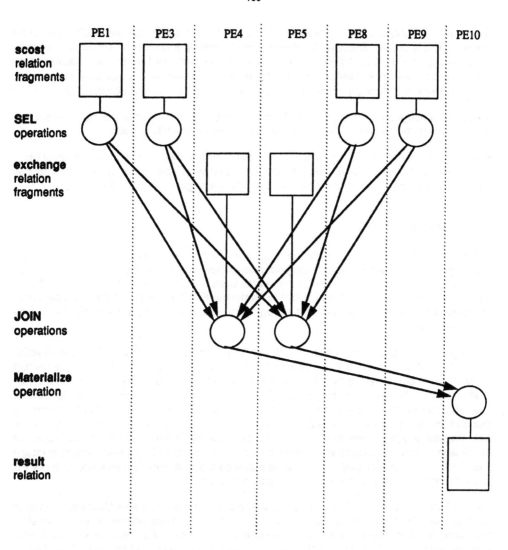

Figure 3: A Plan of the Second Example Query

latency into query execution it is necessary to be able to switch to processing another part of the query when this occurs. Because this may happen frequently, and process switching is relatively expensive, *EMEX* provides light weight threads of computation which share their address space and have low creation and switching cost. It is therefore a thread which executes an operation. If one is suspended during a computation then the processor can switch cheaply to another.

Threads are assigned a scheduling priority, and are pre-emptable by others of higher priority but not by those of the same priority: this prevents unnecessary switching costs.

Each process (named a '*Task*' in *EMEX*) therefore consists of one or more threads each of which can run in a single PE. However, the threads of a Task may be spread over a set of PEs, as may their address space. The set of a process's threads in a single PE is named a *Team*.

4.2   Message Passing

The computational model is relatively communications intensive due to data being streamed between operations. The provision of high performance (low latency and high bandwidth) message passing is therefore a critical factor in the overall system performance. Whilst much of the responsibility for achieving this is borne by the hardware, *EMEX* provides a high level abstraction of message passing which simplifies the programmer's task and assists the hardware in giving high performance.

Messages are sent to ports. Once a port has been created, any thread in the system which knows its identifier may send a message to it; the sender does not need to know where the port is physically. A port is owned by a Team, and any Thread in that team may read a message from it. Message sending/ receiving may be synchronous or asynchronous, and the user has facilities to specify flow control, and whether or not message transmission is ordered (this is required so that sorted data can be sent between operations). To send a message, which can be of any size, the user program gives its address and size to the *EMEX* which sends it to its destination and wakes up any thread suspended waiting for it. As will be seen in the next section, message passing is done in a very efficient manner; a message is transferred from user space in one PE to user space in another without any intermediate copying.

For the integrity of the database computational mode it is important that Message Passing is reliable. The *EMEX* guarantees that: no message is delivered twice, no message is delivered to the wrong place, no message is delivered with incorrect content, if a message is not delivered then the sender is notified, a sender is never told that a message has not been delivered if it has.

An obvious mapping of the database computational model onto the *EMEX* message passing model would be to allocate a port for each operation which consumes a stream of messages. All messages for that operation would be sent to the port. In fact, a different scheme is used: there is one set of ports for the Data Manager instance in a PE (there is an ordered and an unordered communications port for each thread priority level). Each port has a thread which reads messages from it and processes them (if a thread is blocked then a new thread is scheduled for that port to ensure that all processing does not become halted). This scheme has advantages over the more obvious mapping as there are fewer ports (and so fewer port management costs incurred), fewer threads and so also fewer thread suspensions and thread switches.

4.3   Scheduling Control

It has proved desirable to allow the database system to have some control over scheduling and so *EMEX* provides a low level interface to support this. For example, if a high priority thread is suspended on a lock which is held by a lower priority thread, then the database system can increase the priority of the lock holding thread to that of the higher priority thread. This reduces the suspension time for the high priority thread.

4.4   Virtual Store

EMEX has a very flexible virtual store system. It allows the address space of a Task to extend over several PEs and the user is provided with the means of building a variety of coherence mechanisms. For example, the Data Manager instance on each PE is implemented as a separate Task (so that they can all have the maximum address space of 4G bytes) but they all share a code segment which is copied on demand into the stores of the PEs as the pages in it are accessed. For those segments where the latency required to copy whole pages between PEs is considered too expensive because spatial locality is low, each 4k byte page is split into smaller chunks (*sectors*) of 128 bytes and these may be copied individually or in groups as specified by segment level information. The time to copy a 128 byte sector from one PE to another is 37μ as compared to 410μ for a full 4kbyte page.

The Object Manager is able to exploit the flexibility of the virtual store system by providing its own paging algorithms, including those for disk buffering and page discard. These are tuned to the rest of the database system making it more efficient than if it was mounted on a standard operating system (ex. Unix). In particular, the customized paging algorithms allow the database to make good use of the stable main store.

5   HARDWARE SUPPORT FOR THE RDBMS

The EDS machine is a custom built Distributed Store Parallel machine, designed to efficiently support the range of parallel languages and applications being developed under the EDS project. Therefore, as with the *EMEX* Operating System, it is designed to provide a more flexible platform than it would if it was just intended to support the RDBMS. In this section, we describe the hardware of the EDS machine, concentrating on its support for the RDBMS.

5.1   Overview of the Processing Element

The PE Hardware Architecture is shown in Figure 4. It consists of a number of units communicating over a SPARC MBUS. The Processing Element (PU) which runs the user and *EMEX* code is a high performance state-of-the-art RISC microprocessor from the SPARC family. The Store Unit (SU) contains a minimum of 64Mbytes of local store. The System Support Unit (SSU) is a second SPARC processor which removes some *EMEX* work from the PU, for example Message Passing and the copying of store from remote PEs. The Network Interface Unit (NIU) is tightly coupled to the SSU and provides a DMA-like interface from the Store Unit to the Network. The Diagnostic and Control Interface Unit (DCIU) provides the interface from the Diagnostic Element to the PE for low-level hardware control, including reset. The Interrupter, as its name implies, organises all interrupts to the components of the PE. These include clock, timer and SSU-PU interrupts.

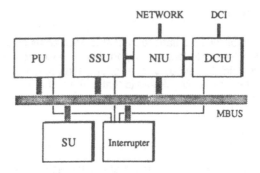

Figure 4: The Hardware Architecture of a PE

By basing the PE around a very fast processor which runs the user code, the basic building block of the EDS machine will have comparable performance to that of a fast serial machine. The System Support Unit ensures that the support of parallelism does not significantly reduce the serial performance of the PU on applications compared to that of a conventional serial processing system. The MBUS is asynchronous and will allow the upgrading of the PU and SSU to faster SPARC processors as they become available, simply by direct replacement of the PU module.

5.2   Storage

The SU contains a large 2-way interleaved semiconductor store constructed from DRAMs. The EDS RDBMS is designed as a main store database taking advantage of the falling price of semiconductor RAM relative to disk storage in order to increase system performance. It is therefore necessary to provide battery back-up for the stores so that any committed data held in them is stable. This will be done by backing up either the individual stores or the whole machine with batteries which will, in the event of a power failure, preserve the contents for as long as it takes to write them out to disk or streamer tape.

Disk storage on an EDS machine is used to hold 'inactive' data and can be provided either by special I-O nodes which are connected to the machine network, or by connecting disks to the PEs.

5.3   Network

In the EDS machine, the PEs are connected by a delta-network [9] built up from 8 by 8 switches: three stages allows 256 elements to be connected. The switches are custom VLSI chips with buffering at each input link. Within the network, a 'virtual cut through' mechanism [10] is used: the transfer of a packet (up to 128 data bytes and 16 header bytes) is a discrete operation.

Each connection to/from a PE has a data rate of 20Mbytes/sec and the nominal latency of a packet through the network is 8μ secs. Simulations have shown that if the network is 30% utilized, an additional delay of 4μ secs is added due to contention; this corresponds to a total throughput of 1.5Gbytes/sec for 256 PEs.

When a thread calls *EMEX* to send a message to a port, the address and length of the message are given to the SSU which determines the location of the target port. It then forms the header for a network packet and gives the NIU the address of the start of the data (which is the start of the message in the case of the first packet). The NIU reads the header and data and sends the packet directly into the network without any intermediate copying. If the message is longer than one packet then the SSU repeats the above process until the whole message has been sent.

At the receiving PE, the NIU reads in the packets and builds up the complete message directly in the address space of the team which owns the port. When the full message has been received, the SSU makes schedulable any threads which are suspended waiting on the port.

By using this method of offloading work, the PU spends very little of its time involved in the mechanics of sending messages. Also, because the messages are send directly from one user address to another, there is no internal buffering to increase latency. The target latency for message passing is 25 μ secs for a 128 byte message.

Similarly, when a read access is made to a page or sector not currently in the local PE, it is the SSU's at the sender and receiver which do the work of requesting the page/sector, sending it through the network, via the NIUs, and updating the address translation tables. These actions are triggered by a store access in which the SPARC MMU finds the accessed page to be invalid. The processor enters a segment level, user defined exception handling routine which forces a page/sector copy and carries out the necessary actions to enforce coherency (if any).

Sometimes during a read access, if sector copying is being used, the page will appear valid to the MMU but a local copy of the sector will not exist. This case is dealt with by special hardware in the SU which, in parallel with the MMU initiating the store read, checks that the sector being accessed is valid (it keeps a bit map showing which sectors are valid for each real page). If it is not valid, then a bus error is forced causing the current access to be abandoned and exception code is executed to force a sector copy.

A thread which executes a store access that results in a remote store copy is suspended for the duration of the access so that another thread can be run to prevent the processor idling during the access.

Remote store writes are added to a remote update queue for ordered transmission and execution. The user program is able to determine when they have been carried out and so synchronise on them, if that is necessary.

The method of implementing remote store accesses was designed so that the SPARC MMU can still process local store accesses, which will be in the great majority, without any degradation in performance over a conventional serial SPARC system. It is only for remote accesses that an exception routine is entered.

5.4   Hardware Integrity

This is clearly important in a RDBMS, and will be provided using well developed techniques. In a product, the PEs will use duplication of the microprocessor chip set with consistency checking between them; parity checking will be used within the ASICs; the mainstore will use hamming techniques; the delta-network will use CRC (it will have parity on its dataflow to aid fault resolution).

The battery back up of main store will also protect the integrity of data.

5.5   Hardware Resilience

Resilience is available at a number of levels:

- **Stand-by machines** This technique dynamically updates a stand-by machine which can be used should the first machine fail. The hardware will provide a high bandwidth interconnect between two EDS machines. The use of stand-by machines is however an expensive solution which may not be suitable for all applications; other levels of resilience are available to be exploited.

- **Replication** Within the EDS machine the next level of resilience is replication. One or more spare PEs can be provided within the machine. These can be configured in as required by diagnostic / *EMEX* support without re-booting. There is also path replication within the network.

- **Local to Processing Element** The next level of hardware resilience is on the processor / mainstore interface. Physically adjacent processing elements can be given access to each others mainstore. This is statically configured by the diagnostic system. Should a processing element fail, then the adjacent processor will be granted permanent access to its store. Within the mainstore, the hamming logic provides protection against single bit failures by correcting them.

6   CONCLUSIONS

The EDS project will run until December 1992. Within it a number of prototype EDS machines, of up to 64 PEs, will be built and used by the partners and their associates to tune and benchmark the RDBMS. One source of benchmarks are the industry standard TP benchmarks, however within the project a number of the participants are porting their own database applications which are of commercial importance to them onto the EDS RDBMS. Some of these were originally written for non-Relational databases, others did not use a database system at all: one was coded in FORTRAN ! These will be a good test not only of the performance of the parallel machine on real applications, but also of the expressive power of relational databases, and in particular ESQL.

The project target performance is 12000 Debit-Credit [12] transactions per second on a 256 PE machine at 30% utilization. A target for complex queries will be defined later in the project (the Transaction Processing Council are currently still in the process of producing standard benchmarks for complex queries). More details of the performance of the EDS machine on complex queries are given in a companion paper in this volume [11].

The machine architecture and operating system of the EDS machine provide a platform for high performance parallel computing. This, along with the fact that each PE can run Unix as an *EMEX* subsystem creates the possibility of producing an interim product by porting a conventional commercial distributed RDBMS onto the EDS machine, mapping one RDBMS instance onto each PE. Parallelism would be exploited in a relatively simple way, probably between queries.

The EDS project has the intention of producing a prototype of a commercial parallel RDBMS. This has forced the project to design a complete system, rather than just an experimental vehicle for demonstration purposes. The prototype will not implement all of the design, but where an omission is made, and this affects performance, a dummy with equivalent performance characteristics will be substituted. By addressing all of the issues rather than just a subset of them valuable lessons should be learnt about running commercial applications on a parallel relational database system.

7 ACKNOWLEDGEMENTS

This paper describes the work being carried out by the partners and associates of the EDS project.

8 REFERENCES

[1] B. Bergsten and R. Gonzalez-Rubio. *A Database Accelerator and its Languages*, CONPAR 88, BCS Workshop Series, CUP, pp. 63-71(1988).

[2] U. Baron, J. Chassin de Kergommeaux, M. Hailperin, M. Ratcliffe, P. Robert, J-C. Syre and H. Westphal. *The Parallel ECRC Prolog System PEPSys: An Overview and Evaluation Results*, Proc. FGCS88, Tokyo, Int. Conf. on Fifth Generation Comput. Sys., (Nov-Dec 1988).

[3] J. Darlington and M. Reeve. *ALICE- A Multi-Processor Reduction Machine for the Parallel Evaluation of Applicative Languages*. Proc. of the 1981 ACM Conf. on Functional Programming Languages and Computer Architecture, (1981).

[4] I. Watson, J. Sargeant, P. Watson and V. Woods. *The FLAGSHIP Parallel Machine*, CONPAR 88, BCS Workshop Series, CUP, pp. 125-133, (1988).

[5] B.J. Proctor and C.J. Skelton. *Flagship is Nearing Port: A Status Report on the Alvey Stage of the Project*, CONPAR 88, BCS Workshop Series, CUP, pp. 100-107,(1988).

[6] G. Gardarin and P. Valduriez. *ESQL: An Extended SQL with Object and Deductive Capabilities*, Int. Conf. on Database and Expert System Applications, Vienna, Austria, August 1990.

[7] H. Boral, W. Alexander, I. Clay, G. Copeland, S. Danforth, M. Franklin, B. Hart, M. Smith, and P. Valduriez. *Prototyping Bubba, a highly parallel database system*, IEEE transactions on Knowledge and Data Engineering, Vol 2(1), (1990).

[8] M. Rozier, V. Abrossimov, F. Armand, I. Boule, M. Gien, M. Guillemont, F. Herrmann, C. Kaiser, S. Langlois, P. Leonard and W. Neuhauser. *CHORUS Distributed Operating System*, Proc. IEEE 6th Int. Conf. Distrib. Compt. Sys., pp. 558-563, (19-23 May 1986).

[9] J.H. Patel. *Processor-Memory Interconnections for Multi-processors*, Proc. 6th Annual Symp. Comput. Arch., pp. 343-354, (1988).

[10] P. Kermani and L. Kleinrock. *Virtual Cut-through: A new Computer Communication Switching Technique*, Comput. Networks 3(4), pp. 267-286, (Sept 1979).

[11] S. Patel. *Performance Estimates of a Join* In this Volume. 1990.

[12] T. Sawer and O. Serlin. *DebitCredit Benchmark - Minimum Requirements and Compliance List*, Codd and Date Consulting Group, San Jose, (June 1988).

PRISMA Contributions

PRISMA, a platform for experiments with parallelism

P.M.G. Apers

University of Twente

L.O. Hertzberger

University of Amsterdam

B.J.A. Hulshof, A.C.M. Oerlemans

Philips Research Laboratories Eindhoven

M.L Kersten

Centre for Mathematics and Computer Science

Abstract

Using a large multiprocessor, consisting of 100 processing nodes, in the area of data and knowledge processing poses challenging research and engineering questions. The PRISMA project presented here has addressed many of the problems encountered by the design and the construction of such a system. Among the results obtained are an implementation of a parallel object-oriented language, a hardware platform with efficient communication, and a distributed main-memory relational database system. Their combination forms a platform for further experimental research in several areas of distributed processing.

1 Introduction

The PRISMA project is a large-scale research effort in the design and implementation of a highly parallel machine for data and knowledge processing. It is organized as a nationwide Dutch research activity with combined forces from four universities, a governmental research institute, and Philips Research Laboratories. It ran from 1986 until end of 1990 and was manned with thirty persons. In this paper we present an overview of the PRISMA project.

The key research issue of the PRISMA project is to study the interaction between a non-trivial application, an object-oriented language, and a multiprocessor machine architecture. For this purpose an experimentation platform has been designed, which enables us to experiment with coarse grain parallelism for applications at many levels of detail. Such as its effect at the hardware level, the basic software such as the distributed operating system, language design and its compilation, and, finally, the construction of applications that exploit the computing power provided by a large multiprocessor system. Our effort has resulted in a prototype system of 100 processing nodes.

Since a multiprocessor system offers many opportunities to improve the performance of database systems, the prime target application selected as a testcase for the PRISMA platform was the construction of a new relational database management system. The DBMS architecture is based on two novel aspects. First, the PRISMA machine is equipped with about 1.5 Gigabyte of direct store, which provided the hardware foundation to focus on a main-memory DBMS architecture. Second, the multiprocessor system leads to a decomposition of the DBMS into functional components and the design of an extensible distributed system architecture. Thus, the research issues focus on exploitation of main-memory as the prime database store and the effective exploitation of the potential parallelism offered by the platform.

The PRISMA project is supported by the Dutch "Stimuleringsprojectteam Informaticaonderzoek" (SPIN)

One way to exploit a multiprocessor system is to augment a traditional implementation language with communication primitives, such as remote procedure calls, and process management. Its potential drawback is that application programs then tend to be bulky with hardwired code that manages process allocation and intra-process communication. To alleviate these problems we developed a Parallel Object-Oriented Language (POOL) that allows the programmer to express the inherent parallelism in an algorithm without concern on its mapping to the underlying system. The experimentation platform then provides the application and the hardware boundaries to study implementation techniques for POOL that show performance improvement over a wide range of multiprocessor system configurations without altering the program source.

The key issues in the design of the multiprocessor system are to choose the level of potential parallelism and the interconnect. To obtain a viable experimentation platform, we aimed for a large system, consisting of about 100 processing nodes equipped with sufficient main-memory to support large applications. Moreover, by focusing on an experimentation platform we needed an architecture that scales without showing step function behavior during performance measurements.

As mentioned before, the outcome of this project is a platform that supports a wide range of experiments to improve our understanding on parallel (symbolic) processing. Instead of focusing on toy problems, we have chosen a non-trivial application that provides an abundance of optimization problems for the language and the system implementation, while at the same time it would benefit from hiding the multiprocessor details. Moreover, by actually building such an integrated platform, we obtained a tool to calibrate performance models in a wide range of research areas.

In addition to the main-stream research and development within the PRISMA project, we fostered exploratory research in various directions. To illustrate, we looked at various techniques to speedup expert-systems, to exploit parallelism in information retrieval [Aalbersberg1, Aalbersberg2], and parallel term rewritting [Rodenburg].

The remainder of this paper is organized as follows. Section 2 describes in more detail the assumptions, questions, and methodology to construct the PRISMA system. Following, in Section 3 we focus on the realization of the platform from three perspectives; the database management system, the object-oriented language and runtime system, and the machine architecture. For each we describe how the component was realized and what lessons we learned in the course of its construction. We conclude with summary and future research in Section 4.

2 Assumptions, Questions, and Methodology

Research on the construction of systems is always characterized by having externally given assumptions and additional assumptions to focus the research. In the following subsections these assumptions and related questions are made explicit for the various layers in the system. Moreover, the assumptions are related to the state of the art in the various fields.

The externally given assumptions stem from the vision we have on the field. First, we expect that homogeneity and scalability are important factors for the production of hardware. Second, by chosing an object-oriented platform we want to prove that this platform provides the right kind of abstraction to easily express parallelism available in the application and to efficiently implement this platform. To prove these points, we have taken a non-trivial application, a database management system, and started experiments for the object-oriented platform and the database management system to gain experience in expressing and implementing parallelism.

2.1 Database Management System

The design and construction of database machines to improve non-numeric processing has attracted many researchers during the last two decades. At one end of the spectrum they have reduced the amount of data to be manipulated by filtering records as they are transferred from disk to main-memory [Ozkarahan] and using several functionally specialized computers linked into a network

[DeWitt1, Gardarin, Leland]. The other end of the spectrum is characterized by attempts to harness the processing power and storage capacity offered by large scale integration [Shaw, Katuka].

An observation is that no single database management system will efficiently support all database applications in the future. There arises a need for a variety of facilities, providing the proper level of abstraction, user interface, and functionality. The consequence is that future database management systems should be designed with functional distribution in mind. That is, a database management system comprises a set of data managers, each providing part of the required overall functionality and coordinated by a distribution manager. Structuring of the database management system as a collection of such data managers (operating on local data) controlled by a distribution manager fits well with the architecture of a (shared-nothing) *multiprocessor system*. Another observation is that the cost for main memory drops rapidly. Therefore, it becomes feasible and cost-effective to keep a major portion of the database in main memory[DeWitt2, Molina]. Our multiprocessor system is equipped with sufficient *main memory* to directly store and manipulate a medium-sized database, and thus avoid the I/O bottle-neck to disk. Two questions have to be answered here. First of all, can "massive" parallelism provided by a 100-node system (or even more) effectively be used in processing queries and, secondly, what are the effects of a main memory approach for data storage. Related to the main-memory approach is the question whether the system can be made reliable enough.

Database management systems are often viewed as interpreters of "unformatted" data on disk. The interpretation problem can be overcome by introducing the concept of a One-Fragment Manager (OFM). Such an OFM can be regarded as a relational algebra machine that handles relations or fragments of one specific tuple type (intuitively, one specific relation schema). This makes it possible to *compile* selections submitted to an OFM into code directly working on the data structures used by the OFM. The question to be answered here is whether the overhead of compilation is small enough to make a performance increase feasible.

One externally given assumption was that the database management system should be implemented in the *object-oriented language* called POOL [America1, America2] [America3]. In a previous project [Bronnenberg] in the area of distributed systems the language POOL (Parallel Object-Oriented Language) was developed. This language was slightly extended to make it suitable as implementation language for a database management system. This language almost completely shields the distribution aspect of the multiprocessor system from the database management system. The question related to this assumption is whether the language POOL provides the right level of abstraction to implement a database management system and whether this implementation can be made efficient. Section 2.2 will elaborate more on this.

To specify distributed processing that is inherent to a database management system it was set up in a strictly *modular* way. At the top level this modular design led to components such as parsers for SQL and PRISMAlog (see below), Query Optimizer, Data Dictionary, Transaction Manager, One-Fragment Manager, and a Data Allocation Manager. All of these components can be assigned to processors rather independently of each other. It is our conviction that fine-grain parallelism is not suitable to implement a database management system; none of the above components has any parallelism in it. The question is whether this *coarse-grain* approach is the right one and what the optimal size is of a relation or fragment to be managed by a One-Fragment Manager.

In Section 3.1 we will come back to these assumptions and corresponding questions.

2.2 The Object-Oriented platform

The main purpose for the platform is to offer a programming paradigm for writing parallel symbolic applications. The DBMS system being a testcase for this platform. The main programming paradigm chosen for the platform was object-orientation. Existing object-oriented languages, like Smalltalk [Goldberg], C++ [Stroustrup], and Eiffel [Meyer1], have shown that the approach is promising for constructing large software systems. Key issues mentioned here are reusability, maintainability and modularity [Brooks, Cox, Meyer2].

Several ways to introduce parallelism into an object-oriented language have been proposed; introduce parallelism as an orthogonal concept, as e.g. in Trellis/Owl [Moss] or allow asynchronous communication between objects, as in actor languages [Hewitt]. The approach taken for our object-oriented platform, called POOL, is that each object is essentially an independent process.

Furthermore, the following features are offered by the platform. The POOL language offers primitives for (synchronous and asynchronous) message passing between objects, however, since each object is an active entity, it determines itself when to answer the messages. In general, messages can have any size. Also, objects can be created dynamically. Since objects can be referred to from all over the system, it is hard to recognize, at POOL programming level, whether it has become redundant. Therefore, a garbage collector is present which will automatically eliminate most of these redundant objects. As a consequence no language features are offered to remove objects explicitly.

In response to the requirements analysis of the DBMS, some facilities have been added to the object-oriented platform. The most important ones are; support for exception handling and error propagation between objects, support for tuples, and support for stable storage. The platform only provides a stable storage medium, where data written to this is guaranteed to survive system crashes. The responsibility to exploit the stable storage facility such that it can be used to recover the state of an application subsequent to a failure, lies with the application itself.

The major question to be answered is whether the language features of POOL can be implemented efficiently enough. In particular, the uniform use of the object from integers, simple record like structures to complicated processes makes it hard to find optimal implementations over the whole range. The key research issues have been efficient scheduling, message passing, garbage collection and optimal allocation control.

2.3 Machine architecture

Two basic assumptions were given for the architecture of the machine. First, it should provide a large amount of memory and processor power. Second, we wanted to investigate parallelism. Therefore we chose a multiprocessor system. In designing such a system, there is constant trade-off between three parameters. These parameters can be used to describe the properties of processor and memory subsystems as is illustrated in Table 1 (including the chosen prototype configuration). Clearly there

Processors	Memory	Prototype
number	number of banks	100 processors, 100 banks
power	size of banks	2 MIPS, 16 Mbyte
connectivity	connectivity	point to point network, non shared memory

Table 1: Parameters of memory and processor system

is an interrelation between choices made in either of the first two parts of the table. As an example the connection machine [Hillis] has chosen for a large number of simple processing elements each element connected to a limited size memory bank, whereas the connectivity of the network between processing nodes is high. In this situation a point to point network exist between processing nodes, therefore, these are called direct connection or distributed memory machine. On the other side of the spectrum we see the development in current super and mini super computers where a small amount (less than 20) of powerful processors are connected towards a small number (less than 20) of memory banks each of considerable size and connected via a low connectivity network. In this example the network is shared between processors and memory elements and, therefore, they are called shared connection or shared memory machine.

Another important issue in designing multiprocessor systems is the flexibility of the system. This is determined by such parameters as:

Extensibility: indicating that it should be easy to add processing power and memory to the system.

Scalability: indicating that an increase in processing and memory should lead to a smooth addition of total system performance.

Modularity: indicating that adding processing or memory should not lead to changes in system homogeneity.

If we take these criteria into account we can observe that shared memory systems score less on the flexibility scale than direct connection machines. Adding processing power to shared memory machines could give rise to step function behavior when the shared resources are exhausted. It is not argued that the extension problem is not present in direct connection machines at all, but because of the point to point connections it is possible to add an almost unlimited number of processing nodes. In practice, the maximum number (degree of the network) is decided during design time. However, this is possible to the cost of a more complex communication problem if processing nodes a non-neighbor.

In case of the PRISMA architecture the following boundary conditions had to be taken into account:

- Optimal support of a virtual Pool machine consisting of a large number of (coarse grain) objects with explicit message passing based communication.

- A strong demand for flexibility in particular homogeneous scalability because we wanted to build a machine with a large (order of 100) number of processing nodes and memory banks. Moreover, the addition of processing power and memory should be smooth.

This leaded us to the conclusion that the architecture for our machine should be a direct connection machine.

2.4 Experimentation

In the previous sections we have formulated the research goals and the boundary conditions of our project. In our research we have chosen for the methodology of performing experiments to verify the correctness of a particular model and to change the implementation dependent on the results obtained. Because of this choice for experimentation we first had to realize the instrumentation of our experimental set-up. Implementing the DBMS on top of the object oriented platform which is built on top of a multiprocessor system was not enough instrumentation to be able to do our experiments. To realize a flexible experimental system, extra facilities were needed at all levels, the DBMS as well as the language implementation and the operating system. Among others they include:

- A more powerful profiler to study the behavior of various software components, such as the objects and message traffic.

- The ability to pass-on object scheduling information from the application towards the O.S., via so-called pragma's offered on the object oriented platform.

With the set of facilities described here it now becomes possible to study the research questions mentioned in Section 2 and give quantitative answers which are a measure for the quality of a particular solution chosen. These results can be the incentive to change part of the implementations or even try another model. In the remainder of the article, we will describe the instrumentation of our experimentation platform, and some preliminary results.

3   Realization and design decisions

Preliminary results and some experiences gained during the construction of our experimental platform are given in the following sections for each of the three layers.

3.1 Database Management System

This subsection discusses the current status of the implementation of the database management system and the preliminary answers to the questions posed in Section 2.1.

3.1.1 Realization

Currently the first version of the database management system, called PRISMA/DB0, runs on the multiprocessor system consisting of 100 nodes. It consist of 35.000 lines of POOL code and is fully documented with a WEB-like documentation system. It consists of the following components: SQL and PRISMAlog parsers, Query Optimizer, Transaction Manager, Concurrency Controller, One-Fragment Manager, Data Dictionary, and Data Allocation Manager (see Fig. 1). For more details on DB0 we refer to [Kersten, Apers1].

The forms of *parallelism* used in the database management system are multi-tasking, pipe-lining, and task spreading. Multi-tasking is used to execute concurrent queries in a parallel fashion if data access allows that. The execution of a query is done in the form of a directed-acyclic graph, where the nodes represent OFMs and the directed edges represent data transmissions. This is done in a pipe-lining manner. As soon as intermediate results are produced, they are sent to the next OFM where they are used as input. Task spreading occurs because the data of the entire database is fragmented and allocated to many OFMs. So, the traditional relational operators can be computed in a distributed manner. It turns out that some of these operators, like sort or join, prevent or diminish the effect of pipe-lining. So, special care has been taken to avoid these operators or to come up with an implementation to improve pipe-lining. In [Wilschut] a hash-based join algorithm is proposed that hashes tuples from both operands as they come in and that computes the output tuples at the same time. It turns out that this join algorithm is slightly more expensive than the traditional hash join algorithm but that it produces its output much earlier, thereby enhancing pipe-lining.

The database management system is responsible for its own *recovery* after hardware crashes using stable storage, a service provided by the object-oriented platform. This means that after a crash the whole database has to be reloaded from disk. The expectation is that the recovery time after a failure is not more than a few minutes. Since disks are spread over the system most of the data can be read from disk into the OFMs in parallel. Currently, various main-memory data structures are studied that make writing to stable storage efficient.

PRISMAlog, a Datalog-like language, is provided as an interface allowing for recursive queries. For the class of *regular recursive queries*, containing the class of linear recursive queries, it was shown that it could be rewritten to a traditional relational algebra program with the transitive closure as an additional operator [Apers2]. Optimization techniques to process the transitive closure of a fragmented relation efficiently have been proposed [Houtsma].

3.1.2 Experience

The prime method to visualize the performance of a database management system is to run a well-known benchmark, such as the Wisconsin benchmark [DeWitt3]. The first series of runs support most of our ideas but they also uncovered several weaknesses in the various layers of the system, which are being corrected now.

Our experiences with the POOL language are that it gave us sufficient facilities to design the database management system in a *modular* way. Furthermore, shielding low level communication from the implementors was one of the most attractive points of POOL. It gave a lot of flexibility in specifying the various forms of parallelism and determining the actual parallelism by allocation pragma's. However, the performance of local computations of the first POOL implementation is rather poor, because every user-defined object is implemented like a process.

First experiments show that the *coarse-grain* approach is the appropriate one. As soon as the system is tuned more extensive experiments will be done to determine the "optimal" fragment size

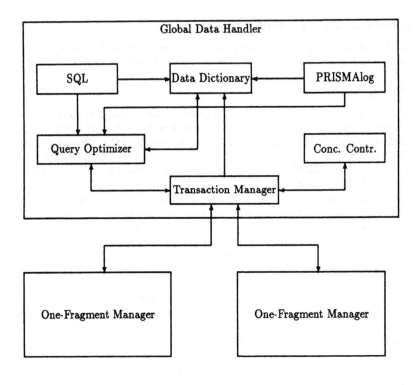

Figure 1: The PRISMA Database Architecture

to gain as much performance as possible given a pool of 100 processors.

In an early stage of the project a C implementation of the OFM has been constructed. This experiment showed that even for small fragments and relatively simple selections the cost incurred by the *compilation* is small compared to the execution time, and almost always results in an improvement [vdBerg].

3.2 The object-oriented platform

This subsection discusses the current state of the implementation of the object oriented platform and the experiences obtained.

3.2.1 Realization

Currently a running implementation is available of the object oriented platform, consisting of a compiler, runtime support, target operating system, and some performance measurements tools.

The POOL compiler is structured in a traditional way; it consists of a frontend, which translates POOL into an intermediate language, and a backend which takes care of the translation into assembly code. The compiler supports separate compilation. The intermediate language is chosen at a relative high level and can be characterized as a declarative typed stack machine combined with procedure, send, answer and create primitives in which it resembles the POOL language itself. In the backend the send, answer, and create primitives are mapped to operating system primitives, possibly via the run time support.

The target operating system [Brandsma] is split into two parts, the nucleus which is POOL independent, and the POOL specific support. The nucleus takes care of the resource management and offers a multi tasking environment as well as some (parameterizable) transport primitives over the network. The operating system itself is also implemented as a collection of communicating processes. All (POOL and operating system) processes share the same address space allowing to implement these as light weight processes and allowing fast exchange of data. The POOL language offers sufficient protection to prevent malicious usage. The memory management is fully implemented in software to allow experimentation with various strategies and to obtain insight into the "typical" allocation behavior of POOL programs. For stable storage the data will be stored twice on different disks, furthermore all disks are attached to different nodes, so no data is lost in case of a single node (disk) crash. The garbage collector which is implemented is a distributed on-the-fly mark and sweep garbage collector [Augusteijn].

3.2.2 Experience

Preliminary experiments with prototype implementations of the object-oriented platform have shown that it is not a trivial task to recognize optimizable objects. A main problem appears to be clustering of objects to increase the granularity of parallelism. Due to the generality of the object and communication constructs, this clustering cannot be done efficiently enough by the compiler for the object-oriented programming language. Therefore the object-oriented platform is extended to support pragma's, to identify objects with a straightforward behavior, such as record like structures. Using these pragma's the compiler can cluster objects and subsequently generate efficient code to be executed on the platform.

The implementation of the clustering pragma's is still under development. Therefore overall performance measurements are not possible, due to the slow local computations.

3.3 Machine architecture

This subsection describes the realized architecture and discusses some results obtained.

3.3.1 Realization

The PRISMA architecture has been realized in four prototype machines. Two smaller prototypes of 4 nodes, one with 8 nodes and one big prototype with 100 nodes. Each node consist of an off the shelf processor board and memory board, connected with the other nodes by a communication processor developed by the DOOM project [Bronnenberg]. The small prototypes are used by the different research institutes involved in PRISMA.

The Communication Processor (CP) takes care of deadlock free routing of packets through the communication network without intervention from the dataprocessor. Each CP has four bi-directional links connected to other CP's, the speed of these (serial) links is 20 Mbit/s in both directions. In addition it has a parallel port to the dataprocessor. The dataprocessor communicates to the network by writing 256 bit packets, containing the destination node, into the CP and by reading the packet at the destination. The CP is capable of adaptive routing, multiple paths to the same destination can be chosen to avoid network congestion areas. This has the consequence that packets can arrive in a different order than they were send. Furthermore the CP is designed for general purpose network routing, it is fully deadlock free, can handle any network with a diameter of up to 8 and connect maximal 4096 nodes.

In the smaller prototypes, the topology of the network (the connections between the CP) is hardwired. The large machine has a 400x400 switch, enabling us to partition machine in one large or more smaller machines. Each machine can be interconnected in a requested topology. The set of topologies that can be chosen is limited to: mesh, torus, chordal ring and an optimal extended chordal ring.

For communication with the host one on every five nodes is equipped with an ethernet board running the standard ethernet protocol layers.

To support fault tolerance, the machine is equipped with disk based permanent storage where the database relations can be stored to survive crashes. The disks are distributed over the machine, half of the nodes each have one 300 Mbyte disk.

An address tracer is constructed to measure the locality behavior of POOL programs as input for future cache support.

3.3.2 Experience

The distributed memory architecture has proven to be a good choice. It has been rather simple to built, because all nodes are equal (except form discs and ethernet) and are connected by an asynchronous network.

The switch gives us the possibility to use the machine optimal (many persons can use small parts to test software), but also to do experiments with network topology, and to measure the effect of the number of processors on the behavior of an application. Each node has 16 Mbyte of memory which allows enough room for experimentation and measurements for a wide range of applications.

The CP is successful although it was more difficult to built than was expected. The adaptive routing capability is currently not used because of the expected overhead at the processor side when packets arrive out of order. Experiments with different topologies have shown no significant differences in performance. For a small 1 packet POOL message only 15% of the time is used by the physical transport layer in the CP.

The optimization of the physical transport layer has been fruitful, but we neglected the interface between the data-processor and the CP itself. The mapping from the POOL messages to the hardware should be implemented more efficient. A separate administration processor between the CP and the data processor is under study [Muller]. Several interface levels are considered, but no choice has been made. One possibility is to make the CP interface stream oriented instead of packet oriented. Another option is that the administration processor takes care of the conversion from POOL messages to packets and vice versa. Still, we also have to keep the flexibility of the system in mind. Would the administration processor prescribe the exact format of messages, it will reduce the possibilities for implementation experiments at the compiler side of the interface. Moreover the interface would become much more detailed, because it has to include a description of memory management, scheduling, and parts of the system that must be accessed atomically such as message queues.

At this moment, we get some feeling about the behavior of POOL and "typical" POOL programs. We are now able to study their behavior further, and start to design a less flexible, more POOL optimized machine. From the experiments we hope to get the required insight in the communication strategy, caching (memory management) support and possibly dataprocessor support to use.

4 Summary

In this paper we have presented an overview of the PRISMA project. The major research question addressed in this national project is to design, to construct, and to experiment with a highly parallel machine for data and knowledge processing. Among the results obtained are an implementation of a parallel object-oriented language, a hardware platform with efficient communication, and a distributed main-memory relational database system.

A prototype PRISMA/DB system has been implemented and is currently subjected to various detailed performance studies. In particular, new query processing strategies, concurrency control techniques, and implementations of data managers are being developed.

The parallel object-oriented language POOL-X has proven to be a decisive factor in this project. Although the construction of a new programming language (and support environment) requires a lot of manpower, it greatly simplified the construction of parallel programs. In particular, the database system software obtained is highly modular and benefits from the computational and typing model offered by the language.

Since, automatic parallelization of programs is beyond the current horizon of technology, we focused on ways to obtain advisory information from the programmer to arrive at an efficient application program without revealing too much of the language runtime detail. This has resulted in a few orthogonal language features that provide the necessary resource control information to the runtime system.

Lastly, we designed and constructed a shared nothing multiprocessor system. A novel aspect included is a separate communication processor to improve the performance of the interconnect.

The hardware and software platform obtained in the PRISMA project provides a basis for experimental research in many areas of research in distributed processing. Its existence can provide the necessary feedback to analytical and theoretical work in this field.

5 Acknowledgement

The following persons have contributed to the PRISMA project. Carel van den Berg, Marc Bezem, Anton Eliens, Martin Kersten, Louis Kossen, Peter Lucas, Kees van de Meer, Hans Rukkers, Jan Willem Spee, Nanda Verbrugge, and Leonie van de Voort, from Centre for Mathematics and Computer Science. Peter Apers, Herman Balsters, Maurice Houtsma, Jan Flokstra, Paul Grefen, Erik van Kuijk, Rob van der Weg and Annita Wilschut, from University of Twente. Marcel Beemster, Maarten Carels, Sun Chengzheng, Boudewijn Pijlgroms, Bob Hertzberger, Sjaak Koot, Henk Muller and Arthur Veen, from University of Amsterdam. IJsbrand Jan Aalbersberg, Pierre America, Ewout Brandsma, Bert de Brock, Huib Eggenhuisen, Henk van Essen, Herman ter Horst, Ben Hulshof, Jan Martin Jansen, Wouter Jan Lippmann, Sean Morrison, Hans Oerlemans, Juul van der Spek, Marc Vauclair and Marnix Vlot, from Philips Research Laboratories. Piet Rodenburg and Jos Vrancken, from University of Utrecht. George Leih, from University of Leiden.

References

[Aalbersberg1] IJ.J. Aalbersberg, *A Parallel Full-Text Document Retrieval System*, Workshop on Object-Oriented Document Manipulation, Rennes, France, pp. 268–279, May 1989.

[Aalbersberg2] IJ.J. Aalbersberg, F. Sijstermans, *InfoGuide: A Full-Text Document Retrieval System*, International Conference on Database and Expert Systems Applications DEXA 90, Vienna, Austria, Springer Verlag, pp. 12–21, August 1990.

[America1] P. America, *POOL-T — A parallel object-oriented language*, In: Akinori Yonezawa, Mario Tokoro (eds.): Object-Oriented Concurrent Programming, MIT Press, 1987, pp. 199–220, 1987.

[America2] P. America, *Issues in the design of a parallel object oriented language*, Formal Aspects of Computing, Volume 1, number 4, pp. 366–411, 1989.

[America3] P. America, *Language definition of POOL-X*, PRISMA Doc. 350, Philips Research Laboratories, Eindhoven, the Netherlands, November 1989.

[Apers1] P.M.G. Apers, M.L. Kersten, and H.C.M. Oerlemans, *PRISMA Database Machine: A Distributed, Main-Memory Approach*, Proc. Int. Conf. on Extending Database Technology; Venice, 1988.

[Apers2] P.M.G. Apers, M.A.W. Houtsma, and F. Brandse, *Processing Recursive Queries in Relational Algebra*, Proc. IFIP TC2 Working conf. on Knowledge and Data, 1986.

[Augusteijn] L. Augusteijn, *Garbage collection in a distributed environment*, Proc. of Parallel Architectures and Languages in Europe, Eindhoven, the Netherlands, 1987.

[vdBerg] C. v.d. Berg et al., *A Comparison of scanning algorithms*, Proc. Parbase90, Florida, 1990.

[Brandsma] E. Brandsma, Sun Chengzheng, B.J.A. Hulshof, L.O. Hertzberger, A.C.M. Oerlemans, *Overview of the PRISMA Operating System*, Int. Conference on New Generation Computer Systems, 1989.

[Bronnenberg] W. Bronnenberg, L. Nijman, A. Odijk, R. v. Twist, *DOOM: A Decentralized Object-Oriented Machine*, IEEE Micro, October 1987.

[Brooks] F. Brooks, Jr., *No silver bullet - essence and accidents of software engineering*, IEEE Computer, April 1987.

[Cox] B.J. Cox, *Object-Oriented programming; an evolutionary approach*, Addison-Wesley, 1986.

[DeWitt1] D.J. DeWitt, *DIRECT - A Multiprocessor organization for Supporting Relational Database Management*, IEEE Transactions on Computers, Volume C-28, number 6, pp. 395–406, June 1979.

[DeWitt2] D.J. DeWitt, R.H. Katz, K. Olken, L.D. Shapiro, M.R. Stonebraker and D. Wood, *Implementation Techniques for Main Memory Database Systems*, Proc. ACM SIGMOD 1984, pp. 1–8, 1984.

[DeWitt3] D. Bitton, D. DeWitt, and Turbyfill, *Benchmarking Database Systems. A Systematic Approach*, Proc. 9th VLDB, Florence, 1983.

[Moss] J.E. Moss, B. Moss, W. Kohler, *Concurrency features for the Trellis/Owl language*, Proc. ECOOP'87, June 1987.

[Gamma]   D.J. DeWitt, *A Performance Analysis of the Gamma Database Machine*, Proc. SIG-MOD 1988; Chicago, 1988.

[Gardarin] G. Gardarin, P. Bernadat, N. Temmerman, P. Valduriez and Y. Viemont, *Design of a Multiprocessor Relational Database System*, IFIP World Congress, Paris, Sep. 1983.

[Goldberg] A. Goldberg, D. Robson, *Smalltalk-80, The language and its implementation*, Addison-Wesley, 1983.

[Hewitt]   C. Hewitt, *Viewing control structures as patterns of passing messages*, Artificial intelligence, 8:323-364, 1977.

[Hillis]   W.D. Hillis, *The connection machine*, MIT Press, 1985.

[Houtsma]   M.A.W. Houtsma, P.M.G. Apers, and S. Ceri, *Parallel Computation of Transitive Closure Queries on Fragmented Databases*, submitted for publication, 1989.

[Katuka]   T. Katuka, N. Miyazaki, S. Shibayama, H. Yokota, and K. Murakami, *The Design and Implementation of Relational Database Machine Delta*, Proc. of the 4-th Int. Workshop on Database Machines, editors D.J. DeWitt and H. Boral, Springer Verlag, page 13-34, 1985.

[Kersten]   M.L. Kersten et al., *A Distributed Main-Memory Database Machine*, Proc. 5th IWDM; Japan, 1987.

[Leland]   M.D.P. Leland and W.D. Roome, *The Silicon Database Machine*, in Proc. of the 4-th Int. Workshop on Database Machines, editors D.J. DeWitt and H. Boral, Springer Verlag, page 169-189, 1985.

[Meyer1]   B. Meyer, *Eiffel: A language and environment for software engineering*, Report TR-EI-2/BR, Interactive Software Engineering Inc., 1987.

[Meyer2]   B. Meyer, *Object-oriented software construction*, Prentice-Hall, 1988.

[Molina]   H. Garcia-Molina, R.J. Lipton and P. Honeyman, *A Massive Memory Database System*, Techn. Report 314, Dep. of Comp Sci. Princeton Univ., Sep 1983.

[Muller]   H. Muller, *Mixed level simulation of the POOMA architecture*, Submitted for publication, March 1990.

[Ozkarahan] E.A. Ozkarahan, S.A. Schuster and K.C. Smith, *RAP- An Associative Processor for Database Management*, Proceedings of the National Computer Conference, Volume 45, page 379-387, 1975.

[Rodenburg] P. Rodenburg, J. Vrancken, *Parallel Object-Oriented Term Rewriting: The Booleans*, , 1988.

[Shaw]   D. Shaw, *Knowledge-Based Retrieval on a Relational Database Machine*, Ph.D. Department of Computer Science, Stanford University, 1980.

[Stroustrup] B. Stroustrup, *The C++ Programming Language*, Addison-Wesley, 1986.

[Wilschut] A.N. Wilschut and P.M.G. Apers, *Pipelining in Query Execution*, Proc. Parbase, 1990.

The PRISMA Experiment

Peter M.G. Apers

University of Twente

L.O. Hertzberger

University of Amsterdam

Ben J.A. Hulshof

Philips Research Laboratories

Abstract

The design of a large database management system on top of an object-oriented platform which is implemented on a tightly coupled multiprocessor system requires a large number of design decisions. There exist no methodology to evaluate the consequences and compare the differences between them. Looking into experimental methodology in physics we find a lot of similarities and techniques we think that are useful to solve our problems. A discussion is presented in which way such experiments have to be set up and of the tools that are required. The status of the project and our experience up till now is presented.

1 Introduction

In the last five years the possibility to build parallel computers has become more and more appealing. On the one hand, switching speed of electronic components has increased to such a height that the speed of light poses severe limitations on the physical length of interconnections in a computer. On the other hand, integration technology of semiconductors will soon reach a point where a complex conventional computer architecture only occupies a fraction of the effective space on a silicon chip. One of the possibilities to fill up the available space on a silicon chip is to design regular parallel computers, where a basic processor and communication design can be copied as often as required.

Although the hardware possibilities are there to build a parallel computer system, the models and the experience to effectively exploit parallelism in computer systems is still to a great extent missing. The Japanese Fifth Generation Computer System Project [1] had a large influence convincing the computer science community that parallel systems had a great potential. This project was aiming at exploiting implicit, more fine-grained parallelism, as was believed to be present in a language as Prolog.

The ESPRIT project 415 [2], headed by Philips Research Laboratory in Eindhoven, also had as its target designing a parallel computer, however, its aim was to exploit explicit, more coarse-grain parallelism as present in application programs. For that purpose a language called Parallel Object-Oriented Language [3] was designed. With the help of this language the user can structure his application programs as a collection of processes (objects), which can only interact explicitly via the exchange of messages. The combination of parallel machine and language provided an object-oriented platform called Distributed Object-Oriented Machine (DOOM) [4].

It was felt that to gain more experience with explicit parallelism, it was necessary to construct large applications. Therefore the PRISMA project [5] was started as a collaboration between Philips Research Laboratory in Eindhoven and a number of Computer Science Departments at Dutch universities and the CWI, the Centre for Mathematics and Computer Science. Although targetting to design a Database and Knowledgebase machine, it became clear in the course of the project that only parallelism in databases was understood sufficiently well to be able to design a parallel implementation.

This paper describes the evolution in our approach and way of thinking about parallelism during the course of the four year PRISMA project. More specifically, attention will be paid to how we think

The PRISMA project is supported by the Dutch "Stimuleringsprojectteam Informaticaonderzoek" (SPIN)

that a better understanding of the exploitation of parallelism in large application can be obtained and what methodologies are necessary. In this discussion the experience gained from the database application on top of an object-oriented platform will serve as a guide-line.

2 Project evolution and constraints

In this section it will be illustrated how our ideas of the project changed over time and what the constraints were the project had to deal with .

When the PRISMA project started the aim was to design a high performance database machine with a maximum of functionality. The major reason for this was, that it was expected that one of the spin-offs of the project would be a commercial product.

The main aim to realize the high performance was to exploit parallelism where and whenever possible. To make optimal use of current technology, the main memory approach was chosen. The further the project evolved, the more we found that the demands of functionality and speed could not be realized in the given time frame. Because of this, and because it was realized that there was not sufficient experience with such highly parallel applications as a database management system to justify our design decisions, we realized that a methodology was required that allowed us to compare and evaluate these decisions. Such a methodology should allow to compare the consequences of different forms and implementations of parallelism in the application. Looking around into other fields of science, like physics and chemistry, we came to the conclusion that an experimental approach (see Section 3) was the best suited methodology.

Before discussing this approach any further, it is important to analyse the consequences of the fact that PRISMA was based on the DOOM project. In the DOOM project the target had been to design a flexible and extensible machine. This had resulted in the choice for a distributed memory machine with a separate Communication Processors (CP) [6] responsible for communication and message routing. This CP was necessary to discharge the Data Processor (DP) from the abundance of message passing as generated by the object-oriented language. When we started, we decided to use the same hardware as the DOOM project and also to make use of the object-oriented platform as provided by POOL where and whenever possible. This was one of the arguments why the total database management system was coded in the POOL language. An additional goal was to evaluate the object-oriented programming style as a rapid prototyping facility.

For the PRISMA project, DOOM mainly set constraints on the language (object-oriented language) and machine level (distributed memory). In addition it was decided to implement issues that are to a large extend dictated by the application (the database system) like memory management, stable storage, etc via the flexible but slower software solutions and not by an inflexible hardware approach. Although we realized that this would imply speed penalties, it offers the flexibility to experiment, also at this level, with different solutions.

3 Why an experimentalist approach

In computer science for a long time the habit has been to design a model or a small experiment (for instance based on Fibonacci numbers) to present this model or some results of an experiment and thereafter conclude that a new idea would work far better and consequently emerge on a completely different track. Such an approach has the following disadvantages:

- there is no continuity built up in a certain research direction.

- it becomes almost impossible to compare results obtained from similar research because results are not obtained with similar techniques or under comparable assumptions.

At this moment it can be observed that a number of research groups have left that track and are looking for a more solid basis to evaluate and compare research results.

We found that research in parallel computing is one of these areas demanding for an approach allowing to better compare results obtained at different locations. Now that the field has left the stage where an elegant theoretical model of concurrency or a complicated design of a network switch will convince the scientific community that parallel computing is an attractive solution, the time has come where large implementations based on real parallel hardware have to prove that parallel computing is as promising as was predicted. It then becomes necessary to develop more solid research methodologies, also allowing comparison of results obtained by different groups.

In the course of the project we decided that to be able to do so it is helpful to look at methodologies used in other areas of science like physics. In particular the methodology and the problems that have to be solved in experimental physics such as high energy or low energy physics show a certain similarity. Although experiments in parallel computing do not require a similar preparation time and are running for a shorter period in time than their physics counterparts, there are similarities and one could learn from their methodology of experimentation.

In physics an experiment is performed to test a certain model or a number of hypotheses. For this purpose an experiment is designed. Such an experiment might require a lot of equipment like detectors (including read-out electronics and data acquisition computing) to measure the phenomena of interest. The design of all that equipment on itself often represents a large effort. Consequently the preparation phase of such an experiment might require a number of years and the experiment is often carried out a number of years after it was prepared. Because it can only partly be foreseen whether the choice for equipment was correct, an experiment must possess the flexibility to allow changes in equipment during the time the experiment is running, which often also could be a number of years. During this period data is collected and analysed. The results of this analysis often will demand a modification of the model. Moreover, this could require to test other properties sometimes demanding considerable modification of the experiment or making a new experiment necessary. In all phases of experimentation simulation plays an important role. Simulation can be used to get a better feeling for the essential parameters to test a model, or a design. This can be either a theoretical model, the design of a detector or the behaviour of the essential parameters one wants to test in an experiment.

So what is the resemblance with parallel computing and what can we learn from the example in physics. The advances in parallel computing have come from the progress in the key technologies of e.g. electronics (in particular chip technology) and computer design. In the last field, processor, memory and network switch design have been the most important issues for the actual realization of parallel computers. Nevertheless, as it was already observed, the progress in the field has not been so fast as was expected a number of years ago. In particular it turns out to be difficult to efficiently exploit the processing power present. Partly this is caused by factors in the hardware like an unbalance in the correspondence between processing and memory or processing and the performance of the network switch. The largest problem, however, is the lack of understanding of the role parallelism plays. More specific the mapping of the parallelism from the application onto the parallel hardware demands for far more research. This research encompasses modelling of parallelism as well as experimentation with parallel implementations. In the PRISMA project we have chosen for the experimentation with different implementations of the parallelism as present in a database management system.

We believe that the problems envisaged during these experiments show a certain similarity with those in physics that were discussed and that consequently we could learn from them. During the planning phase of the PRISMA machine it was realized that a large number of design decisions had to be taken for which no clear insentive existed which solution would be the best under the given circumstances. Moreover, we discovered that our ideas of how to solve the problems we were facing, changed during the time we were building up our equipment. For example, when POOL was designed it was believed that the language should not make any difference between data and code objects, and that the users of POOL should have no influence on the allocation of their objects over the processors of the machine. At the beginning of the PRISMA project we realized that these assumptions resulted not only in severe execution speed penalties, but, what was more important, restricted the possibilities to evaluate different implementation decisions. And, last but not least, also the area of data management itself evolved over time. Therefore a modification to the language became necessary and demanded for flexible solutions.

In conclusion, the ideas about modelling parallel database applications as well as implementing them on a parallel object-oriented platform is similar to designing an experimental facility allowing to perform different types of experiments in parallelism. Like in physics such experiments should show continuity and being designed with sufficient flexibility in mind as to allow series of experiments with different parallel implementations. Also like in physics we have to accept that because of the long development time and the fact that experiments can run for a considerable period in time, the hardware will not always be according to the latest state-of-the art in technology. This does not have to be a disadvantage as long as it is, to a reasonable approximation, possible to scale and callibrate the results of the experiments. In this paper we will further concentrate on how such an experiment should be built and what type of extra tools it will require.

4 Design and realization of an experiment

When we are designing an experiment roughly three groups of questions play a predominant role. These are :

- What is the experiment we want to do?

- What do we want to measure?

- How do we build the experiment?

In Table 1 the three main groups are listed.

In the first group we find the type of questions we have to ask to make sure that we are setting up a correct experiment. In particular that we have given sufficient thought towards the aims and scope of the experiment. In Figure 1 the basic cycle of experimentation is presented. When starting to design an experiment one of the basic questions is which model or what set of assumption do we want to test. When we do not have a sufficiently clear idea, simulation studies of the model under test could help us to get a better feeling towards which parameters would play a crucial role in our experiment. In this phase it is important to study results of others to prevent duplication of effort. Also it is essential that we are able to restrict ourselves and define a clear program for the series of experiments that have to be performed.

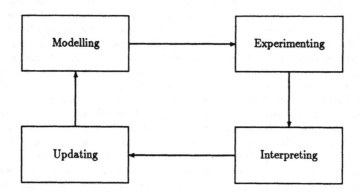

Figure 1: Cycle in experimentation

Design of experimental facility

- What is the experiment I want to do?

  - which model or assumption(s) do we want to test
  - what are results of others
  - where can we do better
  - how can we restrict ourselves

- What do we want to measure?

  - do we measure what we want to
  - what data can we expect
  - what biases do we introduce

- How do we build the experiment?

  - what type of flexibility is necessary
  - what type of tools are required and which are critical
  - which data aquisition chain is required
  - what dataprocessing tools are necessary (visualization)
  - can we build triggers
  - what is the foreseen lifetime

Table 1: Design of experimental facility

In the second group questions related to the actual measurement activities are presented. An important issue there is whether we really measure those parameters which are important for the study of the model under test. And if we know which parameters to measure, the issue is which type of sensors and probes are needed. A question is: are those probes not disturbing the parameters and processes we plan to measure. In that case we are producing data that could contain a lot of biases. To have a better impression of what type of data and what type of biases we could expect we again can use simulation. We can try to simulate the influence our sensor or probe has on the measurement and to find a method to callibrate our measurements for biases we think we will introduce.

In the third group of Table 1 the questions concerning the actual realization of the experiment are listed. Here we have to concentrate on such issues as whether the experiment will run for a large period in time and consequently the type of flexibility that will be required. But also the type of equipment is important. What do we have to develop and what can we buy of the shelf. It has to be stressed here that the more we push technology in our experiment the more we will be obligated to design our own equipment which will result in a longer development time for our total experiment. In almost all types of experiments and specially in computer experiments this device plays a predominant role. This is partly in the read-out and control of an experiment and for the other part in the data processing, data analysis and the visualization of the results. In experiments where the computer is the only equipment of experimentation, such as in parallel computing experiments, the double role of the computer, e.g. as the purpose of the experiment and as an aid in experimentation, has to be realized. This implies that specially during the measurement process additional tools have to be developed (like tracers and profilers) that help us to perform the measurements. However, what is more essential we also have to develop tools that allow the flexibility to do the experiments. In case of experimentation with parallel implementations like in the PRISMA project we had to develop annotations allowing the experimenter to indicate parallelism.

5 Database Experiment

In this section we address the questions "What experiment do we want to perform?", "Which parameters do we need to measure?", and "How do we build the experiment?", related to the database system.

5.1 What experiment do we want to perform?

In this subsection we discuss the assumptions we want to test, compare our approach with others, and indicate how we confined ourselves to set up the experiment.

In very global terms the goal of the PRISMA project was to find out whether the usage of parallelism and main memory as the primary storage medium would increase the performance of a relational database system, and whether this performance would be scalable. This question is of course too general to be tested so we had to be more specific.

The architecture of PRISMA/DB is very traditional, the reason being that simplicity is often the best in a parallel environment. Advances made in centralized environments often do not apply to distributed environments. The only point where we deviated from traditional approaches were the data managers. We choose for data managers that could manipulate only one type of relation, which is a parameter that is given at creation time. These data managers are called One-Fragment Managers (OFM).

PRISMA/DB consists of components such as parsers, (SQL and PRISMAlog), a query optimizer, a transaction manager, a data dictionary, and an OFM. None of these components has parallelism in it. Parallelism is obtained by executing these components on different processors. During execution there might be an arbitrary number of instances of these components depending on the query load, assigned to different processors. This architecture emphasizes medium to coarse grain parallelism.

A database management system as described above can of course be implemented in various programming languages running on top of various hardware configurations. An additional goal of the PRISMA project is to see whether an object-oriented language, to be more specific POOL-X, has the right abstraction level for implementation. POOL-X [3] shields the hardware architecture, a shared-nothing, 100-node multi-processor system, from the database system implementor, including as a matter of fact the main memory aspect. The language provides a way of specifying communication protocols between objects, without having to worry about low level implementation details such as buffering.

The current trend in computer science is to define languages with an increasing abstraction level to make life easier for the application programmer (4 and 5GL). At the same time the burden for the implementor of these languages, to come up with an efficient implementation, is growing. It is our conviction that a separate language is necessary to describe performance knowledge of the application, to make the implementation efficient. Especially, coarse grain parallelism is so inherent to the application that no compiler can ever detect it. Therefore, POOL-X has a language of pragma's to capture performance knowledge of the database management system. We started with pragma's only for allocation directives. But after a first implementation other pragma's were added to indicate that the object is actually a local data structure (see Section 7).

All of these assumptions mentioned above are subject of our experiment, in the sense that we want to find out whether we have taken the right decisions. Some of these decisions can be altered during the project based on experiments, others are so inherent to the project that finding out that they were wrong will lead to new projects with altered assumptions.

As mentioned, comparing computer science research done in different groups is rather difficult. Because there are too many degrees of freedom different groups tend to take different assumptions as their starting point. On very few points there seems to be consensus. Furthermore, there seems to be a tendency to have projects with mixed goals, a functionality goal and a performance goal. Without giving all the references (these can be found in [5]), some of the projects have as functionality goals a standard SQL interface, a logical query language interface, extensibility, etc. while others are restricted to join operators, transaction processing environment, etc. Also the hardware environment might differ enormously, e.g. centralized versus distributed, main memory versus disk based, bus-based network versus point-to-point connections, shared nothing versus shared memory, etc. It is obvious that comparing the performance of systems with different functionality is like comparing apples and pears. Also, the various hardware implementations have different scalability characteristics. Finally, a lot of projects never exit the simulation phase, so one never knows whether the result also holds for real implementations.

The PRISMA project has its own mixture of functionality and performance goals. In spite of the heavy performance goals (we wanted to be significantly faster than other database machines), there were also quite extensive functionality goals: a standard SQL interface to facilitate the support of existing applications and a logic query language interface, called PRISMAlog, to make the support of knowledge-based applications possible. As far as the performance goals are concerned we wanted to take a leap in the number of processors by choosing a 100-node system. Also, because the prediction is that main memory is becoming cheaper, every processor has 16 Mb of memory.

To obtain all the goals set, we of course also had to limit ourselves. Limitations that were given up front were the hardware architecture and the implementation language POOL-X. Other confinements are: choosing a traditional architecture of the database management system, taking simple solutions for some of the functionality aspects, only considering medium to coarse grain parallelism, only considering complex, ad hoc queries, not covering certain topics in detail (e.g. fault tolerance).

5.2   What do we need to measure

In this subsection we look at the parameters to be measured and the consequences of measuring.

If we want to know the overall performance of the database system or if we want to get a better insight in parallel execution of queries we have to determine the relevant parameters. For example, does the amount of communication traffic between objects say anything about the overall performance of the database system. Also, does just running benchmarks and obtaining response time and throughput information give a better insight in parallel execution. The question "which are the right parameters to be measured" is difficult to be answered up front. Seeing the results of one test run, one realizes that other parameters should have been measured to gain better insight. So, the database system and its environment should be set up in such a way that measuring the right parameters should be relatively easy. As in many other projects, also in the PRISMA project this aspect has been underdeveloped. Work in this area will continue after the official termination of the project in October 1990. Another problem is the presentation of the parameters measured. Most of the time one is flooded with data. The presentation problem is addressed in the next subsection.

Based on our current experience we have decided on the following list of parameters to start with: response time of (sub)queries, throughput of the database system, CPU utilization, network utilization, profiler information concerning the activities of objects. Where possible we need a breakdown per database component to get a good idea about the bottle-necks in the system. As mentioned before the parameters may change after the actual testruns.

As with all experiments in physics we have to be well aware of the fact that measuring a system also influences its behaviour. So, there should be a constant validation of results obtained from the measured system.

5.3 Setting up the experiment

In this subsection we look at which parts of the system we want to change and what tools we need to perform the experiment.

Although, many aspects of performance may be a topic for experimenting, here, we focus only on parallelism. Various forms of parallelism are used in the manipulation of the data (queries and updates, including constraint maintenance) and in the handling of queries and updates (parsing, optimization, etc.).

The manipulation of the data can be experimented with by allocating the base OFMs and the intermediate OFMs to different processors or by using different strategies for specific operators, e.g. for the join, or for queries altogether. This experiment can be undertaken by changing the query optimizer such that it produces different strategies or different allocation directives.

The handling of queries can be experimented with by allocating the components of the database management system to different processors, or, maybe, splitting up a component to be able to assign its task to several processors. The latter comes close to changing the architecture of the database management system. This experiment can be done by changing the allocation pragma's of the objects that together constitute the database management system.

6 The POOL experiment

In this section we address the questions "What experiment do we want to perform", "Which parameters do we need to measure?" and "How do we build the experiment?" related to the POOL approach. Note that POOL-X can be viewed as a tool towards the PRISMA/DB and the PRISMA/DB as one major application towards POOL-X, therefore there is a strong correlation between experimental aspects concerning the POOL language.

6.1 What experiment do we want to perform?

The main intention of the POOL language is to offer the application programmer a flexible, clear, powerful and safe programming model for parallel application. Flexible in the sense that the programmer must be able to write a large variety of parallel programs, ranging from small to large, from dynamic to static, and from medium to coarse grain. Also a clear model is chosen: the object-oriented approach. Each object protects itself by running its own sequential program. The interaction between objects is realized via message-passing using explicit communication. The approach is made powerful by removing as much resource management from the programmer as possible, so for instance the programmer is not bothered by allocation/deallocation of messages and deallocation of redundant objects. Finally the language offers optimal safety by using a strong typing mechanism. By writing several POOL applications, amongst others DBMS, we want to validate the before mentioned claims on the expressiveness of the POOL language.

Of course the implementation of such a powerful language is not trivial. Therefore we also want to investigate whether the implementation can be made sufficiently fast to compete with other (parallel) languages. Because the performance of several features in the language, such as communication, is very difficult to estimate on beforehand, and also because we wanted to have a real parallel environment for experimentation, we decided not to use simulations, but to build and implement an object-oriented platform, consisting of compiler, operating system and hardware. When starting the implementation the "typical behaviour" of POOL programs was not known. Therefore a mainly software-oriented approach was chosen. Only for the communication special hardware was proposed, since this was expected to be crucial for performance. Furthermore we made a choice to use a distributed tightly coupled hardware platform, since this was expected to best fit the execution model of POOL and is also preferable because of extensibility, scalability and modularity. This complies with the choice already made in the DOOM project. From measurements we hope to derive guide-lines for hardware support in possible second generation systems. For flexibility we chose to implement the operating system fully by ourselves directly on the bare hardware, other reasons were the expected inefficiency of general purpose operating systems and less implementation effort. For similar reasons we also chose to implement the compiler fully by ourselves.

Note that there is a potential conflict between the goal for expressiveness and the goal for efficiency of the implementation.

During the design of the system we have imposed several restrictions on ourselves. First we concentrated on the execution of a single POOL program at a time. Furthermore limited effort was put into fault tolerance. Only error detection is supported for communication, using checksums and sequence numbering. In order for the DBMS to recover after a crash a stable storage facility was offered.

6.2 What do we need to measure?

The expressiveness of the POOL language is not measurable in an ordinary sense. This aspect can only be "evaluated" by writing several applications and interact with the programmer to get some insight into his experiences.

The performance measurement of the POOL approach as a whole can only be done by running several applications on top of the object-oriented platform and derive figures from the behaviour of the applications. These figures can be used to modify the compiler and/or operating system.

Some components of the object-oriented platform deserve special attention, since these are expected to be bottle-necks and/or potential candidates for hardware support. The most important components are :

1. Scheduling

2. Memory management

3. Communication

4. Garbage collection

5. Object allocation

6. Tuple manipulation (only DBMS)

7. I/O system

The garbage collector takes care of removal of redundant objects. The I/O system allows interaction with the disks attached to the machine and some host systems connected via ethernet, it also supports the stable storage.

Note that speed up should be measured from application level, not from the object-oriented platform, since the application is primarily responsible for a proper parallelization of his algorithm. However, the object-oriented platform should give support in two ways. First it should offer some tools to measure the speed up and secondly it should give some characteristics of the implementation (for instance ratio communication/processing speed, communication delay) in order to let the programmer tune its application. But it is not directly clear which characteristics should be provided and this might also depend on the application. A similar difficulty is to relate figures measured in the object-oriented platform to a POOL program.

To provide characteristics of the object-oriented platform, appeared to be a difficult task. Therefore a study was done, to get some insight on how this should be done as input for future systems.

6.3 Setting up the experiment

As already mentioned in Section 1, we chose to follow the DOOM approach at the hardware level. For experimentation the Communication Processor (CP) hardware offers two programmable features. First by installing routing tables, one can select different networks and also exploit dynamic or static routing. Second the ratio of buffers for packets from the node the CP is attached to and packets on the way can be varied.

By fully implementing the operating system and compiler ourselves we also allowed a large degree of experimentation. To measure the performance of the components mentioned in Section 6.2 either a profiler can be used and/or some specific counters/time measurements can be incorporated into the components.

7 Tools for experimentation

In this section we will discuss some of the tools we need to perform the above experiments. First of all, we need the pragma's to explicitly control the parallelism. Furthermore, we need tools to automatically perform testruns with benchmarks and profilers and performance monitors to produce the required data. And, finally, we need presentation tools to present the parameters measured at the right abstraction level. Sometimes, one wants detailed information, and sometimes just global information. Besides this, simulation tools are required to justify design decisions that have far-reaching consequences for the overall architecture.

As was mentioned we consider annotations as additions to the original language, but also as handles to allow us to experiment with different implementations. An annotated program should also run on a sequential implementation of the language. So, in contrast to the additions to other imperative languages to obtain parallelism (e.g. message passing primitives), annotations do not change the result of the computation and can be considered as a kind of comments made by the programmer, that will be passed to the lower levels of the system, where they may be used to generate or speed up parallel execution. Such annotations are said to be transparent.

Apart from the syntactical differences, we can distinguish at least three different levels where parallelism can be annotated [7]:

- At the first level one is concerned with annotating possible parallel computations. These are the most fundamental annotations where the programmer expresses his expectation that a computation may be executed as a concurrent task.

- The second level is where the programmer ensures that parallel computations have a sufficiently coarse grain size. Especially in recursive programs one may start off with coarse grain parallel tasks, but during the recursion the grain size continuously decreases and has to be stopped somehow to prevent the architecture to be flooded with fine grain tasks.

- The third level is concerned with allocation of tasks and loadbalancing. Apart from generating a number of coarse grain parallel tasks by annotations of level 1 and 2, the programmer may know a clever way to distribute those tasks efficiently on the parallel architecture in question. These allocation annotations may be dependent on physical characteristics of the underlying architecture.

Apart form the annotations concerning parallelism it appeared necessary for POOL to include annotations that increase the efficiency of compiled sequential code. In many cases a special behaviour of an object can be annotated such that the compiler can avoid the overhead that is incurred for full blown objects.

As performance handles towards the application level, two facilities are offered, monitoring and profiling:

- The monitor gives a first glimpse of the performance of the system by displaying the CPU, communication and memory occupation of each node in a graphical way during execution of the program.

- Two profilers are supported, the first one measures the system in a usual way, based on function like calls, the second one extends this scheme to the object level.

When using a profiler it is important that the user is able to select that data that is useful for the type of study he is performing. For that reason the profiler consist of a tool collecting all raw data and putting it into a file, as well as some extra facilities that allows the user to wrap around in that part of the data he is interested in. The presentation tools of the profiler allow the user to make among others histograms and present them on any type of terminal.

Some preliminary work has been done on performance modelling of the PRISMA machine. It uses information of the structure of POOL-X programs mapping it on tasks models, with as characteristic input the amount of work and the amount of communication involved in tasks. The parameters for these models will be obtained from the real POOL-X programs, using a trace tool collecting this information.

8   Experience and Status

In this section a short description of the status of the project will be given. In addition some of the experience with PRISMA/DB and POOL-X will be presented.

8.1   PRISMA/DB

Determining the functional specification of PRISMA/DB was harder than expected. There were many design decisions to be taken regarding topics on which there is very little consensus. Not all design decisions can be accounted for. Some were taken in the implementation phase. Looking back there was a constant struggle between functionality requirements and performance requirements. Many design decisions were discussed in a qualitative sense, too few decisions were actually validated by simulation. But we gained a lot of experience in building DB0 and were able to correct some of our mistakes in building DB1.

Building DB1 took a little more than 2 man years. It comprises 40,000 lines of POOL-X code. Most of the tools to perform the experiments are implemented. So, we now enter the experimentation phase. First testruns show that execution on one processor is well within the range of an implementation language like C, except for occasional interrupts of the garbage collector.

8.2   POOL-X

Already in a very early stage of the DOOM project it was recognized that the compiler/operating system was unable to automatically allocate objects over the system in a optimal way. Therefore pragmas were added to the object-oriented platform, to let the programmer explicitly control the allocation. But after the first implementation, the performance of the system was still poor. This was due to the fact that the compiler was unable to optimize on local communication to simple record like objects. Instead of direct access the more expensive communication primitives were used. As a consequence another type of pragma's was introduced to specify some simplified object behaviour types.

Currently the implementation with this new pragma's is finished. Some preliminary measurements show promising results on the performance. More measurements are necessary, however, which might lead to adjustments in the compiler/operating system. To begin with we will use the general profiler, before adding specific facilities to the components. The monitor and first profiler are operational.

In conclusion we can say that during the PRISMA project the emphasis more and more shifted towards the methodology aspects of the project.

References

[1] T. Moto-Oka et al., *Challenge for Knowledge Information Processing*, Fifth Generation Computer Systems, JIPDEC, 1982, pp. 3-92, North Holland.

[2] E.A.M. Odijk, *The DOOM system and its applications: a survey of ESPRIT 415 subproject at Philips Research Laboratories*, in PARLE Eindhoven 1987 part I, LNCS 258, pp 461-479.

[3] P. America, *POOL-T - A parallel object-oriented language*, In: Akinori Yonezawa, Mario Tokoro (eds.): Object-Oriented Concurrent Programming, MIT Press, 1987, pp. 199-220, 1987.

[4] W. Bronnenberg, L. Nijman, E. Odijk, R. v. Twist, *DOOM: A Decentralized Object-Oriented Machine*, IEEE Micro, October 1987.

[5] P.G.M. Apers, L.O. Hertzberger, B.J.A. Hulshof, A.C.M. Oerlemans, M.L. Kersten, *PRISMA: a platform for experiments with parallelism*, to be published.

[6] J.K. Annot and R.A.H. van Twist, *A novel deadlock and starvation free package switching communication processor*, in PARLE 1987, pp 68-85.

[7] L.O. Hertzberger and W.G. Vree, *Mapping explicit parallelism onto distributed memory architectures*, To be published, Workshop on Parallel Processing, February 7-9 1990, Bombay, India.

Back-end Aspects of a Portable POOL-X implementation

Marcel Beemster
Faculty of Mathematics and Computer Science
University of Amsterdam, the Netherlands
beemster@fwi.uva.nl

Abstract

The paper discusses an implementation of POOL-X that aims to be all of available, reliable, portable, modifiable and efficient. This implementation consists of both compiler and run-time-support system. In order to attain the stated goals, the system is kept as simple as possible. Design trade-offs are be discussed, and the final system is evaluated.

1 Introduction

This paper discusses the portable implementation of the parallel object-oriented language called POOL-X [3] on the 100-node PRISMA machine. The tension is described that exists in making an implementation of the programming language POOL-X that is all of available, reliable, portable, modifiable and efficient. An implementation of POOL-X consists of both a compiler and an extensive run-time-support system. In Section 2 an overview is given of the whole language implementation system.

The research is conducted in the context of the PRISMA project, and this is where the demands on the implementation, from availability to efficiency, come from. In Section 3, on the goals of the implementation, these demands will be further discussed.

The first and most important decision taken in the implementation described here, was to compile POOL-X to sequential C-code. This was only done after the techniques described in Section 4 were developed, and it was shown that these techniques incurred no great execution overhead. In Section 5 the language will be looked upon from the viewpoint of a language implementer. Of a number of interesting language constructs implementation alternatives will be discussed.

Sections 6.1, 6.2, 6.3, 6.4, 6.5 concentrate on important and influential implementation issues, as addressing an object in a parallel machine, garbage collection and off-node communication. The abovementioned goals of the implementation are evaluated in Section 7.

This paper not only discusses the Portable Implementation as such. It is also comments on the software engineering aspects of the implementation of a system of this size. And also in some cases the circumstances under which the implementation was made will be described, referring to the complex interplay between language design, language implementation and language use. Where possible, a comparison is made with the other implementation of POOL-X, the Natlab Implementation. From this it will be clear that different goals lead to entirely different solutions for the same problems.

2 Implementation Overview

The POOL-X implementation described in this paper is called the Portable Implementation, also known as PPMX or POOL±X. The Portable Implementation is not an exact implementation of the language definition, due to both technical and non-technical arguments. The author believes the differences have only minor effects for the users of POOL-X, so they will not be a major topic in this paper.

Any implementation of POOL-X will roughly consist of two parts, a compiler and a run-time-support system. The run-time-support system consists of both passive libraries and active components. The passive libraries contain functions for string handling and array manipulation and so on. These are used at the POOL-X programmer's specification.

The active components are much less visible from the language's surface. These are components like the garbage collector and the synchronization detector. They are vital for the actual implementation of POOL-X. And this is an important point where POOL-X differs from a language such as C that requires no active components at all.

In the Portable Implementation compiler and run-time-support system are closely integrated. It is often possible to move pieces of implementation from compiler to run-time-support or the other way round, and this was often done. There is no sharp interface between the two. The reason for this close integration is most likely that the Portable Implementation was designed and largely implemented by a single person. This allows great flexibility.

This is not to say that the Portable Implementation is a mess. The portable part of the Portable Implementation consists of some 57000 lines of C-code, by no measure a small system. This, together with the fact that the system works is proof that it reasonably well structured. For more proof, see the section on reliability, 7.2.

The Portable Implementation had two important predecessors, the POOL-X interpreter, from which the front-end was taken, and the sequential portable POOL-X compiler, from which the compilation strategy and the standard Classes were taken, although both of these have been substantially rewritten. Yet the major effort in the development of the Portable Implementation was the development of the parallel pieces of run-time-support, and the addition of the atomic data pragmas.

2.1 The compiler

The compiler of the Portable Implementation consists of three parts. The first part is the the so-called front-end. It was originally written and used for the POOL-X interpreter, a predecessor of the current systems. It performs all syntax and context dependent checks, and does type-checking. Its output is a highly orthogonal and canonical representation of the translated POOL-X Unit.

The orthogonal representation is then read by the so-called code-generator. It compiles the POOL-X program into C. Unlike the front-end, the code-generator was especially written for the portable implementation.

The third step is compilation of the generated C-code into machine language. Of course, a standard C-compiler is used for this step. It is this what makes the Implementation portable.

2.2 The run-time-support system

The passive parts of the run-time-support system are the standard Classes. They are used when the programmer uses them in the POOL-X program. Only the Classes that make up the I/O system are less passive. This is because the I/O system must take care of routing the I/O throughout the network of nodes.

The active parts of the run-time-support are centralized around the scheduler. The scheduler performs polling on the active parts in order to let them run.

2.3 The Natlab Implementation

The Natlab Implementation was made by the POOL-X implementation team of Philips Research Laboratories in Eindhoven. It is also described in this proceedings. From the beginning, speed of execution of the compiled POOL-X program has been the goal of this implementation. All other factors, mentioned in the next section were of secondary importance.

The Natlab Implementation is a much less integrated and compact system than the Portable Implementation. The active parts of the run-time-support system are taken apart of the rest of the system and form the so called Operating System. It has a well defined, POOL specific interface to the rest of the implementation. Whereas the Portable Implementation is uniformly implemented in one language, the Natlab system uses no less then five: Modula-2, extended POOL-X, dialects of Elegant, C, and IPXC.

Whenever possible, comments will be made on the implementation choices in the Natlab Implementation as well as the Portable Implementation. It will be clear that speed has always been the design motive for the Natlab Implementation, where in the Portable Implementation often simplicity was valued higher.

3 Goals in the Portable Implementation

The goals on the Portable Implementation of POOL-X were, in order of importance, availability, reliability, portability, modifiability and efficiency.

Availability The first and most important aspect of a language implementation is its availability. The PRISMA project is divided into separate sub-tasks that are assigned to the project partners. As in the case of all useful parallelism these tasks are not independent. In this particular case, there is the database implementation group that could independently start thinking about parallelism in the relational DBMS. But at a certain point in the project this group had to start implementing their ideas. At that very moment, an implementation of POOL-X had to be available.

Reliability In computer science, nothing is worse than a tool that cannot be trusted. For a computer scientist, errors that are made, discovered, found and corrected, are a fact of life. The most time-consuming step in the life-cycle of a *bug* is finding it. This pin-pointing of the source of a bug is a search process. The search space in which the POOL-X programmer, the user of the compiler, has to look should be as small as possible. When the POOL-X programmer knows that the problem is in the POOL-X program, he or she will not give up looking. On the other hand when the POOL-X programmer suspects that the bug might be introduced by the compiler, he or she will quit debugging much earlier. The language implementation has to be reliable enough for the programmer to be trusted.

Portability The PRISMA project aims at the parallel implementation of a relational database. This implies POOL-X must run on parallel hardware. But because this hardware is also being developed inside the project we cannot assume that it is available at all times for the database-developers. Hence, the implementation should not only run on this hardware to be developed, but also on developer's workstations.

In addition, the system should survive future upgrades to new hardware.

Modifiability In a project such as PRISMA nothing is fixed. The hardware can change, the language can change—POOL-X has gone through many formal and informal revisions—and the expected and actual use of the language may differ considerably. The language implementation acts as the glue between all these different pieces of project. As such, it is so important that a little consideration from these three "users" of the glue might be expected. From the hardware, this has been the case. Within the first half-year the target processor was decided upon.

But between the compiler, the language design, and the POOL-X programmers, a complicated interaction has existed. Programmers demanded more language features and higher speed, the language design had to stay clean enough to remain understandable and yet provide the demanded support, and the compiler implementation demanded that changes to the language could be integrated into the system.

The most recent changes to the language were due to the introduction to the atomic data pragmas in 1989. The final specification was not finished before 1990. In the summer of 1989 it was clear that the expected performance of POOL-X programs compiled with the Natlab implementation would be much worse than comparable C programs. In order to improve this situations, the atomic data pragmas were developed. These allow the compiler to make use of a much more efficient implementation model for annotated Classes, but at a considerable increase in program design effort.

Efficiency Some would claim that efficiency, or speed of execution, should be the goal to be haunted by the language implementation. Especially in the (originally) performance oriented PRISMA project. But in this list of five demands, efficiency necessarily comes last. Without all of the previous four being satisfied, it would not be useful to have a language implementation at all.

But it is not to say efficiency should be ignored. Efficiency falls apart into several pieces: Absolute speed of the compiled program, memory utilization, compile efficiency, and relative performance of language constructs.

Besides absolute speed of the program, memory utilization is of importance. Other than is the case for C, there is no direct relation between a certain language construct and its memory usage. POOL-X is too abstract a language for this, and leaves a lot of room for implementation choices.

Efficiency should also be achieved in the implementation of the compiler itself. A POOL-X program should compile withing reasonable time.

But as important as absolute speed of language constructs is their relative speed. There has to be a balance between the implementation characteristics of the elements that make up the language. In POOL-X there is often more than one choice of implementing a certain algorithm. The language provides a multitude of partially and completely overlapping primitives, differing in, for example, generality towards extension to parallelism.

In order for the POOL-X programmers to make the correct choice of primitives to use, they must either know all about the efficiency of all primitives, or *the POOL-X programmers must be offered a set of primitives that provides no surprises on the point of efficiency.* Only in the second case, a choice can be made purely based on functionality (or taste).

Some of the demands on the language implementation are conflicting, especially in the case of efficiency and the rest. The solution lies in adopting a method that is best described as:

"The RISC approach to software development"

Although the RISC-principle, see [7], is a design technique for microprocessors, which is hardware, its ideas can be very well applied on software development. It all boils down to the rule: Keep it simple until analysis shows that complexity really pays off. And this is what is done for the implementation of a portable POOL-X compiler. Strive for the simplest of implementations for POOL-X, and then see what needs to be fixed.

4 Basic Technology, Concurrency in C

This section describes how concurrency is implemented in portable C, in a reasonably efficient manner. With efficiency taken care of, it is easy to see that compilation to C offers enormous advantages concerning the other four demands posed on the implementation.

When an object, or process in more familiar terms, is scheduled out, its state must be saved in such a way that it can be restarted. State consists of two parts, the data and the program counter. The data of an object consists—among other things—of the instance and local variables. It is not possible to allocate any of this data on the C-stack. This is because the C-stack cannot be manipulated as an *thing* in C. It is not possible to change the stack-state of a C program into another stack-state in a fully portable manner. Of course, with machine specific extensions—probably written in assembler—it would be possible, but that is what portability is trying to avoid.

So, if data cannot be left on the C-stack it must be located on the heap, the dynamically allocatable memory. An object is a data-structure allocated on the heap. Associated with an object is a stack, which is also allocated on the heap.

The second problem is the program counter associated with an object. When an object does a send, its program counter should be recorded in such a way that the object continues its action at the right place when the reply arrives. In C, the program counter is also not manipulatable as a *thing*. Fortunately function addresses can be moved around as values in a C-program. This solves part of the problem, the problem of globally indicating what the program counter is. Now in addition, the specific place within a function must be indicated. This is done by means of a number that is used as a switch label inside the function.

As a result, the representation of a program counter consist of two values, the function address and the local switch statement label. This solves the basic problems of concurrency in C. The following describes the basic schema of how the Portable Implementation operates.

4.1 The object

Assume two data-structures for the process-object and its stack. There are many kinds of object-records in the Portable Implementation. The one described here is for user defined POOL-X objects. Other kinds are for Arrays, Strings, I/O objects and so on. The object-record described here holds the data such as instance variables and message queue of the object. In addition there are fields that are needed for the run-time-support system. It looks like:

```
struct object {
    int             typ ;          /* Generic header */
    struct object   *alllink ;     /* Generic header */
    int             offloc ;
    struct ptype    *pooltype ;
    struct object   *rque ;
    struct frame    *stack ;
    int             *answset ;
    struct frame    *head, *tail ;
    int             ivarlen ;
/*int               ivar[n] ;*/
}
```

The first field in the object's record is an identification field. At run-time, it will be instantiated with a value that identifies this object as a real user-defined POOL-X object. This field and the next one is shared by all data-structures for all kinds of objects. It is used by the garbage collector. The second field links all objects together such that the garbage collector can find them.

The offloc field holds the off-node identification number of the object. Normally, an object does not have an off-node identification. Its reference is only known within the node. But at the moment the reference to the object is sent outside, it gets assigned a slot in the off-node reference table. The reference outside the node is a concatenation of the node number and the index into the off-node reference table. When the object's reference is no longer known outside the node—the garbage collector detects this—its slot in the table is freeed. The offloc field is shared by all object data-structures that can have a reference from outside the node. Value data-structures do not have an offloc field.

Other fields in the object-record hold the message queue, the answer set and a reference to the object's stack. The pooltype field holds a reference to an object that represents the type of the object. It is used in dynamic type expressions. The rque is used in the linked list that is the ready queue of the current node.

The ivarlen holds an integer that tells the garbage collector how many instance variables the object has. It is used by the garbage collector to know how many references to scan. The amount of instance variables determines the final size of the object's record. The ivar array is not really a part of the C-structure. It indicates that the instance variable-store directly follows the object-record in heap memory in an actually allocated object.

4.2 The stack

The stack of a process-object is a data-structure consisting of a number of linked stack-*frames*. For each invocated procedure, which can be a body, method or routine, there is one stack-frame. It hold run-time-support data and also parameters, local variables and expression stack of the procedure. It looks like:

```
struct stackframe {
  int flags ;
  struct stackframe *next ;
  func funaddr ;
  int local_pc ;
  struct ptype *pooltype ;
  int methnum ;
  struct object *sender ;
  int retoff ;
/*int parlocexp[0] ; */
}
```

The stackframe is no object, so its initial word does not have to be an identification. Nevertheless the first word in the structure contains some flags that identify the state of the frame. It can be either a body, method, routine or special type of frame. The special frames have no corresponding language construct, they are used to implement concurrency in the I/O system. Also a method frame can still be in rendez-vous, or in asynchronous mode.

The next field identifies the next frame deeper in the stack. The last frame in this list is always the body-frame. The object's reference to the stack is always the top-of-stack frame, the last activated procedure.

The two next items form the program counter. Funaddr holds the address of the C-function of the current procedure, local_pc the switch-index. It is important to note that these values are only updated when the frame is suspended in some way, by procedure calling or descheduling.

The pooltype field is valid only if the current procedure is a routine. Because a routine is executed on behalf of the current object but can be of some other Class, it can have a different type-context than the current object. A routine must bring its own type with it.

The methnum field is only used in the message passing protocol. It hold the index number of the method in the answer set of the Class. The sender field holds the reference to sender of the current method while the method is in rendez-vous. If the current procedure is no method, the field is unused. When the method sends its reply, the sender reference is used to find out where the reply value must go to.

The retoff field is used for two purposes at once. Basically it holds the return address for a value that comes back from a procedure call, this can be a routine or method call, or a synchronous send. When the called procedure returns, or replies, its result value is placed at the position in the stack-frame that the retoff field points to. This is always in the expression stack-part of this stack-frame.

Its second purpose is as a marker for the garbage collector. The garbage collector scans through the, variable sized, parlocexp array until, and including, the word pointed to by the retoff field. The parlocexp array is a variable length array of words at the end of the frame record. Its configuration is determined by the current procedure. Its lower addresses, [0..p-1], holds the parameters of the current procedure invocation. Inside a body, where there are no parameters, p is simply zero. The range [p..p+1-1] holds the local variables of the procedure. And the range [p+1..p+1+e-1] is used for the expression stack. Since the garbage collector scans through the parlocexp array from reference zero until the retoff indicated word in the expression stack, it scans the parameters, the local variables and a part of the expression stack.

The expression stack is used for the evaluation of nested expressions. Consider the POOL-X expression s!m1(p1, r!m2(p2, p3)). It send a message to object s with method m1 and two parameters. The first one simply p1, the second one is the result of a nested send. At the moment that the send to r will be done, the evaluation stack contains:

$$e[0]:s, \quad e[1]:p1, \quad e[2]:r, \quad e[3]:p2, \quad e[4]:p3, \quad e[5]:?, \quad \ldots$$

The send to r will be done by passing the address of e[2] to the run-time-support send-function. It knows that the address points to the destination object, and subsequent addresses the parameters. In order for the evaluation stack to have the correct configuration for the send to s, the reply value of this send must arrive at position e[2] in the stack. This is accomplished by letting the retoff field point to e[2], at the moment of sending and consequent descheduling.

The result is, that when the garbage collector scans this frame while it is descheduled, it will scan the evaluation stack up to and including e[2], and that is exactly what is needed. The e[0] and e[1] words contain valid data that is to be used in subsequent action by the frame, this data must be scanned. After the rendez-vous e[2] contains the result of the action. And this result must be scanned because it will be used in future. And that is precisely what is not done with the values in e[3] and higher up. The parameters are already send to somewhere else, and will be kept alive there. There is no use for them in the current frame.

The nice thing about the retoff field is that with a minimum of administrative overhead both the return address and the minimum upper address for the garbage collector is maintained.

4.3 The scheduler

With the information on the general format of the object and stack-frame records, it is now time to examine the scheduler-code:

```
while( 1 ) {
  poll() ;
  pxcobj = headq() ;
  if( pxcobj != NULL ) {
    pxframe = pxcobj->frame ;
    do {
      (*pxframe->funaddr)() ; /* Call object's function */
    } while( pxstopper == SCHCONT ) ;
  } else {
    /* Termination detector for parallel machine */
  }
}
```

And that is basically the code for the scheduler in the Portable Implementation. It actually includes an optimization in the inner loop. It uses three global variables, pxcobj to hold the pointer to the currently active object. Pxframe contains the pointer to the top stack-frame of the object. And pxstopper contains a return status for the scheduler.

The scheduler's code is two nested loops. The outer loop is an endless loop. It terminates when the termination detector does an exit() call, in the else-branch of the if. The first that happens in the outer loop is a call to a polling function. It checks on the status of the garbage collector, the in-coming I/O channels, and in a parallel implementation on the in-coming network channels.

The first thing to do next is take the first object from the scheduling queue. The if checks whether there is an object. NULL signals that the queue was empty. This is the easy case. The branch then jumps to the else. In a single node implementation an empty scheduling queue means that no more objects want to run. And consequently that the execution run is finished. Exit() is called, and the run stops. In a parallel environment, an empty queue means just that there is no more work to do on *this* node. But objects on other nodes that are still running may send messages—meaning work—to this node. So at this point the complex process of termination detection begins, see Section 6.4.

When the scheduling queue was not empty—the normal case—the object must be activated. Before starting the object, the environment is set to the correct state. It consist of the two global variables pxcobj, meaning current object of POOL-X, and pxframe, for current stack-frame of that object.

With the environment set, the inner loop is entered. The inner loop is an optimization that is not really necessary. It is also used to give some more control over the scheduling order. What is does is to allow *underwater scheduling*, scheduling without the top-scheduler—the one discussed now—being aware of it. Suppose a synchronous send is executed by an object. Then the logical thing to do is directly transfer control to the destination object, in such a way that it can handle the message immediately. Then the running of the destination object does not have to wait for countless other objects that come first in the scheduling queue. And this is what *underwater scheduling* does. It just changes the global variables for current object and frame, sets the pxstopper variable to SCHCONT, and tells the currently running object to return to the scheduler. The inner loop of the scheduler detects a SCHCONT and jumps to the function of the *newly* installed frame.

Although *underwater scheduling* is an optimization, and could have been left out, it provides faster scheduling and a more natural scheduling policy than would otherwise be the case. So at this point some simplicity in the implementation is sacrificed.

A normal scheduling action is slightly simpler. For example, an object does an answer and detects that there are no more messages directed to it. It then returns to the scheduler after setting pxstopper to SCHWAIT. The scheduler will then fall back to its outer loop and try the next object in the scheduling queue.

And now the code for the framework of the procedures that are called when the scheduler does its (*pxframe->funaddr)() call. This typically looks like:

```
struct s_Tping_Pong_batje {
  struct pxfrax f ;
  int          s[2] ;
} ;

m_Tping_Pong_batje()
{
  struct os_Ping_Pong *co = (struct os_Ping_Pong *)pxcobj ;
  struct s_Tping_Pong_batje *t =
                    (struct s_Tping_Pong_batje *)pxfrax ;

  switch( t->f.local_pc ) {
    case 0:
      /* some code */
    case 1:
      t->s[0] = co->v[2] ;       /* Put instance variable v[2] on
                                    expression stack */
      if( pxnsend( im_Tping_Ping_batje, &t->s[0] ) ) {
        t->f.local_pc = 3 ; return( 1 ) ;
      }
    case 3:
      /* more code */
    default:
      panic( "Scheduling error\n" ) ;
  }
}
```

The example code is for a method batje inside a Class Pong within a Unit of the name Tping. This information is concatenated into the name of the method. Every procedure has its own layout of local variables, parameters and expression stack. So before the procedure's code, a definition of its frame is given. It includes the generic frame definition pxfrax, and additionally declares space for a two element expression stack. There are no parameters or local variables in this particular method. There is a similar definition for the record of the object, with the name struct os_Tping_Pong.

When entered, the first thing to do is putting the current object and frame into local variables. This requires some type-casting. Local variables are usually faster to access in C.

The second thing to do is jump to the correct local_pc. It is taken from the current frame, and then used for the switch. When a frame is first installed, the local_pc is always set to zero.

In the translated POOL-X code, C-procedures of process-objects can have only two return values, zero and one. When a procedure returns zero, it means that it has been able to do its task without any scheduling. This is for example what happens often in the library procedures for I/O. The I/O call can be directly executed without scheduling and returns zero. The caller can continue its execution.

A return value of one means that a scheduling action is taking place. The current procedure should immediately save its state and return to the scheduler—or its caller—with a return value of one. And this is what is shown in the code for doing a send operation. In the example, the actual send is embedded in a the test for scheduling. With a return value of zero, the code just continues after the case 3:, there are no breaks in between the case-statements. With a return value of one, the code inside the if is taken. It has to save the state of the current object, data and program counter. As mentioned, all data is stored in the object and stack-frame records on the heap. No special precautions are needed for these, they stay where they are. Of the two parts of the program counter, the function address pointer is already in the stack-frame, after all that was used by the scheduler to get to this function in the first place. Only the local switch value has to be updated. And that is what happens, it is set to the next case where execution has to be continued after the synchronous send has finished. Then the current function has to continue the scheduling operation to the next function higher-up by passing on the return value of one.

4.4 On-node message passing

This section discusses the handling of messages that are send from one process-object to another. It will only discuss the single-node case where sender and receiver are allocated on the same node.

Consider an object that sends a synchronous message—the asynchronous case is a straightforward extension—to another object. The sender takes care of placing the parameters and the destination in an array, and passes that array together with a method-identification to the run-time-support function pxsend(). The first entry in the array is the reference to the destination object. The rest are the parameters, and from the method-identification the run-time-support knows how many there are.

At this point the run-time-support checks on the destination object-handle. First to see if it is NIL, in that case an error is generated. Then to see if it is allocated on the current node. We assume that it is.

Then in the sending object the retoff fields is set to point to the correct entry in the sender stackframe where the return value is to be stored.

The run-time-support now creates a stack-frame for the method that is to be executed. It can do that with all the information it finds in the method-identification. Number of parameters, number of local variables and length of the expression stack. The parameters are copied from the array into the parameter area of the stack-frame, and the local variable stack is cleared to contain only NIL values—the initial value of any unused variable in POOL-X. The expression stack is not explicitly cleared, but left as the memory was allocated. The retoff field of the stack-frame is set to point to the last parameter, the garbage collector needs not look beyond that for references.

After this the other fields of the stack-frame are initialized; the sender fields is set to point to the sending object, the flags are initialized to tell that this is a method's stack-frame. From the method-identification the method's function is determined and put into the funaddr field. The local_pc is set to zero, its initial value.

And at this point the stack-frame is ready to run. Now the question is whether the destination object is ready to actually answer the method. For this to be the case it must be stopped in an answer state and have the correct set of methods to be answered.

In case the object is ready to answer the method, the run-time-support can link the stack-frame in the stack of the object and perform the *underwater scheduling* act. The pxsend returns 1 to the original sending object to signal that it must deschedule itself, and the scheduler will start the destination object with running the newly created stack-frame.

In the case the destination object is not ready to answer the method, the stack-frame becomes a suspended message. It is linked into the message queue of the object. The methnum field is filled with a method index—a bit-number in the answer set. When the destination object does an answer somewhere in the future it will scan the message queue for a stack-frame with a method index that fits the answer set. When it finds one—which will usually be immediately with an answer ALL—it can load the stack-frame onto the stack, and jump to it.

This implementation of using a stack-frame both for the stack and the message was developed after an idea coined by Carel van der Berg and Martin Kersten in the autumn of 1988.

5 POOL-X Through a Language Implementer's Glasses

POOL-X is an object-oriented language and offers many of the advantages that are attributed to object-oriented languages, see for example [12]. But it also has many other features that in combination make the language rather unique and a challenge to implement. In this section a number of these is discussed. Also described are the implementation choices that are available, and which one is used in the Portable Implementation.

5.1 Message passing

In Section 4 it is already described how the basic message passing mechanism operates. But it does not tell why it exactly looks like that. Here a number of variations on the basic synchronous send mechanism are described that must also be handled. The reader can straightforwardly check that the mechanism does indeed do so.

The basic message passing mechanism is the synchronous send. One object **sends** to another that **answers** the message. At that point the objects are said to be in rendez-vous. After executing the method, the receiver **replies** the return value and both objects can continue concurrently.

A POOL object is a process that runs completely independent of other objects until it expresses the desire to communicate with other objects. It does so with either the **answer** or **send** primitive. With an **answer**, the object signals that it is ready to accept messages that are **sent** by other objects. The receiving object cannot discriminate between different senders of messages. On the other hand, the sender does pinpoint the exact destination of its message. The communication pattern is thus many-to-one.

The **answer** primitive accepts exactly one message that is sent to the object. When there is no message for the object, it stops executing until a message comes along. At answering the message, the parameters in the message are transferred to be the parameters of a specific method that is also designated by the message. This method is than executed by the receiving object. At the sender side, much less is going on. The sending object stops execution after sending the message until it gets a reply back from the destination object. The reply is sent back by the receiving object when the method finishes and the receiver continues after the **answer** code. From the moment that the receiver starts answering the message until the reply is sent back, we say that the objects are—in ADA terminology—in rendez-vous.

But POOL-X is not as simple as this. There are many complications that make the message passing mechanism expensive to implement:

- The **answer** can provide a mask to select between different methods to answer. It can say that some messages that are designated to particular methods should remain queued. This is needed to be able to express a semaphore-like object elegantly. The semaphore object can specify that it first wants to answer a V method before it can let any P message-sending objects continue.

- The language features a **conditional answer**. It is a variant of the normal answer that does not stop the object when there are no messages to answer. In this way, polling of the message queue is achieved.

- Message passing does not always have to be synchronously. With the **asynchronous send** sending object can continue right away when it has send its message. No rendez-vous status is reached, and no reply is sent back at the end of the method. This is very useful for certain algorithms, because a less strict communication pattern can be used.

  The POOL-X definition places no restriction on the size of the buffer for non-answered asynchronous messages. A sending object can send as many asynchronous messages as it wants, until memory runs out.

- The method that answers the message can do an **early reply**. While in the middle of the method, the reply message can be returned to the sending object. From that moment on, the objects are no longer in rendez-vous. This is useful for increasing the parallelism in a program because both sender and receiver continue doing work concurrently. Note that an early reply is quite different from asynchronous sending. With an early reply, the communicating objects are still synchronized at a certain point in time.

- The language permits **recursive answers**. While very naturally and elegantly expressed in the language definition, it is a problem for the implementation. It means that inside a method, which is answered on behalf of a message sending object, another answer can take place. When that happens, the object, which was originally executing the method, is in rendez-vous with two objects at the same time. It requires objects to have an unbounded stack.

- Methods are not only used for answering messages. They can also be **called** as local procedures within the object, without any other object involved at all. So the same method code can be executed in two totally different situations. The main difference being where to put the result value of the method, and which object to wake up when. Local method calling also allows recursion within the object.

- The message passing mechanism is **universal**. It is used for the most trivial operations on integers, to the heavy coarse grain communication between process like objects. The expression for adding the integers (i + 3) is syntactic sugar for i!add(3), which means send the message add, with as parameter a reference to the object 3, to object i. Both forms can be used by the POOL-X programmer, and can be readily interchanged without any change of meaning. Therefore, the compiler's front-end transforms all syntactic sugar to the canonical format, the message passing form. Similarly, the expression a[5] is syntactic sugar for a!get1(5). It is typically used in array operations, although the transformation is purely syntactic and can be applied in other environments as well. A third example is the expression left!stop(), which is already in canonical form. This form is typically used in real communication between concurrently running objects.

We now have three examples of send statements:

```
i!add( 3 )
a!get1(5)
left!stop()
```

These all look quit similar, but they are not. The first form should be compiled into inline code for the addition of two integers. The second form, array access, should be compiled to a procedure call at most, without any interference from the run-time-support system. (POOL-X's arrays are quite heavy compared to arrays found in other languages.) The third communication is between two objects that are completely process-like, so the complete message passing mechanism as comes into play.

With all the variations on the basic scheme described above, tens to hundreds of different specializations on the message passing mechanism are possible, each optimized for its own task.

The critical questions here are how many different specializations of the message passing the implementation must make, and how to distinguish them from each other from the program code alone. Before summer 1989, the answers to these questions were: As much as possible in order to make communication fast, and, by making the compiler very smart.

But the compiler writers found the task harder than was thought, the potential POOL-X programmers were unhappy with the projected performance, and the language designers decided that faster progress was needed. With the introduction of the family of atomic data pragmas the smart-compiler attitude had disappeared. From that moment on the POOL-X programmer could see from the program text at what places what specialization of message passing is used. There are three of them, and they correspond to the three examples above. Inline code for value access, procedure calls for atomic data access, and the full message passing overhead for process to process communication.

The pragmas changed the language at its root, the message passing mechanism. Since then, POOL-X has got a totally different feel, although its looks stayed the same: The POOL-X programmer can now talk to the compiler about how a piece of code should be implemented. The programmer gets control, whereas previously there was no control at all, and the programmer gets an idea of what is going on at run-time. But in order to make use of the opportunities offered, the programmer must plan far ahead and know a lot about both the language and the machine specific implementation.

For this reason, the Portable POOL-X Implementation tries to keep some of the old feel. It tries hard to make message passing as efficient as possible. It tries to offer a **balanced** implementation, one that doesn't immediately go astray—performance wise—when the programmer does not force the optimal implementation.

5.2 Typing

POOL-X features strong, mostly static typing, and unlike many other object-oriented languages, lacks inheritance and sub-typing. From the language emplementers point of view, constructs that are not incorporated in the language are a Good Thing. It means less work and less errors.

Strong typing implies that a program cannot "go wrong" at run-time. Static typing means that many checks can be left out of the generated code and run-time-support. In an addition, the add does not have to check first whether both arguments are actually integers. Strong and static typing implies static binding. When a message is sent, there is no need to go search for the method's code, it can be determined at compile time.

But POOL-X also contains some features that make the implementation of the whole typing scheme rather complex.

5.2.1 The NIL value

Objects are the instantiations of a Class. A Class is the template for the objects of a Class. There can be many objects of the same Class. But for every Class there is one special object, the NIL-object. It acts as a bottom element for the Class, one cannot do anything with the NIL object, except use it in a comparison, and move it around. At the entrance of a scope, all local variables of that scope are initialized with NIL.

It is not possible to send any messages to a NIL-object, it leads to an exception. For the normal message passing mechanism this check on the NIL value is not very expensive. A single pointer comparison is sufficient, which is not too much overhead in the whole process of message transfer.

This is different for the optimized operations. As already mentioned, all Classes have a NIL object. This also holds for the Integer Class. Besides ..., $-1, 0, 1, 2, ...$ it also contains the NIL object. And every operation with NIL should lead to an exception. So, when the expression $a + b$ is executed, there should be a check on NIL for both operands of the addition. And in this case it means that the operation can become three times as expensive, a non-neglectable overhead.

There are three solutions to the problem. The first one is a hardware solution that is provided by some microprocessors (notably the SPARC). Instead of the normal 32-bit word size, in the hardware solution only 31 bits are used for the basic processor operations. The 32nd bit is used as a tag. When the processor detects that an operand has its tag set, it signals an exception that can be handled by software. In this way, the check on NIL does not cost any extra processor cycles in the normal mode of execution, which is computations without NIL.

The second solution is a compiler solution. It consists of flow-analysis of the program's code. As already said, most NIL-values are introduced by the initial values of local variables. It can be easily established that most expression's return values that are not NIL, this is certainly the case for the majority of library methods and routines. A rather straightforward use-def analysis [1] on the code can compute that most of the operands used in operations can never be NIL. This analysis technique was however never implemented for POOL, so no results are available on the success-rate of the optimization.

The third solution is the one chosen in the Natlab compiler, it consists of a compiler flag that can be used to tell the compiler that it should not generate code for NIL-checks. The POOL-X programmer must make sure that NIL exceptions do not occur, otherwise the NIL exception semantics of the program would change. This is because a NIL exception might be caught in the program and be fixed. Without the check, the exception handler is never triggered and the program would go astray with wrong results.

In the Portable Implementation, nothing is done to optimize NIL-checks, the overhead is accepted.

5.2.2 Parametrized Classes and the id-routine

POOL-X offers parametrized Classes. Parametrization of Classes gives the type-system comparable capabilities as polymorphic typing found in modern functional languages, see for example [8]. It fills up part of the hole that is left by leaving inheritance and sub-typing out of POOL-X. Parametrized Classes allow the programmer to define a Class Stack(Elem). The stack is parametrized with a type-parameter Elem. It allows the programmer to create a Stack(Int) or a Stack(Char), and only have to write the code for the Stack once.

Inside the Class Stack(Elem), there is not much that can be done with objects of the type Elem besides keeping references to the in local variables. It is not possible to send messages to objects of the Elem type, because the type-checker cannot determine whether the object has the right method with the correct parameters. But there is one exception, objects of type Elem can be compared to each other with the id-routine.

The id-routines take a very special place in POOL-X. Every Class—and therefore every object—is obliged to have one. The id-routine has a fixed signature. For a Class C, the id-routine has the declaration ROUTINE id(o1,o2:C):Bool. The default functionality of the id-routine is to establish the equality of two objects, and can especially determine if an object is equal to the NIL.

The problem is that id-routines can be redefined by the programmer. Without redefinition being allowed, the id-routine could always for every Class be the same piece of run-time-support system. With redefinition, a specific piece of code can exist for a Class. Now the problem is how to find the id-routine of an object of type Elem in a parametrized Class.

Two solutions are possible. One is to let all objects carry around their type, or any other way to establish the id-routine at run-time.

The other is to generate specialized code for every type-instance of a Class that may ever exist at run-time. This is used in the Natlab-compiler. In the example above, separate code is generated for both the Stack(Int) and the Stack(Char), the compiler acts as a macro-expander. The POOL-X definition explicitly forbids programs that generate an unlimited amount of type-instances. Although not very elegant, it is not a limitation in practice. A second potential problem might be that still very much code is generated for certain programs. But again it turns out that for existing real programs—written in DOOM, PRISMA and POOMA—parametrized Classes are never used for many different types.

5.2.3 Routines as objects

Routines can be used as objects in POOL-X. In this way not only data can be moved around in the program, but also procedures that act on data. For example, it is possible to write a parametrized sorting Class that acts on unknown objects that it has to sort. To do comparisons between the objects, the caller of the sorter provides the comparison routine together with the data to be sorted.

As useful as it may be, with routine objects full static binding is not possible. Every routine, including the routines in the standard libraries and the special id and new-routines, can be dynamically passed around and called from unknown places. To implement this flexibility, every routine has to conform to a standard calling interface. Improvements are possible through global analysis but this process is complex and compile-time inefficient. There are no simple local optimizations based on local analysis.

In the Portable Implementation five of these different calling strategies are distinguished. To find out which to use at the dynamic calling side, some run-time checks are performed.

5.2.4   Dynamic typing and the tuple compiler

Dynamic typing in POOL-X is integrated into the static, strong typing strategy. This sounds difficult, and it is. POOL-X is extended to make the Database Management System Implementation on a parallel machine possible. In a DBMS, the end-users—not the POOL-X programmer—determine the types of the data to be manipulated. It is possible to implement such a system in a fully statically typed environment through full interpretation of every DBMS operation. The PRISMA designers did not want this, and the run-time tuple-operation *compiler* was developed as a solution. Operations to be performed on large batches of data can be compiled at run-time. In this way, the inner loops of the DBMS do not have to consist of interpreted operations.

To integrate this dynamic compiler with the statically type-checked language requires the use of some unconventional tricks based on run-time type-case analysis. The interested reader is referred to [2]. The implementation is required to manipulate types on-the-fly. Types can be created and manipulated at run-time, just like any other objects. There is a close interaction between this type-manipulation and the type-manipulation required in the parametrized Classes as described above. The Portable Implementation has chosen for a fully dynamic type-manipulation, where each object carries its own type. The Natlab Implementation has chosen for the faster but more complex static parametrization and dynamic tuple-type manipulation.

All this type-manipulation is needed to dynamically construct and check to-be-compiled tuple-expressions of arbitrary type. Tuple-expressions are compositions of a number of simple operations on tuple-objects and the basic objects of type Integer, String, Boolean and Float. The expressions cannot contain if-then-else or loop constructs, and they can operate on only one tuple at a time. The result of the compilation of an expression is a routine object that can be applied to a tuple. To the POOL-X programmer, this routine object looks like any other routine object in POOL-X.

The range of implementations for the run-time tuple-expression compiler contains the following three points:

- Full interpretation of the expressions at run-time. While attractive because of its simplicity and portability, this alternative does deny the major motivation for the tuple compiler: Speed of execution for inner loop operations.

- The other extreme is the construction of a piece of straight line code by really compiling the expression into machine code. The code generator can then even take care of optimal register assignment. While this certainly could provide the highest speed, it is the least portable. Only if speed is the only concern, this is the way to go.

- The Portable Implementation uses a much more portable method. It constructs the expression's code by putting together a number of templates, and filling in some code addresses and constants in the templates. The interesting aspect is that the templates are written in C themselves. The tuple-expression compiler finds out the structure of the templates by scanning the code that is generated by the C-compiler. This code is then copied into the compiled routine.

Care must be taken that both direct and relative offsets to code addresses are recognized and generated. Also one must make sure that the processor instruction cache is coherent with the constructed instruction stream in main (heap) memory. To achieve this, the instruction cache is flushed at the time of garbage collection. This is enough since memory is not reused in between garbage collection cycles. The final performance is estimated to be not more than three times slower than the fully machine dependent code. In the Natlab compiler a comparable method is used, but then written in POOL-X with some extensions for peeking and poking memory.

5.3 Exception handling

The exception handling mechanism is capable of catching exceptions generated by the run-time-support, library procedures or a SIGNAL statement. The run-time-support, for example, generates an exception when an object tries to send to NIL. The division procedures check for a zero-divisor, when it occurs an exception of the name illegal_value is generated. With a SIGNAL, an exception can be generated explicitly at a point in the POOL-X execution. Exceptions can have names, and the exception handlers can specify which exceptions they wants to handle. A handler can also specify that it wants to handle all exceptions with the OTHERS designator.

When the exception is generated, the run-time-support will search for the closest surrounding exception handler. When it is not found within the current procedure, the exception propagates. In the case of a method or routine call, it propagates to the place where the method or routine call was done—it goes higher up in the dynamic calling stack. But in case a rendez-vous is encountered by this propagation, the exception is propagated to two places. At the sender object the exception propagates from the place where the send was executed. At the receiver side it propagates at the ANSWER. When an object runs out of calling stack and the exception is not even handled by the body, the POOL-X program stops with an error. So, exceptions do not get lost when they are not handled.

Exception handling is a method for handling errors, strange or exceptional situations in a program. As such, it *seems* to provide the programmer with convenient tools to do so. Instead of doing all of checking for NIL, division by zero and loop-boundary conditions, the programmer can place one exception handler around the code considered, and catch all anticipated errors. The problem is, the exception handler will also catch all unanticipated errors, real bugs. This makes exception handling the GOTO of structured programming. Actually exception handling is worse than GOTO because exception does not specify where the control should go to. At least the GOTO points to something. And the handler itself also does not specify where the control came from.

The net result is harder debugging for POOL-X programmers and programs that are hard to read and maintain. Among the many valid bug-reports for the implementation of the POOL-X interpreter, there have also been a number of false alarms caused by misinterpreting the exception handling mechanism. Most were caused by the default exception handler that ate all OTHER exceptions that propagated to the default body. Fortunately this feature is removed from POOL-X since then.

Back to the implementation then. In principle it is possible to implement the exception handler installation mechanism without run-time overhead. To do so, the run-time-support system must be able to map the current program counter at the moment of the exception to the installed handler. This can be supported by a static table containing the position of all handlers and beginning and ending of all procedures.

In the Portable Implementation exception handling is not implemented at all. For a large part due to the software engineering reasons described above, for another part due to implementation restrictions. New mechanisms had to be developed to implement exception handling in the Portable Implementation. And because examination of existing POOL-X programs showed that these hardly ever used exception handling in a consistent way, it was decided not to implement it. The RISC approach to engineering is applicable here as well.

5.4 Garbage collection

POOL-X is a language without user programmed memory management. The programmer does not allocate an object's memory. Instead the whole creation process is handled by the Class' new-routine that takes care of allocation, initialization and startup. Destroying objects is not even visible to the programmer at all. When an object is inactive, either because it is waiting for an in-coming message or has finished its body code, and no other active object knows—directly or indirectly—about the object, it is garbage and subject to removal by the run-time-support. In no way the object could have contributed to the progress of the program.

This is great for the programmer, but is does come at a price. The phrase "*no active object knows about the object*" implies that all references that any object has to any other object must be retrievable by the Garbage Collector. The garbage collector must somehow know about the layout of the data-structures representing the objects, and must know where to find the references.

An important design choice in the Portable Implementation has been to allow garbage collections inside the execution of so-called atomic procedures. This means that also inside these atomic procedures, references must remain visible to the garbage collector, and the C register-variable mechanism could not be used to great extend.

Sometimes optimizations are possible. For example, it is not always necessary for the garbage collector to scan through the parameters of a procedure, the references in the parameters are also known at the calling side. This particular optimization is used to pass the parameters to atomic data procedures directly with the C parameter passing mechanism. While ideal for a simple implementation as ours, such a *caller saves* mechanism might not be of great benefit in an implementation that would optimize on more global grounds: When it is sure that no garbage collection can happen inside an atomic data procedure call, there is no need for saving references at all. More about garbage collection in Section 6.5.

5.5 Parallelism

The most special thing about POOL-X is that it is a language that explicitly supports parallelism. Objects run by definition in parallel. Even in a sequential implementation, all objects should get a share of the CPU-time. In POOL-X, this is called fairness. It means that any object, which can make progress, gets some processor time sometimes.

Note explicitly that the definition does not require that objects should get an *even* share of the processor-time, just that no object can get stuck infinitely long.

To implement fairness special precaution is taken to prevent an object to run forever. At every end of loop instruction, a check is placed to see if the object is not running too long. If it is, it is descheduled, and put at the tail of the active-objects queue. In this way other objects also get a chance to run. It does make DO-loops rather more expensive than their C equivalent, but that is the price of fairness.

It must be clear now that the programmer can do very little about exact scheduling points and amount of processor-time that an object gets. It is not possible for a POOL-X programmer to assume that an asynchronous sender and its receiver run equally fast and do not require further scheduling. There is no way for the programmer to establish relative speeds of objects, and even when this would be done for a particular implementation of POOL-X on a particular processor, it might turn out to be very different on another. In the example, when the receiver runs faster, there is no problem, it will wait when there are no messages. When the sender runs faster, the queue of waiting asynchronous messages will fill up memory and finally abort the application.

Therefore, not explicitly implementing any synchronization between an asynchronous sender and its receiver in the POOL-X program can be considered an error. But the language does not treat it as such. Instead it requires the implementation to repair such an error but providing an *elastic buffer*. The elastic buffer is infinite, but must make sure that the sending object gets less and less processing time, and the receiver more time to process the pending messages. By definition of POOL-X, it is not allowed for the implementation to completely stop the sender.

For the Portable Implementation, this mechanism was not implemented. For two reasons, obviously it is too costly, and secondly, when the program contains an error, the programmer must get notification as soon as possible. The Portable Implementation does nothing to prevent queue overflow, but exactly the opposite. By not considering the asynchronous send as a scheduling point, a simple asynchronously sending loop will not be scheduled out until the looping-check will do so. This will cause the sender to run *much* faster than the receiver and the error be detected earlier.

Unfortunately the problem carries much further than just the asynchronous send. For parallel programming to be cost effective, the programmer must be aware of memory and CPU resource consumption of the program. The programmer must be able to estimate cost of operations to take care of workload distribution. With a language as high as POOL-X, this is *simply not possible*. Optimizing a POOL-X program by the programmer is an experimental enterprise that is valid for one combination of hardware/compiler/run-time-support at a time. The problem is unlikely to be limited to POOL-X. It is a general problem for parallel implementations.

5.6 Conclusions on language complexity

The language contains many interesting experiments in the field of language design. The question is whether all these experiments were really needed, especially when the language was to be used in the project itself. For example, for exception handling the answer is a definite no, although of course there are people debating even this. The point is that each extra piece of language is going to cost in the implementation. If not in speed, then somewhere else.

Being a language implementer, the author finds it debatable whether so much richness is required for one single language. It is time to advocate "the RISC approach to language design".

6 Implementation Aspects

6.1 Addressing an object

This section is on the addressing and object-handle schemes used in the Portable Implementation. The object-handle is the address that is used to get to the objects data. When a piece of POOL-X code does an assignment as in a:=b;, it is the object-handle that is transferred into the variable a. For a user defined object it is the pointer, either local or off-node, for an integer it is the, slightly modified, value of the integer itself.

In the Portable Implementation, the rule is simple. All object-handles fit into one machine word of 32-bits, a C integer. This is not always the most speed-efficient representation, but is by far the simplest.

There are two potential problems that are solved by this data-representation-scheme, these concern the parametrized Classes and the garbage collector. When the object-handling scheme does not solve these problems, they must be solved by more complicated means.

6.1.1 Parametrized Classes and the object-handle

Consider the Class Array(C), it is a parametrized Class. It can be used to store and retrieve object-handles of any type. In the Portable Implementation the Array-Class is written in C because it is a standard Class, part of the library. The problem is whether the actual type-parameter makes a difference to the implementation. Since the array only has to be able to store the parametrized object-handles, the only thing that matters is the size of the object-handle. And in the Portable Implementation this size is always the same, 32-bits. As a result there is only one generic piece of code that handles all types of arrays.

On the negative side, there is the memory overhead for arrays of booleans and arrays of characters. In principle, a character would fit into 9 bits—including NIL-encoding—and a boolean in 2 bits, so the arrays could be packed much denser. This is the price of simplicity.

For all other parametrized Classes including the user defined parametrized Classes the same holds. All that is needed to be done with the objects that have the type of a Class parameter is to move them around and store them. The universal 32-bit format suffices for this. Also note that the String-Class is not a parametrized Class. In a String, characters take only 8 bits. The characters are converted when they come in and go out of the String. Especially in a database implementation language Strings should not cause too much memory overhead.

In the Natlab Implementation the choice is made for more costumized arrays and user defined parametrized Classes. Several versions of the array Class available for different sizes of object-handles. These are generated from a template. To handle this for user defined Classes, a complicated two-step compilation scheme is used.

6.1.2 Garbage collection and the object-handle

Consider the situation where the garbage collector has to scan through the instance variable store of an object. The garbage collector knows where to find the instance variables and how many there are, but what about the question which of them are pointers to objects that have to be scanned and which of them are values, integers and the like, and do not have to be scanned.

In the Portable Implementation the garbage collector scans along all elements of a variable store, and all object-handles are tagged. The garbage collector looks at the tags to find out what to do with them. The tagging scheme is as follows:

- The NIL value of all Classes is represented as zero, 32 bits of 0.

- Characters have a 1-tag in the least significant bit, bit 0. The eight bits that represent the character are put into bits 1 to 8, one bit shifted from their normal position. The other bits, 9 to 31, are zero.

- The same holds for booleans. A 1-tag at position 0, and bit 1 signals the truth value. As a result the object-handle value for **true** is 3, and for **false** it is 1.

- Integers are also encoded in this way. Bit 0 is a tag of 1, and the integer representation is stored one bit-position to the left. Special about integers is that this implies that only 31 bits of integer representation are available.

- Floating point numbers are required to have a 64-bit IEEE-representation by the POOL-X definition. And all these bits definitely do not fit into the object handle. So floating point numbers are not represented by value, they are stored as objects on the heap. The object-handle is a pointer to the record.

- Local pointers do not require conversion. Their object-handle is the same as their C representation. To make this possible, care is taken that all heap-allocated records are allocated on an 8-byte boundary. This makes sure that the pointer always ends with 000.

- Non-local pointers end with the bit-pattern 010. A non-local is needed when the object that the object-handle points to is allocated on a node different from the current node. The conversion between local and non-local pointers takes place by the message handler. All non-local pointers point outside the node. This is used to circumvent a large number of checks and conversions in the run-time-support.

  The representation of the non-local pointers fits in the 29 bits that are left. The upper 9 bits—31 to 23—are used to denote the node number, a maximum of 512 nodes. The remaining 20 bits are an index into the off-node reference table. This table contains an entry for all objects of which there is a non-local pointer floating around on another node. When an object is only known at the current node, only its direct pointer is used and the object has no entry in the table.

Entries into the table are made by the message handler when it sends object-handles outside. The entries are wiped out by the garbage collector that computes the validity of all off-node reference tables on all nodes at every garbage collection cycle.

Note that off-node references are dealt with dynamically. It can occur that an object's handle is sent out, and the object gets an entry in the off-node reference table. Then after a while the garbage collector may detect that the handle outside the node is no longer present and clears the entry in the table. When then again the object's handle is sent outside, it is again allocated an entry in the table, which may well be another one.

With these representations for the object-handle, the garbage collectors task becomes trivial. First it is checked if the object-handle under inspection is zero. If it is, the handle is a NIL value and no more action is needed. The next check is on bit 0 of the object handle. If it is set, the handle is a by-value representation of an object, and needs not to be scanned. Then the check on the 010 pattern distinguishes local and non-local pointers. With a local pointer, the object that it points to is known, and can be scanned. For a non-local pointer, a message is sent to the home-node of the object-handle—obtained from the first 9 bits—that the object should be scanned there.

6.1.3 Non-tagging schemes

It is obvious that the tagging scheme does not allow for a maximum performance of integer operations unless there is, rather unusual, tagging hardware. The current scheme requires at least a doubling of the cost of many integer operations. An integer addition of two values a and b must be performed as $a + b - 1$. And this does not include overflow checking which is not implemented at all in the Portable Implementation, because it is too costly.

The integer operations account for most of the overhead of the tagging scheme. The overhead for floating point operations depends very much on the program. For typical information processing tasks that POOL-X is designed for, there is very little overhead for floating point handling because these do hardly any floating point operations.

When the POOL-X implementer would decide that the cost is too high, another scheme is needed for the garbage collector to know which object-handles are references and which are not. In the following is assumed that all object-handles still fit 32-bits. Would they not—e.g. for floating point numbers—than the problem becomes just bigger, but not basically more complicated.

Two schemes have been used for non-tagged implementations:

- The two-stack scheme is used in the Natlab Implementations. Basically all object-handle stores, e.g. for the expression evaluation stack, are divided into two regions, one containing all references and one containing all values. This solution is far from trivial. It requires some administration to be performed twice, for both stacks. Likewise it causes some problems in dynamic typing and the handling of parametrized Classes.

- The second solution is to let all object-handle stores carry around a bit-mask that denotes which items in the object-handle store are values and which are pointers. In this way, the garbage collector can walk through the object-handle store while in the mean time interpreting the bit-mask.

The parametrized Classes problem is solved by making the bit-masks an attribute of the type, not the code. So for a parametrized Class only one piece of code needs to be generated. At run-time the bit-masks are manipulated that come with the actual type.

The bit-mask scheme is probably the most run-time efficient for a version of POOL-X including dynamic typing and parametrization. The problem lies with the compiler. It needs to generate bit-masks as well as code, and this is not trivial to implement. It was done for the POOL-X interpreter, and it was one of the reasons why it was delayed.

The conclusion must be that non-tagging schemes potentially offer faster execution of POOL-X programs, but that this comes at a high price to be paid in the implementation of compiler and run-time-support. Also it must be noted that in both non-tagged schemes there is a lot of room for shifting complicated compiler work to the, easier to implement but slower at run-time, dynamically maintained schemes. And this practice would loose part of the advantage.

For these reasons, for the Portable Implementation the simple, dynamically maintained, tagged representation was chosen.

6.2 Atomic data objects

Since the addition of pragmas in 1989, a POOL-X compiler is required to support four kinds of object implementations: The process, server, data and value implementations, also called object models. See [4]. Although it was originally intended that the use of pragmas should not incur changes to the semantics of POOL-X, this could not be maintained. It makes the pragmas an essential part of the language definition.

- A process object is the full blown object with full message passing capabilities. It can communicate with any other object kind, and do answers at any point in its Class code, also recursively.

- A server is restricted in its answering capabilities. A server object does not have a user defined body. Instead it has a *default* body, which is an endless loop containing a single ANSWER ANY statement. Also a server can only have synchronous methods. It can however send to any other object. Since this includes blocking synchronous sends, a server object must still have the capability of scheduling and saving state. Because of this it is implemented in exactly the same way as the process objects in the Portable Implementation.

  In the Natlab Implementation advantage is taken of the fact that a server cannot do recursive answers and has only synchronous methods, it can have only a single thread active at any time. This allows the server's methods to be executed on behalf of the sender, without message passing through the operating system. When the sender is not at hand, when it lies on another node, the operation defaults to the process mechanism.

- Data object implementations are referred to as atomic data objects in this paper. While executing a method, a data object is not allowed to deschedule. To enforce this the same restrictions apply as to server objects. Additionally a data object may only do synchronous sends to other data or value objects. This ensures that a data object can execute requests made to it atomically, without any scheduling. Note that asynchronous sends to any other kind of object are still allowed, since these do not require descheduling. Because of this atomicity, the fairness rule of the language definition has now become void.

- A value object is restricted so much in its activities that it can savely be replicated throughout the system. To make this possible, it is not allowed to have any changing state. Once initialized, its instance variables can no longer be modified.

  In the Portable Implementation value user-defined value objects are not implemented. Tuples can be used instead.

6.2.1 The implementation of atomic data objects

Atomic data objects allow a more efficient implementation than the general process objects. Executing atomically means executing sequentially, without taking care of structuring data-stores in such a way that there contends are not lost on scheduling. In the Portable Implementation, stack-frames of methods of atomic data objects no longer have to be allocated on the heap. Instead, they can be allocated on the C-stack.

No descheduling is one thing, no garbage collection is another matter. Suppose an application is written that makes very good use of the more efficient object models. To run, the application starts one job on on each processor. These jobs do not require any communication when running, but at the end of all jobs there is small phase where all results are integrated into the final answer of the application run. This is the ultimate divide and conquer type of application.

But now consider the jobs in themselves. Since they can run without any communication, they can be implemented sequentially, using the atomic data objects to do the work, and relying on the more efficient implementation of atomic data objects for speed. *The most efficient implementation for the single jobs is to make each job run as a single atomically running task.* And since a running job produces garbage, it is unavoidable that garbage collection must take place while running an atomic data object.

Being able to do garbage collection while running an atomic data object means that the garbage collector must have access to all the local data of the—possibly recursive—method invocations. So, data is allocated on the C-stack, but it must be accessible from the run-time-support, and it must be subject to Portable Implementation. The solution is to put local data into a linked list structure. When the garbage collector walks through the list it will find all references. The following code fragment shows an example method of an atomic data object:

```
dm_Bool_Tester_test( lockit, co, p0, p1 )
int lockit ;
struct os_Bool_Tester *co ;
int p0, p1 ;
{
  struct {
    int *atom_next ;
    int atom_len ;
    int v[2] ;
    int s[5] ;
  } s ;

  s.atom_next = atomlink ;      /* Link list of frames */
  atomlink = (int *)&s.next ;
  s.atom_len = 7 ;                        /* For GC */
  bzero( &s.v[0] , sizeof(int) * 7 ) ;  /* Init NIL */
  if( lockit && (!co || isremote(co) || co->lock++) ) {
    pxdatsenderr( co ) ;                 /* At error */
  }

  /* some atomic code */

  s.s[0] = s.v[0] ;            /* Prepare return value */

  atomlink = s.atom_next ;     /* Unlink frame */
  return( s.s[0] ) ;
}
```

The most interesting aspect is that for passing parameters and return value, the normal C mechanisms can be used. For atomic data methods, a caller-saves protocol is used for garbage collectable references. This means that the caller must have the parameters stored at some place where the garbage collector can find them.

The first parameter signals whether the method is called in a method call (lockit false), or via an atomic message (lockit true). The difference lies in checking for cyclic send that are done for the message. This can be seen in the if satement. With lockit false, no checks are made. Otherwise, the current object is checked for NIL-ness, locality, and cyclic calling respectively.

The second parameter, as will be clear now, is a reference to the current object. After that follow the parameters, untouchable for the garbage collector because they are allocated on the C-stack.

The method declares its local variables and expression stack inside a structure. This forces them to be allocated in a contiguous piece of memory, albeit allocated on the C-stack. The first two statements in the method link this structure into a globally known list rooted at the atomlink variable. The third statement is to tell the garbage collector that the scannable variable store is seven words long. The following statement sets the whole variable store to NIL. This to make sure that the garbage collector will not encounter any unexpected references.

After the if statement the method is ready to run. There is no switch statement because the method is atomic and cannot deschedule.

At the end of the method the variable-structure is unlinked from the global list, and the return value is returned with the C mechanism.

When such a method is called from within a process-object, that object must take care of saving the parameters, because of the caller-saves convention used here. The caller does so by setting the retoff-field of its current stack-frame to point to the last of the parameters.

Inside the atomic data methods themselves, there is no such thing as the retoff-field, the garbage collector simply scans the whole of the expression stack.

6.3 The Off-Node Communication Handler

The off-node communication handler takes care of the off-node communication in the POOL-X execution. In addition it also handles the off-node communication that takes place inside the run-time-support, for example for the garbage collector or I/O-system. Basically the off-node communication handler takes a message apart, puts in into a stream of bytes, send the stream over a communication link to another node, and rebuild the message at the receiver side.

The off-node communication handler is one of the most complicated pieces of run-time-support. It could have been simpler but that would be at the cost of speed. This is one of the very few places in the Portable Implementations where demands on speed have led to a more complicated implementation. The reason is that in a parallel machine such as the PRISMA machine speed the off-node communication is one of the important research topics.

And although complicated, the communication handler is also kept as portable as much. To enable porting, the off-node communication handler is split into an upper an lower level part. And because the lower level is the part that must be ported towards different hardware, it is kept rather simple.

Portability to different parallel hardware is achieved while retaining performance. Ports have been finished to the PRISMA machine, a Transputer machine and a Unix network. Of course in a Unix based network implementation jobs are subject to the Unix' scheduling policies. Speed of a rendez-vous drops therefore below 10 rendez-vous' per second. Maximum bandwidth does not suffer that much from Unix.

Performance on the 68020-based PRISMA hardware is rather impressive. A complete rendez-vous at the POOL-X level involving two objects at different nodes takes about 700 micro-seconds. This is less than both the Natlab Implementation and the time reported for Amoeba [11]. Both of these implementations require about 1.5 milliseconds.

The maximum throughput through the PRISMA network is more than 1 megabyte/sec for a node. This cannot be reached for a single object to object connection for reasons discussed below. It is achieved for a single object sending (not too big) messages to three objects on three different nodes. For receiving, when three objects send to a single receiving object, the same figure is attained.

The reason for this high performance is that the off-node communication handler software directly converts the POOL-X data formats into data given to the communication processor, and vice versa. Although the off-node communication handler is internally split into two layers, no internal copying of data is involved in the process.

6.3.1 The communication processor hardware

The communication processor [5], developed in the DOOM project, is the most impressive piece of hardware in the PRISMA machine, both in appearance and in performance. It consists of two closely connected VME-boards and consumes 80 Watts of power. As of functionality, it is the building block of a deadlock free network of any topology with a maximum degree of four, and a maximum diameter of 8[1]. The maximum single direction throughput on a wire is measured to be some 500 Kbytes per second. Since each communication processor has four in-coming and four out-going links, the total network bandwidth of the 100 node PRISMA machine is 200 Megabytes per second. This is reasonably balanced considering the total computation performance of some 300 to 400 MIPS.

---

[1]Actually the diameter can be much larger. To understand why requires substantial knowledge of the routing algorithm. A diameter of 8 is a save *minimum* maximum.

The communication processor handles packets of 256 bits each. Sending a packet from one CP to the next takes 50 micro-seconds, this is the *hop*-time. The first 16 bits of a packet are used for destination addressing and internal CP-administration.

The CP consists of five in-coming and out-going links. Four of the links are used for the network, the fifth is the connection with the computational board, the processor. Packets can come in at any link. The destination address of an in-coming packet goes through the routing-table internal to the CP. It determines a set of out-going links that the packet might take to go its destination. The set may contain only one out-going link, in that case the packet has no choice. This is the case for example when a packet has reached its destination node, the only feasible link then is the link to the computational board.

But the CP was designed to handle the multi-link case. The packet chooses *whichever link is free first*. The reason behind this is that it allows a packet to avoid heavily used links, in this way increasing throughput. This feature is called dynamic routing. Dynamic routing has also drawbacks. One of them is the implementation complexity of the CP, its 80 Watts power requirements is an indication to this. Another indication is the single link throughput of 500 Kbytes/sec, because the physical wires run at 20 Mbits/sec, allowing for 2 Mbytes/sec bandwidth. The difference must lie in the handling of deadlock freedom and dynamic routing complications.

An even more severe problem caused by dynamic routing is the complications it enforces to the outside world. Since packets coming from a certain node going to a single destination might take different routes across the network, *they might arrive in reversed order!* It is then up to the software to reorder packets. See [13] for implementations of sliding window protocols. Needless to say, these protocols cost performance. It is then up to the designer to decide where the performance bottlenecks lie, in the raw network bandwidth, or in the network handling software. The RISC approach to engineering applies here as well.

Fortunately the communication processor offers great flexibility. It is possible to configure the routing tables in such a way that static routing is implemented. By giving only one possible out-going link per destination, it is impossible for packets to choose different routes and overtake each other. This configuration is used in the Portable Implementation on the PRISMA hardware. It is thus ensured that packets always arrive in the same order as they were sent.

6.3.2 Communication handler, overview

The following terminology is used: The low level off-node communication handler is called the *commpart*. The upper level of the off-node communication handler is called the *upppart*. The commpart calls functions provided by the upppart, these are the input communication handler functions, called *inmess* functions.

The whole Portable Implementation is based on the idea of one sequential C-process running on each processor in a parallel machine. To keep it sequential, the communication handler is implemented by means of polling on the in-coming network link. There is no need for separate interrupt driven processes, although they may turn out to be convenient on particular hardware. The number of times a poll is performed depends on tunable parameters. Polling occurs at two places, in the scheduler, see Section 4.3, the call to poll()) and in the test-for-branch of every DO-loop. A counter takes care that the polling routine is called every so many times a test-for-branch is done. This mechanism ensures that an object that would monopolize the processor cannot interfere too much with the communication handler needs.

Inside the poll() function several checks are done. These are a check for garbage collection, a check for user and file-I/O, and a call to the pxmpoll() function, the entry to the commpart. In addition to this polling-by-count mechanism there is also support for interrupt driven implementations by the provision of a global variable called pxyoehoe. In this variable, bits may be set to enforce the polling function to be called before the counter runs to zero.

There are five major calling functions from the upppart to the commpart. The already introduced pxmpoll() takes care of in-coming messages in combination with pxreciv(datap, len), more about this later. The functions pxstsend(destnode, imfuncid), pxdosend(datap, len), and pxendsend() are called to send a message to a destination node. At any time, no more than one out-going message is handled. Upppart takes care a message is send as an atomic action in as short as possible time, no garbage collection or scheduling will occur in the mean time.

6.3.3 The out-going communication handler

First the out-going communication handler is described. It is the simpler part because no scheduling is involved in the sending of a message. The protocol for sending a single message by the upppart is as follows:

- A call to pxstsend(destnode, imfuncid) initializes the message transfer action. The first parameters tell the commpart to what node the message should go, it is just a number that uniquely identifies the node. The second parameter is an index into a table of inmess functions. It is used at the receiving side to recreate the message from the stream of bytes.

- Then any number of calls to pxdosend(datap, len). Each time adds len words pointed to by the pointer datap to the byte-stream that constitutes the message.

- The last function call to finish this message is to pxendsend(). When this call is done, commpart has the obligation to send the whole data-stream to the destination node. It may not keep some bytes buffered for a next message for that destination because a next message may never come.

  Also the integrity of the data passed to pxdosend is ensured until the call to pxendsend. This means that if the commpart needs to buffer the data-stream because the communication processor is busy, it may keep the pointers to the data, and needs not copy the data itself. But after pxendsend is finished, the upppart and other parts of the run-time-support may change the data. If commpart wants to retain the data after pxendsend, it must copy anyway.

When the communication processor is so busy that it cannot accept the data to be send at the call to pxendsend, a few strategies are possible for commpart.

- The simplest is to keep waiting in pxendsend until the network is available. And while it is waiting for the out-going link to be free, commpart is required also to monitor the in-coming link, and eat any in-coming data immediately. Otherwise deadlock could occur.

- A second strategy is to copy the whole stream into buffered memory and return from the call to pxendsend. Then at every subsequent call to pxmpoll, it can be checked whether the out-going link is ready to accept some more data.

- The preferred refinement of the two strategies is to buffer up to a certain amount of data, e.g., fifty Kbytes. When there is more than this amount of data waiting to be sent away, generation of even more out-going messages might as well be prevented, and the commpart can then block in pxendsend until the pressure is lowered.

With all this talk about buffering unaccepted data it is interesting to know the actual behavior at message sending. Actually the Portable POOL-X Implementation is quite slow, say some 10 to 20 times slower than comparably structured C-programs. The chance that a running POOL-X program will saturate the network in therefore minimal, except under special conditions.

Under ordinary conditions, messages will be rather small, from some tens of bytes to maybe a message containing a tuple of a few hundred bytes. The calls to pxdosend mostly refer to data that is only a single word long. Consider the sending of a 64 byte string. It consists of three calls to pxdosend. The first one to send a single word tag to tell that it is a string coming. A second single word to tell the length of the string. And the third call for the actual data of the string, 16 words long. This process of turning a string into a stream of data is commonly known as marshaling.

From this it will be clear that commpart is not allowed to optimize pxdosend with large data at the expense of pxdosend with small data.

Under special conditions is is possible to saturate the communication processor, even from a POOL-X program. For example by sending a single large string of a million characters. Commpart will start throwing the one Megabyte to the communication at the maximum copying speed of an MC68020 to the VME-bus where the CP is located. This copying speed is more than two times higher than the 500 Kbyte/sec link to the destination node, and the CP will soon fill up.

To measure the maximum sending throughput of commpart and CP together from a POOL-X program, it is required to know some more of the internals of the CP. Since a single link can only handle 500 Kbyte/sec, all four out-going links of the CP must be used. This can be done by sending messages to four different objects on four nodes. The CPs have an internal buffering capacity of 8 Kbytes. Of this only a limited percentage, say 50%, may be used by the local node. So 4 Kbytes available for the local node. To keep all links busy, there must be messages in this buffer to all the out-going links, it is therefore unwise to send single very large (> 4 Kbytes) messages, since then one message would occupy the whole buffer-space in the CP. Best throughput is obtained by sending in turn messages of 1 Kbytes to other nodes. Under these conditions a sustained throughput of over 1 Megabyte/sec is obtained. Since these measurements were done from running a POOL-X program, it includes the overhead of the garbage collector that regularly has to remove all those unused strings.

6.3.4   The in-coming communication handler

This section describes how in-coming messages are handled. To enable commpart to do so, upppart calls the pxmpoll() function. When a message arrives, commpart determines from what node it comes, and what the imfuncid is. Remember that this imfuncid is the second parameter of the pxstsend-call. An important observation is that from a given node, only one message at a time can come in. This is because a message is send in one transaction of pxstsend-pxdosend...pxdosend-pxendsend, and because pieces of messages cannot overtake each other. But on the other hand, it is very well possible that pieces of messages coming from different nodes come in *mixed through each other*. In the PRISMA network, the basic unit of this mixing is the packet. Packets come out of the CP one at a time, but may come from any of the four in-coming links of the CP.

To make this work without intermediate buffering of complete messages—non-buffering was one of the design goals—upppart implements a rather complicated scheme that can handle the concurrent receipt of messages coming from different nodes. As said there can be no more than one in-coming message per node, so in a 100 node machine, upppart must be prepared to handle up to 99 concurrent in-coming messages. Concurrency in C requires status to be saved, and for this reason there are 99 status-vectors allocated for message handling, one for each node. Because of the one-node/one-message correspondence we can also say that a status-vector is associated with a message.

When the first packet of a message arrives, commpart uses the imfuncid as an index into a table of inmess functions provided by upppart. It then calls the indicated function with a single parameter, the status-vector. The status vector will be in a clean initial state, and the inmess function will know that a new message is to be received.

There are about ten different inmess functions. The most important one is for the real POOL-X-level messages, receiving user defined messages from other nodes. Other inmess functions are for receiving the reply value, requests for creating a new object on a node, handling off-node array accesses, deep-copies, and other housekeeping tasks. Based on the inmess function, it is known what has to happen with the message once it is received.

The general shape of a message is a tree. Take for example a message with two parameters, a tuple and an integer. The message contains a destination object-handle, the sender object-handle, a method identification, then the tuple and the integer. But because the tuple is send by value, it is itself a branch in the message tree containing a number of entries. This tree-shape is not limited, neither in breadth, consider an array of 20.000 tuples, nor in depth, as in a deep_copy. The tree structure is hence recursive, and the status-vector must be able to cope with these kinds of complicated status.

6.3.5 Concurrency in the in-coming communication handler

For the message to be built by the inmess function it needs to receive the data from the commpart. To get it, it calls the pxreciv(datap, len) function of the commpart. This function is the counterpart of the pxdosend function. But unlike the pxdosend, pxreciv can fail to deliver data. It then retuns a failing status, instead of signaling with a success-status that it has filled the block.

The reasons for such failure can be twofold. The first possibility is that the CP can provide no more in-coming data. This means that the rest of the message is hold up in the network, or that the sending node is a bit slow. A slow sender can occur when sending a remote deep-copy, which requires a lot of administration to be maintained. When the CP runs dry like this, the local node—actually commpart—may decide not to stop and wait for the data, but instead save the receiving status and wait for the next pxmpoll, while doing some useful local computations in the mean time. So pxreciv returns failure then.

The second reason for failing to comply to pxreciv is that there may be data—a packet—coming in for a different message. In that case, if copying of data is to be avoided, the receipt of the current message must be suspended by returning a failure status to pxreciv. The inmess function receives the failing status, saves itself on the status-vector, and returns. Commpart itself keeps track of which inmess functions are active with which status vectors, because the inmess function identification is only send at the very beginning of a message. Additionally, commpart keeps track of the last—non-satisfied—call to pxreciv and its data-buffer and required length. When more data comes in for the suspended message, commpart first puts it into this saved buffer. When this is full, commpart re-activates the inmess function by calling it. The inmess function will restart itself *after* the last call to pxreciv as if it succeeded, which is now indeed the case.

6.3.6 The suspension mechanism

The mechanism for suspension could have been similar to the process-scheduler of POOL-X objects. That is with all data always maintained on heap-allocated data. This heap-allocated data makes the context switch cheap. Only the program counter has to be saved. But the inmess functions are optimized for the other case, where context switching is expensive but local processing cheap. In the inmess functions, data is actually allocated on the C-stack, and can be put into registers at the C-compiler's command. When a suspend action must be done, all the data is copied from the local stack into the status vector. At the point of restarting, all data is copied from the status-vector onto the local stack. Although the amount of status to be saved and restored is not very much for typical messages, some 20 to 50 bytes, the cost of suspension is higher than the cost of POOL-X object scheduling.

The reason to justify preferring local processing costs over suspension costs is that suspension is not expected to happen that often. The two reasons for suspension given, the CP running dry and mixed messages are not supposed to happen frequently. The first only occurs when either the sender is very slow, or the network is very crowded. The sender usually has a much easier job than the receiver, just a recursive tree-walk, except in the case of a deep-copy, so it is not supposed to be slow. The deep-copy is a special case, a highly complex action that *may* be some slower in operation. In the unlikely case that the network is very crowded, it is the network that is the bottleneck, and not the processor, and some lost CPU-cycles do no harm.

The second reason that suspension might occur is that two messages are coming in from different nodes. This type of clash is expected to be rare, a coincidence. The reason is that the network is expected to be quite empty because of its high total bandwidth. And with an almost empty network, clashes do not occur often. In the current Portable Implementation this is certainly the case—although it also depends on the application—because the rather low POOL-X processing speed prevents sending of too many messages at a time.

6.3.7 Finishing up

The ending of a message is fully determined by the inmess function. Commpart has at no point in time any idea how long a message is. It can only find out that a message terminated when the inmess function terminates without the last pxreciv that occurred failed. When this is the case, commpart finishes up the message by removing anything left of the last packet that was not yet read by pxreciv.

The amount of administrative overhead added to the packet stream by the commpart is minimal. A packet in the CP consists of 8 words of 4 bytes each. The first half word, 16 bits, are used by the administrative overhead of the CP hardware itself. The other 16 bits are used by the commpart to store the identification of the sending node and the inmess function-id. And since a node can only send one message at a time, this is all administration needed by the commpart for each packet. So seven out of eight words in a packet are available for message data.

6.3.8 Garbage collection and the communication handler

To make the garbage collector and off-node communication handler cooperate well, some special measures are taken. Two potential problems are partially finished in-coming messages and messages that still hang around in the network. The first, unfinished messages, can cause a problem because these incompleted messages are inconsistent data-structures and can thus not be scanned by the garbage collector. Would such unscanned message contain a vital reference, things go wrong.

In case a message still hangs around in the network, it may also contain a vital reference, and of course, the garbage collector would not be able to get to it.

The two potential problems are solved by the synchronization detector, see Section 6.4, that is used at the beginning of a garbage collection cycle. The synchronizer is used in the Portable Implementation to make all nodes agree on the fact that they are synchronized. It is used to decide on termination, garbage collection, and debugging. Part of the work that the synchronizer does is to send a message from all nodes to all other nodes, and wait for them to arrive at the destination nodes. This action takes care of *sweeping* the network. All paths in the network that are used in any possible communication are used. And because of the order-preserving properties of the network as configured under the Portable Implementation, after sweeping there can be no more unfinished or complete messages in the network. Both potential problems are thus effectively removed.

6.4 The synchronization detector

The synchronization detector is one of the most complicated pieces of code in the run-time-support system of the Portable POOL-X Implementation. Although the size of the code is only 300 lines, it has taken about a month to develop. This time was not spend in writing code, but in debugging. Also the time was not spend in a single period, but errors kept creeping out. The reasons for this are that the code has some intimate connections with the rest of the system, notably the, already complicated in itself, off-node communication and I/O handlers. A second reason is that the code is a parallel algorithm. And thirdly and most importantly, the code has evolved over time from a *termination* detector into a *synchronization* detector. Whereas a termination detector has to fire only once, the synchronization detector has to be restartable time after time. And finally, as all pieces of parallel code in the run-time-support, the synchronization detector lives under a polling regime.

The exact use of the synchronization detector is to bring all nodes into a synchronized state at either garbage collection or termination time. And when all nodes agree on synchronization, the network may not contain any messages from before the synchronization. To simplify the algorithm, it is always node zero that plays the leading role in the synchronization process. When a certain node is nearly out of memory and wants to garbage collect, it send an asynchronous message to node zero to notify it. Node zero will then take measures to get all nodes agree on garbage collection.

The algorithm will be described as if it runs for termination detection. The garbage collector synchronization runs in a comparable manner. The synchronization process consists of the following phases:

1. When node zero has nothing to do, it send an *initial-probe* message to node 1. Node 1 will receive the initial-probe, and store it until itself has nothing to do. Then node 1 sends the initial-probe to node 2, and so on until the initial-probe returns to node zero.

   In this way, it can take quite a while until the initial-probe returns to node zero. When it does, it is established that all nodes at some time have had nothing to do.

2. Node zero receives the initial-probe, and checks on itself whether it "did" anything since the initial-probe was first send. In a node that has nothing to do, there are two sources of work. The first is messages coming in from the other nodes, the second is the—user and host-file system—I/O connection with the host. Both of these systems take care of setting a bit in a global variable. The synchronization detector takes care of the resetting. By inspecting the bit, the synchronization detector knows whether something has been "done". When something was done, the synchronization detector restarts itself and starts with the initial-probe again at step 1.

   When nothing was done, node zero sends the *second-probe* to node 1. At node 1, the check for work since the initial-probe is made. When no work is done in the mean time, node 1 sends the second-probe to node 2, and so on.

   When something was done in the mean time, node two sends through the *notidle-probe*, thereby converting the probe into another one, and notifying that the synchronization process has failed. When node zero receives the notidle-probe, it will restart the synchronization procedure.

   When node zero receives the second-probe, it is established that there is a good likelyhood that the machine is in idle state. But this is not completely assured yet because there may still be pending messages hanging around in the communication network. This is a very unlikely occurrence, but is is very hard to give upper bounds on the time that a packet spends in the network.

3. The next step is that node zero sends a *clear-network-probe* to all nodes but itself.

   This establishes that the communication-network paths from node zero to all nodes do not contain packets anymore from before the synchronization. Because of the static routing, packets cannot overtake each other.

4. At receipt of the clear-network-probe from node zero, all nodes will send a clear-network-probe to all other nodes except itself and node zero. The nodes will then wait until they receive $n - 2$ clear-network-probes.

   This establishes that almost all communication paths in the network do not contain old packets anymore. Except possibly for the messages on the paths to node zero.

5. At this point all nodes except node zero repeat the check on "doing" work. After all, there might have been work in the network that has just popped up. In case there is no work, the node sends the final clear-network-probe to node zero. Otherwise, a notidle-probe is send to node zero.

6. At the receipt of $n-1$ clear-network-probes, node zero checks for itself on doing work again. If there is one in-coming notidle-probe, or node zero itself has done work in the mean time, the synchronization process restarts.

Otherwise, termination is established and the network is empty. At least, node zero knows this. One remaining thing to be done is to notify the other nodes of this fact by sending an asynchronous *finitermi-probe* to all nodes. This notification is necessary to make the synchronization process restartable.

The algorithm for synchronization detection seems pretty straightforward. It is not. The problem does not lie in the simple case that it succeeds. It is almost trivial to see that it is correct when the steps simply follow one another from the first to the last state. The problem lies in the cases where synchronization fails to be established, and the algorithm must restart.

A second problem lies in the embedding of the algorithm in the polling run-time-support system. The synchronization detector is not alone. It is called from the polling system, must check whether anything happened since the last poll, save its state, and return to the polling system, which may then in turn poll the user-I/O and off-node message handler. In case the Portable Implementation runs on a network of workstations in parallel operation, it is unwanted for a piece of the POOL-X system to eat up all processor time with polling, without actually doing anything. For this case, a piece of the POOL-X system can go into a sleeping state, where it waits for any in-coming I/O. Again this must be correctly integrated with the synchronization detector.

Yet another problem was the change in specification of the synchronization detector. When it was first designed to be the termination detector, it was a one-shot process. It did not need to be re-run after the last step was reached. When it turned into the synchronization detector, the implementation had to be much more careful in the administration of the final moment where synchronization is detected. For example each node should exactly once determine that the point of synchronization is reached for every succeeded run of the synchronization detector. Suppose the synchronization detector is run successfully twice in a row. After the success of the first run, node zero sends out finitermi-probes to all nodes, asynchronously. So it never knows when these actually arrive. Now node zero immediately starts sending the initial-probe around. At node 1, nothing can go wrong because the finitermi-probe will always arrive before the initial-probe of the next synchronization. But at node 2, the initial-probe has taken a different route across the network and may arrive *before* the finitermi node. Although extremely unlikely, this situation does actually occur in a network of workstations POOL-system, and is now—after many hours of debugging—correctly handled by the portable system.

In the Natlab Implementation, the communication network is not order preserving and other measures must be taken to ensure that the network is empty at synchronization. This involves careful counting of packets, but this had already to be done to implement the sliding window protocols.

6.5   The parallel garbage collector

The garbage collector in the Portable Implementation is an intermittent one. An description of a non-intermittent, on-the-fly, garbage collector for POOL is given in [6]. The implementation described here has in common that it is also a mark and sweep algorithm, but is simpler because it stops the normal execution of POOL at all nodes at the same time in order to collect garbage.

Garbage collection is the process that removes all unneeded objects from the system to free their memory for later use. To determine which are the unwanted objects, the garbage collector must find out which objects can no longer contribute to the the the running program. This is necessarily a conservative process. The garbage collector can never exactly find out which objects are not used anywhere in the future. The definition of the garbage objects is the set of objects that are not "known" by the active objects. The "knowing" relation is a transitive closure over all references—object handles—starting with the references of the active objects.

The garbage collector determines the transitive closure with the mark and sweep garbage collection algorithm. At first, all objects except the active objects—those that are in the scheduling queue, waiting to be run—are put into the set of garbage objects. The active objects are put into the set of grey objects. These are the objects that are alive, but may still have references to objects in the garbage set.

Then the mark phase starts. The objects are taken from the grey set one at a time. All references of such object are examined. When the reference points to a grey or alive object, nothing happens. But when it points to an object in the garbage set, that object is transferred from the garbage set to the grey set. After all references of a grey object are examined in this way, that grey object is moved into the set of alive objects. When the set of grey objects is empty, all active objects and all objects "known" by the active objects are in the alive set. All objects still in the garbage set are then removed in the so called sweep phase.

The algorithm is almost trivial to extend to a parallel version. The three sets are distributed across the nodes, or rather each node has its own three sets of garbage, grey and alive objects. Remember that the garbage collector can see from the object-handles where an object resides. When an object-handle—reference—points to a local object, the garbage collector acts as described above, moving the object around in the local sets. When an object-handle points outside the node, a message is sent to the node where the object resides to notify the garbage collector over there that the object should be moved out of the garbage set. This message also sets a bit with the entry of the object in the off-node reference table. After the garbage collection, all entries in the off-node reference table without the bit set, are removed, even if the object that it points to is kept alive by a local reference.

From this simple description it appears that the garbage collector is not a complicated piece of code, and in fact, it isn't. The problem with garbage collectors are the invariants that must be maintained by the program execution to enable the garbage collector to find all references. One single missed reference can cause an alive object to be removed. It is this maintenance of invariants that makes garbage collected languages difficult and often run-time inefficient to implement.

The garbage collector is very fast. Although it stops execution of the program for garbage collection, this is often not even noticeable.

7 Evaluation

In this section we evaluate to what degree the five goals of the Portable Implementation of POOL-X, availability, reliability, portability, modifyability and efficiency, have been met.

In addition, in Section 7.6 an idea is given of the amount of code that is involved in the Portable Implementation.

7.1 Availability

The Portable Implementation has been available since February 1, 1990. This is only slightly more than half a year before PRISMA is finished. This is clearly too late, but for reasons outside the scope of the implementation of the Portable Implementation. The actual implementation of the system—starting from the sequential portable implementation—took only five months since October 1990, when the definition of the pragmas was about settled.

Since its first distribution a lot of effort has gone into keeping the Portable Implementation available. Beside fixing the bugs that came in to be repaired, most effort has gone into not doing anything. Already from the beginning it was clear that the Portable Implementation could do a lot on optimizing the generated code. Especially in the handling of simple arithmetic, arrays and types. It was decided not to incorporate all these optimizations for reasons of availability. In order to keep the system stable, no more major development was done since the release date.

7.2 Reliability

For reliability of the Portable Implementation of POOL-X we have only one objective measure:
Number of bug-reports. Since the first distribution of the Portable Implementation on February 1,
1990, an accurate report has been kept of all the problems that were encountered by the DBMS and
Expert system implementers and other users of the Portable Implementation.

Since the first distribution of the system until the time of writing this paper, at the end of August
1990, a total of 39 bugs have been reported for a system of over 57000 lines of code. There is not
much that we can compare this to. In Knuth's report on TeX in [9], he describes the errors that were
found in TeX. Counting the real errors, not the enhancements, in the seven months starting from
September 1, 1978, he found 18 bugs in a system of 4600 statements. The date, September 1, 1978
is chosen because Knuth indicates that as the time that TeX was starting to be used by a number
of local users. It was already in March, 1978 that Knuth felt that his system was "finished".

Of the 39 bugs in the Portable Implementation, one has not been repaired. It is a bug concerning
routine objects of a complicated dynamic type. It is introduced in the front-end and was already
present when the front-end was used for the interpreter implementation of POOL-X. Because the
front-end type-checking is quite complex, it has not been possible to exactly locate the source of the
error. In addition it is unwanted to make an unreliable fix in the front-end because it might introduce
new bugs. Since the complicated routine object types are not really needed it was decided to leave
the bug.

But the other 38 bugs have been repaired. It is interesting to examine the frequency with which
they were reported. If the total amount of bugs diminishes in time—which is the expected effect of
solving bugs—than we can expect that the frequency of bug-reports drops with time. And this has
fortunately happened:

Month	Nr. of reports
February	17
March	8
April	4
May	3
June	6
July	0
August	1

Actually one must also take into account how much the system is used by different people. It
is likely that no new programs were written during the last months of PRISMA when evaluation
was performed. So although the above figures show a trend towards a highly reliable Portable
Implementation, this is not really sure.

It is also interesting to look at the type of bugs that are reported:

Part of the system	Nr. of reports
Front-end	3
Code generation	9
Standard Classes	8
Garbage collector	2
Termination detection	0
Off-node communication	1
I/O system	4
Debugger	1
Run-time-support, other	4
Introduced by fix	2
Portability	2
Other	3

The entry for portability is for two bugs that were caused by changes in the Sun-OS concerning signal handling and floating point support. The entry for "Introduced by fix" is for a bug that was introduced by fixing another bug. Surprising is the high number of bugs in the standard Classes since these were already used in the sequential predecessor of the Portable Implementation. These problems are mostly caused by the changes in the calling interface, which were evidently not carried out carefully enough.

Even more important than actual reliability of a system is the perceived reliability by the POOL-X programmers. When the programmers know that there are bugs floating around in the system, they will loose confidence in it. This will considerably hinder software development.

It is therefore very important that bugs can be fixed with the shortest possible delay. For the Portable Implementation this has been achieved by distributing the system in source form, in such a way that the fixes can be applied by the local system administrator. Because of this the turnaround time for a fix of a bug-report was usually within one or a few days, and sometimes within hours.

7.3 Portability

The portability of the Portable Implementation is claimed to be high, especially for an implementation of a parallel system. The system runs on VAX, MC68020, SPARC, MC88000, and transputer machines with Unix-like I/O capabilities. It assumes a 32-bit pointer and integer representation, which is nowadays quite common.

The core of the system, fully written in C, runs unmodified on all of these machines. The only parts that require changes are the interfaces to peripheral functions, especially those handling communication between parallel nodes. This was done for the PRISMA machine, UNIX-network, and a 64-node Transputer machine.

7.4 Modifiability

Although the language definition was largely fixed after the implementation of the Portable Implementation started, still some changes had to be made. In particular the Fixed-Arrays were introduced, implemented, and removed from POOL-X again. And later it turned out that the deep_copy could not be implemented correctly in the Natlab Implementation. In order to remain compatible with that implementation, the error was mimicked in the Portable Implementation.

More interesting were the development of the source level debugger and a simulator system. The source level debugger was a successful addition to the Portable Implementation just because the implementation was not optimized. Because all types of all objects are maintained at run-time, it is easy for the debugger to get to them. The debugger also works on all parallel implementations, since it was built on top of the communication handler and synchronization detector. With it, it is possible to inspect objects and data-structures on all nodes. The portability of the debugger is equal to that of the rest of the system. Only the optional windowing interface is SUN-specific.

The simulator was developed by Petter Moe, it simulates the execution of a parallel machine on a single node-system. It is also completely integrated with the Portable Implementation. It is based on saving the complete state of the scheduler and subsystems for node-switching. This state consists of a number of global variables. The simulator includes the simulation of the upppart of the communication handler. This is done by replacing only the commpart. This gives rise to accurate simulation for off-node communication. Unfortunately the simulator was not maintained after its initial implementation. It has to be tuned to give reliable results for a specific parallel implementation.

7.5 Efficiency

The speed of a compiled POOL-X program in the the Portable POOL-X Implementation is not very impressive. In the worst case, it is about 20 times slower than a comparable compiled C program. But as mentioned before, a balance in the implementation is also important. For this reason, care has been taken to make inter-process communication between process-model objects not extremely more expensive than between the more optimized object models. Memory efficiency and the speed of the compiler itself are quite satisfactory.

There are some parts of the Portable Implementation, notably the experimental parts like the communication-handler and the distributed garbage collector, that run at high performance. But the development of these parts have been at the expense of optimization in other important parts of the Portable Implementation. It is especially the C-code generator that must be optimized to such extend that the Portable Implementation will give adequate performance, at all levels. It is likely that this goal can be attained, but only at the investment of considerable effort, and the introduction of more complexity.

7.6 Actual code size of the implementation

The figures given here actually give only a very shallow picture of the complexity of the Portable Implementation. The reason is that programming styles may vary widely across programmers. And even in the Portable Implementation quite a large amount of programmers have contributed code.

The code generator part is about 850 Kbytes or 31000 lines. Two thirds of which were written by Juul van der Spek for the front-end that translates POOL-X into the pnull-code, the normalized parse tree representation. The front-end was later modified by the author (of this paper) to include the atomic data pragmas. The rest of the code generator part mainly consists of the driver program that coordinates the compiling process—a make facility—and the C-code generator. It translates pnull-code into C-code.

The portable part of the run-time-support system is some 560 Kbytes larges, or 26000 lines. Most of it written by the author, some changes and additions were made by Mark Tucker, mostly in the debugger, and Petter Moe provided numerous "ifdef"ed pieces of code to make his simulator run.

Three hardware specific libraries account for 34 Kbytes of code. Of this code 37 lines are needed to make a single node UNIX version run, 681 lines for a network of UNIX machines, and 907 lines are used to make the simulator tick. All of this is written in C.

The fourth machine implementation runs on top of bare hardware, the PRISMA machine. It consists of 90 Kbytes or 3500 lines of code for the UNIX I/O implementation and low level off-node message handler. It does contain some pieces of assembler. This code was written by Henk Muller for the Natlab Implementation and adapted for the Portable Implementation, except for the message handler that was written from scratch (660 lines, 24 Kbytes). In addition there are 125 Kbytes of code, or 4500 lines, for the disk filing system. It was taken from the Natlab Implementation to make the disk formats of the Natlab and Portable Implementation equal. It was written by Sun Chengzheng who did the filing interface, and Marnix Vlot made the low level SCSI interface. Henk Muller did the adaptation of these parts for the Portable Implementation.

8 Conclusion

With an experimental language as large as POOL-X, the first aim in implementing it must be simplicity. With this aim, the Portable Implementation has succeeded in being available, reliable, portable and modifiable. It has not succeeded in being a high performance implementation, but even the performance of the system can be called promising. This is most certainly the case for a number of research topics such as the distributed garbage collector and the off-node communication handler.

Not only can the RISC approach be applied to processor design, but also to software engineering and language design.

9 Acknowledgements

The research in this paper was supported by the SPIN, the Dutch Stimuleringsprojectteam Informatica. I want to thank the PRISMA team headed by Huib Eggenhuisen of Philips Research Laboratories in Eindhoven for the offered possibilities and support for this implementation of POOL-X. I am also grateful for the many pleasant and stimulating times I spend at the Natlab in Eindhoven. I especially want to thank the DBMS development teams at the Technical University of Twente and CMCS, the expert system development team at the CMCS, and all other developers for actually using my systems and providing me with encouragements and bug-reports.

References

[1] Alfred V. Aho, Ravi Sethi, Jeffrey D. Ullman, *Compilers Principles, Techniques, and Tools*, Addison-Wesley, 1986.

[2] Pierre America, *A proposal for tuple types in POOL-X*, PRISMA document 0037, Philips Research Laboratories Eindhoven, 1987.

[3] Pierre America, *Definition of POOL-X*, PRISMA documents 0350, 0351, 0352, and POOMA document 0019, Philips Research Laboratories Eindhoven, 1990.

[4] Pierre America, Lex Augusteijn, Ben Hulshof, *Annotations for data object support in POOL-X*, POOMA document 0019, Philips Research Laboratories Eindhoven, 1990.

[5] Jan Koen Annot, Rob A. van Twist, *A Novel Deadlock Free and Starvation Free Packet Switching Communication Processor*, Parallel Architectures and Languages Europe, LNCS 258, Springer-Verlag, pp 68-85, 1987.

[6] Lex Augusteijn, *Garbage Collection in a Distributed Environment*, Parallel Architectures and Languages Europe, LNCS 259, Springer-Verlag, pp 75-93, 1987.

[7] John L. Hennessy, David A. Patterson, *Computer Architecture: A Quantitative Approach*, Morgan Kaufmann Publishers, Inc., 1990.

[8] Paul Hudak, Phil Wadler, *Report on the Programming Language Haskell, A Non-Strict, Purely Functional Language*, 1990.

[9] Donald E. Knuth, *The Errors of TEX*, Stanford Report STAN-CS-88-1223, 1988.

[10] Frank G. Pagan, *Converting Interpreters into Compilers*, Software—Practice and Experience, Vol. 18(6), 1988.

[11] Robert van Renesse, *The Functional Processing Model*, Phd thesis, VU Amsterdam, 1989.

[12] Bjarne Stroustrup, *What is object-oriented programming*, IEEE Software, May 1988.

[13] Andrew S. Tanenbaum, *Computer Networks*, Prentice/Hall, 1981.

Logging and Recovery in PRISMA

C.A. van den Berg

M.L. Kersten

CWI

P.O. Box 4079, 1009 AB Amsterdam, The Netherlands

Abstract

The recovery methods for main-memory database systems are mostly based on maintaining a disk based log and checkpoint. The information written to the log usually consists of low level information, before-after images or single tuple updates. In this paper we examine the effect of writing higher level update information to the log. This results in less logging overhead during normal processing, but an increased replay overhead during recovery.

We introduce a cost model for analyzing the effect of higher level logging on the transaction throughput, and present the results of a performance analysis based on this cost model.

Key Words & Phrases: main memory database machines, logging and recovery, performance analysis

1985 Mathematics Subject Classification: 69H22, 69H26, 69C40, 69C24

1990 CR Categories: H.2.2, H.2.6, C.2.4, C.4

1 Introduction

An advantage of main-memory DBMS over disk-based systems is the performance gain that results from ignoring one level in the storage hierarchy during retrieval. However, to ensure stability either its memory should be non-volatile, i.e. safe RAM, or disks should be used to keep logs and checkpoints. PRISMA [1] follows the latter approach; using multiple disks to realize a stable storage subsystem.

The overhead involved in maintaining a log and checkpoint pair has been identified as a limiting factor for the transaction throughput. Traditionally logging takes place at the physical record level, which reduces the time spent in reconstructing the actual database from the most recent checkpoint. Logging at a logical level, for instance of SQL update statements, can greatly reduce the amount of log information stored, and therefore reduce the IO cost involved in reading the log. The price being paid is an increased CPU cost, due to longer log replay. This cost may be reduced considerably by the exploitation of parallel hardware. In general a tradeoff must be made, between the overhead of logging during normal processing and the time spent in crash recovery.

Several techniques are proposed to reduce the overhead for logging and checkpointing , including parallel logging [AD85], using stable log storage [DKO+84, Eic87], and database partitioning [LC87]. It is for memory resident databases not entirely obvious at which level the logging process should take place. In this paper we present a cost model, which is used to examine the effect of the logging level. This model is also used to study the effect of parallel logging, and database partitioning on the transaction throughput in the context of the PRISMA architecture.

The remainder of this paper is organized as follows. Section two contains a short introduction to the PRISMA architecture and gives an indication of related work. In the third section the PRISMA recovery architecture is presented. A cost model for this architecture can be found in section four and, finally, we present the results of some experiments based on this cost model.

---

[1] The PRISMA project is a SPIN project, partially funded by the Dutch government, and is a joint effort of Philips Research Labs, the CWI and several Dutch universities for the development of a parallel inference and storage machine.

2 Background and scope

2.1 PRISMA and POOL

The PRISMA database management system is developed for a prototype multiprocessor machine, which consists of 100 processing nodes interconnected through a dedicated packet switching network. Each processing node is based on a MC68020 with 16 Mbyte of non-stable memory. Every two nodes share a 150Mbyte disk (See elsewhere in this volume).

The PRISMA database system is implemented in POOL-X [Ame88] a parallel object oriented language designed to simplify the construction of parallel applications. The language provides a stable storage class for data persistency. This class offers the same operations as an ordinary typed file (à la Pascal), but the implementation ensures that writes are atomic and that they survive system crashes and disk failures.

The language does not provide a low level interface to disk, which would allow reading and writing pages directly and fancy disk allocation algorithms for minimizing average seek time. Furthermore, the DBMS designer has no control over the physical records, nor direct access to the system buffers to speedup checkpointing. Everything below the simple file interface is hidden. Consequently logging and checkpointing can only be implemented in terms of POOL objects.

2.2 Related work

In [LC87] Carey and Lehman propose to perform the log and checkpointing operation on database partitions. A partition is used to store a variety of information, ranging from indices to tuples. The logfile and checkpoint file for a partition contains enough information to allow for an independent recovery of the partition. Using demand recovery improves the average response time of transactions further. The undo records for update transactions are stored in volatile memory. A separate recovery processor is used to write the redo log entries of committed transactions to stable storage.

In PRISMA the database relations are already partitioned into fragments. In many respects, the fragment storage can be seen as a partition in terms of [LC87] and, thus, could be the level of the recovery and logging process.

In [DKO+84] DeWitt compares several recovery schemes for disk-resident multi-processor database machines. Methods based on logging, shadowing, and differential files are compared. The experiments show that a recovery scheme based on parallel logging is most suited for multiprocessor database machines. In particular it proves to be an effective technique for improving the transaction throughput. Although PRISMA is foremost a main memory machine, the observation of DeWitt is still relevant, because the I/O overhead involved in gathering the recovery information is considered.

The paper by Eich [Eic87] gives a classification of recovery architectures for main memory database systems. The different classes are compared on transaction throughput and transaction cost (response time). The classification is based on: (1) the amount of stable memory (none, only log, and all), (2) availability of logging hardware (yes, no), (3) checkpointing overhead (yes, no) and (4) commit policy (immediate, group and precommit). From a simple analytical model the following general conclusions are drawn: (1) group commit is bad for response time for an individual transaction, (2) stable memory and log processor is good for both response time and throughput, (3) if there is no stable memory, use group commit to improve throughput. The cost model presented, ignores the effect of the level level at which the logging takes place.

In the remainder, we investigate the influence of the logging level on the transaction cost and throughput. Our primary goal is to find a recovery architecture suitable for the PRISMA machine. Thus, we have to ignore the evidently good approaches to equip the system with some safe RAM [CKKS89]. The software techniques like partitioning and parallel logging can be used, however.

The next section presents the considerations for the design of the PRISMA recovery architecture.

3 Recovery architecture

In this section we describe the general architecture of PRISMA and describe how the ideas of parallel logging, database partitioning, and choosing a different logging level work out in the PRISMA context.

We start with a brief description of query processing within PRISMA. A more detailed description of the architecture can be found in [KAH+87]. Then we define the causes for transaction failures and, finally, we present three alternative logging techniques for PRISMA, which are based on varying the level at which logging takes place.

3.1 PRISMA query processing

The PRISMA database system is designed as a distributed relational database system. The database relations are fragmented and stored in data managers, called One Fragment Managers (OFM). A fragmentation rule tells how the relation can be reconstructed from its fragments. Currently, horizontal fragmentation is supported only. Following the fragmentation rules a query on a relation is translated to queries on its composing OFM's, which can be executed in parallel.

Transactions are translated by an SQL parser to its equivalent form in XRA, which stands for eXtended Relational Algebra. A description of this language can be found in [WG89]. Apart from the ordinary set of relational operators like select, join, group an project, XRA offers operators for handling recursive queries and operators to express and control parallel execution of subqueries.

The Query Optimizer transforms the XRA statements to a semantically equivalent but less costly set of XRA statements. The optimizer uses the fragmentation rules to expres the query in terms of operations on fragments. In the sequel we refer to the two forms of the XRA query as XRA-R (on relations) and XRA-F (on fragments).

The Transaction Manager takes the XRA-F transaction, requests locks for the involved fragments and passes the individual OFM's the required XRA-F statements. Before a transaction commits, the Transaction Manager checks the integrity constraints, which must hold for the database relations. Transaction atomicity is ensured using a standard two phase commit protocol.

The individual OFM's execute the XRA-F statements on their fragment data. Each XRA-F update operation, which is set oriented, can result in a sequence of tuple insertions and deletions.

3.2 PRISMA transaction failures

The recovery mechanism of a database system must be able to recover from different causes for transaction abort. Following the overview on transaction oriented recovery given in [HR83], we distinguish between transaction failures, system failures and media failures.

Transaction failures are likely to happen frequently, about 1% - 10% of all update transactions [Reu84]. The recovery from these failures should therefore be fast. In PRISMA, like other main memory database systems, we keep the *undo* logrecords in volatile memory, which results in a fast recovery from these failures.

System failures are caused by hardware failures, operating system failures, and database system software failures. Estimations based on the failure rate of the hardware components in PRISMA, indicate that a hardware caused system crash occurs every three days [Mul87]. For the other causes of system failure we can not give a reliable estimation. The machine recovers from a system crash by performing a cold restart, which is followed by reloading the database from stable storage. Thus in the event that one processing node fails, the whole system is rebooted. [2]

The database is protected against media failures by using replicated files as a backup storage for the fragment data. The replicas are allocated by the operating system to different disks. After a system crash, the operating system restores the file system into a consistent state. Thus recovery from media failures is performed by the operating system.

---

[2]The problem of building a fault tolerant system was considered to be out of the scope of this project.

3.3 PRISMA logging and recovery

A transaction is any sequence of XRA (update) statements bracketed as such. The Transaction Manager is in charge of guarding the transaction semantics, i.e. atomicity, consistency, isolation and durability. The recovery mechanism assures that the effects of committed transactions survive system crashes.

The recovery mechanism for PRISMA maintains a log file, where the update statements for a transaction are recorded. The logfile is also used to record the transaction status information. The transaction status can be aborted or committed. In the event of a system crash, the updates of all committed transactions, which are recorded on the logfile are replayed. To reduce the replay time, the database is checkpointed once the log size reaches a certain threshold value. A low threshold value incurs too much checkpointing overhead during normal processing. However, if the treshold value is chosen too large, log replay during recovery becomes too time consuming [CBDU75]. Clearly, we need a threshold value for which the overhead is minimal.

In PRISMA a two phase commit protocol is used to obtain transaction atomicity [CP84]. For the design of the recovery mechanism, which is integrated in the two phase commit protocol, two choices have to be made:

- Which processes are involved in logging ?

- What information is logged ?

The logging process can either be centralized or distributed. In centralized logging the Transaction Manager could log all the update information. In distributed logging, both the OFM's and the Transaction Manager could be involved in the logging process. For distributed logging the Transaction Manager records the global abort or commit decision on the transaction log only. The OFM's record the updates performed on behalf of the transaction, the local abort or commit decision, and the global decision.

The design of the logging and recovery scheme for PRISMA aims for the best possible transaction throughput. That is, we do not optimize the logging procedure or the recovery procedure in isolation, but together in relation to the expected mean time between failure (MTBF). The choice of what is logged has a direct influence on the crash recovery time and the logging overhead. Evidently, logging at the highest level in PRISMA leads to small amounts of log info. But the cost associated with recovery could become so high that the effective transaction throughput remains low. So there is a tradeoff between IO and CPU cost.

In the following overview we consider, the influence of a given log level on the replay cost and logging cost for a transaction. Three different logging levels are considered: XRA-R, XRA-F and Tuple level. We illustrate the effect using the following update transaction:

$$UPDATE \quad R$$
$$SET \qquad salary = salary * 1.10$$
$$WHERE \quad dept = ``CS''$$

3.3.1 XRA-R

The SQL transaction is translated by the SQL parser to the following XRA-R transaction:

$$update(R, select(R, dept =" CS"), salary = salary * 1.10)$$
$$commit/abort$$

The logging process is controlled by the Transaction Manager, which writes the transaction commit or transaction abort decision to the log. A checkpoint operation is initiated by the Transaction Manager, whenever the log size reaches a certain threshold. Update operations are only written to the log if all the locks for the operation have been acquired. This ensures that during replay the transactions are reexecuted in the correct order.

The recovery process requires that all OFM's reload their latest checkpoint and that the Transaction Manager, in charge of the recovery, replays the operations of committed transactions found on the log. The replay cost includes the translation of the XRA-R statements to XRA-F statements.

3.3.2 XRA-F

Logging at the XRA-F level is just like logging at the XRA-R level a form of centralized logging. The advantage is that the XRA-F statements are already optimized. The amount of log information., however, is larger. The single example XRA-R statement is translated to n_f XRA-F statements, if the relation R is stored in n_f fragments. [3]

$$update(F_i, select(F_i, dept =" CS"), salary = salary * 1.10) \quad i = 1, \ldots, n_f$$
$$commit/abort$$

The Transaction Manager records the XRA-F statements and the transaction commit and transaction abort decisions on the log. The checkpoint operation is again initiated by the Transaction Manager.

The recovery process involves reloading the latest checkpoint in the OFM's and replaying the XRA-F log. [4]

3.3.3 Tuple

Logging at the tuple level is a form of distributed logging. It is basically the technique described in [CP84]. Each XRA-F statement results in a list of tuple updates. The exact amount depends on the selectivity of the update and the size of the fragment s_f. In PRISMA a hash-based fragmentation scheme is used, thus each fragment has on the average the same amount of tuple updates.

$$update(tuple_i, f(tuple_i)) \quad i = 1, \ldots, \sigma s_f$$
$$precommit$$
$$commit/abort$$

The OFM's write the list of tuple updates to a private log. If the size of the log becomes too large, a checkpoint of the fragment data is made. Because the One Fragment Manager has complete control over the updates on the fragment it is also possible to perform a 'fuzzy' checkpoint operation. By keeping a copy of the data of completed transactions, the checkpoints can be written to disk, while new update transactions are in progress. This process is described in a little more detail in [DKO+84].

For recovery it is necessary that the OFM records both the precommit, as well as the global commit or global abort records for the two phase commit protocol. The Transaction Manager writes the global decision on a system log, because a crash may occur before the global decision is recorded on the logs of all OFM's involved.

The recovery of an OFM then involves reloading its most recent checkpoint and replaying the updates of completed transactions from its private logfile. Transactions, which have entered their precommit phase, but which have not yet run to completion are either aborted or committed, depending on the information on the system log.

Because the logging and checkpointing information involves only a single fragment, it is possible to recover fragments individually. This makes on demand recovery of fragments possible.

---

[3] This number of logrecords is a pessimistic value and probably too high in practice.

[4] It is possible with this scheme to recover fragments on demand by analyzing the dependency graph for fragments and transactions. This analysis delivers a subset of the transactions on the transaction log, which is minimally required to recover the database to a correct state. In general, it is unlikely that this subset is smaller than the complete collection of completed transactions on the transaction log.

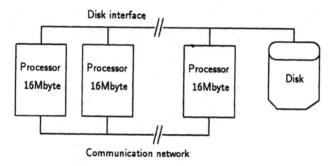

Figure 1: The architecture for the cost model

4 Cost model

In the previous section, we have discussed in general terms the recovery mechanisms for each logging level and argued that there is a tradeoff between logging overhead during normal processing and recovery time. In this section, we want to substantiate this claim by deriving a simple cost model for a memory resident database system. Our model is based on the one proposed by Eich [Eic87] for main memory database systems to experiment with different logging policies. The main difference is that we model the recovery time explicitly, as it influences the throughput.

The cost model is based on a simplified PRISMA architecture consisting of several processors connected by a communication network and sharing a single disk (see figure 1). The effect of using several disks in parallel can be modeled by reducing the time to read or write to disk. The fragments of a relation are allocated to different processors and we assume that an update transaction affects a single relation only. This means that the tuple modifications, during normal processing and log replay can be performed in parallel for each fragment.

The procedure for determining the proper logging level is as follows. First, we express the transaction throughput as a function of the checkpointing frequency. Next, we determine the checkpointing scheme that maximizes transaction throughput. Finally, this cost formula is used to determine the maximum transaction throughput for different logging levels, using some typical cost estimates for the basic operations, like writing log records and copying memory.

4.1 The basic cost model

A summary of the parameter setting is given in table 1. In the remainder σ represents the update selectivity; that is the fraction of the relation, modified by an update transaction.

The transaction throughput r_t depends on the MTBF T_f, the recovery time c_R and the average transaction time c_t. We assume that the recovery must be finished before normal processing can begin.

$$r_t = \frac{T_f - c_R}{c_t T_f}$$

The recovery cost is determined by the cost for reloading the latest database checkpoint and the cost for replaying the log records. The reload cost depends on the database size s_{db} (in pages) and the time to read a page from disk c_{io}.

The checkpointing policy for all logging levels considered is that L_{max} log records are written, after which a new checkpoint is produced. The replay cost consist of the IO cost for reading a log record c_l and of the CPU cost for re-executing the log record c_{replay}. Obviously c_{replay} depends on the logging level.

SQL	0.6	SQL level execution overhead
$XRA-R$	0.4	XRA-R level replay overhead
$XRA-F$	0.2	XRA-F level replay overhead
$Tuple$	0.0	Tuple level replay overhead
f_u	0.25	the fraction of update transactions
f_t	0.03	the fraction of failing update transactions
s_l	0.1	the size of a log record in pages
s_t	0.5	the size of a tuple in pages
n_t	1000	the number of tuples in a fragment
n_f	10	the number of fragments in a relation
n_r	30	the number of relations in the database
T_f	259200	MTBF
c_{io}	0.03	time to read/write a page to/from disk
c_{qry}	0.8	average cpu time per read transaction
c_{tuple}	0.001	tuple update cost

Table 1: The parameter setting

$$c_R = s_{db}c_{io} + \frac{L_{max}}{2}(c_l + c_{replay})$$

$$s_{db} = n_r n_f n_t s_t$$

The average transaction time c_t is determined by assuming that a fraction f_u of all transactions are update transactions. We assume that the cpu cost involved in read transactions can be estimated by constant cost c_{qry}. The effect of parallel execution is already included.

$$c_t = (1 - f_u)c_r + f_u c_u$$

$$c_r = c_{qry}$$

The cost for an update transaction depends on the cost for updating the data c_{upd}, the number of log records produced by the transaction n_l, on the proportional overhead required for the checkpoint operation c_{chk}, the checkpoint frequency f_c and the fraction of transaction failures f_t. Note that the number of log records produced in a transaction depends on the log level.

$$c_u = c_{upd} + n_l c_l + f_c c_{chk} + f_t c_{undo}$$

The update cost consists of a fixed amount for translating the SQL update operation to tuple updates and on a variable cost for modifying the selected tuples. The latter depends on the update selectivity σ and the fragment size n_t.

$$c_{upd} = SQL + \sigma n_t c_{tuple}$$

Every time the total number of log records written to the log exceeds the threshold value L_{max}, a checkpoint is generated. This results in a fraction of $\frac{n_l}{L_{max}}$ checkpoint operations per update transaction.

The time spent in the checkpoint operation depends on the amount of dirty pages produced during normal processing. We make the assumption that the (tuple) updates are equally distributed over all the database pages. Using probabilistic arguments we find an expression for the expected amount of dirty pages after k tuple updates.

	XRA-R	XRA-F	Tuple
n_l	2	$1 + n_f$	$1 + 2n_f + \sigma n_f n_t$
c_{level}	$XRA - R$	$XRA - F$	0
logging method	centralized	centralized	distributed

Table 2: Parameter setting for different logging levels

Between two checkpoints run $\frac{L_{max}}{n_l}$ update transactions, which produce together $k = \sigma n_f n_t \frac{L_{max}}{n_l}$ tuple updates.

$$c_{chk} = (1 - (1 - \frac{1}{s_{db}})^k)) s_{db} c_{io}$$

The cost for undoing the result of a transaction is determined by the amount of updates already performed on a fragment. As the list of undo records is kept in memory, no IO cost is involved. Therefore, the update selectivity σ determines the amount of tuple modifications, which have to be undone.

$$c_{undo} = \sigma n_t c_{tuple}$$

Given the formula for the transaction throughput can determine the maximum throughput for each logging level by filling in the n_l and c_{replay} parameters and differentiating the transaction throughput.

$$\frac{d}{dL_{max}} r_t = 0$$

As the solution of this equality is analytically intractable, we have solved the equality numerically.

4.2 Analysis of the logging levels

The cost formula $r_t(L_{max})$ is parameterized by the replay cost c_{replay} per log record and the number of log records per transaction n_l.

The replay cost depends on the number of transactions, which can be replayed and the cost per transaction. On the average about $\frac{L_{max}}{2n_l}$ update transactions have to be replayed after a system crash. This is per log record $\frac{1}{n_l}$.

The transaction cost for each logging level depends on a level dependent overhead c_{level} and replay cost for the tuple updates, which depends on the update selectivity. The replay of the tuple updates can be performed in parallel for each fragment and therefore only depends on the size of the fragment.

$$c_{replay} = \frac{c_{level} + \sigma n_t c_{tuple}}{n_l}$$

For the XRA-R level 2 log records are produced per transaction. The replay cost per log record involves the translation of the XRA update statement and the subquery execution in the OFM, which are performed in parallel.

The XRA-F level produces $1 + n_f$ log records. The replay cost per log record is again composed of a fixed overhead for translating the XRA-F statements and the actual tuple updates.

At the tuple level for each tuple update a log record is produced. The replay cost per log record is simply the cost for performing a single tuple update. As the log records for the n_f fragments can be replayed in parallel. An overview of the parameter settings for the different logging levels can be found in table 2.

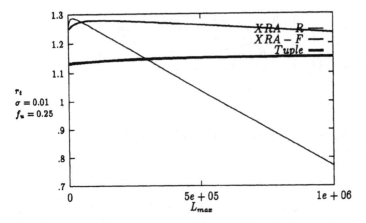

Figure 2: The transaction rate as a function of L_{max}

5 Experiments and results

The cost model presented formed the basis for some experiments to increase our understanding of the parameter settings. These experiments show that choosing a higher log level as the basis of the recovery architecture improves the transaction throughput of the database system. Additional experiments were conducted to validate that this conclusion holds even when the parameters for the hardware change an order of magnitude, and if the ratio read/update transaction shifts. All calculations are based on the default parameter settings, which can be found in table 1.

Critical in optimizing the recovery mechanism is the choice of the threshold log value. This value is different for each log level, because it is determined by the replay cost and the log cost. For tuple level logging the maximum transaction throughput is reached at much higher values for the log size threshold, than for XRA-R and XRA-F level logging. This is caused by the checkpointing overhead. For tuple level logging, the threshold value L_{max} is reached sooner than for XRA-R and XRA-F level logging, which results in more checkpointing overhead per transaction. An increase in the update selectivity necessarily results in a reduced transaction throughput, but has no effect on the optimal threshold value. The results of this experiment can be found in figure 2.

Given the optimal threshold value for each logging level we determined the effect of changing the update selectivity for a transaction on the maximum transaction throughput. (See figure 3).

The transaction throughput for tuple logging degrades more quickly as a function of update selectivity than the other methods. This is caused by the logging overhead during normal processing. We expected that for low values of the update selectivity, the recovery mechanism based on tuple logs would beat a recovery mechanism based on XRA-R or XRA-F logging. However, even for update selectivity values, where only a single tuple was updated, XRA-R and XRA-F logs give the highest performance. This effect can be explained by considering that the transaction throughput is dominated by the logging overhead during normal processing. The replay overhead, which is higher for XRA-R and XRA-F logging, is negligible for large values of MTBF. Experiments with values for the MTBF, which were an order of magnitude smaller, however, showed that tuple logging neither beats XRA-R logging.

By varying the ratio f_u between read and update transactions, we can get an impression of the overhead involved in logging. The results on transaction rate can be found in figure 4. It highlights the considerable influence of the read/update transaction ratio. To find out whether this is should be attributed to the logging overhead or only by the amount of tuple updates, we have run the same experiment with the overhead for logging and checkpointing set to zero. This situation corresponds with a database system equipped with safe ram and a separate checkpoint processor.

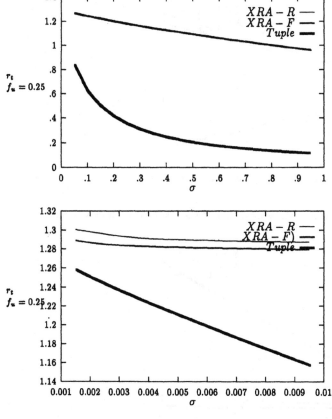

Figure 3: The maximum transaction rate as a function of the update selectivity σ.

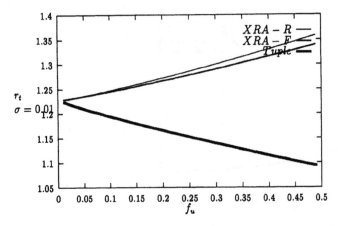

Figure 4: The maximum transaction rate as a function of the read/update transaction ratio, f_u.

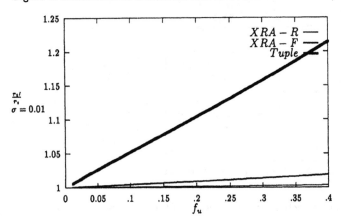

Figure 5: The ratio $\frac{r_t\prime}{r_t}$, where $r_t\prime$ represents the maximum transaction rate in a stable memory environment

The result of this experiment is shown in figure 5. As expected, tuple level logging performs under these circumstances (only marginally) better than XRA-R and XRA-F level logging. The maximum transaction throughput, however, is hardly influenced. This indicates that the overhead is primarily determined by the tuple updates and the overhead caused by transactions failures. Although this effect is at first sight in conflict with the results reported in [Eic87], the different findings can be explained. In that paper only tuple level logging was considered. If we only look at the effect of stable memory on the transaction throughput for tuple level logging, we observe a similar increase of transaction throughput.

6 Conclusion

In this paper we have considered the impact of choosing a higher logging level for memory resident database systems. The cost model, although very simple, indicates that for transactions with a high update selectivity, logging at an algebraic level does improve the transaction throughput over tuple level logging. This method results in a performance gain of about the same order of magnitude as using stable memory to keep the log tables, and parallel checkpointing hardware. The reason is that the cost for log replay after a system crash has decreased considerably, when the database is stored in memory.

In the current implementation of PRISMA, the recovery mechanism is based on logging at the tuple level. Provided that the evaluation of the cost model using the PRISMA architecture does not lead to contradictory results, the next version of PRISMA should seriously consider XRA logging.

7 Acknowledgements

We would like to thank all persons involved in the PRISMA project for the stimulating cooperation and the effort they have put into making this project a success.

References

[AD85]   Rakesh Agrawal and David J. DeWitt. Recovery architectures for multiprocessor database machines. In *Proc. SIGMOD*, 1985.

[Ame88]   P. America. Language definition of pool-x. PRISMA document Doc. Nr. 350, Philips Research Laboratories, September 1988.

[CBDU75]   K.M. Chandy, J.C Browne, C. Dissly, and W.R. Uhrig. Analytic models for rollback and recovery strategies in database systems. *IEEE Transactions on Software Engineering*, 1, March 1975.

[CKKS89]   G. Copeland, T. Keller, R. Krishnamurthy, and M. Smith. The case for safe ram. In *Proc. of the 15th International Conference on Very Large Databases*, 1989.

[CP84]   S. Ceri and G. Pelagatti. *Distributed Databases, Principles and Systems*. McGraw-Hill, 1984.

[DKO+84]   D.J. DeWitt, R. Katz, F. Olken, L. Shapiro, M. Stonebreaker, and D.Wood. Implementation techniques for main memory database systems. In *Proc. ACM SIGMOD Conference*, pages 1–8, June 1984.

[Eic87]   Margaret H. Eich. A classification and comparison of main memory database recovery techniques. In *Proc. of the 1987 Database Engineering Conference*, pages 332–339, 1987.

[HR83]   Theo Haerder and Andreas Reuter. Principles of transaction-oriented database recovery. *Computing Surveys*, 15(4), December 1983.

[KAH⁺87] Martin L. Kersten, Peter M.G. Apers, Maurice A.W. Houtsma, Erik J.A. van Kuyk, and Rob L.W. van de Weg. A distributed, main-memory database machine. In *Proc. of the Fith International Workshop on Database Machines*, pages 353–369, October 1987.

[LC87]   Tobin J. Lehman and Michael J. Carey. A recovery algorithm for a high-performance memory-resident database system. In *Proc. SIGMOD*, 1987.

[Mul87]   H. Muller. Hardware aspects of fault tolerance. PRISMA document P121, University of Amsterdam, June 1987.

[Reu84]   Andreas Reuter. Performance analysis of recovery techniques. *ACM Transactions on Database Systems*, 9(4):526–559, December 1984.

[WG89]   A. Wilschut and P. Grefen. Xra definition. PRISMA document P465, Twente University, September 1989.

Parallel Handling of Integrity Constraints

Paul W.P.J. Grefen   Jan Flokstra
Peter M.G. Apers
University of Twente

Abstract

Integrity constraints form an important part of a data model. Therefore, a complete integrity constraint handling subsystem is considered an important part of any modern DBMS. In implementing an integrity constraint handling subsystem, there are two major problem areas: providing enough functionality and delivering good performance in constraint enforcement. In the PRISMA project, an integrity constraint handling subsystem for a relational DBMS is developed, that meets both requirements. Functionality is reached through a modular and extensible architecture of the subsystem. Performance is reached through extensive use of parallelism in various constraint enforcement algorithms.

1 Introduction

In databases a part of the real world is modeled. The real world model consists of structures, operations, and constraints [Tsich82]. The structures represent the real world entities and relations between them. The operations allow manipulation of the structures to model changes in the real world. The constraints guarantee the validity of the real world model represented by the database, by constraining the allowed operations on the database. As such, the constraints describe (part of) the semantics of this model [Tsich82], or, in other words, the knowledge of application properties [Simon87].

Especially in the relational data model integrity constraints are necessary to describe the semantics of the applications, because this data model has very little implicit semantics [Tsich82]. The growing complexity of modern database applications further increases the need for powerful constraint handling mechanisms. Therefore, a complete constraint handling mechanism is considered an important part of any modern DBMS, and is thus included in the PRISMA DBMS, called PRISMA/DB.

There are two general problem areas in implementing a constraint handling mechanism in a DBMS. At the first place, performance of constraint enforcement is a great problem. At the second place, providing a complete functionality is a problem. Solutions for these two problems are the goal of the research towards constraint handling in the PRISMA project:

- high performance of the constraint enforcement mechanism is achieved through extensive use of parallelism in various algorithms;

- complete functionality is reached through a very modular design of the constraint handling subsystem, guaranteeing a high degree of flexibility and extensibility.

---

[0]The work reported in this document was conducted as part of the PRISMA project, a joint effort with Philips Research Laboratories Eindhoven, partially supported by the Dutch "Stimuleringsprojectteam Informaticaonderzoek (SPIN)"

There has been some research in the field of integrity constraint handling already for centralized and traditional distributed database systems, e.g. [Stone75, Zloof78, Simon85, Morg84, Simon87]. In the context of parallel database systems the topic is new. This paper combines the theory of integrity constraint handling with the theory of query execution in parallel database systems, and adds some new ideas to obtain a full-fledged integrity constraint handling mechanism for parallel database systems with fragmented relations.

The paper starts with a discussion of the ideas that form the basis for constraint handling in PRISMA/DB; these ideas lead to the approach taken for design and implementation of the constraint handling subsystem in PRISMA/DB. Next, the architecture of the constraint handling subsystem is described in the context of the full DBMS architecture. Then, the various algorithms for constraint enforcement are discussed. The combination of these algorithms provides a good combination of functionality, flexibility and efficiency. The paper ends with some conclusions.

2 PRISMA approach to constraint handling

In this section the approach to constraint handling as taken in the PRISMA project is discussed. We start with a short discussion of the PRISMA/DB context. Next, the requirements to constraint handling are identified. From these, the approach chosen in the project follows.

2.1 The PRISMA/DB context

In the PRISMA project a parallel, main memory database management system is developed, called PRISMA/DB [Kers87, Apers88]. The system is designed to run on a shared-nothing multi-processor hardware architecture [Bron87]. To support parallelism in query execution, PRISMA/DB uses horizontally fragmented relations. Figure 1 shows the simplified base architecture of PRISMA/DB. The following components can be identified:

Data Dictionary (DD) the DD forms the central storage of all system information, such as information on relations and their fragments; the DD is also responsible for the creation and deletion of new fragments (OFMs);

Concurrency Controller (CC) the CC is responsible for the serializability of concurrent transactions; a two-phase locking protocol is used with fragments as the locking granularity [Date83];

User Interface (UI) the UI is the interface that enables interactive communication with one of the user language parsers of the system (here only the SQL interface is shown);

SQL Parser (SQL) the SQL parser translates SQL queries into the internal relational language of PRISMA/DB; further, the SQL parser informs the DD about the creation and deletion of relations;

Query Optimizer (QO) the QO deals with resolving fragmentation transparency, view removal, translation of recursive expressions, and, of course, the traditional optimization of queries;

Transaction Manager (TM) the TM manages the execution of schedules produced by the QO; for this purpose, the TM builds execution infrastructures out of OFMs and tuple transport channels; the TM also provides transaction serializability through locking and transaction atomicity through a two phase commit protocol [Date83];

One Fragment Manager (OFM) the OFM manages a single base fragment or intermediate result in the database; all fragment data is kept in main memory; disk storage is used for logging and checkpointing only; the OFM also executes all relational operators.

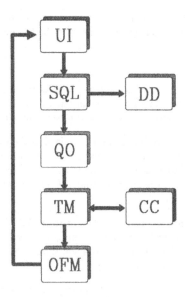

Figure 1: PRISMA/DB base architecture

An important role in PRISMA/DB is played by its internal relational language, called eXtended Relational Algebra (XRA) [Wils90a]. As its name suggests, XRA is an extension to the normal relational algebra; the extensions allow using the language as an operational language. XRA is used as the interface language for the interfaces between SQL Parser, Query Optimizer, Transaction Manager and One Fragment Manager.

2.2 Requirements

The PRISMA project provides an experimental research environment for the development of a DBMS. In this research two main issues can be identified. At the first place, the use of parallelism to improve the performance of a main memory relational DBMS is investigated. At the second place, the feasibility of the implementation of a full blown DBMS in a high level object oriented programming language is an issue under investigation.

The main goals in the field of integrity constraint handling can be deduced from these general project goals. At the first place achieving high performance through the use of parallelism in constraint enforcement is important. Further, using the implementation environment to obtain a complete functionality is considered a main topic. So, the constraint handling subsystem in PRISMA/DB has to meet the following requirements:

- the subsystem must be able to make extensive use of parallelism in the enforcement of constraints to obtain high performance;

- the subsystem should allow a high degree of expressiveness in constraints, to be able to model complex applications;

- as experimenting with the functionality is considered very important, a high degree of flexibility and extensibility should be available;

- as the base architecture of PRISMA/DB already exists, the subsystem must fit easily into the modular PRISMA/DB architecture;

- since integrity constraint handling is one of several research topics in the PRISMA context, the implementation effort for the subsystem should not be too large.

2.3 Approach taken

As lined out above, the approach to constraint handling as taken in the PRISMA project is based on performance on the one hand and on functionality and flexibility on the other hand.
To achieve high performance, a two track approach to parallelism is employed:

- parallelism in constraint enforcement can be obtained in the same way it is obtained in regular query execution if constraints can be translated to normal query constructs in XRA; in this case constraint enforcement is controlled explicitly by the Transaction Manager; therefore, we call this form of enforcement *explicit constraint enforcement*; this approach allows a high degree of functionality and flexibility;

- parallelism can be obtained by having a 'self-checking' data layer; in PRISMA/DB terms this means that the One Fragment Managers containing the base fragments enforce their constraints autonomously; this form of constraint enforcement is called *implicit constraint enforcement*; this approach allows a high degree of efficiency.

Good functionality and flexibility are achieved by having a strict decomposition of the tasks involved in constraint handling; the following tasks are identified:

- *translation* of constraints from the form as specified by the user to the form fit for dircet enforcement by the system;

- *storage* of constraints in both source as translated form;

- *enforcement* of the translated constraints within the transaction mechanism.

3 Architecture for constraint handling

The architecture of the constraint handling subsystem is deduced from the approach described in the previous section. Below we first describe how this architecture is integrated into the existing PRISMA/DB architecture. Next, attention is paid to the constraint translation module, the only fully new module needed for constraint handling.

3.1 Global architecture

As mentioned before, there are three important tasks to be performed for constraint handling in our approach:

- constraint translation

- constraint storage

- constraint enforcement

Because a two way approach to constraint enforcement is adopted in PRISMA/DB, we can split up the last task into explicit and implicit constraint enforcement. So, in total four tasks can be identified. These four tasks and their allocation in the PRISMA/DB architecture are discussed below. Figure 2 shows the modifications to the base architecture as shown in Figure 1.

Constraint translation is considered a fully new task with respect to the base architecture of PRISMA/DB. Therefore, a new component is designed for this task; this module is called the Constraint Compiler (abbreviated as C2, to avoid confusion with the abbreviation for the Concurrency

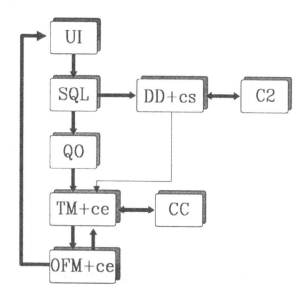

Figure 2: PRISMA/DB extended architecture

Controller component). The C2 component receives constraint specifications at the relation level in source format as its input from the Data Dictionary (DD), and returns optimized constraint specifications at the fragment level in internal format to the DD.

Constraint storage is considered part of the storage of data definitions. Since this task is already allocated with the Data Dictionary, constraint storage is also handled by this component. The DD receives constraint specifications at relation definition time and stores them. Further, the DD activates the C2 module to obtain constraint definitions in internal format. Performing the translation at constraint definition time avoids large overhead at constraint enforcement time. As shown in the figure, the DD is extended with a constraint storage module (cs).

Explicit constraint definitions are stated in XRA, just like ordinary queries. Therefore, it is obvious that explicit constraint enforcement is handled in the same way as regular queries. So explicit constraint enforcement is handled by the Transaction Manager (TM). The TM is extended with a constraint enforcement module (ce) for this purpose. The TM retrieves the constraint definitions in XRA format from the DD, as shown by the thin arc in the figure.

Implicit constraint enforcement is performed at the data level in the DBMS. Therefore, this task is allocated with the OFMs managing the base fragments in the system. The OFM component is extended with a constraint enforcement (ce) module. This module contains special purpose algorithms for local constraint enforcement. Constraint specifications are passed to the OFM at its creation time.

3.2 Constraint compiler

The Constraint Compiler (C2) performs the translation and optimization of constraints in external format at the relation level to constraints in internal format at the fragment level. Since PRISMA/DB employs two different kinds of constraint enforcement, there are two internal constraint formats:

- for explicit constraint enforcement, the constraints are translated to XRA constructs; these constructs are optimized to avoid query optimization overhead at constraint enforcement time; further, constraints are labeled with triggers that indicate when they have to be enforced to

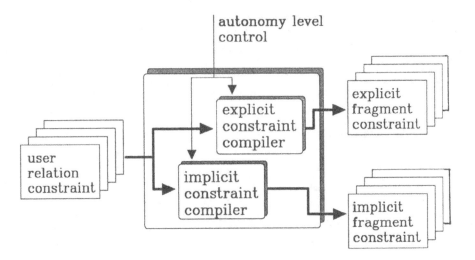

Figure 3: Constraint compiler architecture

avoid unnecessary constraint enforcement; the translation from external form to XRA is treated in detail in Sections 4.2 and 4.3;

- for implicit constraint enforcement, the constraints are translated to special purpose data structures for the OFM components; these data structures are interpreted by the OFMs; the translation from external form to OFM constraints is described in Section 5.1.

To obtain maximum flexibility, both translation types are fully separated in the C2 component. This may be inefficient, but since constraint translation is done statically (at constraint definition time only), performance is not an issue here. The way constraints are split up into explicit and implicit constraints is fully dynamically controllable by the user of the system. So, per relation one can decide what part of the constraints should be enforced explicitly or implicitly. The architecture of the constraint compiler is depicted in Figure 3.

4 Explicit constraint enforcement

For explicit constraint enforcement, constraints specified by the user are translated to XRA constructs; this involves the following two steps:

- translation of the constraints to the fragment level;

- mapping the translated constraints to XRA constructs;

The XRA constructs are executed by the Transaction Manager at the end of a transaction to enforce the constraints. The whole process of translating and enforcing explicit constraints is illustrated by two important classes of example constraints, domain constraints and referential integrity constraints; these constraints are presented below.

4.1 Example constraints

Constraints are denoted as a pair $I = [t, r]$, with the following elements:

- t is the set of *triggers* of the constraint; this set specifies the update types that may violate the constraint;

- r is the rule of the constraint; the rule is a boolean function with a part of the database schema as its domain.

A more formal description of this notation can be found in [Gref89, Gref90a].

Using this notation, a domain constraint is defined at the relation level as follows:

$$
\begin{aligned}
I1_{rel} &= [t1_{rel}, r1_{rel}] \\
t1_{rel} &= \{INS(R), UPD(R)\} \\
r1_{rel} &= (\forall x \in R.i)(c(x))
\end{aligned}
$$

in which $c(x)$ is some boolean condition over x. The trigger set of this constraint states that constraint enforcement is necessary whenever a transaction performs an insert or update operation on relation R; clearly, a delete operation cannot violate a domain constraint. The rule of the constraint specifies that each value in attribute i of relation R has satisfy condiction c.

A referential integrity constraint as defined in [Date81] can be formulated in our notation as follows:

$$
\begin{aligned}
I2_{rel} &= [t2_{rel}, r2_{rel}] \\
t2_{rel} &= \{INS(R), UPD(R), DEL(S), UPD(S)\} \\
r2_{rel} &= (\forall x \in R.i \mid x \neq null)(\exists y \in S.j)(x = y)
\end{aligned}
$$

In this definition, $S.j$ is a key (unique attribute) of relation S. The constraint states that every foreign key in relation R that is not equal to null, must have its counterpart in relation S.

4.2 Translating constraints to the fragment level

Constraints defined by the user are formulated in terms of relations. Because enforcement of constraints takes place at the fragment level of the system, a translation to this level is necessary. The translation of constraints is comparable to the translation of queries from the relation to the fragment level [Ceri84]. The objective of the entire translation is to obtain a specification of the constraints that can straightforwardly be used for constructing efficient enforcement algorithms for the constraints.

The constraint translation is accomplished in the following steps:

- translation of the constraint at the relation level into canonical fragment form; this step brings the definition of the constraints from the external specification level (stated in terms of relations) to the internal level (stated in terms of fragments);

- distribution of the canonical form to the fragments; this step makes the semantics of the constraint fragment oriented; the result of this step is a set of constraints;

- optimization of the distributed fragment form; this step tries to obtain possibilities for a more efficient enforcement of the constraints;

These steps are treated in detail in [Gref89, Gref90a]. Here we limit ourselves to an illustration of the translation by means of the two example constraints.

4.2.1 Translation from relation to fragment level

Constraints specified in terms of relations have to translated to constraints specified in terms of fragments. The first step is translation to the canonical form. Assuming that relation R is fragmented into n fragments, the canonical form for domain constraint $I1$ is the following:

$$
\begin{aligned}
I1_{can} &= [t1_{can}, r1_{can}] \\
t1_{can} &= \{INS(R_1), \ldots, INS(R_n), \\
&\quad\; UPD(R_1), \cdots, UPD(R_n)\} \\
r1_{can} &= (\forall x \in (R_1.i \cup \cdots \cup R_m.i))(c(x))
\end{aligned}
$$

This constraint is defined in terms of fragments, but the semantics are still relation-oriented. To obtain fragment-oriented semantics, the canonical form is distributed to a set of fragment constraints, containing one constraint for each fragment in the relation. The constraint for fragment R_k obtained by distributing $I1_{can}$ is the following:

$$
\begin{aligned}
I1_{R_k} &= [t1_{R_k}, r1_{R_k}] \\
t1_{R_k} &= \{INS(R_k), UPD(R_k)\} \\
r1_{R_k} &= (\forall x \in R_k.i)(c(x))
\end{aligned}
$$

The same steps can be applied to referential integrity constraint $I2$. The construction of the canonical fragment form is straightforward; the construction of the distributed fragment form is different, however. In constraint $I2$ two relations are involved that play different roles: introduction of new values in relation R may cause a constraint violation, whereas deletion of existing values in relation S can violate the constraint. Therefore, separate constraints are constructed for the fragments R_k of relation R and S_k of relation S:

$$
\begin{aligned}
I2_{R_k} &= [t2_{R_k}, r2_{R_k}] \\
t2_{R_k} &= \{INS(R_k), UPD(R_k)\} \\
r2_{R_k} &= (\forall x \in R_k.i \mid x \neq null) \\
&\quad (\exists y \in (S_1.j \cup \cdots \cup S_n.j))(x = y)
\end{aligned}
$$

$$
\begin{aligned}
I2_{S_k} &= [t2_{S_k}, r2_{S_k}] \\
t2_{S_k} &= \{DEL(S_k), UPD(S_k)\} \\
r2_{S_k} &= (\forall x \in (R_1.i \cup \cdots \cup R_m.i) \mid x \neq null) \\
&\quad (\exists y \in (S_1.j \cup \cdots \cup S_n.j))(x = y)
\end{aligned}
$$

The rule of $I2_{S_k}$ cannot be simplified in the general case, due to the fact that referenced values from S_k may be inserted again into another fragment of S within the same transaction (i.e. tuple migration between the fragments of a migration to keep the fragmentation consistent).

4.2.2 Optimization of constraints

The constraint definitions that are the results of the translation as described above are not very efficient for enforcement. Therefore, optimization of these constraints is necessary. Constraints at the fragment level can be optimized in a number of ways:

- the amount of data to be checked can be reduced by checking only those parts of fragments that have been changed in a relevant way; this method has already been described as differential test [Simon85, Simon87, Gard89];

- constraint rules can be algebraically manipulated to obtain forms that are cheaper in execution; this technique is similar to regular query optimization by expression rewriting [Ceri84];

- constraint rules can be simplified in some cases if knowledge about the fragmentation of relations is used; this is similar to removing 'empty' subtrees from query trees in query optimization [Ceri84].

As an example, we show how referential integrity constraint $I2_{R_k}$ as defined above can be optimized. The amount of data to be checked is reduced by replacing R_k by the differential set containing only the new values in R_k; this differential set is denoted as R_k^+. Next, the rule is manipulated by pushing the existential quantor through the union operation; this makes it possible to perform the existence check local to the fragments (opening the possibilities for parallelism). These optimizations result the following constraint definition:

$$
\begin{aligned}
I2_{R_k} &= [t2_{R_k}, r2_{R_k}] \\
t2_{R_k} &= \{INS(R_k), UPD(R_k)\} \\
r2_{R_k} &= (\forall x \in R_k^+.i \mid x \neq null) \\
&\quad (\bigvee_{w=1}^{w=n}((\exists y \in S_w.j)(x = y)))
\end{aligned}
$$

If relation R is fragmented using fragmentation constraints defined only on attribute $R.i$, and relation S is fragmented using the same fragmentation constraints defined only on $S.j$, we know that references from R_k are always to S_k; therefore, we can simplify the referential integrity constraint $I2_{R_k}$ as shown above to the following:

$$
\begin{aligned}
I2_{R_k} &= [t2_{R_k}, r2_{R_k}] \\
t2_{R_k} &= \{INS(R_k), UPD(R_k)\} \\
r2_{R_k} &= (\forall x \in R_k^+.i \mid x \neq null)(\exists y \in S_k.i)(x = y)
\end{aligned}
$$

It is clear, that enforcement of this constraint is much easier (and cheaper) than the enforcement of the constraint in its previous form. This leads to the observation, that integrity constraints should be taken into account in relation fragmentation design.

4.3 Translation to XRA constructs

Constraints are specified by the user in a non-procedural form. To be able to execute the constraints, they are translated to a procedural form in XRA. The XRA necessary for this is only a minimal extension to the XRA needed for normal query execution.

The use of XRA as an enforcement vehicle gives several important advantages over specialized hard coded algorithms:

- XRA provides an abstraction level that makes straightforward translation of constraints into enforcement algorithms possible;

- enforcement via XRA makes use of modular building blocks for the enforcement algorithms, thus ensuring flexibility and extensibility;

- for enforcement via XRA software building blocks are used that are already available for regular query processing to a large extent; this minimizes implementation overhead for integrity constraint handling on the one hand, and maximizes the use of parallel algorithms on the other hand.

4.3.1 Basic XRA constructs

For constraint enforcement in XRA, we make use of the regular relational algebra operators, such as union and difference. Further, we make use of a few extensions to the normal relational algebra. Apart from one, the *alarm* operator, all these extensions are also used for normal query processing in PRISMA/DB.

XRA contains two operators that take care of distributing tuples of a source operand to several destination operands; these operators are functionally equivalent to a combination of regular relational algebra operators, but, as is shown below, operationally extremely important for obtaining parallelism. The first of these operators, *copy*, copies the source operand to each of the destination operands:

$$copy\ (src, dst_1, \cdots, dst_n)$$

This operation is functionally equivalent to the following sequence of assignments:

$$
\begin{aligned}
dst_1 &\leftarrow src \\
&\vdots \\
dst_n &\leftarrow src
\end{aligned}
$$

The second distributing operator, *split*, splits up the source operand over the destination operands given the fragmentation constraints of the destination operands:

$$split\ (src, dst_1, cond_1, dst_2, cond_2, \cdots, dst_n, cond_n)$$

In this operation, all conditions $cond_i$ are mutually disjoint and together complete with respect to the source relation src; in other words, the conditions define a partition of the source relation. This operation is functionally equivalent to the following sequence of assignments:

$$dst_1 \leftarrow \sigma_{cond_1} src$$
$$\vdots$$
$$dst_n \leftarrow \sigma_{cond_n} src$$

Finaly, we have an operator that has as its sole functionality that it causes a transaction abort if its operand is not empty:

$$alarm\ (oper)$$

Using the XRA operators, logic constructs as appearing in constraint definitions can be translated to XRA constructs. Transformation rules as shown below are used for this. These rules give a few examples that can be used in the context of the example constraints of this paper.

$$(\forall x \in R)(c(x)) \qquad\qquad \rightarrow \quad alarm\ (\sigma_{\neg c(x)}(R)) \qquad\qquad (1)$$

$$(\forall x \in R)(\exists y \in S)(x = y) \quad \rightarrow \quad alarm\ (unique(R) - S) \qquad\qquad (2)$$

$$(\forall x \in R)(\bigvee_{i=1}^{n}(\exists y \in S_i)(x = y)) \quad \rightarrow \quad copy\ (unique(R), T_1, \cdots, T_n) \qquad (3)$$
$$alarm\ ((T_1 - S_1) \cap \cdots \cap (T_n - S_n))$$

4.3.2 Translating constraints to XRA

Here we show how the example constraints can be translated to XRA constructs. Domain constraint $I1$ is taken as a first example; the definition of this constraint is:

$$I1_{R_k} = [t1_{R_k}, r1_{R_k}]$$
$$t1_{R_k} = \{INS(R_k), UPD(R_k)\}$$
$$r1_{R_k} = (\forall x \in R_k^+.i)(c(x))$$

The rule of this constraint can easily be mapped onto the following XRA construct using transformation 1 as shown above:

$$alarm\ (\sigma_{\neg c(x)}(\pi_i(R_k^+)))$$

We take referential integrity constraint $I2_{R_k}$ as a second example; the form based on general fragmentation of the involved relations was described above as follows:

$$I2_{R_k} = [t2_{R_k}, r2_{R_k}]$$
$$t2_{R_k} = \{INS(R_k)\}$$
$$r2_{R_k} = (\forall x \in R_k^+.i \mid x \neq null)$$
$$(\bigvee_{w=1}^{w=n}((\exists y \in S_w.j)(x = y)))$$

Using transformations 1 and 3 as listed above, we can map the rule of this constraint onto the following XRA construct:

$$copy\ (unique(\pi_i(\sigma_{i \neq null}(R_k^+))), temp_1, \cdots, temp_n)$$
$$alarm\ ((temp_1 - \pi_j(S_1)) \cap \cdots \cap (temp_n - \pi_j(S_n)))$$

Note, that the $copy$ operator takes care of distributing the differential set of R_k; this is used to obtain pipeling parallelism, as discussed below. The form of constraint $I2_{R_k}$ that was optimized with respect to matching fragmentation of the involved relations is the following:

$$I2_{R_k} = [t2_{R_k}, r2_{R_k}]$$
$$t2_{R_k} = \{INS(R_k), UPD(R_k)\}$$
$$r2_{R_k} = (\forall x \in R_k^+.i \mid x \neq null)(\exists y \in S_k.j)(x = y)$$

In this case, the resulting XRA construct can be:

$$split(unique(\pi_i(\sigma_{i \neq null}(R_k^+))), temp_1, f_1, \cdots, temp_n, f_n)$$
$$alarm(temp_1 - \pi_j(S_1))$$
$$\vdots$$
$$alarm(temp_n - \pi_j(S_n))$$

The differential set R_k^+ is not sent completely to every fragment of S, but is split up over the fragments of S, thereby reducing tuple transport; further, the costly intersection operation is not necessary here.

4.4 Enforcing constraints

The XRA constructs used for explicit constraint enforcement as presented in the previous section can straightforwardly be implemented using XRA execution infrastructures in PRISMA/DB. This section discusses the way this is realized and the possibilities for parallelism in this method.

4.4.1 Building the infrastructure

The infrastructure for constraint enforcement at the OFM level consists of three types of building blocks:

- permanent OFM : used for the storage of fragments of permanent relations (base fragments);

- temporary OFM : used for execution of relational operators and storage of intermediate results of operations;

- channels : used for the transportation of tuples between OFMs.

The permanent OFMs contain the fragment data on which integrity constraints must be enforced. These OFMs contain algorithms to automatically maintain the differential sets; this means that these sets are already constructed during transaction execution on a local basis in the fragments. The temporary OFMs are used for the execution of the XRA operators needed for the constraint enforcement structures. These OFMs can be created dynamically by the Transaction Manager when needed. The channels are used as communication means to transport tuples from one OFM to another. Both OFMs and channels are designed to make optimal use of pipelining in executing XRA [Wils89, Wils90b].

To obtain complete transaction semantics with respect to atomicity, all constraints are enforced at commit time in PRISMA/DB; note, that the techniques as presented in this paper can be used for other approaches equally well. Enforcing constraints at the end of a transaction consists conceptually of two phases:

- *setup phase*: in this phase the transaction manager builds the execution infrastructure needed for constraint enforcement; actually, this phase can already start during transaction execution;

- *execution phase*: in this phase the execution infrastructure processes the data to be checked; similar to the execution of regular user queries, this operates in a fully parallel, pipelined fashion [Wils90b].

The setup phase makes use of the same mechanisms that are used for setting up normal query execution infrastructures in PRISMA/DB; this implies that constraint enforcement does not require any architectural changes at the execution level [Gref90c]. Especially, the Transaction Manager does not have to deal with any part of the database extension, thus avoiding a possible bottleneck in the enforcement algorithms.

The previously presented example of the XRA construct used for enforcement of referential integrity constraint *I*2:

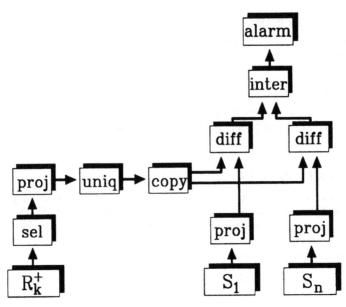

Figure 4: XRA constraint enforcement infrastructure

$$copy\ (unique(\pi_i(\sigma_{i \neq null}(Rk^+))), temp_1, \cdots, temp_n)$$
$$alarm\ ((temp_1 - \pi_j(S_1)) \cap \cdots \cap (temp_n - \pi_j(S_n)))$$

can straightforwardly be implemented by the execution infrastructure as shown in Figure 4.

4.4.2 Parallelism in explicit constraint enforcement

We have seen that constraint enforcement is executed by an XRA infrastructure. The relational operators in these infrastructures are all independent processes, so parallelism can be employed easily. Within the explicit constraint enforcement mechanism we can distinguish three types of parallelism [Gref88, Wils89]:

- several independent constraints can be checked at the same time; this is possible because after the setup phase, the enforcement process is fully asynchronous; at the constraint enforcement level, we can consider this a form of *multi-tasking*;

- at the same level in a XRA infrastructure, several OFMs operate on the data of several fragments in parallel; in the example of figure 4 we can see that all difference operators can work in parallel; this kind of parallelism is called *task spreading*;

- because all operators operate in a pipelined fashion, several stages of the XRA infrastructure can work in parallel too; we call this *pipelining* parallelism [Wils90b].

Further, improvements in response time for the entire transaction can be reached by executing normal queries of the transaction and constraint enforcement queries in parallel. As such, an overlap is created that shortens the overall transaction execution time. Take as an example a transaction that first insert some tuples into two distinct fragments managed by OFMs OFM_1 and OFM_2, and thereafter computes the join of both fragments on a third OFM $OFM3$. In this case the activity of the OFMs can be as depicted in Figure 5.

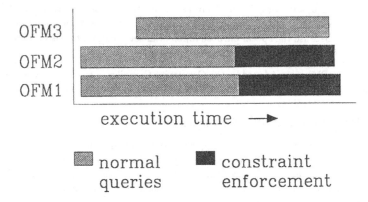

Figure 5: Regular query execution and explicit constraint enforcement

5 Implicit and hybrid constraint enforcement

In the previous section explicit constraint enforcement is discussed. This approach to constraint enforcement has a high degree of functionality and flexibility. This approach has however two drawbacks with respect to high efficiency:

- there is overhead at constraint enforcement time in creating the necessary XRA execution infrastructure and in passing the XRA commands to the One Fragment Managers involved in constraint enforcement;

- no specialized algorithms in the OFMs can be used for constraint enforcement to obtain high efficiency, because all constraints are stated in regular XRA.

To overcome these drawbacks, PRISMA/DB also employs implicit constraint enforcement. This form of enforcement is characterized by a high degree of autonomy of the involved One Fragment Managers: the OFMs enforce constraints without intervention of the Transaction Manager. Implicit constraint enforcement is however only applicable to very limited forms of integrity constraints. Therefore, PRISMA/DB employs a third technique which is a combination of explicit and implicit constraint enforcement; this form of enforcement is called hybrid constraint enforcement.

5.1 Translating constraints for OFMs

As shown in Figure 3 the compilation process in the Constraint Compiler component is directed by the autonomy level control. Four levels of OFM autonomy are distinguished by the C2 component [Gref90b]:

1. The lowest level of autonomy is called *no autonomy*; in this case all constraints are handled by *explicit enforcement* as described in the previous section; the OFM has no knowledge about constraints.

2. In the case of *strictly local* autonomy, the OFM enforces standard constraints having a strictly local scope with respect to the fragment managed by the OFM; this is a form of *implicit constraint enforcement*.

3. If *data reduction* autonomy is used, the OFM also offers special purpose differential sets for explicit constraint enforcement; the OFM constructs these sets by performing a filtering technique on the standard differential sets; this is a form of *hybrid constraint enforcement*.

4. The highest level of autonomy is called *process reduction* autonomy; in this case the OFM uses built-in logic, that can decide that explicit constraint enforcement for a specific constraint is not necessary, because the specal purpose differential set is empty; this is also a form of *hybrid constraint enforcement*.

Constraint sets for OFMs are produced by the Constraint Compiler in special purpose data structure format. These constraints are passed to the OFMs at their creation time by the Data Dictionary.

5.2 Implicit enforcement of constraints

In implicit constraint enforcement, an OFM enforces local constraints without any intervention from the TM. The constraint enforcement is triggered by the standard two-phase commit protocol; as such, the enforcement is treated as a part of the local commit decision making in the OFM and does not need any special communication with the TM. Implicit constraint enforcement can be applied to the following types of constraints:

- domain and nonull constraints: if the OFM is aware of the domains of the attributes of the fragment it manages, it can easily check if the values in the tuples of the fragment match with these domains;

- general tuple constraints: the same holds for constraints describing relations between values within one tuple;

- local uniqueness constraints: the OFM can enforce an uniqueness constraint if the relation to which the OFM belongs is not fragmented, or the relation is fragmented on the attributes on which the uniqueness constraint is defined.

5.3 Hybrid enforcement of constraints

In hybrid constraint enforcement, local activities of the OFM are used to alleviate the process of explicit constraint enforcement. The key to this is the maintenance of special purpose differential set for specific constraints. These differential sets can then be used in two ways:

- the sets can be smaller than the general purpose differential sets; this reduces the amount of data to be processed in explicit constraint enforcement; this used in *data reduction* autonomy;

- the OFM can check whether a special purpose differential set is empty, thereby making explicit constraint enforcement superfluous; this is used in *process reduction* autonomy.

The first of these protocols does not need any changes in the communication protocol between TM and OFM. The only necessary change at this level, is to make both TM and OFM aware of the fact that a special purpose differential set is used for a specific constraint. Because the Constraint Compiler generates both the information for TM and OFM, this is rather easy.

The process reduction protocol is somewhat more complicated. The TM has to request a status report from the OFM about the constraints used with process reduction. The OFM produces a status report indicating the constraints having non-empty differential sets. These constraints are then enforced by the TM in the usual way via XRA. And as usual, constraint violation will lead to a transaction abort. The necessary communication primitives between TM and OFM are depicted in Figure 6 [Gref90c].

We illustrate the idea of hybrid constraint enforcement with an example. Suppose we have a relation *Employer* of which the attribute *dept* is a foreign key referring to the attribute *name* of relation *Department*. Then we have the following constraint I:

$$
\begin{aligned}
I &= [t, r] \\
t &= \{INS(Employer), UPD(Employer), DEL(Department), UPD(Department)\} \\
r &= (\forall x \in Employer.dept \mid x \neq null)(\exists y \in Department.name)(x = y)
\end{aligned}
$$

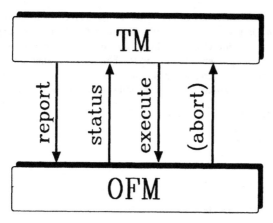

Figure 6: Communication for process reduction

To use hybrid enforcement for this constraint, all fragments of relation *Employer* are notified that attribute *dept* forms a foreign key in a referential integrity constraint. Now suppose fragment $Employer_k$ contains the following tuples:

name	empnr	dept
johnson	64576	sales
smith	64537	staff
richardson	24356	sales
crosby	48675	admin

If a transaction inserts two new tuples (jackson,34567,sales) and (dundee,76545,prod) into $Employer_k$, the general purpose differential set contains two tuples. If data reduction is used, the OFM can decide locally that the first of these two tuples can never violate the referential integrity constraint, because the foreign key value of this tuple is already present in the fragment. So, the amount of data to be checked in explicit constraint enforcement can be reduced. If a transaction inserts two new tuples (jackson,34567,sales) and (hilbilly,32224,admin), the general purpose differential set contains two tuples again. If data reduction is used, the OFM can decide locally that it can reduce the differential set for the referential integrity constraint to an empty set. If process reduction is also used, the OFM can inform the TM that the constraint does not need any explicit enforcement.

6 Conclusions

In this paper we have lined out an approach to parallel handling of integrity constraints on fragmented relations in a relational database system. The approach is designed such, that it meets both the requirements of a high degree of functionality and flexibility as well as high performance.

The first requirement is met by using a strictly modular design of the integrity constraint handling subsystem, in which a separate constraint compiler plays a central role, and by using regular query execution techniques for the enforcement of constraints. This approach results in a clear separation of constraint definition preprocessing, constraint enforcement protocol handling and constraint enforcement data processing.

The requirement of performance is met by having a two way approach to constraint handling that heavily uses the possibilities of parallelism. In *explicit constraint enforcement*, constraints are enforced using relational algebra operators, employing the same means for parallelism as in normal query execution. In *implicit constraint enforcement*, a high degree of autonomy of the data management layer of the DBMS is used to obtain parallelism and to use special purpose algorithms. For maximum flexibility, a integration of both techniques is found in *hybrid constraint enforcement*.

The techniques have been implemented in the PRISMA/DB parallel main memory DBMS. The integration of the constraint handling subsystem has been easy due to the modular design of this subsystem. Currently, the subsystem supports the following types of constraints:

- domain constraints
- general tuple constraints
- nonull constraints
- uniqueness constraints
- referential integrity constraints

These constraint types cover the structural constraints of the relational data model [Gard89].

There are two main issues to be investigated in the future. In the first place, the performance of the various constraint enforcement protocols has to be evaluated. This will enable tuning the overall integrity constraint enforcement process. Further, the evaluation should make clear the advantages of parallelism in constraint enforcement in a quantitative sense. In the second place, the usability of the presented techniques for a broader range of constraint types has to be investigated, thus showing the general applicability of the approach.

Acknowledgements

We wish to thank the PRISMA project members for providing a challenging environment and productive cooperation with the teams from Philips Research Laboratories Eindhoven, the University of Amsterdam and the Centre for Mathematics and Computer Science Amsterdam in the development of our DBMS. In particular, Carel van den Berg is acknowledged for his ideas about local constraint enforcement in the One Fragment Manager component. Further, we wish to thank dr. A.J.Nijman for bringing academia and industry together, dr. H.H.Eggenhuisen for providing good project management and for stimulating the interaction between the various subprojects.

References

[Apers88]   P.M.G. Apers, M.L. Kersten, H.C.M. Oerlemans; *PRISMA Database Machine: A Distributed Main Memory Approach*; Proceedings International Conference on Extending Database Technology; Venice, Italy, 1988.

[Bron87]   W.J.H.J. Bronnenberg, L. Nijman, E.A.M. Odijk, R.A.H. v. Twist; DOOM: A Decentralized Object-Oriented Machine; IEEE Micro; October 1987.

[Ceri84]   S. Ceri, G. Pelagatti; *Distributed Databases, Principles and Systems*; McGraw-Hill, 1984.

[Date81]   C.J. Date; *Referential Integrity*; Proceedings of the 7th Conference on Very Large Data Bases; Cannes, France, 1981.

[Date83]   C.J. Date; *An Introduction to Database Systems, Volume II*; Addison-Wesley, 1983.

[Gard89]   G. Gardarin, P. Valduriez; *Relational Databases and Knowledge Bases*; Addison-Wesley, 1989.

[Gref88]   A.N. Wilschut, P.W.P.J. Grefen, P.M.G. Apers, M.L. Kersten; *Implementing PRISMA/DB in an OOPL*; Memorandum INF 88-69; University of Twente, The Netherlands, 1988.

[Gref89]   P.W.P.J. Grefen; *Integrity Constraint Handling in a Parallel Database System*; Memorandum INF 89-59; University of Twente, The Netherlands, 1989.

[Gref90a]   P.W.P.J. Grefen, P.M.G. Apers; *Parallel Handling of Integrity Constraints on Fragmented Relations*; Proceedings DPDS'90; Dublin, Ireland, 1990.

[Gref90b]   P.W.P.J. Grefen; *Design Considerations for Integrity Constraint Handling in PRISMA/DB1*; PRISMA Document P508; University of Twente, The Netherlands, 1990.

[Gref90c]   P.W.P.J. Grefen, C. v.d. Berg; *PRISMA/DB1 TM-OFM Interface*; PRISMA Document P517; University of Twente, Centre for Mathematics and Computer Science, The Netherlands, 1990.

[Kers87]   M.L. Kersten et al.; *A Distributed Main Memory Database Machine*; Proceedings of the 5th International Workshop on Database Machines; Karuizawa, Japan, 1987.

[Morg84]   M. Morgenstern; *Constraint Equations: Declarative Expression of Constraints with Automatic Enforcement*; Proceedings of the 10th Conference on Very Large Data Bases; Singapore, 1984.

[Simon85]   E. Simon, P. Valduriez; *Integrity Control in Ditributed Database Systems*; MCC Technical Report Number DB-103-85; MCC, Austin, USA, 1985.

[Simon87]   E. Simon, P. Valduriez; *Design and Analysis of a Relational Integrity Subsystem*; MCC Technical Report Number DB-015-87; MCC, Austin, USA, 1987.

[Stone75]   M. Stonebraker; *Implementation of Integrity Constraints and Views by Query Modification*; Proceedings of the 1975 SIGMOD Conference; San Jose, USA, 1975.

[Tsich82]   D.C. Tsichritzis, F.H. Lochovsky; *Data Models*; Prentice-Hall, 1982.

[Wils89]   A.N. Wilschut, P.W.P.J. Grefen, P.M.G. Apers, M.L. Kersten; *Implementing PRISMA/DB in an OOPL*; Proceedings of the 6th International Workshop on Database Machines; Deauville, France, 1989.

[Wils90a]   A.N. Wilschut, P.W.P.J. Grefen; *PRISMA/DB1 XRA Definition*; PRISMA Document P465; University of Twente, The Netherlands, 1990.

[Wils90b]   A.N. Wilschut, P.M.G. Apers; *Pipelining in Query Execution*; Proceedings of the ParBase'90 Conference; Miami Beach, USA, 1990.

[Zloof78]   M.M. Zloof; *Security and Integrity within the Query-by-Example Database Management Language*; IBM RC 6982; Yorktown Hts., USA, 1978.

Performance Analysis of a
Dynamic Query Processing Scheme *

M.L. Kersten

S. Shair-Ali

C.A. van den Berg

Centre for Mathematics and Computer Science
P.O. Box 4079, 1009 AB Amsterdam
The Netherlands

Abstract

Traditional query optimizers produce a fixed query evaluation plan based on assumptions about data distribution and processor workloads. However, these assumptions may not hold at query execution time. In this paper, we propose a dynamic query processing scheme and we present the performance results obtained by simulation of a queueing network model of the proposed software architecture.

Key Words & Phrases: database machines, dynamic query processing, performance analysis.
1985 Mathematics Subject Classification: 69C40, 69C24, 69H24, 69H26, 69H33
1990 CR Categories: C.4, C.2.4, H.2.4, H.2.6, H.3.3, I.6.3

1 Introduction

Exploitation of distributed processing capacity provided by large multi-processor systems remains one of the cornerstones to improve the performance of database management systems. The key to achieve this goal lies in the architecture of the query optimizer and the query execution strategy. To illustrate, several large research groups have produced research prototypes that attack the problem from a different angle. To name a few:

The distributed query processing technique of Bubba [ea90] is a multi-stage set-at-a-time technique. That is, the levels in the query plan lead to several stages at run time, where the transport of intermediate results between the layers in the plan is based on declustering the tuples first. Moreover, the program components to solve the query are dynamically loaded upon need at each processing step.

The query processing techniques of PRISMA [KAH+88] and GAMMA [DGS+90] are based on a pipelined query processing technique. During query optimization the pipe layout is determined and its junctions are mapped to processing nodes. Subsequently, the query is solved in a dataflow driven manner.

Although each prototype has demonstrated performance improvement over centralized query processing, they are mostly based on the same hidden assumptions, which may still block a potential leap in performance for large scale multiprocessors.

The predominant assumptions are that a query optimizer generates the single optimal plan of action and that it does not take into account the possibly disastrous effect of concurrent running

---

*The work reported in this paper was conducted as part of the PRISMA project, a joint effort with Philips Research Eindhoven, partially supported by the Dutch "Stimuleringsprojectteam Informaticaonderzoek (SPIN)".

queries. For example, concurrent queries may have an exclusive lock on a relation fragment, which may cause a delay in the estimated response time. This knowledge could be used to switch to an alternative plan at runtime, which would exploit the waiting time to produce a partial result already in another way.

Furthermore, the query plan is based on simple estimates about the data distribution. A plan is normally not adjusted when these estimates turn out to be wrong. At best a query processor aborts the query when one of the subqueries produce an empty result or the query optimizer regularly refreshes its statistics. Ideally, the query processor could dynamically adjust the plan upon recognition of major deviations from the statistics maintained. An approach in this direction is also presented by [GW89].

The query plan generated in PRISMA (to a lesser extend in Bubba and Gamma) is based on an a priori known number of processors. For example, a query that joins three relations can be assigned 5 processors for pipelined processing. Equally, the query optimizer can design a plan that uses tens of processors using a declustering scheme on the relations and intermediate results. Unfortunately, either plan is fixed, which means that all resources should be conceptually acquired during query startup to guarantee the response time aimed for. In particular, the database should be properly declustered before, such that parallel execution for a large class of queries pays off.

Fixing the number of processors within the query plan also ignores the relative speed by which the operands produce their (partial) answers. For example, to deal with a bursty behavior of the processes involved, it would be better to automatically acquire more processors when work is available and release processors when nothing is left to be processed.

The dynamic query processing scheme described in the sequel is based on the observation that the strong relationship between query plan and query execution should be weakened. Instead, we propose to consider query processing a dual problem. First, how to solve a query when you have a (small) portion of the database within the query program buffers. The techniques for this can be borrowed from centralized query processing. Second, how to collect the interesting portions and how to distribute the work over the available processors using a centralized scheduler.

The core of this paper is an investigation in the potential performance bottlenecks that might arise from this scheme. We have constructed a queueing network model, to gain insight in the behavior of our query processing scheme. Using a parameter setting that reflects the properties of a reasonably tuned distributed operating system and main-memory DBMS implementation, we conclude that a central scheduler does not become an immediate bottleneck.

Our architecture also indicates an alternative caching strategy for database systems, based on dynamic replication of database fragments during query processing. Finally, the model indicates that reasonable linear speedup for processing join queries on a PRISMA-like database machine is attainable.

The remainder of this report is organized as follows. In Section 2, we describe a global architecture for our dynamic query optimization scheme. Section 3 describes the performance model and the simulation parameters. The basic queueing model is introduced in Section 4, while an improved model to deal with distributed caching is given in Section 5. We conclude with a summary and an indication of future research.

2 The Qstar architecture

In this section, we give a system architecture for our dynamic query processing scheme. Its main purpose is to show an evolutionary path for the PRISMA system architecture in sufficient detail. Furthermore, this architecture is used as a reference model for the performance analysis and a mock-up implementation to validate our approach. The system's nickname is Qstar, which indicates the central role of individual queries.

The Qstar design objectives diverge from the PRISMA approach in several aspects. First, we do not assume that there exists a query optimizer that produces uniformly good, yet static query plans.

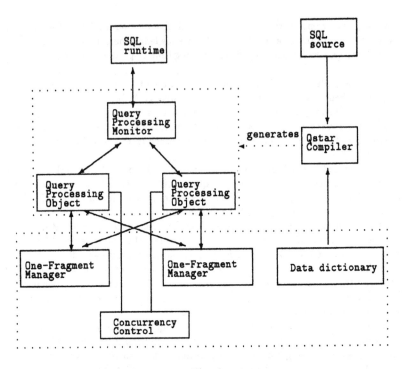

Figure 1: The Qstar architecture

Rather, we aim for a dynamic query optimization strategy.

Second, we favor repetitive queries over ad-hoc, i.e. one shot queries. That is, we believe that most queries in practice are recurrent in nature. That is, successive calls only differ in the constants included. This warrants a compiled approach to gain performance.

Third, we foresee that most applications are browsing in nature, i.e. selecting a few tuples followed by a lengthy delay during which the user (application) absorbs the data. This calls for mechanisms that not only control the order and speed of presenting the tuples to the application program (i.e. cursor control), but also those that control the actual query resolution without blocking resources in the database (i.e. memory and processors) for lengthy periods.

The global system architecture is modelled after PRISMA and consists of three layers (Figure 1). The bottom layer is a collection of One Fragment Managers (OFM) and a concurrency controller. Each OFM is a relational data manager geared towards supporting a single horizontal relation fragment. In particular, it provides a relational algebra interface and a checkpoint/recovery facility. The OFMs do not contain any knowledge about other OFMs. Rather, their orchestration is handled at the distribution level.

The distribution level of Qstar differs from PRISMA in the following aspects. The query entered by the user is processed by the SQL parser, analyzed for semantics errors, logically optimized, and, finally, a code generator produces a Query Processing Monitor (QPM) and a Query Processor Object (QPO). A QPO contains the algorithms to solve the query under the assumption that (all) data is available within the local address space of the process, i.e. a main-memory buffer pool. Moreover, it contains an interface with the One Fragment Managers to extract (replace) portions from (in) the database. Each QPO can thus be seen as a query specific server. Several may be active in handling a single request, while any number of QPOs may have been installed on a processor pool.

The QPOs are managed by a single Query Processing Monitor, which contains a strategy to obtain database portions from the OFMs and which distributes the workload over the QPOs. The QPM, comparable with a transaction manager, is also given the responsibility for distributed integrity- and concurrency- control. A more detailed description of the OFM, QPO, and QPM is given below.

2.1 One-Fragment manager

The base relations are managed by a so-called One Fragment Managers (OFM). Like in PRISMA they are always optimized towards supporting a single relation fragment. That is, an OFM is ideally compiled from a single (extended) SQL create statement.

Each OFM is implemented as a server object, that contains at least two kinds of threads. A communication thread and a storage thread. The communication thread handles the communication with the clients, such as queues incoming requests for execution and enquiries. The storage thread deals with storage subsystems, such as the file servers, and it evaluates the relational subqueries.

To illustrate, consider the case that a QPM requests a range selection on the base table. That is, the OFM receives the message *select segment*, which is queued upon arrival. Once a storage thread is scheduled for execution, it picks a request from the queue of pending queries and prepares a local processing plan. This plan is subsequently taken into execution and the qualifying tuples are copied into a tuple segment. Once the tuple segment is full, the client is notified with the message *segment cached* .

The tuple segment itself is not being sent, but it remains cached in the OFM. It can be obtained by interested parties later on by issuing a *get segment* message, which is handled directly by the communication thread. The tuple segment is set up such that no additional copying is needed to reply.

Associated with each tuple segment we keep reconstruction information, such as the range query, the base table portion being used, and the cost involved in re-producing it. When a tuple segment should make room for a new one, this information can be used to decide whether to copy the partial result to disk or to reconstruct it when need arises.

2.2 The Query Processing Object

The prime task of a Query Processing Object is to evaluate a query upon receiving the message *reduce vector* from the Query Processing Monitor. A segment vector consists of a list of tuple segment id's, one for each database variable mentioned in the query. Upon receipt, the QPO first acquires copies of the tuple segments mentioned in the message. This involves communication with one or more OFMs when the tuple segment was not already cached in the workspace of the QPO itself.

The QPO algorithm should be designed such that partial results are produced as quickly as possible with minimal space consumption. For example, a hash-index can be associated with each incoming tuple segment. When all segments have arrived the join algorithm can use them to quickly discard non-qualifying tuple combinations.

Following, two strategies can be applied to produce a result. First, the traditional approach is to actually construct an intermediate relation, which contains only the target tuples. This involves joining the tuple segments, and copying the qualifying tuples into tuple segments. This intermediate is presented to the outside world analogous to the base tables.

Second, result construction is delayed until it is actually needed in the application. Therefore, for each database variable a new segment is produced that contains the tuples that participate somehow in the result. The final phase, i.e. construction of the target tuples, is done within the application workarea.

The prime advantage is that the communication overhead for emitting the result is never greater than the sum of its input. The drawback is that the actual relationship among the tuples should be reconstructed by building indices again. We expect that re-construction is less expensive than shipping indices.

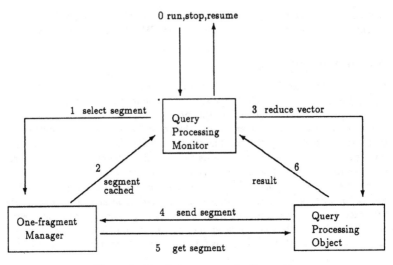

Figure 2: The Qstar communication pattern

2.3 The Query Processing Monitor

The prime task of the Query Processing Monitor (QPM) is to distribute the workload over the OFMs and the available QPOs to produce the partial results. The communication pattern is shown in Figure 2. The *run*, *stop*, *resume*, and *abort* are user commands. The message *select segment* tells the OFM to produce a new tuple segment. The OFM replies with the message *segment cached*, when it has read a segment from disk. The message *reduce vector* tells a QPO to produce a reduced copy of the operands, such that no tuples are retained that provably will not be part of the final result. When the QPO has completed this task it will respond with the message *result*.

The QPM itself is divided into three major components; the pairing-, the filter-, and the schedule - component. They will be discussed in following paragraphs using the query to join two Wisconsin 10K relations, relA10k ⋈ relB10k.

Assume that the OFMs involved in maintaining the base relations have received a request to produce a tuple segment. Then, in due time, they will notify the QPM that such a segment has been *cached*. Say, the first segment of relA10k is cached, denoted by relA10k[1], which is recorded by the QPM.

When the message *segment cached* arrives from the other OFM, say relB10k[1], then all possible pairings are made with previously cached relA10k segments. In this case, a task *reduce vector* is formulated to reduce the tuple segments by evaluating the query for relA10k[1] and relB10k[1]. This task is stored in a work table. Once the result becomes available its status is turned into *cached*. This pairing algorithm is applied to all segments being cached. The effect is formation of the Cartesian product over all relations operands in the query, i.e. a nested-loop over tuple segments. To illustrate, the table below contains a portion of the administration kept by the QPM.

cached	relA10k[1]
cached	relB10k[1]
select	relA10k[2]
cached	relB10k[2]
select	relB10k[3]
reduce	relA10k[1] relB10k[2]
cached	relA10k[1] relB10k[1]
...	

To improve the response time of a query considerably we could filter the tasks to avoid firing useless (sub)tasks. This filter uses semantic knowledge to reduce the Cartesian search space generated by the pairing component. For example, we might use min/max values over the join attributes supplied by the OFM to drop vectors that do not overlap. The net effect is to take only those tasks into execution that contribute to the query result.

The filtered vectors are handed to the scheduler that maintains a table of available QPOs. For each QPO it knows the segments already stored there and the amount of slack resources. Thus, it can direct the vector to the least costly QPO, i.e. cheapest in communication.

3 Performance Analysis Method

The performance analysis of the Qstar architecture is based on modelling it as a queueing network. In particular, for each component in the system architecture we could identify an arrival time distribution function (A), a service time distribution function(B), the number of services(n) and the service discipline(d). This leads to an element of the queueing model space (A/B/c/d), using Kendall's notation [Kle75].

Unfortunately, queueing theory does not yet provide answers to all possible combinations, nor is it possible to cast the behavior of Qstar in a set of closed formula. Therefore, we have used the queueing network model as a basis for a discrete event simulation, where the characteristics are partly described by distribution functions and partly described by algorithms. Following, the simulation scheduler can collect the relevant measurements of the interesting performance indicators.

The queueing network modelling package QNAP2[1] version 5.0 has been used [CII84]. This package contains algorithms for discrete event simulation and algorithms for analytic solutions. The analytic solvers yield exact and approximate steady-state solutions provided the simulation model satisfies some severe constraints, such as, mutual independence between stations.

The major limitation of a simulation is its production of average indicators instead of exact or approximation results and the processing time involved to gain stable results, which limits the number of cases that can be covered. (Some of the runs lasted for days.) Furthermore, the complexity of the QPM is reduced by ignoring the filtering component. The result on our simulation is that the performance figures indicate a 'worst-case' situation, because there is no semantic feedback in the system to reduce the amount of work generated within the QPM.

3.1 Performance measurements

The focal point of our performance analysis are the questions *what is the Qstar system utilization* and *will Qstar exhibit a linear speed up for large number of processors*. To answer these questions we acquired several performance factors from our simulation.

The prime simulation variable is the number of QPO centers, because it relates to the fraction of the PRISMA machine that could have been used. Furthermore, we are interested in the following output measures:

- system measures

  - system throughput (in terms of processed segment vectors per second)
    This will be an indication for query response time. The number of vectors estimated during query compilation divided by the system's throughput yields the response time.

  - average number of messages in system
    This will be an indication for the network load. Too many messages cause network congestion.

- service center measures (QPM, OFM, QPO)

---

[1]QNAP2 (Queueing Network Analysis Package 2) is copyrighted by CII HONEYWELL BULL and INRIA 1981,1982

- utilization of a center
  This will be an indication for a possible bottleneck in the system. A relative high utilization percentage, that increases with each additional QPO, will limit the performance in the long run.

- average residence time
  This represents the waiting time in a queue and in the service center of a station.

- throughput
  This highlights centers for further improvement

- average queue length
  A high performance implementation will be infeasible, if this is accompanied by large queues at stations and show insufficient buffering capacity.

We limited the amount of data gathered from the simulation to the messages that requested joined segment vectors.

3.2 The parameter settings

The parameter settings for our simulation are not directly derived from the PRISMA machine, because no stable figures were available at the time of writing. Instead, we have used parameter settings that reflect a reasonably optimized distributed operating system and we used our experience in writing a main-memory OFM early on in the project. As such, the parameter settings reflect a system that could emerge within the next few years. A more detailed validation of the parameter settings for the queueing model is underway.

The test query we will be working with is as follows:

$$\textbf{relA10k} \bowtie \textbf{relB10k} \bowtie \textbf{relC10k}$$

We begin with the mean time to transport data over the network. These values are based on Amoeba network characteristics [MvRT+90].

The setup costs for communication	1.0	ms
Transfer costs of data (per Kb)	1.1*S	ms
Total costs for communication	$1 + 1.1 * S$	ms

The parameter 'S' represents the data size in Kb. Since communication is negatively influenced by small blocks, we use a segment size of 32 Kb. Although the Qstar query processing scheme could request the OFMs to project out the unwanted attributes from the relations, we assume in our simulation that this has not been done. Consequently, each segment contains about 160 tuples.

We further assume rather lengthy RPC messages of 250 bytes. These are needed to send the segment vectors around. The corresponding delays introduced by the network are:

for a segment transfer	32*1.1+1	=	36.2	ms
for a RPC	1 + 0.25*1.1	=	1.3	ms

The mean time for an OFM to prepare a segment, i.e. local query optimization and index lookup, is related to the segment size and pre-selection cost within the OFM. For the latter aspects we used a fixed cost of 20 ms. During selection the qualifying tuples are be copied into a result tuple segment. The processing time is calculated as follows:

Time to prepare a tuple segment	20.0	ms
Time to move data around in memory (per Kb)	0.2 * 32	ms
Total costs for preparing a segment	26.4	ms

The task of a QPO is to handle a M-way join. The costs involved are based on a hash-join algorithm that consumes 0.1 ms per tuple. We assume that each QPO produces a single segment that contains 5% of the input tuples. The processing time of a QPO over M relations becomes:

M * hash-index construction	M * 160 * 0.1	=	16.0 * M	ms
one join scan to collect result		=	0.1 * M	ms
5% tuple construction	M * 0.2 * 0.05 * 160 * 0.200	=	0.32 * M	ms
Processing time to join M relations			16.42 * M	ms

The delay from the network for transferring the result becomes:

$$
\begin{array}{ll}
\text{Transfer of result} & \text{5\% from 160 tuples} \\
\text{Size of result} & 8 * 200 * M \text{ bytes} \\
& 1.6 * 1.1*M + 1 \quad = \quad 1.8*M + 1 \quad \text{ms}
\end{array}
$$

The experiments are conducted with 3 OFMs (3-way relation join), thus:

$$
\begin{array}{llll}
\text{Time to join 3 relation segments} & 3*16.42 \text{ ms} & = & 49.26 & \text{ms} \\
\text{Time to transfer result over the network} & 1.8*3 + 1 \text{ ms} & = & 6.4 & \text{ms}
\end{array}
$$

The PRISMA machine has a fully interconnected network architecture, where each link has a bandwidth of 20 Mbits/sec. The simulations are performed under these network assumptions.

4 Qstar queueing model

In this section we describe the general queueing network layout of Qstar, the message classes and the modelling assumptions. In the remaining sections we illustrate an analytic model for the components involved. The outcome of this section is a basic model that captures the message flows and the processing characteristics of the basic Qstar implementation. Some illustrative performance figures are given to highlight its behavior under the parameter settings. In the next section we will improve the basic model by using the caching of segments within QPOs to enable segment exchange between QPOs.

4.1 Message classes

The components of the Qstar architecture are mapped to service centers in the queueing network. That is, we have a single service center to model the QPM, a fixed number (m) of OFM service centers that hold the query operands, and a variable number (n) of service centers for the QPOs. In addition, we assume a service center that mimicks the user input, called SRC, and a service center for the communication network, that models the network delays. The corresponding message classes and propagation paths are as follows:

- *class-0 $SRC \rightarrow QPM$*
  This class marks the beginning of a new vector evaluation.

- *class-1 $QPM \rightarrow OFM_i \rightarrow QPM$*
  The QPM produces m *class-1* messages for each *class-0* messages to request a selection by the i-th OFM.

- *class-2 $QPM \rightarrow QPO_j \rightarrow QPM$*
  The QPM converts the answers by the OFM into segment vector evaluation requests to be sent to the QPOs. Upon receipt of the answer it marks the vector as being cached.

- *class-3 $QPO_j \rightarrow OFM_i \rightarrow QPO_j$*
  In a QPO the vector request is turned into a request to the OFMs to deliver the necessary segments for processing.

To avoid unnecessary complications we have not included the network component in this list. Actually all paths go through the network service center. The exception is the $SRC \rightarrow QPM$ link which is internal to the QPM.

Furthermore, the SRC includes a heuristic to avoid over- and underflowing the QPM center with (user) requests. That is, the source will keep on supplying requests until the number of segments already at the QPM center exceeds twice the number of idle QPOs. Thereafter, it reduces to a slow rate to avoid overflowing QPM.

4.2 Model assumptions

The analytic models derived for the system components are based on the assumption that service times for all classes within a service center are exponentially distributed and the service discipline is First Come First Serve. Furthermore, the communication is asynchronous, which avoids blocking the individual service centers (deadlock as well). Finally, we assume infinite buffering capacity and sufficient bandwidth to handle the requests. The latter assumptions are quantified in the subsequent simulations, which show that indeed this assumption holds for PRISMA-like machines.

4.3 Analytical model

The Qstar components can be individually characterized with an analytic model. For brevity we will illustrate the modeling of QPM only. The models for OFM QPO, and network have been obtained in a similar fashion.

The QPM center deals with three message classes. The *class-2* messages communicate with the QPO and the *class-1* messages with the OFM. Furthermore, it receives the *class-0* messages produced by an internal source to mark the start of a new vector evaluation.

We assume that the system consists of independent Poisson processes, thus the total input process will be a Poisson process as well [Kle75]. Therefore, the overall interarrival time distribution of input messages is exponential with factor λ_{qpm}. We further assume that the service time distributions for the message classes is exponential, that is

$$s_i(x) = \mu_{qpm,i} \; e^{-\mu_{qpm,i}x}.$$

The parameter $\mu_{qpm,i}$ models the following aspects:

- $\frac{1}{\mu_{qpm,0}}$: the mean time to prepare a request for a vector for the OFM.

- $\frac{1}{\mu_{qpm,1}}$: the mean time to prepare an evaluation request for the QPO.

- $\frac{1}{\mu_{qpm,2}}$: the mean time to register a join of the segments within a vector.

The choice of our distribution functions makes the service time of the QPM center hyperexponential (H_3) [Kle75] namely:

$$b(x) = \sum_{i=0}^{2} \alpha_{qpm,i} \; \mu_{qpm,i} \; e^{-\mu_{qpm,i}x}$$

The distinct $\alpha_{qpm,i}$'s denote the fractions of the messages of the corresponding calls-i in the input stream. The average interproduction time is:

$$\overline{x}_{qpm} = \sum_{i=0}^{2} \frac{\alpha_{qpm,i}}{\mu_{qpm,i}}$$

The resulting output rate will be:

$$\mu_{qpm} = \frac{1}{\overline{x}_{qpm}}$$

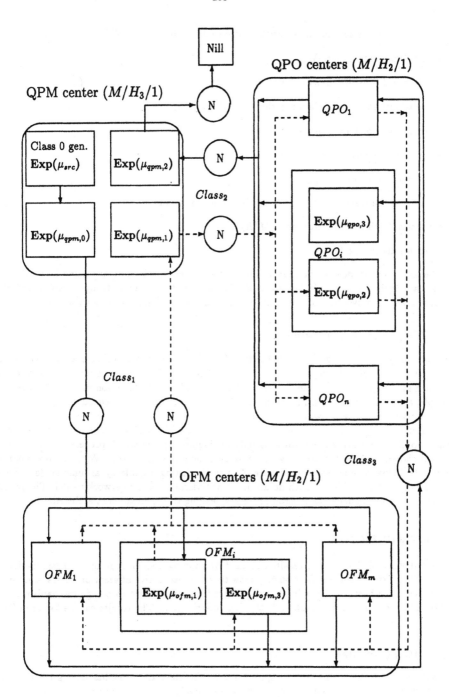

Figure 3: Basic model

To summarize the specifications for the QPM center (with $i = 0, 1, 2$):

- total input rate factor: λ_{qpm}

- the arrival time distribution function : $\exp(\lambda_{qpm})$

- probability message of class i in the input stream : $\alpha_{qpm,i}$

- service time distribution class i message : $\exp(\mu_{qpm,i})$

- total service distribution: *hyperexponential* (H_3)

- average output rate : μ_{qpm}

- per class the messages are directed to an unique destination

- we classify the QPM center as : $(M/H_3/1)$

- service discipline: FCFS

The analytical models for the OFM and QPO are developed along the same line. The input streams are again considered independent Poisson distributions leading to hyperexponential distributions as well. An overview of the resulting queueing model is shown in figure 3.

4.4 The network service

The network service process represents the transfer delay encountered during interprocess communication. A routing mechanism for messages has been implemented in the simulator. The mechanism is needed for modelling the communication, such as to impose a delay upon message transport. For example, a *class-2* message send from the QPM to a QPO process must encounter a different delay than the returning message, which contains data and is larger.

All processes at a center will have the same probability of being chosen as a destination process. This simplifies the routing mechanism by only distinguishing centers. A process in the destination center is chosen randomly by the network to become the receiving process. Without this assumption every path between processes should have been made distinguishable by an unique class, because routing can not be specified in such details in an analytical queueing network model. The processes involved are again modelled as Poisson processes, leading to hyperexponential distributions.

5 Evaluation

In the following we present the results obtained by running a simulation of the basic model. The results of this experiment (see Section 5.1) show that the load of the different processes is not equally distributed. The basic model is improved by introducing a segment exchange mechanism between QPOs. This extended model shows a better load distribution. The results can be found in Section 5.2.

5.1 Basic model

The simulation results are shown in Figure 4 and 5. The simulated time has been set high, so as to obtain statistical measures with a 95% confidence intervals of $\pm$ 10% around the mean.

Figure 4 shows the utilization levels for the three system components. In this architecture, the load on the OFMs is much higher than on the QPM and QPO. In particular, its reaches 90% utilization with 20 processors already. The underlying cause is that the ergodic constraint at the OFMs reaches equality at this point ($\frac{\lambda}{\mu} \approx 1$). That is, the expected number of arrivals (λ) at a center reaches the serving capacity (μ).

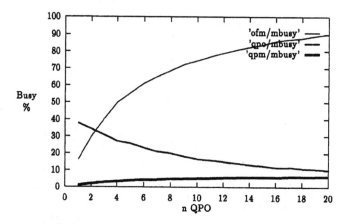

Figure 4: Utilization level

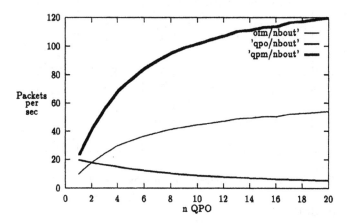

Figure 5: Throughput of messages

An indication of the total throughput for each process is given in Figure 5. The central role of the QPM is highlighted by the throughput of messages through this center. Furthermore, the bottleneck is the OFM which can not adequately handle an increasing number of QPOs. Therefore the throughput for QPOs decreases.

5.1.1 Network measures

The assumption that the network will not limit the system still holds, as can be seen in table 2. Using the message type distribution, obtained from the simulation, and the size of each message type (Table 1), we have calculated in this table the total data throughput for each process. It turns out that for all process types the required bandwidth is much lower than the network limit of 2 Mbytes/sec. Thus the capacity of a single network link is not exceeded. Under the assumption that a fully interconnected network is used, we conclude that the global network bandwidth is not exceeded either.

Message type	size
RPC	0.5 Kb
Data	4.8 Kb
Segment	32.0 Kb

Table 1: Messages sizes

Process	I/O	Description	Type	Messages/sec	Kb/sec
QPM	IN	*segment cached* from OFMs	RPC	82.5	
		result from QPOs	Data	27.0	
					170.9
	OUT	*reduce vector* to QPOs	RPC	27.0	
		select segment to OFMs	RPC	82.5	
		partial result to user	Data	27.0	
					184.4
					355.3
QPO	IN	*reduce vector* from QPM	RPC	0.7	
		get segment from OFMs	Segment	2.1	
					67.6
	OUT	*result* to QPM	Data	0.7	
		send segment to OFMs	RPC	2.1	
					4.4
					72.0
OFM	IN	*select segment* from QPM	RPC	27.5	
		send segment from QPOs	RPC	27.0	
					27.3
	OUT	*segment cached* to QPM	RPC	27.5	
		get segment to QPOs	Segment	27.0	
					877.8
					905.1

Table 2: Network requirements for the basic model

5.2 Extended model

In the previous section we observed that the OFM forms the potential bottleneck in the system. The congestion of the OFMs can be avoided by also using the QPOs as a cache for the tuple segments, thereby spreading the load for accessing tuple segments over both the QPOs and OFMs. To simplify the model, we assume unbounded caching resources at the QPOs. In the remainder of this section we show the results of a simulation of this model.

This model was simulated under the same conditions as the previous model (i.e. accuracy, simulation time). The results from these runs are presented in Figure 6 - 8.

In Figure 6 the utilization level of the three system components is shown. The bottleneck has been shifted towards the QPM, which reaches saturation with 60 QPOs. However, the throughput peak of the QPM is reached for a much lower number of QPOs (43), which means that between 43 and 60 one already faces a reduced payoff of parallel execution.

Compared with the simple model we have doubled the effective number of active QPOs and we obtained a 5 times higher throughput (20 QPOs) by better utilization (See figure 8). Furthermore, the model displays linear speedup in processing up to 30 QPOs.

5.2.1 Network measures

As with the simulation of the basic model we verify the network assumption using the simulation results. The calculations of the required network bandwidth for each processor link can be found in Table 3. We see that although the maximum vector throughput has increased considerably (Figure

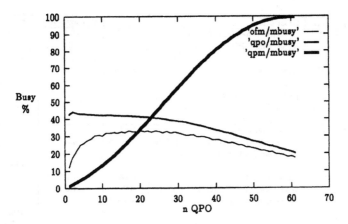

Figure 6: Utilization level

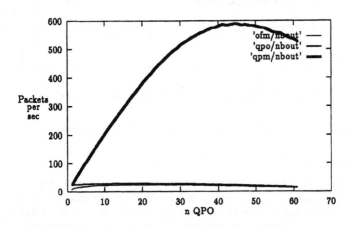

Figure 7: Throughput of messages

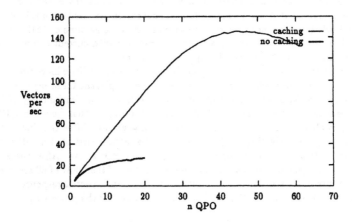

Figure 8: Total number of joined vectors for both models.

Process	I/O	Description	Type	Messages/sec	Kb/sec
QPM	IN	*segment cached* from OFMs	RPC	26.9	
		result from QPOs	Data	75.2	
					374.4
	OUT	*reduce vector* to QPOs	RPC	75.2	
		select segment to OFMs	RPC	26.9	
		partial result to user	Data	75.2	
					412.0
					786.4
QPO	IN	*reduce vector* from QPM	RPC	1.6	
		get segment from OFMs and QPOs	Segment	4.8	
		send segment from QPOs	RPC	10.5	
					159.7
	OUT	*result* to QPM	Data	1.6	
		send segment to OFMs and QPOs	RPC	4.8	
		get segment to QPOs	Segment	10.5	
					346.1
					505.8
OFM	IN	*select segment* from QPM	RPC	9.0	
		send segment from QPOs	RPC	9.1	
					9.1
	OUT	*segment cached* to QPM	RPC	9.0	
		get segment to QPOs	Segment	9.1	
					295.7
					304.8

Table 3: Network requirements for the extended model

8), that the network throughput for each process does not exceed the maximum link bandwidth.

5.3   Response time

The simulation results can be used to obtain an indication of the response time for the example query. Recall that it represents a three-way join over the Wisconsin relations without support of access paths and without reduction of the operands by pre-selection. Each relation contains 10K tuples, which leads to about 60 segments per operand. Thus, a naive implementation of the QPM would produce 216000 segment vectors (60^3).

This job can be handled with 20 parallel QPOs without overloading any of the processors. Their utilization level is about 30-40%. For this system configuration we need about 11ms per vector (Figure 8), which leads to a response time of 2376 seconds. A response time of 1512 seconds can be obtained, if 40 QPOs are used. Clearly, this is not competitive with current commercial systems, because it is essentially based on the nested-loop join algorithm.

Yet, the response time can be improved dramatically when we spent little more time in preparing the work within the OFM using well-known techniques. For example, the OFM may be requested to hash-partition the relation into batches of 10 segments. This leads to an initial delay of 0.26 second before the first segment batch becomes available. The advantage is that now the QPM filtering component can drop all vectors that have incompatible hash values. After the first batch of each OFM we can form 10 tasks, activating 10 QPOs as well. The second burst of each OFM will expand the vector table to 10.2^3, generating enough work to keep 40 QPOs active. After the k-th burst it will be $10.k^3$. In our example, we can hash partition the contents of the OFM of 60 segments into k= 6 batches. This results in a total amount of 2160 vectors with an expected response time of about 15 seconds. (The work within the OFM after $k = 2$ is overlapped by the processing in the QPOs.)

6 Summary

In this paper, we have presented an alternative approach for query processing on large multiprocessors. Our approach is based on breaking the query into two smaller problems, namely, how to solve the query for a small portion of the database and, how to schedule a large number of tasks, which together form the query program. The hypothesis is that the combination leads to better system utilization and smooths the fluctuations normally encountered in parallel query processing.

A queuing network model has been constructed that captures the processing aspects of our architecture. It has been used to drive a discrete event simulation to experiment in a time efficient way with two processing strategies, i.e. a central and decentralized caching of tuple segments.

The two simulations show that the central scheduler does not lead to an immediate bottleneck. The linear speed-up curve flattens before the scheduler becomes overloaded. That is, the speedup from parallelism becomes neglectable before the QPM becomes saturated. Furthermore, the decentralized caching of segments proved effective.

The system utilization in both cases is still limited, mainly due to the network activities, which are modelled as independent processes. Thus, once a QPO has issued a request for a tuple segment it has to wait for delivery; it does not take part in handling the communication protocols.

Designing the filter algorithm as well as query specific scheduling is an open-ended track. The filter can do a better job once more feedback information is passed to the QPM about the contents of the segments being cached. For example, as part of the message *cached* one could also return the min/max over the join attributes. This would enable the filter to precompute the overlap of a proposed segment pairing (and drop it when no such overlap exists). Furthermore, one can easily configure a more static evaluation plan within the QPM to enforce a specific order of vector evaluation.

A lot more has to be done. The current activities are focussed on a validation of our simulation in the 'real' multiprocessor environment. Furthermore, a comparison with architectures based on static query plans is under way.

References

[CII84]   CII Honeywell Bull and INRIA. *QNAP2*, 1984. Introduction to QNAP2 and Reference Manual.

[DGS+90]   D. J. DeWitt, S. Ghadeharizadeh, D.A. Schneider, A. Bricker, H. Hsiao, and R. Rasmussen. The gamma database machine project. *IEEE Transactions On Knowledge and Data Engineering*, 2(1), March 1990.

[ea90]   H. Boral et al. Prototyping bubba, a highly parallel database system. *IEEE Transactions On Knowledge and Data Engineering*, 2(1), March 1990.

[GW89]   Goetz Graefe and Karen Ward. Dynamic query evaluation plans. In *Proc. SIGMOD*, 1989.

[KAH+88]   M.L. Kersten, P.M.G. Apers, M.A.W. Houtsma, E.J.A. van Kuyk, and R.L.W. van de Weg. A distributed, main-memory database machine; research issues and a preliminary architecture. In M. Kitsuregawa, editor, *Database Machines and knowledge Base Machines*, pages 353–369, 1988.

[Kle75]   Leonard Kleinrock. *Queueing Systems, Theory*, volume 1. John Wiley & Sons, 1975.

[MvRT+90]   S.J. Mullender, G. van Rossum, A.S. Tanenbaum, R. Renesse, and H. van Staveren. Amoeba - a distributed operating system for the 1990s. *IEEE Computer Magazine*, May 1990.

Evaluation of a Communication Architecture by means of Simulation *

H.L. Muller

University of Amsterdam,
Kruislaan 403, 1098 SJ Amsterdam, The Netherlands
henkm@fwi.uva.nl

Abstract

The Oyster evaluation framework is developed to support high level simulation of computer architectures. A designer can make a simulation model of a proposed architecture, and gets feedback in the form of performance figures, and an analysis of the architecture. Oyster has a layered structure, allowing for both high level descriptions, low level specifications and the possibility to incorporate existing switch level simulators.

As a case study, the framework is used to examine the interface between the data processor and the communication network of a distributed memory architecture, the PRISMA machine. A small parallel machine is simulated, the network is modeled at the packet level, the data processor is modeled at the instruction level. To get realistic results, the software running on the data processor is also simulated (application program plus run time support and operating system). In this experiment, the architecture is extended with specialized message passing hardware, and the potential benefits are evaluated. Both the models and the outcomes of this simulation experiment are presented.

1 Introduction

Experimentation with architectures gets more important today. The explosively increasing density of VLSI-techniques, together with the new possibilities how these transistors can be used to increase the performance of an architecture, and the new insights in the potentials of compiler technology lead to a need for early design evaluation: during the first stages of the design, the designer needs performance figures of the architecture. At the same time, the correctness of the architecture should be verified to prevent time consuming mistakes.

Three ways are open to verify and evaluate an architecture. One can make a mathematical proof of the correctness and an analytical estimate of the performance, one can simulate the architecture and observe the correctness and the performance characteristics of the simulation run, and one can implement the architecture in hardware.

Since the designer of an architecture should be encouraged to experiment with the architecture, the evaluation of the design must be cheap and fast. Building the architecture is neither cheap, nor fast. An analytical performance estimate of the architecture is a time consuming business. The simulation of an architecture is easy, cheap and takes almost no implementation time. This is the preferred way to evaluate an architecture. We should keep in mind that the simulation of an

---

*This research was sponsored by PHILIPS and the SPIN, the Dutch stimuleringsprojectteam informatica.

architecture gives different results from building the architecture, since there are always details which influence the performance, but which are not modeled.

An interesting field to study the evaluations of designs is the development of communication architectures for parallel machines. Looking at existing distributed memory MIMD machines, we see that most machines implement the packet transport and routing layer in specialized hardware. The exact nature of the hardware varies. Cut through routing, deadlock freedom and (fixed) packet size are some design decisions influencing the ease of programming and the performance of the network. On top of this networking hardware, there are one or more layers of software providing a suitable level of abstraction to the user (the compiler or the programmer). The hardware and the software layers together form the communication architecture as seen by the user. The important issues in the design of such a communication architecture are the questions if the network will function correctly, and if the performance of the network is satisfying, under varying circumstances (long messages, many short messages).

Three recent designs in this field are the Torus Routing Chip (or TRC, [Dally86]), the Adaptive Routing Chip (the ARC, [Mooij89]), and the DOOM Communication processor (or CP, [Annot87]). These three communication processors have all been analyzed, simulated and built. The analysis was made to prove the correctness of the network (deadlock freedom) or to analyze the networks performance behavior (queuing models). The simulation was used to observe the network performance under non analyzable conditions. Eventually all the three communication processors have been realized. The ARC and TRC on single chip, the DOOM CP is first implemented using TTL Logic and is currently being integrated into a single chip version. At the moment the DOOM CP was really used it came out that the software overhead was underestimated. Sending messages from A to B takes 350 μs instead of the 30 μs needed in the network. The reason that this was not foreseen during the design phase was that both the analysis and the simulation of the design only took the packet level into account. The abstractions above packet level running outside the communication processor have not been simulated or analyzed. It can be expected that both the ARC and the TRC have the same problems; they are both extremely fast communication processors, but to exploit this speed for general purpose messages an extra layer of software or hardware is necessary, restricting the speed. In general (not only for communication architectures) it can be stated that the simulation of the design should not stop at some level from which on everything is expected to be trivial (the software layers in the case of the communication processor).

Another observation is that most simulations are made on an ad-hoc base. Someone wants to simulate an idea, so a new simulator is built. The last years simulation systems are becoming popular in the world of micro electronic engineering and spring up like mushrooms. Verilog, Dacapo, Helix and NDOT are examples of recent hardware simulation systems. A drawback of these systems is that they are developed to check the correctness of an implementation, and do not *evaluate* a design. In the world of computer architects attempts have been made to make evaluation systems. The AWB [Bray89] and PARET [Nichols88] are examples of such systems. These systems give good results, but they evaluate specific details of an architecture (cache/register design and networking respectively).

The simulation system developed at the university of Amsterdam is made to evaluate architectures in general. Both high level parts (the application –compiled to assembler–, the processor) and low level details (communication hardware) are simulated. This framework, called Oyster, is described in section 2. Several serious, complete architectures have been evaluated using Oyster. We describe the experiment with the the simulation of the communication part of the PRISMA architecture (based on the DOOM CP, section 3.1) and is described in section 3. A number of architectural options have been evaluated ranging from a complete software implementation of the higher communication layers (which is also used in a prototype machine and is used as a calibration point) to an implementation containing some specialized hardware. The results of these simulations are presented in section 3.3. Finally an evaluation of the simulation framework is presented in section 4.

2 The evaluation framework: Oyster

The considerations above about the ad hoc simulations and the necessity to simulate the architecture as a whole instead of a part of the architecture were the inspiration for the creation of an evaluation framework. By means of simulation this framework should provide computer architects with an environment for obtaining performance figures from an architecture. The way the architecture is specified must be simple, allowing to make quick changes to evaluate alternative architectures. Since each designer eventually implements the architecture in hardware, the simulation framework should be integrated with simulation systems found in existing VLSI design packages.

It is not a goal to build a simulator for checking the functional correctness of the design. However, the design must function correctly before it can be evaluated. It is still not required that the model is an exact implementation of the proposed hardware. As an example, a fully associative cache can be modeled as an array with a linear or tree search, instead of the parallel matching. As long as the functional behavior and the behavior in simulated time are identical, no one will notice the difference. When the functional behavior of the cache is incorrect, the simulation will not give sensible performance figures.

In short, four points in designing an evaluation framework are critical:

Evaluation Output. The simulation results in two kinds of output: besides the normal functional output of a simulation (with which a sanity check of the design can be made, i.e. simulation of the addition of 12 and 13 should give 25), an evaluation framework must provide the designer with output regarding the performance of the architecture. Section 2.2 elaborates on this topic.

Flexibility. Designers should be encouraged to ask "what-if" questions [Krishnakumar87]. Given an architecture, the designer will modify it a bit and try to see what the result is. As an example, one may try to insert an extra cache in an architecture and watch the effects on the performance. To support this kind of experiment, the framework should allow the designer to specify the architecture flexibly, so changes can be made easily.

Open. Most simulations systems are closed in the sense that they do claim they are the only simulator in the world. A good simulator should be open-ended, so that existing VLSI switch level simulators can be connected to it.

An open system has another advantage, it allows the designer to modify the evaluation framework. For certain architectures it might be necessary to change the framework a bit to get better evaluation outputs or to ease the modeling of the architecture. One might think of making a small change in the simulation language, or in the generated evaluation output.

Reliability. The figures coming from the simulator are use to optimize the architecture. Consequence of this is that these figures should be reliable. By using the right level of abstraction to specify the design, the designer is discouraged to make errors, as will be seen in section 2.1.1.

The simulation system developed at the University of Amsterdam, called *Oyster*, fulfills the above mentioned requirements. A question the reader may ask is why we developed our own simulation framework and language instead of buying one of the existing systems like NDOT or one of the VHDL-derivates. The answer is twofold and is argued below: Other systems do not fulfill the requirements above, and we want to experiment with the simulation framework itself.

Many of the available simulation systems model hardware. They realize this by giving primitives for wires, clocks and gates. The designer has to think in terms of hardware before he will be able to model the architecture. Only some general purpose simulation systems use an object oriented approach like SIMULA. The problem with these systems is that they do not exploit the special limitations and possibilities in architecture evaluation. The existing architecture evaluation systems finally evaluate one specific item of an architecture. Furthermore, most of these systems have an enormous complexity which makes it unfeasible to add the features mentioned in section 2.1 onwards.

As can be read in the sections below, we are interested in evaluation output which can be obtained from the simulator. We are interested to try to connect other simulators to our system. For both reasons, we need to have a system which is small enough to experiment with. Oyster is a small system, so it can easily be adapted to our needs. Moreover, the restricted simulation language is one of the issues we are experimenting with: Is it possible to model architectures reliably using this restricted set of possibilities, or do we need more features, and if so, which features? These experiments can only be done if we have full control over the simulation system.

Therefore Oyster has been developed. The rest of this section gives an overview of the structure of Oyster and a brief description of the evaluation output produced by it (2.2).

2.1 Structure of Oyster

Oyster has a layered structure as sketched in figure 1. At the bottom layer, a discrete event simulation kernel provides the basic simulation primitives, other simulators and languages (C) can be hooked on at this layer. The middle layer is the *Pearl* layer. Pearl is an object oriented programming language designed for architecture simulation and evaluation. The top layer supports standard models, it is a library of components frequently found in architectures. The components specified at this layer are compiled to Pearl. Pearl is compiled into C, which is the implementation language of the bottom layer. Oyster is fully portable to any machine with a C-compiler.

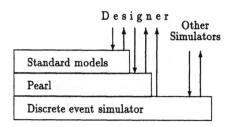

Figure 1: structure of Oyster

The specification of the architecture made by the designer is input for the top and middle layers. The top layer is used for modeling all components which are available in the library, the Pearl layer is used to model all components that are not in the library. All the layers provide the designer with evaluation output. Below, the three layers are discussed in more detail top down, section 2.2 contains a description of the output generated by the various layers.

2.1.1 Standard Model layer

The top layer supports several parametrizable standard models. Eventually, this layer will contain models of most components frequently used in computer designs: memories, busses, arbiters, (hierarchical) caches and processors. The models are parametrizable to fit the particular requirements in a certain architecture. As an example the cache parameters are word size, line size, number of sets, set-size, the replacement algorithm and three timing parameters. By defining these eight parameters, a cache is defined. Internally, the cache is implemented straight forward. It maintains a two dimensional array of tags and values, one dimension is looked up using the address, the other dimension is searched for the right tag. The dimensions of the array depends on the associativity and the size of the cache.

For the memory and the busses, fewer parameters are needed. The processor parametrization poses interesting problems. The current implementation allows only a specification at the instruction set level. For each instruction, its semantics, the number of parameters, the timing characteristics, and the needed program size are specified. These parameters have defaults; the default semantics of the instruction ADD for example is the addition of the parameters. Orthogonally on the instructions, the allowed addressing modes are specified; again with their timing characteristics and needed space in the instruction space. The specification of the addressing modes includes the specification of the memory port(s) and register bank(s). From these instruction and addressing mode specifications, a simulation model of the processor is generated. The processor is programmed in assembler. An assembler program is interpreted by the processor model (for efficiency the assembler program is tokenized) in a fetch and execute cycle. The current assembler instruction is fetched from a stream internal in the processor, the instruction fetch is simulated to the memory, and the instruction is executed. The instruction decoding as found in hardware is not simulated, this means that the instruction format needs not to be specified, only the size of the instructions is important to simulate the right instruction fetches.

This processor model is only a first step in the development of a general processor model, which will also maintain interesting statistics. The model of the data processor used in section 3.2 is based on the simple model described above.

Since the designer only has to specify relatively few parameters at this level, and does not have to worry about the correctness of the implementation, an architecture can be modeled and changed in short time. Furthermore, the designer makes fewer errors in specifying eight parameters than in the specification of a complete model. This leads to fewer mistakes and thus to more reliable simulation results.

2.1.2 Pearl layer

Pearl provides the designer with an object oriented programming level. It is known that an object oriented environment is well suited for simulation [Dahl66]. (The ancestor of the object oriented languages is SIMULA [Birtwistle73], an ALGOL 60 derivative developed for programming simulation problems.) Object oriented programming is a natural way to model both concurrency and interaction between various components.

A Pearl program consists of a set of concurrently executing objects. These objects communicate by sending messages to each other. In the object oriented paradigm messages are sent to a method of an object. An object that wants to receive a message has to wait explicitly for a message on one or more methods. Note that message passing is the *only* way of communication, this leads to clear, well understandable, programs.

Like SIMULA, the Pearl run time system maintains a virtual clock. This clock always maintains to the current simulation time. Computations in objects and message passing do not influence the virtual clock, they are executed in zero time. When an object wants to wait some simulation time, it asks the run time system to be suspended for a period. When all the objects are suspended, the clock is advanced to the lowest point in time some object(s) have work to do, and the corresponding object(s) are restarted.

Objects can be waiting for two reasons. They are waiting for a message to arrive, or they can be waiting for the simulation clock to pass time[1]. Objects waiting for the clock are modeling activity. These objects are said to be "busy". Objects waiting for a message to arrive, cannot run because some other object should first send a message. These objects are said to be in an "idle" status. Note that the time is also passing for these idle objects. To clarify the way an architecture is modeled in Pearl, figure 2 contains an example of an architecture with a processor, a cache, and a memory. The objects are denoted by the boxes, the messages by the arrows between the boxes. The time is increasing from top to bottom.

In this example, the processor is an object which does two accesses, first it fetches a word on address 0x1414. The cache does a lookup, waits 5 clock ticks to model the time needed for the lookup

---

[1]In fact, they can also wait for either of both events to happen. This is an important feature needed for time-outs. For reasons of simplicity this is not elaborated in this article.

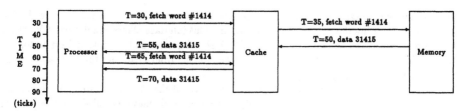

Figure 2: Example of communicating objects

and decides to query the memory for that word, since it was not in the cache. The memory gets the request and needs 15 clock ticks to fetch the data. The data (31415) is sent to the cache that stores the data and sends it back to the processor after a small delay (5 ticks). The second access to the processor goes to the same address and is handled by the cache. After the lookup, the cache immediately sends the data back to the processor. In this example, the processor is idle during the time interval 30..55 and 65..70, because it is waiting for the cache's reply. The memory is idle before time 35 and after time 50, when waiting for a request from the cache. Note that the time is measured in ticks, it is the designers responsibility to scale these ticks to for example μs or clock cycles.

The architecture sketched in this example does not exhibit any concurrency, all actions are executed sequentially. In figure 3 the example architecture is extended with a second processor and cache, there is only one memory that is shared by the two processors and caches. The memory is not dual ported, it handles one request at a time.

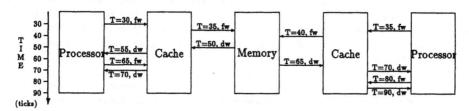

Figure 3: The previous example with an extra processor and cache, "FW" means fetch word, "DW" means data word reply.

The right-hand processor tries to access the memory at time 40, when the latter is handling the request of the left-hand processor. The memory blocks this call and handles it after the other request has been finished. The consequence is that the right processor gets its data 10 ticks later than expected. The architecture modeled here is a simple shared memory architecture with two nodes on one memory. It can be extended to complex architectures, but there are restrictions in the language. The language does not permit run time creation of objects. This makes the language unusable for general purpose simulation, but it is no restriction for architecture modeling since computer architectures are fixed. This restriction makes the language implementation and the implementation of some statistical features simpler. There are no restrictions in sending messages, both the amount and the size of the messages are unlimited. They are buffered in potentially unbounded buffers.

Pearl as seen from the language point of view is a restricted subset of POOL[America89] enriched with a restricted form of subtyping, a virtual clock, some low level features found in C and a function call interface to the language C.

2.1.3 Discrete event kernel

The discrete event kernel gives the support needed to run a Pearl program. It is normally not seen by the architecture experimenter. This layer is entirely programmed in C and implements primitives for process handling, message passing and clock synchronization. Besides this interface to the Pearl compiler, there is an interface to low level simulators. This interface allows simulators of VLSI tools to be connected to Oyster and guarantees that the Oyster simulator and the external simulator agree on the simulation time. It also converts the messages coming from Pearl and the bus-values coming from the external simulator properly.

Clock driven[2] external simulators are treated as a slave of the Pearl simulator. At the moment the Pearl simulation time would pass a clock-edge, the external simulator is called to settle its circuit in a stable state for the next clock phase. After this, the newly generated events (caused by the external simulator) are inserted into the Pearl event lists, and the pearl simulation proceeds until the next clock edge of the external simulator.

Fully event driven[2] external simulators are called as a co-routine. Each time one of the simulators attempts to advance the clock, it passes control to the other simulator. Only when both simulators are ready to advance their respective clocks, the clock is advanced and the simulator with the earliest virtual time is allowed to run again.

Note that in both cases the interface of the external simulator should also be well defined. Currently, we are experimenting by coupling the Oyster simulator to the MULGA VLSI design environment [Weste81] and the COSMOS simulator [Bryant87]. Both are clock driven simulators with a well documented interface.

2.2 Evaluation output

The evaluation output is the collection of all information being relevant for the performance of the architecture. The output is split into "evaluation messages", each evaluation message reports about a specific topic of a part of the architecture. Example topics are the absolute performance (the time needed to do X), the relative performance (Y is 4 times faster than Z) but also figures not directly related to the "time" like the hit rate of a cache or the instruction set usage of a processor. These parameters cannot be quantified in seconds, but the designer should be able to judge their influence.

At all three layers, the simulation framework generates evaluation messages. At the top layer, model specific evaluation output is generated. At the Pearl layer, the designer is responsible for the evaluation output. The Pearl library provides some help by supporting standard statistical functions. At the bottom layer, model independent evaluation outputs are generated.

2.2.1 Standard model evaluation output

Each standard model has its own specific type of evaluation output. In the case of the cache example, the hit rate of the cache and the number of reads and writes are maintained. This should give enough information to judge the quality of the cache. The memory model outputs the number of reads and writes and information about the locality of subsequent reads and writes. The current model of the processor only records the effective instruction execution rate (MIPS). Future processor models will maintain more relevant information.

2.2.2 Discrete event kernel evaluation output

The output coming from the discrete event simulation kernel is the most interesting. Because of the chosen object oriented model with message passing communication, there is at this level still a clear

---

[2]Two kind of simulators are distinguished *Clock driven* and *Fully event driven*. A clock driven simulator uses the phases of the architecture's clock as the time step. When simulating a circuit, the system simulates the logic until it is stable, before advancing the clock to the next phase. On the contrary, fully event driven simulators do not treat the architecture's clock as special. It is considered as a normal input switching regularly between 0 and 1 at moments the simulation time says so. In the mean time, the logic is updated and the simulation time is incremented for each traversal of a block of logic. The Pearl simulator is fully event driven, most switch level VLSI simulators are clock driven, see also [Bryant84].

separation between the activities of the various objects. The interactions between the objects is also visible at this level. Two of the numbers which are measured are explained below: the activity of objects and a number measuring the contention in parts of the architecture. Other measurement strategies are in a preliminary research stage.

The *activity* is measured as the fraction of the total simulation time that the object was "idle", and the fraction of the time the object was "busy". These two percentages are a measure for the time this object was waiting for other objects. The idle and busy times of the example in figure 3 (section 2.1.2) are summarized in the table below:

Object	Idle	Busy
left processor	60%	40%
left cache	70%	30%
memory	50%	50%
right cache	80%	20%
right processor	70%	30%

These percentages were calculated in a time window from 30 to 80 ticks. The part with the highest *busy*-percentage is the first candidate to be optimized (*how* it is optimized is left to the designer). The parts with the highest *idle*-percentages are candidates to be eliminated from the architecture, since they may not be cost-effective.

As a measure for 'hot spots' in the architecture, a distribution of the message queue length is maintained for each object. Objects which are a bottleneck are not only busy the most of their time, but depending on the "temperature" of the hot-spot, they will also have several messages waiting to be handled in their queue. By maintaining a distribution of the queue size over the time, the number of waiting objects can be measured. The memory in the example above is a centralized object. In this example, the memory had a queue distribution with 20% one message, 80% no messages. When the architecture is extended with another 8 processors making frequent accesses to the memory, the distribution will shift and show a large number of pending messages. Objects with many pending messages are subject to optimization or replication. The mean of the distribution is an indication how much extra service is needed.

2.2.3 Output ordering

All types of evaluation output described above are produced for each object in the architecture. For a medium sized architecture, this rapidly comes to more than 500 evaluation messages. The risk with this large number of messages is that the 10 important messages get lost in the 490 unimportant messages. For this reason, the evaluation output is filtered and ordered. The ordering is on base of an "importance" criteria, a number telling the importance of an evaluation message. By observing the top 20 of the evaluation output, the designer gets an idea which part of the architecture need to be optimized.

The importance of an evaluation message depends on the type of that message. As said, messages about **very** busy and **very** idle objects are important. Messages about objects with a long queue are important, cache hit rates between 90 and 95 % are *not* important, hit rates of 10% *are* important. With a simple calculation an importance value is created for each of these messages. Even though the algorithm for calculating the message's importance depends on the type of the message, the importance is never completely correct. There are components which are idle on purpose, and which are vital for the architecture. As an example, a reset circuit of a computer should be idle for 99.999% of the time. The ordering is thus only a help to ease the selection of potential important messages, it is not an absolute criterion.

The filtering procedure allows the designer to reduce the number of evaluation messages by deleting (sub)classes of non interesting evaluation messages. As an example, all messages from one specific component, like that of the reset circuitry above, can be ignored, or the number of reads and writes of *all* memories (gets boring after you have seen them once).

2.3 Using the layered model

The three layers of Oyster are not used at the same frequency. The top layer is for specifying real standard components. After the parameters of these components are specified, Pearl modules are generated, representing the top level components. The interconnection architecture of the architecture, and the models which could not be modeled at the top level are programmed in Pearl, by the designer. The Pearl modules are compiled into C, and are linked to the discrete event system by the Pearl compiler. At this point, user supplied C-functions and other simulators can be linked to the system. All modules are then linked together by the C-compiler, the resulting executable is the simulator.

Running this simulator results in the output of the simulation run (generated by ordinary I/O statements from the simulator) and in the desired simulation output, ordered on base of the importance and filtered according to the users wishes.

Note that the four requirements presented in section 2 are in agreement with this layered structure. The flexibility stems from the fact that all levels can be used as input, the system is open because of the bottom layer, all layers provide evaluation output, and the restrictiveness of the layers (the upper layer models only a cache, not a *faulty* cache, the Pearl layer allows only one form of communication and synchronization), significantly reduces the amount of errors in the modeling actions.

In the experiment described below, four components are described using a standard (top level) model, the processor, register bank, memory, and cache. The other components are modeled in Pearl. No external simulators are used.

3 An experiment: enhancing PRISMA's communication architecture

The simulation experiment described in this section involves the evaluation of the communication part of the PRISMA architecture (PRISMA stands for PaRallel Inference and Storage MAchine [Apers90] and is also called POOMA –Parallel Object Oriented MAchine– or DOOM –Decentralized Object Oriented Machine– [Bronnenberg87]). The whole architecture is simulated, only the communication part is evaluated by trying three implementation strategies. After a short description of the architecture (see the references above and [Vlot90] for a concise description) the used models (3.2) and the results of the simulation are given (3.3). Section 3.4 presents the conclusions which can be drawn from this experiment.

3.1 The PRISMA architecture and implementation

PRISMA is a distributed memory architecture, interconnected by a packet switching network. A node of the machine consists of a data processor, a memory and a communication processor (CP). Some nodes are equipped with a disk or an Ethernet board for communication with the host machine. Figure 4 gives a sketch of the relevant parts of a node.

The CP implements a deadlock and starvation free, packet switching network [Annot87]. A packet consists of a 16-bits header (specifying the destination node and some administration) and 240 data bits. The CP's are interconnected by serial links in some topology (mesh, torus, chordal ring, ...), through which the packets are routed to the destination using a store and forward protocol.

The PRISMA machine is programmed using POOL [America89], a Parallel Object Oriented Language. A running POOL program consists of objects that communicate and synchronize by sending messages to each other. In general, neither the destination of a message, nor the size is known at compile time.

A 100 node prototype of the machine has been built [Vlot90]. Each node has 16 Mbyte of memory, an MC68020 data processor, equipped with memory management unit, instruction cache and floating point co-processor, and a prototype version of the communication processor. Every other node has

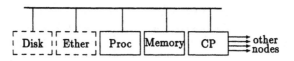

Figure 4: A PRISMA node

a 300 Mbyte SCSI disk, and one out of five nodes is equipped with a self-contained Ethernet board. The Ethernet is not used for communication inside the machine but for host communication. Both the disk and the Ethernet board are not relevant for the communication performance, and are not taken into account.

The data processor and communication processor are connected by a (slow) VME-interface. Via a memory mapped interface, the data processor (DP) reads and writes packets from and to the CP. There is no DMA (Direct Memory Access) in a node, the data processor does the data transport to and from the communication processor itself. Several POOL implementations have been made [Beemster90, Spek90], the one which is used in these experiments [Beemster90] translates POOL into C and uses a C-compiler to generate the code for a specific processor. The run time support system of the compiler, with routines for sending and receiving messages is written completely in C. The structure of this implementation is sketched in figure 5.

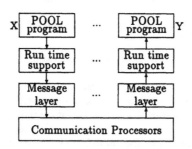

Figure 5: The communication layers

At the top level, the POOL code is executing and sending/receiving POOL messages. The level below is the POOL run time support system. It extracts the destination node of the message and flattens the POOL-message (which is a tree-structure) to a flat message, a stream of bytes. These byte streams are handled by the message layer that converts a byte stream to packets, and puts them in the communication network. At the receiver side, the packets are glued together, structured to a POOL message and finally delivered at the destination object.

The interface between the message layer and the communication processor is a polling packet oriented interface. A packet is written to, or read from the CP by sending eight 32-bit words. If only a part of a packet is needed, zero words need to be written to the CP, waisting bandwidth. In the same way, partly empty packets should be read completely from the communication processor. The interface between the message layer and the run time support layer consists of six functions, three for sending and three for receiving messages. At the sender side, the processor first calls a 'start-of-message' function. The data is sent by (repeatedly) calling a function to send a block of bytes. At the end of a message an end-of-message function is called. This function terminates half-filled packets. At the receiving side, the run time support layer polls for a message, by calling a function 'is-there-a-message?' When a message is available, (multiple) blocks of memory are filled with the data portions of the message. When the message is ready, an end-of-receive function is called which flushes the rest of the packet. The interface between the POOL compiler and the runtime support consists of functions for generically sending and receiving a complete graph of POOL-objects.

An example POOL program is shown in figure 6. It consists of two objects X and Y that are located on different nodes. Object X continuously sends synchronous messages to object Y, which are immediately answered by Y. This program is trivially short and is used to demonstrated one important performance-parameter of the implementation: the latency introduced by sending messages. The latency is defined as the time needed to completely execute a synchronous send to another node. It is thus the time for a message in figure 5 above traveling from top left via the bottom communication part to top right (marked Y) and back to X again. In the prototype POOL implementation, this rendez vous takes 700 μs. It is this delay (or latency in network terminology) which is one of the major problems in exploiting fine or medium grain parallelism, since frequent synchronizations take more time than the computations in between. For an efficient parallel implementation of POOL, this delay needs to be reduced.

```
Object x:              Object y:
...                    ...
                       METHOD pingpong( a : Int ) : Int
BODY                   BEGIN
   DO                     RESULT a * a ;
      i := y!pingpong( 3 ) ;   END pingpong
   OD
YDOB   %% end of body   %% Default body
```

Figure 6: POOL application

This delay is only partially caused by the communication processor. The major reason for the overhead is the interface between the CP and the data processor, and the software layers running on the data processor. A rough calculation shows that 85% of the time is spent while the communication processors are idle, as is sketched in figure 7, where the message transport between X and Y is depicted. This suggests that it could be fruitful to introduce special interface hardware between the data processor and the communication processor. This so called *message processor* should relieve the data processor from tasks like packet assembly and memory transfers. The lowest level of the POOL runtime support (which implements a message passing layer) is then implemented in this specialized message processor.

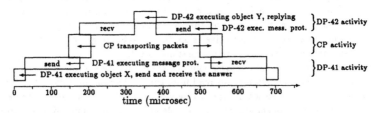

Figure 7: Schematical drawing of the data processor and CP activities in a node while running the POOL ping pong program. X is located on node 41, Y on node 42.

This message processor could give more benefits. The other important performance characteristic of the network, the throughput, could possibly also be improved. The peak throughput of the network is defined as the maximum number of bytes per second which can be transported through the network. The throughput measured over a single link of the prototype machine is high, 500 KB/seconds, taking all software layers into account. This throughput is not only bounded by the software layers, but also by the communication network, as they run in parallel, see figure 8. It is thus not expected that an improvement in the interface will have a dramatic impact on the throughput. However, since the data processor currently needs all its capacity to send a message, the overhead in sending messages can be reduced greatly by adding a message processor before the CP. We will use the latency of the network as our optimization criterion and come back on the throughput in the conclusions.

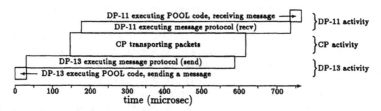

Figure 8: Schematical drawing of the various activities in a node while sending a large message from node 13 to node 11, without result. The throughput is bounded by CP *and* DP.

The message processor is not the only possible upgrade of the PRISMA machine. The current prototype machine has been built using outdated technology. We will simulate the message processor therefore in an technological upgraded machine. The data processor will be faster than the currently used MC68020 and the entire node will fit on a single board, so the slow VME bus is eliminated from the machine. Below, the two machines are referred to as '1985-technology' and 'new-technology'. Note that the architecture itself is not different, only the timing parameters of the model are changed.

3.2 The simulation model

A two node version of the PRISMA machine has been modeled using Oyster. One node is modeled as four parts, the memory, a small instruction cache, the communication processor and the data processor. The memory, cache and processor model are taken from the standard library. The memory is a standard dynamic RAM with a size of 65536 words (just enough for these experiments). The instruction cache is a direct mapped cache, with one word per line and 512 lines. There is only one set in the cache.

The communication processor is modeled as depicted in the dashed box in figure 9. All the objects can be recognized literally from [Annot87]. Four input machines "Ⓘ" receive data from neighboring communication processors. Four output machines "Ⓞ" send data to these neighboring nodes. The central store manages the internal buffer space. Two special input and output machines (marked SI and SO) handle the packets going to and coming from this node. An input queue and output queue decouples the data processor.

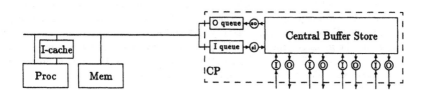

Figure 9: The PRISMA model

The algorithms used in the model are partly different from the algorithms used in the hardware version of the CP, however their external behavior remains the same. The buffer management in the central store is normally a unit consisting of four queues. These four queues contain references to the packets which should be sent over the four links. A rather complicated but efficient protocol ensures that each packet travels over exactly one link. We model this for the sake of simplicity as a single queue. Both the FIFO order and the timing of the original queuing scheme are preserved. The input and output machines are also implemented radically different from the hardware. They are normally running using a polling protocol. During a simulation, this takes an arbitrary amount of CPU-time. The protocol is therefore changed into an event driven protocol, again with preservation of the external behavior.

The data processor is a three address register oriented processor, with the capacities of approximately an MC68020. The instruction set is enriched with a few instructions like "printf", "readtimer" and "printtimer" which do not take any execution time, nor any space in the program (no instruction fetches are simulated for it) but which are very practical in debugging simulators, compilers and assemblers and for getting performance figures from a simulator.

To simulate the software, the GNU C-compiler [Stallman] is used to translate the POOL run time support system and the compiled POOL program of figure 6 (note that the POOL compiler translates POOL into C) into the assembler needed by our processor. We choose the GNU compiler because of its portability. Targetting the compiler to the processor in this architecture was rather easy since the processor is highly orthogonal, and has absolutely no nasty implementation caused non-orthogonalities. Such a processor is hard to build, but the performance characteristics of a real-world processor are not very different, it is only more work to build the compiler and the simulator.

Since the POOL program, run time support and message handling library are compiled to our processor, the full message trajectory is simulated, *including* the software overhead. Using this simulation, trade-offs between hardware and software can be made.

Note that some parts of the architecture are not modeled. The floating point unit, memory mapping (virtual to physical address translation which causes interesting problems when passing physical references to the coming message processor), and possible cache coherency problems are not taken into account. These points do not have a performance influence, they only introduce complexity in the design and are thus not interesting in this *evaluation* study.

3.3 Measurements and Results

The model described above has been verified first, by doing a simple check. All parameters are set to the values which are measured in the hardware prototype. The results should match the experimental results implemented on the prototype machine[Beemster90]. After this trivial verification, the parameters are upgraded to values which are reasonable for new technology. This upgraded model gives the performance which could be expected if the same architecture is implemented with current state-of-the-art technology. These performance figures serve as a reference point for evaluating the benefits of adding two architectural features.

A major performance improvement in terms of latency is expected when adding the message processor. This is done in two steps, the addition of an output message processor (does DMA from processor to network) and the addition of the input message processor (handles messages destined to the processor). This message processor needs to allocate memory for buffering of messages. Since the memory is managed by the data processor, this would lead to a complex interface between the data processor and the message processor. This problem is circumvented by incorporating a special purpose *allocation processor*. This unit manages the memory for both the message processor and the data processor, and has a clear well defined interface.

3.3.1 Verification

The model is roughly verified by simulating the prototype hardware exactly. To do so, the values of the parameters of the prototype need to be found. For the most simple components, this value is not hard to find. The values of the link-speeds of the CP and the speeds of the internal state machines of the CP are known, so all the times of the CP are known exactly. The memory waits states, cache parameters and the bus latency are also known exactly.

The situation with the data processor is worse. The model is not an exact copy of an MC68020, but a highly orthogonal three address machine. By restricting the amount of registers, and by tuning the allowed addressing modes to look like the MC68020, and by teaching the compiler to use these addressing modes, the model already looks like an MC68020 with respect to the amount of memory references and computations. To make the speed of the modeled processor and the MC68020 comparable, the instructions times needed for the various instructions are set to the time needed by an MC68020. By setting the clock speed to the value used in the prototype machine, the processor executes around 3 millions instructions per second, which is also the speed obtained by the MC68020 in the prototype machine. It is clear that this model is still radically different from an MC68020, so that MIPS measurements have not much relevance, but it seems that the modeled processor can do about the same work as an MC68020 in the same time. Most important is that the basic architectural differences do not have big performance consequences (three address mode) and there are no architectural differences (like separate instruction and data spaces, a data cache, or a special pipelined implementation) that *have* consequences for the performance.

When running the simulator with the parameters sketched above, it predicted a rendez vous time of 690 μs. Considering the measured value of the real prototype machine of 700 μs, the error is only 1.4%. This error is so insignificant that it seems to be ordinary luck: all the errors made in the modeling process compensate each other. We did our best to eliminate all possible sources of systematical errors, so there is a reasonable chance that the distribution which parts of the architecture are responsible for which part of the delay is not too different in reality and in simulation. This is absolutely an important condition because tradeoff's between various hardware and software solutions will be made in the coming pages.

3.3.2 Technology update

Upgrading the internal parameters of the CP to a more comfortable internal and link speed, and upgrading the speed of the internal algorithms gives a latency of 655μs. Reducing the access time of the communication processors IO-queues from 1 μs (introduced by the VME-bus) to 50 ns, gives a message rendez-vous time of 625 μs. This could have been expected, since 32 accesses are accelerated by about 1 μs each. The next step is to increase the clock frequency of the data processor. In figure 10[a] the delay time is plotted against the processor frequency. In this figure, it can be seen that the step from 25 to 33 Mhz did not give much improvement in delay time. This is an indication that other components are more and more becoming a bottleneck. This can also be observed by plotting the MIPS rate (in figure b). It is increasing faster than the latency is decreasing, which indicates that the processor is doing tasks which has nothing to do with computation: Being idle. The other thing to learn from the MIPS curve is that it does not increase fast (in a first order approximation, MIPS equals the clock frequency divided by the clocks per instruction, which comes to 5.2 MIPS for a 33.3 Mhz clock) enough from 25 to 33.3 Mhz. This is caused by the slow memory.

Figures from Oyster show that the memory system was utilized for 92% during the rendez vous when the data processor was set to a clock frequency of 33 Mhz. The small instruction cache did not give a sensible hit rate (about 40%, of which the major part caused by the idle loop of the POOL run time support system). After increasing the cache size by a factor 8 (which is not unreasonable as technology upgrade), the delay time improves to 450 μs. The memory is still utilized for 80%. This can be explained because a part of the idle loop refers to global variables in the memory, causing lots of accesses. This idle loop causes more problems: the processor is running like crazy and seems to be busy, while it actually is idle. Oyster's idea of idleness is thus disturbed by it. It is clear that both the MIPS rate coming from the simulator and the idle-detection should be interpreted carefully.

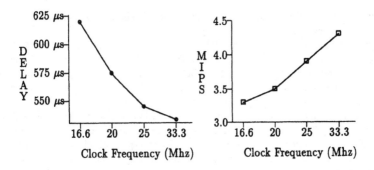

Figure 10: Clock frequency vs delay (a) and clock frequency vs MIPS (b)

3.3.3 Adding the allocation processor

The allocation processor handles memory allocation requests. It is not introduced to increase the performance, but because it makes the design of the message processor simpler. The interface of this allocation processor as seen from the data processor exactly resembles the C-library malloc()/free() calls. Allocation of memory is done by asking the allocation processor for a certain amount of bytes. A block of memory is freed again by passing the address of the first word to the allocation processor. The allocation processor itself maintains multiple linked lists of free blocks. This processor can be extended with capabilities for coalescing free blocks during idle periods, but that is a separate research issue.

There are some issues involved here posing nasty implementation problems when building real hardware. For example, when the data processor asks for a block of memory which is not yet available, the data processor should release the bus so the allocation processor can access the memory to search for a block. This bus-release need not to be simulated since it is only an implementation difficulty and has no influence on the performance. The performance is bounded by the speed of the memory and the allocation processor itself. Only if the bus switch between the data processor and allocation processor would take considerably more time than a memory reference, a complete simulation of it would be necessary.

The result of adding this allocation processor to the PRISMA node is that the delay time of a message decreases with about 40 μs. This is caused by the fact that parallelism is introduced (memory management activities are carried out in parallel with execution of the program) and because the allocation processor is dedicated to this job. During the total rendez vous, four calls are made to the allocation processor. This speedup is a nice side effect, but it is questionable if the hardware pays off.

3.3.4 Adding the message processor

The message processor implements the message layer of figure 5 in hardware. The interface as seen from the run time support is not changed, but 99% of the functions code is now implemented in hardware. Functions for start-message, end-message, send-data etcetera are all two or three assembler instructions. These assembler instructions pass the function parameters to the message processor via a memory mapped interface.

In figure 11 is a sketch of the complete architecture including the allocation processor and the input and output message processor (Input MP, Output MP). The input and output message processors itself are dual ported, one port is dedicated to talk to the communication processor, the other to communicate with the memory and to get commands from the processor. The message processor does not only transport data from one bus to the other, it also generates the headers required by the communication processor at the start of each packet, and removes these headers when retrieving the packet from the network. Additionally, the input message processor unravels the various streams coming from all nodes of the machine into separate byte streams.

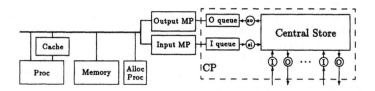

Figure 11: The model of the enhanced PRISMA architecture

The result of adding the output side of the message processor (from DP to CP) is that the rendez vous time dropped with another 80 μs, to 325 μs. When sending larger messages the benefits are higher, since the message processor is dedicated to transport data from memory to the CP over two busses.

Placing the input side of the message processor in the stream from network to data processor saves less, only 25 μs, bringing the latency to 300 μs. In more complex POOL programs, where multiple objects are communicating, messages from different nodes interleave. In that case a larger gain can be expected. Further simulations are necessary to get insight in the behavior at higher loads.

3.4 Conclusion

Figure 12 summarizes the delay times for varying processor speeds in the case of the original architecture (figure 10), with message and allocation processor (figure 11) and one with message processor, but with a small instruction cache (to observe the cache's influence). The first two lines of this table contain the measurements of the prototype machine and the results of the first simulation run, using the parameters of the prototype PRISMA machine.

Clock	16.7 Mhz	20 Mhz	25 Mhz	33.3 Mhz
Measured on Prototype	700 μs			
model, 1985-technology	690 μs			
new-technology	615 μs	575 μs	550 μs	533 μs
with MP, small cache	425 μs	400 μs	380 μs	375 μs
with MP, large cache	360 μs	330 μs	310 μs	300 μs

Figure 12: Delay of prototype, first model, introduction of a small processor cache, introduction of the message processor and with a larger cache. The four columns represent 4 clock speeds.

The latency introduced in executing a synchronization can be reduced from 690 to 300 μs. 75 μs are caused by a technology upgrade of the memory, cache, CP and DP-CP interface. 60-80 μs is saved by a higher clock speed of the data processor, 160-180 μs by the special extra hardware and 75 μs by the bigger instruction cache.

When the table in figure 12 is extended with lower clock frequencies, the latency is increasing linearly with the cycle time of the clock. This is because the processor is the slowest component of the system and is then completely responsible for the delay. At clock frequencies higher than 20 Mhz, the latency is bounded by other parts of the architecture, notably the memory, cache and bus.

The rate at which the latency increases for low clock frequencies is a measure for the amount of instructions executed in the critical path of the message transfer. In the two cases with and without MP, these rates are respectively 40 and 30 μs per 10 ns clock cycle time. From this, we learn that the data processor spends 4000 ($40\mu s/10ns$) and 3000 cycles executing critical code, a reduction of 1000 cycles. 3000 cycles remain to be optimized.

When the latency is measured as a number of data processor instructions instead of in micro seconds, the difference in latency between 16 Mhz and no message processor, and 33.3 Mhz with message processor is smaller. Due to the higher clock frequency the latency is 2000 and 1500 instructions respectively. This indicates that a machine with a message processor allows applications with a smaller grain size to run. Note that the architecture without message processor, but with a 33.3 Mhz data processor requires a larger grain size.

Because of the the large remaining grain (1500), further reduction of the remaining 300 μs are an important research issue. These microseconds are partly spent in the flattening procedure, which converts a POOL message to a stream of bytes. This task can theoretically be done in hardware, but that takes all flexibility out of the implementation, and generates a horrendous interface between the compiler and the hardware, which is not an attractive alternative. Other optimization points might be the introduction of a cache for data accesses (which is troublesome because of coherency) and a second port on the memory for the message passing hardware.

As explained in section 3.1 above, the throughput of the network could not be improved since the communication hardware is the bottleneck. However the processor overhead in sending messages decreases dramatically when sending large flat POOL messages, like arrays of integers, large strings or code segments. Since the memory is shared by the data processor and the message processor, the data processor is stopped sometimes due to memory contention. The effect of this is less than a 10% slow down of the processor because of memory conflicts.

The next step in a real world situation should be an estimation of the costs to see if the hardware is cost effective, but that is outside the scope of this paper. The only conclusion drawn from these experiments is that the latency can be reduced to 300 μs give or take an error introduced in the simulation.

4 Discussion

Despite some minor inconveniences, we are very satisfied with the simulation environment so far. The modeling of the PRISMA architecture (including the port of the GNU compiler) took 2 man weeks work, and gives promising results; we conclude that the Oyster simulation system is adequate for rapid prototyping. The abovementioned results are simulation results and thus less reliable than measurements on a real machine, but the most common sources of errors have been circumvented since we simulate not only the hardware communication layer but also the interaction with the software.

That the modeling time was short is partly because the designer was familiar with the simulation system and the architecture to be simulated, but also due to the facilities provided by Oyster. Especially the standard models for caches, memories and processor, the message passing approach in Pearl and the close interface to the C-programming language make life easy. Comparing this to the situation in using a standard hardware simulator, we saved lots of work.

Despite the overhead of the message passing language, the execution times of the simulator were short (a few seconds). This was mainly due to the fact that we used mixed level simulation, where the algorithms are simulated at a high level and the interface hardware was simulated at a low level. Together with the good experiences so far, it encourages us to continue the research in this direction.

4.1 Future work

Oyster is not finished, currently it is extended at two sides. The model of data processors is too simplistic. It is upgraded to a model including pipelining and other forms of internal parallelism. This new data processor model will maintain more important statistical outputs like the pipeline usage, the dynamic instruction usage, the dynamic branch frequency and distance, and so on. The evaluation output coming from the bottom layer of Oyster is further extended with measurements correlating activities of various objects. These figures will better point out *why* objects are idle, instead of only recording their idleness. Because of the clear communication structure, the interdependencies between objects can be monitored easily.

5 Acknowledgements

The author likes to acknowledge the support of the PRISMA project headed by Huib Eggenhuisen and the DOOM project, especially the architecture group and Eddy Odijk. Rutger Hofman, Wim Vree, Bob Hertzberger, Pieter Hartel and Marcel Beemster made valuable comments to earlier versions of this article. The Pearl compiler was developed by Gert Jan Stil and Benno Overeinder.

References

[America89] P.H.M. America, *"P0350: Definition of POOL-X"*, PRISMA document 350, Philips research laboratories, Eindhoven, The Netherlands.

[Annot87] J.K. Annot and R. van Twist, *"A novel deadlock free and starvation free packet switching communication processor"*, Proceedings of PARLE pp 68-85, June 1987.

[Apers90] P. Apers, L.O. Hertzberger and B.J.A. Hulshof, *"PRISMA: A Platform for experiments with parallelism"*, Proceedings of the PRISMA workshop on parallel databasesystems (this proceedings), Noordwijk, The Netherlands, September 24-26, Springer Verlag 1990.

[Beemster90] M. Beemster, *"Back end aspects of the portable POOL implementation"*, Proceedings of the PRISMA workshop on parallel databasesystems (this proceedings), Noordwijk, The Netherlands, September 24-26, Springer Verlag 1990.

[Birtwistle73] G.M. Birtwistle, O.-J. Dahl, B. Myhrhaug, and K. Nygaard, *"SIMULA begin"*, 1973.

[Bray89] B. Bray, K. Cuderman, M. Flynn and A. Zimmerman, *"The computer architect's workbench"*, Proceedings of IFIP '89.

[Bronnenberg87] W.J.H.J. Bronnenberg et al, *"DOOM: a decentralized object oriented machine"*, IEEE micro, Vol 7, No 5, pp 52-69, October 1987 .

[Bryant84] R.E. Bryant, *"A Switch level model and simulator for MOS systems"*, IEEE Transactions on computers, Vol C-33, No 2, pp 160-177, February 1984.

[Bryant87] R.E. Bryant, et al, *"COSMOS: A compiled simulator for MOS circuits"*, 24th Design Automation conference, pp 9-16, 1987.

[Dahl66] O-J. Dahl and K. Nygaard, *"SIMULA and ALGOL based simulation language"*, Communications of the ACM, Vol 9, No 9, pp 671, 1966

[Dally86] W.J. Dally and C.L. Seitz *"The torus routing chip"*, Distributed computing 1, 1986.

[Inmos86] *"IMS T800 architecture "* INMOS technical note 6, 1986.

[Krishnakumar87] A.S. Krishnakumar, "*ART-DACO: Architectural research tool using data abstraction and concurrency*", Proceedings of the international conference on computer design, October 1987.

[Mooij89] W.G.P. Mooij, "*Packet Switching Communication Networks for Multiprocessor Systems*" Ph.D. Thesis, University of Amsterdam, December 1989.

[Nichols88] K.M. Nichols and J.T. Edmark, "*Modeling multi computer systems with PARET*", IEEE computer, May 1988.

[Spek90] J. vd Spek, "*Back end aspects of the portable POOL implementation*", Proceedings of the PRISMA workshop on parallel databasesystems (this proceedings), Noordwijk, The Netherlands, September 24-26, Springer Verlag 1990.

[Stallman] R.M. Stallman, "*Using and Porting the GNU C-compiler*", Free Software Foundation Inc., Massachusetts.

[Vlot90] M. Vlot, "*The POOMA architecture*", Proceedings of the PRISMA workshop on parallel databasesystems (this proceedings), Noordwijk, The Netherlands, September 24-26, Springer Verlag 1990.

[Weste81] N. Weste, "*MULGA- An interactive symbolic layout system for the design of integrated circuits*", The Bell System Technical Journal, Vol 60, No 6, 1981.

A Parallel Implementation of the EQUIP Expert System

J. W. Spee*

PTT Research Tele-Informatics Laboratory

P. O. Box 15.000, 9700 CD Groningen, The Netherlands

Abstract

We describe a parallel implementation of a subset of the EQUIP expert system. In EQUIP, diagnostic reasoning is applied to the domain of silicon chip production control. In order to diagnose all probable process faults that occurred in the manufacturing of IC's, the necessary computations in the inference part of the program become very time-consuming. To reduce this computation time, a parallel inference algorithm has been developed. We describe this inference algorithm and its parallel implementation in POOL-X. In the end some results will be shown using a multi-node computer.

1 Introduction

The work presented in this report concerns the parallel implementation of a part of an expert system called EQUIP, developed by H.J. ter Horst at Philips Research Laboratories in Eindhoven (PRLE) [1]. EQUIP stands for 'Expert system for the **QU**alitative Interpretation of PCM-data'.
EQUIP is used at Philips' integrated circuit (IC) production plants. It is capable of deducing the possible causes of faults in the manufacturing of IC's.

Constructing an integrated circuit is a difficult process, involving many process steps. Every step takes place under stringent conditions, which must be satisfied, to obtain a satisfactory result in the end.
For deciding whether the IC production process has performed properly, a number of tests is performed using a test chip called 'Process Control Module', or PCM for short. The test data is first analysed statistically to obtain a set of parameters which is interpreted to find out what possibly went wrong during some stage in the process. EQUIP contains a knowledge base which describes possible process faults and their consequences as observable in the PCM data at the end of the process.
Given the results of measurements done by the PCM, EQUIP is able to derive the possible process faults which may have caused them. This is done in a qualitative way.
This means that the qualitative results yielded by statistical analysis, like 'transistor parameter xxx shows too large spread between wafers', is interpreted by EQUIP to derive something like 'temperature in process step yyy not stable', a process fault.

---

*The work described in this document was conducted at the Centre for Mathematics and Computer Science (CWI) in Amsterdam as part of the PRISMA project, a joint effort with Philips Research Eindhoven, partially supported by the Dutch "Stimulerings-projectteam Informatica-onderzoek" (SPIN).

process dist.   structure dist. measurement dist.

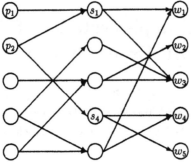

Figure 1: structure of the knowledge base

The current operational version of EQUIP is a LISP program. A problem with that program is that the necessary computations become time-consuming. Therefore research has been carried out to assist in the inference process using parallelism, in order to keep the response time of the system feasible.

This parallel implementation is done in POOL-X, a member of the family of POOL languages [5,7] developed at PRLE, and has been evaluated using the POOMA machine, a 100-node coarse-grain multiprocessor computer.
The remainder of this report gives a precise description of the basic search procedure, an overview of the improvements to this algorithm, the design issues involved in the POOL-X implementation and the results obtained by experimenting with the program on the POOMA machine.

2 Diagnostic Problem Solving

We start by giving a more formal description of the problem, and also a sequential procedure for solving it. In the next section it will be shown how this procedure can be parallelized using POOL.

Faults in the IC's produced are usually a consequence of some disturbance of the environmental conditions under which they manufactured. The consequences of a process disturbance consist of deviations from the normal range of measurements performed on the PCM. These are stored in a knowledge base, which has a three-layered structure. The first layer consists of process disturbances and is linked to so-called 'structure disturbances', the second layer. These are disturbances that are a direct consequence of a process disturbance. For example, the process disturbance 'temperature too high' causes the structure disturbance 'silicon layer too thick'.

Each structure disturbance is linked to a collection of measurement disturbances, the third layer. These correspond to the measurements made by the PCM. The structure of the knowledge base is given in figure 1.

In this figure, disturbances are represented by circles, and when two disturbances in different layers are causally related, they are connected by an arrow.

Given a knowledge base, all the consequences of a process disturbance can be computed in advance.

In order to reduce the number of possibilities without losing information, all the consequences of one such a process disturbance are clustered. Given a set of observed measurement disturbances, each cluster is restricted to its intersection with this set. If the clusters of two process disturbances have become the same, that is, these process disturbances result in the same set of observed measurement disturbances, they can be regarded as equivalent. This induces an equivalence class on the set of all process disturbances. Each equivalence class is characterized, and will be identified with the resulting set of observed measurement disturbances, which we call a cluster. For example in figure 1 all consequences of process disturbance p_1 are w_1 and w_3: the only consequence of p_1 is structure disturbance s_1 and its consequences are w_1 and w_3. So w_1 and w_3 are clustered. The consequences of process disturbance p_2 are w_1, w_3, w_4 and w_5. If $\{w_1, w_2, w_3\}$ is the set of observed measurement disturbances, then $\{w_1, w_3\}$ is a cluster, and p_1 and p_2 are members of the equivalence class of process disturbances associated with this cluster.

Now given some measurement disturbances, all the possible sets of clusters that can cause these measurement disturbances can be computed. From such a set of clusters the associated process disturbances follow directly.

After that in the LISP version all those sets of clusters are ordered according to some likelihood criterion. Such a set, which is an explanation for the measured disturbances, will be called a diagnosis.

Definition 2.1 *Given a set W of measurement disturbances and a set of clusters $C = \{X_1, \ldots, X_n\}$. A* **diagnosis D** *of W, $\mathbf{D} = \{X_{i_1}, \ldots, X_{i_m}\}$ is a minimal subset of C covering W, which means $\bigcup\{X_{i_1}, \ldots, X_{i_m}\} = W$, and no strict subset of $\mathbf{D}$ covers W.*

If any cluster is omitted from a diagnosis, then not all measurement disturbances are still explained. In case of a non-minimal cover, there must be some cluster redundant, which can be neglected without losing completeness of the explanation.

So we are not only interested in a cover of W with a minimal cardinality, but in all minimal covers of W. Now we will present an advanced algorithm to find these minimal covers, or equivalently, these diagnoses.

3   Sequential Algorithm

In this section we will concentrate on the problem of finding all minimal covers.

First we will give some important definitions. Then we will show a basic algorithm, using *implicit enumeration*. This algorithm is proven correct. Hereafter we demonstrate three search space reductions, two of which have been presented in literature about the Set Covering Problem (cf. for example [13,17]), in which some minimum cover is searched for. We will prove completeness properties of two of these reductions for our minimal cover problem. Finally we will present a formal property of a heuristic that has shown its value in practical situations.

Definition 3.1 Let $W = \{w_1, \ldots, w_n\}$ be a finite set of observations, and $C = \{X_1, \ldots, X_k\}$ a set of sets, such that $X_i \subseteq W$, $i = 1, \ldots, k$. C **covers** W if $\bigcup C = W$, that is, $X_1 \cup \ldots \cup X_k = W$, or, in other words, C is a **cover** of W. S **minimally covers** W if C covers W and $\forall X \in C$ $\bigcup(C - \{X\}) \neq W$. In this case C is called a **minimal cover** of W.

Definition 3.2 Let C be a set of sets.
C is **independent** if $\forall X \in C$ $\bigcup(C - \{X\}) \neq \bigcup C$.

It follows immediately that
- A minimal cover of a set is independent.

- An independent cover of a set is a minimal cover of that set.
- Every subset of a minimal cover is independent.

Definition 3.3 A **partial cover** of a set W is an independent set, the union of which is a subset of W.

Definition 3.4 Let D be an independent set of sets, and C a set of sets of the same type. Then $D' = D \cup C$ is an **extension** of D.
D' is an **independent extension** of D if D' also is independent.

Definition 3.5 Let W be a set and C be a set of sets that covers W. Then $MC(D', C)$ is the set of all minimal covers D of W, such that:
- D' is a subset of D.
- the independent extension D of D' is formed using a subset of C.

So the set of all minimal covers of W, using a set of sets C that covers W, is $MC(\emptyset, C)$.

It turns out that we need an algorithm to compute $MC(\emptyset, C)$, that is, we have to find all independent extensions of the empty set that are covers of W.

In the rest of this section we shall use the following standard identifiers:
W is the set of elements to be covered, C is the given set of sets that can be used to cover W, D is a partial cover of W.

When no confusion arises, we shall sometimes say that an element of W is covered, meaning that the singleton set containing this element is covered.

3.1 Basic Enumeration Algorithm

The *search space* of the SCP consists of all subsets of C. Simply enumerating all subsets is not feasible, for $2^{|C|}$ sets have to be considered.

A more efficient enumeration method must be used, that still finds all minimal covers, but that needs to check a minimal number of subsets.

A well-known technique to achieve this is *implicit enumeration*, a strategy that leads, as the enumeration proceeds, to the exclusion of large parts of the search space that do not need any further consideration.

In our approach, which we call "increasing cover search", an element of the set to be covered is taken, and the current partial cover is extended with a set that covers this selected element. The basic algorithm looks as follows:

```
Increasing_Cover_Search( W', C', D'):
begin
    C" := C';
    select an element w ∈ W';
    for all X ∈ C' such that w ∈ X
    do
        D" := D' ∪ {X};
        W" := W' - X,
        C" := C" - {X};
        if W" ≠ ∅
        then
            C'" := {X ∈ C" | D" ∪ {X} independent };
            if ∪C'" ⊇ W"
            then Increasing_Cover_Search(W", C'", D")
            fi
        else report D"
        fi
    od
end
```

The initial call to this algorithm is "Increasing_Cover_Search(W, C, $\emptyset$)". We assume that W and C are initially not empty.

The algorithm acts as follows:

First a not yet covered element $w \in W'$ is chosen. Then for all sets $X \in C'$ that contain w, the current partial cover D' is extended with X. For such an extension D'', if there are still not yet covered elements, that is $W'' \neq \emptyset$, the algorithm is called recursively with sets that are independent of D'', because only such sets can be useful in the construction of a minimal cover. But this happens only if the union of these remaining sets can cover W'', for otherwise a minimal cover will never be found.

Also X is removed from C'', the local copy of C'. This guarantees that every minimal cover will be found exactly once. This important optimization appears to be new.

If, on the other hand, all elements have been covered, then a minimal cover is found, which is reported.

This algorithm can be proven correct:

Theorem 3.1 The improved increasing cover algorithm finds every minimal cover exactly once.

The actual proofs of all theorems in this section can be found in [2].

3.2 Search Space Reductions

If it would be possible to reduce C, such that no minimal covers are lost, and only partial covers are generated that can be extended to a minimal cover, then we would have an implicit enumeration algorithm, which is in some sense optimal: it would simply construct all minimal covers, without doing any redundant processing.

This can be achieved if at each recursive instance of the algorithm with partial cover D' and remaining set of sets C', the two following sets can be identified:

the set $\bigcap(MC(D', C')) - D'$, which contains all sets that occur in every minimal cover containing

D', and the set $C' - \bigcup(MC(D', C'))$, which contains all sets of C' that occur in no minimal cover containing D'.

The former set can simply be added to the partial cover D', because any of its members is part of every minimal cover containing D'. Every set contained in the latter set will not appear in any minimal cover containing D'. So these sets can be eliminated from C' without any further consideration.

At each recursive instance of the algorithm these two sets should be computed exactly. We exhibit two *reductions*, which can also be found in literature [9,11,12,13], in which they are applied to the Set Covering Problem. We shall prove that these reductions identify $\bigcap(MC(D', C')) - D'$ and $C' - \bigcup(MC(D', C'))$ exactly if D' is empty and $C' = C$, and otherwise subsets of these, which is still useful.

We will also introduce a third reduction, namely *partitioning* the remaining set of sets.

3.2.1 Computing $\bigcap(MC(D', C')) - D'$

If a set X in C contains an element that is not contained in any other set in C, then X is needed in any minimal cover, otherwise this element in X would never be covered. So X is a member of every minimal cover and therefore X is also in the intersection of all minimal covers.

These sets, which contain some element exclusively, exactly define $\bigcap(MC(\emptyset, C))$, but in general they only form a subset of $\bigcap(MC(D', C'))$, if D' is not empty.

Definition 3.6 Let C be a set of sets. The **cover rate** *of an element* w *in* C, denoted as $\text{cov}(w, C)$, is the number of sets in C of which w is an element, that is, $\text{cov}(w, C) = |\{X \in C | w \in X\}|$.

It turns out that $\bigcap(MC(\emptyset, C))$ consists of exactly those sets that contain some element exclusively:

Theorem 3.2 Let X be an element of C'. If $D' = \emptyset$ and $C' = C$, then
$X \in \bigcap(MC(D', C')) - D'$ iff $\exists w \in X \; \text{cov}(w, C') = 1$.

If the partial cover D' is not empty, then the *only if*-part does not longer hold: it can happen that elements in W' are covered by sets that cannot be element of an independent extension of D'.

Now we can incorporate the following reduction procedure in our basic algorithm:

Reduction 1 Given a recursive instance of the algorithm with parameters W', C' and D'. In every iteration of the for-loop, let D'' be the extension of D' and C''' the remaining set of sets. for all $X \in C'''$, such that
$\exists w \in X \; \text{cov}(w, C''') = 1$, do $D'' := D'' \cup \{X\}$, $C''' := C''' - \{X\}$ and
$W'' := W'' - \{X\}$.

3.2.2 Computing $C' - \bigcup(MC(D', C'))$

Suppose, for some recursive instance, that for some $w_1, w_2 \in W'$, for every X set in C', $w_1 \in X$ implies $w_2 \in X$. Then whenever w_1 is an element of the union of an extension of the current partial cover, then also is w_2.

In literature [13,17] this is called *domination* and defines a relation "$<_{C'}$".

Definition 3.7 Let $<_{C'} \subseteq W' \times W'$, such that $w_1 <_{C'} w_2$ (w_1 *dominates* w_2) iff $\forall X \in C' \; w_1 \in X \to w_2 \in X$.

In the algorithm only minimal elements of W' in the partial order "$<_{C'}$" are needed. So every non-minimal (that is, dominated) element can be omitted from W'.

Definition 3.8 Let in every iteration of the for-loop in the algorithm C''' be the remaining set of sets and W'' the remaining set to be covered. **Dominated elements removal** consists of removing every element $w \in W''$ such that there is another element $w' \in W''$ and $w' <_{C'''} w$. Such a w is removed from W'' and from each set in C'''.

In every recursive instance of the algorithm we could start searching for dominated elements. When a set in C' only consists of such elements, this set need not be used in any extension of a partial cover. So this set can be removed.

It can be shown that $C - \bigcup(MC(\emptyset, C))$ is exactly defined by such sets. Whenever $D' \subset C$ is not empty, they form only a subset of $C' - \bigcup(MC(D', C'))$. In this case, all sets in C' that cannot be used in an independent extension of D' are also in $C' - \bigcup(MC(D', C'))$.

Theorem 3.3 Let X be an element of C'. If $D' = \emptyset$ and $C' = C$, then $X \in C' - \bigcup(MC(D', C'))$ iff $\forall w \in X \, \exists w' \notin X$, $w' \in W$, such that $w' <_{C'} w$.

If the partial cover D' is not empty, the *only if*-part does not longer hold. We can incorporate the following reduction procedure:

Reduction 2 In every iteration of the for-loop in the algorithm with C''' as remaining set of sets, apply *dominated elements removal*. For all $X \in C'''$, if $X = \emptyset$, do $C''' := C''' - \{X\}$.

3.2.3 Partitioning the Remaining Search Space

If in a recursive instance of the algorithm, with parameters W', C' and D', the set C' can be partitioned into $C'_1, \ldots, C'_k$, such that $\bigcup C'_i \cap \bigcup C'_j = \emptyset$, for all pairs i, j, $1 \leq i, j \leq k$, $i \neq j$, then all minimal covers of W' can be found by combining all minimal covers of all partitions, and omitting the ones that are not independent. Now at most $2^{|C'_1|} + \ldots + 2^{|C'_k|}$ subsets have to be generated, which is less than $2^{|C'|}$, for $k > 1$.

Theorem 3.4 Let $\bigcup C' \supseteq W'$, and $C' = C'_1 \cup \ldots \cup C'_p$, such that $\bigcup C'_i \cap \bigcup C'_j = \emptyset$, for all $i, j = 1, \ldots, p$, $i \neq j$. Then for all $D \in MC(D', C')$, $D = D' \cup D_1 \cup \ldots \cup D_p$, such that $D_i \subseteq C'_i$ and D_i is a minimal cover of W'_i.

If the set C' can be partitioned, then finding all minimal covers comes down to computing every possible combination of D' with a partial cover D_j of each partition, $j = 1, \ldots, p$, provided that such a combination is independent.

Reduction 3 In a recursive instance of the algorithm with D' as partial cover of W' and C' as set of sets, if $C' = C'_1 \cup \ldots \cup C'_p$, such that the $\bigcup C'_i$ are pairwise disjoint, then report as a minimal cover every D, such that $D = D' \cup D_1 \cup \ldots \cup D_p$, where D_j is reported as a minimal cover by a recursive instance of the algorithm with parameters $\bigcup C'_j$, C'_j, $\emptyset$, for each $j = 1, \ldots, p$, provided that D is an independent extension of D'.

3.2.4 Example

Consider the following example, in which the set $C = \{X_1, \ldots, X_6\}$ is represented by a matrix, such that $C_{i,j} = 1$ iff $w_i \in X_j$, where $W = \{w_1, \ldots, w_5\}$.

$$C = \begin{pmatrix} 1 & 1 & 0 & 0 & 0 & 0 \\ 0 & 1 & 1 & 0 & 1 & 0 \\ 0 & 1 & 0 & 1 & 1 & 0 \\ 0 & 0 & 1 & 0 & 1 & 1 \\ 0 & 0 & 0 & 1 & 1 & 1 \end{pmatrix}$$

We omit the subscript from the domination relation "$<$", as long as no ambiguity occurs.

Assume element w_1 (represented by the first row) is selected first. Look at the recursive instance of the algorithm where $\{X_1\}$ is taken as partial cover. Then $\{X_1, X_2\}$ is not independent, so X_2 is omitted, that is, $X_2 \in \{X_2, \ldots, X_6\} - \bigcup(MC(\{X_1\}, \{X_2, \ldots, X_6\}))$. Now $w_2 < w_4$ and $w_3 < w_5$, therefore w_4 and w_5 are dominated elements and are removed. But now X_6 has become empty, so it is removed. Assume w_2 is selected next, and the partial cover is extended to $\{X_1, X_3\}$. Then $\{X_1, X_3, X_5\}$ is not independent, so X_5 is removed. As a consequence, $\text{cov}(w_3, \{X_4\}) = 1$, so $X_4 \in \bigcap(MC(\{X_1, X_3\}, \{X_4\}))$, and the partial cover is extended to the minimal cover $\{X_1, X_3, X_4\}$.

This example shows that applying the reductions as described in the previous subsections can reduce the search space very quickly.

3.3 A Heuristic

Now we introduce a heuristic, which has shown to reduce the number of recursive instances of the algorithm considerably in practical cases (cf. [3,17]). This heuristic selects some special element of W' in the "increasing cover search" algorithm.

Good results are obtained by chosing an element of W' that has a minimal cover rate in C'. Informally, this can be justified as follows: in each recursive instance another element of W is covered. When to achieve this, a minimal number of recursive instances is generated, it seems plausible that for the whole cover of W a number of recursive instances is generated that is nearly minimal. Although we are not able to prove this, we show that by applying this strategy dominated elements are removed automatically. Therefore, sets that consist of dominated elements only, which are element of $C' - \bigcup((MC(D', C')))$, are never used to extend a partial cover. This forms a possible explanation for the success of this heuristic in practice.

Heuristic 1 *Greedy Search*: In each recursive instance of the algorithm with parameters W', C' and D', select an element in W' with a minimal cover rate in C'.

To prove the theorem, we need the following lemma:

Lemma 3.1 Let C' and W' be given, and $\bigcup C' \supseteq W'$.
Then for all $w_1, w_2 \in W'$ $w_1 <_{C'} w_2$ implies $\text{cov}(w_1, C') < \text{cov}(w_2, C')$.

Theorem 3.5 Given a recursive instance of the algorithm with parameters W', C' and D'. If Greedy Search is applied, then D' is never extended to $D' \cup \{X\}$, $X \in C'$, such that X only consists of dominated elements.

This theorem follows from the observation that if Greedy Search is applied, an element in W is chosen that is not dominated by any other element. Therefore any set in C' that is used to extend the current partial cover, does contain at least one not dominated element.

It seems that when Greedy Search is applied, reduction 2 becomes redundant. Actually, this is not the case. If, using reduction 2, sets consisting of dominated elements are removed, possibly more partitions can be found, which reduces the search space. Therefore reduction 2 is still useful.

3.4 Some Remarks about the Algorithm

We have shown an algorithm to find all minimal covers of a set, consisting of a basic enumeration algorithm, reduction procedures and a heuristic.

The reductions can identify $\bigcap(MC(\emptyset, C))$ and $C - \bigcup(MC(\emptyset, C))$ completely. However, if D' is not empty, they only find subsets of

$\bigcap(MC(D', C')) - D'$ and $C' - \bigcup(MC(D', C'))$, so probably some redundant processing is still performed.

If the partial cover D' is not empty, the effectiveness of the reductions can be order dependent. It seems wise to start applying a reduction that removes as much redundant sets as possible, that is, apply reduction 2 first. Hereafter reduction 1 can be applied. Reduction 3, the partitioning reduction, can be applied before or after the other reductions.

4 Parallel implementation of the search procedure

A parallel implementation of this search procedure is not really straightforward. The POOMA machine is a MIMD machine, consisting of 100 processing units, each with its own memory. In such a computer the cost of communication is relatively high compared to local computation. Therefore an efficient parallel computation on this machine should be rather coarse grained, that is, the ratio between local computation and interprocessor communication should be high enough.

In our case this can be achieved by mapping different instances of the search procedure on different processors. Then communication is only necessary when a new search node is generated or when a diagnosis has been found, and the rest of the computation is done locally.

Collecting all diagnoses and sorting them is a difficult task in a parallel implementation. Sending all diagnoses to one special processor that sorts them gives rise to a bottleneck: this processor will still be sorting diagnoses when searching has already been finished. So a distributed approach has to be used.

4.1 The POOL programming language

We shall present the main features of the POOL programming language.

POOL (Parallel Object Oriented Language) is developed at PRLE [5,6,7]. It combines parallelism with object oriented programming. In an object oriented language, computation is performed by objects, these are independent units consisting of private data and program code. An object interacts with other objects by means of a communication mechanism.

Objects are grouped into classes. Objects of the same class have the same program code and the same type of data. Objects of a certain class are called *instances* of that class.

Communication is done by sending messages consisting of a message name and some arguments. This comes down to a request to execute one of the procedures of the receiving object, identified by the message name. Such a procedure is called a method.

Objects are created by calling a special routine. After creation they start executing their program code directly. An object terminates as soon as it has executed its last program statement. When all objects have terminated, the computation has finished.

In POOL objects can be executed in parallel, thus introducing parallelism. At the moment of creation of an object, it can be allocated on a specified processor. If objects run in parallel, communication can be used not only for exchanging information between objects, but also for synchronizing them.

4.2 POOL implementation

The POOL implementation there are four major parts: initializing, searching, load balancing and sorting.

The POOL program mainly consists of the following four class definitions:

- an **initializer** that first reads the input file and makes a compact representation of the clusters read. Then it creates in parallel an n-dimensional hypercube structure, which is used for load balancing purposes, and a search node, the root, to activate the search procedure.

- a **hypercube structure** that is used for load balancing purposes by collecting and exchanging workload information of processor nodes.

- an **AVL-tree** that sorts all diagnoses which are found by search nodes and were sent to this tree. All diagnoses i.e. sets of clusters, are ordered first on length and then lexicographically on cluster number.

- a **search node**. An object of this class executes the search algorithm presented in the previous section. If a diagnosis is found, this diagnosis is sent to an AVL-tree which is situated on some processor, according to some sorting criterion.

4.3 The Initializer

There is only one instance of this class. This instance reads the name of the input batch as well as clusters which have a nonempty intersection with the measurement disturbances of this batch.

All these clusters are restricted to their intersection with the measurement disturbances, because we are not interested in explanations for disturbances that did not occur.

Then it creates in parallel a hypercube structure and the root search node.

4.3.1 Data compaction

Often it is possible to make the sets that have been read more compact:

if there are two measurement disturbances that occur in exactly the same sets, it has no use to distinguish them any more. In this way one measurement disturbance can be eliminated, without loosing any solution. In this way the maximum set size could be reduced by maximally 40 %.

This can be stated more formally:

If two elements w_1, w_2 do not need to be distinguished we write it down as $w_1 \sim w_2$.

Definition 4.1 $w_1 \sim w_2 \iff \forall$ *clusters* X, Y $(w_1 \in X \cap Y \leftrightarrow w_2 \in X \cap Y)$.

It is clear that this defines an equivalence relation.

The size of the messages between search nodes are proportional to the maximum set size. So data compaction gives a serious reduction in the message size. When all diagnoses have been found, the root search node sends a message to the initializer, which on its turn sends messages of this kind to all AVL-trees.

4.4 The Hypercube structure

On each processor node a hypercube-object, that is, a hypercube node in a hypercube structure, is created that keeps notice of the current workload on its processor and on its neighbour processors in the hypercube structure. When a new search node is created, the local hypercube object is consulted to decide on which processor node this search node has to be allocated. Using workload information from its neighbour hypercube objects, it determines the processor node with the currently lowest work load. On that processor the search node will be allocated. Using this strategy a very satisfactory load balancing has been obtained [4].

4.5 The AVL-trees

On every processor an AVL-tree is allocated. Diagnoses are sent to the AVL-trees according to an order preserving function. This is a kind of hash function, that guarantees for all diagnoses d_a and d_b, that, if d_a is sent to AVL-tree c_i and d_b is sent to AVL-tree c_j, then $i < j \Rightarrow d_a < d_b$. At every AVL-tree the diagnoses are inserted into a balanced binary AVL-tree. In this way, a total ordering on all diagnoses found is obtained automatically.

The diagnoses are sorted first on length and then lexicographically. The diagnosis with the shortest length gives the most simple explanation for all disturbances. The diagnosis are further ordered lexicographically for readability purposes only.

4.6 The Search Nodes

The recursive search algorithm gives rise to a natural parallel implementation:
each instance of the algorithm is seen as an object. Each recursive call is translated into the creation of a new search object, possibly running on (another) processor node. Such an object is called a child node.
In this way many search nodes (objects) are created on all processor nodes.
If a search node has found a diagnosis it sends this diagnosis to an AVL-tree.
A search node terminates if it has no children and it has sent all diagnoses found to the AVL-trees, or when all its children are terminated. Then it signals its father object. At the moment that the root search node has received termination messages from all its children it is known that all diagnoses have been sent to the AVL-trees (this is guaranteed by the synchronous nature of communication).
In figure 2 we see the search nodes of the search tree. Now the diagnoses are sent to an AVL-tree (the triangulars) according to the order preserving function. When all diagnoses have been inserted into the AVL tree, they have at the same time been sorted.

5 Evaluation of Parallelism

After having tested the program thoroughly using a POOL simulator, we also evaluated the program on a real parallel platform, the POOMA machine. The measurements are taken using the PPMX compiler [8] on the 4-node baby-POOMA in Amsterdam, and the POOL-X 2.1 compiler [6] on the POOMA machine in Eindhoven.

6 PPMX Measurements

In table 1 we see the run time of our program in seconds for different input batches and various combinations of active and inactive reduction procedures.
An 'h' means that the heuristic was used, and 'rXY' means that reductions X and Y were active.
This leads to the following observations:

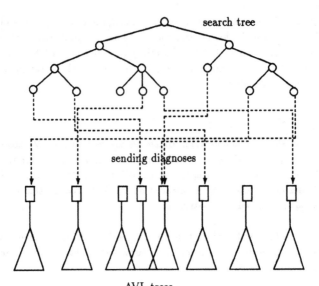

AVL-trees
Figure 2: communication structure of second version

	A278		A277		E027		E112	
Scheme	4	1	4	1	4	1	4	1
r123h	41	52	32	56	541	577	om	-
r123	37	45	35	41	524	575	689	812
r12	33	94	26	70	546	om	340	1158
no red.	94	315	75	211	om	-	-	-
r12h	34	75	27	65	479	om	359	-
r1h	54	141	37	85	om	-	776	-

Table 1: run time in seconds with PPMX, om = out of memory, - = not measured

1. The optimal scheme of reductions and heuristics that minimizes the run time on 4 nodes consists of reductions 1 and 2 and possibly the heuristic.

2. The optimal scheme for one node consists of all three reductions, possibly augmented with the heuristic.

3. If we define the *effective speed up* to be the optimal run time on 1 processor divided by the optimal run time on the number of processors currently used (in this case 4), we see that we do not gain much from parallelism. This is due to the fact that reduction 3 can be used effectively on 1 processor, but not on more than 1. We will explain this later on.

7 POOL-X 2.1 Measurements

We applied only the two most promising reductions schemes to two of the largest input batches (called 'SZ9E027.SB' and 'SZ9E112.SB') and one medium sized input batch ('SZ8A278.SB'). The results are given in table 2. We can make the following observations:

1. Comparing the performance of the two compilers, we see that POOL-X 2.1 is roughly two times as fast as PPMX.

2. The reductions scheme r123h results in an almost constant run time in spite of adding more processors. This can be explained as follows: reduction 3, the partitioning reduction, reduces the search space considerably, in such a way that only a relatively few number of search nodes are generated. As a consequence, only a limited number of processors can be activated to execute these objects. Therefore it makes no use to add more processors.

   On the other hand, reduction 3 involves a lot of communicational and computational overhead: all partial covers that are found for each part of the partition are sent to one sink, in which all these parts are combined and sent to the AVL-trees. This was suspected to be a bottleneck. Therefore another implementation of reduction 3 has been developed, that distributes the computational load of combining these partition parts equally among all processor nodes. However, this involved a lot of additional communication and turned out to slow down the overall run time by a factor 2 on the average. Therefore it has been decided to include this new combining strategy only as an option in the program.

   We conclude that it is difficult to parallelize reduction 3 effectively, resulting in relatively high run times.

3. With reduction scheme r12 an almost linear speed up can be obtained for the largest inputs. This is caused by the fact that the active reduction procedures are relatively cheap and, even more important, they can be applied locally in every search node, so no additional communication is necessary. With this scheme the algorithm, like in previous versions, becomes a divide-and-conquer type of algorithm.

8 Conclusions

- An acceptable response time can be obtained using this parallel inference algorithm on the POOMA machine.

# procs	SZ8A278.SB		SZ9E027.SB		SZ9E112.SB	
	r1234	r123	r1234	r123	r1234	r123
1	24	49	290	808*	319	474
4	23	16	269	265	255	154
8	22	12	267	123	252	78
16	23	8	263	67	251	45
32	23	8	267	43	252	30

Table 2: run time in seconds with POOL-X 2.1, * = due to much garbage collection

#procs	A278	E027	E112
4	1.5	1.1	2.1
8	2	2.4	4.1
16	3	4.3	7.1
32	3	6.7	10.6

Table 3: effective speed up with POOL-X 2.1

- In a sequential implementation of the search procedure all four reductions should be applied, especially reduction 3, which turns out to be very powerful.

- In a parallel implementation only reduction 1 and 2 should be applied, not reduction 4, which introduces a lot of communicational overhead.

- Using the heuristics does not improve the performance in all cases.

- With reductions 1 and 2 active an almost linear speed up can be achieved, if the input batch is large enough.

- The effective speed up that can be obtained with the largest input batches can be considered acceptable. See table 3.

- The currently largest input batches can be handled very well if enough processors (for example 32) are put to work.

References

[1] H.J. Ter Horst (1990). *Paper on EQUIP*, Philips Research Laboratories Eindhoven, The Netherlands, to appear.

[2] J.W. Spee (1990). *Finding All Minimal Covers of a Set Using Implicit Enumeration*, technical report of the Centre for Mathematics and Computer Science CS-R9007, Department of Software Technology, The Netherlands.

[3] J.W. Spee (1989). *A Parallel Implementation of a Part of EQUIP in POOL2*, PRISMA doc. nr. P0459, Philips Research Laboratories Eindhoven, The Netherlands.

[4] J.W. Spee (1989). *A Dynamic Load Balancing Strategy for POOL Programs*, PRISMA doc. no. P0464, Philips Research Laboratories Eindhoven, The Netherlands.

[5] P. America (1989). *Language Definition of POOL-X*, PRISMA doc. nr. P0350, Philips Research Laboratories Eindhoven, The Netherlands.

[6] P. America, L. Augusteijn, B, Hulshof, (1990), *Annotations for Data Object Support in POOL-X*, POOMA doc. nr. 0019, Philips Research Laboratories Eindhoven, The Netherlands.

[7] P. America (1988). Definition of POOL2, a parallel object-oriented language, Esprit 415A, doc. nr. 364.

[8] M. Beemster (1990), *POOL±X*, PRISMA doc. nr. P0522, Philips Research Laboratories Eindhoven, The Netherlands.

[9] Y. Peng (1986). *A Formalization of Parsimonious Covering and Probabilistic Reasoning in Abductive Diagnostic Inference*, Ph.-D. Thesis, Department of Computer Science, TR-1615, University of Maryland.

[10] J.A. Reggia, D.S. Nau, P.Y. Wang (1985). A Formal Model of Diagnostic Inference I. *Information Sciences*, vol. 37, pp. 227-256.

[11] J.A. Reggia, D.S. Nau, P.Y. Wang (1985). A Formal Model of Diagnostic Inference II. *Information Sciences*, vol. 37, pp. 257-285.

[12] A.M. Geoffrion (1967). Integer Programming by Implicit Enumeration and Balas' Method, *SIAM Review*, Vol. 9, No. 2, pp. 178-190.

[13] N. Christofides (1975). *Graph Theory, An Algorithmic Approach*, Academic Press, New York, pp. 30-57.

[14] C.E. Lemke, H.M. Salkin, K. Spielberg (1971). Set Covering by Single Branch Enumeration with Linear-Programming Subproblems, *Operations Research*, vol. 19, pp. 998-1022.

[15] R. Garfinkel, G.L. Nemhauser (1972). *Integer Programming*, John Wiley & Sons, New York. Class of Set-Covering Algorithms, *SIAM Journal of Computing*, Vol. 12, No. 2, pp. 329-346.

[16] V. Lifschitz, B. Pittel (1983). The Worst and the Most-Probable Performance of a Class of Set-Covering Algorithms, *SIAM Journal of Computing*, Vol. 12, No. 2, pp. 329-346.

[17] M.H. Young, S. Muroga (1985). Minimal Covering Problem and PLA Minimization, *International Journal of Computer and Information Sciences*, Vol. 14, No. 6, pp. 337-364.

[18] F. Sijstermans & J.M. Jansen (1988). Parallel branch- and bound algorithms, Esprit 415A doc. nr. 413.

POOL-X and its Implementation

J. van der Spek

Philips Research Laboratories
Eindhoven, The Netherlands

Abstract

This paper presents an overview of the problems encountered in implementing POOL, a parallel object-oriented language, along with solutions found for them. In order to get insight in the problem domain, also a short introduction to the language has been supplied.

1 Introduction

1.1 Scope

In the framework of both ESPRIT Project 415, DOOM [Bro87], and the PRISMA project [Ape86] it has been investigated how the parallelism offered by a specific type of multiprocessor computer can be exploited by means of a general purpose programming language.

The specific type of multiprocessor computer that was designed in these projects, was a *message passing* computer: a multiprocessor computer which consists of several nodes, each built up as a ⟨*processor, local memory, communication processor*⟩ triple, that are connected by a sparse (i.e. not fully connected) message passing network. Separate processors can exchange information only by sending messages via the network. This kind of configuration is *scalable*, which in this context means that additional processors (nodes) can be added to the machines without sudden degradation of machine complexity and/or performance. Such scalable machines are attractive because they allow simply "plugging in" of processing power, to fit the needs of the applications.

A parallel object-oriented language, POOL-X, [Ame89b, Ame89c, Ame89d] has been designed as a language to develop large and well designed systems, exploiting the parallelism offered by multiprocessor machines. As usual in Object Oriented languages, program execution is carried out by so called *objects*. Such objects are encapsulations of local data that are protected by direct access from the outside (i.e. other objects); however, objects can indirectly influence the contents of other objects by sending *messages*. A message consists of an identification of a procedure, as well as some data, upon reception of which the receiver reacts by associating an actual procedure to the procedure identification, and invoking it with the data serving as parameter. Often, some resulting data will be sent back to the sender of the message. This protocol actually is a form of *remote procedure calling*. New in POOL-X is the integration of processing capabilities with objects: each object has a separate activity assigned in which it usually accepts all incoming messages; however, more inspiring behaviour is possible.

Using the resulting object oriented language to program a parallel computer seems promising because the integration of processing capabilities with objects easily delivers the desired parallelism: a collection of such separate process objects can be distributed over a collection of processors. Moreover,

---

The work described here was done as a part of the PRISMA project, supported by the Dutch "Stimuleringsprojectteam Informaticaonderzoek" (SPIN).
Author's current address: BSO, P.O. Box 1444, 3430 BK Nieuwegein, The Netherlands.

it is increasingly recognized that objects correspond with similar entities occurring during software design (see e.g. [You85]). This makes object oriented languages attractive to program reliable software systems in, because the final result (the program) tends to be close to the specification.

It is interesting that it now becomes possible for objects to explicitly accept or refuse certain messages, "going to sleep" when no acceptable one has arrived. Because objects thus exactly know *when* and *where*, *which* types of messages will be served, the amount of protection offered by the object metaphor is increased. Also it appears possible to avoid the need for additional process synchronization primitives such as semaphores: synchronization very often will automatically result from proper use of message acceptance.

A parallel object-oriented machine, POOMA, has been built as prototype computer. POOMA consists of 100 nodes, each containing a MOTOROLA MC68020 processor and 16Mb of memory. Also an implementation of POOL-X has been delivered, and several larger applications have been developed to investigate the usefulness of the system.

The most important application forms a parallel main memory Data Base Management System (DBMS) [Ape88], for which some specific provisions have been included in the language (*dynamic typing, exception handling facilities* and a *mini-compiler*).

Furthermore, a VLSI circuit simulator, a VLSI component placement optimization algorithm and a parallel document retrieval system have been implemented.

1.2 About the document

This paper describes run-time issues of the implementation of POOL-X on top of POOMA. It is assumed that the reader has some knowledge about object oriented programming. More on this can be found in e.g. [Mey88].

The structure of this paper is as follows: first some introduction to POOL-X will be given, followed by an enumeration of previous POOL languages and various implementations that have preceded the one described here (sections 2 and 3); a description of the goals of the implementation is presented in Section 4, followed by an enumeration of new aspects of the language. After a presentation of several implementation issues (Section 6), the paper will be concluded with an enumeration of some results (Section 7) and final remarks (Section 8).

As can be discovered in Section 2, there exist several versions of POOL; although this paper covers a POOL-X implementation, the suffix "-X" will often be dropped in contexts that do not deal with problems specific to POOL-X. Furthermore, the following abbreviations and notions will be used:

- *OS*: Operating System.

- *LI*: Language Implementation.

- *GC*: Garbage collector.

- *machine*: computer.

- *reference*: an identification (name) of a run-time object structure. These identification are especially important during garbage collection (see Section 6.3).

1.3 Related system components

Descriptions of related system components can be found elsewhere: OS in [Bra89], [Hul90] and the language implementation specific interface of the OS in [Hul88]. More detailed information than presented here and a description of the compiler structure itself can be found in [Spe89]. A description of the I/O system, which is implemented as run-time support, can be found in [Sun88], [Sun90].

2   Overview of POOL(-X)

2.1   Introduction

POOL languages are strongly typed, object oriented and parallel. At first sight, they can best be compared with Smalltalk [Gol83], in that activity is carried out by *objects*, encapsulations of data, stored in *instance variables* of the object, and can interact with each other by sending *messages*. Receiving a message, an object responds by executing a corresponding local procedure called a *method* with the contents of the message serving as parameters. Such objects are described by a kind of blueprint, called a *Class*, containing descriptions of the instance variables, and the code that the described object can execute. Classes can be thought of as types, and they also provide a neat description of the world from the point of view of the objects that belong to this class. This latter makes it relatively easy to reason about individual object behaviour.

Just as in Smalltalk, objects are of very dynamic nature: they can be created at any time and in any amount, and they can mutate during execution. Also, POOL relies upon automatic garbage collection: there is no way for the programmer to explicitly remove objects from the system (and typical POOL programs create enormous amounts of objects that become obsolete very rapidly). POOL languages provide a large amount of safety, in that the language definitions state pre- and postconditions for many operations. These result in e.g. overflow checking for arithmetic operations, bound checking for array access, as well as checking whether operands of certain operations are not NIL, a bottom element in the language which represents the absence of a value.

A closer look reveals some important differences with Smalltalk, which are listed below. Most differences originate from the demand that POOL should be a language to program large, reliable software systems that can efficiently run on parallel machines, while Smalltalk is intended for rapid prototyping.

- POOL languages are strongly typed.

- The POOL type system does not contain inheritance or subtyping, which avoids the need for dynamic association of a message *name* to a *method* (the procedure to be executed as response).

- Classes are not considered objects themselves.

- POOL objects each contain a separate activity, or *thread of control*, and this makes it possible to temporarily (and selectively) refuse to accept received messages, which will be queued in such case. This feature gives an object exclusive control over its local object invariant. Note that in this way parallelism is nicely integrated in an object oriented language.

Although a collection of POOL objects act in parallel to each other, each separate object internally shows sequential, single threaded, behaviour.

2.2   Language elements

2.2.1   Classes

As explained above, a Class is a description of the behaviour and contents of a collection of objects. It contains an enumeration of instance variables and methods for which the object can receive messages. It also contains a *body*, i.e. a small program that the object starts executing just after creation and initialization. A creation routine, called *new*, is implicitly present (i.e. without explicitly being declared), but one can explicitly specify the parameters that it expects. These parameters, called new-parameters, are copied into the object at initialization, and further play a role similar to instance variables. Also a comparison routine *id* that checks for equality of two objects is implicitly supplied.

It is important for the dynamic part of the type system (see Section 2.2.4), that values bound to parameters of routines, methods, and also new-parameters cannot be altered (i.e. such parameters are *read-only*).

In order to support a certain amount of *code sharing*, classes may be generic in certain types, called *class parameters*, which must be enumerated in the class header. For example, the class described in Figure 1 shows a description of a class with one parameter (P); this class is subsequently used.

Generic types are restricted in their use: to avoid the need for dynamic binding of class features, only the *id* routine and the *NIL* value belonging to parameter classes can be used.

2.2.2 Communication

Object communication is the basic way to get things done, because, as even e.g. integers are considered objects, with addition, subtraction and so on as methods, objects can in essence only send and receive messages and change the contents of a private locations (variables).

Objects can explicitly specify when they are prepared to answer (accept) messages by means of a so-called ANSWER statement. Such a statement contains a list of methods for which the object wants to serve messages. As a result, the object will wait until any of those messages has arrived; other arriving messages will be queued for later processing. Exactly one message will be processed after which the ANSWER terminates.

Communication can be either *synchronous*, in which case the sender will wait until the receiver has answered the message, or *asynchronous*, in which case the sender merely sends without waiting. As the most intersting form, we will only deal with synchronous communication in this paper.

The case of a receiving object answering a message (with the sender waiting for the result) is called a *rendezvous*.

To be able to read the examples in this paper: the notation for sending a synchronous message m with parameter p to object o is

$$o!m(p)$$

where m must be the name of one of the methods described in o's class.

```
GLOBAL
  val1:= st ! get()
  val2:= st ! put("hello world")
  st  := Store(String).new(1)

CLASS Store(P)
  NEWPAR (name: Int)

  VAR cont: P

  METHOD put(p:P): Store(P)
  BEGIN cont:= p; RESULT SELF END put

  METHOD get(): P
  BEGIN RESULT cont END get

  BODY
    ANSWER(put);
    DO ANSWER(get) OD;
  YDOB
END Store
```

Figure 1: *Sample POOL-X program.*

2.2.3 Globals

Normally, an object can only access values that are contained in variables or parameters within the object itself. While experimenting with earlier POOL versions, it appeared convenient to make certain objects globally known (for instance the standard input/output files), and thus obtainable by any object. For this purpose, *globals* have been introduced: identifiers bound to values of specified expressions. These global expressions will be evaluated at application startup, while reading the corresponding values will be synchronized on availability of these values. The value of a global will remain fixed after evaluation. However, although a global then refers to a fixed object, this object itself can of course be mutated, as in:

$$GLOBAL \quad arr := Array(Int).new(0, 10)$$

where *arr* refers to an array whose elements can be updated.

The fact that global expressions are evaluated instantaneously ('out of nothing') is used for *application startup*: POOL execution must be started by the creation of initial (global) objects.

See Figure 1 for a sample POOL program. It describes a generic store object that can only be read out *after* it has been filled, due to the order of selective message answerings. One store object is created as a global value, while a second global fills it with a string value. This value will subsequently be found within the store by the last global.

Due to synchronous access to globals, the order of creation, put and get will automatically be sequentialized; the textual order of global declarations is therefore irrelevant: in Figure 1, evaluation of both the value for *val1* and *val2* need the value of *st*, and therefore have to wait. After *st*'s value has become available, it will refuse to answer the *get* method until a value has been *put*.

2.2.4 Dynamic typing

Dynamic typing is a form of typing that allows postponing the binding of type identifiers to actual types to run-time. It must not be confused with *weak* typing, since the manipulation of dynamically typed objects can still be subject to the same type restrictions as for normal objects.

An experimental form is included in POOL-X as one of the special provisions for the development of the (relational) database management system: such a system has to manipulate *relations*, tables consisting of *tuples* of which the types cannot be known at compile time. Without a form of dynamic typing, these tables would have to be represented in a very cumbersome way, due to the strong type system of POOL. The language contains only a minimal form of dynamic typing: it is sufficient that only tuples can be dynamically typed. However, this restriction is not fundamental.

Since little compile time knowledge is generally present about such types, most operations to dynamically typed objects need to be preceded by investigation of the types in order to make sure that they are allowed. An often used approach makes this investigation part of the operation itself, which is unacceptable for the DBMS since such a system often operates on large sets of identically typed objects. Without several kinds of optimizations, the system probably would spend large amounts of time investigating the same type over and over again. Rather, as we will see, the type system allows for factorizing similar type investigations out of an entire context.

In POOL-X, dynamic types can be introduced in the scope of a routine- or method body as *TUPLETYPE* parameter (see Figure 2). Being parameters, such type values cannot be changed during the lifetime of the corresponding scope. This is important, since such a type can still describe an object in the context; altering the type then would cause inconsistencies.

Types can be *inspected* in a so called *type-case* statement, which behaves similar to a normal CASE statement in MODULA-2, or a *switch* in C: a type case matches an unknown type against several other types. The smart idea is that every case branch forms a new scope, in which the two matched types (the 'header' type and the type corresponding with the branch) are assumed to be equal.

In the example Figure 2, a routine is described that is able to sum the components of the elements of an array, provided that it is an *Array([Int])*. The summation loops between the lower- and upper

```
ROUTINE sum (a: Array(T), T: TUPLETYPE): Int
TEMP s:= 0
BEGIN
  CASE T OF [Int]
    FOR i FROM a@lb TO a@ub DO s:= s + a[i]@1 OD
  ESAC;

  RETURN s
END sum
```

Figure 2: *Separation of type matching and operations.*

bound of the array, with the type investigation, that provides safety, factorized out of the loop, thereby showing that there is no hard relation between objects and dynamic types.

The selection of the first component of elements of a and adding the result to an integer variable, in

$$s + a[i]@1$$

is allowed here since the compiler knows that

$$T = [Int]$$

As additional advantage, all necessary type investigations in POOL-X are explicitly performed by means of type-case statements, thus avoiding performance surprises due to hidden dynamic type checks.

2.2.5 Routine values

In POOL, routines are also considered objects. Although the routine classes do not contain methods, their values (i.e. the routines) can be *called* with a proper parameter list. In order to prevent routine objects from being fundamentally different from other objects, *calling* is considered to be syntactic sugar for a send to the routine object.

There is some difference between POOL routine objects, and routine values in e.g. MODULA-2, or C. In POOL, routine denotations (or *inline* routines) are a special kind of expression (see Figure 3), and therefore the body of the routine denotation has some values in scope (the parameters t and T of the outer routine, in the example) that do not belong to the direct scope of the routine. This is a potential problem, because the denoted routine may outlive the scope in which it was created. Furthermore, in a parallel environment, the routine may be activated on another node, in which case it may be hard to access the elements of this outer scope. Because of the first problem, MODULA-2 forbids non top level routines to be assigned to routine variables; in C, the problem is not present, because C does not allow static nesting of routines.

In POOL, the problem is solved by defining the value of a routine denotation to be a *closure*, i.e. a package in which values from outer scope have been copied at creation time. The elements are referred to as the *routine environment*, and are read-only for the routine.

Routine objects can be useful because they can remember values from the context in which they have been created, as is shown in Figure 3. Here a routine is presented that can hide values of any type into a "box", implemented as an inline routine. The returned routine is able to reproduce the hidden object, but only after the "key", the type of the object, has been used as parameter. Otherwise, NIL (no result) will be returned.

```
ROUTINE pack(t: T, T: TUPLETYPE):
                    ROUTINE(TT: TUPLETYPE): TT
BEGIN
  RETURN

    ROUTINE(Q: TUPLETYPE): Q
    BEGIN
      CASE Q OF
        T THEN RETURN t
          ELSE RETURN NIL
      ESAC
    END

END pack

    :
    :

VAR
  r: ROUTINE(X: TUPLETYPE): X
  i: Object
    :
r:= pack( [3],              [Int]    ) ;
r:= pack( [Object.new()],  [Object] ) ;

i := r( [Object] ) @ 1;
```

Figure 3: *Sample use of dynamic types and of inline routines*

2.2.6 Exception handling

In POOL-X, statements can be protected against exceptional situations (or errors) by means of *exception statements*. They bracket a list of statements with a list of *exception handlers*. Figure 4 shows an example of an exception statement.

Although generally applicable for anticipation on exceptional situations, the reason for the presence of exception handling in POOL-X is, again, the DBMS application. This application has to be robust against errors in processing the large amounts of input, which without provisions for exception handling would require flooding the source code with very many tests (e.g. on overflow situations) and constructs to propagate the results of these tests. See [Mey88] for comments on this.

Exceptions can be explicitly raised, as in

$$SIGNAL\ some\_problem$$

But also implicitly, e.g. the standard exceptions *nil_error*, *bound_error*, *value_error*, *case_error*, *overflow* can be raised in case of use of NIL argument of certain operations, array index out of bounds, no appropriate entry in CASE statement or arithmetic overflow, respectively.

After occurrence of an exception, nested invocation of methods and routines will recursively be aborted until an appropriate handler is found. During this process, aborting a synchronous method in rendezvous will cause a copy of the exception instance to be signalled within the sending object.

In case an appropriate handler is found, this handler will be invoked, after which the object resumes execution just behind the protected statement. The absence of a handler will cause the system to crash.

```
EX
   a:= 1/a

   EXCEPTION value_error
   BEGIN
      write("oh-oh, 'a' was 0")
   END value_error
XE
```

Figure 4: *Example of exception statement.*

2.2.7 Tuple expressions

To facilitate efficient operations on sets of tuples in the DBMS, a standard unit *Tuple_Expressions* is available in POOL-X. Such expressions define operations on the components of tuples, and they can be dynamically constructed.

Five classes of expressions exist, according to the type of the result of application, which can be *Char*, *Bool*, *Int*, *String* and *Float*.

For example, a value of type *Int_Expr* is an expression which, upon evaluation (i.e. upon *application* to a tuple), produces an integral value. Such (unevaluated) expressions can be assigned to variables, used as parameters, evaluated and used to build more complex expression values. Basic expressions can represent constants, such as the result of

$$Float\_Expr.constant(5.0)$$

or they can represent component selections out of tuples, as in

$$Int\_Expr.field(3)$$

which will select the third component.

Other expressions can be built according to relevant operations on values of type *Char, Bool, Int, String* and *Float*; e.g. the expression *expr*, defined by

$$expr := Int\_Expr.field(1) + Int\_Expr.field(3)$$

represents a summation of the first and third component. Note that the + operator is not used in its usual arithmetical meaning, but as an operator which constructs expressions.

Expressions can directly be applied to tuples by means of a method *eval*. Such application involves interpretation of the expression as well as a check whether the basic field selections are allowed (i.e. the specified component exists and has the correct type), such that apart from the tuple to be used as argument also its type has to be provided. As an example, let *expr* be the above defined expression in:

$$expr \ ! \ eval(\ [3, 'a', 1], \ [Int, Char, Int] \ )$$

It will be clear that due to repeated expression interpretation and tuple type checking, application of the same expression to each element of a large database of tuples will involve a considerable overhead. Therefore the tuple expressions can also be compiled into routines by means of a method *compile*. In this case, interpretation and type checking will once be done at expression compile time. The resulting routines can then be called with tuples of the proper type as arguments. Figure 5 shows an example, describing a routine that receives as parameters some array of tuples (dynamically typed), and an integer expression. An activation of this routine will compile the expression once, after which the result will be applied many times, namely to each of the array elements.

```
ROUTINE tabsum(a: Array(T),
               T: TUPLETYPE,
               e: Int_Expr
              ): Int
TEMP
  s: Int                  := 0
  r: ROUTINE(t:T): Int    := e ! compile(T)
BEGIN
  FOR i FROM a@lb TO a@ub DO
    s:= s+r(a[i])
  OD;
  RESULT s
END tabsum
```

Figure 5: *Sample usage of the mini-compiler.*

These expression compilers are called *mini-compilers*.

3 History

3.1 POOL languages

The first of the POOL languages was POOL1 [Ame85a], rather designed as inventory of concepts that should be present in a full-fledged Object Oriented programming language. Since POOL1 was too complex for an experimental parallel implementation, a drastically simpler version was designed: POOL-T [Ame85b], based solely upon (unparameterized) object classes, and synchronous message passing as communication mechanism. Apart from a few standard classes, some syntactic sugar served as programmer comfort. After some implementation experience both in- and of POOL-T (see Section 3.3), a more mature POOL version was defined again: POOL2 [Ame88], including class parameterization, routines as first class objects, asynchronous communication, and several forms of syntactic sugar and language constructs to please POOL-2 programmers. POOL-X [Ame89b] was derived from POOL2 by adding some requisites for the DBMS implementation.

Initially it was considered undesirable to offer explicit means for object allocation and controlling object implementation, since it was believed that the compiler could do a good job on these topics automatically. However, after initial implementation of both POOL2 and POOL-X opinions changed and it appeared both very difficult and undesirable to let the compiler control allocation and implementation all by itself.

Difficult because it requires too much information that is hard to deduce automatically from the program text, and undesirable because the impacts on performance are too large and too unpredictable: an unaware programmer could easily reduce (or improve) the performance of his program by an order of magnitude by simply changing some of his source code.

For this reason, some annotations have been proposed to explicitly influence the default implementation strategy of the compiler [Ame89a]. This effectively introduced a new language that sometimes is referred to as POOL-XP (POOL-X with pragmas). This version has been implemented.

Until recently, although often considered as the essence of a real object oriented language, inheritance was not included in any of the POOL languages. This was because the real meaning of inheritance and subtyping was still unclear [Ame85c]. However, a recent model of subtyping as means of specialization and inheritance as means of code sharing has resulted in an experimental language POOL-I (POOL with Inheritance and subtyping, [Ame90]). POOL-I has not yet been implemented; only a front end has become available recently.

3.2 Ancestors

The design of POOL has been influenced by earlier (Object Oriented) languages [Ame85c], such as Simula [Bir80], Smalltalk-80 [Gol83], various LISP-based Object Oriented systems, CSP [Hoa85] and Ada [Ada83]. For instance, systems of independent activities interacting via messages occurred in CSP, and one can easily trace the message passing paradigm back to Smalltalk and Ada (rendezvous between two tasks), while also the exception handling mechanism originated from Ada.

3.3 Implementations

Very soon after the design of POOL-T, *SODOM* [Oer86] was implemented. Being a POOL-T to VAX/MODULA-2 compiler, SODOM was implemented to get insight in the implementability of POOL-like languages. However, it was a full implementation complete with garbage collection and soon used by a community of POOL-T programmers, experimenting with the language.

Somewhat later *pl* [Bee89a], a POOL-T interpreter was released, and, because of its portability (written in C), short compile/edit cycle and good performance, was easily picked up by the POOL-T community.

At the same time, *FLIP* [Lav89], a (still sequential) MC68000 code generating POOL-T compiler was written. FLIP was originally written for an ATARI-ST, and later on ported to a SUN-3 environment, but at that time POOL-X became popular already, due to the implementation of *plx*, a *pl*-style POOL-X interpreter [Bee89b].

Both FLIP and plx are ancestor of POOL-X compilers: *poolx*, the compiler described in this paper originated from FLIP ideas, while the interpreter back-end of plx has been replaced by a C code generator (*ppmx*, [Bee90]). Both *plx* and *ppmx* have been extended with multinode simulators. The only implementations that actually could make use of the parallel machine are *poolx* and *ppmx*; the latter also runs on other multiprocessor machines, since it was relatively easy to link the generated code (C) to other environments. *Poolx* also contains a sequential implementation of the OS, but due to the specific assembly generation (MC68020 only) the sequential system currently only runs on a Sun-3.

4 Objectives

The main goal of the design of *poolx*, the POOL-X compiler, was to get insight in the implementability and the impact on efficiency of constructs that contribute to the safety- and expressibility of a new parallel language, and to show by implementation that such a language could actually be implemented with reasonable efficiency.

Of course, such efficiency can only be related to state-of-the-art implementations of 'competing' languages. Therefore, we tried to show that *on the average, execution of some algorithm running under our implementation should not be more than a few factors slower, say five, than the same algorithm similarly encoded in C on the same processor.*

The 'few factors' should 'encode' the difference in compiler technology between our implementation and that of the SUN compiler (e.g. we did not plan to implement traditional low level optimizations, since this would require a large amount of additional implementation effort), as well as the differences between the two languages: POOL-X language constructs often are more general and always safe[1], and therefore more expensive to implement than similar C constructs.

An evaluation of the implementation is much work, since it requires many representative programs to be similarly encoded in both POOL and C. Some results are already referred to in Section 7.

5 Topics and new aspects

This section is devoted to a list of new topics from the implementation point of view. For each topic, a brief summary of the relevant problems to solve will be given.

5.1 Very light weight processes

Early POOL programs showed that the possibility to create large amounts of powerful objects was eagerly used by the POOL community. This resulted in high scheduling rates[2] during execution of typical POOL programs. Rather than forcing programmers to use object models of restricted functionality (see Section 6.1), which could be implemented in a cheaper way but would result in a misuse of the language, we decided that effort had to be put into efficient implementation of the process scheduler.

5.2 Communication

Also POOL communication needed special attention, because of the fact that conceptually *every* object interaction involves a message send in POOL. Such communication is a powerful, and therefore potentially expensive operation.

An object whose class has the most general form must be implemented by means of a process, and communicated with by sending messages. It will be clear that, however general message communication is implemented, it always will result in too much overhead for communication with simple data abstractions such as record objects or array objects since such communication should have to compete with a simple record access in other languages.

---

[1] Which means that no unnoticed errors can occur.

[2] Typical: about 1000 per second.

5.3 Garbage Collection

The system's ability to automatically remove unused objects from the system required some form of *garbage collector*. It was chosen to use an *on the fly, mark and sweep* garbage collector [Aug90]. The implications for the language implementation where threefold:

1. All *references* stored within objects have to be able to be found in some generic way. So objects have to be *traceable*.

2. Certain *Garbage Collector Invariants* have to be maintained. For our garbage collector these invariants imply, in short, that references can only be transferred between objects after having informed the garbage collector. Note that reading out some record object is some form of data transfer, but this would suffer too much overhead from such interaction with the garbage collector. However, we were able to exploit special cases of the garbage collector for such record access [Aug89].

3. Any location which can contain a reference created during execution (in new procedure context or new object), has to be initialized with some legal value.

5.4 Exception handling

As mentioned before, objects have the ability to dynamically *install* various handlers for specific kinds of exceptions. *Signaling* such an exception, either explicitly or automatically due to violating preconditions of operations, will have to result in abortion of processing, *propagation* of the exception within and possibly between objects, and *restoring* an old state in case of the presence of an appropriate handler.

The fact that exceptions can be raised every few instructions require that certain implementation invariants have to be maintained in a very fine-grained fashion. Also additional information has to be administrated within objects, in order to cleanly abort certain states that the object is in. To illustrate this, we can give two examples:

- For any allocated block of memory, e.g. to prepare a message or to implement some object with, the creator is responsible for its final deallocation. This can be done by making it known to the garbage collector, deallocating the block itself, or transferring the responsibility to another object. When exceptions can occur during such deallocation responsibility, the involved object has to take precautions to delegate this responsibility to the exception propagator.

- Similar holds for the responsibility to reset a semaphore[3] while accessing a protected data structure, when exceptions can occur during the access.

In traditional languages without exception handling these topics are irrelevant: cases corresponding to our exceptions are considered errors which lead to program abortion instead of the necessity to cleanup-and-resume.

5.5 Globals

Globals values are defined by means of a POOL expression. Several aspects need attention: due to possibly unknown data dependencies between the globals (global values may be referenced while evaluating others), they have to be evaluated in *parallel* to prevent deadlock. Also, since the value bound to a global will never change after it has been evaluated, it is attractive to *distribute* them over all nodes such that cheap access is possible.

---

[3]semaphores are not known as such in POOL, but they can be introduced by the implementation

It can occur that an object tries to access the global value while it is still being evaluated, in which case it will have to wait: access to the value has to be *synchronized* on the availability of the value.

However, global expressions can be declared to be *atomic* (see Section 5.8), in which case reading out the corresponding global is not allowed to block. For such globals, the implementation has to take precautions to ensure that their values have been evaluated before the first access.

5.6 NIL

In POOL, values of any type can be NIL, while most operations on NIL are disallowed: they result in the signalling of some exception. In the implementation, we are faced with the *representation* of the NIL values, and the implementing of the *investigation* of operands to check whether they are NIL. Since such investigation may occur frequently (operands of arithmetics, dereferenced pointers), it is of certain importance that they are of low cost.

Due to the fact that values may have non-uniform representations (e.g. characters are represented different from object names), separate solutions have to be found for each representation class.

5.7 Replicable objects

Some object types, such as *Strings*, are immutable, i.e. their values will not change over their lifetime. When additionally a copy of such an object cannot be distinguished from the original (by means of the identity operation, in POOL), it can be transparently copied by the run-time system. This can be exploited by the implementation by either inlining them into the data space of other objects, or by always copying such objects when they occur in internode messages, having the effect that references to such objects always are *local* and thus permitting cheap access. Since such objects also may contain immutable objects themselves, copying may lead to replication of entire graphs.

5.8 Pragmas

The most general way to implement objects and object communication (by means of processes sending messages) appeared to be rather costly. For reasons described in Section 3.1, it was decided to supply specific information to the compiler by means of *pragmas*, i.e. annotations to a POOL program that can be interpreted as implementation guidance. Pragmas only state some properties of the annotated program, which in order to be used of course must be verified by the compiler. They appear in three kinds (see also [Ame89a]):

1. *Atomicity pragmas*

    These pragmas are used to state that method- or routine bodies, or global expressions can be evaluated atomically with respect to object scheduling. The *atomic* pragma mainly is used in combination with *object pragmas* (see below).

2. *Locality pragmas*

    Object names that are statically known to refer to local[4] objects allow relatively cheap object access: there is no need to dynamically find out the node on which the corresponding object resides (it is the current node), and therefore they can be represented by means of a pointer to the local object data structure instead of some encoding of a $<node,index>$ pair. *Locality* pragmas can be used as a kind of type attribute to indicate local values. E.g. as in

$$VAR\ a:\ (*LOCAL*)Array(Int)$$

or

$$VAR\ a:\ Array((*LOCAL*)Object)$$

---

[4]i.e. relative to an object that contains such names

3. *Object pragmas*

Several levels of restrictions on object behaviour where identified, resulting in possibilities for cheaper implementations:

(a) Server objects are objects that repeatedly answer any message (the default body in POOL) and have only methods which

- are synchronous,
- do not ANSWER messages themselves, and
- RESULT at the end of their bodies

An example is an *Array* object, which is sequentially answering *get-*, *put-*, or *take_size* messages (a *take_size* alters the array's bounds). During execution of one of the methods, no other may become active.

Due to these properties, server objects never show activity parallel to objects that communicate with them. This can be exploited by representing these objects by means of the instance data plus some semaphore, instead of a full process. During a rendezvous, the server then can borrow the processing capabilities from the sender, since this object cannot proceed until the rendezvous terminated. This practice will be called *serve yourself.*

Note that with such implementation the integration of objects and processes, carefully brought in by the language, is undone: there is no simple correspondence between processes and objects any more, since processes dynamically multiplex their activity between multiple objects. However, this separation will be hidden in the implementation; the programmer is still provided with a uniform object view.

Of course, serve yourself can only be applied by an object that wants to communicate with another object on the same node; other cases have to escape to a message send anyway.

(b) Data objects. These objects are server objects that have *atomic* methods. Actually this class of objects is defined in order to be able to make recursive structure copies in POOL: the standard method *deep_copy* recursively copies *local* data objects. Data objects have the nice property that at moments of copying, they either are

- (conceptually) answering, (due to the atomic methods) and therefore can be safely copied, or
- (conceptually) in rendezvous, and therefore not allowed to be copied without fundamental problems. However, in these cases one can show that the deep_copy operation will cause deadlock and the implementation then is allowed to block the copying process forever (and print some warning to the user).

(c) Value objects. These are immutable data objects which can *automatically* be copied by the implementation, when suitable.

Object pragmas are tagged to the class definition.

5.9 Class parameterization

When dealing with parameterized classes, some implementation properties are dependent on the actual binding of the class parameters. Figure 6 shows an example; one can imagine that List(Int) and List(String) will behave slightly different in the implementation: because String objects will probably be subject to automatic garbage collection, the *heads* of the latter must be able to be found, while the Int *heads* are not visible for the garbage collector. Furthermore, the Int.id routine call will result in an equality test on the two integers (one machine instruction?), while the String.id call requires the entire contents of the string operands to be matched.

```
CLASS List(P)
  NEWPAR( head GETTABLE: P,
          tail GETTABLE: List(P)
        )

  METHOD element(p: P): Bool
  BEGIN
    IF P.id(p,head) THEN
      ...
    FI
  END element
END List
```

Figure 6: *Generic list class.*

5.10 Dynamic typing

The dynamic typing scheme in POOL-X is new, and therefore its impact on the implementation was not a priori known.

One apparent complication was that it seemed necessary that at least the POOL-X front end should be able to manipulate *type equivalences* introduced by *type CASE* statements, with some limited theorem proving capabilities in order to do type inferencing.

Because of the large overhead involved, the necessity for such functionality during run-time was unwanted.

5.11 Mini-compiler

The implementation of the mini-compilers involves the dynamic generation of machine code, and dynamic linking of this code to the running program. This linking is necessary because also during execution of such code, calls to the run-time system will be necessary. The generated code also must be *relocatable*, since the routine object that is the the result of compilation must be able to be copied to other nodes.

6 Implementation

We will present some flavour of the current POOL-X implementation in this section, following the same structure as in the previous section. Detailed information can be obtained from [Spe89].

First, an enumeration of some a *priori* design decisions will be given:

- *The role of the operating system.* The higher layer of the POOMA operating system (further called *OS*) actually forms a lightweight process package with rudimentary support for POOL. The idea was that all object interaction, such as process scheduling, object creation, garbage collection, termination detection, message handling, and the propagation of exceptions to other objects would be the responsibility of the OS. On top of this basis, POOL could be implemented.

  Reason for the OS's exclusive right to 'do' object interaction is not only caused by software modularity, but also by the severe invariants of the on-the-fly garbage collector[Hul89]: this complex component is in this way mainly hidden within the OS.

  The efficiency of this layer was also made possible because, due to the safeness of POOL, no separate address space per process was necessary since objects need not be protected against each other.

- *Minimal self description.*

  Almost all data structures manipulated by the application will be known by the OS as well. Either because they are subject to garbage collection (objects), or because they can be transferred to OS services (messages). Therefore, such data structures are divided into two parts: one part for OS administration, and one part that can be used by the application. None of the parties has explicit knowledge about each others administration.

  However, several OS activities require moreless detailed information about the application's part of several data structures. Examples of these activities are:

  - *Object initialization*: initializing the application's part of the object's data structures just after creation.
  - *Scanning*, i.e. reporting all object names contained within the application's part of the data structure during garbage collection.
  - *Destruction* of the data structure (by the garbage collector or message handler).

  Rather than exposing these details to the OS, data structures contain a (pointer to) an *object info record*, which contains routines for certain generic tasks.

  See Figure 7 for an illustration.

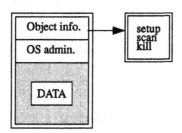

Figure 7: *Uniform object layout.*

- *Non blocking access routines.*

  In contrary to conventional operating systems, the POOMA OS offers services, called *access routines*, that are all but one atomic with respect to process scheduling. The exception is the switching routine itself.

  This has several advantages:

  1. The potentially many processes do not need to reserve stack space to execute the access routines on: the atomic routines can make use of a shared system stack, thereby saving memory.
  2. The compiler has a clear view on the scheduling behaviour of objects. It will be indicated below how this can be exploited.

  Of course, some OS services require process blocking now and then, e.g. the memory manager, when a memory request could not be honoured. This requires a somewhat elaborate usage of such services. In these cases, a special return condition indicates the need for waiting. See Figure 8, where a calling sequence is showed in a C like notation.

```
'Switch to system stack';
 mem = noh_alloc(size); /* access rout call   */
'Switch from system stack';
 if (mem == NULL)  /* ..not available:         */
 { pmswitch();      /* wait for retry after GC */
   mem = 'get from data transfer area';
 }
```

Figure 8: *Use of nonblocking access routines.*

- *Compiler determined scheduling.*

  Running objects in the POOMA OS will only be switched out at their own request; no timer-based scheduling strategy is used. This introduces a notion of *atomicity* with respect to process scheduling for free, since only calls to the process scheduler can cause objects to switch (see next section). Code that contains no scheduler calls can therefore be executed atomically.

  Because of this, the access to various shared resources need not be protected by semaphore-like entities, which would otherwise have caused additional overhead.

  Also, since the compiler knows when the scheduler will be called, it can cause only the relevant part of the volatile process context to be saved and restored around the process switch. This generally results in a cheaper context switch than in cases where the scheduler itself saves and restores the entire volatile process context (including the (often many) unused registers).

  Of course, for fairness, the compiler will have to guarantee that processes will switch now and then. This can be done by generating preemptive calls to the scheduler.

6.1 Object models

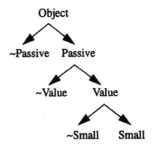

Figure 9: *Object taxonomy.*

Figure 9 presents an object taxonomy, based on properties we used for object representation decisions:

- Objects that can do without private processing capabilities are called passive. Such objects do not need to be implemented by means of the most general object type, a process, but can be represented in a simpler and more efficient way.

- Passive objects that cannot be modified after creation are called value objects. Such objects can be transparently copied without the application to know.

- Value objects that can be represented by means of little memory, are called small. 'Small' objects do not need private memory, but their value can be encoded within their *name*. This has the effect of *inlining* the representation in the data space of other objects. E.g. this can be done for Integers (see next).

It shall be clear that these properties are very implementation dependent (e.g. what exactly is 'little' memory; when do objects need processing capabilities).

In our implementation, the following decisions were made:

- Objects of several standard classes, such as *Int, Float, Bool, Char, Node* are considered *small*.

- Objects of classes (also including some standard classes) that have been assigned the *VALUE* pragma are considered non- small *value* objects. Objects of class *Tuple_n* are also *value*, but they will not be considered *small*. This in order to obtain a uniform representation of dynamically typed (tuple) objects.

- Objects of classes (also including some standard classes) that have been assigned the *DATA*- or *SERVER* pragma are considered *passive* non- *value* objects. Such classes are intended as POOL equivalents of abstract data types.

- All other objects are considered non- *passive*.

Apart from the *small* objects, all objects can be represented by means of two kinds of generic system objects: *process objects* (used for all non-passive objects) and *non process objects* (used for all passive objects).

These objects will be manipulated by both the operating system and the code generated from the POOL application: they are created on application's request by the operating system, after which they are animated by the application and it is the responsibility of the operating system again to remove them from the system after they have become obsolete.

Of course, they have the general layout as depicted in Figure 7. In the next sections, we will elaborate on the application's data part.

6.1.1 Passive objects

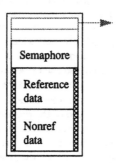

Figure 10: *Data layout of passive object.*

As can be seen in Figure 10, passive objects have a rather simple layout of the application's data part. They only contain data (instance variables) which optionally need to be protected by means of a semaphore, to administrate a rendezvous with other processes that take the liberty of "serving themselves" (see Section 6.2).

As will be explained in Section 6.3, it is necessary for the object *scanning* strategy to separate all references from the object data.

6.1.2 Processes

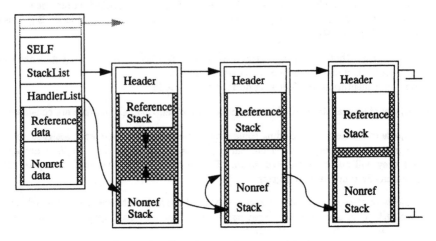

Figure 11: *Data layout of process object.*

Process objects are more interesting (Figure 11). Their application data areas contain several parts:

- *SELF*, i.e. the name of the object that currently owns the process's processing capabilities. Due to a *serve yourself*, this can be temporarily altered to some other (passive) object (see Section 6.2).

- A *process stack*:

  1. Because of GC strategy reasons (Section 6.3), the process stack has been split: a *reference* stack, and a *non-reference* stack.

  2. Large amounts of (process) objects can be created by POOL applications, each of which possibly in need for unbounded stack space due to recursion. In conventional multiprocess environments (multitasking operating systems) such problems are solved by assigning a separate address space to each process, which is too expensive in our case. See e.g. remarks in Section 5.1 about scheduling rates. An second solution, assigning a large area of address space to each process also can cause problems, since the potential large amount of processes makes even virtual memory a scarce resource.

     Instead, we experimented with a process stack that is itself mapped upon a stack of *stack segments*. At each moment, the top of the process stack resides in the top of the segment stack. Regularly, the topmost stack segment is checked against stack segment *overflow*, which may result into the allocation of a new segment. In our case, "regularly" means "at the start of each procedure", where the free space is checked against the maximal stack needs for the respective procedure. This has the advantage that the top of the non-reference stack is a return address, which can be altered into the address of a stack segment deallocation routine, thus avoiding the need for regularly checking stack segment *underflow*.

     Note that, because the two object stacks grow into each direction in the same stack segment, leaving the free space in the middle, overflow checks for both stacks can be done in one action by checking the difference of the stack pointers against the sum of the two stack needs (a compile time constant in our case). Because both the stack pointers will be cached in registers, such a check has minimal overhead.

This stack implementation usually behaves very well: a slight additional overhead (usually about 5 percent) is caused by stack overflow checking and occasional segment extension. However, due to the lack of hysteresis in this scheme, frequent routine invocations on an almost full stack segment (each separate invocation responsible for extension and shrinking of the stack) can easily cause considerable overhead.

- A *handler list* of marks within the process stack. Such a mark usually corresponds with the installation of a collection of exception handlers (exception statement), but also it can be a registration of a specific object state (e.g. rendezvous) that has to be untimely undone during exception propagation. More on stack marks in Section 6.4.

6.1.3 Object naming

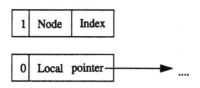

Figure 12: *Object name encodings.*

Names of objects are represented in a 32-bit word. Such a name must encode the following information:

1. the *node* that the object is allocated on, and

2. its *local name* on that node.

Therefore, in its most general form, the object name is a concatenation of a node identifier and an *object index*, which is a unique name of the object on its node. An index is used instead of its address in memory, because it is more compact.

Due to proper use of locality pragmas, we often know (statically) that certain object names refer to local objects, in which case the node part of the name is redundant. For these cases, a second representation is allowed: a mere pointer to the object representation in memory, thereby allowing cheaper access.

It will be clear that conversions between these representations are necessary when object names are transferred between contexts with different knowledge about locality.

For reasons of genericity, the two name encodings can be kept apart by the high order bit (see Figure 12).

6.2 Communication

Contrary to most object oriented languages (Eiffel[Mey88], Smalltalk, C++[Str86]), there is a static correspondence between messages, sent to objects, and methods. This is due to the fact that POOL does not contain inheritance. Because of this, no run-time provisions will have to be taken for the mapping of messages to the code to be invoked (dynamic binding).

Care has been taken to implement trivial communication types in an efficient way. Of course, operations like the addition mentioned are implemented in the 'traditional' way, using the machine instructions available, but also communication with passive objects has obtained a 'special' implementation.

6.2.1 Process communication

Communication between processes takes place by means of *messages*, blocks of memory filled with the parameters of the corresponding method plus some system data (e.g. destination, message type). Messages are structured, again, in the self descriptive way that is depicted in Figure 7, and can be transported and received by means of calls to the OS.

Contrary to objects, (memory for) messages must be allocated by the sending objects, and also they will not be deallocated by the garbage collector. Instead they can be explicitly deallocated, thereby saving some GC overhead, because at each moment they are known by exactly one process: either sender, destination or OS.

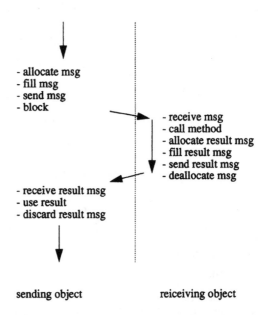

- allocate msg
- fill msg
- send msg
- block

        - receive msg
        - call method
        - allocate result msg
        - fill result msg
        - send result msg
        - deallocate msg

- receive result msg
- use result
- discard result msg

sending object   reiceiving object

Figure 13: *Synchronous send to process.*

The synchronous process send protocol is depicted in Figure 13. Major causes of overhead form the allocation and deallocation of message and result message, and the need for at least two context switches. The (de)allocation needs could in principle be prevented in case of synchronous sends by mapping the messages on the stack of the senders of the respective messages, but the current garbage collector implementation does not allow this practice at the moment.

When no *non-small value objects* (see Section 6.1) are present among the message parameters, interprocess communication is straightforward, as is shown in Figure 13.

In Section 6.7, we will describe how we deal with *non-small value objects* as parameters.

6.2.2 Non- process communication

Communication with non- process objects (passive objects) is more interesting. These object kinds have been introduced because their simple communication behaviour allows a more efficient implementation of the synchronous send.

First examine the control flow of a synchronous send in Figure 13, and observe that during rendezvous, the sender does not execute in parallel with the receiver. This means that, when sender and receiver of a synchronous message are allocated on the same node, the sending process can temporarily modify itself into the destination object and execute the method corresponding to the message by itself. This saves two calls to the scheduler, as well as the construction, sending and deallocation of two messages.

This practice can in principle be used for each synchronous send[5].

However, before applying 'serve yourself', the sending object must wait until the destination indeed is ready to accept the particular message, while afterwards one of the possible other objects that are waiting for the destination must be unblocked. Since this requires a rather elaborate and costly protocol in general, 'serve yourself' is only applied to objects that are declared to be either *Server* or *Data* by means of the object pragmas.

Such objects show *server* behaviour, which means that their only activity consists of repeatedly answering any message that has arrived. Therefore, for these kinds of objects, a semaphore can be used to administrate the 'answering' state, resulting in a simple serve yourself protocol by mere P and V operations.

Figure 14 contains a sketch of this protocol, with as illustration the MC68020 code that will be generated by the current compiler. As can be seen, the actual method body is surrounded by object transformations and semaphore operations, as explained above.

One POOL-X specific complication exists however, due to the fact that exceptions can be raised during execution of the method body whose propagation can result into an early abortion of the method by the exception propagator. In order to cleanly abort the method, the semaphore has to be properly reset and therefore it must be able to be found by the propagator. Therefore, it will be administrated on the stack of the current process by means of one of the *stack marks* (Section 6.4). As can be seen in the machine code, this registration will cause a significant overhead in case of simple methods. Two solutions are currently being used to avoid this overhead:

1. Application wide exception propagation analysis can reveil that exceptions raised in certain method bodies will never be caught by a handler, and therefore will lead to application abort. In such cases the semaphores that have to be reset will not be used any more and registration is not necessary.

2. Much simple method bodies (in which case the registration overhead is relatively large) are also *atomic* with respect to the process scheduler. This can be exploited by moving the P operation before the method body, and combining it with the corresponding V. In such a case, the semaphore is reset before execution of the body and need not be administrated. Also the combined PV operation is even simpler than each of the separate P and V. Note that *other* methods of the same class still can have non- atomic bodies and thus can cause the semaphore to be closed, so that the combined PV actually can happen to block.

When the method is very simple, as is the case for methods that merely read or update one of the instance variables, the object modifications can be avoided and the resulting method can be inlined when used. This practice will result in access costs that are comparable to conventional record access.

As mentioned earlier, application of 'serve yourself' requires the destination object to reside on the same node as the sender. This can be statically known, due to proper use of locality pragmas, or it can be checked at run-time. When sender and receiver do not reside on the same node, a message has to be sent anyhow. This seems to be a problem because messages can only be sent to objects with processing capabilities, which passive objects do not have. In order to resolve this, each node has a *node server* installed. This is a process object that will receive any message to passive objects that arrives on its node, installs a new node server in that case, and executes the method instead of the passive destination object. The installation of a fresh node server is necessary to prevent deadlock. Because the current implementation maintains a dynamic pool of processes that are candidates for node servers, it is not necessary to create a process each time a message to a passive object arrives.

---

[5]We here neglect the possibility in POOL that rendezvous can be terminated before the method has been finished, still resulting in parallelism between sender and receiver

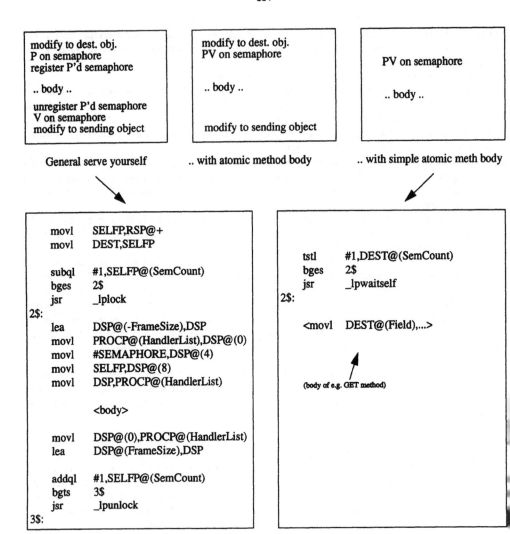

Figure 14: *Synchronous sends to passive objects.*

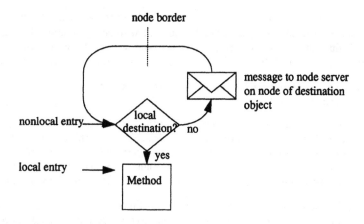

Figure 15: *Using remote node servers.*

Upon termination of the method, the serving object simply returns itself to the pool, after which it is available for installation again.

Figure 15 shows a sketch of the structure of methods for passive objects. They will be compiled into a routine with two entries: one called in case of a send to an object that is statically known to be local, while the other is used in all other cases. This last does a dynamic check to find out if the destination actually happens to be local, in which case it 'falls through' to the local case. Otherwise a message will be constructed and sent to the node server on the node on which the destination object resides; this node server then again uses the 'nonlocal' entry although it knows that now the destination resides on the same node. The reason for this is that in the current implementation the locality test has some necessary side effects.

6.3 Garbage Collection

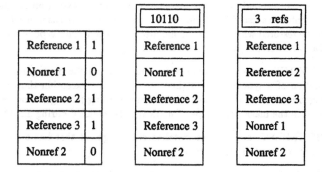

Figure 16: *Three ways to identify references.*

For garbage collection purposes, provisions have to be taken to be able to find references within data spaces. We took a choice out of three solutions (depicted in Figure 16) that were already used in earlier POOL implementations:

1. *tagging*, i.e. offering one bit of each machine word in the data space for description: object name or not. This solution requires each atomic *value* to be representable by exactly one word, which is difficult for e.g. floating point values, and wasteful for values from a small domain (characters, booleans). Also, during a *scan*, each word in the data area has to be investigated.

2. *masking*, i.e. maintaining a bit vector in the data area header; each bit describing one word: reference or not.

3. *two- stack model*, named to its implication that the process stack has to be split into two parts (see the process description in Section 6.1.2). Generally, using this model the data space has to be divided in *three* parts: a reference area, a non-reference area, and a small header indicating the start- and end of the reference area. This solution has the advantage that references can very quickly be extracted from objects. Disadvantage is the more complex data mapping.

While in principle the several solutions could be used intermixed, due to the self descriptiveness of objects in this respect, we only choose one of them; the reader might already have guessed that it is the third: the two stack model. This model was used because of its larger efficiency: no tags or masks to be maintained, and no non-references to be taken into account during scanning.

6.4 Exception handling

Signalling of exceptions can be done either explicitly or implicitly, as side effect of some built-in operation. Most implicit signals apply to *nil_errors*, after testing operands of built-in operations for being NIL. This kind of test can be performed in a rather simple way (see Section 6.6).

After the signalling of an exception, the *exception propagator* takes control of the current process. This run-time support routine tries to find an appropriate exception handler which, when found, has to be be invoked in the context in which it was installed. To restore this context, generally several recursive calls to routines and methods will have to be aborted which at least involves the truncation of the stack in order to get rid of the corresponding stack frames; however, sometimes also some other administration has to be reset.

Information that is needed by the propagator is encoded in a list of *handler marks*, information records woven within the process stack (see Figure 11). Several types of such marks are being used:

- **HANDLER**: corresponds with the installation of a set of exception handlers. Such a mark contains a pointer to a list of (*exception id, handler*) pairs, as well as a saved copy of information that has to be restored when one of the handlers is invoked. This type of mark will be installed during POOL-X 'EX' statements (see Figure 4).

- **RENDEZ_VOUS**: marking a rendezvous, indicating to the propagator that it is about to abort execution of a synchronous method; a copy of the exception that is being propagated must be signalled within the sender of the corresponding message. The name of this sender can be found in the mark. This type of mark will be installed during an ANSWER.

- **STACKSEGMENT**: marking an installed stack segment that has to be deallocated when the propagator encounters such a mark.

- **SEMAPHORE**: marking a 'serve yourself' for whose abortion the corresponding object semaphore has to be reset, *and* the old notion of 'SELF' has to be restored within the current process. Both can be found in the mark. This type of mark will be installed during a 'serve yourself' of a non-atomic method.

- **STACKFRAME**: used for debugging purposes only, to link all stack frames. This mark contains a symbol table describing the parameters and temporaries of the corresponding stack frame. It will be installed for each routine- or method invocation when the application was compiled with the debug option.

An example of a SEMAPHORE handler mark installation can be found in Figure 14.

The advantage of the current implementation of the propagator is that no detailed stack layout knowledge is necessary: it only knows about the handler list, and abortion of invocations automatically takes place when the information stored in the appropriate HANDLER frame will be restored: old values of stack pointers and SELF (resulting in truncating of the stacks), and a new value of the program counter, which is the code address of the handler to be entered.

6.5 Globals

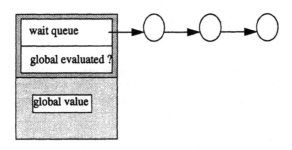

Figure 17: *Global record.*

POOL *globals* are represented by a global variable on each node, combined with a semaphore-like entity that indicates the availability of the *global*'s value (see Figure 17).

Objects that want to access the value first have to test for availability, which will result into blocking if the test fails; access to an already evaluated global is in this way almost as efficient as access to a global variable in conventional languages (C, MODULA-2): additional overhead is caused by a succeeding availability test on a boolean field.

At application startup, a process is created for each global that will evaluate the global's expression, place the resulting value into a message and call an access routine to let the OS distribute the resulting value over the parallel machine.

Upon arrival of a copy of this message on a specific node, the value will be copied into the global record after which the objects that were waiting for this value will be released.

Atomic globals need a slightly different treatment: in order to prevent later accesses to such globals to block because of unevaluated values, these globals will be evaluated just before actual application startup. Because all such global expressions can be evaluated atomically with respect to scheduling, this special treatment is possible since evaluation is guaranteed to terminate within bounded time.

6.6 NIL

POOL objects are represented roughly in five different ways, each with its own representation of *NIL*:

1. *object names*: the general 32-bit object name encoding (see Figure 12). The NIL representation is a zero word, which can be detected by a simple test.

2. *pointers*: 32-bit local names of objects that allow cheaper access. The NIL representation also is a zero word.

3. 1-, 2- or 4 byte *numbers*, used for encoding objects of class *Int, Char, Bool, Node* and for any user-defined enumeration class. Values will be tagged with a NIL tag, as shown in Figure 18. Extracting the value out of such representation, just before an operation, merely involves an arithmetic shift right. On the MC68020, this shift has the pleasant side-effect of copying the tag into the processor's condition code word so that the *test* on NIL has already been performed.

Figure 18: *NIL tagging of enumeration objects.*

4. *floats* are required to conform to the IEEE double precision floating point standard (64 bit, [Mot88]). NIL is represented as one of the special values, according to that standard: a *nan*. Using the MC68881 mathematical coprocessor, testing for NIL can be performed *after* an operation, by investigation its *ordered* condition.

5. POOL *unions* carry an additional ordinal value, encoding the *case*. A NIL union has a NIL case (see above).

6.7 Replicable objects

In order to serve cheap access, references of *non-small value object* (see Section 6.1) will be kept local by always making recursive copies when they occur as parameter in non-local messages. This practice makes message handling more involved than the case in which only a simple block of memory has to be transmitted: complete graphs of value objects have to be identified, copied and reconstructed on another node, while matters are complicated because due to information hiding, the message handler does not have any knowledge whatsoever about the representation of the structure.

Such copying is performed by making use of a specific feature of the message handler, *compound transport*. To any message, a so called *compound table* can be linked. Such a table is an array of pointers to mere blocks of uninterpreted memory, which will be copied along with the message to the destination node.

To each internode message that contains value parameters (e.g. a String), a generic compound constructor will be applied just before sending. This routine determines which objects are part of the value structure that is to be copied, and places their pointers into an allocated compound table that is subsequently linked to the message. In this way, a flattened view of the structure is presented to the message handler. This is illustrated in Figure 19 in which the solid part depicts a message containing a reference to a value structure; the shaded part depicts the compound table, which is additional information about the value structure to be used by the message handler. The dashed box surrounds all that logically belongs to the message.

After arrival at the destination process, the structure will be rebuilt by turning the copied memory blocks into objects and patching the new object references into their contents.

Care has been taken that multiply referenced objects within the structure will not be duplicated during transformation, and that the entire transformation runs in bounded stack space.

6.8 Class parameterization

As explained in Section 5.9, objects of parameterized classes need to know the value of the current class parameters. Two solutions solutions have been proposed:

.. ! m ([[1,'a'],"string"]) ..

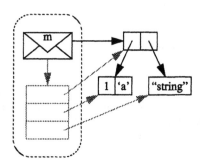

Figure 19: *Transmission of value structure.*

1. class expansion: For each usage $C(T_{11},\ldots,T_{1n}),\cdots,C(T_{m1},\ldots,T_{mn})$ of a certain parameterized class $C(P_1,\ldots,P_n)$, generate separate code instances. The parameter specific information then will be implicitly present in the code that is executed by a certain object.

2. interpretation: Generate only one code instance per class, but make sure that each context has access to a descriptor of the *current* class parameters. These descriptors will have to be investigated at various moments at run-time, e.g. at procedure invocation (to create variable spaces).

It will be clear that both solutions have their advantages and disadvantages: using solution 1, the size of the generated executable can explode when many different parameterizations of a same class are used, solution 2 can result in large interpretation cost. As for the former: existing POOL applications show that code explosion due to class expansion seems to occur very rarely.

Two additional problems for class expansion are the possibility to construct programs that use an infinite number of parameterizations, resulting into the need for infinite code instances, and the fact that in POOL-X the exact value of certain class parameters are not statically known since they may be dynamic types, resulting in too little information for generating the proper code instance. However, we still favoured the more efficient class expansion, and therefore we currently use a mixture of both class expansion and interpretation: expansion for class parameters with known value, and interpretation for dynamic tuple type class parameters. Because already certain information is present about such dynamic types (they are tuple types, which will always be represented by a reference to a passive object), there will already be less need for descriptor investigation at run-time. The only information occasionally needed to be dynamically found out is the proper tuple comparison routine $P_i.id$, when used, for tuple type class parameter P_i, or its complete type value, which can be needed for type case statements.

Dynamic descriptors currently take the form of a type descriptor of the current class, which will be kept within objects (in an additional instance variable) and in the environments of routines belonging to such class. The latter is necessary since any object can call such routines.

Figure 20 contains an example of a program where information about the current class parameter is needed at various points.

```
    ... TT: TUPLETYPE ...

  b:= C(TT).r()   %% pass 'C(TT)' via env of 'r'
       ...


CLASS C(T: TUPLETYPE)

  ROUTINE r(): Bool
  BEGIN
    CASE T OF          %% value 'T' from C(T) out of rout env
    [Int] THEN RETURN TRUE
          ELSE RETURN FALSE
    ESAC
  END r

  METHOD m(t: T): Bool
  BEGIN
    CASE T OF          %% value 'T' from C(T) out of instvar
    [Int] THEN
      RETURN t==[3]    %% 'T.id' stored within descriptor of 'T'
    ESAC
  END m

END C
```

Figure 20: *Type descriptors.*

6.9 Dynamic typing

Apart from the problem how to make the dynamic class parameter values explicit, as mentioned in the previous section, dynamic typing as occurring in POOL-X does not pose severe implementation problems; most of the dynamic type semantics can be statically dealt with by the compiler front end. This is not surprising, considered that the type system was designed for a minimal amount of run-time consequences. The most complex part is the maintenance by the compiler front end of an equivalence relation that is induced by nested type case statements.

An abstract data type *Type_descriptor* has been designed, with constructor operations and an equality test.

6.10 Mini-compiler

The mini-compiler has been written entirely in POOL-X. Although this did not result into the most efficient implementation, it has the advantage that it is simple and portable, and is an interesting exercise in POOL.

The mini-compiler takes as input an arithmetic expression and delivers a routine object that is the root of a tree of routine objects, one routine for each node in the expression tree.

```
METHOD compile(T : TUPLETYPE) : ROUTINE (T) : Int
TEMP
  r1, r2 :ROUTINE(T) : Int
BEGIN
  CASE case

      ...

  OR int_exp_add THEN
    r1 := left_operand  ! compile(T) ;
    r2 := right_operand ! compile(T) ;
    RESULT
        ROUTINE(t: T) : Int
        BEGIN
          RESULT r1(t) + r2(t) ;
        END
      ...
  ESAC
END compile
```

Figure 21: *Part of the mini-compiler in POOL-X.*

Figure 21 shows part of the implementation, which compiles an integer addition expression node by recursively compiling the operand expressions, and resulting a routine that calls these expressions and returns the sum of their results. It shall be clear that this compiled code suffers routine calling overhead for each node in the expression tree. An actual compiler can however be written that produces stretched, efficient machine code, but this will require much more work due to its complexity.

Only when the code delivered by the current mini-compiler appears to be a bottleneck, a real machine code generator will be considered.

7 Results

7.1 Implementability

Many conventional programming languages have been designed with ease of language implementation in mind, resulting in a straightforward mapping of language constructs and data types to the facilities of the target machine.

POOL languages, in contrary, were designed with ease of language *use* in mind (uniformity, complexity and safety of many language constructs), resulting in an implementation challenge where the larger gap between language and implementation often had to be bridged using more involved solutions.

Although reasonable solutions could be found to implement the entire language, its complexity and uniformity resulted in a very lot of implementation work (about 4 man-year for the compiler with support).

A relatively large amount of time has been lost during this implementation by the introduction of pragmas and different object types in POOL halfway the implementation. Not because they were that hard to implement, but because they had to be quickly included, thereby ruining part of the compiler design.

7.2 Memory requirements

A few remarks about memory usage:

- code size: POOL defines a lot of syntactical sugar, requires a lot of run-time checks, defines many predefined class features (*new* routines, *(deep_)copy* method), complex object behaviour (initialization protocol, default bodies). This results into POOL code to be very dense compared to the generated executable. Where typical MODULA-2 compilers generate about 30 bytes of binary code per line of source code, POOL compilers can easily generate twice as much. Class expansion (see Section 6.8) is only partly responsible.

- object size: Due to the need for e.g. self description and garbage collection, even the simplest passive object (the *value* object) needs an implementation overhead of about 30 bytes of memory. More involved passive objects that can be known on other nodes and require a semaphore, need about 50 bytes. This is a considerable overhead for small objects. It is not expected that these memory requirements can be easily reduced.

7.3 Performance

Unluckily, since the major application, the parallel DBMS is still under development at the delivery of this paper, no measurements on this system have been performed yet.

Some studies and implementation experiences have already resulted in reports, e.g.:

- [Dij90a], [Dij90b]: an investigation of local execution efficiency, related to C, by comparing single language constructs and several complete programs, coded in both POOL-X and C

- [Bau90]: a report on the implementation of a parallel sorter for very large data files, coded in C and in POOL-X.

- [Nau90]: The implementation of a placement algorithm for VLSI circuit components, only in POOL.

- [Aal90]: a document retrieval system

These reports, as well as earlier experiences, generally show that POOL-X is pleasant to use, offering a high level programming model to control parallel parallelism and relieving the programmer from (tricky) tasks as memory management and termination detection. Also controlling parallelism, which very often appears to be difficult using semaphores, monitors, etc, turns out to be relatively easy using synchronous communication.

However, performance measures in the reports mentioned above still show that under the current POOL-X implementation POOL-X programs can run up to an order of magnitude slower than similar programs in C[6], even when proper use has been made of pragmas:

- Experiences with the parallel sorter in [Bau90] showed a performance difference of about a factor of 10.

- [Dij90b] compared the performances of smaller programs, implemented in both C and POOL, running on a single node. The programs used were a list sorter and an implementation of two problem solvers, one solving a little puzzle, and the other solving instances of the travelling salesman problem, all with varying inputs. Since the author was interested in the best possible performance, the programs were run without run-time checks (but this gained less than 10 percent).

Figure 22, Figure 23 and Figure 24, showing the running times of the C and POOL implementations, are extracted from [Dij90b]. The time intervals reflect the different inputs.

The figures show that the performance of the POOL sorter is within a factor of two from the C version, while the POOL problem solvers appear to be much slower (also factor 10) than the C versions.

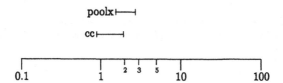

Figure 22: *Time (in s) for sorting 500 elements*

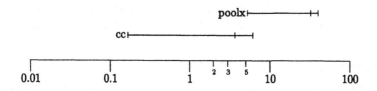

Figure 23: *Time (in s) for the Blackwhite application*

---

[6]Compiled with Sun3 OS3 C compiler using -O optimization flag

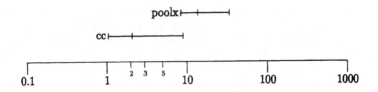

Figure 24: *Time (in s) for the Salesman application*

The POOL performance of the parallel sorter does not seem too bad, considered that the C version has been optimized by hand for maximal performance (it even used custom disk drivers). The performance of the problem solvers is more alarming.

To explain this, first have a look at Table 1, built with data from [Dij90b] and showing execution costs of basic language constructs in C and POOL on the POOMA. The POOL versions have been timed with and without run-time checking (*poolx* and *poolx-* respectively).

The table reveals that, although most basic constructs are implemented in a reasonably efficient way compared to their C counterparts, both object creation and interprocess communication have large overhead (see Table 1). This explains the difference in relative performance between the sorter and the problem solvers: the POOL sorter allocates few objects, and then spends a relatively large time sorting, while the problem solvers in POOL frequently allocate objects.

These figures indicate that protocols for communication and object creation need attention: although garbage collection provisions will stay to cause some overhead in both, they can be implemented more efficiently.

8   Conclusion

A Parallel Object Oriented Language has been designed and implemented on a message passing machine. Early tests have shown that POOL programs already can run with reasonable performance, despite the run-time costs implied by

- frequent run-time checks

- less advanced compiler technology

- large functionality of POOL objects

- language level

However, implementation of several topics need attention since they currently easily become execution bottlenecks. They are *process communication* and *object creation*.

We feel confident that similar effort in improving POOL implementations as resulted in current optimizing C implementations will result in very acceptable future POOL implementations.

9   Suggestions for future work

The described compiler offers a rather straightforward implementation of POOL-X, while already exploiting pragmas to use several object models and communication types. Several topics deserve more attention:

cc	poolx-	poolx	construct
2.4	3.5	5.3	while iteration
2.3	4.2	4.7	for iteration
4.6	4.5	4.9	routine call
5.2	7.3	9.0	recursive routine call
1.2	2.6	6.0	integer addition
7.1	21.9	26.2	floating multiply
-.-	3.6	3.6	EX statement
38.9	60.4	64.8	string compare
1.7	3.1	16.6	array access
-.-	6.2	10.7	data method send
-.-	1.0	3.4	data put or get)
1.1	-.-	-.-	record access
-.-	7.6	11.0	local server method send
-.-	478.0	480.0	local process method send
11.9	-.-	-.-	RECORD creation
-.-	377.7	377.7	data object creation
-.-	508.3	508.3	process object creation
-.-	1999.9	2025.8	remote data send
-.-	1999.9	1999.9	remote process send
-.-	3553.6	3553.5	remote data creation
-.-	1748.0	1761.4	remote process creation.

Table 1: *Time (in μs) of some basic constructs in C and POOL*

- Research has to be done on the influence of exception handling and garbage collection on traditional optimizations.

- More specific higher-level optimizations have to be investigated. For instance dataflow analysis can reveal objects with limited lifetime, which then can be deallocated directly or can be immediately reused. These topics are an issue in all languages which rely on garbage collection, and have already been studied in LISP contexts (see e.g. [Ino88]).

- Application wide dataflow analysis should also be used to minimize the overhead of the often frequent run-time checks. A limited form of such analysis is already implemented for exception propagation, but also e.g. NIL propagation analysis can result into less frequent nil checks.

- The current implementation is closed, in the sense that it is not intended to link code written in other languages to POOL applications. Work on a clean external interface is necessary to make the system more open.

- Irrespective copying of value objects at internode communication can result in the creation of copies that never will be used. A form of *lazy loading*, i.e. sending a placeholder that will be expanded upon first access, can make message handling more efficient.

- Using machine traps, instead of explicitly checking, to detect rarely occurring situations was not considered because during development of the implementation this would result in erroneous situations due to implementation errors (e.g. bus errors) to be disguised. However, it seems a useful mechanism, because it lessens the need for run-time checking while preserving safety. One could think of trapping on *overflow* or *nil_error*, and let the trap handler invoke the exception propagator, but also in the above suggestion of *lazy loading* placeholder-detection could be implemented by means of trapping-upon-access.

References

[Aal90]   IJsbrand Jan Aalbersberg and Frans Sijstermans, *InfoGuide: A Full-Text Document Retrieval System*, POOMA Doc. 0133, February 1990.

[Ame85a]   Pierre America, *POOL1 Language Definition*, DOOM Doc. 0003, February 1985.

[Ame85b]   Pierre America, *Description of POOL-T*, DOOM Doc. 0075, May 1985.

[Ame85c]   Pierre America, *Rationale for the design of POOL*, DOOM Doc. 0053, October 1985.

[Ame88]   Pierre America, *Definition of POOL2, a parallel object-oriented language*, DOOM Doc. 0364, April 1988.

[Ame89a]   Pierre America, Lex Augusteijn, Ben Hulshof, *Annotations for data object support in POOL-X*, POOMA Doc. 0019, November 1989.

[Ame89b]   Pierre America, *Language definition of POOL-X*, PRISMA Doc. 0350, December 1989.

[Ame89c]   Pierre America, *Standard classes for POOL-X*, PRISMA Doc. 0351, December 1989.

[Ame89d]   Pierre America, *Standard units for POOL-X*, PRISMA Doc. 0352, December 1989.

[Ame90]   Pierre America, Frank van der Linden, *A Parallel Object Oriented Language with Inheritance and Subtyping*, Nat Lab Technical Note No. TN11/90, May 1990.

[Ada83]   ANSI, *Reference manual for the Ada programming language*, Document ANSI / MIL-STD 1815 A, United States Department of Defense. January 1983

[Ape86]   P.M.G. Apers, J.A. Bergstra, H.H. Eggenhuisen, L.O. Hertzberger, M.L. Kersten, P.J.F. Lucas, A.J. Nijman, G. Rozenberg, *A Highly Parallel Machine for Data and Knowledge Base Management : PRISMA*, PRISMA Doc. 0001, October 1986.

[Ape88]   P.M.G. Apers, M.L. Kersten, and A.C.M. Oerlemans, *PRISMA Database Machine: A Distributed, Main-Memory Approach*, Proc. Int. Conf. on Extending Database Technology; Venice, 1988.

[Aug89]   Lex Augusteijn, Ben Hulshof, *Garbage collection and data objects*, POOMA Doc. 0021, June 1989.

[Aug90]   Lex Augusteijn, *A distributed on-the-fly garbage collector*, DOOM Doc. 0137, January 1990.

[Bau90]   B. A. W. Baugstø, J. F. Greipsland, J. Kamerbeek, *Sorting Large Data Files on POOMA (for the CONPAR '90 conference, Zürich)*, POOMA Doc. 0109, May 1990.

[Bee89a]   Marcel Beemster, *Implementation of the POOL-X interpreter*, PRISMA Doc. 0438, May 1989.

[Bee89b]   Marcel Beemster, Edwin de Jong, Juul van der Spek, *User manual of the POOL-X interpreter*, PRISMA Doc. 0258, September 1989.

[Bee90]   Marcel Beemster, *POOL±X*, PRISMA Doc. 0522, February 1990.

[Bir80]   Graham M. Birtwistle, Ole-Johan Dahl, Bjorn Myhrhaug, Kristen Nygaard, *Simula BEGIN*, Chartwell-Bratt Ltd, Bromley, England, 1980.

[Bra89]   E. Brandsma, Sun Chengzheng, B.J.A. Hulshof, L.O. Hertzberger, A.C.M. Oerlemans, *Overview of the PRISMA Operating System*, Proc. Int. Conf. on New Generation Computer Systems, pp.369-379., 1989.

[Bro87]   W.J.H.J. Bronnenberg, L. Nijman, E.A.M. Odijk, and R.A.H. van Twist, *DOOM: A Decentralized Object-Oriented Machine*, IEEE MICRO, Vol.7, No.5, pp.52-69, 1987.

[Dij90a]   Henk Dijkstra, *Time measurements of some constructs of POOL-X implementations*, POOMA Doc. 0140, March 1990.

[Dij90b]   Henk Dijkstra, *Time measurements (an update of M0140)*, POOMA Doc. 0147, May 1990.

[Gol83]   Adele Goldberg, David Robson, *Smalltalk-80, The Language and its Implementation*, Addison-Wesley, 1983.

[Hoa85]   C.A.R. Hoare, *Communicating Sequential Processes*, Prentice-Hall, 1985.

[Hul88]   Ben Hulshof, *LI-OS interface*, PRISMA Doc. 0353, November 1988.

[Hul89]   Ben Hulshof, *Overview of implementation of new GC*, POOMA Doc. 0049, August 1989.

[Hul90]   B.J.A. Hulshof and R.H.H. Wester, *Run-Time System for POOL-X Support*, Proc. of the PRISMA Workshop on Parallel Database Systems, Noordwijk, the Netherlands, September 24-26, 1990.

[Ino88]   Katsura Inoue, Hiroyuko Seki, Hikaru Yagi, *Analysis of functional programs to detect run-time garbage cells*, ACM Transactions on Programming Languages and.Systems, Oct 1988.

[Lav89]   B. Laverman, *Porting and Optimizing the POOL-T compiler*, PRISMA Doc. 0493, February 1989.

[Mey88]   Bertrand Meyer, *Object Oriented Software Construction*, Prentice Hall, 1988.

[Mot88]   Motorola, *MC68881 Floating-Point Coprocessor User's Manual*, MC68881UM/AD, January 1988.

[Nau90]   W.M. Naus, *A parallel implementation of a genetic placement algorithm*, Nat Lab Technical Note No. TN81/90, April 1990.

[Oer86]   Hans Oerlemans, *SODOM, Rationale*, DOOM Doc. 0181, November 1986.

[Spe89]   Juul van der Spek, *The POOL-X run-time model on POOMA*, POOMA Doc. 0087, October 1989.

[Str86]   B. Stroustrup, *The C++ programming language*, Addison-Wesley, 1986.

[Sun88]   Sun Chengzheng, *The structure of the POOMA I/O system*, PRISMA Doc. 0455, August 1988.

[Sun90]   Sun Chengzheng, *Stable Storage in a Parallel Environment*, Proc. of the PRISMA Workshop on Parallel Database Systems, Noordwijk, the Netherlands, September 24-26, 1990.

[You85]   Edward Yourdon, Larry L. Constantine, *Structured design; fundamentals of a discipline of computer program and systems design*, Prentice-Hall, 1985.

Automatic recovery of a parallel stable file system

Sun Chengzheng   L.O.Hertzberger

University of Amsterdam

Abstract

This article describes the automatic recovery algorithm and its implementation for the POOSS stable file system. The recoverable faults by our scheme include non-consecutive disk loss, single duplication loss, single duplication corruption, and duplication inconsistency. The recovery algorithm is implemented on the 100-node parallel machine (POOMA). One important feature of the recovery algorithm is that it is node-independent and can be executed simultaneously on different nodes, resulting in a highly parallel recovery procedure.

1   Introduction

In the context of PRISMA project [1, 2], a parallel object-oriented stable storage system (POOSS) [9] has been designed and implemented for the PRISMA-DBMS [5] to store log files in order to recover itself by roll-back in case of system crash. The environment in which the POOSS system is built is the POOMA machine[3], which consists of 100 nodes, with each node containing a CPU, a substantial amount of locally accessible memory (16 MBytes) and a special communication processor (which implements a packet switching network[4]). 50 nodes are equipped with a local disk of 300 Mbytes (with maximum speed of 1.2 MB/ps).

The POOSS system is constructed as a multiple layering system (as shown in Fig. 1), so that different issues, including object-orientness and atomicity, fault tolerance, parallelism and load-balance, and fast file system, can be attacked at different layers. Each layer provides a restricted set of UNIX compatible interface routines, which can be accessed by the upper layer and other C programs running on the POOMA machine.

This article concentrates on the issue of automatic recovery of the POOSS system. This issue is attacked at the stable file system (SFS) layer, which provides the abstration of files of byte-sequence and could survive system crash. Moreover, this layer inherents from the global file system layer the feature of parallel access of multiple files on different disks. For detailed description of the stable file system layer and the POOSS system as a whole, readers are referred to [9].

The rest of this article is organized as follows: In Section 2, strategies for duplication maintenance are introduced. Then, the automatic recovery scheme is presented in Section 3. The recoverable faults by our scheme are analyzed and proved in Section 4. The implementation issues are discussed in Section 5. Finally, the conclusions are given in Section 6.

2   Strategies for duplication maintenance

The fault tolerance effect of the stable file system is achieved by transparently maintaining two duplications for each (stable) file. One of the duplications is called the **primary copy** and the other is called the **secondary copy**. The association of a stable file with its duplications is based on the following naming scheme:

Duplication naming scheme:
If **stable** is the name of a stable file, **stable.org** will be the name of the primary copy, and **stable.cpy** will

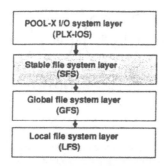

Figure 1: The hierarchy structure of the POOSS system

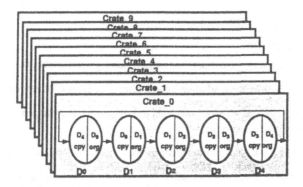

Figure 2: The crate-ring distribution of stable file duplications

be the name of the secondary copy.

In the POOMA machine, the 100 machine nodes are configured into 20 crates, with each crate consisting of 5 nodes. The 50 disks are connected to 10 crates. As an experimental parallel machine, the 100 nodes could be partitioned into smaller clusters, with each cluster consisting of a number of crates. To match the machine level partition, it is required that the distribution of stable file duplications be localized within every crate, i.e., if one copy of a stable file is stored in one disk of a crate, the other copy must be also stored in some disk of the same crate. Furthermore, in order to process the maximum number (50) of different stable files simultaneously, each disk in the system should be able to store both the primary copies and the secondary copies of different stable files. The following distribution strategy is used to meet the above requirements:

Duplication distribution strategy:

Let D_i ($0 \leq i < 5$) be a disk in one crate. For any stable file, if its primary copy is storied on disk D_i, the secondary copy will be stored on disk $D_{i+1 \pmod 5}$.

In this way, every 5 disks in the same crate forms a crate-ring in terms of duplication distribution, as shown in Fig 2. In the context of a crate-ring, disk $D_{i+1 \pmod 5}$ is called the partner disk of disk D_i.

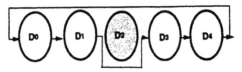

Figure 3: The partnership after restructuring

3 Automatic recovery

The recovery procedure is divided into two subprocedures: the restructuring procedure and the recovering procedure. By restructuring, we mean the reestablishment of the partnership between the disks. By recovering, we mean the recreation of lost files and the repairing of the corrupted and inconsistent files.

3.1 Restructuring procedure

Definition 1 Effectively lost disk

A disk is regarded as an effectively lost disk if one of the following situations happens:

1. The connection of this disk to the machine node is disabled, damaged, or removed.

2. The administration information of the low level disk file system is corrupted so that all the files on this disk are not accessible any more.

3. The connection of the machine node to the network is disabled or damaged.

Assumption: The fault of an effectively lost disk is detectable by the underlying disk driver (disk faults), the local file system (file system administration corruption), and the message handler (network faults).

Restructuring algorithm

for disk D_i $(0 \leq i < 5)$ in a crate of the system.
$k = i + 1$ (mod 5);
while $k \neq i$
    if D_k is an effectively lost disk
    then $k = k + 1$ (mod 5); **continue** ;
    else D_k will be the partner disk of D_i; **exit.**
panic("there is only one disk in this crate !").

As the example shown in Fig 3, if D_2 is lost, D_1 will has D_3 as the new partner after the restructuring procedure.

3.2 Recovering procedure

for any disk D in the system.
1.   **Initialization**
    $S_o = \{$ name $|$ file **name.org** is stored on D $\}$
    $S_c = \{$ name $|$ file **name.cpy** is stored on the partner disk of D $\}$
2.   **Detect lost files and possibly corrupted files**
    $S_i = S_o \cap S_c$ (the set of stable file names with possibly corrupted copies).
    $S_{o-i} = S_o - S_i$ (the set of stable file names with lost secondary copies).
    $S_{c-i} = S_c - S_i$ (the set of stable file names with lost primary copies).
3.   **Recreate lost files**
    for any name $\in S_{o-i}$,

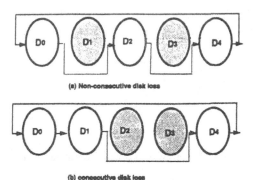

(a) Non-consecutive disk loss

(b) consecutive disk loss

Figure 4: Different disk loss situations

    create a file **name.cpy** on the partner disk;
    write the contents of **name.org** to **name.cpy**;
  for any name $\in S_{c-i}$,
    create a file **name.org** on D;
    write the contents of **name.cpy** to **name.org**;
4.   **Repair corrupted and inconsistent files**
  for any name $\in S_i$,
  (1) read **name.org** and **name.cpy** ;
  (2) **if**   both readings return failure values
    then   system crashes (unexpected situation !)
    else if reading **name.org** returns a failure value
    then   repair the corrupted **name.org** with the contents of **name.cpy**;
    else if reading **name.cpy** returns a failure value
    then   repair the corrupted **name.cpy** with the contents of **name.cpy**;
    else   compare the contents of **name.org** and **name.cpy**.
            if the contents are different.
            then write the contents of **name.cpy** to the **name.org**.

4 Recoverable faults

4.1 Non-consecutive disk loss

Definition 2 Non-consecutive disk loss fault

Let S_{ld} be the set of effectively lost disks in one crate of the system, D_i be any disk in this crate. The non-consecutive disk loss fault is the situation that if $D_i \in S_{ld}$, then D_{i+1} must not belong to S_{ld} (see Fig. 4-(a)). Otherwise, the situation is called the **consecutive disk loss fault** (see Fig. 4-(b)).

Assertion 1 The non-consecutive disk loss fault is recoverable.

Proof: Let D_i be any one of the effectively lost disks. Considering the recovery procedure for disk D_{i-1}:

1. After restructuring, disk D_{i-1} will have a new partner disk D_{i+1}.

2. After the initialization of the recovering algorithm:

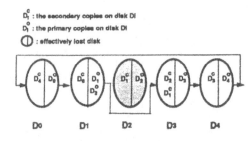

D_i^c : the secondary copies on disk DI
D_i^o : the primary copies on disk DI
⦶ : effectively lost disk

Figure 5: The recovery of a non-consecutive disk loss

    (a) S_o will contain the stable file names with primary copies on disk D_{i-1}.

    (b) S_c will contain the stable file names with secondary copies on disk D_{i+1}.

3. After the detecting phase of the recovering algorithm:

    (a) S_i must be empty, because for any **name** $\in S_o$, if **name** $\in S_c$, then before D_i was lost, **name.cpy** must be on both D_i and D_{i+1}, which is impossible since the global file system ensures the uniqueness of file names in the system (see [7]).

    (b) S_{o-i} is equal to S_o, which indicates all the lost secondary copies on D_i;

    (c) S_{c-i} is equal to S_c, which indicates all the lost primary copies on D_i;

4. After recreating the lost files, the following is done:

    (a) the lost secondary copies indicated by S_{o-i} will be recreated on the disk D_{i+1}.

    (b) the lost primary copies indicated by S_{c-i} will be recreated on the disk D_{i-1}.

5. In the phase of repairing the corrupted and inconsistent files, there is nothing to with disk D_{i-1} since S_i is empty.

According to above recovery procedure, the lost secondary copies on D_i will be recreated on disk D_{i+1}, and the lost primary copies on D_i will be recreated on disk D_{i-1} (as illustrated in Fig 5). Thus, our claim is proven.

4.2 Single duplication loss

Definition 3 Single duplication loss fault

The single duplication loss fault is a situation that either the primary copy or the secondary copy of a stable file is lost.

The single duplication loss fault could happen in the following situations:

1. System crashes during creating/deleting the duplications of a stable file (the crash happens after creating/deleting the primary copy but before creating/deleting the secondary copy).

2. The administration for one of the duplications of a stable file is corrupted, so that this file is not accessible any more.

The single duplication loss faults are detected by the recovering algorithm by computing the name set of S_{o-i} and S_{c-i} (see section 3.2).

Assertion 2 The single duplication loss fault is recoverable.

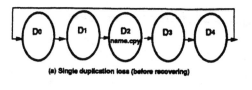

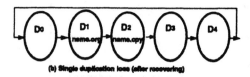

Figure 6: The recovery of single duplication loss

Proof: Let **name** be any stable file on disk D_i in the system. Assume the primary copy **name.org** was lost, then the followings are held for disk D_i (according to the recovering algorithm):

1. **name** is not in S_o (from the assumption);

2. **name** $\in S_c$ (from the precondition);

3. **name** is not in S_i (from $S_i = S_o \cap S_c$)

4. **name** $\in S_{c-i}$ (from $S_{c-i} = S_c - S_i$ and **name** $\in S_c$)

Therefore, the **name.org** will be recreated on disk D_i (as illustrated in Fig 6). Similarly, we can prove the secondary copy **name.cpy** can be recreated on disk D_{i-1} if it was lost. Thus, our claim is proven.

4.3 Single duplication corruption

Definition 4 Single duplication corruption fault

The single duplication corruption fault is a situation that both copies of a stable file are existing but one of duplications has been corrupted.

The single duplication corruption fault could happen in the following situations:

1. System crashes during writing one of the copies of a stable file.

2. The data for one of the duplications of a stable file is corrupted by any source of damage.

The single duplication corruption fault is detected by the underlying disk driver (reading a corrupted disk file will always get a failure result).

Assertion 3 The single duplication corruption fault is recoverable.

Proof: Let **name** be any stable file on disk D_i in the system. Since the two duplications are existing in the system from the precondition, the followings are held for disk D_i (according to the recovering algorithm):

1. **name** $\in S_o$;

2. **name** $\in S_c$;

3. **name** $\in S_i$ (from $S_{c-i} = S_c - S_i$ and **name** $\in S_o$ and **name** $\in S_c$);

In the repairing phase of the recovering algorithm, if **name.org** was corrupted, then reading of **name.org** will return a failure value. Thereafter, the corrupted **name.org** will be repaired with the contents of **name.cpy**. Similarly, we can prove the secondary copy **name.cpy** can be repaired if it was corrupted. Thus, our claim is proven.

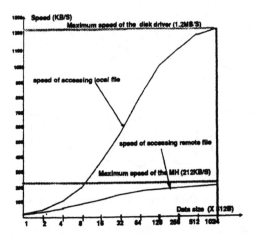

Figure 7: Performance curv of the underlying global file system

4.4 Duplication inconsistency

Definition 5 Duplication inconsistency fault

The duplication inconsistency fault is a situation that both copies of a stable file are existing but the contents of the primary copy and the secondary copy of a stable file are not the same.

The duplication inconsistency fault could happen in the following situation:

System crashes after modifying the primary copy of a stable file but before updating the secondary copy of this stable file.

The duplication inconsistency fault is detected by the recovering algorithm by comparing the contents of the two copies of a stable file (see section 3.2).

Assertion 4 The duplication inconsistency fault is recoverable.

Proof: Let **name** be any stable file on disk D_i in the system. Since the two duplications are existing in the system from the precondition, the followings are held (according to the recovering algorithm):

1. **name** $\in S_o$;

2. **name** $\in S_c$;

3. **name** $\in S_i$ (from $S_{c-i} = S_c - S_i$ and **name** $\in S_o$ and **name** $\in S_c$);

In the repairing phase of the recovering algorithm, the readings of both **name.org** and **name.cpy** will return successful value. If the contents in these two duplications are different, the contents of **name.cpy** will be copied to **name.org**, resulting in two consistent duplications of stable file **name**. Thus, our claim is proven.

5 Implementation issues

- **On-line/off-line recovery**
  The stable file system recovery could be started by a detected system error without crashing the system (**on-line recovery**), or by a dedicated recovery running session (**off-line recovery**). The current implementation supports only part of the on-line repairing of the corrupted files in reading stable files but full and selectable off-line recovery. A file system tool utility command **mksfs** is provided to facilitate the off-line recovery [8].

- **Stable file server and underlying system supports**

  There is one stable file server on each disk node, which is responsible for the stable file system recovery.

  In the POOMA system, machine nodes are connected by a reconfigurable packet switch network [4]. Each time the system is started, a machine node is identified by a logic node number, which could be different in different running sessions. To determine the partnership between disks, each disk should have an identifier which is physically and logically independent of the machine node to which it is attached. This identifier is stored on the disk so that it is always the same for every running session. An interface routine $gfs\_get\_id(nodenr)$ is provided to get the identifier of the disk on machine node **nodenr**. In executing $gfs\_get\_id()$ routine, if all the tests are successful, the identifier of this disk is returned; otherwise, a failure result is returned. In the restructuring phase, each stable file server first has to get the state information about all the underlying disks in the same crate by calling $gfs\_get\_id()$ routine. Then, according to the state information of each disk, the stable file server can reestablish a new partnership with one of the disks in the same crate.

  In the recovering phase, the stable file server first has to get all the file names suffixed by **.org** from the local file system and all the file names suffixed by **.cpy** from the partner file system (extra supports from the underlying file system is needed here). Then, the rest of the recovering algorithm can be implemented by making normal underlying file system calls.

- **Buffering and parallelisms**

  Since the performance of the underlying file system is dependent on the size of the data (see Fig. 7), and in the dedicate recovery running session sufficient main memory (16MB) is available to the recovery procedure, the stable file server uses a very large buffer size (0.5 MB) to obtain the highest speed of reading/writing the primary copies of the stable files (about 1.2MB/ps). However, the speed of reading/writing the secondary copies (about 180KB/ps) is limited by the current low speed of the message handler (as shown in Fig 7).

  The recovery algorithm is node-independent in the sense that each disk node can be recoveried independently and there is no need for recovery procedures on different nodes to do communication and synchronization with each other. This feature is exploited by implementing a stable file server on each disk node so that all the stable file servers can execute the same recovery algorithm on different nodes in parallel.

6 Conclusions

The automatic recovery algorithm and its implementation for the POOSS parallel stable file system have been described in this article. The recoverable faults by our scheme include non-consecutive disk loss, single duplication loss, single duplication corruption, and duplication inconsistency. One important feature of the recovery algorithm is that it is node-independent and can be executed simultaneously on different nodes of the parallel machine, resulting in a highly parallel recovery procedure.

7 Acknowledgements

The authors wish to acknowledge the contributions of all PRISMA project members involved, and in particular the operating system group. The work described in this article is the result of a stimulating cooperation between a number of research groups headed by H.H. Eggenhuisen of Philips Research Laboratories.

References

[1] P.M.G. Apers, J.A. Bergstra, H.H. Eggenhuisen, L.O. Hertzberger, M.L. Kersten, P.J.F. Lucas, A.J. Nijman and G. Rozenberg, *A Highly Parallel machine for Data and Knowledge-base Management: PRISMA*, Doc. Nr. 1, PRISMA Project, Philips Research Laboratories, Eindhoven, The Netherlands, 1986.

[2] E.Brandsma, Sun Chengzheng, B.J.A.Hulshof, L.O.Hertzberger, and A.C.M. Oerlemans, *Overview of the PRISMA Operating System*, Proc. of the International Conference on New Generation Computer Systems 1989, pp.369-379.

[3] M.C. Vlot and R.A.H. van Twist, *The Parallel Object Oriented MAchine POOMA*, Esprit project 415-A, doc.no.0502, Philips Research Laboratories Eindhoven, The Netherlands, 1989.

[4] J.K.Annot and R.A.H. van Twist, *A Novel Deadlock Free and Starvation Free Packet Switching Communication Processor*, Proc. PARLE Conf., Springer Lecture Notes in Computer Science, Part 1, 1987, pp.68-85.

[5] P.M.G.Apers, M.L.Kersten, A.C.M.Oerlemans, *PRISMA Database Machine: A Distributed, Main-Memory Approach*, Proc. of International Conference on Extending Data Base Technology, Feb. 1988.

[6] Sun Chengzheng, *The POOMA local file system*, POOMA document.nr. 0126. March 2, 1990.

[7] Sun Chengzheng, *The POOMA global file system*, POOMA document.nr. 0126. March 2, 1990.

[8] Sun Chengzheng, *The POOMA file system tools*, POOMA document.nr. 0129. March 2, 1990.

[9] Sun Chengzheng, L.O. Hertzberger, B.J.A.Hulshof, Rogier Wester, *POOSS: A Parallel Object-Oriented Stable Storage*, POOMA document.nr. 0152. 1990.

Duplicates and Translation
of Nested SQL Queries into XRA

N.Th. Verbrugge

CWI

Kruislaan 413, 1098 SJ Amsterdam

Abstract

The PRISMA/DB system[1] contains a parser to translate the database language SQL into eXtended Relational Algebra (XRA). The early definition of XRA, which has a multi-set semantics, proves inadequate for translating SQL according to its nested-iteration semantics. The prime cause is that no distinction is made between original and generated duplicate tuples during nested query handling. To achieve a correct translation, tuple identifiers were introduced into XRA and the system.

Keywords: Duplicates, SQL, XRA, nested query evaluation, nested-iteration method, tuple identifiers, syntax-directed SQL translation.

1 Introduction

The PRISMA/DB system [Kersten] supports two query languages, SQL and PRISMALOG (a logical language). SQL [SQL] was chosen since it is the standard database query language, and PRISMA-LOG adds knowledge base characteristics through its inference techniques. Both languages are translated into the internal language of the PRISMA/DB system, an extended relational algebra called XRA [Wilschut]. The XRA structure is then passed to the Query Optimizer, which is responsible for deriving an optimal query execution schedule.

Our primary goal is to develop a general translation heuristic, or even better, a syntax-directed translation from SQL to XRA.

It is striking that many systems do not support the full power of SQL, especially its nesting capabilities. These systems avoid nested queries for several reasons: (1) the asymmetry of the query biases the query optimizer to a nested query handling strategy, using for-loops which may not be optimal, (2) translation problems concerning duplicates (tuples of a table with equal values for all their attributes) in relational algebra translations of SQL, and (3) block notation is hard to learn for non-programmers ([Astrahan], referring to psychological studies).

In this paper, we present a solution to the first two problems, i.e. we present a correct translation of a nested SQL query into XRA. This translation distinguishes duplicate tuples by using artificial primary keys for relations, called tuple identifiers. Except maybe for handling "unknowns", which is *the* other SQL problem [Date2], nested queries can always be handled correctly now.

The asymmetry is removed by translating the nested predicate to a (symmetric) join. The join can be optimized taking the relative sizes of the joined relations into account. Other opportunities for query optimization in relational algebra are described by [Ullman] and [Hall].

Concerning the third reason to avoid nesting, in our opinion, nested queries can be quite useful for programming SQL, as e.g. [Date] shows. While we do not fully deny block notation complexity,

---

[1]The research for this article is conducted in the context of the PRISMA project, which is supported by the Dutch "Stimuleringsprojectteam Informaticaonderzoek" (SPIN).

nesting may ease query formulation by users considerably. A system should at least provide for the option, letting the user decide whether to nest the query or not.

The next section explains the multi-set semantics of SQL and XRA. Before we present our solution, we first show that XRA cannot be used to translate SQL. This is primarily caused by the semantics of nested queries, which require a distinction to be made between generated and original duplicates in relations. In section 4, we give the solution to the translation problem: tuple identifiers. Tuple identifiers are not only implementation handles to ease database system construction, they also prove to be essential to support multi-set oriented processing of nested queries. The general characteristics of the correct nested predicate translation which uses tuple identifiers in XRA are discussed, and an example translation is given. (The results propagate to SQL2 and SQL3 as well [SQL2].) A syntax-directed translation of the nested predicates into XRA is provided after that. It is the key to the complete syntax-directed translation of SQL into XRA with tuple identifiers. Section 5 presents our conclusions.

2 Nested query semantics

To understand the translation problems caused by nested queries, the main characteristics of SQL and XRA concerning the translation process and the key role of duplicates must be understood. Therefore, the semantics of SQL and XRA are explained, and a sample nested query translation is given.

2.1 SQL: the nested-iteration semantics

The database relations on which SQL operates are multi-sets, i.e. the set may contain duplicates. SQL queries typically contain *(sub)query blocks* of the well-known form: SELECT-FROM-WHERE. A *nested (sub)query* in SQL is a (sub)query block containing one or more subquery blocks. The semantics of query and subquery blocks are equal.

We first give a simple example of an SQL nested query. It shows what the inner subquery and outer query blocks are. The database schema is the same as the schema of the suppliers-and-parts database by [Date]. It contains the relations S(snr, sname, status, city), P(pnr, pname, color, weight, city), and SP(snr, pnr, qty).

SQL query nr. 1:

SELECT sname		
FROM S		*outer block*
WHERE S.snr IN	(SELECT snr	
	FROM SP	*inner block*
	WHERE pnr = 1);	

The query is handled by *conceptually* doing the following: for each tuple in the outer block, see whether it satisfies the search condition(s) given. We have to keep in mind that for every tuple, nested predicates (boolean expressions containing a subquery) may come out differently, depending on the tuple's own values. Therefore, the inner block may have to be evaluated again for every outer block tuple.

This way of (sub)query handling is called a *nested-iteration method*. It is applied recursively, and another formulation is the following:

```
FOR every outer block tuple (FROM S)
DO
        recursively evaluate the inner block(s);
        IF WHERE-condition
        AND HAVING-condition hold THEN
                add the outer block tuple to the result
        FI
OD;
apply aggregate functions and project the SELECT columns.
```

The outer block tuples are formed by taking the Cartesian product of the relations mentioned in the FROM-part. (Grouping can also be incorporated; this is not done here for simplicity.)

The result of the example query contains those S-tuples for which there is an SP-tuple with both "S.snr = SP.snr", and the "SP.pnr" value equals 1.

Most systems which allow nested SQL use a nested-iteration-like strategy for nested query handling. Query execution time can be long in these systems because of the asymmetry of the query. The SQL standard [SQL] leaves the evaluation strategy to the system implementor, as long as a system obeys the same semantics. This is what we do in PRISMA/DB: we translate SQL into XRA, which includes optimization techniques to improve system response time.

2.2 XRA: algebraic multi-set semantics

The database relations on which XRA operates are multi-sets as well. The basic operations in XRA are relational expressions, consisting of a relational operator and its arguments. The result of any relational expression has the form of a relation again. This relation may contain duplicate tuples (also called duplicates for short), and therefore is a multi-set. This shows that XRA has a multi-set semantics.

In XRA, a database relation is an elementary relational expression (*rexpr*), e.g. "SP". An example of a relational operation is "uniq(*rexpr*)", which removes the duplicate tuples from *rexpr*. Another operation, "select(%1 > 10, *rexpr*)", selects only those tuples from *rexpr* of which the first attribute's value[2] is greater than 10. Table 1 shows some of the XRA operations used in query translation, along with roughly corresponding SQL constructs.

Function	SQL	XRA
project columns from *rexpr*	SELECT	project(*plist, rexpr*)
condition must hold for tuple	WHERE/HAVING	select(*cond, rexpr*)
Cartesian product	FROM	cp(*rexprlist*)
relational join	FROM/nesting	join(*rexpr1, cond, rexpr2*)
eliminate duplicate tuples	DISTINCT	uniq(*rexpr*)
grouping and aggregate funcs	GROUP BY, MAX, etc.	gb(*grlist, funcs, rexpr*)
sort tuples	ORDER BY	sort(*sortlist, rexpr*)

Table 1. The function of some operations in SQL and XRA.

2.3 Simple nested query translation

In this section, we give a correct XRA translation of the aforementioned nested SQL query, *SQL query nr. 1*, provided that S does not contain duplicates. In this case, S is a set rather than a multi-set of tuples. Moreover, to give a simple translation, we also assume that S has the primary key snr.

---

[2]In the PRISMA/DB system, columns are referred to by their relative position number in the table or subexpression(s). Column number calculation is not essential to this article. Therefore, from now on the names are used instead of numbers.

Under these two assumptions, an XRA translation of SQL query nr. 1 using column names becomes:

Dupl. translation nr. 1key:

```
?project(S.sname,
        uniq(project((S.sname, S.snr),
             join(  S,
                    S.snr = SP.snr,
                    select(SP.pnr = 1, SP)))))
```

The *join* operation joins table S and SP. The combination *uniq-project* projects over the columns **sname** (the supplier's name) and **snr** (the supplier's number), and discards the duplicates. The result of the outermost *project* produces the names of the suppliers of parts with number 1, without discarding duplicates. The question mark denotes a query.

3 Duplicate problem analysis

As we will inductively show in this section, the current definition of XRA [Wilschut], is not expressive enough to translate SQL nested queries correctly. The problem concerns tuple duplicates and translation of nested predicates. The analysis naturally leads to an extra construct in XRA to control removal and retention of duplicates, i.e. the tuple identifier. The role of the tuple identifier in the XRA translation will be deferred to section 4.

Other authors have recognized this SQL processing problem as well. [Kim] and [Kiessling] worked on SQL unnesting, to ease query optimization. They did not develop a complete solution; otherwise, we could have used it. [Murali] also uses primary key knowledge, assuming its presence in each relation, to obtain a dataflow algorithm for nested query execution. [Ceri] made a relational algebra translation which is limited to tuple sets. Therefore, concerning duplicates, our XRA and their Relational Algebra differ as follows:

- Their Relational Algebra does not deal with duplicates, while our XRA does. Therefore, in their approach duplicates are always eliminated. Queries and subqueries are viewed as if they were always written "SELECT DISTINCT...". They pointed out that extensions to their Relational Algebra with control over duplicates are feasible.

- They only allow GROUP BY in a query if it applies to the outermost query block, whereas we allow grouping in all (sub)query blocks. This is a good decision in their case. Namely, control over duplicates in subqueries (and in relational algebra joins) is essential for correctly translating grouping and aggregate functions.

3.1 Duplicate elimination and preservation

Why is it so important that the result of a nested predicate evaluation (and therefore a nested query) in XRA complies with the semantics of SQL? It is needed for aggregate evaluation.

For example, consider a query in which the original relation was $O = \{a, a, b\}$, where a and b are tuples, and a has a duplicate since it occurs twice. Suppose also that a nested WHERE search condition and a GROUP BY operate on O, and the result of the former is incorrect, e.g. $\{a, a, a, a\}$. Then the XRA gb-operation in combination with e.g. a SUM aggregate function will have a result which is two times the SQL result if the SUM is calculated over a non-zero column of the a-tuples. Having duplicates in an answer can be overcome easily by users, but faulty calculations of functions will generally not be detected by them.

The semantics of XRA expressions is defined such that the result of the (sub)expression is a multiset of tuples. Duplicates can be eliminated from the (intermediate) result explicitly by applying the "uniq" operator. In SQL, duplicate tuples can be removed with the "DISTINCT" option in the

SELECT-list of a query block. Similarly, "UNION" removes duplicates, in contrast to "UNION ALL".

Less obvious is the fact that some kinds of nested SQL queries also require duplicate removal, while others require duplicate preservation. Notable is the use of aggregate functions in combination with grouping, of which we gave an example. Always removing duplicates would cause aggregates requiring duplicate preservation to behave wrongly, as Kiessling noted [Kiessling]. Always retaining duplicates would be a bad strategy for aggregates requiring duplicate elimination. However, even without aggregate functions and grouping, wrong results are easily produced. Actually, for correct duplicate handling, we must be able to distinguish between:

- "original" duplicates, which were present in the original relation(s) used. They must be preserved in a result. And

- "generated" duplicates, which are formed by projections, or projections on joins (or Cartesian products). They must be removed from a result.

This problem concerning correct duplicate handling will be called the *duplicate problem*.

It may look as though *primary keys* can always serve to solve the duplicate problem, like in the translation in the previous section. This is not true, since some tables, such as intermediate tables and tables with duplicates, do not have primary keys. Next to that, especially if the primary key is a multi-valued key (i.e. contains multiple attributes [SQL]), we should answer the following questions: Do any primary key attributes participate in the intermediate result (=XRA subexpression)? Are they used in arithmetic or aggregate functions? Which of these attributes should then be eliminated from the result?

3.2 XRA cannot solve duplicate problem

We now want to show that XRA cannot translate SQL correctly if it has no tuple identifiers at its disposal.

For nested query translation, all XRA operators which have some effect on duplicates must be considered. They are: join, cp, project, uniq, gb, as well as (multi-set) union, intersection, and difference. The first five can be used for nested predicate translation, the last three for AND, OR, and NOT in search conditions containing one or more nested predicates. Nested predicate translation will be covered first. If nested predicates are not correctly translated, and thus the duplicate problem is not solved, then union, intersection, and difference for search conditions also yield incorrect results. Furthermore, we show why correct nested predicate translation is crucial to aggregate evaluation in nested queries.

A nested predicate in SQL has the form:

```
<nested predicate> ::=
            <lvalexpr> <nesting compop> <subquery>

<subquery> ::=
            ( SELECT [DISTINCT] <valexpr>
            FROM <table list>
            [WHERE <where sc>]
            [GROUP BY <grouping attrs>]
            [HAVING <having sc>] )
```

Nested predicate translation cannot be done correctly in XRA. Namely, in terms of XRA, a nested predicate in SQL requires:

1. a cp or join over the outer(O) and the inner(I) block tuples, including a condition which must hold. The O tuples come from the SQL query containing the <nested predicate>. The I tuples are the Cartesian product of the subquery's <table list> tables. The condition compares <lvalexpr> and <valexpr>.

2. sometimes: grouping and aggregate function calculation, and selections for WHERE and HAV-ING search conditions on the group or the aggregates.

3. extraction of the outer(O) tuples from the (possibly grouped) product of O and I.

4. that the duplicate problem must be solved. That is, the result should contain just as many duplicates for a tuple as O had, or none at all, because any search condition either holds for all tuple duplicates or for none.

Especially the last point cannot be accomplished. Namely, we can combine the XRA operators cp/join, project, uniq, or gb to form the result. The effects of cp and join are the same, except that a join also incorporates a search condition for the resulting tuples, and thus a tuple and its duplicates are either all kept or all removed. In general, cp/join and project generate duplicates and preserve generated duplicates. On the other hand, gb and uniq eliminate all duplicates of a tuple; one tuple is saved. To translate a nested predicate, we have to start out with a **join** of two or more multi-sets. (Join stands for cp as well here.) The join is needed because the predicate itself, and possibly a WHERE condition in the subquery as well, compare O-attributes with I-attributes. XRA can only compare attributes from O and I by means of a join, or by a combination of a Cartesian product cp and a selection.

For the second and further operations, we have more choice. Selections and other XRA operations which do not structurally change the number of duplicates for a tuple are not shown.

An important thing to keep in mind is that, in general, O and I both contain duplicates. Such duplicates cannot be removed from O or I by XRA in all cases. Namely, suppose we have an aggregate or GROUP BY over O or I *in the subquery*. Without the duplicates of O and I, a gb operator could return an incorrect result compared to SQL nested query semantics. Even if duplicates were first removed from O and/or I, by doing uniq(O) and/or uniq(I), duplicates of the O-tuples (and I-tuples) can be introduced again, that is generated, by the join. We are looking for a solution which works for all cases, since during query translation we cannot determine whether an intermediate result will contain duplicates relative to a subset of its columns (e.g. its O-tuple part). After the join, what can follow is:

- **project**: project(O-attributes, join(O, I)).
  Suppose for one O-tuple there were more than one joinable I-tuples, that is tuples which satisfied the join condition. Then the result is too large: it contains (extra) duplicates for the joinable O-tuples. A third operator could work correctly, but not in all cases:

  - **uniq**: uniq(project(O-attributes, join(O, I))).
    This works correctly only if O contains no joinable tuples with duplicates; this cannot be guaranteed. Otherwise, the result contains only one tuple out of a group of duplicate tuples from O, which is incorrect. [Ceri] also observed this, since set-semantics were used in their Relational Algebra. This is the same as always applying a uniq operator to every intermediate result in our XRA.

  - **join**: join(O, project(O-attributes, join(O, I))).
    This is a join again, which has the same structure as the join we started off with. Analysis of the cases therefore is done already.

  - **gb**: gb(O-attributes, O-aggregates, project(O-attributes, join(O, I))).
    This has the same shortcomings as uniq(project(O-attributes, join(O, I))).

- **gb**: gb(OI-attributes, OI-aggregates, join(O, I)).
  To extract the outer(O) tuples, a **project** should follow (after a select for some search condition was performed):
  project(O-attributes, gb(OI-attributes, OI-aggregates, join(O, I))).
  This has the same characteristics as project(O-attributes, join(O, I)).

- **join:** could have been incorporated in the first join.

- **uniq:** uniq(union(O, I)) serves no purpose for nested predicate calculation.

This shows that such a nested predicate translation cannot be duplicate correct. Note that an extra join and project with the original O (or I) will not help, again because the join generates duplicates. Also, deeper nesting through a subquery inside the inner block sometimes prohibits this, especially if it contains aggregate calculations. Moreover, multi-set union, intersection, and difference cannot be of help either, since the operands should be duplicate correct first. This also implies that AND, OR, and NOT in search conditions containing nested predicates cannot be translated according to SQL semantics.

4 SQL translation into XRA with TIDs

If we add an artificial primary key to all tuples, we *can* make correct translations for nested queries. The *tuple identifier* or *TID* is a unique number, relative to the TIDs of the other tuples in a specific relation.

4.1 Example translation

We will give a taste of the solution using TIDs in this subsection. The translation of the following problematic nested SQL query with grouping and with an aggregate function SUM will be discussed:

SQL query nr. 2:
```
        SELECT *
        FROM R
        WHERE R.b >  (SELECT SUM(S.c)
                     FROM S
                     WHERE R.x = S.x);
```

Suppose the database contains the tables R and S as given here (note that R contains a duplicate tuple). The result of the SQL statement is shown as well:

R.x	R.b
1	40
1	40

S.x	S.c
1	10
1	20

$\Rightarrow$

R.x	R.b
1	40
1	40

The SQL query result is calculated according to the nested-iteration method. For every tuple in the relation R, we calculate the subquery. The sum over the column S.c is 30 for each of the two original R-tuples.

To show how TIDs work, the correct translation into XRA with TIDs (see the tid column in the grouping construct) is:

Dupl. translation nr. 2tid:
```
            ?project((R.x, R.b),
                select(R.b > SUM(S.c),
                    gb((R.tid, R.x, R.b), (SUM(S.c)),
                        select(R.x = S.x,
                            cp(R', S')))))
```

We show the tables R' and S', which are R and S each with an added *tid* column, as well as the temporary table after the "cp" and "select" operation, that is the last two lines. (S instead of S' gives a correct result as well. This is not so if the subquery in its turn contains a subquery again.)

R.x	R.b	R.tid
1	40	1
1	40	2

S.x	S.c	S.tid
1	10	1
1	20	2

R.x	R.b	R.tid	S.x	S.c	S.tid
1	40	1	1	10	1
1	40	1	1	20	2
1	40	2	1	10	1
1	40	2	1	20	2

When grouping is done on R.tid, then for every R-tuple the SUM over S.c is calculated separately. This is exactly what the SQL semantics prescribes. The TID serves to distinguish duplicates (for the SUM calculation), and to remove duplicates which were generated in the Cartesian product. The latter removal is done through the grouping columns in the "gb", which works just like "uniq(project(...))", except for aggregate function calculation.

If we did not group on R.tid, but only on R.x and R.b, then the XRA result would have been empty (no tuples), and therefore wrong. This was exactly the case gb-join in the previous section's analysis.

4.2   General XRA with TIDs translation

The general characteristics of the nested predicate translation are covered in this subsection.

We consider the evaluation of a nested predicate, with a subquery at level n. Let I', the inner tuples, contain the Cartesian product of this subquery's FROM relations, including their TIDs. Let O', the outer tuples, contain the Cartesian product of all its ancestor (level 1 through n-1) query blocks FROM relations plus TIDs. The TIDs in O' are called O-tids.

When we have TIDs at our disposal, we use either

- uniq(project((O-tids, O-attributes), join(O', I')))

- or, if we need to group:
  uniq(project((O-tids, O-attributes), gb((O-tids, OI-attributes), OI-aggregates, join(O', I')))).

to translate nested predicates in both WHERE and HAVING clauses.

Selection of tuples is not shown for simplicity, like in the previous section. The result now does satisfy the constraints for SQL results. Also notice the simplicity of the solution.

Why does the first option with uniq-project work?

First, the outer tuples O' are joined with the inner tuples I'. Then, O-tids and O-attributes (satisfying some search condition) are projected out. It is very likely that duplicates are among the resulting tuples from O'. They are both generated and original duplicates; generated duplicates were formed by the combination project-join. The O-tids form an artificial key for O'. The uniq operator therefore returns the original duplicates, and eliminates the generated duplicates. This is exactly what SQL requires.

An extra project is needed to remove the O-tids. Only the other columns are meaningful to the user and SQL. Those columns need not be all O-attributes, but can be some value expressions using O-attributes only. These value expressions come from the SELECT clause of the outermost query block. If the nested predicate was part of a more complex search condition or of a subquery, or if another nested search condition (HAVING) is to be applied, then the TIDs are still needed.

Why does the second option with uniq-project-gb work?

The grouping operator gb can be caused by a GROUP BY clause in the subquery, and/or an aggregate function over either O or I tuples within a subquery. Per tuple in the outer block, grouping will be performed. Namely, we group on O-tids as well. If generated duplicates of O-tuples were present, the columns are *not* counted several times by the aggregates. This is as SQL requires. The uniq-project serves the same purpose as in the first solution, and an extra project may be needed as before.

The example in the previous subsection uses the second option. There, the grouping attributes are just O-attributes. Therefore, the extra uniq-project is not needed, and the project alone suffices.

Complex nested search conditions can be translated correctly too, now. The translation uses the TIDs in A' and B', the results of the partial nested search conditions scA and scB, respectively. For comparison, unnested search conditions "scA" are translated thus: select(scA, O').

"ScA AND scB" is translated into intersection(A', B'), or select(scA, B') if scA was not nested.

For "scA OR scB" we could use uniq(union(A', B')). This is likely to perform better than: union(diff(A', B'), B').

"NOT scA" becomes diff(O', A').

4.3 Syntax-directed translation of nested predicates

In this subsection, a general framework for the translation of nested predicates is given, to show how the TIDs are used in the complete translation. Not all details are covered. For the complete syntax-directed SQL to XRA translation, see [Verbr1].

4.3.1 Nested predicates

Nested predicates in SQL are all translated the same way, except the nested quantified predicate with ALL. For ALL, "$\forall x\ Pred(x)$" is equivalent with "$\neg\exists x\ \neg Pred(x)$". The latter form can be translated into XRA multi-set operations.

SQL syntax	XRA syntax	C
<nested predicate>	<XRA nested sc(subexpression)> ::= uniq(project(*allcolumns*(subexpression), select(<XRA simple sc from nesting>, <XRA subquery(subexpression)>)))	 4 3 2 1

Numbered comments:

1. This is the subquery translation into XRA (see next translation). The subexpression tree was passed down by the translation process as a parameter. It contains the translation of the outer (sub)query: an XRA expression over O', containing the O-tids.

2. This is the search condition from the <nested predicate>, joining O' with I'. For example, for *SQL query nr. 2*, this condition is "R.b > SUM(S.c)", when we use column names.

   The expression "select(...)", now, has as a result columns from O' *and* from I'.

3. The function *allcolumns* returns all columns of O' including the O-tids.

4. The "uniq-project" is needed for extracting the O' columns and removing duplicates. Now the result contains only the O' columns satisfying the conditions.

4.3.2 Subqueries

SQL subqueries look like SQL queries, except that ORDER BY and a <select list> of length more than one are not allowed in subqueries.

SQL syntax	XRA syntax	C
<subquery>	<XRA subquery(subexpression)> ::=	1
SELECT [DISTINCT] <valexpr> FROM <table list> [WHERE <where sc>] [GROUP BY <grouping attrs>] [HAVING <having sc>]	<XRA having sc(gb((*allcolumns*(subexpression), <XRA grouping attrs>), *grouping_functions*, <XRA where sc(cp(subexpression, <XRA table list>))>))>	2 1

Most parts of the translation, except cp, are only needed if a corresponding part was present in the original SQL statement. Care should be taken for grouping: aggregate functions can be used in <valexpr>, or in the HAVING search condition (even in subqueries within it).

Numbered comments:

1. The "cp" is always needed. The subexpression contains the translation of the outer subquery. The translation of <table list>, a Cartesian product which forms I', is joined (or cp-ed) with the subexpression.

2. Also, we must group over the O' columns, including O-tids, from outer subqueries. Otherwise, the nested-iteration semantics are not simulated.

5 Conclusions and further research

Nested predicate translation into an extended relational algebra, e.g. XRA, is not feasible. Namely, XRA cannot distinguish between original duplicates, which must be kept, and generated duplicates, which must be eliminated. Correct duplicate handling appeared crucial to aggregate function calculation.

With an extra artificial primary key added to each tuple of a relation, called the tuple identifier, a syntax-directed translation can be made.

Further research includes the performance effects of tuple identifiers on the database system.

6 Acknowledgements

The database group at the CWI in Amsterdam, especially Arno Siebes and Martin Kersten, are thanked for their suggestions to improve this article.

References

[Astrahan] M.M. Astrahan, M.W. Blasgen, D.D. Chamberlin, et al. (1976) System R: Relational Approach to Database Management. ACM Transactions on Database Systems 1(2), pp. 97-137.

[Ceri]   Stefano Ceri, and Georg Gottlob. Translating SQL Into Relational Algebra: Optimization, Semantics, and Equivalence of SQL Queries. IEEE Trans. on Softw. Eng., Vol. SE-11, No.4, April 1985. pp. 324-345.

[Date]   C.J. Date. An Introduction to Database Systems. Volume I. 3rd Edition. Addison-Wesley Publ. Company. 1981. Page 129.

[Date2]   C.J. Date. Be careful with the SQL EXISTS function! In *Informatie*, December 1989, pp. 977-979.

[Hall]   P.A.V. Hall. Optimization of a Single Relational Expression in a Relational Data Base System. IBM J. R. & D. 20, No. 3 (1976).

[Kersten]   M.L. Kersten, P.M.G. Apers, M.A.W. Houtsma, H.J.A. van Kuijk, and R.L.W. van de Weg. A Distributed, Main-Memory Database Machine. In Proc. of the 5th Int. Workshop on Database Machines, Karuizawa, Japan, Oct. 5-8, 1987; and in Database Machines and Knowledge Base Machines, M. Kitsuregawa, and H. Tanaka (eds.), Kluwer Academic Publishers, 1988, pp. 353-369.

[Kiessling] Werner Kiessling. On Semantic Reefs and Efficient Processing of Correlation Queries with Aggregates. Proceedings of VLDB 85, Stockholm. pp. 241-249.

[Kim]   Won Kim. On Optimizing an SQL-like Nested Query, ACM Transactions on Database Systems, Vol.7, No. 3, September 1982, pp. 443-469.

[Murali]   M. Muralikrishna. Optimization and Dataflow Algorithms for Nested Tree Queries. In Proc. 15th Int. Conf. on Very Large Data Bases, Amsterdam 1989, pp. 77-85.

[SQL]   SQL standard, according to documents "Final Draft ISO 9075-1987(F) Database Language SQL", and "SQL Addendum-1 Error Log and corrected version".

[SQL2]   "(ISO-ANSI working draft) Database Language SQL2 and SQL3", ANSI X3H2-89-110, February 1989.

[Ullman]   Jeffrey D. Ullman. Principles of Database and Knowledge-Base Systems, Vol. II: The New Technologies. Computer Science Press, 1989. pp. 633-733.

[Verbr1]   N.Th. Verbrugge. Translation of Nested SQL Queries into eXtended Relational Algebra. PRISMA document nr. 501, 1989.

[Wilschut] Annita Wilschut, Paul Grefen. PRISMA/DB1 XRA Definition. PRISMA document nr. 465. Sept. 1989.

The POOMA Architecture

M.C. Vlot[1]

Philips Research Laboratories
P.O.Box 80.000
5600 JA Eindhoven, The Netherlands

Abstract

This article contains an overview of the POOMA hardware architecture and its prototype implementation, as developed within the machine subproject of the PRISMA (PaRallel Inference and Storage MAchine) project. The prime objective of the POOMA (Parallel Object Oriented MAchine) architecture is to support high performance database applications. These applications are both data-intensive and processing-intensive. Optimal support is achieved by using a large main memory in order to make access to large amounts of data very fast, and by using parallelism in order to obtain the required processing capacity. The POOMA architecture is based on a network of computing 'nodes'; each node consisting of a Data Processor, a memory and a Communication Processor. This approach leads to a scalable multiprocessor with distributed memory, the network being the most novel part of the architecture. Secondary storage in the form of disks is intended only for archiving purposes. A 100-node prototype has been implemented and is currently in use for software implementation and experiments. The implementation of the system, the nodes, the network, Communication Processor and the software environment for using the machine are described in some detail. Some evaluation results and comparisons with other systems are presented, confirming the potential of the hardware architecture as such.

1 Introduction

The PRISMA project started in October 1986, and aims to exploit parallelism in databases in order to speed up such applications. The machine platform developed for this purpose offers a general purpose parallel object oriented programming model for implementation of the database, in the form of the programming language POOL-X (Parallel Object Oriented Language, eXtended). The machine subproject has developed a platform, which consists of three parts: the POOL-X compiler, the Operating System and the Machine Architecture. This paper discusses the machine architecture of the PRISMA hardware, called POOMA (Parallel Object Oriented MAchine), its prototype implementation and presents some evaluation results. The effort of defining and implementing the architecture has been shared with subproject A of ESPRIT 415: the Decentralized Object-Oriented Machine (DOOM).

The PRISMA machine subproject aims to deliver a parallel hardware platform, supported by an Operating System and a POOL-X compiler. The hardware architecture does not contain dedicated hardware support for these applications in particular, since the applications are considered far too irregular and too complex to be supported by hardware directly. Furthermore standard microprocessor technology would offer similar performance gains in matter of a few years. Other efforts

---

[1]The work of this author was conducted as part of the PRISMA project, supported by the Dutch "stimuleringsprojecten informaticaonderzoek" (SPIN).

of providing dedicated or specially tuned general purpose platforms for databases can be found in [DeWi79, Lela85].

The POOMA architecture aims at using current advances in microprocessor and main memory technology, and use cheap replication of these standard components to build a cost-effective and powerful general purpose parallel processing platform. Its large distributed main memory allows large data structures to be kept in main memory all time. Multiple general purpose processors allow fast manipulation of the data. Yet the platform will be usable as a general purpose parallel computer, so that it offers a complete solution in other application areas, which may or may not incorporate one of the specific PRISMA applications.

The POOMA architecture defines a loosely coupled parallel computer. It is comprised of many so called *nodes*. A node consists of a Data Processor (DP), a memory, a Communication Processor (CP) and I/O devices, most notably a disk for permanent storage of data. The Communication Processors transfer packets via serial point-to-point connections, thus forming a store and forward packet switching communication network that allows all nodes in a system to exchange messages. Both the architecture and its prototype implementation have been developed in close cooperation with the ESPRIT-415A DOOM project. See [Annot89b, Odijk87] for an overview of the DOOM project. Similar machine architectures are described in [Kung89, Seitz85, Arl88, Nug88, Dally89]. The programming language POOL-X [Amer89] allows the programmer to specify parallelism explicitly by specifying parallel running objects (generalized to processes) which communicate via messages. The POOL-X language model and the POOMA machine model correspond closely. Each node executes a number of objects. The objects communicate by messages that are sent over the network of Communication Processors in the form of packets. Mapping of a POOL program onto the architecture is the task of the compiler [Spek90] and the Operating System (OS) [Brand89, Huls90]. The Operating System directly supports processes and messages as required by POOL-X.

The POOMA architecture has been implemented in the form of a 100 node 'physical' prototype. The software, comprising the Operating System, and the applications [Kerst87, Apers88, Aalb89] written in POOL-X, have been implemented on this machine. Testing of software (especially the Operating System) also takes place on the machine. Special facilities have been added to the POOMA machine in order to make software development easier.

In Section 2 the POOMA architecture and its underlying principles are described. The next section (3) describes the prototype implementation of the architecture and the additional features that were added to make the prototype flexible. Some evaluation and comparison results are presented in Section 4. The last section (5) gives a perspective on the potential of the POOMA architecture.

2   The POOMA architecture

The backbone of the POOMA architecture consists of a loosely coupled network of computing nodes with distributed memory. Communication between the nodes is performed by means of a packet-switching point-to-point network. In that way, the available communication bandwidth is well scalable to several tens or even hundreds of nodes without requiring very high-bandwidth interconnection links.

In the following sections, various aspects of the POOMA hardware architecture are described. First, in Section 2.1 the node architecture is described, followed by Section 2.2 discussing the network topology. It was decided that not one network topology should be adopted; instead, the hardware support for communication is made flexible enough to handle many different topologies. This hardware support, the Communication Processor (CP), is the most innovative part of the POOMA architecture. Its principles of operation are presented in Section 2.3. Section 2.4 describes the fault handling strategy adopted in the PRISMA architecture, and the consequences of this strategy to the architecture. The memory architecture and the motivation for the presence of an MMU are discussed in Section 2.5. Some aspects of message handling and the overhead caused by it are described in Section 2.6. The I/O philosophy is addressed in Section 2.7.

2.1 Node Architecture

The structure of a POOMA node is depicted in Figure 1. It consists of a Data Processor (DP) with Memory Management Unit (MMU), a Communication Processor (CP), a memory subsystem and I/O interfaces.

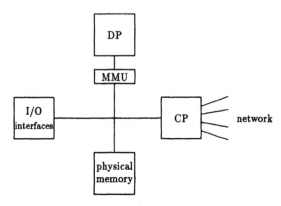

Figure 1: The structure of a POOMA node

The *Data Processor* (DP) executes the code of the objects residing on the node. Each POOMA node is able to execute several (presumably some 10 to 100) processes simultaneously. The processor architecture therefore supports multi-tasking. Efficient process switching is an important requirement, due to the relatively small grain size[2] of the processes. Close investigation of suitable DP architectures has not been an important issue in POOMA. It was felt that standard high performance microprocessors would offer suitable functionality and performance.

The *memory* is used to store the code and data of the Operating System and the code, stacks and message queues of the objects residing on the node. The memory and the function of the Memory Management Unit (MMU) are discused further in Section 2.5.

The *I/O interfaces* are not necessarily available on all nodes. I/O interfaces can be LAN-controllers, disk controllers etc. They are connected directly to the bus of the Data Processor.

The *Communication Processor* (CP) establishes the communication between the nodes. When a message is sent from a source DP to a destination DP on another node, the source DP divides the data into one or more fixed-size packets, and transfers each packet to the local CP. Each packet is forwarded via a path of CP-to-CP connections to the CP on the destination node, where it is transferred to the destination DP. The destination DP re-assembles the packets to obtain the original message. Using CPs avoids interrupting the DPs on intermediate nodes and hence provides a powerful and efficient communication mechanism for the DPs.

2.2 Network Topology

An important aspect of any distributed computer architecture is its communication support. Each POOMA node has only a few[3] direct neighbour nodes. The graph formed by nodes and the communication links between them is called the topology of the network. Compared to a shared memory architecture using busses or multi-stage networks, the POOMA network has longer communication

---

[2] Execution time between process switches
[3] In principle between 3 to 8, in the POOMA prototype: 4

delays; therefore, the grain size of the parallelism should be large enough such that it does not require very low latency communication facilities.

As the POOMA architecture is not dedicated to the execution of any specific algorithm, we must determine a topology suiting the general case in which communication patterns are of an irregular nature and may vary during program execution. Several selection criteria can be defined for networks, for example:

- The **diameter** d (maximum distance between any two nodes) of the network.

- The **regularity** of the network.

- The number of connections per node, called **degree** or δ.

- The **extensibility** of the network.

- The **average distance** d_{av} to be traveled by a packet.

- The number of different minimum length paths between any two nodes in the network (paths not sharing any edge).

- The tolerance of the network to defective nodes or connections.

If the (minimum) distance between two nodes u and v is defined as $d_{u,v}$, and the number of nodes defined as N, then the average distance d_{av} between two nodes is defined as:

$$d_{av} = \frac{\sum_{\text{all nodes } u} \sum_{\text{all nodes } v} d_{u,v}}{N^2}$$

Note that the path from a node to itself is also considered a proper path in the definition of d_{av}. In order to disregard this path use $\frac{N}{N-1} d_{av}$.

In this network study we use the terminology of graph theory: the POOMA nodes are considered as vertices, the communication links as edges of the network graph. In graph theory a graph is defined to be regular if all its vertices have the same degree. A stronger characteristic is *vertex-transitivity*, or *homogeneity*. Informally, a graph is homogeneous if, when inspecting the graph starting at some vertex, the result of the inspection is independent from the starting vertex. More formally, homogeneity means that for every pair of vertices u, v an adjacency-preserving permutation $P_{u,v}$ of vertices exists such that $P_{u,v}.u = v$. Homogeneity of a communication network implies that all nodes have the same "view" of the rest of the network, so that various distributed functions are identical at all nodes; moreover, there are no inherent congestion areas in the communication network.

To construct large graphs from small graphs several classical methods can be used, e.g. join, union, Cartesian product and composition [Har72]. Especially the Cartesian product has several nice properties: (1) the product of homogeneous graphs is again a homogeneous graph, and (2) given two graphs G_1 and G_2 with number of vertices, degree, average distance and diameter equal to $(N_1, \delta_1, d_{av1}, d_1)$ and $(N_2, \delta_2, d_{av2}, d_2)$ respectively, then the corresponding numbers for the product graph $G_1 \times G_2$ are equal to $(N_1.N_2, \delta_1 + \delta_2, d_{av1} + d_{av2}, d_1 + d_2)$. Examples of cartesian products are shown in Figure 2.

Note that for the average distance and diameter an upper bound for N can be found as a function of the (maximum) degree of a node and the diameter of the network, by regarding that each node can access all other nodes via an optimally balanced tree-subgraph of the topology. In case of a network with diameter d, with $d > 1$, the maximum number of nodes in such a network is $N_{max} \leq 1 + \delta + (\delta - 1)^{(d-1)}$; which is called the Moore-bound [Bigg74]. Similarly a lower bound for the average distance can be found. Only three such graphs with $d \geq 2$ and $\delta > 2$ exist, all with $d = 2$ and $\delta = 3, 7$ or 57, on $10, 50$ and 3250 nodes respectively. Since our target architecture has $\delta \leq 8$ and $N > 50$, and should feature scalability, using graphs with N equal to the Moore-bound

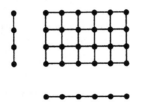
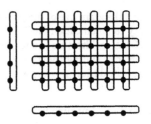
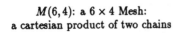

$M(6,4)$: a 6×4 Mesh:
a cartesian product of two chains

$T(6,4)$: a 6×4 Torus:
a cartesian product of two rings

Figure 2: Examples of chain, mesh, ring and torus topologies

only would be impractical. But many "suboptimal" alternatives remain.

Trivial examples of homogeneous graphs are the ring and the fully connected network (FCN). For a detailed study of elementary homogeneous graphs and their properties we refer to [Twist87b]. Here we confine ourselves to some 'practical' example graphs of vertices with degree 4 or less. The graphs are not necessarily homogeneous. We use $\oplus_k$ and $\ominus_k$ to denote modulo k addition and subtraction respectively.

Mesh: In a mesh the vertices are placed in a regular grid of dimensions n and m. It can be characterized as $M(n,m)$. The "outer" vertices have a degree of 3 (or 2 if they are at the corners of the graph). A mesh is a non-homogeneous, non-regular graph. It is the cartesian product of two chains of vertices. If the nodes of $M(n,m)$ are denoted as (i,j), with $0 \leq i < n$ and $0 \leq j < m$, then node (i,j) is connected to nodes $(i+1,j)$ if $i+1 < n$, $(i-1,j)$ if $i-1 \geq 0$, $(i,j+1)$ if $j+1 < m$, and $(i,j-1)$ if $j-1 \geq 0$. An example is sketched in Figure 2.

Torus: A torus can be described as a mesh in which the outer vertices are connected to the opposite outer vertices. This gives rise to rings in both horizontal and vertical directions. A torus is characterized by $T(n,m)$ where n and m again give the two dimensions of the grid. A torus is a homogeneous, regular graph. It is the cartesian product of two rings. If the nodes of $T(n,m)$ are denoted as (i,j), with $0 \leq i < n$ and $0 \leq j < m$, then node (i,j) is connected to nodes $(i \oplus_n 1, j)$, $(i \ominus_n 1, j)$, $(i, j \oplus_m 1)$, $(i, j \ominus_m 1)$. An example is sketched in Figure 2.

chordal ring $CR(8,3)$ chordal ring $CR(8,2)$ chordal ring $CR(12,3)$

Figure 3: Three chordal ring examples

Chordal ring: A chordal ring, characterized by $CR(N,c)$, consists of N vertices, connected in a ring. We identify the vertices by the numbers $0 \dots N-1$ such that two neighbour vertices on the ring have a number, differing by one. The remaining edges form connections between any two vertices that differ by the chordal distance c. A chordal ring is a regular, homogeneous

Type	nodes	Diameter	Av. dist.
M(3,3)	9	4	1.78
T(3,3)	9	2	1.33
CR(10,4)	10	2	1.40
ECR(10,1,0,0,0,1)	10	3	1.50
M(10,10)	100	18	6.60
T(10,10)	100	10	5.00
CR(100,18)	100	7	4.69
ECR(100,1,8,13,15,9)	100	5	3.29

Table 1: Some examples of practical graphs and their properties

graph. If the nodes of $CR(N,c)$ are denoted as (i), with $0 \leq i < N$, then node (i) is connected to nodes $(i \oplus_N 1)$, $(i \ominus_N 1)$, $(i \oplus_N c)$, and $(i \ominus_N c)$. Several examples are sketched in Figure 3.

Extended chordal ring: The concept of a chordal ring can be generalized to a ring with more than two chordal distances (The normal chordal ring $CR(N,c)$ is considered to have two chordal distances: 1 and c). For k chordal distances, nodes of degree $2k$ are needed. Such nodes can be implemented as a subnetwork, consisting of k nodes of degree 4 connected in a ring; this leaves 2 links per node, i.e. $2k$ links per ring, to be used for connections to other rings. We have chosen to fix k to 5. An extended chordal ring can be characterized by $ECR(N,c_0,c_1,c_2,c_3,c_4)$, where N is an integer multiple of 5. Its nodes are denoted by (i,j), with $0 \leq i < \frac{N}{5}$ and $0 \leq j < 5$. i is the number of the subnetwork to which (i,j) belongs, and j is its position in the subnetwork. Let the number of subnetworks $n = \frac{N}{5}$. Node (i,j) is connected to nodes $(i, j \oplus_5 1)$ and $(i, j \ominus_5 1)$ (connections to the direct neighbours of (i,j) in subnetwork i) and $(i \oplus_n c_j, j \oplus_5 2)$ and $(i \ominus_n c_{(j \ominus_5 2)}, j \ominus_5 2)$ (connections to other subnetworks).
The extended chordal ring is an interesting topology because its average internode distance (and diameter) is very small if the chordal distances are chosen properly.

The network types have different characteristics in, particularly, their diameter and average distance. Some typical values are listed in table 1 for small and large examples of each of the four networks. Note that the "Moore" lower bound for the average distance for any topology with 100 nodes of degree four is 3.24: so the average distance of the $ECR(100,1,8,13,15,9)$ is very close to this theoretical lower bound indeed.

2.3 The Communication Processor

The network of Communication Processors (CPs) in POOMA establishes a communication system via which every Data Processor can communicate with every other Data Processor. Communication is performed in terms of fixed size[4] packets of information. The network of CPs has to meet the following requirements [Annot87]:

- Absence of deadlock and starvation. Deadlock can be intuitively seen as a situation where progress is impossible and starvation as a situation where progress is possible but not guaranteed.

- Independence of network topology or network size.

- High data throughput.

- Efficient usage and administration of packet storage space.

---

[4]Prototype: 256 bits.

- Dynamic routing, i.e. packets can be forwarded to the same destination via different routes; the decision on which route a packet will follow must be postponed as long as possible.

- Independent operation. A Data Processor should not be involved in the forwarding of packets not yet arrived at their destination.

- Implementability in VLSI.

Basic operation

The task of the CP of a node is best described as that of routing packets through the network, without any involvement of the DP of the node. The connection to (or from) the DP of the node is in principle identical to a connection to (or from) a neighbouring CP.

The routing function in the CP uses a routing table which is down-loaded into the CP upon initialization of the POOMA architecture. Each packet contains a destination field. When a packet arrives in a CP, the routing table of the CP is indexed with the destination field of the packet to find the so-called routing vector for the packet. The routing vector is a vector of bits, one bit per CP-to-CP output of the CP, each bit indicating whether or not the packet may be forwarded via the corresponding output. If multiple bits are true, different paths are allowed. If all bits are false, the packet has reached its destination and it must be forwarded via the CP-to-DP output.

With each output of a CP, a queue of references to packets is associated. When a packet arrives in the CP, it is stored internally and its reference is added to the queues associated with the outputs indicated by the bits in the routing vector of the packet. When an output wants to transmit a packet, a reference is taken from the queue associated with that output, the reference is removed from all queues, the packet is read from where it was stored and the packet is transmitted.

The concepts of a routing table and multiple queues together allow the required independence of topology and size of the network and the required dynamic routing.

Deadlock freedom

To meet the negatively stated requirement of absence of deadlock and starvation, we first translated it into the positive requirement of guaranteed progress. We introduced a new strategy, called *class climbing*[5], to guarantee progress of all the packets in the network. To every packet a class is assigned and for every class an acyclic directed graph is superimposed on the physical network graph. After each step of a packet its class is updated; when the step was according to the direction of the acyclic directed graph associated with the packet's class, the class is unchanged. Otherwise it is incremented by at least 1. This way, a partial order is created of all the states in which a packet can be:

- A packet with class c is "farther" [6] than a packet with class less than c.

- A packet in CP P is "farther" than a packet of the *same* class c in CP Q if there is a directed path in the acyclic directed graph associated with class c from Q to P [7].

During its route through the network a packet should get "farther" on every transition from CP to neighbouring CP. To prove progress of all packets in the network, first progress is proved for the packets which are the "farthest" of all packets according to the above created partial order. This is proved using the assumptions that those packets must have arrived at their destination, and are removed from the network, without any precondition on the network state. Arrival at the destination is guaranteed if the diameter of the network is less or equal to the number of classes, since a packet only has to climb at most one class per hop.

---

[5]The term "class" in "class climbing" is not related to the concept of "classes" in the POOL family of languages.

[6] "Larger than" in the partial order sense.

[7]The transitive closure of the acyclic directed graph of a class directly represents the partial order relation between packets of the same class in different CPs.

Then progress is proved for an arbitrary packet, using as a presupposition that progress has been proved for all packets which are "farther" (than the arbitrary packet) according to the partial order. Finally, using induction, progress is concluded from the above two proofs. Of course, guaranteeing progress requires that packets are routed to their destination and that packets that have arrived at their destination are consumed by the DP.

Buffer store management

Another requirement found in a formal proof of deadlock freedom [Annot89a] is a restriction on the use of packet storage space. In order to guarantee progress for packets of class i or higher at least $c - i$ buffers for packets should be dedicated for storing packets of those classes (c being the number of classes).

The restrictions class-climbing puts on the use of storage space can be explained in an operational way. All available packet-buffers are given a 'guard' number, representing the minimum class of a packet that may reside in that buffer. So in a buffer with guard 3 only packets of class 3 or higher may be stored, and a packet of class 5 may only be stored in a buffer with guard number 5 or lower. For each class c larger than 0 (the lowest class) in the network there is (at least) one buffer in each CP having c as a guard number. For class 0 there may be more than one. So if there are 10 classes (0 to 9) and 25 buffers in a CP, the CP has 9 buffers with guard numbers 1..9 and 16 buffers with guard number 0. It is clear that a packet may only be accepted by a CP if it has a free buffer with a suitable guard number, or if it can reshuffle the packets in the buffers in such a way that such a 'suitable' free buffer becomes available.

Actual implementations do not have to reshuffle packets. They merely have to test if such a reshuffle is possible. This can be done efficiently by keeping track (for each class) of the number of packets of a particular class in the CP. Such an administration can be updated 'incrementally' on arrival and departure of a packet.

Flow control between CPs and the class climbing algorithm are combined. Packets are only forwarded between CPs *on-demand*, i.e. only when a *request* for a packet arrives, indicating the availability of a buffer at the receiving end, a packet may be forwarded. When a receiving CP sends out a request for a packet, it will mention the "guard number" of the buffer reserved for receiving a packet in the request. The sending CP will then have to send a packet with a class higher or equal then the guard number in the request. In case no such packet can be found a cancel-packet is sent indicating that the buffer can be used to store packets coming from other CPs.

Conclusion

The above described functionality of the CP was worked out to algorithms completely implementable in hardware, such that no involvement of the DP is needed for the execution of the algorithms, thus allowing a high data throughput. The bread-board implementation of the CP in the current POOMA prototype does not attempt to "reshuffle"; the VLSI implementation of the CP, which is currently underway shuffles "optimally". More information on networks, Communication Processors and deadlock freedom can be found in [Annot87, Annot89a, Dally86, Dally87, Gun81, Merl80a, Merl80b]

2.4   Fault Tolerance Strategy

The PRISMA machine contains many components. Hard and soft failures are likely to appear during the life-cycle of a single application (the PRISMA-DBMS has a long life time). This makes full restart of the application upon detection of a failure infeasible. Fully transparent fault tolerant computing is no trifle and this holds even more for distributed computing. Therefore we have decided to follow an application controlled approach to rollback. This means that the OS and the

POOMA hardware support mainly error-detection, e.g. detection of parity errors on memory and communication network. Upon detection of a (non correctable) error the PRISMA machine will automatically reconfigure (hardware plus software) and restart the DBMS which recovers itself with the help of the PRISMA-OS. To enable this, a facility for the DBMS to write essential data to stable storage is built into the standard units of POOL-X and implemented by the PRISMA I/O system. Summarizing, the fault-tolerance strategy consists of four elements:

- Error Detection

- Reconfiguration of the machine (isolating faulty parts).

- Restarting the application (DBMS) from stable storage.

- Updating stable storage by the application (DBMS) during operation.

Error Detection

Decisions concerning the error detection strategy for the POOMA architecture have been taken according to an analysis of the expected error rates of specific parts of the architecture. Table 2 below, derived from [Mull87] presents the estimates of the various parts in KFIT: 1 error in 10^6 hours of operation. The error rates of the communication-links of the CP are rather dependent on

Node component	1 node [KFIT]	100 nodes [KFIT]	MTBF [days]
RAM, soft-error, 128 1Mbit chips	500	50000	0.8
RAM, hard-error, 128 1Mbit chips	8	800	50
disk (50 disks only)	33	1650	25
Communication Processor	100	10000	4
links of Communication Processor	see text		
(VLSI) Data Processor	10	1000	40
random logic	10	1000	40
power supply	20	2000	20

Table 2: Estimates of hardware error rates

the electro-magnetic environment and the design of the link drivers.

From this table it is clear that error detection for RAM and the CP[8] is most helpful. The error detection for the network (both CPs and links) is provided in the Operating System by checksums and timeouts. The RAM memory can be checked using parity circuitry. Error correction on the memory may be used if one recovery approximately every day is not acceptable.

Reconfiguration

The reconfiguration algorithm allows the machine to isolate (partially) faulty nodes and links from the rest of the machine. Since links are the only physical connections between the nodes, propagation of electrical problems between nodes is small and confined. The lack of central resources in the machine suits the fault-tolerance approach ideally. Furthermore faulting peripheral devices like disks can easily be isolated from the system. The reconfiguration algorithm is complicated by the lack of a global synchronization mechanism. Due to some peculiarities in the link circuits of the CP it also relies quite heavily on time-outs.

---

[8]The figures in table 2 are derived for a breadboard implementation comprising over 150 standard integrated circuits. A VLSI version of the CP would be as reliable as the Data Processor.

Intermezzo: Reconfiguration algorithm details

This intermezzo has been derived from PRISMA project documents [Brand87] and [Vlot87].
Any node which detects an error will reset its CP first. Neighbouring nodes will detect loss of
communication with this node (by polling their neighbours regularly), and reset their CP as well.
After a limited amount of time[9] all nodes have put their CP in the reset state. In a similar fashion
all nodes put their CP in a halt state and subsequently go into *neighbour-to-neighbour mode*[10] to
find out to which functionally correct nodes they are directly connected. After discovery of the
faulting node or link the node or link is isolated from the rest of the machine by ignoring the
faulting link or all links to a faulting node. Then all CPs are reset again to remove superfluous
packets from the network and to disable irrelevant links (only possible at initialization time).

The locally gathered information of the new topology of the system is then propagated to every
node, which then computes a new routing table using a shortest path algorithm. The routing
tables are installed, communication is restored and normal communication can start.

Stable storage

Stable storage of data is implemented using replicated files stored on disks connected to different
nodes. Techniques as described in [Patt88, Reddy89] can also be used for the implementation of
stable storage. Essential is that failure of one node does not destroy all copies of one file. It is also
desirable that in case more than one node fails, the remaining nodes have a high probability of having
access to all files. Design aspects of the stable file system of POOMA are discussed in [Cheng90]
and [Huls90]. Since disk access will be necessary for every update action on the database update
intensive databases may benefit from using battery backed-up memory instead of disks as stable
storage medium.

Hardware consequences

The consequences for the POOMA architecture are:

- Error detection (or error correction) on main memory.

- Error checking of the communication network by the Operating System.

- Enough secondary storage support (disks) in order to allow for replication in the file system.

- A physical node number attached to each node, in order to allow nodes to identify themselves
  uniquely during reconfiguration.

- CPs be able to shut down (ignore) certain links.

- CPs be able to support various network topologies (subgraphs of the original topology).

2.5 Memory Management Aspects

POOMA is intended to be equipped with a large main memory. Since the memory is the most
expensive resource in the machine, management of memory is an important function of the system.
Managing the memory of the POOMA machine has several aspects:

---

[9]Limited by the diameter of the network times the maximum error detection time between neighbours.
[10]This mode allows a node to communicate with its neighbours only.

1. The memory of the system is distributed. This has been a starting point when the architecture was defined. It has several advantages, such as simple memory system design, fast access time for the local Data Processor, high memory bandwidth, and easy scalability. But proper allocation of objects to nodes is a considerable problem when an application is designed, and therefore the distributed character of the memory is the primary cause of inefficiency. In PRISMA the POOL programmer is responsible for proper allocation of the objects (data-items) in the system. In case of a very unbalanced allocation a program will abort quickly[11]. For a database application, which manages the resources of the machine explicitly anyway, such a policy was considered favourably over Operating System management of allocation.

2. In order to prevent that shortage of memory on one node leads to a system crash one has to have a *node-overflow* strategy. This problem is especially eminent since no paging strategy to secondary storage is used in the Operating System. This subject is discussed more extensively in 2.6.

3. POOL programs use many small memory blocks to store their data and administration. Occasionally large blocks are required. Within the memory of one node this leads to fragmentation.

4. POOL programs request and release memory blocks at very high rates. This requires an execution-time efficient implementation of the request and release algorithms.

The last two issues are further discussed below.

At the design time of the architecture it was uncertain what kind of demands the applications would pose on the memory management system, in terms of size and lifetime distribution of memory blocks. It was clear that providing dynamic 'segments' in virtual memory for the implementation of stacks, strings and dynamic arrays for instance, is desirable, but can not be supported efficiently in hardware for several reasons:

- The *address space* of 32-bit processors is (usually) limited to 2^{32} or less. Providing dynamic segments for most data-structures would lead to a shortage in address space, since for each segment the maximum size should be claimed in the virtual address space. All assuming that a segment is located in a fixed position in memory during its lifetime.
  Allowing segments to be moved in the virtual address space in order to provide for compaction in the virtual address space would mean an extra indirection in accessing a segment, and extra administration to be maintained. Most advantages of the initial dynamic segment scheme would be lost.

- The *size of the administration* of a page-oriented scheme that would efficiently implement a dynamic-segment scheme is very large in case the minimum block size (very small) is equal to a page, and a straightforward (multilevel) table-lookup is used to provide address translation. Only inverted lookup tables, that allow administration to be maintained for mapped pages only, can be used to implement such a page-oriented scheme efficiently. Such hardware was considered too exotic.

Therefore it was decided that a "fixed segment" scheme should form the basis of implementation. A fixed segment scheme is a simple heap: one can claim and release memory blocks of fixed sizes. It can be inefficient due to internal fragmentation (more memory is allocated than required), external fragmentation (free memory is available only as (very) small blocks) and administration overhead. Two schemes were considered:

1. A straightforward standard memory allocation technique is used, like first-fit, buddy algorithm, or quick-fit variants [Knu73, Stand80]. Different algorithms will trade between internal fragmentation, external fragmentation and execution speed.

---

[11]The PRISMA Operating System will signal memory overflow exceptions via a special object to the database system, allowing the database to change its allocation policy.

2. A (standard) MMU is used for mapping really large blocks onto pages (smaller blocks). For large blocks external fragmentation problems are most likely to occur. For smaller blocks one of the above stated algorithms is used. Using the MMU in such a way, and choosing the most appropriate page size is considered an experiment. The usefulness of the strategy will be rather dependent on the behaviour of the application and the implementation of POOL-X with respect to large blocks.

Note that, unlike more conventional systems, the MMU is not used to implement a paging strategy to background memory. It is only used to map available foreground memory into the address space at suitable points.

2.6 Message Handling support

Message handling has several aspects. Some of these have been the subject of studies to see if they can be supported in hardware efficiently. The following issues have to be dealt with when designing the message handling component for the POOMA architecture. They are mentioned in approximate order of functionality:

- Packet buffering for in and out going packets, for reducing the service frequency requirement of the CP by the DP.

- Flow control of packets between CP and DP.

- Computing and checking check sums, and adding and checking sequence numbers for error detection purposes.

- Packet (re)ordering.

- Packet level end-to-end flow control.

- Packetizing and reassembling.

- Message (re)ordering.

- End-to-end (message level) flow control.

- Complete handling of message-buffering at sending and receiving end. This should include a strategy dealing with the requirement that shortage of memory on one node does not lead to a halt of Operating System communication.

Several design studies have been directed towards message handling. The most important conclusions are mentioned below.

Node overflow handling consequences: low and high network

The consequence that memory on a node is limited, and that shortage of memory on one node should not lead to a breakdown of Operating System communication has had some influence on the design of the CP. The number of classes supported by the CP has been extended so that it is guaranteed that a message can be sent from any source to any destination, and a return message can be sent back again, provided that the original source wants to accept the returned message without precondition on the availability of memory. The latter is most often guaranteed by reserving memory for the result before sending the message.

The extended number of classes supported can be viewed as actually implementing two virtual networks: a *high network*, using packets with high class numbers, and a *low network*, using packets with low class numbers. Progress of the high network is guaranteed if all destinations remove the packets without precondition. Progress in the low network is guaranteed only if progress in the high network is guaranteed, and if all destinations guarantee consumption possibly with the precondition that as a result a message has to be sent through the high network. Note that a similar concept with two "virtual networks" is used in the J-Machine [Dally89].

Alternatively the Operating System can use a combination of preclaimed administration memory and a node-to-node flow-protocol in order to guarantee similar functionality. Such a protocol requires that every node keeps an administration record and reserves data space for receiving a message from every other node in the system. For a 100-node PRISMA configuration this is reasonable, provided the amount of memory per node remains limited. For machines with more than 1000 nodes such administration may become prohibitively large.

Dynamic vs. static routing

The CP allows packets to be forwarded via alternative routes, called dynamic routing, or via only one route, called static routing, depending on the initialization of the routing tables. There is a tradeoff between dynamic routing and static routing based on the following arguments:

- Dynamic routing allows lower latency and higher throughput communication. This is especially the case when multi-packet messages are sent between nodes (typical PRISMA DBMS behaviour), which tend to use the network rather 'uneven' if static routing is used. Dynamic routing will send packets of one message over alternative routes (if available), thereby using the resources of the network much more efficiently, and reducing the transfer time of a message significantly. Simulation studies [Essen87] showed these differences to be considerable. So at network level dynamic routing leads to higher performance.

- Static routing will guarantee order preservation of the packets sent from one node to another. Therefore checking for missing packets (sequence number check), reassembling a message from several packets, and keeping messages in order between nodes is significantly simplified. So at message handling level static routing leads to better performance.

Note that the topology can be optimized for either a dynamic routing strategy (more alternative paths) or a static routing strategy (low average distance). See Section 4.3 on this subject.

It was noted that a mixture of the two strategies is worthwhile considering. Small messages can be sent using static routing. This allows the overhead for most messages to be small. Furthermore small messages are not considered to be the bulk of the packet-traffic, and their destinations are likely to be distributed uniformly in the network. So their load is reasonably homogeneous and low. A special data transfer service is offered, which uses dynamic routing to allow for optimal use of the network for the bulk of all packets transferred. The inhomogeneous behaviour of this type of traffic is less of a problem in case dynamic routing is used. Such a mix of routing strategies may be implemented in the current routing table using two entries (destination numbers) per node: one for dynamic and one for static routing.

Minimal hardware support for message handling

In order for the DP to perform message handling with minimal hardware support, the required service frequency of the CP by the DP should be low enough thus causing not too much overhead on the DP, and still allowing high network throughput. The CP packet store is quite small for this purpose, and contention for it by communication links will slow down access to it by the DP. Therefore some form of dedicated input and output packet buffering is a minimal requirement for interfacing a CP to a DP. It can be implemented quite efficiently, using either dedicated FIFO buffers or DMA-based solutions.

Extended hardware support for message handling

Apart from shipping packets from source to destination node by CPs there is quite a lot of processing involved at both the sender and the receiver end of a message exchange. In order to reduce the costs of message transport, further hardware support for the various message handling functions mentioned above has been considered. Some of the thoughts and ideas on this subject can be found in PRISMA project document [Vlot89].

In order for a hardware solution to be effective, the algorithms to be executed by the hardware should be sufficiently simple since otherwise the implementation will be too expensive. Furthermore the interface to the Operating System should not be too complicated[12], since otherwise the overhead of communication between the OS and the message support hardware will offset the initial advantages of having message support hardware. For this reason only packet buffering and checksum handling have been considered appropriate for hardware support up to now. Decisions on further hardware support will require experimental justification for their cost/effectiveness first. See [Mull90] for a study on this subject.

2.7 I/O architecture

Every computer has to do I/O with the user, other computers or peripheral storage units in order to be useful. Here we confine ourselves to I/O interfaces to local area networks (LANs) and secondary storage. The approach chosen is thought to be general enough to handle almost all other types of interfaces in a similar fashion.

The approach in POOMA to I/O has been pragmatic. Considering the backbone of the architecture (nodes in a network) it is plain that I/O interfaces can in principle be added to every node. Another approach is to connect I/O interfaces directly to the CP, but this approach seems impracticable because most I/O interfaces need CPU attention at low latency. This can not be guaranteed by the network.

Once decided to connect I/O interfaces to the node-bus (or an extension of the node-bus), it remains to be decided whether to equip all nodes with I/O interfaces, to provide the possibility on every node to be extended with I/O interfaces or to equip only particular nodes with actual interfaces or provisions for them. Basically there is a cost/convenience tradeoff here. For cheap standard I/O interfaces provisions on every node seem reasonable (SCSI interface to disk or tape-unit, serial terminal connections, even Ethernet nowadays). For more expensive and special purpose interfaces a standard bus extension (VMEbus or Multibus) seems a better solution.

Note that the absence of a single bus in the system creates the possibility to develop systems with a very high aggregate I/O bandwidth. No special facilities like I/O-processors are required. It is reasonable that (some) DPs spend a part of their time servicing I/O interfaces. Every CPU can access all I/O interfaces of the system by message passing over the network. Since the network provides a very high bandwidth only its delay can be an obstacle. In case very low delay interaction with I/O interfaces is required, the part of the software involved is required to run on the DP controlling the I/O-interface. Such software can therefore not be distributed.

A notable disadvantage of a distributed architecture like POOMA occurs for applications which require very high bandwidth I/O over one channel, like video applications. The bandwidth of four to eight links may not be sufficient for such very I/O intensive applications.

3 Implementation of POOMA

3.1 Implementation overview

It was felt from the start of the PRISMA project that having an actual machine running realistic applications is a necessity to show the feasibility of the concepts underlying the project. Therefore a plan was made to arrive at a prototype with a decent performance, incorporating as many of the concepts devised as possible. In order to keep the building effort down, most of the hardware should be commercially available.

---

[12]Not require many interactions between the Operating System and the message support hardware.

Since it is not possible to commercially buy the CP it was decided that a bread-board version should be developed. Furthermore an effort is made to implement the CP in VLSI technology, since it is the most innovative part in the architecture. Development efforts for both CP implementations were mainly done in the DOOM project. An initial effort to implement the CP on Inmos Transputers showed such a poor performance that it was abandoned. A further study into the suitability of a Transputer as implementation platform for a Communication Processor [Roeb89] showed that reasonable performance can be obtained, if the routing and deadlock prevention algorithms are changed to suit the Transputer.

The Motorola MC68020 was selected to be the processor, since at the time it was the standard 32-bit micro-processor, and a very flexible MMU, the MC68851 was available. Furthermore it was clear that a flexible connection with the host computer was needed. Here Ethernet was adopted. It was decided to use a standard VMEbus backplane to interconnect the processor board, the bread-board Communication Processor and Ethernet board. Furthermore a disk was added to the node architecture: SCSI based disks were most convenient. So a rough outline of the node architecture emerges: a commercial processor board with the MC68020 and MC68851, a bread-board Communication Processor, a commercial Ethernet board interconnected via VMEbus, and a disk connected via a SCSI bus. Extra memory has been added to the VMEbus.

In the sequel of this section several important aspects of the implementation are described. In Section 3.2 the different prototypes are discussed briefly. The subsequent section (3.3) describes global construction of the 100-node POOMA prototype system. It is followed by a description of typical operation of the prototype (3.4). Section 3.5 contains the implementation details of the CP. Section 3.6 describes the network switch implementation and Section 3.7 mentions some of the software facilities that were implemented in order to make the system workable.

3.2 Prototypes series

Even though commercial boards were chosen it was decided that the implementation should be done in phases in order to reduce the risks involved. Three phases can be distinguished for the prototype machines:

Single node prototype :
This is a single processor machine. Its purpose is testing and evaluation of the commercial boards (and software). Furthermore the software environment necessary for using the prototype machines was developed using this machine. The system consists of:

- Processor board.
  The Philips PG2100 was selected.
- Ethernet controller board, including TCP-IP software.
  The CMC ENP-10[+] was adopted.
- Disk drive.
  The CDC WREN-III disk drive was selected.

MN1 prototype :
This machine is an 8 node prototype. It is a platform for the Operating System and the language implementors to develop their software. Furthermore the first real experience with the Communication Processor should be obtained with this prototype. Its node implementation is equal to the POOMA prototype described below.

POOMA prototype :
A 100-node machine; it is the platform for applications. A network switch that can manipulate the network topology has been added to this machine. The switch can split the machine into smaller parts so more than one user can use it at the same time, and can be used for experiments with topologies. The 4 Mbyte memory of the processor board has been extended

using 12 Mbyte of VMEbus based memory. Furthermore 50 disks have been connected to 50 nodes. The type of the disk was changed to CDC WREN-IV. The outline of the POOMA machine is sketched in Figure 4.

Furthermore two small 4-node prototypes were constructed for software development by project partners outside Philips Research Laboratories in Eindhoven.

The Communication Processor was also implemented in three phases, which correspond closely to the three prototype phases mentioned above:

Prototype CP :

A wire-wrapped version, basically used to test the functionality of the logic of the CP. It has been tested using a dedicated interface to a processor board, and not in the single node prototype mentioned above, since the latter was not available in time, and because the prototype CP has no VMEbus interface.

First series production CP :

The prototype CP was extended with VMEbus interface and some small items, like performance counters, and provisions for testability. This series was used in the 8-node MN-1machine.

Second series production CP :

This is the series used to populate the 100-node POOMA machine.

It was felt by all people that contributed to the implementation that completion of a phase gave confidence for success in the next phase of the implementation. Skipping a phase would not have been feasible nor "desirable".

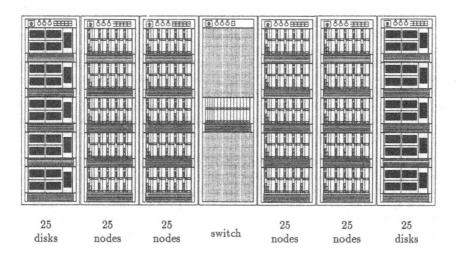

| 25 disks | 25 nodes | 25 nodes | switch | 25 nodes | 25 nodes | 25 disks |

Figure 4: Front view of the POOMA prototype

3.3 POOMA prototype construction

The POOMA prototype has been constructed in a very modular way using standard construction materials. The whole machine is housed in seven cabinets with castors. A sketch of the prototype machine is presented in Figure 4.

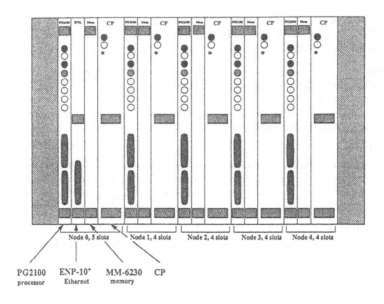

Figure 5: A crate with 5 prototype POOMA nodes

The hundred nodes are housed in four cabinets. One cabinet contains five identical units called *crates*. Each crate is a more or less self-contained unit containing five nodes. Each crate has its own power supply. The layout of a *crate* is sketched in Figure 5. Note that one crate houses five separate VMEbusses, one for each node. The VMSbus, a small serial bus, is crate-wide however. It is used in combination with Ethernet to make every node accessible from the host or user workstation, without using the communication network of POOMA (see Section 3.4). Each crate contains a reset-circuit that can be controlled by the host of the machine via an RS-232 connection. Furthermore there are two signaling lines called "Hold" and "Sync" which implement a global interrupt mechanism within one crate. The construction details of a node are sketched in Figure 6.

The fifty disks of the machine are occupying two cabinets at the outer sides of the machine. A disk cabinet itself contains five identical units, each unit containing five disks. Each disk has its own SCSI interface that is connected to the processor board of a node. The 50 disks are connected to the 50 outer-most nodes.

The four 'node-cabinets' are grouped around the central *switch* cabinet. The links of all CPs are connected to the switch. The switch implements a remote controlled partial crossbar. It dynamically connects input and output links of CPs. The switch also connects the global interrupt signaling lines of crates dynamically, so that sub-machines can be equipped with their own independent global interrupt mechanism. Note that the switch is not a conceptual part of the machine architecture. It is only used to allow the prototype to be used by several users concurrently and to facilitate experiments with the topology.

Each cabinets has its own 380/220V power connection. The cable connections between the various cabinets can be connected and disconnected very easily. The physical interface of the machine to the outside world is via one Ethernet cable (for all I/O) and one RS-232 cable (for remote resetting). The whole machine is protected against overheating. A crate that is overheated is switched off automatically. Due to the modular structure and the use of standard construction materials POOMA is easy to move (break-down and build-up), easy to repair, and easy to maintain.

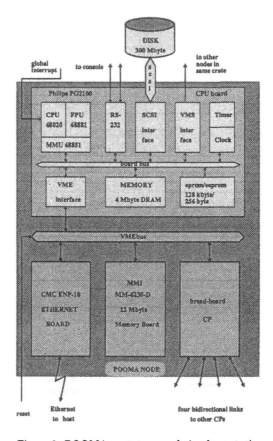

Figure 6: POOMA prototype node implementation

3.4 An example session on the POOMA prototype

During a user session the machine will operate in one of three modes: download mode, execution mode and monitor mode. These are discussed below.

Download mode

A user that wants to run a program specifies the desired sub-machine configuration: the number of nodes, the desired network topology, the number of disks, and monitor-mode requirements. This specification is put as a request to the server-process running on the host of the POOMA machine. The server will allocate a number of crates to the user. The nodes in these crates will be reset by the reset circuits of the crates involved, which are controlled over an RS-232 connection by the server. Furthermore the network and the global interrupt are set up by the switch on command of the server.

The server responds to the user with the network addresses of the Ethernet-nodes in the crates. The user then downloads code on every node of the system using Ethernet and the VMSbus. After the code has been downloaded, the user sends a start-execution command to the nodes over Ethernet and VMSbus. The communication lines involved are illustrated in Figure 7.

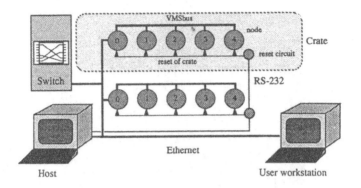

Figure 7: POOMA prototype configuration during download mode

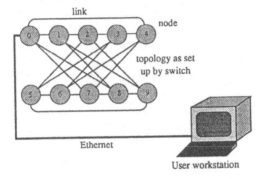

Figure 8: POOMA prototype configuration during execution mode

Execution mode

In execution mode the program sends messages over the network of CPs. Furthermore it communicates with the user over Ethernet. This is illustrated in Figure 8. The nodes have been given consecutive numbers by the network boot program: an implementation of the reconfiguration-algorithm as described in 2.4. Note that some Ethernet nodes may not be used for communication between POOMA and the user, since they are to be used during monitor mode.

Monitor mode

During execution one node can interrupt all nodes in the system, using the global interrupt mechanism set up by the switch during download mode. All nodes will receive a high level interrupt, halt normal execution and turn their CPs into a halt state, thereby freezing the network state completely. The user can inspect the state of the machine, using Ethernet connections to nodes that do not use their Ethernet during normal execution, the VMSbus in each crate and a dedicated RS-232 link to a crate which uses its Ethernet node during execution mode. In order to guarantee that each node can be reached, crates are allocated in pairs if monitor mode is required by the user: each pair of crates has a dedicated RS-232 connection between the nodes on position zero in those crates.

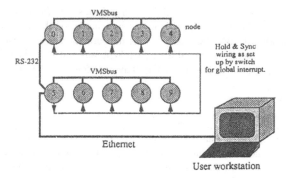

Figure 9: POOMA prototype configuration during monitor mode

If the user has finished he can restart normal execution mode. The global interrupt mechanism is used for restarting all nodes of the sub-machine very precisely. The important communication lines during monitor mode are illustrated in Figure 9. Note that neither the monitor mode nor the global interrupt are part of the architecture. They have been added to the prototype to facilitate experiments.

3.5 Bread-board Communication Processor implementation

In this section the implementation of the bread-board CP is discussed. A complete users manual of the CP can be found in [Twist87a].

The CP consists of two 'extended double eurocard' bread-boards. The two boards are interconnected via two large connectors. Both boards are packed with standard components. One bread-board CP occupies two 'slots' of 21 available in a standard 19 inch rack.

Each CP has four serial *packet-input* machines, four serial *packet-output* machines, one parallel *packet-input* machine and one parallel *packet-output* machine. The latter are used for connection to the DP. The serial links are implemented using Inmos C001 link adapters. These are able to transfer data at an effecive rate of 3 Mbit/s running at 10 MHz, and at 5.5 Mbit/s running at 20 MHz. Since the packet size is 256 bits the link transfer time of a packet is 85 μs at 10 MHz and 45 μs at 20 MHz. The link speed has been set to 10 Mhz, which is enough for all current applications presently running.

The DP-CP link, via the VMEbus interface of the CP is decoupled via FIFOs. The FIFOs increase the minimum service time of the CP by offering an extension of internal packet buffer of the CP for the input and output links. Note that refusal of one DP to remove arrived packets from the network can in principle block the whole network. There are two FIFOs for sending packets and two FIFOs for receiving packets: one called *low* and one called *high* in each direction. Each FIFO can contain 64 packets. The two separate FIFOs are necessary to guarantee deadlock-free execution of, for instance, remote procedure calls, as mentioned in Section 2.6.

The central packet store can contain 255 packets, of which 240 are available for buffering packets with class 0, since there are 16 classes. The number of buffers can be reduced under software control in order to do experiments with CPs having less than 255 buffers. Another feature under software control is a limit counter for the number of packets arrived over the DP-link. The parallel link can transfer packets at a much higher rate than the serial link. So if a DP puts a 'burst' of packets in the FIFOs of the CP, the CP soon runs out of buffers. This inhibits the rest of the traffic through this CP. By limiting the number of buffers occupied by packets that arrived over the parallel (DP to CP) link, this 'congestion' phenomenon can be avoided.

In order to measure the traffic on each link, each link has a *traffic-counter* associated with it. Another feature is the facility to put the CP in the halt mode. If this is done globally the whole network can be frozen almost instantaneously[13]. The network state can be inspected and the traffic-counters can be read and reset. Additional data-path logic was added to the CP in order to improve the observability of the internal state of the CP. This was found to be necessary in order to test production CPs decently.

3.6   The network switch

The switch, situated in the center cabinet shown in Figure 4, makes it possible to divide the machine into several smaller 'submachines', which operate completely independent from one another. A user can request the system for a new submachine and specifically state the number of crates to be used and the type of network that the submachine will have.

The main task of the switch is therefore to dynamically rearrange the connections between the Communication Processors in such a way that the new submachine is created while existing submachines are not disturbed in any way. The obvious solution is to compose the switch from one crossbar switch for each type of signal in the Communication Processor links. In order to achieve a manageable solution (especially in terms of the physical size), some restrictions have been imposed on the functionality of the switch, which can be summarized as follows.

The CPs are divided into five different types, A, B, C, D and E, depending on the position in their crate[14]. The four links on each CP are marked as link0, link1, link2 and link3. The switch only allows two kinds of connections between different CPs: either between link0 and link1 or between link2 and link3. The first kind is restricted to the following CP combinations: A↔B, B↔C, C↔D, D↔E, E↔A, whereas the second kind is restricted to: A↔C, B↔D, C↔E, D↔A, E↔B. Since in each one of the ten connection kinds four different signals are involved (for each direction a packet signal and a request signal), ten groups of four 20×20 crossbar switches are needed. Each group of four 20×20 switches has been implemented on one board.

Beside the Communication Processor signals two other signals have to be switched in order to properly construct separate submachines. Each submachine has its own pair of so-called *hold* and *sync* lines, which are used for global interrupts in a submachine. Two switches are used to setup the connections for these lines between the crates forming a sub-machine. These two switches are mounted on an additional board. All eleven boards are placed in another crate together with a dedicated Processor board and Ethernet controller board. In this way submachine installation requests from the host are received in the Processor, where they are converted into appropriate switch configuration commands to be sent to the switches. Like in the rest of POOMA, the VMEbus is used as backplane communication means. The switch boards are controlled by Inmos serial links. A conversion between VMEbus signals and Inmos signals is performed on the Hold/Synch switch board.

All standard topologies mentioned in Section 2.2 are offered, but some restrictions are posed on the parameters of these networks:

Meshes $M(m,n)$: $m \times n \leq 100$, since only 100 nodes are available. No further restrictions hold.

Torusses $T(m,n)$: both m and n should be integer multiples of 5, and $m \times n < 100$. This leaves: $M(5,5)$, $M(5,10)^{15}$, $M(5,20)$ and $M(10,10)$.

Chordal rings $CR(n,c)$: n a multiple of 5, $c \bmod 5 \in \{2,3\}$ and $n < 100$.

Extended chordal rings : the restrictions are mentioned in 2.2.

The implementation of the switch is described extensively in [Essen88].

---

[13]Using the global interrupt facility.

[14]Actually node 0 maps to A, 1 to B etc.

[15]$M(5,10)$ and $M(10,5)$ are 'isomorphic' graphs.

3.7 Software facilities

Although the architecture effort is mainly directed at development of hardware (concepts), software development has played an important role in the architecture team during the project. Test software has to be generated, and code has to be loaded on the processor board. Therefore the architecture team has developed the following software facilities:

Boot code : Code to allow the processor board to receive code over Ethernet or the VMSbus (and therefore contains the 'drivers' for these two networks). This code has been put in EPROM. It also contains a small monitor for very low level debugging, for handling crashes during the boot process, and for installingnode specific boot parameters like Internet address and node-id.

POOMA-server : The access management system that grants access of users to the machine. It is a *server* process that runs on the host of the machine. Users can request (over Ethernet) parts of the machine. Requests may be queued if they contend for the resources of the machine. The server resets processor boards, sets up the network and global interrupt switch, and allows the user to download code on the sub-machine allocated for him. When the program terminates the user will indicate this to the server, which can then reallocate that part of the machine. There is a library of functions that gives access to the server. It is used by the Operating System for the construction of their download facilities.

Ethernet driver : The device driver necessary for operating the Ethernet board was partially adapted from the sources delivered by the manufacturer of the board in order to fit the Operating System.

Disk driver : The device driver necessary for operating the disk in a reliable way.

Other device drivers : Small device drivers for the VMSbus and RS232 interfaces.

Reconfiguration algorithm : A "configuration" program for a network of nodes (see 2.4). The topology is 'explored', the routing tables of the CPs are set according to the shortest paths in the network discovered and the nodes are numbered consecutively, starting with 0.

Test program : A program that tests all hardware of the machine. Such a program is very useful. Unfortunately good test programs are hard to make: one has to make sure all components are tested as well as possible. The current POOMA test program has almost succeeded in that.

All higher layer software is part of the Operating System, or generated by the POOL-X compiler..

4 Some evaluation results

Doing an evaluation of a machine architecture is not a simple task. Several general criteria can be used to characterize an architecture or a specific implementation, and allow it to be compared to others:

- Functionality (largest program, size of secondary store, I/O facilities, fault-tolerance, expandability, programmability).

- Performance (very much application and implementation dependent).

- Economic lifetime: can cost-effective implementations be made now and in the future?

In this section an attempt will be made to give a partial answer to some of these questions. In spite of all the figures presented in this section, the most important question will not be answered: is the POOMA architecture offer a high performance for database applications, and is it cost effective in doing so.

Some simple qualitative assessments that can be made are:

- The architecture is easily expandable due to the decentralized network architecture.
- A low cost fault tolerance approach is possible due to decentralized network architecture.
- A high total performance can be obtained.
- The archiotecture can easily be programmed.
- The cost effectiveness of implementations seems quite good at present.
- A machine can be scaled up quite easily with respect to processing power, memory and network bandwidth, simply by adding nodes.
- The distributed processing power is difficult to use.
- Distributed memory is difficult to manage.

4.1 Some typical POOMA prototype performance figures

Table 3 below presents a summary of the most characteristic raw performance figures of the POOMA prototype. Compared to sequential machines these figures present an upper limit of the performance, since they do not account for inefficiency due to the parallel and loosely coupled nature of the machine architecture. The MIPS rating of the CPU has been measured using the memory of the processor board only. In case off-board VME extension memory is also used, this figure will drop to 1.3 MIPS/processor.

property	node	POOMA
Integer performance (68020/16MHz)	2 MIPS	200 MIPS
Floating Point performance (68881/16MHz)	0.1 MfLOPS	10 MFLOPS
Main memory	16 Mbyte	1.6 Gbyte
Communication network (20 Mbit/s)	3.2 Mbyte/s	320 Mbyte/s
Disk bandwidth (8 bit SCSI)	1 Mbyte/s	50 Mbyte/s (50 nodes)
Disk capacity	300 Mbyte	15 Gbyte (50 nodes)
Gateway (Ethernet 10 Mbit/s)	-	0.625 Mbyte/s
I/O (VMEbus)	8 Mbyte/s	800 Mbyte/s

Table 3: Some characteristic performance figures of POOMA

4.2 Integer performance comparison

A fair and simple way to compare the integer performance figures of one node of POOMA with the performance of other sequential computers is by means of the standard Dhrystone benchmark. This is a benchmark program that is reasonably characteristic for the integer performance of a processor. Table 4 gives the Dhrystone figures for some commercial available computers. The Philips PG2100 is used in the nodes of POOMA. The hardware of this board is comparable with the hardware of a Sun 3/50. The reason why the PG2100 runs the Dhrystone benchmark 1.5 times faster than a Sun 3/50 is due to the better memory system of the PG2100. The same compiler is used for the Suns and the PG2100. One processor of a large IBM 3090 mainframe runs roughly ten times faster than a PG2100.

The performance figures of POOMA in Table 3 and 4 are based on single processor performance. A more suitable integer performance benchmark has been devised: a factorial program. It computes the factorial of a very large number in full integer precision. Table 5 contains the performance

system	Dhrystones/s
PG2100 (68020/16.67MHz, Sun C compiler 3.4)	3649
Sun 3/50 (68020/15MHz, SunOS 3.4, Sun C compiler)	2581
Sun 3/280 (68020/25MHz, SunOS 3.4, Sun C compiler)	6374
Transputer (T414/20MHz, Penquin 0.9, Stack in ext. memory)	2171
Transputer (T414/20MHz, Penquin 0.9, Stack in int. memory)	3317
VAX 8820 (VMS C Compiler)	10416
IBM 3090/200 (Amdahl UTS C compiler 1.22)	31250

Table 4: Dhrystone figures of some well known computer systems

results of executing a parallel version of the factorial problem on POOMA for increasing number of nodes. The parallel program is written in "C" and uses the communication facilities of POOMA without involvement of an operating system. The implementation can compute factorial 0 up to 400,000 maintaining full precision of the result (roughly 2 million digits for factorial 400,000). As a reference for speed-up calculations a sequential version of the factorial problem, with the same precision requirement, is executed on one node of POOMA.

number of nodes	execution time (sec.)	speed up
1 (seq. impl)	816.2	1.0
2	620.6	1.3
5	249.0	3.2
10	124.2	6.5
25	49.6	16.4
50	25.0	32.6
75	16.4	49.7
100	12.7	64.3

Table 5: Execution time and speed up for factorial 10,000 on POOMA

Factorial 10,000 performs 1.3 times faster on a two node system than on a one node system. A linear speed-up from 1 to 2 nodes can not be obtained, because the parallel version of the factorial problem can not be implemented as efficient as the sequential version. Some extra administration must be maintained and a lot of communication and synchronization is involved. Although the required communication bandwidth increases linearly with the number of nodes that are involved in the parallel execution of the factorial the resulting speed-up from 2 up to 100 nodes is still fully linear. This is mainly due to the nice scalability properties of the communication network.

Parallelism is obtained by pipelining. The intermediate result, of the factorial to be computed, is split in a dynamicly growing number of portions of 16 bits. These portions are distributed, as a chain, over the nodes. Each portion executes the following loop: receive packet with carries from previous portion, compute new value of this portion (using the correct multiplier) and the values of the new carries, put these carries in a packet and send them to the next portion. The first portion does not receive carries. It simply takes the value zero instead. The last portion in the chain has to create a new portion if it produces carries unequal to zero. The number of portions is much larger than the number of nodes. Factorial 10,000 creates roughly 9,000 portions. On each node a special scheduler, which is driven by the receipt of packets, takes care of the invocation of the correct portion. An invoked portion executes its loop once and returns control.

The time it takes to execute the loop once can be seen as the grain size of this program. The grain size has been chosen such that the data space of a packet is efficiently utilized. This is the case if one combines five carries in one packet. So during the first step of the loop five carries are received. In the second step the new value of the portion is computed in five sub-steps using the correct multiplier (multiplier is initialized with value 1 when the portion is created and incremented by one after each sub-step) and the corresponding received carry. During the third step the five carries that are produced during each sub-step of step 2 are stored in a packet and sent to the next portion.

The grain size of the parallel factorial is 125 μs. During each 125 μs a packet is received and sent which costs roughly 20 μs. The amount of packets that are received and sent by each node is 8,000 per second. The total amount of communication bandwidth required for executing factorial on 100 nodes is 800,000 packets per second which is equal to 25.6 Mbyte/s

Table 6 presents the execution of the sequential version of the factorial problem on some commercially available computers. The POOMA machine performs 5.4 times faster than the IBM 3090 (one processor).

system	execution time (sec.)
PG2100 (SUN C compiler)	816
Sun 3/50 (SUN C compiler)	970
Sun 3/280 (SUN C compiler)	580
VAX 8820 (VMS)	286
IBM 3090 (UTS compiler)	69

Table 6: Execution time of factorial 10,000 on some commercial computer systems

4.3   Network and Communication Processor Performance

An important aspect of the POOMA architecture is the performance of the communication network, and if it matches the demand for communication well in typical applications. The first aspect, a characterization of the network performance, has been undertaken. Extensive results are published in [Twist90]. The most characteristic results are repeated here.

The performance of the network can be characterized by the delay as a function of the throughput, given some additional characterization of the traffic. We have measured the delay caused by traffic of messages sent from every source to every destination, at random, with every source/destination pair having equal probability: so called homogeneous traffic. The total throughput and the message length distribution have been varied. The following two message length distributions have been considered:

Type A 100 % of the messages consist of 1 packet.

Type B 50 % of the messages consists of 1 packet
    30 % of the messages consists of 4 packets
    15 % of the messages consists of 8 packets
    3 % of the messages consists of 32 packets
    2 % of the messages consists of 64 packets
    This is considered a typical load for the network.

Furthermore both static and dynamic routing have been considered, and two topologies: a 10 × 10 Torus, and an Extended Chordal Ring ECR(100,1,18,13,15,9) on 100 nodes. These two are extremes with respect to the tradeoff between average distance and alternative paths. See table 1. The average

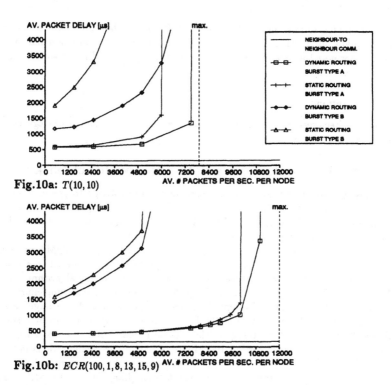

Fig.10a: $T(10,10)$

Fig.10b: $ECR(100,1,8,13,15,9)$

Figure 10: Average packet delay as a function of network throughput

number of alternative links per destination in case of $T(10,10)$ is 2.02, for the $ECR(100,1,8,13,15,9)$ this is 1.24. Figures 10a and 10b show the results. The "max" asymptotes are computed from the total link bandwidth divided by the average distance, which is a good measure in case the network topology is "edge-symmetric": the edges can not be distinguished, and thus carry equal load. The Torus is edge-symmetric, the ECR not, but link traffic is almost homogeneous.

The following important conclusions can be reached from the result:

- In case of dynamic routing a Torus can surpass an ECR for typical (Type-B) traffic.

- For static routing the ECR is superiour.

- The message length distribution has a considerable influence on the average delay and maximum throughput, especially in case of static routing.

4.4 Specific aspects

Fault tolerance

The POOMA prototype is operational since May 1989, and has proven to be very reliable. No exact records have been kept of failures and repairs, but the bread-board Communication Processor is the largest cause of failures, followed by disks and processor boards. Parity errors seems to occur much less, but one has to remember that these are soft-errors. They only occur when the prototype machine is actually used, which is a fraction of the time a real production machine is running programs. Furthermore the disk driver should be enhanced with handling of soft-errors on the disk, which occur quite regularly.

Memory management

No conclusion has been reached yet on the effectiveness of the page-mapping strategy, as implemented in the POOMA Operating System.

4.5 Sorting large data files: a data-intensive benchmark

Most programs that could be used as benchmarks for the POOMA prototype have been written in POOL. Due to the still quite moderate performance of the POOL compiler, it would be unfair to use POOL programs as typical loads for the POOMA machine. Almost all would show that processor performance is the bottleneck of the current prototype system.

A real database machine benchmark has been implemented on the POOMA machine: a sorter program for large data files. This benchmark, due to [Anon85] is considered to give a reasonable performance characterization for database like applications. The sorting algorithm implemented on POOMA is described in [Baug90] based on [Baug89]. The sorter has been implemented in "C", on top of the kernel of the Operating System. The benchmark specifies that a large data file, stored on secondary storage, containing tuples of 100 bytes, has to be sorted on a 10 byte key. The result file should be stored on secondary storage (disks). Table 7 shows results of the benchmark for some experimental database machines, sorting 100 Mbyte of data. The configurations indicate the processing capacity, the total disk bandwidth and the aggregate end-to-end communication bandwidth. The figures for ARBRE stem from [Lorie89], HC-16 from [Baug89] and JASMIN from [Beck88]. The results show that the POOMA prototype even in a 45-node configuration outperforms other experimental database platforms easily.

machine	configuration	time	sorting speed
POOMA	processors: 45× 2.0 MIPS disks: 45×1 Mbyte/s communication: 14 Mbyte/s	40 sec.	2500 kbyte/s
ARBRE	processors: 6× 3.5 MIPS disks: 3 communication: ?	104 sec.	960 kbyte/s
HC16-186	processors: 16× 0.9 MIPS disks: 16×0.8Mbyte/s communication: 40 Mbyte/s	180 sec.	550 kbyte/s
JASMIN	processors: 5×0.6 MIPS disks: multiple communication: 10 Mbyte/s	1066 sec.	47 kbyte/s

Table 7: Sorting performance of some machines

The average network bandwidth used by the sorter has been computed (almost equal to the sorting speed) to be 2.5 Mbyte/s. The maximum bandwidth offered by the network on 45 nodes is 14 Mbyte/s. The maximum bandwidth to the disks is 45 Mbyte/s, of which approximately 10 Mbyte/s is actually used. So the bottleneck in this application seems to be the processing power[16].

---

[16]Main memory size is of minor importance in this benchmark

Keeping in mind the fact that peak-loads on the network during sorting are higher, we may conclude that for this application the network of the machine seems to match the processing capacity reasonably well. Disk bandwidth seems to be adequate as well, but no file replication was used in this benchmark (reducing effective disk bandwidth by a factor of 2). POOMA performance could be enhanced by approximately 20 % if a DMA is used for disk data transfer. For further information on the sorting performance of POOMA the reader is referred to [Baug90].

Note that POOMA was designed to be a main memory database machine. In case the data should have been located in main-memory in stead of on disks, a higher performance could surely been achieved, but communication bandwidth may become a bottleneck then.

5 Concluding remarks

Currently the POOMA prototype has been operational for over one and a half year now. Apart from some small 'freak' errors, it works perfectly. The machine is used quite heavily by software developers and evaluators.

One can state that the implementation of the architecture is quite straightforward because most of the functionality required by the architecture can be implemented using standard board technology. The architecture is well suited however to be implemented in VLSI technology because implementation basically comes down to a reproduction of one standard component: a node. Especially for the Communication Processor implementation in VLSI technology is worthwhile, because of the high number of standard components required for it in board technology. A VLSI implementation of the Communication Processor currently underway offers a 6 times improvement over the current bread-board version of the prototype.

The absolute performance of the prototype system is still very good, although the Data Processor is now outdated compared to the latest RISC processors. The latest RISC processors offer a CPU performance which is less than an order of magnitude smaller than a mainframe. There seems enough technological "room" for a continuing increase in performance of microprocessors. Therefore there is a very promising growth path with technology for the POOMA architecture. An important advantage of this architecture over single processor architectures is that performance ranges of computers can be offered, using the same cheap basic technology. Unfortunately there are no concrete experimental results yet that prove that the raw power of the architecture can be exploited efficiently for database applications.

Acknowledgements

This article is an overview of work carried out in two projects: DOOM and PRISMA. The author wishes to thank all project members, especially the members of the architecture subgroups: J.K. Annot, H.A.v. Essen, G.W.T.v.d. Heyden, H. Muller and R.A.H.v. Twist. Furthermore the author would like mention B.A.W. Baugstø and J.F. Greipsland for porting the sorting benchmark (Section 4.5) on the POOMA machine.

References

[NOTE:]   The ESPRIT project 415, PRISMA and POOMA documents can be obtained from:
           F. Stoots
           Philips Research Laboratories
           P.O. Box 80000
           5600 JA Eindhoven
           The Netherlands

[Aalb89]   IJ.J. Aalbersberg, *A Parallel Full-Text Document Retrieval System*, Workshop on Object-Oriented Document Manipulation, Rennes, France, pp. 268-279, May 1989.

[Amer89]   P. America, *Language Definition of POOL-X.*, PRISMA Doc. 350, Philips Research Laboratories, Eindhoven, the Netherlands, Nov. 1989.

[Annot87]   J.K. Annot and R.A.H. van Twist, *Deadlock Freedom in Packet Switching Networks*, Proc. PARLE, Lecture Notes in Computer Science 258, pp.68-85. Springer, Berlin, 1987.

[Annot89a] J.K. Annot, *A deadlock free and starvation free network of packet switching communication processors*, Parallel Computing, Vol. 9, pp.147-162, North Holland, 1989.

[Annot89b] J.K. Annot and P.A.M. den Haan, *POOL and DOOM, the Object-Oriented Approach*, in: P.C. Treleaven (ed.), *PARALLEL COMPUTERS: Object-Oriented, Functional and Logic*. Wiley, pp.47-79, 1989.

[Anon85]   Anon.et al., *A Measure of Transaction Processing Power*, Datamation, April 1985.

[Apers88]   P.M.G. Apers, M.L. Kersten, and A.C.M. Oerlemans, *PRISMA Database Machine: A Distributed, Main-Memory Approach*, Proc. Int. Conf. on Extending Database Technology; Venice, 1988.

[Arl88]   R. Arlauskas, *iPSC/2 System: A Second Generation Hypercube*, Proc. of the Third Conf. on Hypercube Concurrent Computers and Applications, pp.33-36, 1988.

[Baug89]   B.A.W. Baugstø and J.F. Greipsland, *Parallel Sorting Methods for Large Data Volumes on a Hupercube Database Computer*, Proc. os the 6'th Int. Workshop on Database Machines, Deauville, France, 1989.

[Baug90]   B.A.W. Baugstø, J.F. Greipsland and J. Kamerbeek, *Sorting Large Data Files on POOMA*, To appear in: Proc. Joint Conf. on Vector and Parallel Processing, Zürich, Sept. 1990.

[Beck88]   M. Beck, D. Bitton and W.K. Wilkinson, *Sorting Large Data Files on a Backend Multiprocessor*, IEEE Trans.on Computers, vol.37, no.3, pp.769-778, 1988.

[Bigg74]   N. Biggs, *Algebraic Graph Theory*, Cambridge University Press, 1974.

[Brand87]   E. Brandsma, *A distributed algorithm for network recovery*, PRISMA Doc. No. 120, Philips Research Laboratories Eindhoven, Nov. 1987.

[Brand89]   E. Brandsma, Sun Chengzheng, B.J.A. Hulshof, L.O. Hertzberger, A.C.M. Oerlemans, *Overview of the PRISMA Operating System*, Proc. Int. Conf. on New Generation Computer Systems, pp.369-379., 1989.

[Cheng90]   S.Chengzheng, *Stable Storage in a Parallel Environment*, Proc. of the PRISMA Workshop on Parallel Database Systems, Noordwijk, the Netherlands, September 24-26, 1990.

[Dally86]   W.J. Dally and C.L. Seitz, *The Torus Routing Chip*, Distributed Computing, Vol. 1, No.4, pp. 187-196, 1986.

[Dally87]   W.J. Dally, *A VLSI Architecture for Concurrent Data Structures*, Kluwer Academic Publishers, Boston, 1987.

[Dally89]   W.J. Dally, A. Chien, S. Fiske, W. Horwat, J. Keen, M. Larivee, R. Lethin, P. Nuth, S. Wills, P. Carrick, and G. Fyler, *The J-machine: A Fine-Grain Concurrent Computer*, Information Processing 89 (IFIP 1989), pp.1147-1153.

[DeWi79]   D.J. DeWitt, *DIRECT - A Multiprocessor Organization for Supporting Relational Database Management*, IEEE Trans. on Computers, Vol.C-28, no.6, pp. 395-406, 1979.

[Essen87]   H.A.van Essen, *Simulation Studies with Packet Bursts*, PRISMA Doc. no. 95, Philips Research Laboratories Eindhoven, May, 1987.

[Essen88]   H.A. van Essen and R.A.H van Twist, *Construction of the switch in the POOMA machine*, PRISMA Doc. no. 401, Philips Research Laboratories Eindhoven, 1988.

[Gun81]   K.D. Gunther, *Prevention of deadlocks in packet-switched data transport systems*, IEEE Trans. on Comm. Vol.29, No.4, pp.512-524, 1981.

[Har72]   F. Harary, *Graph Theory*, Addison-Wesley, 1972.

[Huls90]   B.J.A.Hulshof and R.H.H.Wester, *Run-Time System for POOL-X Support*, Proc. of the PRISMA Workshop on Parallel Database Systems, Noordwijk, the Netherlands, September 24-26, 1990.

[Kerst87]   M.L. Kersten, P.M.G. Apers, M.A.W. Houtsma, H.J.A. van Kuijk, and R.L.W. van de Weg, *A Distributed, Main Memory Database Machine*, Proc. of the 5th Int. Workshop on Database machines, 1987.

[Knu73]   D.E.Knuth, *The Art of Computer Programming, vol.1: Fundamental Algorithms*, second edition, Addison Wesley, 1973.

[Kung89]   H.T.Kung, *Network-Based Multicomputers: Redefining High Performance Computing in the 1990s*, Proc. of the Decennial Caltech Conf. on VLSI, March 1989.

[Lela85]   M.D.P. Leland and W.D. Roome, *The Silicon Database Machine*, in Proc. of the 4-th Int. Workshop on Database Machines, ed. D.J. DeWitt and H. Boral, Springer, pp.169-189, 1985.

[Lorie89]   R.A. Lorie and H.C. Young, *A Low Communication Sort Algorithm for a Parallel Database Machine*, Proc. of the Fifteenth Int. Conf. on Very Large Databases, Amsterdam, 1989.

[Merl80a]   P.M. Merlin and P.J. Schweitzer, *Deadlock avoidance in store and forward networks I: store-and-forward deadlock*, IEEE Trans. on Comm., Vol.28, No.3, pp.345-354, 1980.

[Merl80b]   P.M. Merlin and P.J. Schweitzer, *Deadlock avoidance in store and forward networks II: Other deadlock types*, IEEE Trans. on Comm., Vol.28, No.3, pp.355-360, 1980.

[Mull87]   H. Muller, *Hardware Aspects of Fault Tolerance*, PRISMA Doc. no. 121, Philips Research Laboratories Eindhoven, Nov. 1987.

[Mull90]   H. Muller, *Evaluation of a Communication Architecture by means of Simulation*, Proc. of the PRISMA Workshop on Parallel Database Systems, Noordwijk, the Netherlands, September 24-26, 1990.

[Nug88]   S.F. Nugent, *The iPSC/2 Direct-Connect Communication Technology*, Proc. Concurrent Supercomputing 1988, pp.59-76.

[Odijk87]   W.J.H.J. Bronnenberg, L. Nijman, E.A.M. Odijk, and R.A.H. van Twist, *DOOM: A Decentralized Object-Oriented Machine*, IEEE MICRO, Vol.7, No.5, pp.52-69, 1987.

[Patt88]   D.A. Patterson, G.Gibson and R.H.Katz, *A Case for Redundant Arrays of Inexpensive Disks (RIAD)*, ACM SIGMOD Conf., Chicago, IL, pp.109-116, 1989.

[Reddy89]   A.L. Reddy and P. Banerjee, *An Evaluation of Multiple-Disk I/O Systems*, IEEE Trans. on Computers, vol.38, no.12, pp.1680-1690, 1989.

[Roeb89]   H. Roebbers and M.C. Vlot, *A Communication Processor on the Transputer*, Proc. 10th OCCAM User Group Enschede, the Netherlands, Publ. North Holland, Amsterdam, pp.143-151, 1989.

[Seitz85]   C. Seitz, *The Cosmic Cube*, Communications of the ACM, 1985.

[Spek90]   J.v.d. Spek, *POOL-X and its implementation*, Proc. of the PRISMA Workshop on Parallel Database Systems, Noordwijk, the Netherlands, September 24-26, 1990.

[Stand80]   T.A. Standish, *Data Structure Techniques*, Addison Wesley, 1980.

[Twist87a]   R.A.H. van Twist, *Functional Specification of the Prototype Communication Processor*, Esprit project 415-A, Doc. no. 0363, Philips Research Laboratories Eindhoven, 1987.

[Twist87b]   R.A.H. van Twist and E.A.M. Odijk, *Networks for Parallel Computers*, Proc. VLSI and Computers, COMPEURO 87, pp.779-782, 1987.

[Twist90]   W.J.van Beek, R.A.H. van Twist and M.C. Vlot, *Evaluation of the Communication Network of POOMA*, to appear in Proc. 19th Annual Int.Conf. on Parallel Processing, 1990.

[Vlot87]   M.C.Vlot, *Minimum hardware support for reconfiguration*, PRISMA Doc. no. 190, Philips Research Laboratories Eindhoven, Oct. 1987.

[Vlot89]   M.C. Vlot and F. Hopmans, *Preliminary definition of the Message Processor*, PRISMA Doc. no. 424, Philips Research Laboratories, Eindhoven, Mar. 1989.

The POOMA operating system

R.H.H. Wester, B.J.A. Hulshof

Philips Research Laboratories
P.O.Box 80.000
5600 JA Eindhoven, The Netherlands

Abstract

The POOMA operating system, together with the POOL-X compiler, is responsible for the execution on the POOMA hardware of parallel programs written in the parallel object oriented language POOL-X. This article contains two parts, firstly it gives an overview of most of the facilities which are offered by the POOMA operating system, and secondly relevant system components are evaluated. The POOMA operating system has a nucleus and a POOL-X run time support in which the POOL-X dependent parts are concentrated. However, POOL-X characteristics influenced some design decisions for the (POOL-X independent) nucleus. In the first part we present some design decisions and discuss them for the OS components. We also give some implementation details for interesting or non-standard implemented components. The second part of the article gives performance figures of parts of the nucleus and of the run time support, from which we may conclude that fast execution of POOL-X programs is possible.

1 Introduction

In this article the POOMA operating system is discussed, which has been implemented as part of the PRISMA[1] project. The operating system, together with the POOL-X compiler [Spek90] and the 100 node POOMA architecture [Vlot90] form a platform for the parallel execution of POOL-X programs. One of the major POOL-X applications implemented within the PRISMA project is a database management system [Apers90].

The main target of the operating system is to support the efficient execution of a single POOL[2] program. The POOMA operating system falls apart in a POOL independent *nucleus* and a *POOL-X run-time support library* written on top of it. Although the nucleus is POOL independent, the design is influenced by some POOL characteristics. The nucleus deals with the basic resource management and offers (at the moment) a parallel, message passing, single user, single program execution environment. The nucleus is also suitable for writing C-programs on top of it. The interface between compiler and run time support has been chosen in such a way that the run time support is responsible for all POOL distributed tasks. It therefore contains primitives for object allocation, POOL communication, garbage collection and exception handling. This makes it possible to run the same POOL program on a different number of nodes, without recompilation.

Besides the nucleus and the run time support library the POOMA operating system contains a *programming environment* which supports execution and low-level debugging of POOL and C programs as well as profiling and monitoring for performance measurements.

In the remainder of this article we firstly discuss the design decisions taken for guiding and limiting the scope of the implemented operating system. After that, we discuss the important components

---

[1]The PRISMA project is supported by the Dutch "Stimuleringsprojectteam Informaticaonderzoek" (SPIN).

[2]We use POOL, instead of POOL-X, in this article, since the operating system is able to support any language from the POOL family.

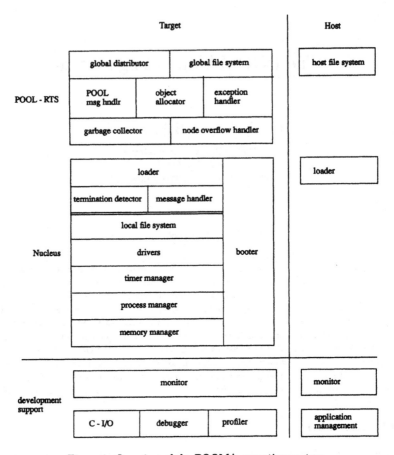

Figure 1: Overview of the POOMA operating system

(see Figure 1 which gives an overview of all parts of the operating system). At the end of the article some performance measurements are given after which we end with some concluding remarks.

In the sequel we will use the terms LI, OS and AR, to denote the language implementation (compiler), operating system and (hardware) architecture.

2 Design decisions

The design decisions which have been taken for the OS implementation are summarized in this section. Firstly we discuss some characteristics of the OS concerning the POOMA hardware and its purpose, after that we discuss some implications for the OS which result from POOL.

The POOMA machine [Vlot90] is a 100 node parallel message passing architecture. Each node is a stand alone computer with 16Mbytes of main memory. Some nodes have a disk attached and some nodes have an ethernet board which connects them to a host machine. Each node has a communication processor which performs the message passing to other nodes. The POOMA machine is reconfigurable by software. The communication network is reconfigurable to certain topologies at initialization time, which means before downloading the OS. Also at download time the 100 nodes machine can be divided into several smaller machines.

The POOMA machine is seen as a server machine. This means that operating system tasks such as a programming development environment do not have to be provided. Also a much simpler file system on the disks can be provided. The OS is downloaded for each program run, for flexibility reasons. In that way, experiments with different networks and different number of nodes are easily established. The programming environment was designed to deal with all configurable items of the POOMA machine and its OS in a flexible way. Some items are: a system debugger, for remote debugging, tools for monitoring and profiling distributed applications and a downloader of the OS dealing with switches to reconfigure the hardware.

The POOMA hardware offers a large amount of main memory on each node (16 Mbytes) and programs are supposed to fit in this memory. Therefore, swapping is not done by the OS. One of the major applications written in POOL is a main memory data base system [Apers90] which shows that swapping is indeed not necessary.

Limited effort was put on fault tolerance. The OS finds at initialization in its initialization all nodes attached to the by the downloader configured network. Nodes that remain unreached are usually faulty nodes. During program execution we only support fault detection. Fault detection of the communication processors by check sum and memory faults by parity checks. A stable file system is offered to support recovery from hardware errors.

In first instance we limited the scope of the operating system by restricting it to single user, single program executions.

Other design decisions are related to POOL. POOL is a parallel object oriented language. These objects communicate with each other by message passing only. Within an object execution is strictly sequential and the parallelism is obtained from multiple objects on multiple nodes.

All objects share the same data area for program efficiency. In this data area objects are light weight processes. Protection between objects is guaranteed by the POOL language definition due to the strong typing mechanism, therefore the OS does not provide protection.

Due to the object oriented approach we expect a large amount of objects residing on a single node and therefore a lot of schedule points during execution. Special attention was paid to minimize the scheduling overhead. One feature already mentioned is that we use light weight processes, but we also chose for *compiler determined schedule points*. This means that the compiler has full control over the descheduling of objects and there are no hidden schedule points in OS access routines. If a schedule action was required in a spooling strategy was used, see Section 3.3. The advantage is that the compiler can minimize the context to be saved at schedule points and also does not need to save and restore the context when calling OS access routines.

POOL offers full control of allocating object to nodes. Therefore the OS will not employ a sophisticated allocation strategy to obtain a good load balance, nor will the OS do reallocation.

Due to the dynamic behavior of POOL and because we only use main memory, special measures have been taken to deal with temporary memory shortage, which we call *node overflow*. For instance, the OS will only use preclaimed memory to store its administration and offers some primitives to wait for memory. A special communication protocol is set up to deal with memory overflow at the receiving node and finally a special *node overflow handler* was implemented which contains strategies (like starting the garbage collector) to recover from these overflow situations.

3 Nucleus

3.1 Overview

The POOMA hardware consists of a number of processing nodes connected via a tightly coupled network [Vlot90]. Each processing node consists of a processing capability (PG2100 board with a.o. a Motorola MC68020 and a MC68851 floating point processor), a local RAM memory (16 MBytes per node) and a communication capability which allows for the communication between nodes. Some nodes have a disk and a few nodes have an ethernet.

The POOMA machine is connected via the ethernet to a host computer (SUN 3, running the UNIX operating system). For a description of the ethernet and disk drivers we refer to [Vlot90].

On the POOMA hardware runs the POOMA nucleus in which we distinguish the following components:

Memory Manager	which handles allocation and deallocation of memory blocks
Process Manager	for scheduling, interrupt handling, creation of OS processes and a name service
Timer Manager	which handles timeouts and provides a local clock
Drivers	for ethernet and disk
Local File System	which handles local IO to disk and/or host
Message handler	which handles communication between nodes
Termination Detector	which detects termination of a program
Loader	which offers program loading on top of the nucleus
Booter	which boots the OS
Debugger	which offers kernel debugging IO and a post mortem core inspection

In the following sections each component will be described in more detail.

3.2 Memory Manager

The memory manager plays an important role in the OS implementation. Due to the dynamic features offered by the POOL language a lot of allocations and deallocation are expected of mostly small blocks with a few large one. Therefore we made the implementation as simple and efficient as possible. Only simple alloc and dealloc primitives are offered, together with a compaction facility. However the OS will not reallocate memory blocks, the compaction is only related to the chosen paging scheme.

The current implemented memory management employs a buddy algorithm [Knuth73] combined with a virtual paging strategy. Each buddy is assigned a free list of two-power number of pages for sizes larger than the pagesize or a free list of pages divided by a two-power number for sizes smaller or equal than the pagesize. The compaction routine walks trough the buddys smaller than or equal to the pagesize and reclaims all pages in which no memory block is used. The PMMU of the PG2100 is used for the virtual mapping. The current pagesize is 4 Kbyte. The reason for using a virtual memory management is to prevent external fragmentation, it is not used for swapping and for dynamic extentable memory blocks.

For statistics and allocation control, the total amount of free memory is maintained by the memory manager.

3.3 Process Manager

The process manager encloses facilities for scheduling, interrupt handling, the creation of OS processes and an object name service.

Since the grain size of parallelism in POOL, i.e. the average number of processing instructions per communication action, is expected to be medium to small scheduling will occur rather frequently. Apart from having light weight processes, we also use *compile-time determined scheduling* to exploit knowledge about context sizes of processes in schedule points.

To decrease stack needs for blocking OS activities all OS calls are made non-blocking. Activities that would have blocked will return a status that indicates that the caller should schedule out until a certain event occurs. The caller's resumption is guaranteed by the OS after the event occurred. The main advantage of this approach is that all OS calls can execute on the same stack. POOL objects do have a local stack and with this approach no stack size calculations are required for OS calls.

These were starting points at the beginning of the design of the OS. With the revised language definition of POOL less POOL processes with activity are expected. Therefore there now is a lower stack need than initially was expected and thus probably less need for non blocking OS calls.

3.3.1 Scheduler

Processes represent independent activities, as well for the operating system itself (OS processes) as for user processes. The scheduler provides primitives for suspension and resumption of execution of processes. The schedule primitives are directly called by the compiler generated code.

The scheduler maintains a ready queue and a priority queue. The priority queue is necessary to give priority to some OS processes (e.g. the message handler when input/output queues become full). For scheduling a *round robin* strategy is used. Besides the priority scheduling this strategy is fair.

The process manager distinguishes two types of processes, namely OS processes and user processes (usually POOL processes). In case of a suspend of an OS process (which is implemented in C) all the machine registers have to be saved, whereas for POOL processes only the stack pointer has to be saved (the other context will be saved by the compiler).

3.3.2 Synchronization

Basically the OS is synchronous, this means that interrupts are handled synchronously and processes communicate synchronously.

Some POOMA hardware capabilities generate asynchronous interrupts (e.g. disks, ethernet, timer). These interrupts are handled on an interrupt stack. The interrupt routine executed on an interrupt only sets a flag which is checked at the next schedule point. If set the process that will handle the interrupt is scheduled in.

For synchronization between processes a facility is offered to put processes asleep until a certain "event" occurs (see also section 3.5). On a wake up a process is put in the ready queue.

3.3.3 Process creation

OS processes are created by the process manager, they have their own execution stack and will never be removed. POOL processes are created by the POOL RTS. Each process with activity has a process descriptor made by the process manager. The process descriptor provides information such as the state of a process, the type of the process, queue links, space for context etc..

3.3.4 Name service

The process manager provides a global name service to uniquely identify processes over the system. The name service is implemented by maintaining a process name table which contains the local pointer to a process descriptor. A process name is made by encoding the node identification and the index in the process name table.

3.4 Message Handler

The message handling in the nucleus is restricted to a *transport layer*. This layer takes care of copying the data from source node to destination node. It offers an order preserving message switching virtual network build on top of the packet switching hardware. The message transport is order preserving because of fairness and for easy support of the POOL order preserving demand of messages.

Furthermore it simplifies the implementation of other OS components. The order preservation of messages is implemented by using the Communication Processor (CP) in such a way that it preserves the order of packets from one node to the other node. This is done by initializing the routing tables in the CP such that there is only one path between two nodes.

Now we discuss how transport is handled in general, after that we discuss three transport types that are supported.

3.4.1 Transporting a message

The transport layer performs three actions.

- packetizing i.e. splitting messages in fixed size packets,

- reassembly i.e. construction of the message out of packets at the receiving side and

- fault detection.

We discuss now the transport of a message. All three aspects will be mentioned.

The transport layer checks the order preservation of the CP by adding a sequence number to every packet. Besides the sequence number also a checksum is added to a packet. When a packet arrives out of order or when an error is detected in the checksum the system panics.

In the transport layer we made the abstraction from synchronization and buffer management by means of function parameters. These functions parameters (and some other information) are grouped into *message types*. During system startup a number of *actual message types* can be defined. For all actual message types a *send_done* and a *signal* function must defined. The *send_done* function is invoked at the source node when the message data has been copied to the network. This function can be used to perform the required synchronization and/or buffer management actions after a message has been sent. The *signal* function is invoked when a message has been reassembled at the destination node. This function can be used to perform the required synchronization action such scheduling of the destination process.

Depending on the transport type (see below) an actual message type can have additional parameters, such as a *get_buffer* function. The *get_buffer* functions are invoked when the transport layer at the destination node requires a new piece of memory for storing message data. The functions may fail in allocating memory. In that case the transport layer will throw away the message data which will be sent again later.

Functions which are parameter of an actual message type are executed by the handlers of the transport layer. Therefore these functions may not block the execution (deadlock) and should have a short execution time.

3.4.2 Transport types

The transport layer supports three transport types:

RSI The remote synchronous interrupt message. It contains maximal 6 long words (32 bit) of data (the size of a packet). The signal function is invoked with a pointer to the data. The data is discarded after termination of the signal function. The RSI messages are used for small system messages in which case the signal function usually performs the required remote action.

COPY With the COPY transport type any part of the local memory can be copied to a preclaimed buffer at the receiving node. The signal function is invoked with a pointer to the preclaimed buffer.

TOBUF The TOBUF transport type is used for buffer to buffer communication. The message contains two areas: a *data* area which is copied to the destination node and a *scratch* area (which is not copied to the destination node). The scratch area can be used for storing local information about the message buffer (e.g. links for queuing a message). There are two variants: the TOBUF_NC (for *non-compound*) and the TOBUF_C (for *compound*). A compound message is a message that copies a number of memory blocks from source node to destination node.

3.4.3 Implementation

The functionality of the transport layer is distributed over two handler processes: the *Output Message Handler* (OMH) and the *Input Message Handler* (IMH). When a message is sent the message is queued in the queue of the OMH and the OMH is activated. As long as the OMH is busy with the sending of the message, it may not be modified. The send done function can be used to signal the sending process that the message may be used again. The IMH accepts packets from the network, performs the checks and reassembly. When the message is sent to dynamic storage it invokes a get buffer function when the first packet of a message or component arrives. When all packets are arrived it invokes the signal function.

For the implementation of node overflow handling (a node has a temporary lack of memory) and the debugger a second virtual network is used. The CP offers the features for a second virtual network, which has functionally the same interface as the normal network. Therefore this second virtual network is implemented in the transport layer by adding a second OMH and IMH for that network which has the same functionality as for the normal network. The second network allows that the get buffer and signal functions for message sent through the normal network may block on sending message through the second network. The second network concept is needed to guarantee the deadlock free routing of the CP. For an actual message type it is indicated which network must be used.

The functionality of the transport layer offers a good language independent platform for the implementation of language dependent communication protocols. The transport types offer the basis for transporting a single word (RSI) up to complicated data structures (TOBUF_C). The actual message type concept offers the possibility of implementing a set of multiform communication primitives all sharing the transport layer. This can be used in optimizing communication protocols for dedicated situations (e.g. remote array access).

3.5 Timer Manager

This section describes the timer facilities provided by the OS. The main functionalities are the handling of timeouts, providing a current time and handling periodically OS calls such as the inspection of the (synchronous) communication processor and profile sampling.

The timer manager provides primitives to implement timeouts. An action can be attached to a time interval and is performed after the time interval expires. Timeouts in the OS are mainly used to time out on disk IO and for debugging.

Some periodic calls are executed by the timer interrupt such as inspection of the communication processor status and program counter sampling for profiling.

Depending on the value of the status register of the communication processor the input or output message handler is awakened. This is done to prevent the need for the scheduler to inspect these registers at each schedule action.

For profiling periodic program counter sampling is required. The timer interrupt will pass the program counter of the interrupted process to a profile routine.

3.6 Drivers

There are two major drivers in the system. One is the ethernet which is standard software and one is the disk driver. For a description of the disk driver we refer to [Vlot90].

3.7 Local File System

The file system is split up in two parts, the local file system which is part of the nucleus and a global file system on top of this. The global file system will be discussed later.

The local file system handles all local IO. It contains two basic components, the local disk file system and the local host file system (for nodes with disk and nodes with ethernet respectively). Communication to the disk is via the disk driver, communication to the host is socket based.

The local file system has a UNIX like interface. It performs the basic operations like open, close, unlink, stat fstat, read and write. All file control functions (all but read and write) accept a type parameter which indicates disk or host file. For read and write calls the local file system provides no buffering.

Each local disk file system has an independent file name space and guarantees uniqueness of file names on the local disk. The disk directory structure is flat and is kept in main memory during execution. No user protection for files on disk is offered yet. The disk file system is parameterizable to the number of files that can be created on a disk and the number of consecutive blocks that is allocated for one file. The system limitations are the file name length and the number of open host and disk files.

Unlike all other OS calls the file system calls are blocking.

A file system tool is made to maintain the files on disk. It offers file information (sizes, names), copy from/to host, recovery, reinitialization etc..

3.8 Termination Detector

The termination detection algorithm straightforward variant of the termination detector described in [Dijkstra83, Goertz].

Locally, each node keeps track of the fact, whether it contains some activity or not. Activity could be ready processes or activity in peripheral devices.

Special measures must be taken for the activities of the termination detector itself. These should not be considered program activities.

3.9 Debugger

In the OS some internal checking is provided and a debugger is added to support post mortem core inspection. Also simple kernel IO is provided.

The debugger offers the handling of magic numbers and checkings at various debug levels. The debugger is also responsible for panic situations (for instance an unhandled POOL-X exception). In this case it will try to stop the system gracefully and afterwards supports inspection of the memory from the host.

3.9.1 Dynamic "type" checking

Since all processes share the same address space, it is very easy to program malicious processes, without directly noticing them. Therefore a dynamic "type" checking strategy is by implementing magic numbers. By checking these mingled administration can be found. For efficiency reasons this checking is debug level depending. Four levels (0..3)are supported:

0: No checking.

1: Only checking of incoming parameters.

2: Checking of incoming parameters and also internally maintained data structures.

3: As 2, but with expensive internal consistency checks.

These levels can dynamically be changed. The OS programmer is responsible for usage of the debug levels in an appropriate way. By inspecting the current value of the debug level he can decide whether checking should be done or not. An example of a level 3 consistency measure is to overwrite a released memory block by a special magic number, which is useful for noticing dangling references.

3.9.2 Panic situation

If a panic[3] situation occurs the system is stopped in a graceful manner in the following way:

1. all local POOL activity is frozen. This means that no POOL objects or POOL related object (like the garbage collector) is allowed to be entered into the ready queue any more.

2. a sweep message is sent to all other nodes.

3. locally await the sweep messages from other nodes.

4. send quiet message to gateway node.

This algorithm makes use of the order preservingness of the nucleus message to guarantee that there are no more message in the network. Furthermore since this algorithm makes use of the OS nucleus, a crash in the OS nucleus itself might prevent this algorithm to work properly. In practice this occurs only rarely. If all quiet message have arrived at the gateway node a debug process is started for memory inspection, see further on.

If a panic situation occurs, the debugger will call a print routine for each relevant OS component. The corresponding OS components can use this routine to verify its consistency and report on failures. After that it starts the local debugger to handle requests from the host. The current debug server is able to find all user and OS processes processes, provides backtraces of C processes, displays message queues of user processes and displays plain pieces of memory in hexadecimal format.

3.9.3 C input/output

In order to assist in debugging and to be able to print some diagnostic information, the standard C input/output is also supported. These C-I/O calls are caught in the OS at the read/write level and then redirected to the host. If the current node has no gateway to the host, first the data is sent to a gateway node using the nucleus message handler. On the gateway node a spooler process is present to pass on the off-node data to the host.

The C-I/O knows two modes :

Non-blocking mode: In this mode the output does not block the current process. This is useful because then the synchronization between processes is not influenced by print statements. A copy of the string is made in a dynamically allocated piece of memory and a spooler process is activated to send the data to the host or to the gateway node.

Blocking mode: In this mode the process waits until the output has been processed. This mode is useful in a crash situation where the memory manager does not function properly any more. It is typically used by the debugger.

Due to the spooling of the data, it might happen that although a print statement was executed its data never arrived because of a crash. This makes it hard to localize errors. Therefore the OS programmer can flush the output, which blocks the current process until all output data is processed.

---

[3]A panic situation may vary from an unhandled exception up to an ordinary bus error.

3.10 Loader

The loader loads the program code from the host and distributes the code to all nodes. Therefore on each node a local code loader is created at booting time. The handler on the gateway node (a node with ethernet connected to the host) creates a communication channel with the host after which the code is read in. Then the code is distributed to all nodes and execution is started on all nodes.

3.11 Booter

The booter initializes all OS components. First the interrupts routines are set, then the initialization of the memory manager is done. After that the communication network is initialized. Roughly this is done by each node finding its neighboring nodes and initializing the routing tables such that static routing is guaranteed. After this the system knows how many nodes are available in the system. Now other components such as the process manager, global name server, timer server, ethernet and disk drivers are initialized. The hardware configuration is distributed to all nodes. The message handler is initialized, as well as the file system and debugger. After this the timer, termination detector and loader are started. The program code is loaded and execution starts.

4 POOL Run Time Support

4.1 Introduction

The POOL support part of the OS mainly deals with distributed POOL tasks. The following tasks are directly related to the POOL language constructs:

1. On top of the nucleus message handling a specific *POOL message handler* is built.

2. New POOL processes and objects are allocated with help of the *object allocator*.

3. The propagation of POOL exceptions to other objects is done by the *exception handler*.

4. For distribution of POOL global values over all nodes as well as for global synchronization[4], access routines are offered by the global distributor.

The following two activities are not directly related to POOL language constructs.

1. The determination and disposal of redundant POOL objects is done by the *garbage collector*.

2. A global file system as support for the POOL I/O standard unit.

3. If a local memory allocation request cannot be honored the node is in so called *node overflow*. Then a strategy is employed in order to let the program continue execution instead of crashing due to a temporary memory shortness.

4.2 POOL message handler

The POOL message handler provides support for various types of POOL messages. Furthermore node overflow is taken into account if a message cannot be stored on the receiver node.

The POOL message handler implements the following primitives: *Synchronous send, Asynchronous send, Return send, Answer* and *Conditional answer*. The answer primitives only extract messages from a queue. The invocation of the associated method is taken care of by the POOL code generation. For the three send primitives there are the variants : *local* and *compound*. A compound message is a message that contains a number of memory blocks, usually objects from an object tree structure.

---

[4]A process has to wait until a global variable is evaluated.

The POOL message handler is implemented on top of the transport layer in the nucleus (see section 3.4), thus only the buffer management and the synchronization have to be implemented.

The synchronization required by the POOL communication primitives results in the following actions:

- When a message arrives at its destination the message is queued. When the destination object was waiting for this message it is activated.

- When a process executes an answer primitive its message queue is searched for an acceptable message. If a message is found, the message is dequeued and returned. If no message is found and it is a non-conditional answer, then the state of the process is changed in waiting for message. A pointer to the answer set (set of methods that the object is ready to answer) is stored in the process descriptor (see section 3.3).

- When a return message arrives, the destination process will be waiting for that message. Therefore the message can be passed directly to the process which is then activated.

The buffer management principle is simple: When a process sends a message the buffer in which the message is stored is passed to the destination process and the sender may not use that buffer any more. For off-node communication the system uses destination buffering which means that all messages sent to an object are buffered on the same node as the destination object. In principle the application programmer has to guarantee that there is memory available.

This responsibility can not always be honored. Programs that have executed many times without crashing can come into a node overflow situation due to asynchronism in a distributed environment. A protocol which has a weaker guarantee about memory availability is the global message buffering protocol.

In the current implementation two variants of the POOL message handling are available: one using global message buffering and one using destination buffering.

4.2.1 Destination message buffering protocol

In this protocol messages are always buffered at the receiving node. The get buffer function (see section 3.4) crashes on a fail to allocate a message buffer. The send done function deallocates the message buffer and the signal function delivers the message.

For messages sent to a local process the nucleus message handling is not used. The send primitive directly invokes the signal function.

This protocol is usable for applications which have recovering features after a system crash (e.g. stable storage, check points).

4.2.2 Global message buffering protocol

The global message buffering protocol (GMBP) is designed with in mind that memory shortage at a node is an exceptional case. Therefore the GMBP is optimized to the situation that there is no memory shortage.

The principle of the global message buffering protocol (GMBP) operates as follows:

1. A sending node start sending the complete message. The sending node then waits for an acknowledge message from the receiving node.

2. When a message arrives at its destination node and

    (a) there is no memory shortage, the message is *accepted*. This means that the message is buffered and the sending node is informed that the original message can be removed from the system.

(b) there is memory shortage, the message is *refused*. This means that some information (msg info) about the message is saved. With this information the destination node can initiate retransmission of the original message in a later stage.

3. The sending node can receive

(a) the information that the message is accepted at the destination node, in which case the message is removed.

(b) a request for retransmission of the message. In this case the message is sent again and removed from the system. When a message is retransmitted the destination node guarantees that the message can be buffered.

When a message arrives at a node it is assumed that the msg info can be stored even if the node is in a memory shortage situation. This can be done in the process data for the first message and in the last queued message for non first messages. This storage of msg info in the predecessor is done by so called link messages. In this way a distributed queue is built.

When a process accepts a message that is not buffered locally it will initiate the retransmission of that message and update the message queue. Before the request for retransmission a message buffer is allocated.

The GMBP also supports compound messages. The message buffer of a compound message contains also a compound table which refers to memory blocks (components) which have to be copied to the destination too. The message buffer and compound components are treated differently. At a destination node a compound message can be :

accepted : The message buffer and all components are allocated at the destination node.

refused : The message buffer and all components are not allocated at the destination node.

partly accepted : The message buffer is allocated at the destination node but not all components are allocated at the destination node.

When a compound message arrives and it is *accepted*, the sending node is informed that the message can be removed from the system.

When a compound message arrives and it is *refused*, the original message buffer is treated as a refused message buffer.

When a process selects a *refused* compound message it has to allocate the message buffer before it is allowed to send the "request for retransmission". This only guarantees that when the message arrives for the second time it will be "partly accepted" at least. Only when the message is *accepted* the destination node is allowed to inform the sending node that the message can be removed.

When a compound message is *partly accepted*, the message buffer at the destination has been allocated and is treated as an *accepted* message buffer. Only a state field in the message buffer indicates that the message is only partly accepted.

When a process selects a *partly accepted* message the compound table contains the sizes for refused components. For all refused components a memory block has to be allocated before a "request for retransmission" may be sent. This guarantees that when the message arrives the next time the message will be accepted. So after retransmitting a *partly accepted* message, the message can be removed from the system.

The GMBP is implemented with a minimal overhead in the normal case (no overflow). Furthermore it implements reliable communication when nodes only temporarily suffer from memory shortage.

4.3 Object allocator

This chapter describes the implementation of POOL object allocation. The object allocation is based on pragmas [Spek90] provided by the POOL programmer. However even with these pragmas some freedom is left for the OS in the allocation of objects in the form of a nodeset. This freedom allows to perform some dynamic load balancing within the constraints of these nodesets and for those objects without allocation pragmas. But because the main responsibility is with the programmer, the load balancing strategy is kept simple.

In the remainder of this chapter first the load balancing strategy is discussed, followed by some implementation issues of the object allocator.

4.3.1 Strategy for load balancing

One can think of numerous strategies. The decisions are based on the following criteria:

- **Local versus off-node.**
  In general it is preferable to allocate a new object at the creator's node, because local communication is faster.

- **Load information.**
  By maintaining some (more or less accurate) load information of other nodes off-node allocation requests can be directed to less occupied nodes.

- **Granularity allocation requests.**
  Allocation requests can be sent to one node or a number of nodes at a time.

- **Selection nodes.**
  Allocation requests can be sent in a specific order to other nodes, for instance according to (virtual) node numbers, random, alternatively from low to high and from high to low node numbers, via a roving index, several times etc.

Because the programmer has the primary responsibility for the allocation a straightforward strategy is chosen:

1. Allocate an object locally (if allowed by the nodeset), if the local memory has not exceeded some threshold.

2. Try off node allocation one node at a time, using a roving index over all nodes.

This way no load information of other nodes has to be maintained and the roving index gives a fair distribution over the nodes for off-node allocations.

4.3.2 Implementation issues

For object allocation (OA) there reside two processes on each node:

1. a Receiving OA process.
   This process handles all incoming allocation requests from other nodes. If an allocation request arrives an attempt will be made to allocate storage for the new object. If this attempt fails this will be reported to the requester. If the attempt succeeds the new process is initialized and started and its global name (see section 3.3) is returned to the requester.

2. a Local OA process.
   This process deals with all allocation requests coming from its own node. It will employ the strategy as described in the previous section, to find a suitable node. If the allocation succeeds it will return the global name of the newly created object to the creator and reactivate the

creator. If an allocation fails NULL is returned. To simplify administration the local OA process only handles one allocation request a time. Due to the expected relative low frequency of object allocation with respect to other actions this is not considered to become a bottleneck.

As optimization the activity of the receiving OA process is taken over by the input message handler.

4.4 Exception handler

When an exception is raised in a POOL object the exception is propagated to the objects that are in rendez-vous with that object. The exception propagates until an exception handler is found. If no exception handler is found in one or more of these objects the program is aborted. The OS is only responsible for the propagation of an exception. The treatment within the objects is done by LI.

In the following sections first the propagation is described, followed by some implementation issues.

4.4.1 Propagation of exceptions

The exception to be propagated has the following properties:

1. An exception start at only one process (called originator).

2. Processes receiving an exception are either running (originator) or performing a synchronous send and are in rendez-vous.

This means that if an exception starts the objects to which it will propagate can be found. Furthermore there is no mutual interaction between different exceptions. Although the objects to which the exception will propagate are known, this set cannot be determined locally. So from the originator the exception will be propagated to the objects with which the rendez-vous is broken. From these objects in turn the exception will propagate to other objects in rendez-vous with these objects etc. If an exception is handled at an object it can continue with execution immediately, since it is guaranteed that the objects with which a rendez-vous is broken will handle the exceptions also. This is due to the fact that these objects are blocked in a synchronous send and cannot perform any activity before the exception is handled.

If in one of the objects no handler is found the program must be aborted. LI can call an OS access routine for this. The abortion of the program leads to entering the debugger, see section (see section 3.9).

4.4.2 Implementation issues

As noticed in the previous section, the propagation is rather simple. On each node there exist two exception handler(EH) processes:

1. Receiving EH process.
   This process handles all incoming request from other nodes. The flow of control of the victim POOL process is changed and the POOL process starts execution of the exception.

2. Local EH process.
   The local EH process handles requests from POOL processes. If the request is an off-node request it will pass on the request to the corresponding receiving EH process. If the request is local it is is handled immediately.

As optimization the activity of the receiving EH process is taken over by the input message handler.

4.5 Global distributor

The global distributor gives support to LI for global distribution and access to globals. Therefore, two mechanisms are supported: local queues and a broadcast mechanism. Furthermore, the notion of a global record is defined, to maintain the state information of a global.

4.5.1 Usage

When a global value is to be accessed, its global record is inspected. For each global, a global record is available at every node. It contains a flag, whether the global value is set. If it is, the value is obtained directly from the global record. Otherwise, evaluation (and distribution) is to be awaited. Therefore, the accessing object calls an OS primitive, to queue itself with the global record concerned. If the global value gets distributed to this global record, the object is awakened again.

If the evaluator for a global finishes (i.e. knows the value of its global), it creates a message containing global id and value. The message is distributed by the OS over all nodes. At each node an LI routine is called, which contains aforementioned message as parameter. The LI routine sets global value and aforementioned flag. Furthermore, all objects waiting for the global are released by means of an OS primitive.

4.5.2 Implementation issues

The global record is allocated by LI in code space, such that it has the same address at every node. This is the global id. The global record contains flag and value (maintained by LI), queue of waiters (maintained by OS) and some fields related to garbage collector: trace routine and link field to link all global records together.

Distribution of global values over the nodes is accomplished by two servers at every node: the global distributer and the global acceptor. The global evaluator (POOL process created by LI) sends aforementioned message to its local global distributer. This one replicates the message and sends a copy to each global acceptor (i.e. on all nodes, including its own). The global acceptor continuously answers these messages and calls the LI supplied routine, passing it as parameter.

4.6 Global file system

The global file system is built on the local file system (see section 3.7). It has the same properties such as blocking interface, no buffering etc. The global file system adds transparent access to disk, stable and host files on any disk or ethernet node. Stable files are files that survive system crashes.

A restricted Unix like interface is provided. For the open, unlink and fstat a type parameter is added to distinguish the three type of files. The open call also accepts a node parameter to indicate the node on which the file has to be opened.

4.6.1 Implementation issues

Some servers are implemented:
Firstly the *file name server*. Each node has a file name server Each access routine with a name in it (open, unlink and fstat) is routed to a node obtained from a hash over the file name. That node serves the request.
Secondly a *remote file server*.This server handles remote access to files. Each node has two remote file servers. One for disk files (also stable files) and one for host files. The servers share the same code. The messages sent to these servers are from file name servers (open, unlink, fstat) or from user processes (read, write, close, lseek and stat).

This layer is POOL independent.

```
WHILE true DO
  await start of GC
  color root objects/messages grey
  WHILE there are grey objects/messages DO
    get grey object/message
    color white descendants grey (called tracing)
    color object/message black
  OD
  remove white objects
  color all (black) objects white
OD
```

Figure 2: Basic algorithm of GC

4.7 Garbage collector

This chapter describes the implementation of the garbage collector (GC). The purpose of the garbage collector is to remove obsolete POOL objects, but not all obsolete objects can be detected by the garbage collector.This is mainly due to the fact that no knowledge is available of the behaviour of a program, thus taking the save assumption that if an object is referred somewhere it could also be used and may not be collected. Even if the behaviour is made known somehow, the effort to verify certain constraints would be too high either at LI or OS. Therefore the programmer should be aware that no longer used variables could hold references, preventing their removal, especially for objects referred to by globals.

The GC which is implemented is a distributed on-the-fly mark and sweep GC. There are a couple of reasons for chosing this implementation. First within POOL objects can be referred to all over the system, this makes it necessary to used a distributed algorithm. Furthermore within POOL cyclic structures are very commonly used, which prohibits the use of reference counting GC's. Due to the distributed nature of the GC and thus possible unbalance in speed on the different nodes, it was expected that an interrupting GC could give a poor parallel performance, therefore we used an on-the-fly strategy, such that local POOL activity can continue if the local GC is waiting for the global GC to finish.

In the next section we discuss the basic algorithm. To execute the GC on a parallel machine, messages have to be send to other nodes in case a remote reference is encountered.

4.7.1 The basic GC algorithm

The basic GC process is given in an informal algorithmic style in figure 2. It is important to notice that messages are also viewed as traceable data entity. However they are not removed by the GC, but are explicitly disposed as soon as they are not needed any more. The node overflow handler does start the GC. The following root objects/messages are identified :

1. POOL processes in the ready queue.

2. POOL processes waiting for any OS service. This might be the object allocator, exception handler, global distributor or I/O server.

3. POOL global values.

4. POOL processes waiting for a global value.

5. POOL messages waiting to be sent to another node.

Special precautions are taken to guarantee the finiteness of the algorithm by imposing restriction on the POOL execution. The most important one are that the POOL execution may nog generate an infinite number of grey objects/messages during execution of the GC (for termination of the algorithm) and also no black to white references might occur (to prevent dangling references if the GC removes the white objects). Furthermore the GC itself executes within preclaimed storage, to prevent it has to wait for itself.

4.8 Node overflow handler

The node overflow handler is activated as soon as some thresholds are exceeded on the usage of the local memory. Two thresholds are used. If the first one is exceeded, the node overflow handler is started, which in turns tries to reclaim some memory by taking straightforward measures. The second threshold triggers the node overflow handler to take more robust measures. To prevent thrashing a minimal amount of memory consumption is required before the node overflow handler is triggered again after it is terminated. The node overflow handler also queues, if requested, failing allocation requests, until sufficient memory is reclaimed.

The optimal thresholds depend on the memory management strategy used as well as the total amount of memory and the memory consumption speed of the program. Currently the thresholds are set to 75% and 90%. The minimal amount of memory consumption varies from 40% to 5%, depending on the amount of available free memory.

The local node overflow handler sends a message to a central node overflow manager, which activates the GC. After the GC is finished the compaction of the memory manager is called. There are no robust measures (for instance prohibiting allocation of new objects on a node exceeding the second threshold) implemented yet.

5 Programming Environment

5.1 Overview

The programming environment deals with issues as program handling, profiling, monitoring and debugging. The other parts of the programming environment, like editing and compilation are done on the host machine. The following components are distinguished :

- In order to run programs on the POOMA machine the OS has to be linked together with the generated POOL code. If the program terminates, the part of the machine used should be released. This task is described at the *program handler*.

- For evaluations a *profiler* and a *monitor* are implemented. The profiler helps to spot performance bottlenecks in the code. The monitor displays the run-time behavior of the program graphically.

- A low level post mortem *debugger* is added to assist in core inspection. This debugger is mainly for kernel/compiler debugging due to its low levelness.

We first give a short overview of these components and next a more precise implementation description in the succeeding sections.

5.2 Program Handler

In order to run programs on the POOMA machine, the compiler generated code and OS code are linked using *ld(1)*. C programs can run on top of the OS similarly. A system configuration can be given to the down-loader to specify the number of nodes, the network topology (e.g. Mesh, Chordal ring etc.) and how many nodes with disk. A part of the machine is claimed and the program is down-loaded. The IO servers running on the host are started. With help of a global termination detector the end of the program is recognized and the part of the machine used is released. If the system crashes or a uncaught POOL exception occurred the debugger is started up. If the code was generated with profile option the profile information is fetched from the machine upon normal termination.

5.3 Profiler

To get some insight into the bottlenecks of the application or system, a node based profile can be made of the code at routine level. The standard UNIX *gprof(1)* facility [Graham82] facility is used. To profile system code, mcount calls should be inserted by the C compiler to count function calls. This is done by supplying the -pg option to *cc(1)*. Mcount calls can be inserted by the POOL compiler as well (e.g. at body, method and routine entry), by supplying the profile option to the POOL makefile generator. Furthermore PC sampling is added to the timer handler.

For POOL code the profiler is of limited use. Firstly the profile is routine based and not object based and secondly the profile information is generated per node although it can be summed over all nodes. Furthermore, since mcount calls introduce quite some additional overhead per function call, the dynamic behavior of the parallel system could significantly change. No global performance can be evaluated with the profiler.

Profile information can be reinitialized, put on and off from a POOL program to support partial profiles.

5.4 Monitor

The monitor is used to display the run-time behavior of the program without interfering with the normal execution. At regular time intervals, the whole system is stopped using a global interrupt (a highest prior interrupt). This interrupt will immediately stop the communication processors and execution of OS or POOL code simultaneously on all nodes. Now some information is gathered. Depending on a frequency set by the user this information is sent to the host. For this purpose an alternative communication path is required since then communication processor is stopped. As alternative path the VMS bus (on one crate) and RS232 connections (between crates) are used and the data is sent to a special gateway node, whose only purpose is to sent monitor data. The latter is necessary to prevent interference with the gateway(s) normally used for POOL I/O. Ultimately the normal execution is continued using the global interrupt again.

At the moment the information sent to the host only contains some system data like the idle time, the link occupation of the network, the memory occupation and some user dependent data. The system data can be displayed graphically. The user dependent data can also displayed graphically if a script is provided to the monitor how to interpret the user data.

The influence of the monitor on the behavior of the program is made as minimal as possible. The largest influence is the disturbance of the host-target communication. Also ethernet drivers are interrupted by the global interrupt at the target side but not on the host side. Furthermore some gateway nodes are claimed by the monitor. All other monitor influences are very small like updating counters.

5.5 Debugger

If a crash occurs (OS crash or unhandled POOL exception), a message is displayed by using the C-IO of the kernel. A debug server on the host communicates with a debug process on the target via a socket. After the connection is established, first some configuration information (like number of nodes) and relevant entry points for finding the processes in the system are retrieved. The debug server on the host displays information about processes (type, stack etc.), message queues and memory. For more information see section 3.9.

	average	small ($<=$ 4K)	large ($>$ 4K)
mmalloc	20 μs	20 μs	67 μs
mmfree	15 μs	15 μs	67 μs

Table 1: performance memory management

6 Performance evaluations

6.1 Introduction

All measurements are done at the POOMA hardware. The CP ran at 10 Mc (10 Mbit/sec.). The debug level in the OS was 0 (fastest).

We firstly discuss the performance aspects of the nucleus, after that some components of the RTS are discussed. Finally some conclusions are drawn from the measurements.

6.2 Nucleus performance

At nucleus level, the performance of the following components is of interest: memory manager (allocate and deallocate a block of memory), process manager (schedule and deschedule a process), message handler (overhead, throughput and/or delay of the transport types offered) and the file system at nucleus level. Other components are not considered essential to overall system performance (e.g. debugger, monitor, timer).

6.2.1 Memory manager

Defining the overhead of memory allocation – mmalloc – and deallocation – mmfree – actions is not trivial. They depend on the sequence of actions offered to the memory manager:

1. How soon is a block freed again? I.e. what is the statistical distribution of the life-time of memory blocks.

2. What is the distribution of block sizes?

It is very hard to give general statements on this. Especially, because our knowledge of POOL program behavior is still limited. Therefore, it is not possible to give some general applicable 'model' of POOL execution. So, instead we decided to measure the figures for a 'typical' application. To what extent these figures are more generally applicable is still an open issue. Investigation of other 'typical' programs could give some idea. However, we expect that for memory management the figures are quite reliable, at least with respect to an 'average' POOL-X application.

The typical application used is a theorem prover. A *gprof(1)* call-graph profile has been made. From this profile, the time spent in mmalloc and mmfree could be obtained, see Table 1.

The allocation of memory blocks is divided over a number of calls. The mmalloc is divided in a call to allocate a small memory block (smaller to a page size which is 4096 bytes at the moment) or a large block which is large than one page. The mmfree is similar built up. The ratio between small and large allocations was roughly 400 to 1. Therefore the average time is dominated by the small allocations.

The POOMA hardware has 4 Mbytes on board memory and 12 Mbytes off board. This last memory is slower in access time. Access times can differ up to a factor two. Measurements have to be done very carefully because this can give some strange effects. The figures are averages but most allocations will fall in the off-board memory because the program and OS code as well as the OS data lies in the on-board memory.

	without cache
pmputinq	13 μs
pmpputinq	14 μs
pmswitch	9 μs
pmccswitch	19 μs

Table 2: performance scheduling

6.2.2 Process manager

The overhead of the major scheduling primitives is measured:

pmputinq : Put the current process at the end of the ready queue.

pmpputinq(process) : Put process at the end of the ready queue.

pmswitch : Deschedule the current process. Only the stack pointer is saved. The caller should save all other context.

pmccswitch : Deschedule the current (C) process. In addition to the stack pointer, all non-volatile registers[5] are saved.

Measuring is performed by repeating the actions, in some fashion, in a small loop. Therefore, the cache is disabled because in normal programs one will usually not run a schedulings loop and exploit cache behavior. The result are listed in table 2.

6.2.3 Message handler

Subsequently, the three basic transport types of the nucleus message service (RSI, COPY and TO-BUF) are considered. RSI messages are used for system level signaling (very small messages). COPY messages have typical bulk applications within the system. TOBUF messages are mainly used to map POOL–X off-node messages upon.

RSI Two performance figures are of particular interest with respect to RSIs: latency and total processing overhead.

Latency is the time that passes between the moment the send primitive is called at the source node and the moment the signal function is invoked at the destination node. This is measured by "ping-ponging" a message between two nodes a large number of times. The total time passed is then divided by the number of times the message got "hit". The latency of a message depends on the number of network hops taken. Therefore, the measurement is performed for several distances and the time per additional hop is presented as well.

Total processing overhead is the total time taken for sending and receiving the message (i.e. the times taken by source and destination node summed together). Overhead is measured by playing "multi ping-pong". This is a novel game, in which ping-pong is played with so many balls (messages) at the same time, that both nodes are busy hitting all the time (i.e. have no idle time). Again the total number of hits is divided by the elapsed time.

In table 6.2.3 the results are presented.

Using implementation knowledge of the network [Vlot90], it can be concluded, that all network latency (in an empty network) is hop latency (i.e. 105 μs per hop). Latency on the parallel DP–CP interface is neglectable. Therefore, the total processing overhead should equal the message latency for one hop minus the network latency for this hop, i.e.: 458 μs - 105 μs = 353 μs. However, the multi ping-pong game suggests an overhead of only 172 μs. The difference is caused by the fact,

---

[5]For the Sun^{TM} C compiler.

Latency (1 hop distance)	458 μs
Additional latency for each extra hop	105 μs
Total processing overhead	172 μs

Table 3: RSI performance evaluation

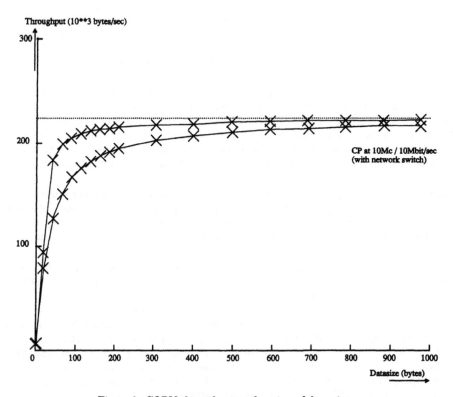

Figure 3: COPY throughput as function of data size

that a lot of scheduling overhead can be amortized over a lot of messages in the multi ping-pong game, whereas in the normal ping-pong game each message gets full scheduling overhead. For each message, the output message handler is scheduled at the source node, and the input message handler at the destination node. This accounts for more than a factor two! So, actually processing overhead is load dependent: many messages make processing cheap. So, the notion of overhead cannot be defined unambiguously, without further specification of the system load.

COPY COPY messages are particularly well suited to transport large amounts of data from one node to another. Therefore, throughput is an important figure to consider. Throughput is defined as the amount of data, which can be transported from one node to another per unit of time. So, for a long time we keep sending messages from one node to another as fast as possible and measure the elapsed time. Then we divide the total number of bytes transported by the elapsed time. The results of this experiment are presented in figure 3.

Data size is expressed in units of bytes, whereas it is actually sent in units of packets (containing 24 data bytes). Therefore, the curves of figure 3 should show some quantization noise. This is depicted by drawing two boundary curves instead of one noisy curve.

Data size (bytes)	latency		overhead
	CP: 10 MHz - 10 Mbit/s (with switch)	CP: 20 MHz - 20 Mbit/s (no switch)	
4	479 μs	414 μs	197 μs
40	565 μs	500 μs	344 μs
400	2.2 ms	1.4 ms	2.2 ms
4,000	18.2 ms	10.7 ms	20.1 ms
40,000	178.3 ms	103.4 ms	199.2 ms

Table 4: TOBUF_NC latency and overhead as function of data size

We see that the curve has an asymptotic behavior. Throughput is limited for small messages, because the fixed overhead per message plays a significant role. For large messages this is neglectable: only the overhead per packet counts. The (breadboard) communication processor can also operate at 20 Mbit/sec[Vlot90], in contrast to our measurements with 10 Mbit/sec. Doing the same experiment on this faster speed, shows that the message throughput is doubled also. From this it can be concluded, that in the 10 Mbit/s case, the network is the bottleneck for larger messages.

TOBUF   At the moment, TOBUF messages are used only to map POOL–X communication upon. Actually, there are two types of TOBUF messages: compound (TOBUF_C) and non-compound (TOBUF_NC) ones. These are treated separately in the following two paragraphs. Notice, the performance figures presented concern the bare transport types: all buffers are preclaimed.

TOBUF_NC   In table 4, latency and overhead figures are presented for increasing data sizes.

We observe that for small messages (4 bytes, i.e. 1 packet), the figures are slightly higher, than for the somewhat simpler RSI message (see section 6.2.3).

For increasing data sizes, the ratio *latency : overhead* decreases. For a single packet message, latency equals total processing overhead, plus network latency (plus additional scheduling overhead). For messages consisting of many packets, sending and receiving proceeds in parallel, keeping latency relatively small[6]. However, latency is somewhat smaller than total processing overhead (178.3 ms vs. 199.2 ms). At first sight, this may appear strange. One expects latency to become somewhat larger than half the total processing overhead (assuming, overhead is reasonably balanced between sending and receiving side). However, transporting 40000 bytes in 178.3 ms means transporting 218 kbytes/sec. So, in this case, latency is determined by the capacity of the hardware network (see section 6.2.3) and not by processing overhead. To illustrate this fact, latency is also shown for a network, which is about twice as fast. In this case, latency indeed is much lower than total processing overhead.

TOBUF_C   One feature distinguishes TOBUF_C from TOBUF_NC messages: their ability to deal with non-consecutive pieces of memory. Therefore, we evaluate TOBUF_C performance (total processing overhead) with respect to this aspect. A message of fixed size (40000 bytes) is chopped up in a variable number of components. The impact on overhead is considered, see table 5.

A one-component compound message of this size is only marginally slower than a non-compound message. The bad performance for very small components (4 bytes) is mainly caused by the quantization effect: each component is disassembled into packets separately. The 20 byte component case is evaluated, because each component exactly fills up one packet. So, the quantization effect is avoided. Then we see, that chopping the 40000 bytes up into 2000 20 byte components costs 60% additional processing overhead.

---

[6]Also, additional scheduling overhead is neglectable.

No. of comps.	comp size (bytes)	overhead	overhead relative to TOBUF_NC
1	40,000	200 ms	1.00
10	4,000	201 ms	1.01
100	400	210 ms	1.05
1,000	40	302 ms	1.52
2,000	20	320 ms	1.60
10,000	4	1.41 s	7.08

Table 5: Total processing overhead for a 40000 byte TOBUF_C message, as function of the number of components

	average	small ($<=$ 4K)	large ($>$ 4K)
POOL alloc	28 μs	25-30 μs	77 μs
POOL free	20 μs	19 μs	71 μs

Table 6: performance memory management

6.3 POOL RTS performance

6.3.1 Introduction

Some figures are presented at the POOL interface. We present only figures for the garbage collector, the POOL communication (destination buffering and global buffering protocol see section 4.2) and the global file system. Other RTS components are not considered to be crucial for POOL performance but will be evaluated at a later stage.

6.3.2 Allocation and Process management

Similar as for the memory manager in the nucleus the performance of the allocation and scheduling primitives can be measured at the POOL RTS level. These are somewhat more expensive due to OS call overhead and facilities like (possibly) waiting for memory. The results are depicted in tables 6 and 7. When a range is specified the timings depend on the RTS environment in which the operation is performed.

6.3.3 Garbage Collector

In general little can be said about garbage collection overhead since this is very application dependent. Some application produce more garbage than others or use more operations with inherent GC overhead than others.

To get some idea of the overhead, we chose an application with produces garbage at quite a high rate, namely a theorem prover Data has been obtained using the profiler. The application was run without run-time checks on 10 nodes with different inputs and thus increasing amounts of garbage. The results are given in Table 8. The garbage collector has a time complexity linear with the amount of non-garbage object (the objects to be marked). Furthermore the frequency of activation depends on the amount of available memory. Therefore the percentage of free memory after the last GC cycle is given for each of the runs. Furthermore the GC overhead is split in two parts, the collect overhead is the time spend to actually free the memory of the garbage objects, the other overhead is due to

	time
POOL putinq	29-32 μs
POOL switch	12 μs

Table 7: performance scheduling

Run	number of GC cycles	amount mem reclaimed	free after last cycle	GC spec overhead	collect overhead
1	1	59 Mb	80%	8.4%	5.3%
2	3	118 Mb	72%	13.3%	6.1%
3	9	242 Mb	57%	23.3%	6.0%
4	20	414 Mb	37%	35.3%	4.9%

Table 8: Garbage collection overhead

POOL communication	on-node		off-node (one hop)	
	normal	gmb	normal	gmb
asynchronous 0 pars	262 μs	266 μs	833 μs	863 μs
asynchronous 17 pars	313 μs	317 μs	1081 μs	1290 μs
synchronous 0 pars	443 μs	467 μs	1714 μs	1783 μs
synchronous 17 pars	491 μs	517 μs	2000 μs	2200 μs

Table 9: communication delay between processes

run-time calls, tracing and the distributed algorithm. The overhead is given as percentage of the effective run-time (= total run-time - idle time). As we can see from table 8, the overhead grows very fast, since both more non-garbage objects occur and the frequency of activation is increased because less memory is available, but at the same time less garbage is collected per cycle.

6.3.4 POOL communication

When considering (off-node) message passing, two performance figures are of interest: latency and total processing overhead (see also section 6.2.3). These are measured using the ping-pong and multi ping-pong games, respectively. The two communication protocols destination buffering and global message buffering (see section 4.2) were taken into account. All measurements were done with full POOL functionality with the debug level of the OS at 0 (no checks).

The communication primitives seen from POOL include memory allocation and preparation of the message before giving it to the message handlers. Therefore the figures in this section should not be compared to the figures for the message handling in the nucleus.

Latency The contribution of parameters to communication cost is only studied for the distinction between the two protocols. Normally only parameterless messages were of interest for latency (see section 6.3.4), but the GMB protocol treats small messages . (up to 64 bytes i.e. 16 parameters) differently. The results are presented in table 9.

synchronous compared to asynchronous We observe that synchronous communication is about twice as expensive as asynchronous communication, since result passing is quite similar to parameter passing.

on-node communication In principle the standard and the GMB protocol act the same for on-node communication. Only coding differences can explain the slight differences. The difference in synchronous on-node communication is larger than expected and can not be explained. Measurements done in C directly on top of the RTS simulating POOL processes do not show these differences. Furthermore the POOL code generated for the two protocols is exactly the same. There are about 20 micro seconds (30 instructions) that can not be explained.

Parameters[a]	total processing overhead
()	620 μs
(Int^6)	772 μs
(Int^{12})	904 μs
(Int^{18})	1.04 ms
(Float^3)	792 μs
(Float^6)	948 μs
(Float^9)	1.11 ms
(User_object^6)	764 μs
(String[0])	1.56 ms
(String[0]^2)	1.96 ms
(String[0]^3)	2.37 ms
(String[24])	1.67 ms
(String[48])	1.80 ms
(String[48]^2)	2.45 ms
(Tuple0)	1.65 ms
(Tuple0^2)	2.16 ms
(Tuple0^3)	2.68 ms
([Int^6])	1.79 ms
([Int^{12}])	1.92 ms
([Float^3])	1.80 ms
([Float^6])	1.96 ms
([User_object^6])	1.82 ms
([User_object^{12}])	1.96 ms
([String[0]])	2.05 ms
([String[0]^2])	2.46 ms
([String[24]])	2.18 ms
([Tuple0])	2.17 ms

[a]Repetition of arguments or tuple fields is denoted by a power notation. String[n] means: an n character String.

Table 10: Total processing overhead for passing asynchronous messages off-node, as function of different parameter lists

off-node communication For small message in external communication the GMB protocol acts like the standard protocol but maintains flow control information. This takes about 30 micro seconds per send/receive action. For large messages (more than 16 parameters) the GMB has to send a system message (RSI) to delete the message buffer at the sender's side. The larger delay is partly due the RSI because this RSI will be sent first from the receiver's node.

Overhead Since synchronous communication is about twice as expensive as asynchronous communication, only the latter is considered. Furthermore, experiments show, that processing overhead for on-node communication more or less equals the latency because no network latency is involved. Playing the multi ping-pong game between two objects on the same node only involves more scheduling overhead than playing the multi ping-pong game on two nodes. But user object scheduling is relatively cheap. Furthermore, adding parameters to an on-node message is relatively cheap, since these messages are passed by reference between objects. Therefore, total processing overhead is considered for (asynchronous) off-node messages, only.

The total processing overhead for (off-node) asynchronous communication is shown in table 10. A multitude of (well-chosen) parameter sets is considered.

Further analysis of these results reveal the possibility to break communication costs down into components. Roughly said: each message has some fixed overhead, plus some variable overhead per

Fixed overhead	
Fixed overhead for async. message	620 μs
Additional 'tax' for compound[a] message	535 μs
Average parameter overhead	
Int	23 μs
User_object	24 μs
Float	55 μs
String (empty)	400 μs
Tuple (empty)	500 μs
Average additional cost per Tuple field	
Int	21 μs
User_object	23 μs
Float	26 μs
String (empty)	410 μs
Tuple (empty)	520 μs

[a]I.e. a message containing one or more string or tuple-like parameters.

Table 11: Model for total processing overhead for off-node asynchronous messages

parameter. The results of this analysis are shown in table 11. The figures presented are approximate averages. In particular, the cost of adding an additional simple parameter or field may deviate from this average, due to quantization noise, caused by the fact that data are transported in units of entire packets (see also section 6.2.3) [7].

From this table, one or two simple formulae can be deduced easily, to give an accurate estimate of communication costs. This model may be very valuable for the construction of simulators for the parallel execution of POOL–X.

Strings, tuples and similar kinds of objects are copied by value, when sent off-node []. This is done using a compound message. This explains the extra overhead for messages containing one or more string/tuple-like parameters (compound table handling). Also, the relatively high costs of these parameters (compared to e.g. Int) are explained by this.

A number of observations can be made, studying these results more carefully:

1. (Empty) strings and tuples, whether shipped directly as parameter, or nested deeper inside some tuple, cost the approximately about 400 μs for a string and 500 μs for a tuple.

2. Int and user object parameters are equally expensive. User object fields in tuples are little more expensive, than Int fields, however. The former are references. So, it should be checked, that they are not references to string/tuple-like objects. Because, these require by value copying.

3. Float fields in tuples are twice as expensive as Int fields: their representation size is twice as large (eight bytes instead of four). The difference is in time (23 compared to 55) is not due to the send but due to time differences at the creation of the tuples. The same holds for float parameters.

6.3.5 Global file system

Here we present some results from results from the POOMA global file system.

The POOMA file system at the interface level reaches the system limits. The limits for the disk file system reach locally the disk driver limit, and remotely the communication processor's limit. The host file system is limited by the ethernet.

[7]Knowing, that the data area of a packet may contain 24 bytes, makes the choice of the parameter sets of table 10 more apparent.

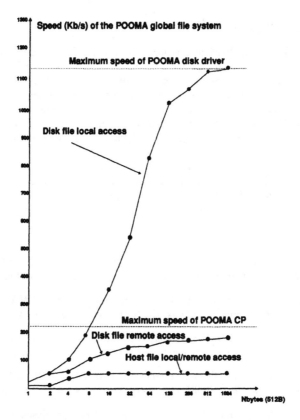

Figure 4: The performance curves of the POOMA-GFS

The speed of the file system is depending on the buffer provided by the user and by the alignment of the buffer to the block alignment on disk. When alignment of the buffers is taken care of (as is done by the POOL file system implementation) and the buffer is a multiple of the blocksize (512 bytes) then the curves as shown in figure 4 can be obtained. When the boundary conditions about size and alignment are not fulfilled the performance drastically decreases mainly due to larger seek times at the disk.

6.4 Conclusions from the performance measurements

Looking at the figures shown in the previous paragraphs we can conclude that the performance of the memory manager and process manager are satisfactory. The garbage collector measurements show that some attention should be paid on the tracing of objects. The simple communication primitives like RSI and COPY show good performance. On the contrary, the more complicated nucleus primitives TOBUF and TOBUF_C, as well as the POOL communication show very poor performance. These will be optimized in future implementations. Finally the performance of the global file system is satisfactory if block size and alignment on the disk are taken into account in the higher layers.

7 Concluding remarks

A lot of small and large design decisions have been taken during design and implementation of the OS. Some of the decisions are based on expected behavior. At the moment the first measurements give a first notion on how good our choices have been. Already in a preliminary stage of the implementation, measurements resulted in changing the memory management and I/O system completely. However, especially with respect to communication and garbage collection some optimizations are still required. Furthermore several parameters of the implementation still have to be tuned to the behavior of the POOL implementation (for instance threshold triggers in the node overflow handler or pagesize in the memory manager).

Also we want to learn from the overall behavior of the POOL program platform, to identify programming and efficiency problems and take appropriate measures in the language definition or propose specific hardware solutions for time consuming actions.

References

[Spek90]   J. v.d. Spek, *POOL-X and its implementation*, Proc. of the PRISMA Workshop on Parallel Database Systems, Noordwijk, the Netherlands, September 24-26, 1990.

[Vlot90]   M.C. Vlot, *The POOMA Architecture*, Proc. of the PRISMA Workshop on Parallel Database Systems, Noordwijk, the Netherlands, September 24-26, 1990.

[Apers90]   P.G.M. Apers, L.O. Hertzberger, B.J.A. Hulshof, A.C.M. Oerlemans, M.L. Kersten, *PRISMA: a platform for experiments with parallelism*, to be published, 1990.

[Graham82]   Susan L. Graham, Peter B. Kessler and Marshall K. McKusick, *gprof: A Call Graph Execution Profiler*, SIGPLAN notices, Vol. 17, No. 6, pp 120-126, 1982.

[Dijkstra83] Edsger W. Dijkstra, W.H.J. Feijen and A.J.M. van Gasteren, *Derivation of a termination detection algorithm for distributed computations*, Inf. Proc. Letters 16(5), p217-219, June 1983.

[Goertz]   Erik Göertz, *A symmetric algorithm for termination detection of distributed computations*, Philips Research Manuscript M.S. 13.278, 198?.

[Knuth73]   D.E. Knuth, *The Art of Computer Programming: Fundamental Algorithms*, Addison Wesley, 1973.

Parallel Query Execution in PRISMA/DB. *

Annita N. Wilschut
Peter M. G. Apers
Jan Flokstra

University of Twente
P.O.Box 217, 7500 AE Enschede, the Netherlands

1 Introduction

In the PRISMA-project, a large multi-processor system has been built, is be used to study the performance gains from parallelism. A parallel, main-memory relational database system (PRISMA/DB) runs on this so-called POOMA-machine. This paper studies the possibilities of using parallelism to improve the performance of relational database management systems. Because the equi-join is an important, and time-consuming operation, queries consisting of a number of equi-joins are used to describe how different forms of parallelism can speed up the execution of such queries.

This paper is organized as follows: First, a brief introduction into PRISMA and the DBMS running on it is given. After that, different forms of parallelism are described and the ways in which they can be used is identified. Using this knowledge, the possible parallelism in the execution of join-queries is discussed. Special attention is paid to pipelining. It is shown, that pipelining needs a new hash-join algorithm and that using this algorithm may yield effective parallelism over a pipeline of join operations. Finally, we discuss the implications of using pipelining as a source of parallelism for the optimization of join queries. The paper is concluded with our plans for future work.

2 PRISMA

The PaRallel Inference and Storage MAchine PRISMA is a highly parallel machine for data and knowledge processing.

The PRISMA-machine contains 100 nodes that each contain a data processor, a communication processor and 16 Mbyte of local memory. 50 nodes have a disk and some nodes have an ethernet card that provides an interface with a host computer. Each communication processor connects a node to 4 other nodes. In this way a fast, high-bandwidth network is provided. This hardware can be classified as a *shared-nothing* multi-processor system.

The machine is designed to support a relational *main memory* database management system PRISMA/DB. An extensive introduction to this system can be found in [Kers87] and in [Wils89]. Here, only the features that are important for this paper are summarized.

PRISMA/DB stores the entire database in main memory. Disks are used for backup only. To gain performance and to make storage in main memory feasible, the tuples belonging to one relation are fragmented over more than one node. A fragment is a set of tuples that belong to the same relation and that reside on the same node. A relation does not necessarily use all available nodes. The fragmentation is disjoint and complete, so each tuple belongs to exactly one fragment.

*The work reported in this document was conducted as part of the PRISMA project, a joint effort with Philips Research Eindhoven, partially supported by the Dutch "Stimuleringsprojectteam Informaticaonderzoek (SPIN)".

A fragment has a process associated with it, that executes operations on that fragment. Such a process is called a One-Fragment Manager (OFM). Both base data and intermediate data are managed by OFMs. OFMs for base-fragments are created at system startup; OFMs for intermediate data are created during query execution. The result of an operation is sent to the OFM that needs it for further processing, if it is an intermediate result, or to the user, if it is an end result. Intermediate results may be fragmented. In that case, the output of an operation is distributed over more than one OFM. After finishing a transaction, the OFMs managing intermediate results are disposed of. The base OFMs stay alive waiting for a next transaction that needs their data.

OFMs are allocated to processors when they are created. Process migration is not supported on the POOMA-machine. In this paper, it is assumed that each OFM has its private processor, because we want to understand the behavior of such a system before the more difficult situation in which different OFMs share one processor is tackled. This assumption implies that each base fragment resides on a private processor, because they each have an OFM. In this way, the data allocation problem is solved for this moment. Data allocation is one of our future research issues though.

3   Parallelism

Before discussing the possibilities of using parallelism for query execution, we start with the definition of some useful concepts: Two sorts of parallelism are relevant to this paper [Bora85, Wils89]:

task-spreading A task is decomposed into a number of similar subtasks that are each executed independently on different parts of the data on different processors. The results of the subtasks are eventually combined to form the result. Task-spreading requires a coordinating process that hands out the subtasks and collects the results if necessary. If the subtasks consist of equal amounts of work, the speedup of task-spreading is expected to be proportional to the number of processors involved. This form of parallelism is called (pure) parallelism in [Bora85].

pipelining A task is decomposed into a number of different subtasks that have to be executed consecutively on the same datastream. The subtasks can be assigned to different processors. Every subtask reads its input from its predecessor and sends its output to its successor. Subtasks are activated, when the first data reach them. When the first data reach the last subtask before the first subtask is done, all subtasks work simultaneously until the first subtask is done. Because of this staging in the execution it is hard to predict the performance gain from pipelining.

Orthogonal to this distinction, the sorts of parallelism that are defined above, can be used in different ways for query execution [Wils89, Schn90]:

intra-operator parallelism One operation in a query tree is distributed over more than one processor.

inter-operator parallelism Different operations in one query tree are executed concurrently.

inter-query parallelism Different queries are executed concurrently. This form of parallelism is not considered in this paper.

Intra-operator task-spreading has been studied extensively during the last few years [Brat89, Schn89, Rich87]. This paper concentrates on using *inter-operator pipelining* and *inter-operator task-spreading*, assuming that each individual operation can be implemented efficiently using intra-operator task-spreading. The next section describes how potential inter-operator parallelism in a query can be identified.

4 Possible Parallelism in Join-queries

In order to describe the possibilities of using inter-operator parallelism for query execution, two query representations are discussed in this section. A join-query can be represented in the following ways.

A *join-graph* is a non-procedural representation of a join-query [Ceri84]. The nodes of the graph represent the relations that participate in the join. Two nodes are connected by an edge if a join criterion connects the relations represented by the edge. Edges are labeled with the selectivity of the corresponding join criterion.

A *join-tree* is a procedural representation of a join-query. The leaves of a join-tree represent the relations that participate in the query. Intermediate nodes are operations on their incoming edges; they send their output via the outgoing edge to the next operation. The root of the tree produces the result of the query. In this way, a join-tree describes an execution plan for a query. Like there are many execution plans for a single join-query, one join-graph can be mapped to several different join-trees.

Figure 1 shows a join-query with its join-graph and two join-trees corresponding with this graph.

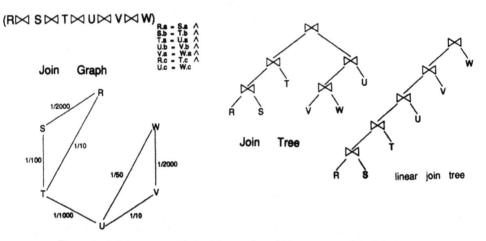

Figure 1: A join-query with its join-graph and two corresponding join-trees.

A join-tree can easily be mapped to the dataflow execution model [Alex88, DeWi88]. In such a model, the data is assumed to flow along the various operation processes, that start processing their input as soon as it is available. The OFMs in PRISMA/DB correspond to operation processes and thus to nodes in a join-tree.

In a join-tree, the potential inter-operation parallelism can easily be identified. Operations that are "next to each other" can be parallelized via task-spreading. Nodes that have a parent-child relationship can possibly execute concurrently via pipelining. Inter-operation task-spreading is used a lot in parallel DBMSs [Ceri84]. In the next section, the possibilities of using inter-operation pipelining to execute join-queries are studied.

5 Pipelining in Join Queries

To find out whether pipelining yields a significant performance gain in join queries, the execution characteristics of the join-tree in figure 2 are considered. This figure shows a join-tree for the four-way join between selections on A, B, C and D. First, the characteristics of the well known hash-join algorithm are described, and then a new version of this algorithm is proposed.

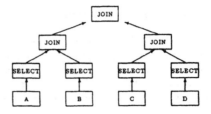

Figure 2: tree representation of $(\sigma A \bowtie \sigma B) \bowtie (\sigma C \bowtie \sigma D)$. The operands are equal in size, the selections have a selectivity of 10%, and the joins operations match one tuple of one operand to exactly one of the other. The operations are executed on a private processor.

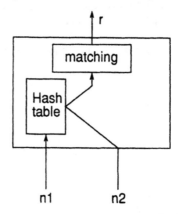

Figure 3: Common main-memory hash-join.

5.1   The common hash-join algorithm

A hash-join algorithm is assumed, because hashing algorithms have proven to perform good compared to other join algorithms [Schn89]. Different hash-join algorithms have been proposed, but they differ mainly in the way in which operands are fetched from disk. The main-memory version of these hash-join algorithms, called *common hash-join* in this text, works as follows (see figure 3):

> In the common hash-join algorithm two phases can be distinguished. First, an in-memory hash-table for one entire operand is built. In the second phase, the tuples of the other operand are hashed and compared to the tuples in the corresponding bucket of the first operand one by one. If a match is found, an output tuple is produced. This algorithm does not need a hash-table for the second operand.

The following can be remarked about this algorithm. Firstly, it is clear that output tuples are only produced during the second phase of the algorithm. Secondly, the algorithm is asymmetric in its operands. This implies that the execution characteristics of $A \bowtie B$ can be very different from the execution characteristics of $B \bowtie A$. Both these properties have important implications for the characteristics of the execution of join queries when the common hash-join algorithm is used. The next paragraph describes the implications of the staging in the algorithm; the asymmetry is discussed further below.

Fig 4 shows the execution characteristics of the join-tree in figure 2, assuming the common hash-join algorithm. The diagrams in this figure plot the processor utilization of an operation against the time. The two phases in the join operation can easily be distinguished in the join-diagrams. It is clear, that the topmost join operation in the tree can only start building its hash-table during

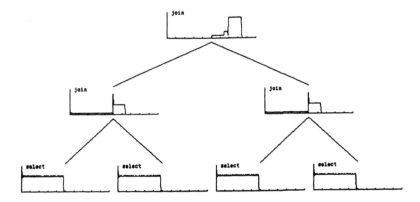

Figure 4: Execution characteristics of the common main-memory hash-join algorithm.

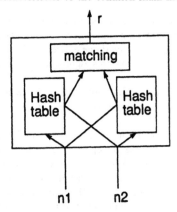

Figure 5: Pipelining main-memory hash-join.

the second phase of the other two join operations. The second phase of the topmost join operation is executed after the other two join operations have finished executing, and so this phase cannot work concurrently with the other two join-operations. So, in a pipeline of join operations that are implemented via this join algorithm, the first phase of a parent join can be executed concurrently with the second phase of the child join operation. Therefore, if a pipeline consists of more than two join operations, at any moment at most two operations can execute concurrently. This means that the staging in the common hash-join algorithm reduces the effective parallelism from pipelining.

5.2 A pipelining hash-join algorithm

To increase the amount of effective parallelism in the execution of the join-tree in figure 2, a new main-memory hash-join algorithm, called *pipelining hash-join* is proposed [Wils90] (see figure 5):

The pipelining hash-join consists of only one phase in which a hash-table for both operands is built. When a tuple arrives of one of the operands, it is hashed and compared to the tuples in the corresponding bucket of the other operand that have already arrived. If a match is found an output-tuple is formed. Finally, independant of the match, the input-tuple is inserted in its own hash-table. As soon as one entire operand has reached the join process, the tuples of the other operand do not need to be inserted in their own hash-table, because this hash-table is not used in the rest of the join process anymore.

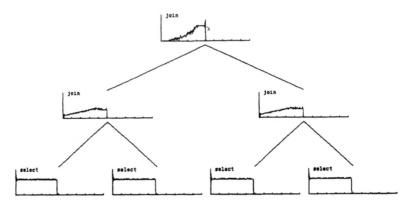

Figure 6: Execution characteristics of the pipelining main-memory hash-join algorithm.

The following properties of this algorithm are important: Firstly, this algorithm already produces its first output tuple as soon as two matching tuples have reached the join operation. Secondly, the algorithm is symmetric in its operands. Finally, if one entire operand reaches the join-process before the first tuple of the other operand is available, this algorithm degenerates to the common hash-join algorithm.

The next paragraph describes how the first property of this algorithm influences the effective parallelism from pipelining. The next subsection is on the (a)symmetry of the hash-join algorithms that are presented in this paper.

Figure 6 shows the execution characteristics of the join-tree in figure 2 using the pipelining hash-join. From this figure it is clear, that all three join operations work concurrently, resulting in a shorter response time for the execution of the complete query. This increased concurrency (with respect to the execution of this join-query using the common hash-join algorithm) is possible, because the result tuples are produced early on the join process. Using the pipelining hash-join algorithm, it is feasible to build join pipelines that consist of several join operations that can all work concurrently. So, using the pipelining hash-join algorithm, both task-spreading and pipelining yield effective inter-operator parallelism.

5.3   The advantage of a symmetric join algorithm

This subsection is a deviation of the main topic of this paper. In the next section, the discussion on parallel query execution is continued with the implications of the pipelining hash-join algorithm for query execution strategies. Here, the advantages of the symmetry of the pipelining hash-join over the asymmetry of the common hash-join are described. It should be realized, that the join operation is a symmetric one in theory; the asymmetry of the common hash-join is merely a consequence of the way in which the tuples of the operands are matched.

The asymmetry of the common hash-join has disadvantages for the determination of a suitable plan for a join-query. Usage of an asymmetric algorithm requires that the decision which operand has to be the left one and which one the right, has to be made thoughtfully. Taking the wrong decision can result in bad execution chararteristics: If for a certain join operation, a common hash-join is planned in which a hash-table is built for the left operand, and the right operand is available earlier than the left one, than the join process sits waiting for the left operand, not doing anything with the tuples of the right operand, that are available for processing. If the pipelining hash-join is used instead, the algorithm itself adapts to the availability of tuples of the operands, because the tuples are processed in the order in which they are available. This adaptation of the algorithm to the availability of the operands makes the task of determination of a suitable query execution strategy easier.

In a paper on query execution strategies, DeWitt and Schneider [Schn90] compare the effective inter-operator parallelism during the execution of linear left-deep and linear right-deep join trees. They conclude that right-deep linear join trees are well suited to process multiway joins. The difference in the execution characteristics of these two strategies is caused by the asymmetry in the hash-join algorithm they use. In a main-memory environment, usage of the symmetric pipelining hash-join algorithm probably yields the same effective parallelism, regardless of the shape of the query tree. In the next section, the implications of the fact that arbitrary shaped query trees can be used for parallel query execution, are discussed.

6 Query Execution Strategies

In this section, the impact of using the pipelining hash-join algorithm on the design of a query execution strategy is considered.

Choosing an execution plan for a query implies that the following two decisions (among others) have to be taken:

- An algorithm has to be chosen for each individual join operation. This choice implies determination of the degree of intra-operation parallelism for each operation.

- A join-tree that corresponds to the join-graph for the query has to be selected from the numerous possible join-trees.

These choices can be fixed (e.g. some systems always use a hash-join algorithm that is distributed over all available processors), or they are made by a query optimizer. To select a join-tree, usually a part of the vast space of join-trees that corresponds to a join-graph is traversed more or less exhaustively searching for the tree that has the best value for some goal-function. The goal-function calculates some execution characteristic of the join-tree using estimates of the costs of the individual operations. Of course, the cost estimates are influenced by the algorithms that are assumed for individual operations.

Many papers on query optimization discuss the process of traversing the space of join-trees and cost functions that are used to estimate the costs of operations and the size of results. In this paper, we assume suitable cost functions to be available and we only try to identify the characteristics of the join-tree that has to be chosen, leaving the way to find that tree for further research.

Now, we will discuss two query execution strategies that are known from the literature, and then an alternative strategy that takes inter-operation pipelining into account, is proposed.

6.1 GAMMA.

GAMMA [DeWi86] uses the approach that is known from System-R [Seli79]. It can be characterized as follows:

- A (non-pipelining) hash-join algorithm is used in which each operation is declustered over all 8 available processors.

- The *linear* tree that has minimal accumulated estimated processing costs is chosen as execution plan for the query.

This strategy has a fixed choice for the join algorithm and for the degree of intra-operator parallelism that is used. The query optimizer only considers linear join trees. Also, this strategy does not use any inter-operator parallelism: each operation occupies all available processors. Therefore, using inter-operator parallelism will not yield any performance gain.

6.2 The Bodorik approach

Bodorik et al.[Bodo88] propose an optimization strategy that chooses a general (not necessarily linear) join-tree in which the accumulated processing time along the longest path is minimal with respect to other join-trees. It is clear, that such an algorithm tends to select wide query-trees that have many possibilities for task-spreading, which is the main source of parallelism in the execution model that is used in this paper. The Bodorik query execution strategy is characterized as follows:

- A (non-pipelining) hash-join algorithm is used in which the degree of parallelism in each individual operation depends only on the fragmentation of the join operands. Before each join operation, one operand is reconstructed and broadcast to the fragments of the other operand.

- The optimization algorithm selects the join-tree in which the total execution time of the operations on the longest path is minimal.

In this strategy, the join algorithm is fixed, and the degree of parallelism in each operation is taken according to the fragmentation of the join operands. The strategy uses both intra-operator and inter-operator task-spreading.

6.3 The PRISMA approach

In PRISMA yet another strategy is used. The execution strategy that is proposed here assumes usage of the pipelining hash-join algorithm. The idea behind it is the following:

- First, the total amount of work that has to be done to evaluate the query is minimized.

- Then, we try to distribute that minimal amount of work equally over the available processors.

If all processes that result from this strategy really execute concurrently, it is clear that this strategy is likely to yield a good response time to the query.

In the previous section, it was stated that both inter-operator task-spreading and inter-operator pipelining yield concurrent join processes, if the pipelining join algorithm is used. So, the idea that is described above can be applied in the following way.

- First, the join-tree is chosen that has the minimal accumulated processing time over all joins that have to be executed.

- Now, the work in the chosen join-tree has to be distributed equally over the available processors. This is achieved by assigning more processors to expensive operations: The available processors are assigned to join operations proportionaly to the costs of those join operation.

So, the PRISMA approach can be characterized as follows:

- A main-memory pipelining hash-join algorithm is assumed. The degree of intra-operation parallelism in each join is determined by the estimated costs for each operation.

- The minimal total estimated processing costs general tree is chosen.

Comparison of the three optimization strategies that are described above leads to the following observations. Firstly, GAMMA only exploits intra-operator parallelism, Bodorik et al. use intra-operator task-spreading and inter-operator task-spreading, and PRISMA exploits intra-operator task-spreading, inter-operator task-spreading and inter-operator pipelining. Secondly, GAMMA and Bodorik set the degree of intra-operator task-spreading heuristically and PRISMA chooses this degree during the optimization process. Finally, different sorts of query trees are chosen. Experiments will have to show which strategy works best.

Of course, the PRISMA optimization strategy has some problems as well. It is clear that two pipelined processes do not yield full concurrency. The effect of the intrinsic delay over a pipeline and the tuning of the speeds in which tuples are generated and consumed need further study.

7 Summary and plans for future work

In this paper, the possibilities for parallel query execution in PRISMA/DB were reviewed. Join queries were considered throughout the paper. It was shown that inter-operator pipelining may yield a source of parallelism in query execution. Exploitation of this form of parallelism affects the characteristics of query execution. An adjusted query execution strategy was proposed.

The material presented in this paper is still is the stage of ideas that need experimental justification. Also, many details of new the algorithms that were proposed need further research. Experiments are carried out in two ways. Firstly, PRISMA/DB is an excellent experimentation platform for the ideas that were presented in this paper. We plan to compare the characteristics of the execution of different query trees for one query on PRISMA/DB. Secondly, a simulator for query execution was developed with which the influence of changes in algorithms can easily be studied. (Figure 4 and 6 were produced by this simulator.) Both PRISMA/DB and the simulator will be used to adjust and validate the algorithms that are presented in this paper.

After that more general queries than just join queries will be considered. Also, process and data allocation will be studied. For that purpose the possibility that more than one data fragment or more than one operation process share one processor is taken into account.

References

[Alex88]   W. Alexander and G. Copeland, *Process and Dataflow Control in Distributed Data-Intensive Systems*, Proceedings of the 1988 SIGMOD conference, Chicago, USA, June 1988.

[Bodo88]   P. Bododrik, J. S. Riordon, *Heuristic Algorithms for Distributed Query Processing*, Proceedings of the first International Symposium on Databases in Parallel and Distributed Systems, Austin, USA, December 1988.

[Bora85]   H. Boral and S. Redfield, *Database Machine Morphology*, Proceedings of the 11th conference on Very Large Databases, Stockholm, Sweden, August 1985.

[Brat89]   K. Bratbergsengen and T. Gjelsvik, *The Development of the CROSS8 and HC16-186 Parallel Database Computers*, Proceedings of the 6th International Workshop on Database Machines, Deauville, France, June 1989.

[Ceri84]   S. Ceri and G. Pelagatti, *Distributed Databases: Principles and Systems*, McGraw-Hill, 1984.

[DeWi86]   D.J. DeWitt, R. H. Gerber, G. Graefe, M. L. Heytens, K. B. Kumar, M. Muralikrishna, *GAMMA - A High Performance Dataflow Database Machine*, Proceedings of the 12th conference on Very Large Databases, Kyoto, Japan, August 1986.

[DeWi88]   D.J. DeWitt, S. Ghanderarizadeh and D.Schneider, *A performance analysis of the Gamma Database Machine*, Proceedings of the 1988 SIGMOD conference, Chicago, USA, June 1988.

[Kers87]   M.L. Kersten, P.M.G. Apers, M.A.W. Houtsma, H.J.A. van Kuijk, R.L.W. van de Weg, *A Distributed, Main Memory Database Machine*, Proceedings of the 5th International Workshop on Database Machines, Karuizawa, Japan, October 1987.

[Rich87]   J. P. Richardson, H. Lu and K. Mikkilineni, *Design and Evaluation of Parallel Pipelined Join Algorithms*, Proceedings of the 1987 SIGMOD conference, San Francisco, USA, June 1987.

[Seli79]   P. G. Selinger, M. M. Astrahan, D. D. Chamberlin, R. A. Lorie, T. G. Price, *Access Path Selection in a Relational Database Management System*, Proceedings of the 1979 SIGMOD conference, Boston, USA, 1987.

[Schn89]   D.A. Schneider and D.J. DeWitt, *A performance Evaluation of Four Join Algorithms in a Shared-Nothing Multiprocessor Environment*, Proceedings of the 1989 SIGMOD conference, Portland, USA, June 1989.

[Schn90] D. A. Schneider and D. J. DeWitt, *Tradeoffs in Processing Complex Join Queries via Hashing in Multiprocessor Database Machines*, Proceedings of the 16th conference on Very Large Databases, Brisbane, Australia, August 1990.

[Ston86] M. Stonebraker, *The case for shared nothing*, Database Engineering 9.1, 1986.

[Wils89] A.N. Wilschut, P.W.P.J. Grefen, P.M.G.Apers, M.L.Kersten, *Implementing PRISMA/DB in an OOPL*, Proceedings of the 6th International Workshop on Database Machines, Deauville, France, June 1989.

[Wils90] A. N. Wilschut, P. M. G. Apers, *Pipelining in Query Execution*, Proceedings of the PARBASE-90 conference, Miami, USA, March 1990.

Lecture Notes in Computer Science

For information about Vols. 1–420
please contact your bookseller or Springer-Verlag